Introductory Readings in Ethics

edited by

William K. Frankena
University of Michigan

and

John T. Granrose
University of Georgia

PRENTICE-HALL, INC. *Englewood Cliffs, New Jersey*

Library of Congress Cataloging in Publication Data

FRANKENA, WILLIAM K   comp.
    Introductory readings in ethics.

    Includes bibliographies.
    1. Ethics—Collected works.
I. Granrose, John T., joint comp. II. Title.
BJ21.F68   170'.8   73-20488
ISBN O-13-502112-X

10   9   8   7   6   5   4   3

PRENTICE-HALL INTERNATIONAL, INC., *London*
PRENTICE-HALL OF AUSTRALIA, PTY., LTD., *Sydney*
PRENTICE-HALL OF CANADA, LTD., *Toronto*
PRENTICE-HALL OF INDIA PRIVATE LIMITED, *New Delhi*
PRENTICE-HALL OF JAPAN, INC., *Tokyo*

CONTENTS

iii

3

UTILITARIANISM, JUSTICE, AND LOVE   127

6

MEANING AND JUSTIFICATION   367

PREFACE

Let no one when young delay to study philosophy, nor when he is old grow weary of his study. For no one can come too early or too late to secure the health of his soul. And the man who says that the age for philosophy has either not yet come or has gone by is like the man who says that the age for happiness is not yet come to him, or has passed away. Wherefore both when young and old a man must study philosophy. . . .

—Epicurus

This volume is dedicated to young men and women "who Aristotle thought unfit to hear moral philosophy" (*Troilus and Cressida*, II, ii). In other words, it is intended to be used primarily in introductory courses in ethics, whether these presuppose previous work in philosophy or not. It is planned as a companion to W. K. Frankena's *Ethics*, second edition, with which it is correlated chapter by chapter and, with only a few exceptions, topic by topic, and which contains further information and discussions on most of the problems and theories presented. It may, however, be used by itself if an instructor so wishes; he may supplement its introductory materials with expositions and discussions of his own. Even so, a student will find it helpful to read Frankena's book in conjunction with this one, since this book repeats as little as possible of that one, though some duplication was, of course, unavoidable.

We have tried to make a book that covers the subject of ethics and yet can itself be covered in a course, with few if any omissions. To this end the selections have been kept to a minimum compatible with the views and topics involved. There is not a full battery of presentations of all points of view on every topic. Often the selections are very short, no longer than necessary for stating a position or argument. Almost all of the essays and passages have been cut and edited to suit the purposes of this volume as we see them, though omissions have been carefully indicated. Though most of the selections are reasonably full, some sections consist entirely of short passages connected by a brief running commentary. Footnotes have generally been omitted, and titles and subtitles of the selections used have sometimes been altered. We have tried not to misrepresent any philosopher's position or arguments, but neither have we tried to present any philosopher's position or arguments in their entirety. This should always be remembered in reading and using this book. Our primary concern is to provide systematic readings for introductory courses in ethics rather than a history of ethical theories or a book for advanced scholars.

In this same spirit, our introductions and supplementary materials have been held to a minimum consistent with clarity and usefulness. We have, however, tried to provide needed introductory information, interpretative guidance, and connecting comment—as well as some study questions and, following each chapter, some suggestions for further reading.

The selections not only vary greatly in length depending on their character and function; they also range over time. Many of them are classical or early modern, some are Christian, some are nineteenth-century, and many again are contemporary. But the ordering is systematic and not chronological, since our purpose is not historical, even if a good deal of history is provided. The chapters can be studied in a different order if that is desired. One might, for instance, study Chapter 5 or 6, or both, before taking up Chapters 2 to 4.

There are many selections, and many different names appear in the course of this book. This could hardly be avoided, given the plan adopted. We believe that readers should remember some of the more important names, and be able to associate views and arguments with them, but, of course, the emphasis in using this volume should be on understanding and thinking about the theories, problems, and arguments, not on learning names and dates.

W. K. F.
J. T. G.

1

MORALITY
AND MORAL PHILOSOPHY

Introduction

The word "ethics" as used in the title of this volume stands for a branch of philosophy, namely, moral philosophy or philosophical thinking about morality and its problems. What is meant by philosophy or philosophical thinking we shall not try to define here; for the most part we shall let that become clearer as we go along. It must be noted, however, that there are three kinds of inquiries about morality: (1) descriptive and explanatory studies such as are made by historians and social scientists; (2) normative inquiries about the principles, standards, or methods for determining what is morally right or wrong, good or bad; and (3) "meta-ethical" questions about the meanings of terms like "right," "good," "responsible," etc., about the meaning of "morality" itself, or about the justification of ethical judgments. Moral philosophy may be equated with inquiries of the second and third kinds.

What is meant by "morality"? This is itself one of the central problems of moral philosophy, and will be touched on now and then in our readings, especially in Chapter 6, but, for present purposes, we may take "morality" to stand, not for any philosophical theory, but for something more like moral practice or moral living. As R. B. Perry puts it,

> Morality is something which goes on in the world. . . . Nothing is more familiar; nothing is more obscure in its meaning. . . . [M]oral philosophy

1

. . . consists in the investigation of this going on. . . . But it cannot be denied that morality exists as a *pursuit*. . . .[1]

He goes on to suggest that "morality is man's endeavor to harmonize conflicting interests," but other philosophers would reject this definition. We may, however, say in general that morality is the business of having an action-guide (an AG) of a certain sort, different in important ways from other (nonmoral) AGs like law, etiquette, or self-interest. Just which AGs are moral ones is, as was indicated, a matter of philosophical debate today, and it should be observed here that the question is not "Which AGs are moral and which immoral?" but "Which are moral and which *non*moral?" However, examples of moral ones would be the things we call moral codes, ideals, or standards. When we speak of "a morality" or "Christian morality" we mean a moral AG of this sort. We also, by the way, sometimes call such an AG an "ethics"; in fact, we often use "ethics" as a synonym for "morality" or "moral code," not just as a word for the branch of philosophy we are now studying. And we usually think of a morality as something that belongs to a group, but actually, an individual may also have a morality and his morality may be different from, even opposed to, that of his society. That is, the pursuit that Perry speaks of may be either a social or a personal enterprise, though originally it is, no doubt, a social one.

We also use expressions like "the principles of morality." This, however, is a rather different use of "morality" from the one just discussed. Here "morality" does not stand for the moral AG of some person or group or for something that is going on in the world, but for something like "the true or valid moral AG." When one says that one of the principles of morality is to treat people equally, one means that treating people equally is part of morality in the sense of true morality, not just that it is part of someone's, or even everyone's, moral AG.

The best way to see or remind oneself what morality (having a moral AG) is, and to begin the study of ethics, is to consider an actual moral problem. In Plato's *Crito* we have a classic discussion of such a problem, one of great interest today, by Socrates (470–399 B.C.), the man who did most to start moral philosophy in the West and was himself its noblest embodiment. The main part of this discussion is reproduced in the first selection. In the *Crito*, Socrates has been condemned to death by the people of Athens for his supposedly dangerous teaching, and he is now in prison but has an opportunity to escape. Personal and family considerations and the feelings of his friends seem to be on the side of escaping, and most Athenians would think he should actually take the opportunity

---

[1] R. B. Perry, *Realms of Value* (Cambridge: Harvard University Press, 1954), p. 86.

of doing so, but Socrates believes there is a moral question involved: "Should he leave when the state has, in effect, commanded him to stay?" In other words, "Is it ever right to disobey the law of one's country?"— the question of civil disobedience.

Socrates' dialogue states very nicely one line of argument for obeying the law—even if the result is one's death. It also illustrates one method of answering ethical questions of that sort, a method that may be applied to other such problems. Even more generally, it expresses the typical spirit of philosophical discussion of moral questions: one should not appeal to authority, one should think for oneself, one should think carefully and logically on the basis of the facts and the soundest basic principles one can find, and one must consider only what is morally relevant. Socrates also made other contributions to moral philosophy that are described in other dialogues; he was the first to ask for careful definitions of ethical terms such as "virtue," and "justice." He also thought that virtue is knowledge, or in other words, that if we know what is right we will do it.

As you read Socrates' discussion with Crito, consider such questions as these: Is Socrates' conclusion that he should not try to escape justified? Do you disagree with his reasoning at any point? If so, where, and why? For example, is Socrates correct in thinking that ". . . neither injury nor retaliation nor warding off evil by evil is ever right"? Also, what do you think of Socrates' claim that one must either obey the government, convince the government of one's point of view (presumably, here, by going through legitimate channels), or leave the country?

Finally, in this, as well as the other selections in this chapter that raise specific moral dilemmas, you might want to ask yourself what *you* would do in a similar situation.

CRITO

Plato

Socrates. Dear Crito, your zeal is invaluable, if a right one; but if wrong, the greater the zeal the greater the evil; and therefore we ought to consider whether these things shall be done or not. For I am and always have been one of those natures who must be guided by reason, whatever the reason may be which upon reflection appears to me to be the best; and now that this misfortune has come upon me, I can not put away the

From The Dialogues of Plato (3rd ed.), trans. Benjamin Jowett (London: Oxford University Press, 1892).

reasons which I have before given: the principles which I have hitherto honored and revered I still honor, and unless we can find other and better principles on the instant, I am certain not to agree with you; no, not even if the power of the multitude could inflict many more imprisonments, confiscations, deaths, frightening us like children with hobgoblin terrors. But what will be the fairest way of considering the question? Shall I return to your old argument about the opinions of men? some of which are to be regarded, and others, as we were saying, are not to be regarded. Now were we right in maintaining this before I was condemned? And has the argument which was once good now proved to be talk for the sake of talking;—in fact an amusement only, and altogether vanity? That is what I want to consider with your help, Crito:—whether, under my present circumstances, the argument appears to be in any way different or not; and is to be allowed by me or disallowed. That argument, which, as I believe, is maintained by many who assume to be authorities, was to the effect, as I was saying, that the opinions of some men are to be regarded, and of other men not to be regarded. Now you, Crito, are a disinterested person who are not going to die to-morrow—at least, there is no human probability of this, and you are therefore not liable to be deceived by the circumstances in which you are placed. Tell me then, whether I am right in saying that some opinions, and the opinions of some men only, are to be valued, and other opinions, and the opinions of other men, are not to be valued. I ask you whether I was right in maintaining this?

Crito. Certainly. . . .

Socrates. Very good; and is not this true, Crito, of other things which we need not separately enumerate? In the matter of just and unjust, fair and foul, good and evil, which are the subjects of our present consultation, ought we to follow the opinion of the many and to fear them; or the opinion of the one man who has understanding, and whom we ought to fear and reverence more than all the rest of the world: and whom deserting we shall destroy and injure that principle in us which may be assumed to be improved by justice and deteriorated by injustice;—is there not such a principle?

Crito. Certainly there is, Socrates.

Socrates. Take a parallel instance:—if, acting under the advice of men who have no understanding, we destroy that which is improvable by health and deteriorated by disease—when that has been destroyed, I say, would life be worth having? And that is—the body?

Crito. Yes.

Socrates. Could we live, having an evil and corrupted body?

Crito. Certainly not.

Socrates. And will life be worth having, if that higher part of man be depraved, which is improved by justice and deteriorated by injustice?

Do we suppose that principle, whatever it may be in man, which has to do with justice and injustice, to be inferior to the body?

Crito. Certainly not.

Socrates. More honored, then?

Crito. Far more honored.

Socrates. Then, my friend, we must not regard what the many say of us; but what he, the one man who has understanding of just and unjust, will say, and what the truth will say. And therefore you begin in error when you suggest that we should regard the opinion of the many about just and unjust, good and evil, honorable and dishonorable.—Well, some one will say, "but the many can kill us."

Crito. Yes, Socrates; that will clearly be the answer.

Socrates. That is true: but still I find with surprise that the old argument is, as I conceive, unshaken as ever. And I should like to know whether I may say the same of another proposition—that not life, but a good life, is to be chiefly valued?

Crito. Yes, that also remains.

Socrates. And a good life is equivalent to a just and honorable one— that holds also?

Crito. Yes, that holds.

Socrates. From these premises I proceed to argue the question whether I ought not to try and escape without the consent of the Athenians: and if I am clearly right in escaping, then I will make the attempt; but if not, I will abstain. The other considerations which you mention, of money and loss of character and the duty of educating children, are, as I fear, only the doctrines of the multitude, who would be as ready to call people to life, if they were able, as they are to put them to death— and with as little reason. But now, since the argument has thus far prevailed, the only question which remains to be considered is, whether we shall do rightly either in escaping or in suffering others to aid in our escape and paying them in money and thanks, or whether we shall not do rightly; and if the latter, then death or any other calamity which may ensue on my remaining here must not be allowed to enter into the calculation.

Crito. I think that you are right, Socrates; how then shall we proceed?

Socrates. Let us consider the matter together, and do you either refute me if you can, and I will be convinced; or else cease, my dear friend, from repeating to me that I ought to escape against the wishes of the Athenians: for I am extremely desirous to be persuaded by you, but not against my own better judgment. And now please to consider my first position, and do your best to answer me.

Crito. I will do my best.

Socrates. Are we to say that we are never intentionally to do wrong, or that in one way we ought and in another way we ought not to do wrong, or is doing wrong always evil and dishonorable, as I was just now saying, and as has been already acknowledged by us? Are all our former admissions which were made within a few days to be thrown away? And have we, at our age, been earnestly discoursing with one another all our life long only to discover that we are no better than children? Or are we to rest assured, in spite of the opinion of the many, and in spite of consequences whether better or worse, of the truth of what was then said, that injustice is always an evil and dishonor to him who acts unjustly? Shall we affirm that?

Crito. Yes.

Socrates. Then we must do no wrong?

Crito. Certainly not.

Socrates. Nor when injured injure in return, as the many imagine; for we must injure no one at all?

Crito. Clearly not.

Socrates. Again, Crito, may we do evil?

Crito. Surely not, Socrates.

Socrates. And what of doing evil in return for evil, which is the morality of the many—is that just or not?

Crito. Not just.

Socrates. For doing evil to another is the same as injuring him?

Crito. Very true.

Socrates. Then we ought not to retaliate or render evil for evil to any one, whatever evil we may have suffered from him. But I would have you consider, Crito, whether you really mean what you are saying. For this opinion has never been held, and never will be held, by any considerable number of persons; and those who are agreed and those who are not agreed upon this point have no common ground, and can only despise one another when they see how widely they differ. Tell me, then, whether you agree with and assent to my first principle, that neither injury nor retaliation nor warding off evil by evil is ever right. And shall that be the premiss of our argument? Or do you decline and dissent from this? For this has been of old and is still my opinion; but, if you are of another opinion, let me hear what you have to say. If, however, you remain of the same mind as formerly, I will proceed to the next step.

Crito. You may proceed, for I have not changed my mind.

Socrates. Then I will proceed to the next step, which may be put in the form of a question:—Ought a man to do what he admits to be right, or ought he to betray the right?

Crito. He ought to do what he thinks right.

Socrates. But if this is true, what is the application? In leaving the prison against the will of the Athenians, do I wrong any? or rather do I not wrong those whom I ought least to wrong? Do I not desert the principles which were acknowledged by us to be just? What do you say?

Crito. I can not tell, Socrates; for I do not know.

Socrates. Then consider the matter in this way:—Imagine that I am about to play truant (you may call the proceeding by any name which you like), and the laws and the government come and interrogate me: "Tell us, Socrates," they say; "what are you about? are you going by an act of yours to overturn us—the laws and the whole state, as far as in you lies? Do you imagine that a state can subsist and not be overthrown, in which the decisions of law have no power, but are set aside and overthrown by individuals?" What will be our answer, Crito, to these and the like words? Any one, and especially a clever rhetorician, will have a good deal to urge about the evil of setting aside the law which requires a sentence to be carried out; and we might reply, "Yes; but the state has injured us and given an unjust sentence." Suppose I say that?

Crito. Very good, Socrates.

Socrates. "And was that our agreement with you?" the law would say; "or were you to abide by the sentence of the state?" And if I were to express astonishment at their saying this, the law would probably add: "Answer, Socrates, instead of opening your eyes: you are in the habit of asking and answering questions. Tell us what complaint you have to make against us which justifies you in attempting to destroy us and the state? In the first place did we not bring you into existence? Your father married your mother by our aid and begat you. Say whether you have any objection to urge against those of us who regulate marriage?" None, I should reply. "Or against those of us who regulate the system of nurture and education of children in which you were trained? Were not the laws, who have the charge of this, right in commanding your father to train you in music and gymnastic?" Right, I should reply. "Well then, since you were brought into the world and nurtured and educated by us, can you deny in the first place that you are our child and slave, as your fathers were before you? And if this is true you are not on equal terms with us; nor can you think that you have a right to do to us what we are doing to you. Would you have any right to strike or revile or do any other evil to a father or to your master, if you had one, when you have been struck or reviled by him, or received some other evil at his hands?—you would not say this? And because we think right to destroy you, do you think that you have any right to destroy us in return, and your country as far as in you lies? And will you, O professor of true virtue, say that you are justified in this? Has a philosopher like you failed to discover that our country is more to be valued and higher and holier far than mother or father or any ancestor, and more to be regarded in the eyes of the gods and of

men of understanding? also to be soothed, and gently and reverently en-
treated when angry, even more than a father, and if not persuaded,
obeyed? And when we are punished by her, whether with imprisonment
or stripes, the punishment is to be endured in silence; and if she lead us
to wounds or death in battle, thither we follow as is right; neither may
any one yield or retreat or leave his rank, but whether in battle or in
a court of law, or in any other place, he must do what his city and his
country order him; or he must change their view of what is just: and if
he may do no violence to his father or mother, much less may he do
violence to his country." What answer shall we make to his, Crito? Do the
laws speak truly, or do they not?

Crito. I think that they do.

Socrates. Then the laws will say: "Consider, Socrates, if this is true,
that in your present attempt you are going to do us wrong. For, after
having brought you into the world, and nurtured and educated you, and
given you and every other citizen a share in every good that we had to
give, we further proclaim and give the right to every Athenian, that if
he does not like us when he has come of age and has seen the ways of the
city, and made our acquaintance, he may go where he pleases and take
his goods with him; and none of us laws will forbid him or interfere with
him. Any of you who does not like us and the city, and who wants to
go to a colony or to any other city, may go where he likes, and take his
goods with him. But he who has experience of the manner in which we
order justice and administer the state, and still remains, has entered into
an implied contract that he will do as we command him. And he who
disobeys us is, as we maintain, thrice wrong; first, because in disobeying
us he is disobeying his parents; secondly, because we are the authors of
his education; thirdly, because he has made an agreement with us that
he will duly obey our commands; and he neither obeys them nor convinces
us that our commands are wrong; and we do not rudely impose them, but
give them the alternative of obeying or convincing us;—that is what we
offer, and he does neither. These are the sort of accusations to which, as
we were saying, you, Socrates, will be exposed if you accomplish your
intentions; you, above all other Athenians." Suppose I ask, why is this?
they will justly retort upon me that I above all other men have acknowledged the agreement. "There is clear proof," they will say, "Socrates,
that we and the city were not displeasing to you. Of all Athenians you
have been the most constant resident in the city, which, as you never
leave, you may be supposed to love. For you never went out of the city
either to see the games, except once when you went to the Isthmus, or
to any other place unless you were on military service; nor did you travel
as other men do. Nor had you any curiosity to know other states or their
laws: your affections did not go beyond us and our state; we were your

special favorites, and you acquiesced in our government of you; and this is the state in which you begat your children, which is a proof of your satisfaction. Moreover, you might, if you had liked, have fixed the penalty at banishment in the course of the trial—the state which refuses to let you go now would have let you go then. But you pretended that you preferred death to exile, and that you were not grieved at death. And now you have forgotten these fine sentiments, and pay no respect to us the laws, of whom you are the destroyer; and are doing what only a miserable slave would do, running away and turning your back upon the compacts and agreements which you made as a citizen. And first of all answer this very question: Are we right in saying that you agreed to be governed according to us in deed, and not in word only? Is that true or not?" How shall we answer that, Crito? Must we not agree?

Crito. There is no help, Socrates.

Socrates. Then will they not say: "You, Socrates, are breaking the covenants and agreements which you made with us at your leisure, not in any haste or under any compulsion or deception, but having had seventy years to think of them, during which time you were at liberty to leave the city, if we were not to your mind, or if our covenants appeared to you to be unfair. You had your choice, and might have gone either to Lacedaemon or Crete, which you often praise for their good government, or to some other Hellenic or foreign state. Whereas you, above all other Athenians, seemed to be so fond of the state, or, in other words, of us her laws (for who would like a state that has no laws), that you never stirred out of her; the halt, the blind, the maimed were not more stationary in her than you were. And now you run away and forsake your agreements. Not so, Socrates, if you will take our advice; do not make yourself ridiculous by escaping out of the city. . . ."

Morality was, of course, going on in the world long before Socrates and the advent of ethical theory. In a more or less unreflective form, perhaps closely associated with myth, religion, and taboo, it must have been in existence from the time men began to live in groups. Even after people started to think philosophically, a great deal of relatively unreflective morality continued to exist and to guide human conduct, even in so-called advanced cultures, as it still does. In fact, it is interesting to ask if it would be desirable that such unreflective morality disappear entirely, or if that is even possible.

In the Bible, as traditionally interpreted, morality is typically represented as divinely instituted, once in the Ten Commandments and again in the Law of Love, and is thought of as a matter either of divine command or of divine revelation. Even in the Judeo-Christian tradition, however, there was a recognition that morality was not entirely dependent on such special divine acts, but was to some extent something that men would naturally develop. Thus St. Paul wrote, "When Gentiles who do not possess the law carry out its precepts by the light of nature, then, although they have no law, they are their own law, for they display the effect of the law inscribed on their hearts" (Romans 2:14–15). This suggests that morality is the work of something natural in man, possibly the expression of an innate knowledge of right and wrong.

In a great myth ascribed to him by Plato, the Sophist Protagoras, who was an older contemporary of Socrates, gives his account of the origin of morality. If his account is interpreted literally, then he is thinking of morality as a special gift of the gods given to man sometime after his coming into the world. But Protagoras was a skeptic about religion and so could hardly have meant his story to be taken literally; it also seems clear that he thinks of morality not as somehow innate in man, but rather as something discovered or invented by him. In any case, his myth contains a very interesting view about the function of, and the necessity of man's having, morality and law in addition to the other arts and sciences. The account of morality implied in the myth of Protagoras is, of course, not the only one which has been given by philosophers. A rather different one, for example, is contained in the writings of Friedrich Nietzsche, some of which are included in Chapter 3.

PROTAGORAS

Plato

Once upon a time there were gods only, and no mortal creatures. But when the time came that these also should be created, the gods fashioned them out of earth and fire and various mixtures of both elements in the interior of the earth; and when they were about to bring them into the light of day, they ordered Prometheus and Epimetheus to equip them, and to distribute to them severally their proper qualities. Epimetheus said to Prometheus: "Let me distribute, and do you inspect." This was agreed, and Epimetheus made the distribution. There were some to whom he gave strength without swiftness, while he equipped the weaker with swiftness; some he armed, and others he left unarmed; and devised for the latter some other means of preservation, making some large, and having their size as a protection, and others small, whose nature was to fly in the air or burrow in the ground; this was to be their way of escape. Thus did he compensate them with the view of preventing any race from becoming extinct. And when he had provided against their destruction by one another, he contrived also a means of protecting them against the seasons of heaven; clothing them with close hair and thick skins sufficient to defend them against the winter cold and able to resist

From The Dialogues of Plato (3rd ed.), trans. Benjamin Jowett (London: Oxford University Press, 1892).

the summer heat, so that they might have a natural bed of their own when they wanted to rest; also he furnished them with hoofs and hair and hard and callous skins under their feet. Then he gave them varieties of food,—herb of the soil to some, to others fruits of trees, and to others roots, and to some again he gave other animals as food. And some he made to have few young ones, while those who were their prey were very prolific; and in this manner the race was preserved. Thus did Epimetheus, who, not being very wise, forgot that he had distributed among the brute animals all the qualities which he had to give,—and when he came to man, who was still unprovided, he was terribly perplexed. Now while he was in this perplexity, Prometheus came to inspect the distribution, and he found that the other animals were suitably furnished, but that man alone was naked and shoeless, and had neither bed nor arms of defence. The appointed hour was approaching when man in his turn was to go forth into the light of day; and Prometheus, not knowing how he could devise his salvation, stole the mechanical arts of Hephaestus and Athene, and fire with them (they could neither have been acquired nor used without fire), and gave them to man. Thus man had the wisdom necessary to the support of life, but political wisdom he had not; for that was in the keeping of Zeus, and the power of Prometheus did not extend to entering into the citadel of heaven, where Zeus dwelt, who moreover had terrible sentinels; but he did enter by stealth into the common workshop of Athene and Hephaestus, in which they used to practise their favourite arts, and carried off Hephaestus' art of working by fire, and also the art of Athene, and gave them to man. And in this way man was supplied with the means of life. But Prometheus is said to have been afterwards prosecuted for theft, owing to the blunder of Epimetheus.

Now man, having a share of the divine attributes, was at first the only one of the animals who had any gods, because he alone was of their kindred; and he would raise altars and images of them. He was not long in inventing articulate speech and names; and he also constructed houses and clothes and shoes and beds, and drew sustenance from the earth. Thus provided, mankind at first lived dispersed, and there were no cities. But the consequence was that they were destroyed by the wild beasts, for they were utterly weak in comparison of them, and their art was only sufficient to provide them with the means of life, and did not enable them to carry on war against the animals: food they had, but not as yet the art of government, of which the art of war is a part. After a while the desire of self-preservation gathered them into cities; but when they were gathered together, having no art of government, they . . . treated one another [evilly] and were again in process of dispersion and destruction. Zeus feared that the entire race would be exterminated, and so he sent Hermes to them, bearing reverence and justice to be the ordering principles of cities and the bonds of friendship and conciliation. Hermes asked Zeus how he should impart justice and reverence among men:—Should he distribute them as the arts are distributed; that is to say, to a favoured few only, one skilled individual having enough of medicine or of any other art for many unskilled ones? "Shall this be the manner in which I am to distribute justice and reverence among men, or shall I give them to all?" "To all," said Zeus; "I should like them all to have a share; for cities cannot exist, if a few only share in the virtues, as in the arts. . . ."

Whether we think of morality as divinely instituted, as expressing an innate faculty in man, or as something discovered or invented by him—and we will encounter all three of these views again—we may think of it as taking different forms or as having different stages—in the life of mankind, in the life of an individual, or in both. It is, in fact, very common for philosophers, psychologists, and social scientists to hold that, both in the history of man and in that of an individual, morality has or may have two forms or stages, one a relatively unreflective, custom or society-directed, heteronomous kind of morality, the other a more reflective, self-directed, or autonomous kind. In the passage that follows, John Dewey (who would agree with Protagoras about the origin and function of morality, except for regarding it as less fixed) adopts this picture of the forms or stages of morality and proceeds to show how moral theory or philosophy arises, and how it is related to moral practice. Incidentally, he indicates the place of Socrates in the rise of moral theory, and he distinguishes two kinds of moral conflict (anticipating Lemmon), and takes the question of fighting for one's country as an example of one of them (anticipating Broad). He also explains why we need moral theory, especially today (though he wrote in 1908), and how it can help us.

Ask yourself when you read Dewey exactly how is it that moral philosophy is claimed to arise out of customary morality? Do you think Dewey gives a plausible account of what moral theory can and cannot do?

REFLECTIVE MORALITY AND ETHICAL THEORY

John Dewey

The intellectual distinction between customary and reflective morality is clearly marked. The former places the standard and rules of conduct in ancestral habit; the latter appeals to conscience, reason, or to some principle which includes thought. The distinction is as important as it is definite, for it shifts the center of gravity in morality. Nevertheless the distinction is relative rather than absolute. Some degree of reflective thought must have entered occasionally into systems which in the main were founded on social wont and use, while in contemporary morals, even when the need of critical judgment is most recognized, there is an immense amount of conduct that is merely accommodated to social usage. In what follows we shall, accordingly, emphasize the difference in *principle* between customary and reflective morals rather than try to describe different historic and social epochs. In principle a revolution was wrought when Hebrew prophets and Greek seers asserted that conduct is not truly conduct unless it springs from the heart, from personal desires and affections, or from personal insight and rational choice.

The change was revolutionary not only because it displaced custom from the supreme position, but even more because it entailed the necessity of criticizing existing customs and institutions from a new point of view. Standards which were regarded by the followers of tradition as the basis of duty and responsibility were denounced by prophet and philosopher as the source of moral corruption. These proclaimed the hollowness of outer conformity and insisted upon the cleansing of the heart and the clarifying of the mind as preconditions of any genuinely good conduct.

One great source of the abiding interest which Greek thought has for the western world is that it records so clearly the struggle to make the transition from customary to reflective conduct. In the Platonic dialogues for example Socrates is represented as constantly raising the question of whether morals can be taught. Some other thinker (like Protagoras in the dialogue of that name) is brought in who points out that habituation to existing moral traditions is actually taught. Parents and teachers constantly admonish the young "pointing out that one act is just, another unjust; one honorable and another dishonorable; one holy and another unholy." When a youth emerges from parental tutelage, the State takes up the task, for "the community compels them to learn laws and to live after the pattern of the laws and not according to their own fancies."

In reply, Socrates raises the question of the foundations of such teaching, of its right to be termed a genuine teaching of virtue, and in effect points out the need of a morality which shall be stable and secure because based upon constant and universal principles. Parents and teachers differ in their injunctions and prohibitions; different communities have different laws; the same community changes its habits with time and with transformations of government? How shall we know who among the teachers, whether individuals or States, is right? Is there no basis for morals except this fluctuating one? It is not enough to praise and blame, reward and punish, enjoin and prohibit. The essence of morals, it is implied, is to know the reason for these customary instructions; to ascertain the criterion which insures their being just. And in other dialogues, it is frequently asserted that even if the mass must follow custom and law without insight, those who make laws and fix customs should have sure insight into enduring principles, or else the blind will be leading the blind.

No fundamental difference exists between systematic moral theory . . . and the reflection an individual engages in when he attempts to find general principles which shall direct and justify his conduct. Moral theory begins, in germ, when any one asks "Why should I act thus and not otherwise? Why is this right and that wrong? What right has any one to frown upon this way of acting and impose that other way?" Children make at least a start upon the road of theory when they assert that the injunctions of elders are arbitrary, being simply a matter of superior position. Any adult enters the road when, in the presence of moral perplexity, of doubts as to what it is right or best to do, he attempts to find his way out through reflection which will lead him to some principle he regards as dependable.

Moral theory cannot emerge when there is positive belief as to what is right and what is wrong, for then there is no occasion for reflection. It emerges when men are confronted with situations in which different desires promise opposed goods and in which incompatibles courses of action seem to be morally justified. Only such a conflict of good ends and of standards and rules of right and wrong calls forth personal inquiry into the bases of morals. A critical juncture may occur when a person, for example, goes from a protected home life into the stress of competitive business, and finds that moral standards which apply in one do not hold in the other. Unless he merely drifts, accommodating himself to whatever social pressure is uppermost, he will feel the conflict. If he tries to face it in thought, he will search for a reasonable principle by which to decide where the right really lies. In so doing he enters into the domain of moral theory, even if he does so unwittingly.

For what is called moral theory is but a more conscious and systematic raising of the question which occupies the mind of any one who in the face of moral conflict and doubt seeks a way out through reflection. In short, moral theory is but an extension of what is involved in all reflective morality. There are two kinds of moral struggle. One kind, and that the most emphasized in moral writings and lectures, is the conflict which takes place when an individual is tempted to do something which he is convinced is wrong. Such instances are important practically in the life of an individual, but they are not the occasion of moral theory. The employee of a bank who is tempted to embezzle funds may indeed try to argue himself into finding reasons why it would not be wrong for him to do it. But in such a case, he is not really thinking, but merely permitting his desire to govern his beliefs. There is no sincere doubt in his mind as to what he should do when he seeks to find some justification for what he has made up his mind to do.

Take, on the other hand, the case of a citizen of a nation which has just declared war on another country. He is deeply attached to his own State. He has formed habits of loyalty and of abiding by its laws, and now one of its decrees is that he shall support war. He feels in addition gratitude and affection for the country which has sheltered and nurtured him. But he believes that this war is unjust, or perhaps he has a conviction that all war is a form of murder and hence wrong. One side of his nature, one set of convictions and habits, leads him to acquiesce in war; another deep part of his being protests. He is torn between two duties: he experiences a conflict between the incompatible values presented to him by his habits of citizenship and by his religious beliefs respectively. Up to this time, he has never experienced a struggle between the two; they have coincided and reënforced one another. Now he has to make a choice between competing moral loyalties and convictions. The struggle is not between a good which is clear to him and something else which attracts him but which he knows to be wrong. It is between values each of which is an undoubted good in its place but which now get in each other's way. He is forced to reflect in order to come to a decision. Moral theory is a generalized extension of the kind of thinking in which he now engages.

There are periods in history when a whole community or a group in a community finds itself in the presence of new issues which its old customs do not adequately meet. The habits and beliefs which were formed in the past do not fit into the opportunities and requirements of the contemporary life. The age in Greece following the time of Pericles was of this sort; that of the Jews after their captivity; that following the Middle Ages when secular interests on a large scale were introduced into previous religious and ecclesiastic interests; the present is preëminently a period of this sort with the vast social changes which have followed the industrial expansion of the machine age.

Realization that the need for reflective morality and for moral theories grows out of conflict between ends, responsibilities, rights, and duties defines the service which moral theory may render, and also protects the student from false conceptions of its nature. The difference between customary and reflective morality is precisely that definite precepts, rules, definitive injunctions and prohibitions issue from the former, while they cannot proceed from the latter. Confusion ensues when appeal to rational principles is treated as if it were merely a substitute for custom, transferring the authority of moral commands from one source to another. Moral theory can (i) generalize the types of moral conflicts which arise, thus enabling a perplexed and doubtful individual to clarify his own particular problem by placing it in a larger context; it can (ii) state the leading ways in which such problems have been intellectually dealt with by those who have thought upon such matters; it can (iii) render personal reflection more systematic and enlightened, suggesting alternatives that might otherwise be overlooked, and stimulating greater consistency in judgment. But it does not offer a table of commandments in a catechism in which answers are as definite as are the questions which are asked. It can render personal choice more intelligent, but it cannot take the place of personal decision, which must be made in every case of moral perplexity. Such at least is the standpoint of the discussions which follow; the student who expects more from moral theory will be disappointed. The conclusion follows from the very nature of reflective morality; the attempt to set up ready-made conclusions contradicts the very nature of reflective morality. . . .

We have already noted in passing that the present time is one which is in peculiar need of reflective morals and of a working theory of morals. The scientific outlook on the world and on life has undergone and is still undergoing radical change. Methods of industry, of the production, and distribution of goods have been completely transformed. The basic conditions on which men meet and associate, in work and amusement, have been altered. There has been a vast dislocation of older habits and traditions. Travel and migration are as common as they were once unusual. The masses are educated enough to read and a prolific press exists which supplies cheap reading matter. Schooling has ceased to be the privilege of the few and has become the right and even the enforced duty of the many. The stratification of society into classes each fairly homogeneous in itself has been broken into. The area of contacts with persons and populations alien to our bringing up and traditions has enormously extended. A ward of a large city in the United States may have persons of from a score to fifty racial origins. The walls and barriers that once separated nations have become less important because of the railway, steamship, telegraph, telephone, and radio.

Only a few of the more obvious changes in social conditions and interests have been mentioned. Each one of them has created new problems and issues that contain moral values which are uncertain and disputed. Nationalism and internationalism, capital and labor, war and peace, science and religious tradition, competition and coöperation, *laissez faire* and State planning in industry, democracy and dictatorship in government, rural and city life, personal work and control *versus* investment and vicarious riches through stocks and bonds, native born and alien, contact of Jew and Gentile, of white and colored, of Catholic and Protestant, and those of new religions: a multitude of such relationships have brought to the fore new moral problems with which neither old customs nor beliefs are competent to cope. In addition, the rapidity with which social changes occur brings moral unsettlement and tends to destroy many ties which were the chief safeguards of the morals of custom. There was never a time in the history of the world when human relationships and their accompanying rights and duties, opportunities and demands, needed the unremitting and systematic attention of intelligent thought as they do at present.

Dewey claims that moral philosophy arises if and when we are faced in practice with troubling moral problems, and he distinguishes two kinds of such problems. In the next essay, John Lemmon distinguishes and studies five types of difficult moral situations. What he does is a nice example of one of the things Dewey says moral theory can do: generalize the types of moral conflicts and thus enable an individual to clarify his own problem by placing it in a larger context. Lemmon also does something to help us to see a way out of these dilemmas if there is one. His discussion of Sartre is worth noting for future use, as are his distinctions between "duty," "obligation," "right," and "ought." It should be observed here that philosophers do not always distinguish these terms as Lemmon does; in fact, they often use them as synonyms, as Broad does in the selection following Lemmon's.

Some questions to ask yourself: In which of Lemmon's various types of moral dilemmas does Socrates find himself in the Crito? How helpful do you find Lemmon's own account of how moral dilemmas (especially of the third sort) are to be resolved? Lemmon's fourth and fifth types of moral dilemmas are serious moral crises which he thinks are rather rare. "There may well be people who have never had to face a moral situation of these dimensions," he writes. Have you, or has anyone close to you, ever faced such a situation? If so, how closely does your experience fit Lemmon's observations?

MORAL DILEMMAS

John Lemmon

In this paper, I attempt to characterize different varieties of moral dilemma. An assumption made throughout is that an affirmative answer can be given to the question: does a human being have free will? With-

From The Philosophical Review, *LXXI (1962). Reprinted by permission of* The Philosophical Review *and Patricia M. Gould.*

out this assumption, in fact, there does not seem to be much for ethics to be about.

There are very many different kinds of moral situation in which a human agent can find himself or put himself. Without making any pretense of defining the distinction between moral and nonmoral situations, let us merely list some kinds of situation which it would be generally agreed can safely be called moral. I shall begin with the most straightforward and gradually move into areas which could be described as "dilemmatic."

1. The first, and it seems the simplest, class of moral situation is this: we know what we are to do, or have to do, or ought to do, and simply do it. Within this class, there are several subclasses, which it will be worth our while to distinguish, depending on the source of our knowledge of what we are to do. What sources are distinguished may well depend on the society to which the agent in question belongs. Thus, if I may stray, like so many philosophers, into the sociology of ethics for a while, our own society tends to distinguish such sources as duties, obligations, and moral principles (Classical Greek society, if we may go by its language, does not seem to have made a clear distinction between obligation and duty). For example, a soldier may receive a battle order, and act on it directly, because he knows that it is his *duty as a soldier* so to do. Or a man may know he is to attend a certain meeting, and do so, because, having given his word that he will be there, he is *under an obligation* to attend. Or a man may know that he ought to tell the truth, and do so, because he holds as a *moral principle* that one should always tell the truth—a slightly unrealistic example, since moral principles tend to be prohibitive rather than compelling: a better example would be that of a man who knows he is not to commit adultery with a certain woman, and does not do so, because he holds it to be a moral ruling that one should at no time commit adultery.

To summarize these three subcases: first, one may know what one is to do, and do it, because one knows it to be one's duty to do that thing; second, one may know what one is to do, and do it, because one knows oneself to be under an obligation to do that thing; third, one may know what one is to do, and do it, because one holds it to be the right thing to do in view of some moral rule.

It follows logically, I would wish to claim, that a man ought to do something, if it is his duty to do that thing. Equally, he ought to do it if he is under an obligation to do it, and he ought to do it if it is right, in view of some moral principle to which he subscribes, that he should do it. But the converse implications do not, I think, hold. It might be true that a man ought to do something, and yet it not be his duty to do it, because rather it is the case that he is under an obligation to do it; or, even though he ought to do it, he is under no obligation to do it, but rather it is his duty to do it; or, even though he ought to do it, it is not that it is right to do it in view of some moral principle which he holds, but rather a case of duty or obligation.

To see that these converse implications fail, it will be necessary to take a closer look at our (rather parochial) concepts of duty and obligation. A man's duties are closely related to his special status or position. It nearly always makes sense to ask of a duty "duty *as what?*" The most straightforward case is that of duties incurred in virtue of a job: thus one has duties as a policeman, duties as headmaster, duties as prime minister or garbage-collector. In many societies, family relationships are recognized as determining duties: thus there are duties as a father, mother, son, or daughter. Less clearly delineated duties, in our society at least, are those of a host, those of a friend, those of a citizen. I do not think there are such things as one's duties as a human being, unless they be duties toward dogs or other members of the animal kingdom, for being a human being is not being in any special or distinguishing position, unless it is vis-à-vis dogs perhaps. The same point emerges from the adjective "dutiful." A dutiful X is someone who does his duties *as an X*; a dutiful parent is one who does his duty as a parent. No clear sense attaches to the phrase "a dutiful bachelor," at least in our society, for the status of bachelor is not thought of as bringing with it certain duties.

If duties are related to a special position or status, which distinguishes the man holding the position or status from others, obligations on the other hand are typically incurred by previous committing actions. Of course, again what actions are regarded as committal will vary from society to society. To us, the most familiar committing actions are promising or giving one's word generally, and signing one's signature. If you swear to tell the truth, from the moment of swearing you are under an obligation to tell the truth. If you promise to attend a meeting, then from that moment you are under an obligation to attend a meeting. If you sign your name to an I. O. U., then from that moment you are under an obligation to return the borrowed money. Less clearly delineated cases of obligations, at least in our society, are the obligation to return hospitality having received it and the obligation to give money to a beggar having been asked for it. This last case illustrates a concept which has relatively rare application for us—that of being put under an obligation to someone by their conduct rather than one's own. In certain societies, I believe, a knock on the door of one's house by a stranger at once puts one under an obligation of a firm kind to provide hospitality and, if necessary, a bed for the night.

If this admittedly sketchy analysis of the notions of duty and obligation is at all correct, it becomes easy to see how a man can be under an obligation to do something, though it is not his duty to do it, or how a man's duty may be to do something though he is under no obligation to do it. For example, it may be true that I ought to vote against a Communist candidate in some election, because it is my duty as a citizen to do this, though there is no clear sense in which I am under an obligation to vote against the Communist (I have made no promises, accepted no bribes, given my word in advance to no one). On the other hand, it could easily be that I am, in a different situation, under an obligation to vote against the Communist just because I have given my word that I shall do so, even though it may not in fact be my duty to do so. This is not, of course, to deny that we may both be under an obligation and have it as a duty to do something. For example, in the witness stand it is my duty as a witness to tell the truth, and I am also under an obligation to tell the truth since I have sworn an oath to do so.

An interesting borderline case between obligation and duty, which when properly understood helps, I think, to mark the watershed between them, is the following. Children are often thought to be under some kind of obligation to help their parents in old age, and it is often thought that it is their duty to do so. Is this more properly to be considered a case of obligation or a case of duty? I suggest that we can consider it both ways, but that thinking of it one way is different from thinking of it the other way. If we regard it as a duty to help our parents, we are thinking rather of our special relationship to them, our status as children. If, on the other hand, we think of ourselves as under an obligation to our parents, it is surely in virtue of what they have done for us in the past, when we were children, that we are under this obligation—that is, it will be a case of our having been put under an obligation in some way by them. This difference in the mode of thought becomes clear if we vary the example slightly. Suppose they turn out to be not parents but foster parents. Then we may well feel that our duty is less because the relationship is less close, but our sense of obligation may be no less great in view of what they have done for us. On the other hand, if our parents have not in point of fact done a great deal for us, we may feel in no sense under any obligation to help them, but our sense of duty may be just as real because of our close relationship with them.

Broadly speaking, then, duty-situations are status-situations while obligation-situations are contractual situations. Both duties and obligations may be sources of "ought's," but they are logically independent sources. And a third source, independent of the other two, is that it is right to do something in view of a moral principle. I have not discussed this here because it is well discussed in almost all contemporary ethical writing, while the concepts of duty and obligation tend to be neglected.

I shall not in fact be very disturbed to learn that there are aspects of the concept of duty or the concept of obligation which I have omitted, or even that I have missed either concept's most central aspect, as we have it. My main concern is rather that there are generically different ways in which it can come to be true that we ought to do something or ought not to do something. While "ought" is a very general word of ethical involvement, "duty" and "obligation" and "right," as I am using them at least, are highly specialized words. . . .

2. A second, slightly more complex, class of ethical situations in which agents find themselves may be described thus: we may know what we are to do, or ought to do, or have to do, and yet in various ways be tempted not to do it, and as a result either do or not do what we are or ought to do, either out of a conscious decision or not. This class includes as a subclass those cases commonly called cases of acrasia, where we know what we ought to do and for various reasons and in various ways fail to do it. There is a clear sense in which all examples in this second class of moral situation are dilemmatic. We are, as we often say, torn between duty and pleasure, or between our obligations and our interests, or between our principles and our desires. Nonetheless, I do not wish to call these cases *moral* dilemmas, because in all these cases our moral situation is perfectly clear. We know where our duties lie or what our obligations are or what our moral principles determine for us here, but for various *non*-moral reasons are tempted not to stick with morality.

It might be as well to say a little here about the so-called problem of acrasia. Some philosophers, notably Aristotle, have found it difficult to explain how someone could know what he ought to do and still not do it. Socrates appears to have adopted the position that acrasia did not occur—that is, if a man acts contrary to what he should do, this can only be because he does not know what he should do, is mistaken or deluded about what he should do, and the like. . . . Of Socrates we can say that as a plain matter of fact he was just wrong—acrasia does occur, or, in Aristotle's phrase, knowledge just is, however sad this may be, frequently dragged about by desire. . . .

3. It is well past time to reach the main topic of this paper. My third class of moral situation constitutes what I take to be the simplest variety of moral dilemma in the full sense. The characterization of this class is as follows: a man both ought to do something and ought not to do that thing. Here is a simple example, borrowed from Plato. A

friend leaves me with his gun, saying that he will be back for it in the evening, and I promise to return it when he calls. He arrives in a distraught condition, demands his gun, and announces that he is going to shoot his wife because she has been unfaithful. I ought to return the gun, since I promised to do so—a case of obligation. And yet I ought not to do so, since to do so would be to be indirectly responsible for a murder, and my moral principles are such that I regard this as wrong. I am in an extremely straightforward moral dilemma, evidently resolved by not returning the gun.

The description of this class of cases may perhaps cause alarm; for it may well be thought to be contradictory that a man both ought and ought not to do something. . . . It seems to me that "ought" and "ought not" may well both be true, and that this description in fact characterizes a certain class of moral dilemma. Indeed, the Platonic example cited would not be a dilemma at all unless it was true that the man both ought to return the gun and ought not to return it. It is a nasty fact about human life that we sometimes both ought and ought not to do things; but it is not a logical contradiction.

My motive for carefully distinguishing some of the sources for "ought's" earlier in this paper should now be apparent. For moral dilemmas of the sort we are at present considering will appear generally in the cases where these sources conflict. Our duty may conflict with our obligations, our duty may conflict with our moral principles, or our obligations may conflict with our moral principles. The Platonic case was an example of a conflict between principle and obligation. A simple variant illustrates a conflict between obligation and duty; the man with whom the gun is deposited may regard it as his duty as a friend not to return the gun, even though he is under an obligation to do so. And duty conflicts with principle every time that we are called on in our jobs to do things which we find morally repugnant.

A natural question to ask next is: how are moral dilemmas of this simple kind to be resolved? There are certain very simple resolutions, known from the philosophical literature, which we should discuss first; but I do not think they are in practice very common. First, we may hold to some very sweeping "higher-order principle" such as "Always prefer duty to obligation" or "Always follow moral principles before duty or obligation." This last precept, for example, at once resolves the Platonic dilemma mentioned earlier, which, as I described it, was a simple clash between principle and obligation. Secondly, and rather less simply, we may have in advance a complex ordering of our various duties, obligations, and the like—putting, for example, our duties as a citizen before our duties as a friend and our duties as a friend before any obligations we may have incurred—in virtue of which the moral dilemma is resolved. But dilemmas in which we are morally prepared, in which we, as it were, merely have to look up the solution in our private ethical code, are rare, I think, and in any case of little practical interest. Of greater importance are those dilemmas in this class where some decision of a moral character is required. And here it must be remembered that the failure to make a decision in one sense is itself to make a decision in another, broader, sense. For our predicament is here so described that, whatever we do, even if we do nothing at all (whatever that might mean), we are doing something which we ought not to do, and so can be called upon to justify either our activity or our inactivity. The only way we can avoid a decision is by ceasing to be any longer an agent (e.g., if we are arrested, or taken prisoner, or kidnapped, or die). This precise situation leads to [a] familiar pattern of bad faith, in which we pretend to ourselves either that no decision is called for or that in one way or another the decision has been taken out of our hands by others or that we are simply the victims of our own character in acting in this way or that, that we cannot help doing what we do do and so cannot be reproached for resolving the dilemma in this way or that. If, however, we are to act here in good faith, we shall recognize that the dilemma is what it is and make the best decision we can.

Now what kind of considerations may or should affect the decision? The situation is such that no moral, or at least purely moral, considerations are relevant, in the sense that no appeal to our own given morality can decide the issue. We may of course consult a friend, take moral advice, find out what others have done in similar situations, appeal as it were to precedent. But again none of these appeals will be decisive —we still have to decide to act in accordance with advice or precedent. Or again we may approach our decision by a consideration of ends— which course of action will, so far as we can see, lead to the best result. (I do not think it is an accident, by the way, that the word "good," or rather its superlative "best," makes its first appearance at this point in our discussion; for it is typically when we are torn between courses of conduct that the question of comparing different actions arises, and hence the word "good," a comparative adjective unlike "right," is at home here; the consequence, admittedly paradoxical, of this view of "good" is that it is not properly a word of moral appraisal at all, despite the vast attention it receives from ethical philosophers; and I think I accept this conclusion.) Thus a consideration of ends determines a solution to the Platonic dilemma discussed earlier. Although I ought to return the gun and also ought not to return the gun, in fact it is evidently best, when we weigh up the expected outcome, not to return the gun, and so to sacrifice one's obligation to utilitarian considerations. Of

course, when I say that this solution is evidently the best, I do not mean
that it cannot be questioned. What I do mean is that it can only be
seriously questioned by someone whose whole attitude toward human
life is basically different from that of a civilized western human being.
Someone who thinks that it would really be better to return the gun
must either hold the importance of a man's giving his word to be fan-
tastically high or else hold human life to be extremely cheap, and I
regard both these attitudes as morally primitive.

4. I shall pass on now to the next, more complex, class of moral
situations which might be described as dilemmatic in the full sense.
Roughly, the class I now have in mind may be described thus: there
is some, but not conclusive, evidence that one ought to do something,
and there is some, but not conclusive, evidence that one ought not to do
that thing.[1] All the difficulties that arose in the way of making a decision
in the last class of cases arise typically here too, but there are now
difficulties of a new kind as well. Moreover, in this class of cases there
can be no preassigned moral solution to the dilemma in virtue of higher-
order principles or a given ordering of one's duties and obligations and
the like, because part of the very dilemma is just one's uncertainty as
to one's actual moral situation, one's situation with respect to duties,
obligations, and principles. For example, it may be unclear whether it
really is one's duty as a citizen to vote against the Communist candidate, and also unclear whether one is under an obligation to vote for
the Communist candidate in view, let us say, of financial help received
from the Communists in the Resistance during the war. Hence one is
in a moral dilemma because there is some evidence that one should vote
Communist and some that one should not, though in neither case is the
evidence conclusive.

A good illustration of the kind of complexity this type of situation
may embrace is . . . from Sartre:

> I will refer to the case of a pupil of mine who sought me out in the follow-
> ing circumstances. His father was quarrelling with his mother and was also
> inclined to be a "collaborator"; his elder brother had been killed in the
> German offensive of 1940 and this young man, with a sentiment somewhat
> primitive but generous, burned to avenge him. His mother was living alone
> with him, deeply afflicted by the semitreason of his father and by the death
> of her oldest son, and her one consolation was in this young man. But he,
> at this moment, had the choice between going to England to join the Free
> French Forces or of staying near his mother and helping her to live. He

---

[1] At this point we bid farewell to the deontological mapping of moral concepts
on which we have partially relied up to now. The new area is not charted enough for
that and perhaps should not be charted in that way at all.

fully realized that this woman lived only for him and that his disappearance—or perhaps his death—would plunge her into despair. He also realized that, concretely and in fact, every action he performed on his mother's behalf would be sure of effect in the sense of aiding her to live, whereas anything he did in order to go and fight would be an ambiguous action which might vanish like water into sand and serve no purpose. For instance, to set out for England he would have to wait indefinitely in a Spanish camp on the way through Spain; or, on arriving in England or in Algiers he might be put into an office to fill up forms. Consequently, he found himself confronted by two very different modes of action; the one concrete, immediate, but directed towards only one individual; the other an action addressed to an end infinitely greater, a national collectivity, but for that reason ambiguous—and it might be frustrated on the way. At the same time, he was hesitating between two kinds of morality; on the one side, the morality of sympathy, of personal devotion and, on the other side, a morality of wider scope but of more debatable validity. He had to choose between these two.[2]

A crude oversimplification of this example might depict it thus: the boy is under some obligation to stay with his mother; or, perhaps better, his mother by her own position has put him under some obligation to stay with her, since she is now dependent on him for her own happiness. Consequently, he is conscious in some degree that he ought to stay with her. On the other hand he feels some kind of duty to join the Free French in England—a duty perhaps to his country as a citizen. But this duty is far from being clearly given; as Sartre stresses, it is felt only ambiguously. It may be his duty to fight, but can it really be his duty, given his obligation to his mother, to sit in an office filling out forms? He is morally torn, but each limb of the moral dilemma is not itself here clearly delineated.

An interesting feature of this case, and of the class of cases in general which we are considering, is that, in attempting to reach a decision, the arguments which try to establish exactly what one's moral situation is are not distinguishable from those which attempt to resolve the dilemma itself. Thus the boy is unclear where his duty lies partly because he is unclear what exactly would be the outcome of his decision to leave his mother, and this outcome is also relevant to the decision itself, as a utilitarian consideration affecting his choice.

Sartre's example has an important further feature, which marks out a particular subclass of the class of moral dilemmas in general: the dilemma is so grave a one, personally speaking, that either decision in effect marks the adoption on the part of the agent of a changed moral outlook. It does not seem to have been much observed by ethical

---

[2] Sartre, *Existentialism and Humanism*, trans. by P. Mairet (London, 1948), pp. 35–36.

philosophers that, speaking psychologically, the adoption of a new morality by an agent is frequently associated with the confrontation of a moral dilemma. Indeed, it is hard to see what else would be likely to bring about a change of moral outlook other than the having to make a difficult moral decision. On the nature of such a change there is time here only to say a few things. First, the change frequently and always in serious cases is associated with a change in fundamental attitudes, such as the change from liberalism to conservatism in politics or the change from Christianity to atheism in the field of religion. And the reasons given for the moral change may well be identical with the reasons given for the change in fundamental attitudes. This last kind of change is neither fully rational nor fully irrational. To persuade someone to change his fundamental attitudes is like getting someone to see an aesthetic point—to appreciate classical music or impressionist painting, for example. Arguments can be given, features of music or painting may be drawn to the person's attention, and so on and so forth, but none of these reasons is finally conclusive. Nonetheless, we should not rush to the opposite conclusion that matters of aesthetic taste are purely subjective. In a somewhat similar way we may persuade someone, or he may persuade himself, to change his fundamental attitudes, and so to change his moral outlook, at a time of moral crisis. Roughly speaking, Sartre's boy has to decide whether to be politically engaged or not, and this decision may well affect and be affected by his fundamental attitudes.

I am not at all saying that this kind of serious case is common; indeed, I think it is rare; but it is still of the greatest importance to ethics to investigate it, because it is of the greatest practical importance in a man's life. There may well be people who have never had to face a moral situation of these dimensions. But for Antigones and others who live faced with occasional major crises, the appropriate reasoning for this kind of moral dilemma is of vital importance. On the other hand, it is not at all clear what the role of the philosopher should be here. If we listen to much of contemporary ethical writing, his role is merely to analyze the discourse in which such reasoning is couched; the task of deciding what are good and what are bad ethical arguments belongs to someone else, though it is never quite made clear to whom. It is my own view that, even though it may be part and an important part of the philosopher's job to analyze the terminology of ethical arguments, his job does not stop there. Perhaps no one is properly equipped to give moral advice to anyone else, but if anyone is it is the philosopher, who at least may be supposed to be able to detect bad reasoning from good. It is a corollary of this view that a philosopher is not entitled to a private life—by which I mean that it is his duty to hold political and

religious convictions in such a form as to be philosophically defensible
or not to hold them at all. He is not entitled to hold such beliefs in the
way in which many nonphilosophers hold them, as mere articles of faith.

5. After this brief digression, I must return to my classification of
moral dilemmas: for there is one more kind that, with some hesitation,
I should like to introduce. This is an even more extreme kind of dilemma
than the last and probably of even rarer occurrence. I mean the kind
of situation in which an agent has to make a decision of a recognizably
moral character though he is completely unprepared for the situation
by his present moral outlook. This case differs from the last in that
there the question was rather of the applicability of his moral outlook
to his present situation, while here the question is rather how to create
a new moral outlook to meet unprecedented moral needs. This case is
in some respects easier for the agent and in some respects harder to
face than the last: easier, if he recognizes the situation for what it is,
because he at least knows that for sure he had some basic moral rethinking to do, which is often not clear in the previous case; but harder,
because basic moral rethinking is harder work in general than settling
the applicability of given moral principles to a particular situation. A
typical, but morally wrong, way of escape from this dilemma is again
to act in bad faith, by pretending to oneself that the situation is one
which one can handle with one's given moral apparatus.

A possible real instance of this kind of moral dilemma is that which
faced Chamberlain in his negotiations with Hitler in 1938. He ought
to have realized that he was dealing with a kind of person for which
his own moral outlook had not prepared him, and that as Prime Minister
he was called upon to rethink his moral and political approach in a
more realistic way. This he failed to do, either because he was genuinely
deceived as to Hitler's real character or, as I suspect, because he deceived himself on this point: if the latter, then he was guilty of the type
of bad faith to which I am alluding.

The main point of this variety of moral dilemma is that, at least
if correctly resolved, it forces a man to develop a new morality; in the
case of the last type of dilemma, this was a possible outcome but by
no means a necessary one. So perhaps this is the place at which to say
a little about what is involved in such a development. Here the analogy
with aesthetics, which Sartre and others have cautiously drawn, may be
useful. There may come a point in the development of a painter, say,
or a composer, where he is no longer able to go on producing work that
conforms to the canons of composition which he has hitherto accepted,
where he is compelled by his authenticity as a creator to develop new
procedures and new forms. It is difficult to describe what will guide him

in the selection of new canons, but one consideration will often be the desire to be (whatever this means) *true to himself*. It may well be that an appropriate consideration in the development of a new moral outlook is the desire to be, in the relevant sense whatever that is, true to oneself and to one's own character. But I will not pursue this topic here, because I confess myself to be quite in the dark as to what the sense of these words is. . . .

Like Socrates in the *Crito*, Broad deals with a current moral problem, also mentioned by Dewey, in a very helpful way. His discussion is, however, very different from that of Socrates. Socrates is trying to answer a moral question about what he should do in a particular situation; Broad is discussing a more general question that does not face him personally. Socrates gives us his answer to his question and his reasons for it, and helps us in two ways: first, by showing us a line of argument we might use ourselves in a similar situation if we agree with it, and second, by setting an example of the way to solve other moral problems. Broad is somewhat skeptical about knowing the right answer to his question, and contents himself in the end with trying to formulate the question clearly and with making a few relevant remarks. The bulk of his essay is not concerned with answering the particular question posed as an example but seeks, rather, to state the general conditions governing all attempts to answer such questions rationally. What he does in this part of the essay is somewhat abstract and technical, but it is important, not only for seeing how to deal with practical ethical problems, but also for further reading in this book. Notice especially his distinctions between:

1. Factual and ethical premises
2. Judgments of obligation and judgments of value
3. Theory of obligation and theory of value
4. Teleological and pluralistic theories of obligation
5. Hedonistic and pluralistic theories of value

All of these distinctions will be adopted in this volume, with a few slight changes and additions. We will also use the expression "ethical judgments," as Broad does, to stand for all of the kinds of normative or value judgments that are relevant to ethics, not just moral judgments. When we mean to talk about specifically moral judgments we will use the word "moral." In other words, we will use "ethical" in a more inclusive sense than "moral."

In addition to the distinctions cited above, Broad also distinguishes universalistic and restricted forms of the teleological theory of obligation. Does either of these forms seem more plausible to you than the other? Is Broad correct that the universalistic form is "flagrantly at variance with common sense"? What helpful insights or distinctions, if any, do you find in Broad's remarks on the specific question, "Ought we to fight for our country?" Can you think of other things he might have added?

OUGHT WE TO FIGHT FOR OUR COUNTRY?

C. D. Broad

The question before us is of the general form: "What ought such and such people (e.g. males of military age) to do under such and such circumstances (e.g. when their country is involved in a war)?" I shall first point out the general conditions which govern all attempts to answer such questions.

Any argument on the subject will have to use premisses of two utterly different kinds, viz. *Purely Factual* and *Ethical*. An ethical proposition is one which involves the notion of good or bad, right or wrong, ought or ought not. A purely factual proposition is one which involves no such notions. That deliberate homicide is wrong is an ethical proposition, true or false. It is a purely factual proposition that, if a man is shot through the heart, he will almost certainly be dead very soon afterwards.

Now the purely factual premisses are of two kinds, viz. (1) Statements of alleged particular facts about the past or the present. These may be called *Instantial Premisses*. And (2) statements of alleged general laws or tendencies. These may be called *Nomic Premisses*. An example of the first kind is the proposition that Japan has spent such and such a proportion of her revenue on her navy for the past ten years. An example of the second is the proposition, true or false, that an increase of armaments tends to produce war. Now everyone admits that what a person ought or ought not to do at a given moment depends *either* on his present state and circumstances and his past history *or* on the probable consequences of the various alternative actions open to him at the time; and most people believe that it depends to some extent on *both*. In order to conjecture the probable consequences of various alternative actions which might be done in a given situation it is always necessary to use both kinds of factual premiss. Therefore everyone would admit that factual premisses of the instantial kind are needed, and the vast majority of people would admit that factual premisses of the nomic kind are also needed, if we are to have any rational argument about such questions as we are asking.

From Ethics and the History of Philosophy *(London: Routledge & Kegan Paul Ltd., 1952). Reprinted by permission of Routledge & Kegan Ltd. and Humanities Press, Inc.*

But it is equally certain that ethical premises are also needed in any argument about an ethical question. Now ethical propositions are of two kinds, which I will call *Pure* and *Mixed*. It is always difficult to be sure that a given ethical proposition is pure, but it is easy to give examples of ethical propositions which are certainly mixed. Suppose I assert that a classical education is a good thing. I mean *(a)* that it is likely to produce in those subjected to it certain experiences and dispositions, which could be described on purely psychological and non-ethical terms; and *(b)* that such experiences and dispositions are good. The first of these two constituents of the original proposition is a purely factual statement of the nomic kind. The second is an ethical proposition. Whether it is *purely* ethical is another question. But, at any rate, the original proposition is certainly a mixed ethical one, and its ethical component is certainly a nearer approximation to a purely ethical one. When mixed ethical propositions are used as premisses in ethical arguments they are always liable to lead to mistakes and misunderstandings. If we are to avoid these, it is essential that we should split up such propositions, so far as we can, into their purely ethical and their purely factual components. For two disputants who agree about one of the components may differ about the other; and, if they fail to recognize and distinguish the two, they are bound to be at cross-purposes and to produce crooked answers.

There is another important division of ethical propositions which cuts across the division into pure and mixed. Ethical propositions are of three kinds, which may be expressed respectively by sentences of the three forms:

"You *ought* (or ought not) to do so-and-so in such and such circumstances."
"Such and such an action would be *right* (or wrong) in such and such circumstances."
"Such and such an experience or state of affairs would be *good* (or bad)."

For the present purpose I shall group the first two together under the name of *Judgments of Obligation*. I shall call the third kind *Judgments of Value*. Now this brings us to a fundamental difference of opinion which it is essential to notice if we are to have any intelligent discussion on such questions as we have before us.

Some people hold that there is one and only one *ultimate* obligation, and that this involves an essential reference to *value*. According to them the one ultimate obligation is to secure the increase and to prevent the decrease of the present amount of good, and to secure the diminution and check the increase of the present amount of evil. All other obligations, such as the duty to keep one's promises or to obey the laws of one's country, are derivative from this one. They are obligations if and only if they are, in the actual circumstances, the most efficient way of fulfilling the one ultimate obligation to conserve and increase good and to check or diminish evil. Otherwise they are wrong. I shall call this the *Teleological Theory of Obligation.*

This theory can, of course, take many different forms. I shall not attempt to distinguish more than two of them, which I will call the *Universalistic Form* and the *Restricted Form.* According to the universalistic form of the theory a person has no special obligation to produce good and diminish evil in one person or community rather than in another. Suppose you have two alternative courses of action open to you. By one of them you will improve the condition of your own countrymen, and by the other you will improve the conditions in another country instead. Then it is your duty, on this view, to avoid the former action and to do the latter, provided that the improvement which you will effect in the foreign country is in the least degree greater than that which you would effect in your own country. According to the *restricted* form of the teleological theory your ultimate obligation still is to conserve and increase good and to check and diminish evil. But you have a stronger obligation to increase the good and diminish the evil in certain persons and communities, to which you stand in certain special relations, than you have towards other persons and communities to which you do not stand in these relations. On either form of the theory the one and only ultimate obligation is that of *Beneficence.* On the universalistic form of it there is only the general obligation to be as beneficent as you can in the circumstances in which you are placed. On the restricted form of it the appropriate strength and direction of the obligation of beneficence is in part determined by the special relations in which the agent stands to certain individuals, institutions, and communities.

Now many people would reject the teleological theory of obligation. They would hold that there are *many* ultimate obligations, and that they do not all involve an essential reference to value. They admit that I am under a general obligation to be beneficent to human beings as such; and they assert that I am also under more special and stringent obligations to be beneficent to my parents, my benefactors, my fellow-countrymen, and so on. But they say that there are many other obligations which are not reducible to beneficence at all, whether general or special. E.g. if a person asks me a question to which I know the answer, the mere fact that I am in this state and that he and I are in this situation gives him a claim on me to receive a *true* answer. On this view there is an obligation of truth-speaking which is not reducible to any obligation of beneficence and which may conflict with one's general or special obligations of beneficence. And there may be other obligations, e.g. an obligation to obey the laws of one's country, which may conflict with the obligation of truth-speaking and with the special and the general obligations of beneficence. I propose to call this theory the *Pluralistic Theory of Obligation.*

On the pluralistic theory a person who is called upon to act in one way or another, or to abstain from action, in a given situation may be subject to many different and conflicting claims or obligations of varying strength, arising out of various factors in his past history and various relations in which he stands to various persons, institutions, and communities. Whichever alternative he chooses he will fulfil some of these component obligations, and in doing so he will necessarily break others which conflict with the former. In such cases the right action is one which makes the best compromise between the several conflicting claims, when due weight is given to their number and their relative urgency. But no general principles can be suggested for deciding what is the best compromise.

Now I cannot attempt here to decide between the universalistic form of the teleological theory, the restricted form of it, and the pluralistic theory. I will content myself with two remarks about them. (1) *Prima facie* the pluralistic theory is in accord with common sense, and the universalistic form of the teleological theory is flagrantly at variance with common sense. And, if we reject the universalistic form of the teleological theory, it seems doubtful whether we can consistently rest in the restricted form of it. It looks as if the restricted form were an unstable compromise between the pluralistic theory and the universalistic form of the teleological theory. (2) However this may be, it is essential to be clear in one's own mind as to which theory one is going to assume before one can argue intelligently about the question at issue. Facts which might prove conclusively, on the universalistic form of the teleological theory, that a man ought not to fight for his country might lead to no such consequence if one held that a citizen is under a special obligation of beneficence to his own nation. And their force would be still further diminished if one held that a man is under a strong direct obligation to obey the laws of his country, good or bad, simply because he is a citizen of it.

It remains to say something about the other kind of ethical propositions, viz. Judgments of Value. Here again there is a profound difference of opinion on a fundamental question. Some people hold that there is one and only one kind of subject of which the adjectives "intrinsically good" and "intrinsically evil" can properly be predicated, viz. experiences. And they hold further that there is one and only one characteristic of experiences which make them good or evil. I will call this the *Monistic Theory of Value*. It might conceivably take many different forms, according to what characteristic of experiences was held to be the one and only good-making or bad-making characteristic. But in practice, I think, nearly everyone who holds the monistic theory of value assumes that the one and only good-making or bad-making characteristic of experiences is their hedonic quality in its two opposed forms of pleasantness and unpleasantness. So, for the present purpose, we may identify the monistic theory of value with the *Hedonistic Theory of Value*. . . .

Now many people would unhesitatingly reject the Hedonistic Theory of Value in whole or in part. . . . [E]ven those who hold that nothing but experiences can be intrinsically good or evil may hold that there are other good-making and bad-making characteristics of experiences beside their pleasantness and their unpleasantness. Anyone who holds [this view] may be said to accept the *Pluralistic Theory of Value*.

Once again I shall not attempt to decide between the rival theories. I will content myself with the following remarks. (1) *Prima facie* the hedonistic theory is flagrantly at variance with common sense. The common-sense view is *prima facie* that persons, at any rate, can be intrinsically good or evil as well as experiences, and that there are many characteristics beside pleasantness and unpleasantness which make experience intrinsically good or bad. (2) If a pluralistic theory of value is admitted, a person who accepts the teleological theory of obligation is faced at the second move with the same kind of problem as faces an adherent of the pluralistic theory of obligation at the first move. He will not, indeed, have to try to find the best compromise between a number of ultimate and conflicting obligations of various degrees of urgency. But he will have to aim at producing the best compromise between a number of ultimate kinds of value and disvalue. He may, e.g. have to weigh the net value of a state of heroic self-sacrifice accompanied by misery and intellectual stupidity against that of a state of clear-sighted and cool selfishness accompanied by comfort. And no general principle can be offered for conducting the comparison. The only person who can avoid such difficulties is one who combines the universalistic form of the teleological theory of obligation with the hedonistic theory of value. And both the elements in this combination seem *prima facie* far too simple to be true. (3) Whatever may be the truth about these rival theories of value, this at least is certain. It is essential to be clear in one's own mind as to which theory one is going to assume before one can argue intelligently about the question at issue. Facts which might prove conclusively, on the hedonistic theory of value, that a man ought not to fight for his country might lead to no such consequence if it were held that heroic self-sacrifice gives value to the persons who practise it just as pleasantness gives value to pleasant experiences. And their force might be still further diminished if it were held that a nation is a persistent collective entity of a peculiar kind, with a characteristic value or disvalue of its own which is determined by the actions and dispositions of its citizens.

This completes what I have to say about the general conditions which govern all rational discussion about such questions as we have before us. I will summarize them as follows. (1) The factual and the ethical premisses must be clearly distinguished; any mixed ethical premisses must be analysed into their purely factual and their purely ethical components; and the instantial and the nomic factual premisses must be separately stated. (2) The theory of obligation which is being assumed by any disputant must be explicitly stated. We must know whether he assumes the pluralistic theory or the teleological theory. And, if he assumes the latter, we must know whether he assumes the universalistic or the restricted form of it. (3) The theory of value which is being assumed by any disputant must be explicitly stated. We must know whether he assumes the hedonistic theory or the pluralistic theory. And, if he assumes the latter, we must know whether he holds that only experiences can have intrinsic value or disvalue, or that only experiences and persons can have it, or that experiences and persons and societies can have it. Unless these conditions are fulfilled, there can be no rational *argument;* there can be only emotional hot-air emitted in argumentative form.

When these conditions have been fulfilled I do not believe that there is much room for argument on such questions except on the purely factual side. We may be able to alter a man's opinions about the probable consequences of fighting or refusing to fight when his country is involved in war, by showing him particular facts which he had overlooked, or by convincing him, from empirical evidence, of laws or tendencies which he had not suspected. But there are no arguments by which we can alter his opinions as to what circumstances do and what do not impose obligations on him, or as to the kinds of things which can have intrinsic value or disvalue, or as to the characteristics which do and those which do not confer intrinsic value or disvalue on the things which possess them. If he is a pluralist about obligation, we cannot by argument alter his opinions about the relative urgency of the various conflicting obligations which he believes to be incumbent on him. If he is a pluralist about value, we cannot by argument alter his opinions as to the various degrees of goodness or badness conferred by the various characteristics which he believes to be good-making or bad-making. We can clear up confusions and indicate possible sources of prejudice; but, when we have done this, we have done all that argument can accomplish in such matters, and, if we still differ, we must agree to do so.

My next business is to try to restate the question in a perfectly clear and concrete form. I shall assume that the war in question is an important one. . . . I shall assume that conscription is in force. And I shall assume that "we" means persons liable under the act to military service, and not exempted by the authorities because of special usefulness in some other form of war-work, such as munition-making. The question is whether such persons, in such circumstances, ought to obey this law or to refuse to obey it. Of course a very similar question would arise for those specially skilled persons, such as research-chemists, who would be exempted from military service in order to apply their special skill to other forms of war-work. Ought they to refuse both to fight and to exercise their abilities in arming those who are fighting?

Now I have no idea what is the right answer to this question, and, if I had, I should not be able to prove it to people who accepted different ethical principles and premises from those which I accept. I am not sure indeed that it is the kind of question to which there is an answer, even laid up in Heaven, as Plato might say. I shall therefore content myself with making a few remarks which are, I think, relevant to it.

(1) There are three and only three cases in which no difficulty can arise. (i) A person may be persuaded that the war in which his country is engaged is the least evil alternative open to it in the circumstances, and he may hold that he has a direct or derived obligation to obey the laws of his country. Such a person will presumably hold that he ought to fight if he is ordered to do so. (ii) A man may hold that there is a direct obligation not to take or help in taking human life, and that this is so urgent that it overrides all other obligations, direct or derivative, which conflict with it. Such a man will have no difficulty in deciding that he ought not to fight, no matter how good the cause may be and even if he admits that war is the only way to bring about a great good or avoid a great evil. (iii) A man may hold that there is a direct obligation to obey the laws of his country, and that this is so urgent that it overrides all other obligations which may conflict with it. Such a man will have no difficulty in deciding that he ought to fight, no matter how bad the cause may be and even if he thinks that war is an inefficient means of securing good or avoiding evil. The second and the third of these opinions seem to me absurd. I do not believe that there is any one obligation which is of such unique urgency that it overrides all other obligations, direct or indirect, that may conflict with it. Therefore the only case that seems to me to be of interest is that of a man who holds that war in general, or this war in particular, is wrong, and who does not

hold that there is an overwhelming obligation either to refrain from taking human life or to obey the laws of his country.

(2) The following fact is very important, and is liable to be overlooked. If one believes that war in general, or a certain particular war, is wrong, this may be a conclusive reason for trying to prevent one's country getting into it and for trying to get one's country out of it if it has entered upon it. But, except on the universalistic form of the teleological theory of obligation, it is *not* a conclusive reason for refusing to fight for your country when, in spite of your efforts, it is engaged in war. There is nothing particularly paradoxical in this. If one is a member of an ordinary partnership or committee, it is often one's duty loyally to help in carrying out a policy which one believes to be wrong and which one has conscientiously opposed while it was still under discussion. No doubt, if the conflict is too extreme, it becomes one's duty to dissolve the partnership or to resign from the committee. But it is just at this point that the analogy breaks down .For you cannot really do anything analogous to resigning from your country. If you are to go on living in England at all during the war, you will be dependent for your food and for such protection as you enjoy on the army, the navy, and the air force; i.e. on the fact that there is a majority of persons of military age whose consciences are less sensitive than yours or work in a different way. Plainly there is a *prima facie* obligation not to put yourself in this situation of one-sided dependence on what you must regard as the wrong actions of people who are less virtuous or less enlightened than yourself. . . .

(3) Refusal to fight in a war is one of those actions whose effects vary greatly with the proportion and the distribution of those who practise them. If a *majority* of persons of military age in *both* belligerent countries simultaneously refused to fight, it would be an extremely good thing, since it would automatically bring the war to an end without either victory or defeat. If a considerable proportion of such persons in England refused to fight, whilst few if any in the enemy country did so, the result would be the defeat of England. Under the conditions of modern war a complete and early defeat might be better even for the defeated country than victory after prolonged fighting. But it is not worth discussing either of these alternatives, because it is as certain as anything of this kind can be that nothing like them will in fact be realized. The actual situation will certainly be that only a quite negligible proportion of those liable to military service, either in England or in any country with which England is likely to be at war, will refuse to fight. The intending refuser can safely assume that, if he refuses, he will be in a tiny minority, and that his action will make no appreciable difference to the duration or the outcome of the war.

Now there are two remarks to be made about this. (i) It is a mistake to suppose, that because refusal *would be* right if most people in both countries were going to refuse, therefore it *will be* right in the actual case where only very few people in either country will refuse. No legitimate inference can be made to what is right in the actual case from what would be right in the widely different hypothetical case. The rightness or wrongness of an action depends, *inter alia,* on the circumstances in which it is done; and one extremely relevant circumstance in the present case is the extent to which other people will perform similar actions.

(ii) Since the large-scale effects of refusing to fight are likely to be negligible, the individual who is debating whether he ought to refuse can confine his attention to the probable effects on himself and his circle of friends and relations when considering the utility or disutility of refusal. This is, no doubt, a great convenience for him. But he will have to reflect that he owes this convenience, as he will owe his food and protection, to the fact that he can count on most other people doing what he judges to be wrong and deciding to fight. Unless he holds the universalistic form of the teleological theory of obligation and the hedonistic theory of value, he may suspect that it is not altogether fitting that his honour should be rooted in the fortunate dishonour of most of his contemporaries. . . .

Suggestions for Further Reading

The following two works contain discussions relevant not only to Chapter 1 but throughout the present book.

GARNER, R. T., and BERNARD ROSEN. *Moral Philosophy*. New York: Macmillan, 1967.
HOSPERS, JOHN. *Human Conduct* (shorter ed.). New York: Harcourt Brace Jovanovich, 1972.

The following works are especially relevant to Chapter 1.

COHEN, CARL. *Civil Disobedience*. New York: Columbia University Press, 1971.
GARNETT, A. C. *The Moral Nature of Man*. New York: Ronald Press, 1952. (Chapters I and IV)
PIAGET, JEAN. *The Moral Judgment of the Child*, trans. Marjorie Gabain. New York: Collier Books, 1962. (Chapter II and Chapter IV, Section 6)
TOULMIN, STEPHEN. *An Examination of the Place of Reason in Ethics*. New York: Cambridge University Press, 1964. (Part III)
WASSERSTROM, R. A., ed. *War and Morality*. Belmont, Calif.: Wadsworth, 1970.

2

EGOISTIC
AND DEONTOLOGICAL
THEORIES

Introduction

In Chapters 2–5, except for parts of Chapter 4, we shall be concerned with normative ethics, not meta-ethics. That is, we shall be occupied with questions about what is morally right or wrong (2–3), what is morally good or bad (4), and what is nonmorally good or bad (5). In Chapter 4 we will recognize that some writers think that the basic judgments in morality are or should be judgments of moral value, not judgments of moral obligation. Now, however, we shall assume, as most philosophers do, that judgments of obligation are basic, and accordingly, Chapters 2 and 3 deal with theories and problems in what Broad calls the theory of obligation or more accurately, the normative theory of moral obligation, which seeks to guide us in making decisions and judgments about what to do in particular situations or kinds of situations.

Philosophers generally distinguish two kinds of normative theories of obligation. A *teleological theory* holds that the sole basic criterion of what is morally right or wrong is the nonmoral value that is brought into being. We ought to do the action or adopt the rule that will produce the greatest possible balance of good over evil. The teleologists may and do differ about what they regard as good or evil; they may be hedonists or nonhedonists. They also differ in their views about whose good it is that we are to promote. Ethical egoism holds that one is to promote one's

39

own good; utilitarianism or ethical universalism asserts, on the contrary, that we are to promote the good (the greatest balance of good over evil) of the world as a whole; a third kind of view would maintain that one should promote the good of his family, nation, or class. The first and third views are what Broad calls "restricted" teleological theories. A *deontological theory* denies what teleologists affirm. A deontologist holds that what makes an action right to do or a rule right to adopt is not just the balance of good over evil produced; there are other factors that may make an action or rule right. For example, an act may be right, other things being equal, because it keeps a promise, because it shows gratitude, or because it is commanded by God. It may even be right sometimes when it (or the rule under which it falls) does not promote the greatest possible balance of good over evil. Deontologists must hold this view about what is right or wrong although, like teleologists, they may hold various views about what is good or evil.

What Broad called pluralistic theories of obligation will obviously all be deontological. But deontological theories may also be monistic, for example, the view that an action or rule is obligatory if and only if it is commanded by God.

This chapter will cover ethical egoism and the main deontological theories. Utilitarianism and some related views will be covered in chapter 3. There will be no separate study of teleological theories of the third kind, even though they have been parts of important ideologies like fascism and some forms of Marxism, and even though many other persons live by such restricted views in practice if not in theory.

2.1

Ethical Egoism

Ethical egoism holds that every individual ought always to do the thing that is most to his interest or for his own greatest good in the long run, or at least not contrary to it. It implies that it is never wrong for one to do something to another if it is for one's own long-run advantage or good. It does not imply that people are never altruistic; it may even recognize that one may be happier if one does something altruistic; but it insists that one ought to do such a thing only if doing it will result in greater good for oneself. Ethical egoists may and do hold different views about what one's interest or good consists in, for example, that it is pleasure, happiness, perfection, power, or self-realization.

Psychological egoism is a factual, not an ethical thesis, namely, that one always does what one thinks will be to one's interest or will give one the greatest balance of good over evil. This does imply that man is never really altruistic, at least not when he acts deliberately or with reflection. It is not entailed by, and does not entail, ethical egoism, but the two usually go together. In fact, ethical egoism is usually defended on the ground that psychological egoism is true.

Egoistic positions were stated by some of the characters in Plato's dialogues, and may even have been held by Plato and Aristotle, but the first clear and full form of philosophical egoism was that of Epicurus and his followers. In their writings, psychological egoism and ethical egoism are combined, and egoism is interwoven with hedonism. Logically, egoism and hedonism are separable, but in debates about egoism they have usually been linked together. Here we are mainly concerned with egoism, leaving hedonism to be dealt with in Chapter 5.

In the following selection from Cicero (106–43 B.C.), one of his characters,

Torquatus, is speaking in defense of the ethics of Epicurus (341–270 B.C.). He argues that each person is basically seeking to gain pleasure and avoid pain for himself, even when he acts virtuously or does great deeds, and that the virtues of wisdom, temperance, courage, and even justice are desirable only because they bring a balance of pleasure over pain to those who have them. He does not believe in "Epicureanism" in the popular sense (eat, drink, and be merry; wine, women, and song), but he is completely egoistic in both psychology and ethics.

Specific questions which you may wish to keep in mind in reading this selection are: According to the Epicureans, is every pleasure to be sought and every pain avoided? What definition or view of the nature of pleasure is suggested by Epicureanism? Is this view adequate? What does Cicero mean by "desires which proceed from nature"? Can you give some examples of them? After reading Cicero, but before reading the selection from Joseph Butler, see what possible objections to both psychological and ethical egoism you can think of and ask yourself if the egoist would have a plausible reply.

THE ETHICS OF EPICURUS: EGOISM

Cicero

IX. We are inquiring what is the final and ultimate good. . . . This Epicurus places in pleasure, which he argues is the chief good, and that pain is the chief evil; and he proceeds to prove his assertion thus. He says that every animal the moment that it is born seeks for pleasure, and rejoices in it as the chief good; and rejects pain as the chief evil, and wards it off from itself as far as it can; and that it acts in this manner, without having been corrupted by anything, under the promptings of nature herself, who forms this uncorrupt and upright judgment. Therefore, he affirms that there is no need of argument or of discussion as to why pleasure is to be sought for, and pain to be avoided. This he thinks a matter of sense, just as much as that fire is hot, snow white, honey sweet; none of which propositions he thinks require to be confirmed by laboriously sought reasons, but that it is sufficient merely to state them. For that there is a difference between arguments and conclusions arrived at by ratiocination, and ordinary observations and statements:—by the first, secret and obscure principles are explained; by the second, matters which are plain and easy are brought to decision. For since, if you take away sense from a man, there is nothing left to him, it follows

From De Finibus, *trans. C. D. Yonge (London: G. Bell and Sons, Ltd., 1878).*

of necessity that what is contrary to nature, or what agrees with it, must be left to nature herself to decide. Now what does she perceive, or what does she determine on as her guide to seek or to avoid anything, except pleasure and pain? But there are some of our school who seek to carry out this doctrine with more acuteness, and who will not allow that it is sufficient that it should be decided by sense what is good and what is bad, but who assert that these points can be ascertained by intellect and reason also, and that pleasure is to be sought for on its own account, and that pain also is to be avoided for the same reason.

Therefore, they say that this notion is implanted in our minds naturally and instinctively, as it were; so that we *feel* that the one is to be sought for, and the other to be avoided. Others, however, (and this is my own opinion too,) assert that, as many reasons are alleged by many philosophers why pleasure ought not to be reckoned among goods, nor pain among evils, we ought not to rely too much on the goodness of our cause, but that we should use arguments, and discuss the point with precision, and argue, by the help of carefully collected reasons, about pleasure and about pain.

X. But that you may come to an accurate perception of the source whence all this error originated of those people who attack pleasure and extol pain, I will unfold the whole matter; and I will lay before you the very statements which have been made by that discoverer of the truth, and architect, as it were, of a happy life. For no one either despises, or hates, or avoids pleasure itself merely because it is pleasure, but because great pains overtake those men who do not understand how to pursue pleasure in a reasonable manner. Nor is there any one who loves, or pursues, or wishes to acquire pain because it is pain, but because sometimes such occasions arise that a man attains to some great pleasure through labour and pain. For, to descend to trifles, who of us ever undertakes any laborious exertion of body except in order to gain some advantage by so doing? and who is there who could fairly blame a man who should wish to be in that state of pleasure which no annoyance can interrupt, or one who shuns that pain by which no subsequent pleasure is procured? But we do accuse those men, and think them entirely worthy of the greatest hatred, who, being made effeminate and corrupted by the allurements of present pleasure, are so blinded by passion that they do not foresee what pains and annoyances they will hereafter be subject to; and who are equally guilty with those who, through weakness of mind, that is to say, from eagerness to avoid labour and pain, desert their duty.

And the distinction between these things is quick and easy. For at a time when we are free, when the option of choice is in our own power, and when there is nothing to prevent our being able to do whatever we choose, then every pleasure may be enjoyed, and every pain repelled. But on particular occasions it will often happen, owing either to the obligations of duty or the necessities of business, that pleasures must be declined and annoyances must not be shirked. Therefore the wise man holds to this principle of choice in those matters, that he rejects some pleasures, so as, by the rejection, to obtain others which are greater, and encounters some pains, so as by that means to escape others which are more formidable.

Now, as these are my sentiments, what reason can I have for fearing that I may not be able to accommodate our Torquati to them—men whose examples you just now quoted from memory, with a kind and friendly feeling toward us? However, you have not bribed me by praising my ancestors, nor made me less prompt in replying to you. But I should like to know from you how you interpret their actions? Do you think that they attacked the enemy with such feelings, or that they were so severe to their children and to their own blood as to have no thought of their own advantage, or of what might be useful to themselves? But even wild beasts do not do that, and do not rush about and cause confusion in such a way that we cannot understand what is the object of their motions. And do you think that such illustrious men performed such great actions without a reason? What their reason was I will examine presently; in the meantime I will lay down this rule,—If there was any reason which instigated them to do those things which are undoubtedly splendid exploits, then virtue by herself was not the sole cause of their conduct. One man tore a chain from off his enemy, and at the same time he defended himself from being slain; but he encountered great danger. Yes, but it was before the eyes of the whole army. What did he get by that? Glory, and the affection of his countrymen, which are the surest bulwarks to enable a man to pass his life without fear. He put his son to death by the hand of the executioner. If he did so without any reason, then I should be sorry to be descended from so inhuman and merciless a man. But if his object was to establish military discipline and obedience to command, at the price of his own anguish, and at a time of a most formidable war to restrain his army by the fear of punishment, then he was providing for the safety of his fellow-citizens, which he was well aware embraced his own. And this principle is one of extensive application. For the very point respecting which your whole school, and yourself most especially, who are such a diligent investigator of ancient instances, are in the habit of vaunting yourself and using high-flown language, namely, the mention of brave and illustrious men, and the extolling of their actions, as proceeding not from any regard to advantage, but from pure principles of honour and a love of glory, is entirely upset, when once that rule in the choice of things is established which I mentioned just now,—namely, that pleasures are passed over for the sake of obtaining other greater pleasures, or that pains are encountered with a view to escape greater pains. . . .

XII. . . . Moreover, the beginnings of desiring and avoiding, and indeed altogether of everything which we do, take their rise either in pleasure or pain. And as this is the case, it is plain that everything which is right and laudable has reference to this one object of living with pleasure. And since that is the highest, or extreme, or greatest good, which the Greeks call $\tau\acute{\epsilon}\lambda os$ [telos], because it is referred to nothing else itself, but everything is referred to it, we must confess that the highest good is to live agreeably.

XIII. And those who place this in virtue alone, and, being caught by the splendour of a name, do not understand what nature requires, will be delivered from the greatest blunder imaginable if they will listen to Epicurus. For unless those excellent and beautiful virtues which your school talks about produced pleasure, who would think them either praiseworthy or desirable? For as we esteem the skill of physicians not for the sake of the art itself, but from our desire for good health,—and as the skill of the pilot, who has the knowledge how to navigate a vessel well, is praised with reference to its utility, and not to his ability,—so wisdom, which should be considered the art of living, would not be sought after if it effected nothing; but at present it is sought after because it is, as it were, the efficient cause of pleasure, which is a legitimate object of desire and acquisition. And now you understand what pleasure I mean, so that what I say may not be brought into odium from my using an unpopular word. For as the chief annoyances to human life proceed from ignorance of what things are good and what bad, and as by reason of that mistake men are often deprived of the greatest pleasures, and tortured by the most bitter grief of mind, we have need to exercise wisdom, which, by removing groundless alarms and vain desires, and by banishing the rashness of all erroneous opinions, offers herself to us as the surest guide to pleasure. For it is wisdom alone which expels sorrow from our minds, and prevents our shuddering with fear: she is the instructress who enables us to live in tranquillity, by extinguishing in us all vehemence of desire. For desires are insatiable, and ruin not only individuals but entire families, and often overturn the whole state. From desires arise hatred, dissentions, quarrels, seditions, wars. Nor is it only out of doors that these passions vent themselves, nor is it only against others that they run with blind violence; but they are often shut up, as it were, in the mind, and throw that into confusion with their disagreements.

And the consequence of this is, to make life thoroughly wretched; so that the wise man is the only one who, having cut away all vanity and error, and removed it from him, can live contented within the boundaries of nature, without melancholy and without fear. For what diversion can be either more useful or more adapted for human life than that which Epicurus employed? For he laid it down that there were three kinds of desires; the first, such as were natural and necessary; the second, such as were natural but not necessary; the third, such as were neither natural nor necessary. And these are all such, that those which are necessary are satisfied without much trouble or expense: even those which are natural and not necessary, do not require a great deal, because nature itself makes the riches, which are sufficient to content it, easy of acquisition and of limited quantity: but as for vain desires, it is impossible to find any limit to, or any moderation in them.

XIV. But if we see that the whole life of man is thrown into disorder by error and ignorance; and that wisdom is the only thing which can relieve us from the sway of the passions and the fear of danger, and which can teach us to bear the injuries of fortune itself with moderation, and which shows us all the ways which lead to tranquillity and peace; what reason is there that we should hesitate to say that wisdom is to be sought for the sake of pleasure, and that folly is to be avoided on account of its annoyances? And on the same principle we shall say that even temperance is not to be sought for its own sake, but because it brings peace to the mind, and soothes and tranquillizes them by what I may call a kind of concord. For temperance is that which warns us to follow reason in desiring or avoiding anything. Nor is it sufficient to decide what ought to be done, and what ought not; but we must adhere to what has been decided. But many men, because they are enfeebled and subdued the moment pleasure comes in sight, and so are unable to keep and adhere to the determination they have formed, give themselves up to be bound hand and foot by their lusts, and do not foresee what will happen to them; and in that way, on account of some pleasure which is trivial and unnecessary, and which might be procured in some other manner, and which they could dispense with without annoyance, incur terrible diseases, and injuries, and disgrace, and are often even involved in the penalties of the legal tribunals of their country.

But these men who wish to enjoy pleasure in such a way that no grief shall ever overtake them in consequence, and who retain their judgment so as never to be overcome by pleasure as to do what they feel ought not to be done; these men, I say, obtain the greatest pleasure by passing pleasure by. They often even endure pain, in order to avoid encountering greater pain hereafter by their shunning it at present. From which consideration it is perceived that intemperance is not to be avoided for its own sake; and that temperance is to be sought for, not because it avoids pleasures, but because it attains to greater ones.

XV. The same principle will be found to hold good with respect to courage. For the discharge of labours and the endurance of pain are neither of them intrinsically tempting; nor is patience, nor diligence, nor watchfulness, nor industry which is so much extolled, nor even courage itself: but we cultivate these habits in order that we may live without care and fear, and may be able, as far as is in our power, to release our minds and bodies from annoyance. For as the whole condition of tranquil life is thrown into confusion by the fear of death, and as it is a miserable thing to yield to pain and to bear it with a humble and imbecile mind; and as on account of that weakness of mind many men have ruined their parents, many men their friends, some their country, and very many indeed have utterly undone themselves; so a vigorous and lofty mind is free from all care and pain, since it despises death, which only places those who encounter it in the same condition as that in which they were before they were born; and it is so prepared for pain that it recollects that the very greatest are terminated by death, and that slight pains have many intervals of rest, and that we can master moderate ones, so as to bear them if they are tolerable, and if not, we can depart with equanimity out of life, just as out of a theatre, when it no longer pleases us. By all which considerations it is understood that cowardice and idleness are not blamed, and that courage and patience are not praised, for their own sakes; but that the one line of conduct is rejected as the parent of pain, and the other desired as the author of pleasure.

XVI. Justice remains to be mentioned, that I may not omit any virtue whatever; but nearly the same things may be said respecting that. For, as I have already shown that wisdom, temperance, and fortitude are connected with pleasure in such a way that they cannot possibly be separated or divided from it, so also we must consider that it is the case with justice. Which not only never injures any one; but on the contrary always nourishes something which tranquillizes the mind, partly by its own power and nature, and partly by the hopes that nothing will be wanting of those things which a nature not depraved may fairly derive.

Since rashness and lust and idleness always torture the mind, always make it anxious, and are of a turbulent character, so too, wherever injustice settles in any man's mind, it is turbulent from the mere fact of its existence and presence there; and if it forms any plan, although it executes it even so secretly, still it never believes that what has been done will be concealed for ever. For generally, when wicked men do any-thing, first of all suspicion overtakes their actions; then the common con-versation and report of men; then the prosecutor and the judge; and many even, as was the case when you were consul, have given informa-tion against themselves. But if any men appear to themselves to be sufficiently fenced round and protected from the consciousness of men, still they dread the knowledge of the Gods, and think that those very anxieties by which their minds are eaten up night and day, are inflicted upon them by the immortal Gods for the sake of punishment. And how is it possible that wicked actions can ever have as much influence towards alleviating the annoyances of life, as they must have towards increasing them from the consciousness of our actions, and also from the punishments inflicted by the laws and the hatred of the citizens? And yet, in some people, there is no moderation in their passion for money and for honour and for command, or in their lusts and greediness and other desires, which acquisitions, however wickedly made, do not at all diminish, but rather inflame, so that it seems we ought rather to restrain such men than to think that we can teach them better. There-fore sound wisdom invites sensible men to justice, equity, and good faith. And unjust actions are not advantageous even to that man who has no abilities or resources; inasmuch as he cannot easily do what he endeavours to do, nor obtain his objects if he does succeed in his en-deavours. And the gifts of fortune and of genius are better suited to liberality; and those who practise this virtue gain themselves goodwill, and affection, which is the most powerful of all things to enable a man to live with tranquility; especially when he has absolutely no motive at all for doing wrong.

For those desires which proceed from nature are easily satisfied without any injustice; but those which are vain ought not to be com-plied with. For they desire nothing which is really desirable; and there is more disadvantage in the mere fact of injustice than there is advantage in what is acquired by the injustice. Therefore a person would not be right who should pronounce even justice intrinsically de-sirable for its own sake; but because it brings the greatest amount of what is agreeable. For to be loved and to be dear to others is agreeable because it makes life safer, and pleasure more abundant. Therefore we think dishonesty should be avoided, not only on account of those dis-advantages which befall the wicked, but even much more because it never permits the man in whose mind it abides to breathe freely, and never lets him rest.

But if the praise of those identical virtues in which the discourse of all other philosophers so especially exults, cannot find any end unless it be directed towards pleasure, and if pleasure be the only thing which calls and allures us to itself by its own nature; then it cannot be doubtful that that is the highest and greatest of all goods, and that to live happily is nothing else except to live with pleasure.

Joseph Butler (1692–1752) was a bishop in the Church of England and his "refutation" of psychological egoism is a classic. In it Butler has in mind primarily Thomas Hobbes (1588–1679) but he was also thinking of the Epicureans, and in some ways what he says fits them better than it does Hobbes. Butler saw psychological egoism as claiming that self-love or a desire for one's own happiness is the basic drive in human nature, the drive from which all other desires and springs of action are derived. In opposition to this, he contends that there are three other forces in our nature that are independent of it and may even oppose it: (1) conscience, (2) benevolent affections, and (3) primary appetites and passions like hunger, curiosity, ambition, resentment, etc., which are aimed, not at one's own happiness, but at particular external objects (here Butler is also attacking psychological hedonism).

Butler was also opposed to ethical egoism, of course, and some of the passages that follow bring this out. His own view was deontological; he thought that conscience ordinarily perceives what is right or wrong without considering either our own or the general good. Among other things, he objects that the Epicurean philosophy of life is not "the moral institution of life," i.e. it is not a morality but something else. If this is correct, we may still adopt ethical egoism as our action-guide but must recognize that in doing so, we are "kicking the habit" of morality. Then the question becomes, "Why should one be moral rather than egoistic", and will be taken up again in Chapter 6.

A "REFUTATION" OF EGOISM

Joseph Butler

[From the Preface]

. . . it is not a true representation of mankind to affirm that they are wholly governed by self-love, the love of power and sensual appetites; since, as on the one hand, they are often actuated by these, without any regard to right or wrong, so, on the other, it is manifest fact that the same persons, the generality, are frequently influenced by friendship, compassion, gratitude; and even a general abhorrence of what is base, and liking of what is fair and just, takes its turn amongst the other motives of action. . . . There is a strange affection in many

From Fifteen Sermons Preached at the Rolls Chapel (*London, 1726*).

people of explaining away all particular affections, and representing the whole life as nothing but one continued exercise of self-love. Hence arises that surprising confusion and perplexity in the Epicureans [1] of old, Hobbes, the author [the Duke de la Rochefoucauld (1613–80)] of *Reflexions, Sentences, et Maximes Morales,* and this whole set of writers—the confusion of calling actions interested which are done in contradiction to the most manifest known interest, merely for the gratification of a present passion. Now all this confusion might easily be avoided, by stating to ourselves wherein the idea of self-love in general consists, as distinguished from all particular movements toward particular external objects—the appetites of sense, resentment, compassion, curiosity, ambition, and the rest. When this is done, if the words "selfish" and "interested" cannot be parted with but must be applied to everything, yet, to avoid such total confusion of all language, let the distinction be made by epithets: and the first may be called cool or settled selfishness, and the other passionate or sensual selfishness. But the most natural way of speaking plainly is to call the the first only "self-love," and the actions proceeding from it "interested"; and to say of the latter that they are not love to ourselves, but movements toward somewhat external: honor, power, the harm or good of another; and that the pursuit of these external objects, so far as it proceeds from these movements (for it may proceed from self-love), is no otherwise interested than as every action of every creature must, from the nature of the thing, be; for no one can act but from a desire or choice or preference of his own.

Self-love and any particular passion may be joined together; and from this complication it becomes impossible in numberless instances to determine precisely how far an action, perhaps even of one's own, has for its principle general self-love or some particular passion. But this need create no confusion in the ideas themselves of self-love and particular passions. We distinctly discern what one is and what the others are, though we may be uncertain how far one or the other influences us. And though, from this uncertainty, it cannot but be that there will be different opinions concerning mankind as more or less governed by interest, and some will ascribe actions to self-love, which others will ascribe to particular passions; yet it is absurd to say that mankind are wholly

---

[1] One need only look into Torquatus's account of the Epicurean system, in Cicero's first book *de Finibus,* to see in what a surprising manner this was done by them. Thus the desire of praise, and of being beloved, he explains to be no other than desire of safety; regard to our country, even in the most virtuous character, to be nothing but regard to ourselves. The author of *Reflexions, etc., Morales,* says, "Curiosity proceeds from interest or pride; which pride also would doubtless have been explained to be self-love" (page 85, ed. 1725). As if there were no such passions in mankind as desire of esteem, or of being beloved, or of knowledge. Hobbes's account of the affections of goodwill and pity are instances of the same kind.

actuated by either, since it is manifest that both have their influence. For as, on the one hand, men form a general notion of interest, some placing it in one thing, and some in another, and have a considerable regard to it throughout the course of their life, which is owing to self-love; so, on the other hand, they are often set on work by the particular passions themselves, and a considerable part of life is spent in the actual gratification of them, that is, is employed, not by self-love, but by the passions.

Besides, the very idea of an interested pursuit necessarily presupposes particular passions or appetites, since the very idea of interest or happiness consists in this that an appetite or affection enjoys its object. It is not because we love ourselves that we find delight in such and such objects, but because we have particular affections toward them. Take away these affections and you leave self-love absolutely nothing at all to employ itself about, no end or object for it to pursue except only that of avoiding pain. Indeed, the Epicureans, who maintained that absence of pain was the highest happiness, might, consistently with themselves, deny all affection and, if they had so pleased, every sensual appetite, too; but the very idea of interest or happiness other than absence of pain implies particular appetites or passions, these being necessary to constitute that interest or happiness.

The observation that benevolence is no more disinterested than any of the common particular passions, seems in itself worth being taken notice of; but is insisted upon to obviate that scorn which one sees rising upon the faces of people who are said to know the world, when mention is made of a disinterested, generous, or public-spirited action. The truth of that observation might be made appear in a more formal manner of proof; for whoever will consider all the possible respects and relations which any particular affection can have to self-love and private interest, will, I think, see demonstrably that benevolence is not in any respect more at variance with self-love than any other particular affection whatever, but that it is in every respect, at least, as friendly to it. . . .

Neither does there appear any reason to wish self-love were weaker in the generality of the world than it is. The influence which it has seems plainly owing to its being constant and habitual, which it cannot but be, and not to the degree or strength of it. Every caprice of the imagination, every curiosity of the understanding, every affection of the heart is perpetually showing its weakness, by prevailing over it. Men daily, hourly sacrifice the greatest known interest to fancy, inquisitiveness, love, or hatred, any vagrant inclination. The thing to be lamented is not that men have so great regard to their own good or interest in the present world, for they have not enough; but that they have so little to the good of others. And this seems plainly owing to their being so much engaged in the gratification of particular passions unfriendly to benevolence, and which happen to be most prevalent in them, much more than to self-love. . . .

Upon the whole, if the generality of mankind were to cultivate within themselves the principle of self-love, if they were to accustom themselves often to set down and consider what was the greatest happiness they were capable of attaining for themselves in this life, and if self-love were so strong and prevalent as that they would uniformly pursue this their supposed chief temporal good, without being diverted from it by any particular passion, it would manifestly prevent numberless follies and vices. This was in a great measure the Epicurean system of philosophy. It is indeed by no means the religious or even moral institution of life. Yet, with all the mistakes men would fall into about interest, it would be less mischievous than the extravagances of mere appetite, will, and pleasure; for certainly self-love, though confined to the interest of this life, is, of the two, a much better guide than passion, which has absolutely no bound nor measure but what is set to it by this self-love or moral considerations. . . .

[From Sermon I]

. . . . there is a natural principle of *benevolence* in man, which is in some degree to *society* what *self-love* is to the *individual*. And if there be in mankind any disposition to friendship; if there be any such thing as compassion, for compassion is momentary love; if there be any such thing as the paternal or filial affections; if there be any affection in human nature the object and end of which is the good of another—this is itself benevolence or the love of another.

[The following two paragraphs appeared as footnotes to Sermon I.]

. . . If any person can in earnest doubt whether there be such a thing as goodwill in one man toward another (for the question is not concerning either the degree or extensiveness of it, but concerning the affection itself), let it be observed that whether man be thus or otherwise constituted, what is the inward frame in this particular, is a mere question of fact or natural history, not provable immediately by reason. It is therefore to be judged of and determined in the same way other facts or matters of natural history are: by appealing to the external senses or inward perceptions respectively, as the matter under consideration is cognizable by one or the other; by arguing from acknowledged facts and actions; for a great number of actions in the same kind, in different circumstances, and respecting different objects, will prove, to a certainty, what principles they do not, and, to the greatest probability, what principles they do proceed from; and lastly, by the testimony of mankind.

Now that there is some degree of benevolence amongst men may be as strongly and plainly proved in all these ways, as it could possibly be proved, supposing there was this affection in our nature. And should any-one think fit to assert that resentment in the mind of man was absolutely nothing but reasonable concern for our own safety, the falsity of this, and what is the real nature of that passion, could be shown in no other ways than those in which it may be shown, that there is such a thing in some degree as real goodwill in man toward man. It is sufficient that the seeds of it be implanted in our nature by God. There is, it is owned, much left for us to do upon our own heart and temper; to cultivate, to improve, to call it forth, to exercise it in a steady, uniform manner. This is our work; this is virtue and religion.

Everybody makes a distinction between self-love and the several particular passions, appetites, and affections; and yet they are often confounded again. That they are totally different, will be seen by any one who will distinguish between the passions and appetites themselves, and endeavoring after the means of their gratification. Consider the appetite of hunger, and the desire of esteem; these being the occasion both of pleasure and pain, the coolest self-love, as well as the appetites and passions themselves, may put us upon making use of the proper methods of obtaining that pleasure, and avoiding that pain; but the feelings themselves, the pain of hunger and shame, and the delight from esteem, are no more self-love than they are anything in the world. Though a man hated himself, he would as much feel the pain of hunger as he would that of the gout; and it is plainly supposable there may be creatures with self-love in them to the highest degree, who may be quite insensible and indifferent (as men in some cases are) to the contempt and esteem of those upon whom their happiness does not in some further respects depend. And as self-love and the several particular passions and appetites are in themselves totally different, so that some actions proceed from one, and some from the other, will be manifest to any who will observe the two following very supposable cases. One man rushes upon certain ruin for the gratification of a present desire; nobody will call the principle of this action self-love. Suppose another man to go through some laborious work upon promise of a great reward, without any distinct knowledge what the reward will be; this course of action cannot be ascribed to any particular passion. The former of these actions is plainly to be imputed to some particular passion or affection, the latter as plainly to the general affection or principle of self-love. That there are some particular pursuits or actions concerning which we cannot determine how far they are owing to one, and how far to the other, proceeds from this that the two principles are frequently mixed together, and run up into each other. This distinction is further explained in the eleventh sermon.

[From Sermon XI]

. . . Every man hath a general desire of his own happiness, and likewise a variety of particular affections, passions, and appetites to particular external objects. The former proceeds from or is self-love, and seems inseparable from all sensible creatures who can reflect upon themselves and their own interest or happiness, so as to have that interest an object to their minds; what is to be said of the latter is that they proceed from, or together make up, that particular nature according to which man is made. The object the former pursues is somewhat internal—our own happiness, enjoyment, satisfaction; whether we have or have not a distinct particular perception what it is or wherein it consists, the objects of the latter are this or that particular external thing which the affections tend towards, and of which it hath always a particular idea or perception. The principle we call "self-love" never seeks anything external for the sake of the thing, but only as a means of happiness or good; particular affections rest in the external things themselves. One belongs to man as a reasonable creature reflecting upon his own interest or happiness. The other, though quite distinct from reason, are as much a part of human nature.

That all particular appetites and passions are toward *external things themselves*, distinct from the *pleasure arising from them*, is manifested from hence—that there could not be this pleasure were it not for that prior suitableness between the object and the passion; there could be no enjoyment or delight from one thing more than another, from eating food more than from swallowing a stone, if there were not an affection or appetite to one thing more than another.

Every particular affection, even the love of our neighbor, is as really our own affection as self-love; and the pleasure arising from its gratification is as much my own pleasure as the pleasure self-love would have from knowing I myself should be happy some time hence, would be my own pleasure. And if, because every particular affection is a man's own, and the pleasure arising from its gratification his own pleasure, or pleasure to himself, such particular affection must be called self-love, according to this way of speaking no creature whatever can possibly act but merely from self-love; and every action and every affection whatever is to be resolved up into this one principle. But then this is not the language of mankind; or if it were, we should want words to express the difference between the principle of an action proceeding from cool consideration that it will be to my own advantage, and an action, suppose of revenge or of friendship, by which a man runs upon certain ruin to do evil or good to another. It is manifest the principles of these actions are totally different, and so want different words to be distinguished by; all that they agree in is that they both proceed from and are done to gratify an inclination in a man's self. But the principle or inclination in one case is self-love, in the other, hatred or love of another. There is then a distinction between the cool principle of self-love or general desire of our happiness, as one part of our nature and one principle of action, and the particular affections toward particular external objects, as another part of our nature and another principle of action. How much soever therefore is to be allowed to self-love, yet it cannot be allowed to be the whole of our inward constitution, because, you see, there are other parts or principles which come into it.

Further, private happiness or good is all which self-love can make us desire or be concerned about; in having this consists its gratification: it is an affection to ourselves, a regard to our own interest, happiness, and private good; and in the proportion a man hath this, he is interested, or a lover of himself. Let this be kept in mind; because there is commonly, as I shall presently have occasion to observe, another sense put upon these words. On the other hand, particular affections tend toward particular external things; these are their objects; having these is their end—in this consists their gratification, no matter whether it be, or be not, upon the whole, our interest or happiness. An action done from the former of these principles is called an interested action. An action proceeding from any of the latter has its denomination of passionate, ambitious, friendly, revengeful, or any other, from the particular appetite or affection from which it proceeds. Thus self-love as one part of human nature and the several particular principles as the other part are, themselves, their objects and ends, stated and shown.

From hence it will be easy to see how far, and in what ways, each of these can contribute and be subservient to the private good of the individual. Happiness does not consist in self-love. The desire of happiness is no more the thing itself than the desire of riches is the possession or enjoyment of them. People may love themselves with the most entire and unbounded affection, and yet be extremely miserable. Neither can self-love anyway help them out, but by setting them on work to get rid of the causes of their misery, to gain or make use of those objects which are by nature adapted to afford satisfaction. Happiness or satisfaction consists only in the enjoyment of those objects which are by nature suited to our several particular appetites, passions, and affections. So that if self-love wholly engrosses us, and leaves no room for any other principle, there can be absolutely no such thing at all as happiness, or enjoyment of any kind whatever, since happiness consists in the gratification of particular passions, which supposes the having of them. Self-love then does not constitute *this* or *that* to be our interest or good; but, our interest or good being constituted by nature and supposed, self-love only puts us upon obtaining and securing it. Therefore, if it be possible that self-love may prevail and exert itself in a degree or manner which is not subservient to this end, then it will not follow that our interest will be promoted in proportion to the degree in which that principle engrosses us, and prevails over others. Nay further, the private and contracted affection, when it is not subservient to this end, private good, may, for anything that appears, have a direct contrary tendency and effect. And if we will consider the matter, we shall see that it often really has. *Disengagement* is absolutely necessary to enjoyment; and a person may have so steady and fixed an eye upon his own interest, whatever he places it in, as may hinder him from *attending* to many gratifications within his reach, which others have their minds free and open to. Overfondness for a child is not generally thought to be for its advantage; and if there be any guess to be made from appearances, surely that character we call selfish is not the most promising for happiness. Such a temper may plainly be, and exert itself in a degree and manner which may give unnecessary and useless solicitude and anxiety, in a degree and manner which may prevent obtaining the means and materials of enjoyment, as well as the making use of them. Immoderate self-love does very ill consult its own interest; and how much soever a paradox it may appear, it is certainly true that even from self-love we should endeavor to get over all inordinate regard to and consideration of ourselves. Every one of our passions and affections hath its natural stint and bound, which may easily be exceeded; whereas our enjoyments can possibly be but in a determinate measure and degree. Therefore such excess of the affection, since it cannot procure any enjoyment, must in all cases be useless, but is generally attended with inconveniences, and often is downright pain and misery. This holds as much with regard to self-love as to all other affections. The natural degree of it, so far as it sets us on work to gain and make use of the materials of satisfaction, may be to our real advantage; but beyond or besides this, it is in several respects an inconvenience and disadvantage. Thus it appears that private interest is so far from being likely to be promoted in proportion to the degree in which self-love engrosses us, and prevails over all other principles, that the contracted affection may be so prevalent as to disappoint itself, and even contradict its own end, private good.

"But who, except the most sordidly covetous, ever thought there was any rivalship between the love of greatness, honor, power, or between sensual appetites and self-love? No, there is a perfect harmony between them. It is by means of these particular appetites and affections that self-love is gratified in enjoyment, happiness, and satisfaction. The competition and rivalship is between self-love and the love of our neighbor, that affection which leads us out of ourselves, makes us regardless of our own interest, and substitute that of another in its stead." Whether then there be any peculiar competition and contrariety in this case, shall now be considered.

Self-love and interestedness was stated to consist in or be an affection to ourselves, a regard to our own private good; it is therefore distinct from benevolence, which is an affection to the good of our fellow creatures. But that benevolence is distinct from, that is, not the same thing with self-love, is no reason for its being looked upon with any peculiar suspicion; because every principle whatever, by means of which self-love is gratified, is distinct from it; and all things which are distinct from each other are equally so. A man has an affection or aversion to another; that one of these tends to and is gratified by doing good, that the other tends to and is gratified by doing harm, does not in the least alter the respect which either one or the other of these inward feelings has to self-love. We use the word "property" so as to exclude any other persons having an interest in that of which we say a particular man has the property. And we often use the word "selfish" so as to exclude in the same manner all regards to the good of others. But the cases are not parallel; for though that exclusion is really part of the idea of property, yet such positive exclusion, or bringing this peculiar disregard to the good of others into the idea of self-love, is in reality adding to the idea, or changing it from what it was before stated to consist in, namely, in an affection to ourselves. This being the whole idea of self-love, it can no otherwise exclude goodwill or love of others than merely by not including it, no otherwise than it excludes love of arts or reputation, or of anything else. Neither, on the other hand, does benevolence, any more than love of arts or of reputation, exclude self-love. Love of our neighbor then has just the same respect to, is no more distant from, self-love than hatred of our neighbor, or than love or hatred of anything else. Thus the principles from which men rush upon certain ruin for the destruction of an enemy, and for the preservation of a friend, have the same respect to the private affection, and are equally interested or equally disinterested; and it is of no avail whether they are said to be one or the other. Therefore, to those that are shocked to hear virtue spoken of as disinterested, it may be allowed that it is indeed absurd to speak thus of it, unless hatred, several particular instances of vice, and all the common affections and aversions in mankind are acknowledged to be disinterested too. Is there any less inconsistency between the love of inanimate things, or of creatures merely sensitive, and self-love than between self-love and the love of our neighbor? Is desire of the love of inanimate things, or of creatures merely sensitive, and self-love than desire of and delight in the esteem of another? They are both equally desire of and delight in somewhat external to ourselves: either both or neither are so. The object of self-love is expressed in the term "self"; and every appetite of sense and every particular affection of the heart are equally interested or disinterested, because the objects of them are all equally self or somewhat else. Whatever ridicule therefore the mention of a disinterested principle or action may be supposed to lie open to, must, upon the matter being thus stated, relate to ambition and every appetite and particular affection, as much as to benevolence. And indeed all the ridicule and all the grave perplexity, of which this subject hath had its full share, is merely from words. The most intelligible way of speaking of it seems to be this: that self-love and the actions done in consequence of it (for these will presently appear to be the same as to this quesion) are interested; that particular affections toward external objects, and the actions done in consequence of those affections, are not so. But everyone is at liberty to use words as he pleases. All that is here insisted upon is that ambition, revenge, benevolence, all particular passions whatever, and the actions they produce, are equally interested or disinterested.

Thus it appears that there is no peculiar contrariety between self-love and benevolence, no greater competition between these than between any other particular affections and self-love. . . .

Many others have since criticized ethical egoism in a variety of ways. In the following passage, A. C. Ewing contends that ethical egoism is unethical. Notice that Ewing supposes that there will be substantial agreement about what we would say in various ethical situations. Might an ethical egoist reasonably take exception to what Ewing considers to be "obvious"?

AGAINST ETHICAL EGOISM

A. C. Ewing

It seems to me indeed that some of the worst acts ever done could be justified if egoistic hedonism were true. In Ibsen's play, *The Pretenders,* there is a well-known scene in which the villain lying on his deathbed has an opportunity of avenging himself on an enemy by giving rise to a misapprehension about the succession to the throne, knowing

From Teach Yourself Ethics (*London: Teach Yourself Books Ltd., 1953*). Reprinted by permission of the publisher.

that if he does so he will gratuitously cause a civil war in which thousands will be slain. The situation in the play is complicated by the fear of punishment hereafter, but we have seen this to be irrelevant unless the proposed action can be seen to be wrong independently of the punishment, and in any case we may suppose the man thus tempted to be an atheist. Now if the sole criterion of the rightness or wrongness of an action is its conduciveness to one's own pleasure, I think one would have to say that the act of revenge was right because it would make the last few moments of his life happier than they would otherwise have been. It is true that he would have been likely to be a happier man on the whole if he had not indulged his vindictive desires to such an appalling extent in the past as he must have done to make such an act even a serious temptation, but it is too late for him to alter this now. We could not say to him—Control your vindictive desires now and your character will be improved so that you will be capable of greater pleasure in the future, for he would reply—I have no future. For the egoistic hedonist to make oneself miserable for the good of another man should be positively wicked in the only sense in which anything could be wicked at all.

But, even if the egoistic hedonist could show that his view was compatible with the ordinary canons of morality as regards the external nature of actions, he would still not have justified his position. For it is not only the external act, but the motive which counts in ethics, and the motive he suggests is one which we must regard as essentially unethical. Suppose a man admitted that he only refrains from stealing for fear of being sent to prison, or from ill-treating his children because he has been promised a sum of money if he does not ill-treat them, and we believed him, should we regard him as morally worthy? Not at all, we should condemn him as much or almost as much as if he had been guilty of theft and cruelty, for we should not recognize his motive as a proper one at all. And if so, why should we regard his conduct as any more moral if he refrains from wrong acts in general merely because he is bribed by the prospect of happiness or deterred by the fear of unhappiness whether in this life or in another, even if the happiness or unhappiness is not viewed as coming in such crude ways and as further removed in time? The best we could say is that he shows prudence and far-sightedness, not that he is good. The occasions when we feel markedly under a moral obligation are just *not* the occasions when we are exercised about our own happiness, but the occasions on which we feel an obligation to somebody else that strikes us as such quite independently of whether obedience to it is or is not conducive to our happiness. If a man sacrifices his own happiness needlessly without apparently harming others, the natural word that springs to the lips of the observer in speaking of him is "foolish"; if he sacrifices the happiness of another to further his own apparent happiness, the natural word is not "foolish" but "bad" (in the moral sense of that word). I do not deny that some egoistic hedonists were good men, but I do say that they had a wrong theory of the motives which determined and ought to determine their conduct.

. . . And is it not plain that it is intuitively at least as obvious that it is wrong to do things which hurt others needlessly as that it is wrong unnecessarily to hurt oneself? There are other ethical intuitions incompatible with egoistic hedonism which might be cited, but this one is sufficient. If it is wrong to do things which hurt others for our own amusement, and we see it to be wrong just because it does hurt them, egoistic hedonism is false. For according to egoistic hedonism the only reason why anything is wrong is because it is not conducive to the agent's greatest pleasure. Even if in fact it is the case that it is never conducive to my own greatest pleasure to hurt others, it should be plain that this is not the main reason why it is wrong. If we can see clearly that our own pleasure is good, we can see just as clearly that the fact that an action needlessly and intentionally hurts another is quite sufficient to make it wrong, whether it also hurts me or not. . . .

It remains to answer the question how it was that such an obviously mistaken view ever acquired an important influence on ethical thinkers. It seems to me that there were two main reasons for this. In the first place it is plain that the fact that a course of action is conducive to one's own happiness, is, as far as it goes, a reason for adopting it. It is a subject for dispute whether this makes it morally obligatory or merely prudent to act in the way proposed, but at least it is a good reason of some sort for doing so. Wantonly to sacrifice one's happiness or incur unhappiness is at least irrational, and that something is rational is a reason for doing it if anything is. Now the project of bringing all Ethics under a single principle so that there is just one kind of circumstance which decides whether an act is right or wrong is very attractive to thinkers, and so when we have found a principle which obviously does give valid reasons for action, there is a temptation to bring all ethical judgements under it. Thinkers have again and again succumbed to such temptations to a premature unification, but knowledge and life are not so simple as that.

Kurt Baier and Brian Medlin have both argued not so much that ethical egoism is unethical, as that it is inconsistent or self-contradictory in one way or another. Their arguments are explained and discussed by John Hospers in the following essay. Hospers argues that once the necessary distinctions are drawn and the position of the egoist is clarified, none of the objections raised by Baier or Medlin successfully refutes ethical egoism. As you study his arguments, ask yourself whether you agree with Hospers. What would actually follow about the truth or falsity of ethical egoism, if he is correct? Finally, consider whether *you* would prefer the way of life that Hospers sketches in this passage toward the end of his essay: "Perhaps the egoist likes to live in a dangerous cutthroat manner, unwilling to help others in need but not desiring others to help him either. He wants life to be spicy and dangerous . . ."

BAIER AND MEDLIN ON ETHICAL EGOISM

John Hospers

In his excellent book *The Moral Point of View,* Professor Kurt Baier attempts to refute ethical egoism—the doctrine that my sole duty is to promote my own interests exclusively—in the following way:

"Let B and K be candidates for the presidency of a certain country and let it be granted that it is in the interest of either to be elected, but that only one can succeed. It would then be in the interest of B but against the interest of K if B were elected, and vice versa, and therefore in the interest of B but against the interest of K if K were liquidated, and vice versa. But from this it would follow that B ought to liquidate K, that it is wrong for B not to do so, that B has not 'done his duty' until he has liquidated K; and vice versa. Similarly K, knowing that his own liquidation is in the interest of B and therefore anticipating B's attempts to secure it, ought to take steps to foil B's endeavors. It would be wrong for him not to do so. He would 'not have done his duty' until he had made sure of stopping B. It follows that if K prevents B from liquidating him, his act must be said to be both wrong and not wrong—wrong because it is the prevention of what B ought to do, his duty, and wrong for B not to do it; not wrong because it is what K ought to do, his duty, and wrong for K not to do it. But one and the same act (logically) cannot be both morally wrong and not morally wrong. . . .

"This is obviously absurd. For morality is designed to apply in just such cases, namely, those where interests conflict. But if the point of view of morality were that of self-interest, then there could *never* be moral solutions of conflicts of interest."[1]

From Philosophical Studies, *XII, Nos. 1-2 (1961). Reprinted by permission of the author and* Philosophical Studies.

[1] *The Moral Point of View* (Ithaca, N.Y.: Cornell Press, 1958), pp. 189–90.

We are to assume at the outset that killing K not only seems to be, but really *is* to B's interest and that killing B really is to K's interest. (If it were to the interest of each to work out a compromise, then no problem would arise.) Operating on this assumption, what can be said of Professor Baier's one-shot refutation of egoism? His argument can be schematized in the following way:

1. Every adequate ethical theory must be able to provide solutions for conflicts of interest.
2. Ethical egoism is unable to provide solutions for conflicts of interest.
3. Therefore, ethical egoism is not an adequate ethical theory.

So much for the argument for the inadequacy of ethical egoism. But his criticism goes even further:

4. Any view which is guilty of self-contradiction is thereby refuted.
5. Ethical egoism is guilty of self-contradiction.
6. Therefore, ethical egoism is refuted.

We may examine the second argument first, since if a theory is guilty of self-contradiction no further refutation of it is necessary.

Let it be admitted that to say that one and the same act is both right and wrong is to be guilty of a self-contradiction, since the proposition that it is wrong entails that it is not right, and an act cannot be both right and not right. (I shall waive any discussion of a point whose truth is presupposed in Baier's argument, namely that rightness and wrongness are properties. I shall also waive discussion of the possibility that even if they are properties they are to-you and to-me properties, e.g., something can be interesting to you and not interesting to me, and rightness might be like interestingness.)

We may admit, then, at least for purposes of the argument, that to say that Brutus killing Caesar was both right and wrong involves a contradiction. But the case presented by Professor Baier is not that of one and the same act being both right and wrong. It is a case of *two* acts, one by B and the other by K. They are two acts of the same *kind*, namely attempted murder (or the attempt to foil the murder-attempt of the other), but there is no contradiction in two such acts being attempted or in both being right. It might well be B's duty to try to dispose of K, and K's duty to try to dispose of B. Since there are two acts here, one by B and one by K, the situation of one and the same act being both right and wrong does not arise, and no contradiction arises either.

So much for the argument concerning contradiction. But the inadequacy argument remains, and it seems much more plausible. It is true that we usually expect an ethical theory to be able to settle conflicts of interest; for example, if husband and wife both want custody of the children, we expect the ethical theory to tell us (in conjunction, of course, with empirical premises) which one's wish should be granted; every judge in a courtroom must make such decisions. The judge in arbitrating such a case could not use ethical egoism as a way of settling it, for if it is the interest of both husband and wife to have the same thing and they can't both have it, he will *have* to decide against the interest of one of them; and egoism, which tells each person to follow his own interest exclusively, can provide no basis for settling the dispute. This does seem to be a very serious criticism.

What would the egoist reply to such a charge? I must first distinguish the *personal* egoist from the *impersonal* egoist. The personal egoist is one who says that *his* sole duty is to promote his own interest exclusively, but makes no pronouncement about what other people should do. (Some would not consider this an ethical theory at all, since it does not fulfill the criterion of generality. And if the theory is restated so as not to talk about duties at all—not "It is my duty to promote my own interest exclusively" but *"I'm going* to promote my own interest exclusively," which is the kind of thing that most practicing egoists say—then of course there is no ethical theory at all, but only a prediction or expression of determination with regard to one's future behavior.) The impersonal egoist is one who says that the duty of *each and every person* (including himself) is to pursue his own interest exclusively.

How will the egoist react to Baier's inadequacy argument? The *personal* egoist will not be disturbed at all. According to him, his one duty is to pursue exclusively his own interest; so if he happens to be B he will try to kill K, and if he is K he will try to kill B (and foil K's attempts to kill him); and if he is neither B nor K he will not concern himself with the conflict of interest one way or the other. Of course if there is something in it for him, he will: if he stands to gain a fortune if K wins, then he will do what he can to assist K's victory in order to gain the fortune. But otherwise he will ignore the matter. "But doesn't an ethical theory have to have a means of deciding what to do or say in cases of conflict of interest? If you had to advise B or K, what would you say?" The answer is, of course, that if there is nothing in it for him the personal egoist will not bother to advise either party or to aid either cause. If asked for advice on the matter, he would probably say, "Get lost, you bother me." (Nor would the personal egoist be likely to engage in philosophical discussion. It would hardly be to his interest to allow other people to plant in his mind the seeds of skepticism concerning his egoistic doctrine.)

So far, then, egoism has not been refuted. It has been shown to be inadequate *only if* you expect an ethical theory to arbitrate conflicts of interest. Thus, it *would* be insufficient for the judge in a divorce court.

The judge has nothing to gain either way, but he has to decide on a matter of conflict of interest between husband and wife. If the judge were a personal egoist, his principle would simply be to follow *his own* interest; but this principle wouldn't help him at all in dealing with the case at hand. Here he needs instructions, not for promoting his own interest, but for settling cases of conflict of interest between *other* people.

And this, of course, the theory cannot provide; but the personal egoist doesn't mind this at all. He has no wish to arbitrate other people's conflicts of interest. He will gladly leave such activities to the "suckers."

What of the *impersonal* egoist? His view is that he should pursue his own interest exclusively, that B should pursue B's, that K should pursue K's, and so on for everyone else. What will he say in the case of B and K? He will advise K to try to win out over B by whatever means he can, and will advise B to try to win out over K by whatever means he can: in other words, to settle the thing by force or craft, and may the strongest or cleverest man win. Does his advice to B contradict his advice to K? Not at all; he is urging each one to try to gain victory over the other; this is not very different from telling each of the two competing teams to try and win the game. His view does not, of course, provide a *rational* means of settling the conflict of interest, but it does provide a means: it tells each party to try to emerge victorious, though of course only one of them *can* emerge victorious.

So far, there seems to be no difficulty for the impersonal egoist. But, as an impersonal egoist, he does have a stake in the general acceptance of his doctrine; for he does say of other people, not just himself, that each should pursue his own interest exclusively. If he sees B, he will urge B to try to win over K (even if he has nothing to gain personally by B's victory), and if he sees K, he will urge K to try to win over B. But there is, while no outright contradiction, a curious *tactical incongruity* in his view. For if the impersonal egoist advises others to pursue their own interest, might not this interfere with the promotion of *his own* interest, and yet is he not committed by his own doctrine to pursuing his own interest exclusively? If he advises B and K, but neither B nor K is a threat to him, there is no problem; but if I advise my business competitor to pursue his own interest with a vengeance, may he not follow my advice and pursue his interest so wholeheartedly that he forces me out of business? For the sake of *my own* interest, then, I may be well advised to keep my egoistic doctrine to myself, lest others use it against me.

An impersonal egoist, therefore, may simply prefer to keep his own counsel and not advise others at all. In this case, he escapes the difficulty just as the personal egoist did. He will pursue his own interest regardless of who else opposes it; and while he does, as an impersonal egoist, advise others to pursue *their own* interests, he will do this only when doing it does not imperil *his* interest.

Thus, *if* you are an impersonal egoist, and *if* as an impersonal egoist you have a stake in advising others—and only then—you will feel a conflict between the promotion of your egoistic doctrine and the promotion of your own interests, which will be damaged if others pursue their interests at the expense of yours. But this hardly *refutes* the impersonal egoist's doctrine; it concerns only a tactical matter of when to publicize it.

But now another objection to ethical egoism presents itself. Suppose you are an impersonal egoist, and are suggesting courses of action to your acquaintances. Acquaintance A asks you what to do, and you say to him, "Pursue your own interest exclusively, and if B tries to get the better of you, cut him down. Even if you could save B's life by lifting a finger, there is no reason for you to do so as long as it doesn't promote your interest." Later on, B asks you what you think *he* should do. So you say to him, "Pursue your own interest exclusively, and if A tries to get the better of you, cut him down. Even if you could save A's life by lifting a finger, there is no reason for you to do so as long as it doesn't promote your interest." And you say similar things to your other acquaintances.

Suppose, now, that an onlooker heard you say all these things. He might wonder (with good reason) exactly what you were advising— what the general drift of your advice was. You tell A to do what is to his interest and ignore B, so our onlooker thinks you are a friend of A's and an enemy of B's. But then you tell B to do what is to his interest and ignore A, and our onlooker now concludes that you are a friend of B and an enemy of A. And in fact what are you anyway? It sounds to the onlooker as if you are pathologically addicted to changing your mind. Perhaps, like some people, you are so impressed by whoever you are with at the moment that you forget all about the interests of those who aren't right there before you. This might explain the sudden shift in attitude.

But the curious thing is that the egoist doesn't consider this a shift in attitude at all, but a consistent expression of *one* attitude, the "impersonal egoistic" attitude. But that is just the point of the objection. *Is* it a single consistent attitude? When you are in the presence of A, it is only A's interest that counts; but a moment later, when you are in the presence of B, it is only B's interest that counts. Isn't this very strange? Can the question of whose interests count really depend on whom you happen to be addressing or confronting at the moment?

The charge, in short, is that the impersonal egoist is guilty of issuing *inconsistent directives.* This charge is made, for example, by Dr. Brian Medlin.[2] According to Medlin, when the (impersonal) egoist is talking to himself he says "I want myself to come out on top, and I don't care about Tom, Dick, Harry . . ."; when he is talking to Tom he says (in effect), "I want Tom to come out on top and I don't care about myself, Dick, Harry . . ."; when he is talking to Dick he says, "I want Dick to come out on top, and I don't care about myself, Tom, Harry . . ."; and so on in a conjunction of an infinite number of avowals. "From this analysis," he concludes, "it is obvious that the principle expressing such an attitude must be inconsistent."[3] (The same conclusion follows if the egoist says to Tom, "You alone count," and to Dick, "You alone count," and so on.)

Now, if this is what the impersonal egoist really means to say, then of course what he says *is* inconsistent. But perhaps that is not what he means to say; at any rate, it is not what he *needs* to say. What else might he mean?

It might be suggested, first, that all that the egoist wants to say is that if you tend to your interests (happiness, or welfare, or whatever) and I to my interests and Tom to Tom's interests, and so on, everyone will be happier (or have more welfare, etc.) than they would if they did not adopt such a completely laissez-faire policy with regard to one another's interests. But two things should be noted about this: (1) If the egoist says this, he is making an *empirical* claim—a claim that human beings will be happier pursuing a policy of splendid isolation with regard to each other than by behaving cooperatively, helping one another in time of need, and so on—and this empirical claim is very dubious indeed; it seems rather to be the case that the welfare of human beings is not independent but *inter*-dependent, and that "no man is an island." If each person pursued his own interest to the exclusion of others, there would be less happiness in the world, not more. But whatever may be said of this empirical claim, (2) when the egoist makes this claim he is no longer an egoist but a utilitarian; he is arguing that the general welfare (or the maximum total fulfillment of human interests) is what should be striven for, and that the best means of achieving it is by a policy of isolation. But in admitting that the general welfare is the end to be aimed at he is already forsaking his egoism.

Is there anything else, then, that the impersonal egoist can be alleged to mean? The charge against him is that his directives to different people are inconsistent with one another. He, Tom, Dick, and

---

[2] "Ultimate Principles and Ethical Egoism," *Australasian Journal of Philosophy*, 35(No. 2):111–18 (August 1957).

[3] *Ibid.*, p. 115.

Harry cannot each be the *only* person who counts, or the only person he hopes will come out on top. Is not the egoist, if he abandons the utilitarian argument (above) and retreats back to his egoism, caught in this web of inconsistency? Is he not saying to Tom that he hopes Tom will come out on top (and by implication that Dick won't), and then the next moment saying to Dick that he hopes Dick will come out on top (and by implication that Tom won't), and so on, thereby patting each one on the back before his face and poking him in the nose behind his back?

The egoist *need* not, I think, be guilty of such duplicity. What if he assembled Tom, Dick, Harry, and everyone else into his presence at the same moment? What would he say to them altogether? He might say, "I *hope* that each of you comes out on top." But in that case, he *is* saying something self-contradictory, since of course each of them cannot come out on top—only one of them can. But he need not say this; suppose that instead he says, "I hope each of you *tries* to come out on top," or "Each of you should *try* to come out the victor." There is surely no inconsistency here. The hope he is expressing here is the kind of hope that the interested but impartial spectator expresses at a game. Perhaps the egoist likes to live life in a dangerous cutthroat manner, unwilling to help others in need but not desiring others to help him either. He wants life to be spicy and dangerous; to him the whole world is one vast egoistic game, and living life accordingly is the way to make it interesting and exciting. It may be that, if our egoist says this, his egoism is somewhat diluted from the stronger and earlier form of "I hope that you all win" or "Each of you alone counts"—but at least, in this latest formulation, he is not caught in an inconsistency.

Whether or not the egoist, then, is caught in an inconsistency depends on what, exactly, we take him to be saying. It should not be assumed that because the egoist in some formulations of his doctrine is guilty of inconsistency, he is therefore inconsistent in all of them.

2.2

Act-Deontological Theories

Deontologists may and do hold rather different sorts of views. Some regard general principles or rules as basic in morality, and take particular judgments or decisions to be derivative from them. This is essentially Socrates' procedure in the *Crito*. Others, however, hold that the basic judgments and decisions in morality are particular ones like "This is what I should do in this situation"; they are act-deontologists. Of these, the more extreme view would be that rules and principles have no place in morality; a more moderate view is that such rules or principles have a place but only as useful, revisable rules of thumb built up on the basis of particular judgments about previous cases, either by oneself or by mankind. Both of these positions, extreme and moderate, are forms of "situational ethics," but a proponent of situational ethics need not be a deontologist at all; he may be an act-utilitarian or an act-agapist, as Joseph Fletcher is. On either view, a particular judgment may be thought of as involving a kind of intuition, seeing, or discovery, or as involving something more like a decision, choice, or creation. In other words, act-deontological theories may be either intuitionist or existentialist.

Butler and Aristotle sometimes sound like act-deontologists. More recently, the position was held for a time by E. F. Carritt, though he later gave it up for a theory more like that of W. D. Ross (a rule-deontologist whose theory is presented in Section 2.3). Notice his references to Butler and Kant. The following passage will also serve as an example of a more existentialist kind of act-deontologism, if one substitutes the idea of decision for that of intuition in reading it.

MORAL RULES

E. F. Carritt

Are there, then, no valid moral rules? It will be agreed on all hands that no number of moral rules will save us from exercising intuition; for a rule can only be general, but an act must be particular, so it will always be necessary to satisfy ourselves that an act comes under the rule, and for this no rule can be given.

First we may notice that if there be such rules they may conflict. So having intuitively apprehended that, of two alternative acts possible for me, one is an instance of promise-keeping and the other an instance of saving innocent life, I should have intuitively to decide which is now "my paramount duty," or, as I prefer to say, "my duty" or "my actual duty." Those who speak of "conflicting duties" seem to mean alternative possible acts, either of which, with very slight change of circumstance, would now be my plain duty, but between which I may well hesitate as to where that duty lies. If they conflict, only one is possible, so I cannot think that both can be my duty; nor should I blame myself for omitting the other. Rules get a specious universality by using dyslogistic terms. "Thou shalt do no murder" meant "Do no killing except justifiable homicide—such as stoning the blasphemer or wiping out the heathen."

But, however they would need to be supplemented by intuition, such rules might be held to have a kind of provisional validity; so we must ask how they are ascertained. Probably all would agree that they are first seen and most clearly seen in individual instances. I may repeat the decalogue, like the multiplication table, by rote, but when any doubt arises as to the universal validity of a precept I must follow the Socratic method and imagine, as definitely as may be, *instances* where my moral judgement would work. But if we can judge an instance without general rules, it might seem, as Butler says, that the inquiry after them is merely an occupation, not without some usefulness, for "men of leisure." The usefulness suggested is, I suppose, that where the right course is obscure or the passions violent, rules may save the ship. So far as this is so I think that their function is that of ballast rather than compass. If the difficulty of acting rightly come from the difficulty of knowing what we now ought to do, whether that difficulty depend upon a real complexity of the situation or upon our own bias in the way of desire or prejudice, then we shall question any constraining rule and must, as a

From The Theory of Morals (*Oxford: The Clarendon Press, 1928). Reprinted by permission of The Clarendon Press, Oxford.*

last resort, fix our attention upon the particular instance, in which, as is admitted, the validity of rules first and most clearly appears. And we shall be right. For since the rules are abstracted from instances and have to be applied to instances, to assume that this rule has been correctly formulated and applies to our present instance is to beg the question. The man who acts on principle is apt to be favourably contrasted with the man of "impulse"; but principles may be wrong and *intuitions* right. We do not hear that Kant ever sacrificed an innocent life by telling the truth, but there is a tale of his condemning the conduct of some sailors who had thrown overboard in a dangerous storm a case of delicacies consigned to him. If the story be true it might be an instance when the idolatry of rules ("never break a promise, even to save life") has worked *on the side of passion* against genuine moral insight. I think it probable that a pedantic desire for consistency with the hedonistic generalization which they thought self-evident has led some men to act wrongly, who would have acted rightly if they had no theory to justify. It has certainly led to the formulation of some very odd maxims. I cannot persuade myself that I first morally apprehend the obligation of several rules, then intellectually apprehend one of alternative actions to be an instance of one and the other of another, and finally, by a second moral intuition, see which rule ought now to be followed. I rather think that I morally apprehend that I ought now to do this act and then intellectually generalize rules.

The real value of Kant's principle of universality is practical, not theoretical; it is a dodge, like asking an angry child to look at its face in a mirror. What is right for me to do in a particular instance is right, not because it would be right for others, but because the situation demands it from me or any one (if any one else could be in this situation), and I may judge more clearly if I imagine the agent to be some *one* else. By "universalizing" my act I see it writ large. To analyse the situation and say that it is the factor A in it which morally demands the action B, and that therefore whenever A is present we ought to do B, is as hazardous as to analyse a work of art and produce those rules and canons of artistic production which pave the road to oblivion. There will always be other factors besides A, and their relevance must be seen, not proved. Perhaps this dispute is only verbal or I have misunderstood the position I am criticizing. Since, as I maintain, it is the situation which determines what I now ought to do, if the character of that situation could be exhaustively described a rule for precisely similar situations could be given. This, of course, is impossible. But, it may be urged, we could thus give a rule for any situation which should differ in no *relevant* fact. I only contend that, for the reasons given, no such rules settle in advance how I ought now to act, and that the preoccupation with such generalities is on the whole apt to mislead us in deciding what is right, just as preoccupation with so-called canons of art is apt to mislead the artist.

But if the formulation of rules does not help us to decide what is now right, may it not help us on the whole to do right in general?—to steady, if not steer the ship? The use of rules may be defended as a very good practical dodge. If I cannot trust myself to choose rightly in the moment of temptation, is it not well to choose in a cool hour beforehand? Even granting that the decision may not always fit the situation when it comes, and that then, in abiding by my rule, I shall err, such errors will be less frequent, probably, than those I should have run into by trying to decide only when all the circumstances were before me, but consequently only when my passions were awake. If I keep a rule always to go to bed at a certain hour, that may on occasion be earlier or later than the circumstances really warrant, but it might on most days prevent me going much too late or too early out of slackness. I cannot imagine a man making rules for his conduct in cases where his passions would not be engaged; for instance, when his conduct would consist in exercising an immediate and unquestioned and disinterested control over the behaviour of another, and when it was not important for that other to know beforehand what would be enjoined. A man may usefully make rules for his own diet and hours of rest. But I suppose that no doctor would determine in advance how much food or sleep or work should be allowed to a given patient through his convalescence. All depends on the case.

This use of rules for my own conduct is just analogous to justice and promise-keeping, as explained by Hume,[1] except that here the question need not be complicated by the expectations of other people. For, when other people depend upon my punctuality, it is not to keep a rule as such but to avoid wasting their time that is right. Hume saw that the individual act of justice may not produce so much pleasure as its omission, but argued that since justice *generally* does so, we should always do just acts.

The weakness of the dodge is that so soon as I recognize that there is no obligation to keep my own rules as such (if others do not rely on my doing so), but only when they really enjoin what I can see is right in this situation, then the fact that I have adopted a rule will leave my choice just as likely to be swayed by desire as if I had not adopted it. I shall be tempted to question the applicability of the rule, at least until I have formed a habit.

---

[1] *Treatise of Human Nature*, III. ii. I only here reproduce so much of his view as suits my context.

This is merely a case of the more general problem as to the nature and value of good resolutions. Really to will is to act. When I do what is called "deciding" or "making up my mind" beforehand, we know well enough that the "decision" will often be abandoned; sometimes it should be. For, in deciding beforehand, not all the circumstances can be known. And when the time for action comes, not only have I to decide whether the decision that I have made applies to this situation, but actually to decide over again; for, after all, I may have changed my mind. Yet, however irrational it may seem, good resolutions are made; and however inexplicable it be, they have some value. They help us to act rightly and so ought to be made. It is something, if not much, to "decide" to get up early to-morrow or even always. So far then as we find rules necessary and useful we shall do well to make them; none of them are without exception, not even the rule not to act on rule; they are not quite rational, but neither are we. . . .

Various criticisms have been made of the kind of theory expressed by Carritt. Earlier it had already been attacked by Henry Sidgwick and Hastings Rashdall, both of whom use "intuitionism" to mean deontologism of an intuitionist sort. What they say, however, applies to act-deontologism of all sorts. Both argue for the necessity of general judgments that are not just rules of thumb.

Bernard Mayo also considers some objections to the philosophy of moral principles. He thinks of the debate as one between existentialists and Kantians and as centering around the question whether a consideration of uniqueness and particularity has any place in morality, a question that is much discussed today.

The question to be kept in mind, of course, in reading each of these three criticisms is whether individually or collectively they provide, to your mind, a conclusive refutation of the act-deontologist's view.

THREE CRITICISMS OF ACT-DEONTOLOGISM

Henry Sidgwick

But though probably all moral agents have experience of such particular intuitions, and though they constitute a great part of the moral phenomena of most minds, comparatively few are so thoroughly satisfied

From The Methods of Ethics, *7th ed. (London: Macmillan & Co., Ltd., 1962).*

with them, as not to feel a need of some further moral knowledge even from a strictly practical point of view. For these particular intuitions do not, to reflective persons, present themselves as quite indubitable and irrefragable; nor do they always find when they have put an ethical question to themselves with all sincerity, that they are conscious of clear immediate insight in respect of it. Again, when a man compares the utterances of his conscience at different times, he often finds it difficult to make them altogether consistent. the same conduct will wear a different moral aspect at one time from that which it wore at another, although our knowledge of its circumstances and conditions is not materially changed. Further, we become aware that the moral perceptions of different minds, to all appearance equally competent to judge, frequently conflict: one condemns what another approves. In this way serious doubts are aroused as to the validity of each man's particular moral judgments: and we are led to endeavour to set these doubts at rest by appealing to general rules, more firmly established on a basis of common consent. . . .

How then can we hope to eliminate error from our moral intuitions? One answer to this question was briefly suggested in a previous chapter where the different phases of the Intuitional Method were discussed. It was there said that in order to settle the doubts arising from the uncertainties and discrepancies that are found when we compare our judgments on particular cases, reflective persons naturally appeal to general rules or formulae: and it is to such general formulae that Intuitional Moralists attribute ultimate certainty and validity. And certainly there are obvious sources of error in our judgments respecting concrete duty which seem to be absent when we consider the abstract notions of different kinds of conduct; since in any concrete case the complexity of circumstances necessarily increases the difficulty of judging, and our personal interests or habitual sympathies are liable to disturb the clearness of our moral discernment. Further, we must observe that most of us feel the need of such formulae not only to correct, but also to supplement, our intuitions respecting particular concrete duties. Only exceptionally confident persons find that they always seem to see clearly what ought to be done in any case that comes before them. Most of us, however unhesitatingly we may affirm rightness and wrongness in ordinary matters of conduct, yet not unfrequently meet with cases where our unreasoned judgment fails us; and where we could no more decide the moral issue raised without appealing to some general formula, than we could decide a disputed legal claim without reference to the positive law that deals with the matter.

Hastings Rashdall

The belief described as unphilosophical Intuitionism in its wildest form is one which can hardly claim serious refutation. If it is supposed that the injunctions of the moral faculty are so wholly arbitrary that they proceed upon no general or rational principle whatever, if it is supposed that I may to-day in one set of circumstances feel bound by an inexplicable impulse within me to act in one way, while to-morrow I may be directed or direct myself to act differently under circumstances in no way distinguishable from the former, then moral judgments are reduced to an arbitrary caprice which is scarcely compatible with the belief in any objective standard of duty; for it will hardly be denied that, if right and wrong are not the same for the same individual on different but precisely similar occasions, they can still less be the same for different persons, and all idea of an objective moral law disappears. It may of course be alleged that the circumstances of no two acts are precisely alike, but they may certainly be alike in all relevant respects. If it be said that Conscience will vary its judgement in accordance with the circumstances of the case, and that other men's Consciences in proportion to their enlightenment will always pronounce the same judgements under similar circumstances, there must be some rule or principle by which it must be possible to distinguish between circumstances which do and circumstances which do not alter our duty, however little this rule or principle may be present in an abstract form to the moral consciousness of the individual. Granted, therefore, that the moral judgements may as a matter of psychological fact reveal themselves first and most clearly in particular cases (just as we pronounce judgements about particular spaces and distances long before we have consciously put geometrical principles into the form of general axioms), it must still, it would seem, be possible by analysis of our particular moral judgements to discover the general principles upon which they proceed. Analytical thought and philosophical language may be inadequate for the accurate expression of the delicate shades and gradations of circumstance upon which, in complicated cases, our moral judgements actually depend; but some approximation to this, some rough rules or principles of ethical judgement, ought, one would think, to be capable of being elicited from a wide comparative survey of one's own and other people's actual judgements. If this be denied, moral instruction must be treated as absolutely impossible. Now it may be quite true that in many ways "example is

From The Theory of Good and Evil, 2nd ed. (Oxford: The Clarendon Press, Reprinted by permission of The Clarendon Press, Oxford.

better than precept," not only on account of its emotional effect but even on account of the intellectual illumination supplied by a good man's conduct in presence of varying practical difficulties. It is true that the contemplation in actual fact or in recorded history of a good life may suggest ideals which no mere system of precepts, abstracted from particular applications, can adequately embody. A general rule is often best embodied in a concrete, typical case. The parable of the Good Samaritan has taught the true meaning of Charity more clearly as well as more persuasively than any direct precept that could be culled from the writings of Seneca or even from the Sermon on the Mount. But still there is a consensus among reasonable men that moral instruction of some kind—however vague, general, and inadequate to the complexities of actual life—is possible, desirable, and necessary. We do not say to a child who asks whether he may pick a flower in somebody else's garden, "My good child, that depends entirely upon the circumstances of the particular case: to lay down any general rule on the subject would be a piece of unwarrantable dogmatism on my part: consult your own Conscience, as each case arises, and all will be well." On the contrary, we say at once: "You must not pick the flower: *because* that would be stealing, and stealing is wrong." Make any reserves you please as to the inadequacy of the rule, its want of definiteness, its inability to meet many problems of life, the necessity for exceptions and the like; yet it must be admitted that if there be any one point about Morality as to which there is a consensus alike among all plain men and nearly all Philosophers it is surely this—that general rules of conduct do exist. Morality cannot be reduced to copy-book headings, but copy-book headings we do and must have. Now, in proportion as all this is admitted, unphilosophical Intuitionism tends to pass into the philosophical variety of the Intuitionist creed [i.e., rule-deontologism] and may be subjected to the same criticism.

Bernard Mayo

Existentialists and Kantians

. . . a moral agent who acted merely in accordance with principles would be in the position of one who merely came to certain decisions, irrespective (to a considerable extent) both of what he happened to be

From Ethics and the Moral Life (*London: Macmillan & Co., Ltd., 1958*). Reprinted by permission of the author and Macmillan London and Basingstoke.

feeling at the time, and of what the particular features of the situation happened to be. All he does is to recognise the situation as having *certain* features and belonging, accordingly, to a certain type of situation which, under a certain rule, requires action of a certain sort. This is held to be an inadequate account, if not a grotesque caricature, of the nature of moral decision. It falsifies both the moral agent and the character of moral experience. The moral agent is not just someone who adopts a rule, recognises a situation as coming under that rule, and decides to act accordingly; he is a unique individual with a particular history, character and emotional state, none of which can be ignored; further, the situation in which he finds himself is itself a unique situation, involving other unique individuals different from himself and each other, and in fact an infinite assemblage of individualising factors. A genuine moral decision, it is argued, must be a response to the uniqueness of the total situation, and not an application of a rule which takes account of only a limited number of general features. Indeed the rule itself, it may be suggested, comes to be formulated only by a sort of inductive procedure; as a result of a series of decisions, each in a unique situation, when certain resemblances among the situations, and among the ensuing actions, have been noted; and even then it serves only as a rough guide for future unique decisions, never as a substitute. We may conveniently use Kantianism and Existentialism as labels for the two sides in this controversy: the extreme Kantians maintaining that generalisation is always, and uniqueness never, relevant to moral decision, the extreme Existentialists maintaining precisely the opposite.

I believe that the Existentialist or counter-Kantian thesis I have just sketched is completely false. . . . the assertion of the "Existentialist" that every situation in which a person has come to a moral decision is a unique situation involving unique persons . . . is perfectly true: what is not true is that this has any bearing on the moral decision. But first some explanation is required of the use of the terms "unique" and "person."

There are two ways of knowing people, and indeed of knowing any kind of object in the ordinary world. These have received the names "knowledge by acquaintance" and "knowledge by description". . . . I use the terms in the ordinary sense in which they correspond to the distinction between *connaître* and *savoir, kennen* and *wissen, novisse* and *scire,* and in English (which is peculiar in not having different verb stems) between knowing somebody or knowing something (being acquainted or familiar with it) and knowing *of* somebody or something, or knowing *that* something is the case, or knowing *about* something or somebody. The fundamental distinction between them is that the second kind of knowledge cannot occur without the use of language. This does not mean merely (what is obvious) that we cannot *formulate* such knowledge unless we have the appropriate words in our language. It means that we could not have such knowledge. If our language happened to have no word for *red*, we not only could not formulate our knowledge that a particular flower was red: we could not know that it *was* red. We might know that it was not green (if we had the words "green" and "not") but nothing could count as knowing the flower to be red. Of course, we might notice something about the flower which suggested the need to have a word describing what that flower had in common with other flowers which resembled it in that respect. But this would not be noticing that the flower was *red*. It could only be after the word became current in the language that we could say *ex post facto* that somebody noticed that the flower was red. And the same is true of all the features of things which we notice or know. We can only notice or know what we have words to describe, or what at any rate we are prepared to find words to describe.

Knowledge by acquaintance, on the other hand, has nothing whatever to do with language. It is indeed only possible for organisms possessing a minimum sensory apparatus, but it is certainly not confined to language-users, that is, to human beings. But human beings, though language-using is the pride of their species, have also inarticulate and inarticulable experiences. The experience of personal relations is one of these. Acquaintance is the minimal element of what I call the personal relation, which is a unique relation between unique persons (or between a person and a thing).

It might be said that this is not very illuminating because all relations are unique since the objects they relate are unique: everything is, in the last resort, different from everything else. This is true but not a valid criticism. The point is that the uniqueness of things is precisely what is ignored or omitted in our dealings with them, except in the case of personal relations, where it just is the uniqueness that matters, that makes the relation a personal one. When I speak of the relation between myself and my wife as a marital relation, I classify it with the similar relation existing between other husbands and wives; and so I do if I call it romantic, or incompatibility of temperament, or anything else whatever. Yet what I classify in this way is, after all, not exactly like that with which it is classified, in every respect; and that of which this is true, is what I call the personal relation. To call this unique is merely to say that, however exhaustively its features are listed, such a list cannot be completely exhaustive. This does not mean that there is a peculiarly unlistable quality called uniqueness. It merely points to the difference between an actual concrete situation, and the possibilities of describing that situation in language, or between knowing that situation by participating in it, and knowing it by being able to describe it.

Personal Relations and Morality

Now such a personal relation cannot be a moral one any more than it can be a legal one, simply because to attend to it as a relation of a certain type is to cease to treat it as a personal relation at all. Nor can a moral decision be one based on attention to the uniqueness of the situation or of the persons involved in it. For if a moral decision is to be a reflective decision—meaning not necessarily the outcome of deliberation, but at least capable of reflective justification (and if it is not even that, it cannot be a moral decision at all)—then it must indeed involve "attention" to certain features of the situation. But the "Existentialist" was mistaken in suggesting that such "attention" could include attention to uniquenesses, or individualising factors. For what can be attended to is necessarily a feature or characteristic; a characteristic is what is named by a universal word or phrase; a universal word is any that is capable of functioning as a predicate; a predicate is necessarily capable of being attached to any subject; therefore what it names cannot be unique. "Unique feature" is a self-contradiction. Hence what is "attended to" in moral (or any other) deliberation or reflection cannot be any kind of uniqueness. Uniqueness can be experienced but it cannot be described.

An example may show how the Existentialist's claim, that moral decisions must take into account particularities, is plausible but false. Suppose my friend has done something illegal and I am wondering whether I ought to report the matter to the police. Here the duty of citizenship is, we may suppose, clear enough, and is obviously capable of being formulated and applied in general terms. But what of the personal claims of friendship? Certainly the relation is a unique one; my relation to my friend is not at all like my relation to the state and the law, and not *just* like my relation to any other friend. But if a moral question arises for me at all, I must necessarily ignore the uniqueness of my friend and of my relationship with him. I must consider my friendship as creating for me certain greater or lesser obligations, comparable with those created by my relations with other people, and in particular with those obligations I accept towards the state. There is no alternative, if I am to act or think morally at all. Of course I may not act or think morally. I may remain fully engaged in the concrete situation, acting unreflectively. My action may be a spontaneous demonstration of friendship (or citizenship). But then it will not be a moral action.

Persons and their predicaments may, then, as the Existentialists claim, be "unutterably particular"; but this does not refute the Kantian universalistic ethics, indeed it serves to sharpen it. But there is a final objection to be considered. . . .

The difference between moral and personal relations can be illustrated by a felicitous remark of a novelist on the difference between loving and liking: "We like someone *because* . . . we love someone *although.* . . ." [1] "Because" introduces a clause mentioning a reason for whatever is asserted in the main clause; "although" introduces a reason against what is asserted in the main clause: a reason, however, which must, to avoid a contradiction, be inadequate or inconclusive. "I like Smith because he has a sense of humour" depends for its force on an assumption that anyone with a sense of humour is likely (other things being more or less equal) to be the object of a favourable attitude on my part; liking is such an attitude; moral approval is another. The force of "I love Jones although he is unkind" is that anyone having the characteristic of unkindness is unlikely to be favoured by me, yet that this reason must be inadequate, since the implied conclusion ("I dislike or disapprove of Jones") is untrue. But the point of the epigram is more subtle. For it may be that the implied conclusion *is* true. I may indeed disapprove of Jones for his unkindness, yet love him all the same. Love is a personal relation which has nothing to do with reasons. Morality has everything to do with reasons.

---

[1] Henri de Montherlant, *Pitié pour les Femmes,* p. 40.

2.3

Rule-Deontological Theories

Rule-deontologists take rules or principles as basic in morality or, at least, consider them to be stronger or more binding than the rules of thumb or general maxims reached by induction from judgments on particular cases. Rules of thumb and maxims based on past experience may not always hold. Rule-deontologists believe that there are moral principles that do always hold— either absolutely or at least *prima facie* in Ross's sense (that is, conditional on not being overridden by other relevant moral principles). They may be monistic, believing there is only one such principle and it is basic, or pluralistic, believing there are two or more of them. Either way, they must maintain that there is at least one basic principle that is nonteleological, i.e., that does not tell us to produce good or to minimize evil, though a pluralist may recognize some teleological principles, as Ross does. Ordinary common sense morality is probably a pluralistic kind of rule-deontologism. So is the Old Testament morality of the Ten Commandments, if taken just as it stands.

The best example of pluralistic deontologism is W. D. Ross. Such pluralists have often talked as if their principles were all absolute, each holding without exception and never being overridden by other principles. But such a view has difficulties and can be maintained only if its principles can never conflict. With this in mind, Ross argues for a set of principles of *prima facie* duty.

It is also necessary to understand that Ross is an intuitionist in meta-ethics (to be explained in Chapter 6), and believes his principles to be self-evident. However, a rule-deontologist need not believe this. He may hold that his principles were divinely revealed or that they are social demands or even that they are just rules he has made for himself.

We include here Ross's criticisms of utilitarianism, which should also be kept in mind in reading Chapter 3. The particular form of utilitarianism that Ross has in mind is pluralistic rather than hedonistic about value; that is, the theory holds that our only duty is to maximize the good, but does not hold that pleasure is the only intrinsic good.

In addition to Ross's statement and defense of rule-deontologism and his criticisms of utilitarianism, he also makes some interesting comments on the way in which concrete situations may involve moral risks.

WHAT MAKES RIGHT ACTS RIGHT?

W. D. Ross

. . . When a plain man fulfils a promise because he thinks he ought to do so, it seems clear that he does so with no thought of its total consequences, still less with any opinion that these are likely to be the best possible. He thinks in fact much more of the past than of the future. What makes him think it right to act in a certain way is the fact that he has promised to do so—that and, usually, nothing more. That his act will produce the best possible consequences is not his reason for calling it right. What lends colour to the theory we are examining [i.e., utilitarianism], then, is not the actions (which form probably a great majority of our actions) in which some such reflection as "I have promised" is the only reason we give ourselves for thinking a certain action right, but the exceptional cases in which the consequences of fulfilling a promise (for instance) would be so disastrous to others that we judge it right not to do so. It must of course be admitted that such cases exist. If I have promised to meet a friend at a particular time for some trivial purpose, I should certainly think myself justified in breaking my engagement if by doing so I could prevent a serious accident or bring relief to the victims of one. And the supporters of the view we are examining hold that my thinking so is due to my thinking that I shall bring more good into existence by the one action than by the other. A different account may, however, be given of the matter, an account which will, I believe, show itself to be the true one. It may be said that besides the duty of fulfilling promises I have and recognize a duty of relieving distress, and that when I think it right to do the latter at the cost of not doing the

From The Right and the Good *(Oxford: The Clarendon Press, 1930). Reprinted by permission of The Clarendon Press, Oxford.*

former, it is not because I think I shall produce more good thereby but because I think it the duty which is in the circumstances more of a duty. This account surely corresponds much more closely with what we really think in such a situation. If, so far as I can see, I could bring equal amounts of good into being by fulfilling my promise and by helping some one to whom I had made no promise, I should not hesitate to regard the former as my duty. Yet on the view that what is right is right because it is productive of the most good I should not so regard it. . . .

In fact the theory of "ideal utilitarianism," if I may for brevity refer so to the theory of Professor Moore, seems to simplify unduly our relations to our fellows. It says, in effect, that the only morally significant relation in which my neighbours stand to me is that of being possible beneficiaries by my action. They do stand in this relation to me, and this relation is morally significant. But they may also stand to me in the relation of promisee to promiser, of creditor to debtor, of wife to husband, of child to parent, of friend to friend, of fellow countryman to fellow countryman, and the like; and each of these relations is the foundation of a *prima facie* duty, which is more or less incumbent on me according to the circumstances of the case. When I am in a situation, as perhaps I always am, in which more than one of these *prima facie* duties is incumbent on me, what I have to do is to study the situation as fully as I can until I form the considered opinion (it is never more) that in the circumstances one of them is more incumbent than any other; then I am bound to think that to do this *prima facie* duty is my duty *sans phrase* in the situation.

I suggest "*prima facie* duty" or "conditional duty" as a brief way of referring to the characteristic (quite distinct from that of being a duty proper) which an act has, in virtue of being of a certain kind (e.g. the keeping of a promise), of being an act which would be a duty proper if it were not at the same time of another kind which is morally significant. Whether an act is a duty proper or actual duty depends on *all* the morally significant kinds it is an instance of. . . .

There is nothing arbitrary about these *prima facie* duties. Each rests on a definite circumstance which cannot seriously be held to be without moral significance. Of *prima facie* duties I suggest, without claiming completeness or finality for it, the following division.

(1) Some duties rest on previous acts of my own. These duties seem to include two kinds, (*a*) those resting on a promise or what may fairly be called an implicit promise, such as the implicit undertaking not to tell lies which seems to be implied in the act of entering into conversation (at any rate by civilized men), or of writing books that purport to be history and not fiction. These may be called the duties of fidelity. (*b*) Those resting on a previous wrongful act. These may be called the duties of reparation. (2) Some rest on previous acts of other men, i.e., services

done by them to me. These may be loosely described as the duties of gratitude. (3) Some rest on the fact or possibility of a distribution of pleasure or happiness (or of the means thereto) which is not in accordance with the merit of the persons concerned; in such cases there arises a duty to upset or prevent such a distribution. These are the duties of justice. (4) Some rest on the mere fact that there are other beings in the world whose condition we can make better in respect of virtue, or of intelligence, or of pleasure. These are the duties of beneficence. (5) Some rest on the fact that we can improve our own condition in respect of virtue or of intelligence. These are the duties of self-improvement. (6) I think that we should distinguish from (4) the duties that may be summed up under the title of "not injuring others." No doubt to injure others is incidentally to fail to do them good; but it seems to me clear that non-maleficence is apprehended as a duty distinct from that of beneficence, and as a duty of a more stringent character. It will be noticed that this alone among the types of duty has been stated in a negative way. An attempt might no doubt be made to state this duty, like the others, in a positive way. It might be said that it is really the duty to prevent ourselves from acting either from an inclination to harm others or from an inclination to seek our own pleasure, in doing which we should incidentally harm them. But on reflection it seems clear that the primary duty here is the duty not to harm others, this being a duty whether or not we have an inclination that if followed would lead to our harming them; and that when we have such an inclination the primary duty not to harm others gives rise to a consequential duty to resist the inclination. The recognition of this duty of non-maleficence is the first step on the way to the recognition of the duty of beneficence; and that accounts for the prominence of the commands "thou shalt not kill," "thou shalt not commit adultery," "thou shalt not steal," "thou shalt not bear false witness," in so early a code as the Decalogue. But even when we have come to recognize the duty of beneficence, it appears to me that the duty of non-maleficence is recognized as a distinct one, and as *prima facie* more binding. We should not in general consider it justifiable to kill one person in order to keep another alive, or to steal from one in order to give alms to another.

The essential defect of the "ideal utilitarian" theory is that it ignores, or at least does not do full justice to, the highly personal character of duty. If the only duty is to produce the maximum of good, the question who is to have the good—whether it is myself, or my benefactor, or a person to whom I have made a promise to confer that good on him, or a mere fellow man to whom I stand in no such special relation—should make no difference to my having a duty to produce that good. But we are all in fact sure that it makes a vast difference.

One or two other comments must be made on this provisional list of the divisions of duty. (1) The nomenclature is not strictly correct. For by "fidelity" or "gratitude" we mean, strictly, certain states of motivation; and, as I have urged, it is not our duty to have certain motives, but to do certain acts. By "fidelity," for instance, is meant, strictly, the disposition to fulfil promises and implicit promises *because we have made them.* We have no general word to cover the actual fulfilment of promises and implicit promises *irrespective of motive;* and I use "fidelity," loosely but perhaps conveniently, to fill this gap. So too I use "gratitude" for the returning of services, irrespective of motive. The term "justice" is not so much confined, in ordinary usage, to a certain state of motivation, for we should often talk of a man as acting justly even when we did not think his motive was the wish to do what was just simply for the sake of doing so. Less apology is therefore needed for our use of "justice" in this sense. And I have used the word "beneficence" rather than "benevolence," in order to emphasize the fact that it is our duty to do certain things, and not to do them from certain motives.

(2) If the objection be made, that this catalogue of the main types of duty is an unsystematic one resting on no logical principle, it may be replied, first, that it makes no claim to being ultimate. It is a *prima facie* classification of the duties which reflection on our moral convictions seems actually to reveal. And if these convictions are, as I would claim that they are, of the nature of knowledge, and if I have not misstated them, the list will be a list of authentic conditional duties, correct as far as it goes though not necessarily complete. The list of *goods* put forward by the rival theory is reached by exactly the same method—the only sound one in the circumstances—viz. that of direct reflection on what we really think. Loyalty to the facts is worth more than a symmetrical architectonic or a hastily reached simplicity. If further reflection discovers a perfect logical basis for this or for a better classification, so much the better.

(3) It may, again, be objected that our theory that there are these various and often conflicting types of *prima facie* duty leaves us with no principle upon which to discern what is our actual duty in particular circumstances. But this objection is not one which the rival theory is in a position to bring forward. For when we have to choose between the production of two heterogeneous goods, say knowledge and pleasure, the "ideal utilitarian" theory can only fall back on an opinion, for which no logical basis can be offered, that one of the goods is the greater; and this is no better than a similar opinion that one of two duties is the more urgent. And again, when we consider the infinite variety of the effects of our actions in the way of pleasure, it must surely be admitted that the claim which *hedonism* sometimes makes, that it offers a readily applicable criterion of right conduct, is quite illusory.

I am unwilling, however, to content myself with an *argumentum ad hominem,* and I would contend that in principle there is no reason to anticipate that every act that is our duty is so for one and the same reason. Why should two sets of circumstances, or one set of circumstances, *not* possess different characteristics, any one of which makes a certain act our *prima facie* duty? When I ask what it is that makes me in certain cases sure that I have a *prima facie* duty to do so and so, I find that it lies in the fact that I have made a promise; when I ask the same question in another case, I find the answer lies in the fact that I have done a wrong. And if on reflection I find (as I think I do) that neither of these reasons is reducible to the other, I must not on any *a priori* ground assume that such a reduction is possible. . . .

It is necessary to say something by way of clearing up the relation between *prima facie* duties and the actual or absolute duty to do one particular act in particular circumstances. If, as almost all moralists except Kant are agreed, and as most plain men think, it is sometimes right to tell a lie or to break a promise, it must be maintained that there is a difference between *prima facie* duty and actual or absolute duty. When we think ourselves justified in breaking, and indeed morally obliged to break, a promise in order to relieve some one's distress, we do not for a moment cease to recognize a *prima facie* duty to keep our promise, and this leads us to feel, not indeed shame or repentance, but certainly compunction, for behaving as we do; we recognize further, that it is our duty to make up somehow to the promisee for the breaking of the promise. We have to distinguish from the characteristic of being our duty that of tending to be our duty. Any act that we do contains various elements in virtue of which it falls under various categories. In virtue of being the breaking of a promise, for instance, it tends to be wrong; in virtue of being an instance of relieving distress it tends to be right. Tendency to be one's duty may be called a parti-resultant attribute, i.e. one which belongs to an act in virtue of some one component in its nature. *Being* one's duty is a toti-resultant attribute, one which belongs to an act in virtue of its whole nature and of nothing less than this. . . .

Some of these general principles of *prima facie* duty may appear to be open to criticism. It may be thought, for example, that the principle of returning good for good is a falling off from the Christian principle, generally and rightly recognized as expressing the highest morality, of returning good for evil. To this it may be replied that I do not suggest that there is a principle commanding us to return good for good and forbidding us to return good for evil, and that I do suggest that there is a positive duty to seek the good of all men. What I maintain is that an act in which good is returned for good is recognized as *specially* binding on us just because it is of that character, and that *ceteris paribus* any one would think it his duty to help his benefactors rather than his enemies, if he could not do both; just as it is generally recognized that *ceteris paribus* we should pay our debts rather than give our money in charity, when we cannot do both. A benefactor is not only a man, calling for our effort on his behalf on that ground, but also our benefactor, calling for our *special* effort on *that* ground.

Our judgements about our actual duty in concrete situations have none of the certainty that attaches to our recognition of the general principles of duty. A statement is certain, i.e. is an expression of knowledge, only in one or other of two cases: when it is either self-evident, or a valid conclusion from self-evident premisses. And our judgements about our particular duties have neither of these characters. (1) They are not self-evident. Where a possibile act is seen to have two characteristics, in virtue of one of which it is *prima facie* right, and in virtue of the other *prima facie* wrong, we are (I think) well aware that we are not certain whether we ought or ought not to do it; that whether we do it or not, we are taking a moral risk. We come in the long run, after consideration, to think one duty more pressing than the other, but we do not feel certain that it is so. And though we do not always recognize that a possible act has two such characteristics, and though there *may* be cases in which it has not, we are never certain that any particular possible act has not, and therefore never certain that it is right, nor certain that it is wrong. For, to go no further in the analysis, it is enough to point out that any particular act will in all probability in the course of time contribute to the bringing about of good or of evil for many human beings, and thus have a *prima facie* rightness or wrongness of which we know nothing. (2) Again, our judgements about our particular duties are not logical conclusions from self-evident premisses. The only possible premisses would be the general principles stating their *prima facie* rightness or wrongness *qua* having the different characteristics they do have; and even if we could (as we cannot) apprehend the extent to which an act will tend on the one hand, for example, to bring about advantages for our benefactors and on the other hand to bring about disadvantages for fellow men who are not our benefactors, there is no principle by which we can draw the conclusion that it is on the whole right or on the whole wrong. In this respect the judgement as to the rightness of a particular act is just like the judgement as to the beauty of a particular natural object or work of art. A poem is, for instance, in respect of certain qualities beautiful and in respect of certain others not beautiful; and our judgement as to the degree of beauty it possesses on the whole is never reached by logical reasoning from the apprehension of its particular beauties or particular defects. Both in this and in the moral case we have more or less probable opinions which are not logically justified conclusions from the general principles that are recognized as self-evident.

There is therefore much truth in the description of the right act as a fortunate act. If we cannot be certain that it is right, it is our good fortune if the act we do is the right act. This consideration does not, however, make the doing of our duty a mere matter of chance. There is a parallel here between the doing of duty and the doing of what will be to our personal advantage. We never *know* what act will in the long run be to our advantage. Yet it is certain that we are more likely in general to secure our advantage if we estimate to the best of our ability the probable tendencies of our actions in this respect, than if we act on caprice. And similarly we are more likely to do our duty if we reflect to the best of our ability on the *prima facie* rightness or wrongness of various possible acts in virtue of the characteristics we perceive them to have, than if we act without reflection. With this greater likelihood we must be content.

Many people would be inclined to say that the right act for me is not that whose general nature I have been describing, viz. that which if I were omniscient I should see to be my duty, but that which on all the evidence available to me I should think to be my duty. But suppose that from the state of partial knowledge in which I think act A to be my duty, I could pass to a state of perfect knowledge in which I saw act B to be my duty, should I not say "act B was the right act for me to do"? I should no doubt add "though I am not to be blamed for doing act A." But in adding this, am I not passing from the question "what is right" to the question "what is morally good"? At the same time I am not making the *full* passage from the one notion to the other; for in order that the act should be morally good, or an act I am not to be blamed for doing, it must not merely be the act which it is reasonable for me to think my duty; it must also be done for that reason, or from some other morally good motive. Thus the conception of the right act as the act which it is reasonable for me to think my duty is an unsatisfactory compromise between the true notion of the right act and the notion of the morally good action.

The general principles of duty are obviously not self-evident from the beginning of our lives. How do they come to be so? The answer is, that they come to be self-evident to us just as mathematical axioms do. We find by experience that this couple of matches and that couple make four matches, that this couple of balls on a wire and that couple make four balls; and by reflection on these and similar discoveries we come to see that it is of the nature of two and two to make four. In a precisely similar way, we see the *prima facie* rightness of an act which would be the fulfilment of a particular promise, and of another which would be the fulfilment of another promise, and when we have reached sufficient maturity to think in general terms, we apprehend *prima facie* rightness to belong to the nature of any fulfilment of promise. What comes first in time is the apprehension of the self-evident *prima facie* rightness of an individual act of a particular type. From this we come by reflection to apprehend the self-evident general principle of *prima facie* duty. From this, too, perhaps along with the apprehension of the self-evident *prima facie* rightness of the same act in virtue of its having another characteristic as well, and perhaps in spite of the apprehension of its *prima facie* wrongness in virtue of its having some third characteristic, we come to believe something not self-evident at all, but an object of probable opinion, viz. that this particular act is (not *prima facie* but) actually right. . . .

Supposing it to be agreed, as I think on reflection it must, that no one *means* by "right" just "productive of the best possible consequences," or "optimific," the attributes "right" and "optimific" might stand in either of two kinds of relation to each other. (1) They might be so related that we could apprehend *a priori*, either immediately or deductively, that any act that is optimific is right and any act that is right is optimific, as we can apprehend that any triangle that is equilateral is equiangular and *vice versa*. Professor Moore's view is, I think, that the coextensiveness of "right" and "optimific" is apprehended immediately. He rejects the possibility of any proof of it. Or (2) the two attributes might be such that the question whether they are invariably connected had to be answered by means of an inductive inquiry. Now at first sight it might seem as if the constant connexion of the two attributes could be immediately apprehended. It might seem absurd to suggest that it could be right for any one to do an act which would produce consequences less good than those which would be produced by some other act in his power. Yet a little thought will convince us that this is not absurd. The type of case in which it is easiest to see that this is so is, perhaps, that in which one has made a promise. In such a case we all think that *prima facie* it is our duty to fulfil the promise irrespective of the precise goodness of the total consequences. And though we do not think it is necessarily our actual or absolute duty to do so, we are far from thinking that any, even the slightest, gain in the value of the total consequences will necessarily justify us in doing something else instead. Suppose, to simplify the case by abstraction, that the fulfilment of a promise to A would produce 1,000 units of good for him, but that by doing some other act I could produce 1,001 units of good for B, to whom I have made no promise, the other consequences of the two acts being of equal value; should we really think it self-evident that it was our duty to do the second act and not the first? I think not. We should, I fancy, hold that only a much greater disparity of value between the total consequences would justify us in failing to discharge our *prima facie* duty to A. After all, a promise is a promise, and is not to be treated so lightly as the theory we are examining would imply. What, exactly, a promise is, is not so easy to determine, but we are surely agreed that it constitutes a serious moral limitation to our freedom of action. To produce the 1,001 units of good for B rather than fulfil our promise to A would be to take, not perhaps our duty as philanthropists too seriously, but certainly our duty as makers of promises too lightly. . . .

Such instances—and they might easily be added to—make it clear that there is no self-evident connexion between the attributes "right" and "optimific." The theory we are examining has a certain attractiveness when applied to our decision that a particular act is our duty (though I have tried to show that it does not agree with our actual moral judgements even here). But it is not even plausible when applied to our recognition of *prima facie* duty. For if it were self-evident that the right coincides with the optimific, it should be self-evident that what is *prima facie* right is *prima facie* optimific. But whereas we are certain that keeping a promise is *prima facie* right, we are not certain that it is *prima facie* optimific (though we are perhaps certain that it is *prima facie* bonific). Our certainty that it is *prima facie* right depends not on its consequences but on its being the fulfilment of a promise. The theory we are examining involves too much difference between the evident ground of our conviction about *prima facie* duty and the alleged ground of our conviction about actual duty.

The coextensiveness of the right and the optimific is, then, not self-evident.

I conclude that the attributes "right" and "optimific" are not identical, and that we do not know either by intuition, by deduction, or by induction that they coincide in their application, still less that the latter is the foundation of the former. It must be added, however, that if we are ever under no special obligation such as that of fidelity to a promisee or of gratitude to a benefactor, we ought to do what will produce most good; and that even when we are under a special obligation the tendency of acts to promote general good is one of the main factors in determining whether they are right.

Writing with both Carritt and Ross in mind, Brand Blanshard criticizes deontological theories, especially pluralistic ones, from a teleological point of view. His general point is that all of our duties finally rest on some kind of consideration of the good or evil that results.

RIGHTNESS AND GOODNESS

Brand Blanshard

. . . "The sense of obligation to do, or of the rightness of, an action of a particular kind," says Prichard, "is absolutely underivative or immediate"; "our sense of the rightness of an act is not a conclusion from our appreciation of the goodness either of it or of anything else." [1] Ross writes: "It seems, on reflection, self-evident that a promise, simply as such, is something that *prima facie* ought to be kept. . . ." [2] "If any one ask us," says Carritt, " 'Why ought I to do these acts you call my duty?,' the only answer is, 'Because they *are* your *duty*,' and if he does not see this we cannot make him, unless by informing him about matters of fact; if he sees they are duties, he can no more ask why he ought to do them than why he should believe what is true." [3]

Now we have granted that the duty of promise-keeping, for example, does not rest merely on consequences; it is better that promises should be kept, even if no later advantage accrues from it. And it may be thought that this is what the deontologists too are saying. That would be a mistake. What they are saying is that promise-keeping is our duty though in fact there is no good in it at all. According to Ross, "If I contemplate one of the acts in question, an act, say, in which a promise is kept . . . and ask myself whether it is good, apart both from results and from motives, I can find no goodness in it. The fact is that when some one keeps a promise we can see no intrinsic worth in that. . . ." And again: "We can see *no* intrinsic goodness attaching to the life of a community merely because promises are kept in it." [4] It is our duty to keep promises, not because, even with other things equal, the life of a community is *better* for promises being kept in it, but because . . . the sentence cannot be completed. It is our duty, but there is no reason why. Our obligation is read off directly, and with self-evident necessity, from a set of neutral facts. So also of such duties as repaying debts, and telling the truth. Indeed most of the *prima facie* duties recognized by the deontologists rest not on the goodness of any state of things, but on the neutral and factual character of the act itself. For this reason, the ancient search of the philosophers for some single characteristic of right acts

From Reason and Goodness (*London: George Allen and Unwin Ltd., 1961*). *Reprinted by permission of the author, George Allen and Unwin Ltd., and Humanities Press, Inc.*

[1] *Moral Obligation,* 7, 9.

[2] *The Right and the Good,* 40.

[3] *Theory of Morals,* 29.

[4] *Foundations of Ethics,* 142–43.

which serves to make them right is set down as misguided. There is *no* one thing that makes right acts right. Sometimes they are right because they are the keeping of promises, somtimes because they are the paying of debts. But between the rightness of an act and its tendency to bring into being any kind or degree of good there is no general relation at all.

Here I must dissent. This conclusion does not seem credible. We are being told that it may be a self-evident duty to choose one rather than another state of affairs even though, in respect to goodness, there is nothing to choose between them. But more; we are being told that state of things A may be definitely and admittedly *worse* than B, and that it may still be our duty to bring A into being. With a choice before us of making the world worse or making it better, we may have a moral obligation to make it worse. This is very hard to accept. A strong case has been carried too far. When the deontologists said that duty is not based always on a goodness that follows the act in time, but sometimes on the character of the act itself, they carried us with them. They did so because it seemed clear that a state of things in which promises were kept, gratitude recognized, and truth told, was a better state of things than one in which these were not done. But when we are now told that such obligations have nothing to do either with the intrinsic goodness of the acts, or of the state of things they institute, let alone the goodness of their consequences, we feel as if the mat on which we had been approaching this school had been pulled out from under our feet. The obligations that were presented to us as rational insights take on an air of caprice.

Can we offer any evidence that we are correct about this and the deontologists not? I think we can, though argument on such ultimate issues is notoriously hard.

(1) Perhaps an *ad hominem* argument may therefore be permitted. Sir David Ross "can see *no* intrinsic goodness attaching to the life of a community merely because promises are kept in it"; goodness attaches only to the motives or consequences of such conduct, not to the state of affairs constituted by its general practice. But when we come to justice, in one of its important forms, Ross is emphatic that this does have intrinsic goodness, regardless of motives or consequences. A community in which virtuous men are happy and wicked men unhappy he considers much better than one in which these allotments are reversed, even though the totals of happiness and unhappiness are the same.[5] Now the goodness admitted to be present here is not the property of anyone's experience,

---

[5] ". . . besides virtue and pleasure, we must recognize, as a third independent good, the apportionment of pleasure and pain to the virtuous and the vicious respectively. And it is on the recognition of this as a separate good that the recognition of the duty of justice . . . rests." *The Right and the Good*, 138.

but of a set of arrangements between experiences. If intrinsic worth can be owned by such a set of arrangements, why should it not also be owned by that other set of arrangements in which promises are kept, or truth told, or debts repaid? If there is any fundamental difference between these situations, which would justify saying that one is self-evidently good and the other self-evidently valueless, I have failed to catch it.

(2) Is it really the case that to ask *why* something is our duty is meaningless? Mr. Carritt says that if we see it is our duty to keep a promise, it is as pointless to ask why we should keep it as to ask why we should believe what is true. In this he is no doubt right. Once we have seen that the keeping of a promise is our duty, it would be idle to ask why we should do it, since we have in our possession already the most conclusive answer that could be given. But then this is not the situation in which the question would be asked. It would be asked, rather, by someone to whom his duty was not apparent and who wanted guidance about it. He might see that keeping a promise would bring pain to someone, and, reluctant to give this pain, he might ask, "What ground is there, after all, for saying that to keep a promise *is* obligatory? You tell me that there is *no* ground, that if I attend and am clear-headed I shall see the obligation immediately. But for the alternative course of breaking the promise there clearly *is* some ground, namely that it will avoid pain. Am I to believe that it is my duty to do something that involves that pain, yet carries no good to counterbalance it? That does not seem to me, on the face of it, reasonable. *Why* should I take it as obligatory to produce that which you own to be without value?" I cannot think this question meaningless, nor the asking of it a sign of obtuseness or failure to attend. I suspect that most people who do attend would agree that it is significant, and also that it has a natural and intelligible answer; namely, "It is your duty to keep promises because the state of things in which they are kept is a better state than one in which they are broken." A critic may rejoin that this is no more obvious to the obtuse than the proposition for which it is offered as a reason. That may or may not be true. But the point is that it *is* significant and does give a reason. It is one thing—and a not very convincing thing—to say that the keeping of promises is a duty because its obligatoriness is self-evident and another thing to say that it is a duty because it is good. If the first account is true, the reason given in the second must be an impertinence—unneeded, untrue, adding nothing to the case. And I do not think it is.

Since the inability to give a reason for duty is ascribed to the "immediacy" of our insight, it may be well to look a little more closely at this immediacy. Take a necessary proposition of an ordinary kind, say "whatever has shape has size." This is an immediate insight because the first attribute entails the second directly; the suggestion that the second follows only through the intermediary of another and omitted term would seem absurd. But the parallel suggestion about promise-keeping and obligatoriness would not seem at all absurd; indeed the absurdity, if there is one, seems rather to lie on the other side, in the suggestion that promise-keeping, described as wholly valueless, should as such be obligatory. And whereas in the shape-size proposition the suggestion of a middle term is a gratuitous complication of what is plain already, the introduction of a middle term in the other clears up a puzzle. "Act A, worthless in itself, should be done"; that seems very dubious indeed. "Act A, *because it is intrinsically good,* should be done"; that is a different matter and makes sense at once. We are not questioning that the obligatoriness of a kind of action may be seen as rational and necessary. We are only contending that the line of necessity does not run straight from a state of things that is utterly grey, so far as worth is concerned, to a duty to produce that state; what carries the obligation is the fact that the state would be worth while, or of some positive value—in short that it would be good.

(3) A further point may be mentioned which has troubled many moralists about this form of intuitionism: the duties with which it presents us are "an unconnected heap." Philosophers and scientists alike have generally felt that they should use Occam's razor whenever they can; it is their business to reduce apparent disorder to law, and diversity of fact to unity of principle. Moral philosophy has proceeded on the assumption that, if we searched resolutely enough, we should discover behind the great variety of acts that we call right and obligatory some unifying principle that made them so. Ethics has consisted very largely of the search for that principle. To be sure, moralists have disagreed in disappointing fashion as to what the principle was; we have been variously advised to order our conduct so as to secure survival, wisdom, self-realization, power, pleasure, the beatific vision, and much else. But the difficulty and disagreement in answering the question have not destroyed the conviction that some principle is there to be found, even if only a very abstract one like the rule of producing the greatest good. Now the new intuitionism says that there is *no* such unifying principle. There is *no* common reason for calling actions right or obligatory. Sometimes they are right because they produce the greatest good; sometimes because, though they produce a smaller good, they have the character of promise-keeping; sometimes because they have the character of debt-paying; and so on. And the deontologists are surely right in saying that we cannot be sure that when we set out in search of unity we shall find it, or even that it is there to be found. The fact that a theory is simpler than another is no proof in itself that it is nearer the truth. The world has not been ordered for the ease of our understanding.

2.4

The Divine Command Theory

Perhaps the oldest monistic deontological theory is theological voluntarism, or the divine command theory, which holds that the sole ultimate standard of right and wrong is the will or law of God, i.e., that an action or kind of action is right or wrong if and only if and *because* it is commanded or forbidden by God. This position has often been taken by religious people in the West, beginning with the Jews and the Greeks, though some of its sharpest critics have also been religious. Even so, it is not easy to find a good clear exponent of the divine command theory. Some who say that the criterion of right and wrong, of moral goodness or badness, is the will of God argue that this is so because, ultimately, what we ought to do is what is in our interest, and God makes it in one's interest to do what He commands. This is basically a kind of ethical egoism. Others defend the position by claiming that God is good, benevolent, or loving, which seems to imply that God's end is the good of his creatures and that, if this is His end, it should be ours and so we should do what He commands. This presupposes as a basic principle that we should be like God and implies that we should obey Him. Yet others reason that we should obey Him because we owe Him gratitude, or because He is our creator; they too are presupposing principles that are more basic than that of doing what God commands.

Emil Brunner, who is included in Chapter 3, takes the will of God to be the source and standard of moral obligation and goodness, but it is not clear that he is a deontologist. A better example for our purposes is C. F. Henry. He does not distinguish, as we have, between the right and the good, but simply equates them and identifies both with the will of God, or rather, with obedience to the will of God. He also has interesting things to say about Kant, utilitarianism, and other views he is opposed to.

THE GOOD AS THE WILL OF GOD

C. F. Henry

. . . The good in Hebrew-Christian theistic ethics is not that which is adapted to human nature, but it is that to which the Creator obliges human nature.

The doctrine that the good is to be identified with the will of God cuts across secular ethics at almost every point. It protests against Utilitarianism, and its validation of the good by an appeal to consequences alone. It indicts Kant's supposition that duty and obligation rest upon a wholly immanental basis. According to Kant, the human will alone imposes man's duties upon him and affirms for him the categorical imperative. This theory of morality mediated to the modern man the artificial hope that the objectivity of the moral order could be maintained by a deliberate *severance* of duty and the good *from* the will of God. The Hebrew-Christian ethical perspective also challenges the many species of humanistic ethics so influential in the Western world today. Biblical ethics discredits an autonomous morality. It gives theonomous ethics its classic form—the identification of the moral law with the Divine will. In Hebrew-Christian revelation, distinctions in ethics reduce to what is good or what is pleasing, and to what is wicked or displeasing to the Creator-God alone. . . .

That the essence of true morality is to be found primarily in complete obedience to the sovereign Lord provided the climate of thought which Hobbes secularized and perverted in the *Leviathan*. His contemporary, Ralph Cudworth (1617–1688), who wrote *Eternal and Immutable Morality*, sought to place all men, including Hobbes and his sovereign, under an obligation to act for the common good. Cudworth argued that the distinction between right and wrong does not depend upon sovereign will, but on the moral order which confronts the whole of reality. Cudworth did not hesitate to insist that the principles of morality are addressed even to the Divine will and hence are determinative of it. By moralists under Cudworth's influence, man's obligation to obey the in-

From Christian Personal Ethics (*Grand Rapids, Mich.: Wm. B. Eerdmans Publishing Company, 1957). Reprinted by permission of the author and publisher.*

junctions of Scripture was no longer suspended exclusively on the fact that God commands obedience, but correlative reasons for man's conformity were introduced, e.g., that obedience involves the common good. British moralists especially contributed to this Platonic rather than Hebraic orientation of values. The erroneous notion gained ground swiftly that the best device for thwarting political Naturalism, and for protecting the idea of duty from arbitrary perversion, is to assert the independent existence of moral values, rather than to defend the good as the will of God. God is himself thereby assertedly obliged to uphold these values, and hence precluded from acting in an arbitrary way. Hence the detachment of the content of morality from the will of God became the optimistic basis of a reply to political Naturalism and all forms of moral autonomy.

Thereafter, the phrase "I ought" no longer means "the sovereign Lord commands." Rather, it is informed by self-evident truths or by intuitions of the moral order, as by the Cambridge Platonists, and finally it loses its connection with a transcendent moral order no less than with the sovereign Divine will. Thus the Christian West enters into a non-Christian orientation of the account of duty, and the outcome of this transition is that the doctrine of obligation is sketched independently of both the will of God and of theism. At first it was thought that, while separated from the will of God, moral obligations were as secure as mathematical axioms. They were safeguarded by universal and necessary implications of conscience or by some other immanentistic device. In place of the God-spoken moral imperative there arose a categorical imperative. This endured as an effective rallying point for ethical Idealism for less than a century. When the empirical and evolutionary movements in modern thought were felt, the attempt to secure the absolute obligation to perform every duty within an autonomous ethics dissolved, and with it the absoluteness of duty. Instead of exhibiting the inner unity of duty and goodness in their ultimate basis in the will of God, it lost the sanctity of moral obligation.

Yet the failure to identify duty and the good with the will of God is characteristic of idealistic ethics both in ancient and in modern times. Even those moral philosophies that professed hostility to an autonomous ethic and championed the transcendent objectivity of the moral order regarded the good as something given to God. They viewed the good as something to which God was bound rather than as something legislated by him. This prepared the way for an objectionable doctrine of the "good in itself." The good then is superior to God. It is a content which is externally addressed to him as it is to us. This thesis runs through Oriental religion as well as early Western philosophy. It underlies the

Zoroastrian notion that Ormazd becomes supreme through his further-
ance of the good. This view assumes the existence of an ethical law
superior to God himself. It is found also in the Hindu conception of the
law of Karma. God is the author of sovereign causality in an impersonal
moral universe. Yet not even he can interfere with its autonomous operation now that it is in movement. The same idea becomes influential in
Western thought through the moral philosophy of Plato, as expressed in
the *Euthyphro.* Plato did not clearly identify the Idea of the Good
with God, but it stood at the apex of the Divine Ideas. Hence the good
can only be regarded as confronting the eternal spiritual world.

This notion of an "intrinsic good" is alien to biblical theology. The
God of Hebrew-Christian revelation is the ground of ethics. He is the
supreme rule of right. He defines the whole content of morality by his
own revealed will. It is not merely because "in God is the perfect realization of the Ideal Righteousness," but because God legislates the nature
of the good that biblical ethics is a radical departure from the pagan
view of the moral order. . . . It is the will of God that defines the
nature of intrinsic goodness. There exists no intrinsic good that is distinguishable from the will of God and to which God must conform.

Therefore the good must be conceived in wholly personal dimensions. The good-in-itself is none other than God-in-himself. . . . Kant's
insistence that there is nothing good in the last analysis but a good will
is formally right. His error was his displacement of the Divine by the
human and his staggering moral optimism about human nature. The will
of God is the source of the ethical law and supplies the content of
morality. It alone is intrinsically good. Man's life is not to be oriented to
impersonal eternal values, to objective norms, to ethical laws, to principles of conduct, to abiding virtues, viewed abstractly or independently
of the Divine will. These place obligation upon men only insofar as they
may be traced to the will of God. . . .

The question whether the good is to be conceived as identical with
the nature of God has supplied fuel for theological debate in numerous
Christian controversies. . . . It is possible to hold a view that transcends
the conflict, yet it is important to rule out dangerous and misleading
views. It is obvious enough that unless there is an ultimate ethical tension
in the being of God, the Divine nature and will cannot be thought of as
in competition with each other, but as morally identical. From this standpoint the good is conformity to God's being and to his will. But the
nature of God must not be regarded as necessarily good in the sense that
it gains its goodness independently of his will, nor that his good nature
determines his will so that the will bows to the good by a sort of
pantheistic inevitability. The good is what God wills, and what he freely

wills. The good is what the Creator-Lord does and commands. He is the creator of the moral law, and defines its very nature.

At the same time no suggestion is conveyed that the good is arbitrary or a matter of Divine "caprice." That term frequently suits the propaganda purposes of those who caricature Divine sovereignty. Biblical morality itself has supplied a perspective from which the capriciousness of the polytheistic gods of Greek mythology may be judged. The moral activity of God is a closer definition of his nature. It is the constancy of God's will in its ethical affirmations and claims that supplies the durable basis for moral distinctions. Hovey declares, "The moral law is a free expression of his will to others, and therefore in the fullest and strictest sense it is from him, under him, dependent on him, and immutable only as he is immutable; while the same law comes down upon us from his mind and will, imposing itself on our consciences, and therefore is over us, and independent of us." [1] In stipulating the moral law, the Creator-God lay under no necessity other than to form it according to his own pleasure, and hence in conformity with his real character and purpose. The will of God so reveals his character that the man who conforms to his commandments will exhibit the image of God in his life. The Hebrew-Christian knowledge of God is a knowledge of the Righteous One. The commandments are manifestations of his character, and righteousness is what he prizes as his special glory (Ex. 33:18f., 34:6f.). . . .

The question what makes an act a duty has been answered ambiguously throughout the whole history of ethics. The view that finds in consequences or good results the obligatory basis of our actions, and conceives the ethical act merely as instrumentally good is inadequate. The view that regards an action itself as intrinsically good with total indifference to its consequences, and derives goodness from obligation, is equally inadequate. Both views fail to grasp the fact that obligation and virtue, goodness and happiness, find their common ground in the Divine will. They also fail to recognize that the notions of duty and goodness cannot be analyzed so as to enforce their interlocking nature when this fundamental reference is ignored. Why should man be obliged to do what is regarded as intrinsically good without regard to the consequences? Why is he obliged to do what leads to good consequences if he is in doubt regarding the basic rightness of his action? Speculative ethics furnishes a running commentary on this tension and fails to resolve it.

Hebrew-Christian ethics centers in the Divine revelation of the statutes, commandments, and precepts of the Living God. Its whole orientation of the moral life may be summarized by what the Holy Lord

---

[1] Alvah Hovey, *Manual of Systematic Theology and Christian Ethics* (Philadelphia: American Baptist Publication Society, 1877), p. 369.

commands and what he forbids: what accords with his edicts is right, what opposes his holy will is wicked. . . .[2]

The moral law that lays an imperative on the human conscience is nothing more or less than the manifested will of God. For man nothing is good but union with the sovereign holy will of God. Sin therefore must not be defined primarily as social irresponsibility. Rather, it is repudiation of a Divine claim. David's words "against thee only have I sinned" (Psa. 51:4) echo the penitent's confession at its deepest level. Since God fashioned man to bear his moral likeness, nothing other than the fulfillment of this Divine purpose is man's supreme good. This purpose of God is the moral standard by which man throughout all history will be judged. Society in all its breadth and depth is responsible to the will of God. According to Christianity, to be morally good is to obey God's commands. The performance of God's will alone constitutes man's highest good. The rule of life is to "seek first the kingdom of God and his righteousness" (Mt. 6:33).

One of the first standard criticisms of theological voluntarism is contained in Plato's *Euthyphro*. In the *Apology* Socrates said that the god Apollo had appointed him to teach the people of Athens and that he would continue to teach, even if they commanded him not to, because a command of the gods takes precedence over a command of the state. He did not believe, however, that actions are pious or right just because they are commanded or desired by the gods, and in the following selection from the *Euthyphro* he explains why.

DISCUSSION OF THE DIVINE COMMAND THEORY

Plato

Socrates. . . . The point which I should first wish to understand is whether the pious or holy is beloved by the gods because it is holy, or holy because it is beloved of the gods.

Euthyphro. I don't understand your meaning, Socrates.

From "Euthyphro," in The Dialogues of Plato, 3rd ed., trans. Benjamin Jowett (London: Oxford University Press, 1892).

---

[2] "The good is what God rewards and the bad is what He punishes." Edward John Carnell, *An Introduction to Christian Apologetics* (Grand Rapids: Eerdmans, 1948), p. 154.

Socrates. I will endeavor to explain: we speak of carrying and we speak of being carried, of leading and being led, seeing and being seen. And here is a difference, the nature of which you understand.

Euthyphro. I think that I understand.

Socrates. And is not that which is beloved distinct from that which loves?

Euthyphro. Certainly.

Socrates. Well; and now tell me, is that which is carried in this state of carrying because it is carried, or for some other reason?

Euthyphro. No; that is the reason.

Socrates. And the same is true of that which is led and of that which is seen?

Euthyphro. True.

Socrates. And a thing is not seen because it is visible, but conversely, visible because it is seen; nor is a thing in the state of being led because it is led, or in the state of being carried because it is carried, but the converse of this. And now I think, Euthyphro, that my meaning will be intelligible; and my meaning is, that any state of action or passion implies previous action or passion. It does not become because it is becoming, but it is becoming because it comes; neither does it suffer because it is in a state of suffering, but it is in a state of suffering because it suffers. Do you admit that?

Euthyphro. Yes.

Socrates. Is not that which is loved in some state either of becoming or suffering?

Euthyphro. Yes.

Socrates. And the same holds as in the previous instances; the state of being loved follows the act of being loved, and not the act of the state.

Euthyphro. That is certain.

Socrates. And what do you say of piety, Euthyphro: is not piety, according to your definition, loved by all the gods?

Euthyphro. Yes.

Socrates. Because it is pious or holy, or for some other reason?

Euthyphro. No, that is the reason.

Socrates. It is loved because it is holy, not holy because it is loved?

Euthyphro. Yes.

Socrates. And that which is in a state to be loved of the gods, and is dear to them, is in a state to be loved of them because it is loved of them?

Euthyphro. Certainly.

Socrates. Then that which is loved of God, Euthyphro, is not holy, nor is that which is holy loved of God, as you affirm; but they are two different things.

Euthyphro. How do you mean, Socrates?

Socrates. I mean to say that the holy has been acknowledged by us to be loved of God because it is holy, not to be holy because it is loved.

Euthyphro. Yes.

Socrates. But that which is dear to the gods is dear to them because it is loved by them, not loved by them because it is dear to them.

Euthyphro. True.

Socrates. But, friend Euthyphro, if that which is holy is the same as that which is dear to God, and that which is holy is loved as being holy, then that which is dear to God would have been loved as being dear to God; but if that which is dear to God is dear to him because loved by him, then that which is holy would have been holy because loved by him. But now you see that the reverse is the case, and that they are quite different from one another. For one is of a kind to be loved because it is loved, and the other is loved because it is of a kind to be loved. Thus you appear to me, Euthyphro, when I ask you what is the essence of holiness, to offer an attribute only, and not the essence—the attribute of being loved by all the gods. But you still refuse to explain to me the nature of piety. And therefore, if you please, I will ask you not to hide your treasure, but to tell me once more what piety or holiness really is, whether dear to the gods or not (for that is a matter about which we will not quarrel). And what is impiety?

Euthyphro. I really do not know, Socrates, how to say what I mean. For somehow or other our arguments, on whatever ground we rest them, seem to turn round and walk away. . . . ,

In the seventeenth century the Platonist Ralph Cudworth (1617–88), who is attacked by Henry but who was a sincerely religious philosopher, gave the following argument against the divine command theory:

Ralph Cudworth

. . . certain it is, that divers modern theologers do not only seriously, but zealously contend in like manner, that there is nothing absolutely, intrinsically and naturally good and evil, just and unjust, ante-

From A Treatise concerning Eternal and Immutable Morality, *first printed in 1731. Reprinted in* British Moralists 1650–1800, *ed. D. D. Raphael (Oxford: The Clarendon Press, 1969).*

cedently to any positive command or prohibition of God; but that the arbitrary will and pleasure of God, (that is, an omnipotent being devoid of all essential and natural justice) by its commands and prohibitions, is the first and only rule and measure thereof. Whence it follows unavoidably, that nothing can be imagined so grossly wicked, or so foully unjust or dishonest, but if it were supposed to be commanded by this omnipotent Deity, must needs upon that hypothesis forthwith become holy, just and righteous.

Arguments similar to those of Socrates and Cudworth have been given many times, for example by A. C. Ewing. Notice the similarity of his argument in part (a) of what follows to that of Cudworth, and that in part (b) to the argument of Socrates. Ask yourself just how the "vicious circle" argument in part (b) arises, and whether the theological voluntarist would have any reply.

A. C. Ewing

(a) If "right" and "good" are themselves defined in terms of the commands of God, God cannot command anything because it is right or good, since this would only mean that He commanded it because He commanded it, and therefore there is no reason whatever for His commands, which become purely arbitrary. It would follow that God might just as rationally will that our whole duty should consist in cheating, torturing and killing people to the best of our ability, and that in that case it would be our duty to act in this fashion.

(b) And why are we to obey God's commands? Because we ought to do so? Since "we ought to do A" is held to mean "God commands us to do A," this can only mean that we are commanded by God to obey God's commands, which supplies no further reason. Because we love God? But this involves the assumptions that we ought to obey God if we love Him, and that we ought to love Him. So it again presupposes ethical propositions which cannot without a vicious circle be validated by once more referring to God's commands. Because God is good? This could only mean that God carries out His own commands. Because God will punish us if we do not obey Him? This might be a very good reason from the point of view of self-interest, but self-interest cannot, as we

From Teach Yourself Ethics (*London: Teach Yourself Books Ltd., 1953*). Reprinted by permission of the publisher.

have seen, be an adequate basis for ethics. Without a prior conception of God being good or His commands being right God would have no more claim on our obedience than Hitler except that He would have more power to make things uncomfortable for us if we disobeyed Him than Hitler ever had, and that is not an ethical reason. A moral obligation cannot be created by mere power and threat of punishment. No doubt if we first grant the fundamental concepts of ethics, the existence of God may put us under certain obligations which we otherwise would not have had, e.g. that of thinking of God, as the existence of a man's parents puts him under certain obligations under which he would not stand if they were dead, but we cannot possibly derive all obligations in this fashion from the concept of God. No doubt, if God is perfectly good, we ought to obey His will, but how can we know what His will for us is in a particular case without first knowing what we ought to do?

What I have said of course constitutes no objection to the belief in God or even to the view that we can have a valid argument from ethics to the existence of God, but these views can be held without holding that our ethical terms have to be defined in terms of God. It has been held that the existence of anything implies the existence of God, but it would not therefore be concluded that the meaning of all our words includes a reference to God. Nor is what I have said meant to imply that religion can have no important bearing on ethics, but I think its influence should lie more in helping people to bring themselves to do what would be their duty in any case and in influencing the general spirit in which it is done than in prescribing what our duty is. While it is quite contrary to fact to suggest that an agnostic or atheist cannot be a good man, the influence in the former respects of religious belief, whether true or false, cannot be denied to have been exceedingly strong.

In the eighteenth century an unknown writer named Thomas Johnson (d. 1737) replied to Cudworth's argument, also used by Ewing. He reasons that God is good, and hence cannot command cruelty, killing, etc.; and then— in answer to Ewing's kind of retort, "But saying that God is good only means that God carries out His own commands"—he replies that "God is good" means "God is benevolent," and that there is, therefore, no circularity or difficulty in his theological voluntarism. Johnson was a utilitarian, but only because he thought that he could prove that what God commands is that we "communicate happiness." The famous utilitarian John Stuart Mill, who is represented by a selection in Chapter 5 of this volume, also argued that if God desires the happiness of his creatures, then utilitarianism is compatible with religious ethics.

Ask yourself as you read Johnson whether his basic commitment is to theological voluntarism or to utilitarianism, and why.

Thomas Johnson

If it be farther asked, why upon our hypothesis God might not as well have made that to be virtue which in the present system of things is vice, or *e contra;* or why two and two are equal to four, rather than to fifteen, or in the improper terms of a late writer, "What makes God command goodness rather than evil"; or why he might not command evil? I answer . . . that 'tis putting an absurd self-contradictory supposition. It is like asking, what if God should cease to exist? For when 'tis said, that whatever God commands, it will be man's duty to perform (which is certainly true), this is built upon a supposition, that God is good, for otherwise there could be no such thing as virtue or vice. Infinite or irresistible power cannot (as Hobbes contended) be sufficient to found a law upon, because the subjects can have no security of a reward for their obedience.

Again he asks, "Why do you suppose God to be good rather than otherwise?" My answer is, because I can prove him so without supposing the thing in question. Not indeed *a priori* or "from the perfection or rectitude of his nature" (which would prove him good from his goodness) but *a posteriori* or by ascending from effect to cause.

By goodness I mean, a disposition to do good, i.e. to communicate happiness. That this is an attribute of the Deity appears from the works of the creation, which is evidently contrived for the good of the whole, or so as to manifest, that the design of the Creator therein must be to communicate happiness. And as he is perfect in wisdom, so we may justly conclude, that he sees and knows all the effects and consequences of his actions, and therefore cannot contradict himself, or sometimes will one thing, and sometimes the contrary; that is, he has a permanent disposition to communicate happiness, can no more cease to be good, than he can cease to exist, or to be what he is. This being granted, let us next suppose, that nothing exists but this infinitely good Being; and then let it be enquired, What could determine him to act, or to create any beings at all. . . .

'Tis evident from what has been said, that the only design of the Creator in any action, must be to communicate happiness, and that if he acts at all, it must be for that purpose. This he can have no possible exciting reason to, extrinsic to himself, or his own internal perfections; because, as he is independent of all other beings, and perfectly happy in himself, he can receive neither advantage nor disadvantage from things

From "An Essay on Moral Obligation: With a View towards Settling the Controversy Concerning Moral and Positive Duties" (London, 1731).

external, or from his creatures, and therefore cannot be determined by them or their supposed relations, habitudes or affections, either to act or not to act. The cause of the existence of things must therefore be referred to his sole will, and terminate in that only; or, which is the same, his goodness or intrinsic desire of communicating happiness, is the only cause assignable for the creation.

In reply to another kind of argument against theological voluntarism, used by P. H. Nowell-Smith and Kai Nielsen, Patterson Brown employs a line of thought that is becoming increasingly popular among theologians today, viz. that the statement "God commands us to do so and so" is not a purely factual statement but a partially moral one, which analytically entails "we ought to do so and so." He believes that, in this way, he can rescue the position under attack, not so much by defining the "right" as "what is commanded by God" as by defining "God" as "He who commands what is right," or rather, as "He whose commanding something makes it right."

Patterson Brown

. . . A number of moral philosophers have argued that God's will cannot indicate what we ought to do, since the factual assertion "God wills x" cannot entail the moral assertion "x is good"; "is" cannot imply "ought." This sort of howler is so widespread and so basic that one may be excused for giving two lengthy examples of such an argument. Professor Nowell-Smith, for one, states that: [1]

> . . . it is a mistake to try to define moral "oughts" in terms of God's commands or "God's will." For the mere fact that a command has been issued by a competent authority, even by God, is not a logically good reason for obeying it. Jones's "thou shalt" does not entail Smith's "I shall"; and neither does God's "thou shalt". . . . For religious people the fact that God has commanded them to do something is a sufficient reason, perhaps the only reason, for thinking themselves obliged to do it. But this is because they have a general pro-attitude to doing whatever God commands . . . the mere fact that God commands something is no more reason for doing it than the fact that a cricket coach tells you to do something . . . the fact that you ought to do it cannot be identified with nor is it entailed by the fact that God has commanded it.

From "Religous Morality," Mind, LXXII (April, 1963). Reprinted by permission of the author and Mind.

------

[1] P. H. Nowell-Smith, *Ethics* (Pelican Philosophy Series), pp. 192–93.

Or, again, Professor Nielsen has argued that:

> . . . there is a crucial *logical* difficulty about basing any morality on re-
> ligion. This difficulty has been noted and ignored again and again ever
> since Plato stated it in the *Euthyphro*. The difficulty . . . is this. No infor-
> mation about the nature of reality, the state of the world, or knowledge
> that there is a God and that He issues commands, will by itself tell us what
> is good or what we ought to do. The statement "God wills x" is not a
> moral pronouncement. Before we know whether we ought to do x, we must
> know that what God wills is good. And in order to know that what God
> wills is good, we would have to judge independently that it is good. That
> something is good is not entailed by God's willing it, for otherwise it would
> be rhetorical to ask "Is what God wills good?" But it is not rhetorical to
> ask that question. "God wills x" or "God commands x" is not equivalent to
> "x is good" in the same way as "x is a male parent" is equivalent to "x is a
> father." "God wills it, but is it good?" is not a senseless or self-answering
> question like "Fred is a male parent, but is he a father?" The moral agent
> must independently decide that whatever God wills or commands is good.[2]

The first point which must be made, surely, is that "God" is ordinarily a partially moral term. In our civilisation, and thus in our language, it would not be strictly proper to call a being "God" whose actions
were not perfectly good or whose commands were not the best of moral
directives. That God is good is a truth of language, and not an ethical
contingency, since one of the usual *criteria* of Godhood is that the
actions and commands of such a being are perfectly good. In referring
to some being as "God," we would in part be saying that he was morally
faultless. (Of course, we would also be saying that that being fulfilled
the other criteria of divinity as well, *viz.* omnipotence, omniscience,
transcendence, being the creator of all other things, and so on.) "God
is good," therefore, is trivially true in the same way as "Saints are good."
We would not in strict propriety call anyone a "Saint" who was not
morally perfect, nor would we call any being "God" if he were not
wholly good. So that "There is a God," like "There are Saints," is in part
a moral statement.

There remains, however, a crucial difference between the necessary
goodness of God and the necessary goodness of Saints. To say that
Saints are by definition morally faultless is to say that we will withhold
the title of "Saint" from anyone who is not perfectly good by Christian
standards. To say that God is by definition perfect, however, is to say
more than this. Not only would we withhold the name "God" from any

---

[2] Kai Nielsen, "Religion, Morality and Bertrand Russell," *The Amherst Review*
(Spring 1959), p. 15. In a more recent article entitled "Some Remarks on the Independence of Morality from Religion" (*Mind*, April 1961) [parts of which are reprinted following this selection], Professor Nielsen has considerably modified and
extended this argument. He adheres, however, to his earlier conclusion that morality
must be logically prior to religion; and this is the point that I wish to contest.

being who was imperfect by Christian standards; in addition, the appellation "God" is reserved for that particular being who is the ultimate Christian *criterion* of the good. The saint is good because he follows God's will; but God is good because he is the standard of goodness. Thus, it is rhetorical to ascribe goodness both to Saints and to God, since only that being is called "God" who is the supreme paradigm of goodness, and no one is called "Saint" unless he is Godly. "God is the ultimate standard of the good" is true by definition, and this entails that "God is good" is trivially true. Therefore, in addition to stating that there is an omnipotent, omniscient, and transcendent Creator and that he is perfectly good, "There is a God" also serves as a moral commitment to that being as the basis of Christian morality. So, quite clearly, the statement "If God commands something, then it ought to be done" is pleonastic. If we are not unconditionally obliged to do whatever x commands, then x is by definition not God. Belief in the Judeo-Christian God, then, can entail normative conclusions just because it presupposes a moral commitment. In becoming a Christian theist, one commits oneself to the will of the Creator—who must first, of course, be assumed to exist—as one's own highest ethical standard.

Apparently, therefore, Nowell-Smith and Nielsen do not include in their rules for the use of "God" that any being so named would be perfectly good, and indeed the standard of all goodness. Unlike Christians, they take "God is good" to be an ordinary moral judgement rather than a truth of language. This no doubt tacit divergence from ordinary religious language enables them to argue that the connection between that which God commands and that which we ought to do is contingent upon our evaluations. Whereas, surely, the actual religious "evaluation," if it can be called such, is that of committing oneself to a God-centred morality in the first place. Subsequently to pass independent judgement on God's actions or commands would be a straightforward abandonment of Christian morality, since some other moral principle would then have been accepted as more fundamental than the Creator's will. So that to judge God is in effect to deny that he is *God*.

Even though the statement "If God commands something, then it ought to be done" is redundant, however, we should not therefore conclude that it cannot serve a central role in moral reasoning. A deontic inference of the following form is basic in the Christian's ethical decision-making:

(1) If God commands something, then it ought to be done (by definition).

(2) There is a God (factual and committal); and he commands y (factual).

(3) Therefore: We ought to do y. . . .

It is worth noting that, since "God is paradigmatically good" is analytically true, it follows that "God is evil" is a contradiction in terms. One could hold *via* a non-Christian morality, however, that the Creator was evil or non-trivially good, for then the moral terms would be predicated of "Creator" rather than "God."

It is clear that one cannot adopt a particular morality for ethical reasons—otherwise the principle by which such a decision was made would itself be one's basic moral standard. But this obviously does not imply that a moral commitment cannot be good or bad; it is not the case that only decisions of morality can be morally evaluated. One's reason for making the commitment must be non-moral, but the commitment may nonetheless be good or evil according to particular ethical standards. Thus, it is supremely good by Christian standards to become a Christian; but one clearly cannot decide to adopt the Christian ethic as a result of feeling morally bound by the Creator's command to do so. For if one feels morally obliged to follow God's commands, then one already holds to Christian morality. The Christian religion cannot be logically posterior to any morality.

For Christians, then, to be moral *is* to adhere to the will of God. Things, actions, persons, and so on are good or evil, right or wrong, according to whether God approbates or condemns them; this is the logic of Christian morality. If God exists, then the good is denoted by what he esteems, and the evil by what he damns.

One of the traditional objections to saying that things are good because God says so, rather than the reverse, has been that this seems to entail God's choices to be arbitrary. A. C. Ewing, for example, recently argued that "if 'obligatory' just means 'commanded by God,' the question arises why God should command any one thing rather than any other.[3] We cannot say that he commands it because it ought to be done, for that would have to be translated into 'God commands it because it is commanded by God.' . . . If what was good or bad as well as what ought to be done were fixed by God's will, then there could be no reason whatever for God willing any particular way. His commands would become purely arbitrary." It does indeed follow from my analysis that there could be no *moral* obligation on God to will one thing rather than another, but this certainly does not imply that God's will is capricious. For God is also defined as perfect in knowledge, justice, and love. He would thus by definition will in accord with these several attributes, and the result would be anything but arbitrary. Those who argue like Ewing neglect that there are other criteria of Godhood besides being

---

[3] "The Autonomy of Ethics," included in *Prospect for Metaphysics,* Ian Ramsey (ed.), p. 39.

an ultimate moral standard; and these necessarily preclude God's choosing without reason.

The Christian has two sorts of ways to find out what is good or what ought to be done according to his morality. Firstly, one can be *told* by God what is best, either directly through personal revelation, or indirectly through the Church or the Bible. (The numerous philosophical difficulties attending these notions would occupy an essay in themselves.) Or, secondly, one can *infer* by means of reason alone, i.e. *via* the Natural Law, what God would command. For we can presumably ratiocinate, at least to some degree, what a supremely intelligent, loving, and just being would will; and that is by definition what God would will, i.e. is morally binding. . . .

We must stop the debate somewhere. Nielsen's replies to people like Johnson and Brown go as follows:

Kai Nielsen

Until recently most analytic philosophers, as well as many other philosophers, have assented to the claim, as old as the *Euthyphro,* that morality and religion are logically independent and that it is impossible in principle to base a morality (any morality) on religion. But of late some Oxford-oriented linguistic philosophers have seriously challenged this claim.[1] While I am completely in sympathy with their overall methodological approach and with their attempt to make detailed and careful explications of the actual functions of religious discourse, I do not find their arguments convincing on this point. It seems to me that the essential logical point that both rationalist and empiricist philosophers, from Plato to Russell, have tried to enforce is sound. I shall try here to vindicate this belief of mine.

The traditional argument may be put as follows. No information about the nature of reality, or knowledge that there is a God and that he issues commands, will by itself tell us what is good or what we ought

From *"Some Remarks on the Independence of Morality from Religion,"* Mind, LXX (April, 1961). Reprinted by permission of the author and Mind.

---

[1] See, for example, D. A. Rees, "The Ethics of Divine Commands," *Aristotelian Society Proceedings* (1956–57); G. E. M. Anscombe, "Modern Moral Philosophy," *Philosophy* (1957); R. N. Smart, "Gods, Bliss and Morality," *Aristotelian Society Proceedings* (1957–58).

to do. The statement, "God wills x," is not a moral pronouncement. Before we know whether we ought to do x, we must know that what God wills is good. And in order to know that what God wills is good, we should have to judge independently that it is good. That something is good is not entailed by God's willing it, for otherwise it would be redundant to ask, "Is what God wills good?" But this question is not redundant. "God wills x" or "God commands x" is not equivalent to "x is good," as "x is a male parent" is equivalent to "x is a father." "God wills it but is it good?" is not a senseless self-answering question like "Fred is a male parent, but is he a father?" The moral agent must independently decide that whatever God wills or commands is good.

Here it is natural for the believer to say, "Well, it isn't just God's saying so or ordering it that makes an action obligatory or good. True enough we moral agents must freely choose or decide what to do. God in his wisdom gives us this choice. Otherwise we would be automata, doing what we do simply on authority. Barth and Brunner are of course right in saying we owe God unconditional obedience, but we owe this to God because he is supremely good and supremely loving. When we reflect on what he must be like, as a Being worthy of worship, we realize he ought unconditionally to be obeyed."

But to say this is really to give Plato and Russell their point. We, as moral agents, form moral convictions and decide that such a Being must be good and his commandments must be followed. But this is so *not* because he *utters* them but because God, being God, is good. But we have here used our own moral awareness and sensitivity to decide that God is *good* and that God *ought* to be obeyed. We have not derived our moral convictions just from discovering what are the commands of God. No command, God's or anyone else's, can simply, as a command, serve as our ultimate standard; and that this is so is purely a matter of logic and not just a result of "sinful, prideful rebellion" against God's law. . . .

. . . if so-and-so is called a "divine command" or "an ordinance of God," then it is obviously something that the person who believes it to be a "divine command" or "ordinance of God" ought to obey, for he would not call anything "a *divine* command" or "an ordinance of *God*" unless he thought he ought to obey it. But we ourselves by our own moral insight must judge that such commands or promulgations are worthy of such an appellation. Yet no moral conceptions follow from a command or law as such. And this would be true at any time whatsoever. It is a logical and not a historical consideration.

Now it is true that if you believe in God in such a way as to accept God as your Lord and Master and if you believe that so-and-so is an ordinance of God then you ought to try to follow this ordinance. But this is not so because we can base morals on religion or on a law conception of morality; rather it is true for just the opposite reason. The man who can bring himself to say "My God" uses "God" and cognate words evaluatively. To use such an expression is already to make a moral evaluation, the man expresses his decision that he is morally bound to do whatever God commands. "I ought to do whatever this Z commands" is an expression of moral obligation. To believe in God, as we already have seen, involves the making of a certain value judgment; that is to say, the believer believes that there is a Z such that Z is worthy of worship. But this value judgment cannot be derived from just examining Z, or from hearing Z's commands or laws. Without a pro-attitude on the part of the believer toward Z, without a decision by the individual concerned that Z is *worthy* of worship, nothing of a moral sort follows. But no decision of this sort is entailed by discoveries about Z or by finding out what Z commands or wishes. It is finally up to the individual to decide that this Z is worthy of worship, that this Z ought to be worshipped, that this Z ought to be called his Lord and Master. We have here a moral use of "ought" that is logically prior to any law conception of ethics. The command gains obligatory force because it is judged worthy of obedience. If someone says, "I don't pretend to appraise God's laws, I just simply accept them because God tells me to," like considerations obtain. This person judges that there is a Z that is a proper object of obedience. This expresses his own moral judgment, his own sense of what he is obliged to do.

A religious belief depends for its viability on our sense of good and bad—our own sense of *worth*—and not vice versa. It is crucial to an understanding of morality that this truth about the uses of our language be understood. Morality cannot be based on religion and I (like Findlay) would even go so far as to deny in the name of morality that any Z whatsoever could be an object or Being worthy of worship. But whether or not I am correct in this last judgment, it remains the case that each person with his own finite and fallible moral awareness must make decisions of this sort for himself. This would be so whether he was in a Hebrew-Christian tradition or in a "corrupt" and "shallow" consequentialist tradition or in any tradition whatsoever. A moral understanding must be logically prior to any religious assent.

2.5

Kant's Ethical Theory

Kant has already been mentioned and discussed. He was against all of the theories we have looked at so far, and was particularly opposed to teleological theories, which he regarded as turning morality into something else—into what he called hypothetical imperatives rather than categorical ones. He was a rule-deontologist and comes out with a number of principles or rules of conduct, but he thought they can and must all be arrived at by using a single more basic nonteleological principle (which he calls "the categorical imperative") without any consideration of the good or evil produced by acting on them.

The selections reprinted here do not present Kant's entire theory of obligation, but only a minimal part of it. In it Kant thinks of himself as moving gradually from common sense to philosophical morality. He begins with some propositions about the good will and moral value, works up to the principle of morality, and then derives four more specific rules of duty, though he believes that others can also be established in the same way.

After our selection ends, Kant goes on to state the principle of morality (the categorical imperative) in two other ways: (a) "So act as to treat humanity, whether in thine own person or in that of any other, in every case as an end withal, never as a means only," and (b) "Act upon a maxim which, at the same time, involves its own universal validity for every rational being." He argues that the three formulae are equivalent and yield the same specific rules.

It will require a good deal of concentration to work your way through the following selection. Among the questions you may wish to keep in mind while reading it are: What does Kant mean by "a good will"? What is Kant's argument for his view that the moral worth of an action does not come from the purpose to be attained by it? What does he mean by "acting from respect for the law"? Finally, once Kant has arrived at his categorical imperative, what do you think of his application of it in the four examples at the end of the reading? Are any of these examples more plausible than the others?

FUNDAMENTAL PRINCIPLES OF THE METAPHYSIC OF MORALS

Immanuel Kant

Nothing can possibly be conceived in the world, or even out of it, which can be called good without qualification, except a Good Will. Intelligence, wit, judgment, and the other *talents* of the mind, however they may be named, or courage, resolution, perseverance, as qualities of temperament, are undoubtedly good and desirable in many respects; but these gifts of nature may also become extremely bad and mischievous if the will which is to make use of them, and which, therefore, constitutes what is called *character*, is not good. It is the same with the *gifts of fortune*. Power, riches, honour, even health, and the general well-being and contentment with one's condition which is called *happiness*, inspire pride, and often presumption, if there is not a good will to correct the influence of these on the mind, and with this also to rectify the whole principle of acting and adapt it to its end. The sight of a being who is not adorned with a single feature of a pure and good will, enjoying unbroken prosperity, can never give pleasure to an impartial rational spectator. Thus a good will appears to constitute the indispensable condition even of being worthy of happiness.

There are even some qualities which are of service to this good will itself, and may facilitate its action, yet which have no intrinsic unconditional value, but always presuppose a good will, and this qualifies the esteem that we justly have for them, and does not permit us to regard them as absolutely good. Moderation in the affections and passions, self-control and calm deliberation are not only good in many respects, but even seem to constitute part of the intrinsic worth of the person; but they are far from deserving to be called good without qualification, although they have been so unconditionally praised by the ancients. For without the principles of a good will, they may become extremely bad, and the coolness of a villain not only makes him far more dangerous, but also

From Kant's Theory of Ethics, *trans. T. K. Abbott (London: Longsmans, Green and Co., Ltd., 1879).*

immediately makes him more abominable in our eyes than he would have been without it.

A good will is good not because of what it performs or effects, not by its aptness for the attainment of some proposed end, but simply by virtue of the volition, that is, it is good in itself, and considered by itself is to be esteemed much higher than all that can be brought about by it in favour of any inclination, nay even of the sum total of all inclinations. Even if it should happen that, owing to special disfavour of fortune, or the niggardly provision of a step-motherly nature, this will should wholly lack power to accomplish its purpose, if with its greatest efforts it should yet achieve nothing, and there should remain only the good will (not, to be sure, a mere wish, but the summoning of all means in our power), then, like a jewel, it would still shine by its own light, as a thing which has its whole value in itself. Its usefulness or fruitlessness can neither add nor take away anything from this value. It would be, as it were, only the setting to enable us to handle it the more conveniently in common commerce, or to attract to it the attention of those who are not yet connoisseurs, but not to recommend it to true connoisseurs, or to determine its value. . . .

We have then to develop the notion of a will which deserves to be highly esteemed for itself, and is good without a view to anything further, a notion which exists already in the sound natural understanding, requiring rather to be cleared up than to be taught, and which in estimating the value of our actions always takes the first place, and constitutes the condition of all the rest. In order to do this we will take the notion of duty, which includes that of a good will, although implying certain subjective restrictions and hindrances. These, however, far from concealing it, or rendering it unrecognisable, rather bring it out by contrast, and make it shine forth so much the brighter. . . .[1]

The second proposition is: That an action done from duty derives its moral worth, *not from the purpose* which is to be attained by it, but from the maxim by which it is determined, and therefore does not depend on the realization of the object of the action, but merely on the *principle of volition* by which the action has taken place, without regard to any object of desire. It is clear from what precedes that the purposes which we may have in view in our actions, or their effects regarded as ends and springs of the will, cannot give to actions any unconditional or moral worth. In what then can their worth lie, if it is not to consist in the will and in reference to its expected effect? It cannot lie anywhere but in the *principle of the will* without regard to the ends which can be attained by the action.

---

[1] [At this point, we omit Kant's discussion of his first proposition, namely, that an action has moral worth only if it is done from duty and not merely from inclination.—EDS.]

For the will stands between its *à priori* principle which is formal, and its *à posteriori* spring which is material, as between two roads, and as it must be determined by something, it follows that it must be determined by the formal principle of volition when an action is done from duty, in which case every material principle has been withdrawn from it.

The third proposition, which is a consequence of the two preceding, I would express thus: *Duty is the necessity of acting from respect for the law.* I may have *inclination* for an object as the effect of my proposed action, but I cannot have *respect* for it, just for this reason, that it is an effect and not an energy of will. Similarly, I cannot have respect for inclination, whether my own or another's; I can at most if my own, approve it; if another's, sometimes even love it; i.e., look on it as favourable to my own interest. It is only what is connected with my will as a principle, by no means as an effect—what does not subserve my inclination, but over-powers it, or at least in case of choice excludes it from its calculation—in other words, simply the law of itself, which can be an object of respect, and hence a command. Now an action done from duty must wholly exclude the influence of inclination, and with it every object of the will, so that nothing remains which can determine the will except objectively the *law,* and subjectively *pure respect* for this practical law, and conse-quently the maxim to follow this law even to the thwarting of all my inclinations.

Thus the moral worth of an action does not lie in the effect expected from it, nor in any principle of action which requires to borrow its motive from this expected effect. For all these effects—agreeableness of one's con-dition, and even the promotion of the happiness of others—could have been also brought about by other causes, so that for this there would have been no need of the will of a rational being; it is in this, however, alone that the supreme and unconditional good can be found. The pre-eminent good which we call moral can therefore consist in nothing else than *the conception of law* in itself, *which certainly is only possible in a rational being,* in so far as this conception, and not the expected effect, determines the will. This is a good which is already present in the person who acts accordingly, and we have not to wait for it to appear first in the result.

But what sort of law can that be, the conception of which must deter-mine the will, even without paying any regard to the effect expected from it, in order that this will may be called good absolutely and without qualification? As I have deprived the will of every impulse which could arise to it from obedience to any law, there remains nothing but the uni-versal conformity of its actions to law in general, which alone is to serve the will as a principle, i.e., I am never to act otherwise than so *that I could also will that my maxim should become a universal law.* Here now, it is the simple conformity to law in general, without assuming any particular law applicable to certain actions, that serves the will as its principle, and must so serve it, if duty is not to be a vain delusion and a chimerical notion. The common reason of men in its practical judgments perfectly coincides with this, and always has in view the principle here suggested. Let the question be, for example: May I when in distress make a promise with the intention not to keep it? I readily distinguish here between the two significations which the question may have: Whether it is prudent, or whether it is right, to make a false promise. The former may undoubtedly often be the case. I see clearly indeed that it is not enough to extricate myself from a present difficulty by means of this subterfuge, but it must be well considered whether there may not hereafter spring from this lie much greater inconvenience than that from which I now free myself, and as, with all my supposed *cunning*, the consequences cannot be so easily foreseen but that credit once lost may be much more injurious to me than any mischief which I seek to avoid at present, it should be considered whether it would not be more *prudent* to act herein according to a universal maxim, and to make it a habit to promise nothing except with the intention of keeping it. But it is soon clear to me that such a maxim will still only be based on the fear of consequences. Now it is a wholly different thing to be truthful from duty, and to be so from apprehension of injurious consequences. In the first case, the very notion of the action already implies a law for me; in the second case, I must first look about elsewhere to see what results may be combined with it which would affect myself. For to deviate from the principle of duty is beyond all doubt wicked; but to be unfaithful to my maxim of prudence may often be very advantageous to me, although to abide by it is certainly safer. The shortest way, however, and an unerring one, to discover the answer to this question whether a lying promise is consistent with duty, is to ask myself, Should I be content that my maxim (to extricate myself from difficulty by a false promise) should hold good as a universal law, for myself as well as for others? and should I be able to say to myself, "Every one may make a deceitful promise when he finds himself in a difficulty from which he cannot otherwise extricate himself"? Then I presently become aware that while I can will the lie, I can by no means will that lying should be a universal law. For with such a law there would be no promises at all, since it would be in vain to allege my intention in regard to my future actions to those who would not believe this allegation, or if they over hastily did so would pay me back in my own coin. Hence my maxim, as soon as it should be made a universal law, would necessarily destroy itself.

I do not therefore need any far-reaching penetration to discern what I have to do in order that my will may be morally good. Inexperienced in the course of the world, incapable of being prepared for all its contingencies, I only ask myself: Canst thou also will that thy maxim should be a universal law? If not, then it must be rejected, and that not because of a disadvantage accruing from it to myself or even to others, but because it cannot enter as a principle into a possible universal legislation, and reason extorts from me immediate respect for such legislation. I do not indeed as yet *discern* on what this respect is based (this the philosopher may inquire), but at least I understand this, that it is an estimation of the worth which far outweighs all worth of what is recommended by inclination, and that the necessity of acting from *pure* respect for the practical law is what constitutes duty, to which every other motive must give place, because it is the condition of a will being good *in itself*, and the worth of such a will is above everything.

Thus then, without quitting the moral knowledge of common human reason, we have arrived at its principle. And although no doubt common men do not conceive it in such an abstract and universal form, yet they always have it really before their eyes, and use it as the standard of their decision.

When I conceive a hypothetical imperative in general, I do not know beforehand what it will contain, until I am given the condition. But when I conceive a categorical imperative I know at once what it contains.[2] For as the imperative contains, besides the law, only the necessity of the maxim conforming to this law, while the law contains no condition restricting it, there remains nothing but the general statement that the maxim of the action should conform to a universal law, and it is this conformity alone that the imperative properly represents as necessary.[3]

There is therefore but one categorical imperative, namely this: *Act only on that maxim whereby thou canst at the same time will that it should become a universal law.*

Now if all imperatives of duty can be deduced from this one imperative as from their principle, then although it should remain undecided whether what is called duty is not merely a vain notion, yet at least we shall be able to show what we understand by it and what this notion means.

---

[2] [For Kant an imperative is a statement in which it is said that someone should or ought to do something. If he is told that he should do it because doing it is conducive to something he wants, then the imperative is *hypothetical,* since it does not hold unless he desires the object in question. If it holds or is binding on him anyway, just because he is a rational being and regardless of his desires, then it is *categorical.* Kant holds that moral imperatives are categorical.—Eds.]

[3] A maxim is a subjective principle of action and must be distinguished from the *objective principle,* namely practical law. The former contains the practical rule set by reason according to the conditions of the subject (often its ignorance or its inclinations), so that it is the principle on which the subject *acts;* but the law is the objective principle valid for every rational being, and is the principle on which it *ought to act* that is an imperative.

Since the universality of the law according to which effects are produced constitutes what is properly called *nature* in the most general sense (as to form), that is the existence of things so far as it is determined by general laws, the imperative of duty may be expressed thus: *Act as if the maxim of thy action were to become by thy will a Universal Law of Nature.*

We will now enumerate a few duties, adopting the usual division of them into duties to ourselves and to others, and into perfect and imperfect duties.[4]

1. A man reduced to despair by a series of misfortunes feels wearied of life, but is still so far in possession of his reason that he can ask himself whether it would not be contrary to his duty to himself to take his own life. Now he inquires whether the maxim of his action could become a universal law of nature. His maxim is: From self-love I adopt it as a principle to shorten my life when its longer duration is likely to bring more evil than satisfaction. It is asked then simply whether this principle of self-love can become a universal law of nature? Now we see at once that a system of nature of which it should be a law to destroy life by the very feeling which is designed to impel to the maintenance of life would contradict itself, and therefore could not exist as a system of nature; hence that maxim cannot possibly exist as a universal law of nature and consequently would be wholly inconsistent with the supreme principle of all duty.

2. Another finds himself forced by necessity to borrow money. He knows that he will not be able to repay it, but sees also that nothing will be lent to him, unless he promises stoutly to repay it in a definite time. He desires to make this promise, but he has still so much conscience as to ask himself: Is it not unlawful and inconsistent with duty to get out of a difficulty in this way? Suppose however that he resolves to do so: then the maxim of his action would be expressed thus: When I think myself in want of money, I will borrow money and promise to repay it, although I know that I never can do so. Now this principle of self-love or of one's own advantage may perhaps be consistent with my whole future welfare; but the question now is, Is it right? I change then the suggestion of self-love into a universal law, and state the question thus: How would it be if my maxim were a universal law? Then I see at once that it could never hold as a universal law of nature, but would necessarily contradict itself. For supposing it to be a universal law that every one when he thinks himself in a difficulty should be able to promise whatever he pleases, with the purpose of not keeping his promise,

---

[4] . . . I understand by a perfect duty, one that admits no exception in favour of inclination, and then I have not merely external but also internal perfect duties.

the promise itself would become impossible, as well as the end that one might have in view in it, since no one would consider that anything was promised to him, but would ridicule all such statements as vain pretences.

3. A third finds in himself a talent which with the help of some culture might make him a useful man in many respects. But he finds himself in comfortable circumstances, and prefers to indulge in pleasure rather than to take pains in enlarging and improving his happy natural capacities. He asks, however, whether his maxim of neglect of his natural gifts, besides agreeing with his inclination to indulgence, agrees also with what is called duty? He sees then that a system of nature could indeed subsist with such a universal law, though men (like the South Sea islanders) should let their talents rust, and resolve to devote their lives merely to idleness, amusement, and propagation of their species, in a word to enjoyment; but he cannot possibly *will* that this should be a universal law of nature, or be implanted in us as such by a natural instinct. For, as a rational being, he necessarily wills that his faculties be developed, since they serve him for all sorts of possible purposes, and have been given him for this.

4. A fourth, who is in prosperity, while he sees that others have to contend with great wretchedness and that he could help them, thinks: What concern is it of mine? Let every one be as happy as heaven pleases or as he can make himself; I will take nothing from him nor even envy him, only I do not wish to contribute anything either to his welfare or to his assistance in distress! Now no doubt if such a mode of thinking were a universal law, the human race might very well subsist, and doubtless even better than in a state in which every one talks of sympathy and good will, or even takes care occasionally to put it into practice, but on the other side, also cheats when he can, betrays the rights of men or otherwise violates them. But although it is possible that universal law of nature might exist in accordance with that maxim, it is impossible to *will* that such a principle should have the universal validity of a law of nature. For a will which resolved this would contradict itself, inasmuch as many cases might occur in which one would have need of the love and sympathy of others, and in which by such a law of nature, sprung from his own will, he would deprive himself of all hope of the aid he desires.

These are a few of the many actual duties, or at least what we regard as such, which obviously fall into two classes on the one principle that we have laid down. We must be *able to will* that a maxim of our action should be a universal law. This is the canon of the moral appreciation of the action generally. Some actions are of such a character, that their maxim cannot without contradiction be even *conceived* as a universal law of nature, far from it being possible that we should *will* that it *should* be so. In others this intrinsic impossibility is not found, but still it is impossible to *will* that their maxim should be raised to the universality of a law of nature, since such a will would contradict itself. It is easily seen that the former violate strict or rigorous (inflexible) duty; the latter only laxer (meritorious) duty. Thus it has been completely shown how all duties depend as regards the nature of the obligation (not the object of the action) on the same principle. . . .

Kant has had many followers and many critics. One of the critics is Ross. It may be doubted that his criticisms are always fair to Kant, but they are worth thinking about. Note that Ross criticizes Kant even though both men are rule-deontologists, and note also the value Ross attributes to Kant's method in the closing paragraph of this selection.

CRITICISM OF KANT

W. D. Ross

. . . Kant next turns to ask what must be the nature of a law, the idea of which is to determine a will that is absolutely good. It cannot be any result to be expected from the following of a law that makes the following of it good; for then the following of it would be a means to an end; it would be something useful and not good in itself. The characteristic of any action which makes it a good action must simply be conformity to law. That is, the principle or maxim on which the action proceeds must be one such that we can will that it should become a universal law, a law for everyone.

Kant is in fact trying to find a characteristic which all particular moral laws must have if they are to be moral laws, and which can be used as a criterion of the correctness of any general principle of action, and therefore of the rightness of the acts which conform to such a principle.

But let us take his criterion as he states it, and see if it will do the work he claims it will do. Let the question be, May I when in distress make a promise with the intention of breaking it? I have only to ask, says Kant, "Can I will that the making of lying promises should be a universal law?" Obviously I cannot. For if this were the law, promises

From Kant's Ethical Theory (*Oxford: The Clarendon Press, 1954*). *Reprinted by permission of The Clarendon Press, Oxford.*

would never be believed, and therefore would cease to be made. My maxim, if made a universal law, would necessarily destroy itself.

It is easy to point out a defect in Kant's statement. For I can no more *will* that truth-telling should become a universal law than that lying should. I cannot will either, since neither is within my power. For his test we must substitute one of two others. (1) Could the maxim in fact become a universal law? This is in effect the test he uses in this case. In saying that the maxim if universalized would destroy itself, he is saying that it cannot become a permanent universal law. It is not the impossibility of my willing the universalization of the law "Always make promises which you do not mean to fulfil," but its self-contradiction when thought of as universalized, that Kant tries to prove. (2) Sometimes he uses another test, viz. whether we could *wish* our maxim to be universalized. And this is made to depend on the goodness of the results that would be produced by the supposed universalization, and thus turns into a teleological view very different from the non-teleological view Kant wishes to maintain. We shall see evidence of this later.

The following comments may be made on Kant's principle. (1) The maxim, "People, when they make promises, shall always make promises they do not mean to fulfil," is not one which would necessarily destroy itself. For if people acted always on this maxim every promise could be relied on to be broken, and this would in many (though not in all) cases serve as well as if it could be relied on to be kept. What Kant in fact supposes to be universalized is not a law but a permission—"Everyone *may* make a deceitful promise when he finds himself in a difficulty from which he cannot otherwise extricate himself." This *would*, no doubt, lead to chaos. Then we should never know whether the maker of any promise meant to keep it or to break it; no attention would be paid to promises, and they would soon cease to be made.

But this objection applies only to the particular case of promise-keeping, and we must look deeper. (2) The principle proves too much. The principle is this. If an act *a* belongs to a class-of-acts A the doing of which by everyone cannot become a permanent law of human society without self-contradiction, act *a* is not right. Now lying, for instance, cannot, so Kant maintains, be a permanent law of human society. Therefore no lie is ever right. And in a similar way we are led to a number of particular moral laws each of which is maintained to be absolute and binding without exception. This leads at once to the problem of conflict of duties, and leads Kant to adopt a paradoxical attitude in face of it. This perhaps comes out most clearly in the essay of 1797 "On a supposed right to tell lies from benevolent motives." He takes there the case of a man A, who is pursuing another, B, with intent to murder him. B takes refuge in the house of C. A comes up and asks C whether B is in his house. Kant maintains that it is C's duty to tell the truth. With his never-failing ingenuity he points out that if C honestly, to the best of his knowledge, answers "Yes," B may meanwhile have gone out unobserved and so escape; while if C with intent to deceive says B is not in the house, and A finds B outside and kills him, C may with justice be called the cause of B's death. But this is not Kant's main ground for saying that C should tell A the truth. His main ground is that the duty of telling the truth is an absolute one, not capable of being overruled by any set of circumstances.

It is one of Kant's most constant claims that his theory is in accordance with plain men's thoughts about moral questions; but most people will feel that he fails in this case to represent normal moral opinion. Most people would have no hesitation in saying, as Benjamin Constant says in the work Kant is here criticizing, that to tell the truth is a duty, but only towards him who has a right to the truth, and that the intending murderer has no such right.

Or again, it is clear that celibacy could not be a permanent law of human society, since it would bring human society to an end. On Kant's principle, that implies that celibacy is a duty for no man. But ordinary moral opinion, not wedded to a theory, would say that for people with certain duties to perform, and for people with serious hereditary disease, celibacy is a duty. In fact the attempt to make any of the particular rules of morality absolute fails when we are faced with the complexity of actual situations. All that can be claimed for them is that they state prima facie duties, definitely arising from certain features of the moral situation, but capable of being overruled by other prima facie duties.

(3) But it is time that we came nearer to the root of Kant's mistake. On the face of it, his principle looks as if it ought to be right. It seems as if it were true to say that a principle of action, if it is correct, must be capable of being applied generally; that that cannot be right for me which would be wrong for someone else; and that therefore the answer to the question "Would it be right for everyone to behave so?" may furnish us with the answer to the question "Would it be right for me to behave so?" Kant's error seems to lie in this: Any individual act is an instance of a class of acts which is a species of a wider class of acts which is a species of a still wider class; we can set no limit to the degrees of specification which may intervene between the *summum genus* "act" and the individual act. For example, if C tells a lie to the would-be murderer, this falls (i) under the sub-species "lies told to murderous persons," (ii) under the species "lies," (iii) under the genus "statements." Kant pitches, arbitrarily, on the middle one of these three classes, and since acts of this class are generally wrong, and are indeed always prima facie wrong, he says that the particular lie is wrong. But

the man who tells the lie may well retort to Kant "Why should the test of universalizability be applied to my act regarded in this very abstract way, simply as a lie? I admit that lying could not properly become a general law of human society. But why not apply the test of universalizability to my act considered more concretely, as a lie told to a would-be murderer, to prevent him from committing a murder? I am willing then to face the test of universalizability. I think that human society would be better conducted if people habitually told lies in such circumstances, than if they habitually told the truth and helped murderers to commit their murders."

We seem, then, to be in an impasse. The test of universalizability applied at one level of abstractness condemns the act; applied at another level of abstractness it justifies it. And since the principle itself does not indicate at what level of abstractness it is to be applied, it does not furnish us with a criterion of the correctness of maxims, and of the rightness of acts that conform to them.

(4) The whole method of abstraction, if relied upon, when used alone, to answer for us the question "What ought I to do?," is a mistake. For the facts we have to choose between, say the telling of the truth or the saying of what is untrue, in some particular circumstances, or the keeping or the breaking of a promise, are completely individual acts, and their rightness or wrongness will spring from their whole nature, and no element in their nature can safely be abstracted from. To abstract is to shut our eyes to the detail of the moral situation, and to deprive ourselves of the data for a true judgement about it. The man who justifies his particular lie by saying "All lies told to murderous persons are right" is abstracting, as Kant is abstracting when he condemns the lie by saying "All lies are wrong." The former is abstracting less than Kant does, and therefore perhaps less dangerously. But still his abstraction is dangerous; for, even if lies told to murderous persons are generally justified, there may be some feature of this lie (e.g. that it endangers the life of a fourth person) that makes it wrong. The only safe way of applying Kant's test of universalizability is to envisage the act in its whole concrete particularity, and then ask "Could I wish that everyone, when in exactly similar circumstances, should tell a lie exactly similar to that which I am thinking of telling?" But then universalizability, as a short cut to knowing what is right, has failed us. For it is just as hard to see whether a similar act by someone else, with all its concrete particularity, would be right, as it is to see whether our own proposed act would be right.

Yet (5) Kant's method has a certain value here, and indeed a great value. Logically we gain nothing by posing the question as a question for everyone rather than for oneself; for it is the same question. But psychologically we gain much. So long as I consider the act as one which I may or may not do, it is easy to suppose that I see it to be right when I merely see it to be convenient. But let me ask myself whether it would be right for everyone else; their advantage does not appeal to me or cloud my mind as my own does. If the act is wrong, it will be easier to see that it would be wrong for them; and then I cannot reasonably resist the conclusion that it is wrong for me. Other writers before Kant had for this reason advocated the adoption of the attitude of the impartial spectator. . . .

Suggestions for Further Reading

2.1 ETHICAL EGOISM

BAUMER, W. H. "Indefensible Impersonal Egoism," *Philosophical Studies,* XVIII, No. 5 (1967), 72–75.

BROAD, C. D. "Egoism as a Theory of Human Motives," *The Hibbert Journal,* XLVIII (1949–50), 105–14. Reprinted in C. D. Broad, *Ethics and the History of Philosophy* (London: Routledge & Kegan Paul, 1952), 218–31.

————. *Five Types of Ethical Theory.* London: Routledge & Kegan Paul, 1930. (Chapter III)

GAUTHIER, D. P., ed. *Morality and Rational Self-Interest.* Englewood Cliffs, N.J.: Prentice-Hall, 1970. See especially the defense of ethical egoism by Jesse Kalin.

WILLIAMS, GARDNER. "Individual, Social and Universal Ethics," *The Journal of Philosophy,* XLV (1948), 645–55.

2.2 ACT-DEONTOLOGICAL THEORIES

GARNETT, A. C. "Conscience and Conscientious Action," *Rice University Studies,* LI (1965), 71–83. Contains an interesting discussion of conscience, part of which is included in the selection from this article in Chapter 4 of this book.

VON HILDEBRAND, DIETRICH. *True Morality and Its Counterfeits.* New York: McKay, 1958. (Chapter X)

2.3 RULE-DEONTOLOGICAL THEORIES

RASHDALL, HASTINGS. *The Theory of Good and Evil* (2nd ed.). Oxford: Clarendon Press, 1924. (Vol. I, Chapter 4)

ROSS, W. D. *Foundations of Ethics.* New York: Oxford University Press, 1939.

2.4 THE DIVINE COMMAND THEORY

EWING, A. C. "Ethics and Belief in God," *The Hibbert Journal,* XXXIX (1941), 375–88.

MERCIER, CARDINAL. *A Manual of Modern Scholastic Philosophy*. London: Kegan Paul, Trench, Trubner and Company, 1917. (Vol. II, Part I, Chapter 3)

PALEY, WILLIAM. *The Principles of Moral and Political Philosophy*. Several editions: first published in 1785. (Book I, Chapter 7 and Book II, Chapters 1–4, 9)

RAMSEY, I. T., ed. *Christian Ethics and Contemporary Philosophy*. London: SCM Press, 1966.

2.5 KANT'S ETHICAL THEORY

BROAD, C. D. *Five Types of Ethical Theory*. London: Routledge & Kegan Paul, 1930. (Chapter V)

WOLFF, R. P., ed. *Kant: A Collection of Critical Essays*. Garden City, N.Y.: Doubleday, 1967. (Part Two)

3

UTILITARIANISM, JUSTICE, AND LOVE

Introduction

This chapter will cover a number of remaining theories and topics in the theory of obligation. The readings in Sections 3.1 to 3.3 will be about utilitarianism, a view that has been widespread in our culture as well as in philosophy, probably as a result of the rise in modern times of the middle class, and of industry, science, and democracy, together with the influence of the Christian ethics of love. There are many kinds of utilitarianism, as we shall see, but they all hold, in one way or another, that we are to determine what is right or wrong by considering what will have the best consequences for the welfare of sentient beings—or, more accurately, produce the greatest balance of good over evil in the world as a whole. All that matters ultimately in the determination of moral right and wrong is the good and evil promoted. The utilitarian does not say only that we are to consider the consequences of our actions and rules; he insists that we are to consider the *good* and *evil* in those consequences—or, rather, the total good and evil brought about —and nothing else. Here "good and evil" means nonmoral good and evil, however this is conceived. Utilitarians may have very different views about what is good or evil in this sense or as an end. Traditional utilitarianism, e.g. that of Jeremy Bentham and John Stuart Mill, was hedonistic, holding that the good = happiness = pleasure. The so-called "ideal utilitarianism" of Moore and Rashdall was nonhedonistic, holding that other things besides pleasure are intrinsically good, e.g. knowledge. Today most utilitarians would probably equate the good with what is desired, needed, or wanted, or with the satisfaction of desires, needs, or wants.

Thus, utilitarians may differ about what is good or evil or about what "utility" and "welfare" are. They may and do differ, also, about the manner in which we are to appeal to consequences in terms of good and evil when trying to determine what we ought or ought not to do. We shall distinguish three forms of utilitarianism on this point: act-utilitarianism (AU), general utilitarianism (GU), and rule-utilitarianism (RU). Some philosophers think that these kinds of utilitarianism are not really all distinct, e.g. some hold that GU and some forms of RU are reducible to AU and hence represent no improvement over AU, as they claim to be. AUs sometimes use this as an argument for sticking to AU, and deontologists sometimes use it as a reason for giving up utilitarianism altogether. However, the arguments for and against such claims about the equivalence of various forms of utilitarianism are too complex and technical to be summarized or reproduced here, and, since no agreement has been reached on these matters, we shall proceed as if the forms are all distinct. The question is, nevertheless, an interesting one to think about in reading what follows.

3.1

Act-Utilitarianism

AU is also called "direct," "extreme," or "unmodified" utilitarianism. It seems, prima facie, the most natural form for utilitarian ethics to take. For, if the end to be promoted is the greatest general balance of good over evil in the world, it seems plausible to believe that each of us ought to aim at that end in each of his actions. This would mean that every time I am faced with determining what I morally ought to do in a certain situation, I must try to determine which action will promote the greatest balance of good over evil. Of course, as Bentham says, I may not have to do this investigating and calculating anew each time. If I or mankind have already learned by past experience that doing A is the best thing to do in a certain kind of situation, then, if I face a situation of this kind, I may simply rely on this past experience. Then, in effect, I use a "rule of thumb" built up in the past, viz., "In such and such situations, do A." But then I must be sure that the situation is of the sort in question, and that the rule of thumb applies to it. It might be that my present situation is different in some way, or it might be that, although the rule of thumb was true for previous cases of the sort in question, it does not hold for this one (i.e., the rule turns out to be false in precisely this case). Hence, for AU, each of us must always be prepared, unless he simply appeals to someone else's authority, to apply the principle of AU in any given situation he may be in. The principle of AU may be stated **thus:**

> An action is morally right for an agent to do in a certain situation if and only if *it* will produce at least as great a balance of good over evil in the world as any other action open to him.

This would mean that, in determining what one should do, one should look at long-run as well as short-run effects, and also, that one should look at indirect as well as direct effects; for instance, one should consider, among other things, the effects of one's action on others who may take it as an example or as an excuse. But one need not and may not ask, "What if everyone did what I propose to do?" for to ask this is to give up AU.

AU has been more recently maintained by G. E. Moore and J. J. C. Smart, among others, but we shall take Jeremy Bentham (1748–1832) as our main example. Even though it is not entirely clear that he is an AU, the selection given below is a good statement of AU (in its hedonistic form), besides being famous in its own right. In it Bentham states "the principle of utility" as he understands it and gives his reasons for adopting it as the standard of morality. He also explains his conception of the way in which we are to calculate the "tendency" of an action, i.e., to determine how great a balance of good over evil it will produce. Bentham does not say we must ask which action would produce the greatest general balance of good over evil in the world as a whole, but only which action would produce the greatest general balance of good over evil for "the party whose interest is in question." But presumably he means by this "those whose interests are affected," which comes to the same thing in practice. In any case he considered only the quantitative dimensions of the pleasures and pains involved; "quantity of pleasure being equal," he said, "pushpin [a child's game] is as good as poetry."

We include also a separate footnote in which Bentham indicates his view of justice.

HEDONISTIC ACT-UTILITARIANISM

Jeremy Bentham

Of the Principle of Utility

I. Nature has placed mankind under the governance of two sovereign masters, *pain* and *pleasure*. It is for them alone to point out what we ought to do, as well as to determine what we shall do. On the one hand the standard of right and wrong, on the other the chain of causes and effects, are fastened to their throne. They govern us in all we do, in all we say, in all we think: every effort we can make to throw off our subjection, will serve but to demonstrate and confirm it. In words a man may pretend to abjure their empire: but in reality he will remain sub-

From An Introduction to the Principles of Morals and Legislation *(Oxford, 1789).*

ject to it all the while. The *principle of utility* [1] recognises this subjection, and assumes it for the foundation of that system, the object of which is to rear the fabric of felicity by the hands of reason and of law. Systems which attempt to question it, deal in sounds instead of sense, in caprice instead of reason, in darkness instead of light.

But enough of metaphor and declamation: it is not by such means that moral science is to be improved.

II. The principle of utility is the foundation of the present work: it will be proper therefore at the outset to give an explicit and determinate account of what is meant by it. By the principle of utility is meant that principle which approves or disapproves of every action whatsoever, according to the tendency which it appears to have to augment or diminish the happiness of the party whose interest is in question: or, what is the same thing in other words, to promote or to oppose that happiness. I say of every action whatsoever; and therefore not only of every action of a private individual, but of every measure of government.

III. By utility is meant that property in any object, whereby it tends to produce benefit, advantage, pleasure, good, or happiness, (all this in the present case comes to the same thing) or (what comes again to the same thing) to prevent the happening of mischief, pain, evil, or unhappiness to the party whose interest is considered: if that party be the community in general, then the happiness of the community: if a particular individual, then the happiness of that individual.

IV. The interest of the community is one of the most general expressions that can occur in the phraseology of morals: no wonder that the meaning of it is often lost. When it has a meaning, it is this. The community is a fictitious *body,* composed of the individual persons who are considered as constituting as it were its *members.* The interest of the community then is, what?—the sum of the interests of the several members who compose it.

---

[1] Note by the Author, July 1822.

To this denomination has of late been added, or substituted, the *greatest happiness* or *greatest felicity* principle: this for shortness, instead of saying at length *that principle* which states the greatest happiness of all those whose interest is in question, as being the right and proper, and only right and proper and universally desirable, end of human action: of human action in every situation, and in particular in that of a functionary or set of functionaries exercising the powers of Government. The word *utility* does not so clearly point to the ideas of *pleasure* and *pain* as the words *happiness* and *felicity* do: nor does it lead us to the consideration of the *number,* of the interests affected; to the *number,* as being the circumstance, which contributes, in the largest proportion, to the formation of the standard here in question; the *standard of right and wrong,* by which alone the propriety of human conduct, in every situation, can with propriety be tried. This want of a sufficiently manifest connexion between the ideas of *happiness* and *pleasure* on the one hand, and the idea of *utility* on the other, I have every now and then found operating, and with but too much efficiency, as a bar to the acceptance, that might otherwise have been given, to this principle.

V. It is in vain to talk of the interest of the community, without understanding what is the interest of the individual. A thing is said to promote the interest, or to be *for* the interest, of an individual, when it tends to add to the sum total of his pleasures: or, what comes to the same thing, to diminish the sum total of his pains.

VI. An action then may be said to be conformable to the principle of utility, or, for shortness sake, to utility, (meaning with respect to the community at large) when the tendency it has to augment the happiness of the community is greater than any it has to diminish it.

VII. A measure of government (which is but a particular kind of action, performed by a particular person or persons) may be said to be conformable to or dictated by the principle of utility, when in like manner the tendency which it has to augment the happiness of the community is greater than any which it has to diminish it.

VIII. When an action, or in particular a measure of government, is supposed by a man to be conformable to the principle of utility, it may be convenient, for the purposes of discourse, to imagine a kind of law or dictate, called a law or dictate of utility: and to speak of the action in question, as being conformable to such law or dictate.

IX. A man may be said to be a partizan of the principle of utility, when the approbation or disapprobation he annexes to any action, or to any measure, is determined by and proportioned to the tendency which he conceives it to have to augment or to diminish the happiness of the community: or in other words, to its conformity or unconformity to the laws or dictates of utility.

X. Of an action that is conformable to the principle of utility one may always say either that it is one that ought to be done, or at least that it is not one that ought not to be done. One may say also, that it is right it should be done; at least that it is not wrong it should be done: that it is a right action; at least that it is not a wrong action. When thus interpreted, the words *ought,* and *right* and *wrong,* and others of that stamp, have a meaning: when otherwise, they have none.

XI. Has the rectitude of this principle been ever formally contested? It should seem that it had, by those who have not known what they have been meaning. Is it susceptible of any direct proof? it should seem not: for that which is used to prove every thing else, cannot itself be proved: a chain of proofs must have their commencement somewhere. To give such proof is as impossible as it is needless.

XII. Not that there is or ever has been that human creature breathing, however stupid or perverse, who has not on many, perhaps on most occasions of his life, deferred to it. By the natural constitution of the human frame, on most occasions of their lives men in general embrace this principle, without thinking of it: if not for the ordering of their own actions, yet for the trying of their own actions, as well as of those of other men. There have been, at the same time, not many, perhaps, even of the most intelligent, who have been disposed to embrace it purely and without reserve. There are even few who have not taken some occasion or other to quarrel with it, either on account of their not understanding always how to apply it, or on account of some prejudice or other which they were afraid to examine into, or could not bear to part with. For such is the stuff that man is made of: in principle and in practice, in a right track and in a wrong one, the rarest of all human qualities is consistency.

XIII. When a man attempts to combat the principle of utility, it is with reasons drawn, without his being aware of it, from that very principle itself.[2] His arguments, if they prove any thing, prove not that the principle is *wrong*, but that, according to the applications he supposes to be made of it, it is *misapplied*. Is it possible for a man to move the earth? Yes; but he must first find out another earth to stand upon.

XIV. To disprove the propriety of it by arguments is impossible; but, from the causes that have been mentioned, or from some confused or partial view of it, a man may happen to be disposed not to relish it. Where this is the case, if he thinks the settling of his opinions on such a subject worth the trouble, let him take the following steps, and at length, perhaps, he may come to reconcile himself to it.

1. Let him settle with himself, whether he would wish to discard this principle altogether; if so, let him consider what it is that all his reasonings (in matters of politics especially) can amount to?

2. If he would, let him settle with himself, whether he would judge and act without any principle, or whether there is any other he would judge and act by?

3. If there be, let him examine and satisfy himself whether the principle he thinks he has found is really any separate intelligible principle; or whether it be not a mere principle in words, a kind of phrase, which at bottom expresses neither more nor less than the mere averment of his own unfounded sentiments; that is, what in another person he might be apt to call caprice?

4. If he is inclined to think that his own approbation or disapprobation, annexed to the idea of an act, without any regard to its consequences, is a sufficient foundation for him to judge and act upon, let him

---

2 "The principle of utility (I have heard it said) is a dangerous principle: it is dangerous on certain occasions to consult it." This is as much as to say, what? that it is not consonant to utility, to consult utility: in short, that it is *not* consulting it, to consult it.

ask himself whether his sentiment is to be a standard of right and wrong, with respect to every other man, or whether every man's sentiment has the same privilege of being a standard to itself?

5. In the first case, let him ask himself whether his principle is not despotical, and hostile to all the rest of human race?

6. In the second case, whether it is not anarchial, and whether at this rate there are not as many different standards of right and wrong as there are men? and whether even to the same man, the same thing, which is right to-day, may not (without the least change in its nature) be wrong to-morrow? and whether the same thing is not right and wrong in the same place at the same time? and in either case, whether all argument is not at an end? and whether, when two men have said, "I like this," and "I don't like it," they can (upon such a principle) have any thing more to say?

7. If he should have said to himself, No: for that the sentiment which he proposes as a standard must be grounded on reflection, let him say on what particulars the reflection is to turn? if on particulars having relation to the utility of the act, then let him say whether this is not deserting his own principle, and borrowing assistance from that very one in opposition to which he sets it up: or if not on those particulars, on what other particulars?

8. If he should be for compounding the matter, and adopting his own principle in part, and the principle of utility in part, let him say how far he will adopt it?

9. When he has settled with himself where he will stop, then let him ask himself how he justifies to himself the adopting it so far? and why he will not adopt it any farther?

10. Admitting any other principle than the principle of utility to be a right principle, a principle that it is right for a man to pursue; admitting (what is not true) that the word *right* can have a meaning without reference to utility, let him say whether there is any such thing as a *motive* that a man can have to pursue the dictates of it: if there is, let him say what that motive is, and how it is to be distinguished from those which enforce the dictates of utility: if not, then lastly let him say what it is this other principle can be good for? . . .

Value of a Lot of Pleasure or Pain, How to be Measured

I. Pleasures then, and the avoidance of pains, are the *ends* which the legislator has in view: it behoves him therefore to understand their *value.* Pleasures and pains are the *instruments* he has to work with: it behoves him therefore to understand their force, which is again, in other words, their value.

II. To a person considered *by himself,* the value of a pleasure or pain considered *by itself,* will be greater or less, according to the four following circumstances: [3]

1. Its *intensity.*
2. Its *duration.*
3. Its *certainty* or *uncertainty.*
4. Its *propinquity* or *remoteness.*

III. These are the circumstances which are to be considered in estimating a pleasure or a pain considered each of them by itself. But when the value of any pleasure or pain is considered for the purpose of estimating the tendency of any *act* by which it is produced, there are two other circumstances to be taken into the account; these are,

5. Its *fecundity,* or the chance it has of being followed by sensations of the *same* kind: that is, pleasures, if it be a pleasure: pains, if it be a pain.

6. Its *purity,* or the chance it has of *not* being followed by sensations of the *opposite* kind: that is, pains, if it be a pleasure: pleasures, if it be a pain.

These two last, however, are in strictness scarcely to be deemed properties of the pleasure or the pain itself; they are not, therefore, in strictness to be taken into the account of the value of that pleasure or that pain. They are in strictness to be deemed properties only of the act, or other event, by which such pleasure or pain has been produced; and accordingly are only to be taken into the account of the tendency of such act or such event.

IV. To a *number* of persons, with reference to each of whom the value of a pleasure or a pain is considered, it will be greater or less, according to seven circumstances: to wit, the six preceding ones; *viz.*

1. Its *intensity.*

---

[3] These circumstances have since been denominated *elements* or *dimensions* of *value* in a pleasure or a pain.

Not long after the publication of the first edition, the following memoriter verses were framed, in the view of lodging more effectually, in the memory, these points, on which the whole fabric of morals and legislation may be seen to rest.

> *Intense, long, certain, speedy, fruitful, pure—*
> Such marks in *pleasures* and in *pains* endure.
> Such pleasures seek if *private* be thy end:
> If it be *public,* wide let them *extend.*
> Such *pains* avoid, whichever be thy view:
> If pains *must* come, let them *extend* to few.

2. Its *duration.*

3. Its *certainty* or *uncertainty.*

4. Its *propinquity* or *remoteness.*

5. Its *fecundity.*

6. Its *purity.*

And one other; to wit:

7. Its *extent;* that is, the number of persons to whom it *extends;* or (in other words) who are affected by it.

V. To take an exact account then of the general tendency of any act, by which the interests of a community are affected, proceed as follows. Begin with any one person of those whose interests seem most immediately to be affected by it: and take an account,

1. Of the value of each distinguishable *pleasure* which appears to be produced by it in the *first* instance.

2. Of the value of each *pain* which appears to be produced by it in the *first* instance.

3. Of the value of each pleasure which appears to be produced by it *after* the first. This constitutes the *fecundity* of the first *pleasure* and the *impurity* of the first *pain.*

4. Of the value of each *pain* which appears to be produced by it after the first. This constitutes the *fecundity* of the first *pain,* and the *impurity* of the first pleasure.

5. Sum up all the values of all the *pleasures* on the one side, and those of all the pains on the other. The balance, if it be on the side of pleasure, will give the *good* tendency of the act upon the whole, with respect to the interest of that *individual person;* if on the side of pain, the *bad* tendency of it upon the whole.

6. Take an account of the *number* of persons whose interests appear to be concerned; and repeat the above process with respect to each. *Sum up* the numbers expressive of the degrees of *good* tendency, which the act has, with respect to each individual, in regard to whom the tendency of it is *good* upon the whole: do this again with respect to each individual, in regard to whom the tendency of it is *good* upon the whole: do this again with respect to each individual, in regard to whom the tendency of it is *bad* upon the whole. Take the *balance;* which, if on the side of *pleasure,* will give the general *good tendency* of the act, with respect to the total number or community of individuals concerned; if on the side of pain, the general *evil tendency,* with respect to the same community.

VI. It is not to be expected that this process should be strictly pursued previously to every moral judgment, or to every legislative or judicial operation. It may, however, be always kept in view: and as near as the process actually pursued on these occasions approaches to it, so near will such process approach to the character of an exact one.[4]

In one of his footnotes Bentham refers to the argument that the principle of utility is a dangerous principle. The point is that the results for society will be bad if each of us always tries, in each case, to see what act will produce the greatest general balance of good over evil. Both deontologists and RUs have used this argument against AU. Objections of another kind are stated by Ross in Chapter 2 and should be consulted again here (see pp. 81–83). Ross is attacking what he calls utilitarianism, but it is really what we now call AU that he has in mind. Very similar objections to utilitarianism were stated by Butler and many others. The following passage is typical, and is interesting partly because it was written by George Ripley (1802–80), the American Transcendentalist who headed the Brook Farm Experiment of the 1840s. His criticisms apply especially to AU, but he mentions the RU of William Paley (1743–1805) and rejects it too. After reading Ripley's comments it would be well worth attempting to put his objections to both AU and RU into writing; then ask yourself if, on balance, you agree with them.

VIRTUE AND UTILITY

George Ripley

What is the criterion by which we may determine whether or not an action or mental disposition is right? It is to be determined by utility, say the advocates of the theory, which we oppose. As soon as it is proved to be useful, it is proved to be right. Let us consider, in the first place, if this criterion will hold in its application to individual actions, for if

From "A General View of the Progress of Ethical Philosophy, Chiefly during the Seventeenth and Eighteenth Centuries, By the Rt. Hon. Sir James Macintosh," The Christian Examiner XIII (1833).

---

[4] Sometimes, in order the better to conceal the cheat (from their own eyes doubtless as well as from others) they set up a phantom of their own, which they call Justice: whose dictates are to modify (which being explained, means to oppose) the dictates of benevolence. But justice, in the only sense in which it has a meaning, is an imaginary personage, feigned for the convenience of discourse, whose dictates are the dictates of utility, applied to certain particular cases. Justice, then, is nothing more than an imaginary instrument, employed to forward on certain occasions, and by certain means, the purposes of benevolence. The dictates of justice are nothing more than a part of the dictates of benevolence, which, on certain occasions, are applied to certain subjects; to wit, to certain actions.

it will not, its importance as a test is at once diminished, since it is individual actions, of which we have the most frequent occasion to determine
the character. Now it is plain, that there are many actions of a moral
nature, which we immediately pronounce to be wrong, of which no one
hesitates to say that they are wrong, yet the actual effects of which have
been beneficial to mankind. If utility were the criterion, such actions
would be right. If the case can be fairly made out that they have done
good to the world, and utility be assumed as the only test of their character, of course, we must admit that they ought to have been done,—
however repugnant to our natural feelings,—since we have pronounced
them useful, we must also pronounce them right. But let us make the
attempt. We shall find it impossible. We might as well hope to move the
sun at our bidding, as to make a wrong action, useful though it be, appear
to our moral faculty as right. Take as an example, the death of Socrates.
The crime against philosophy, which the Athenians committed in his
martyrdom, has never been forgiven, from that day to the present. The
universal sense of mankind is against it. It is unequivocally and unanimously condemned as wrong. But no one can doubt that the ultimate
effects of that atrocious and unjust deed have been eminently useful. It
was a matter of small importance for Socrates to leave the world, though
by a violent death. He was ripe in years and in virtue. He had exhausted
the usual sources of enjoyment which life affords. He could, at best, have
been spared but a little while. He was taken from the world, in the full
possession of all his faculties, neither his mind nor body impaired by the
touch of a loathsome disease, calmly conversing with the troops of friends,
who were faithful to the last, and, finally, yielding to the gentle operation
of the poison, resigned his breath without a struggle. If we were asked
what injury were done to Socrates, we should not know where to look
for a reply. Indeed, it is difficult to conceive a more enviable situation
than that of the martyred philosopher, when, after blessing his executioner, he tasted the fatal cup and surrendered himself to the pleasing
visions of immortality, which hovered around his last moments. But does
all this prove that his condemnation was just? Does it not rather lead us
to regard the crime of his accusers, with deeper indignation? Are we in
the slightest degree reconciled to them, by the assurance of the good
effects which their crime has produced? Of these good effects, there can
be no doubt. The manner of his death, far more than the spirit of his
philosophy, or the beauty of his character, has embalmed the memory of
Socrates, in the hearts of every succeeding generation. The remembrance
of his name has given a charm to his principles, and the efficacy of his
example added strength to virtue. If, then, we judge of the sentence
which doomed him to drink hemlock, by the test of utility, how can we
avoid pronouncing it virtuous? Why do we not praise the Athenian popu-

lace for the incalculable good which they have been the agents in effecting? We hold up the action of Brutus, "who slew his best lover for the good of Rome," as commendable and noble. Yet the death of Julius Caesar has been of far less use to his country and to the world, than the death of Socrates. If utility is the criterion of right and wrong, how do we account for the different feelings with which we contemplate the instances that have been mentioned? We might multiply examples of this kind to an unlimited extent. The blood of the martyrs has in every age been the seed of the church; and if the character of actions is determined by their utility, we must approve of those which have erected the scaffold and kindled the fires; since these have been the means of the promotion of truth and the progress of righteousness.

It may be maintained with regard to such actions, that the good which they have accomplished is incidental, while the intention which prompted them is wrong, and that it is the intention and not the consequence of the action, to which the criterion of utility is to be applied. But this admission concedes the very point in question. It allows that the beneficial effects of an action, are not all at which we are to look, in determining its moral character. So that it virtually renounces the theory of utility as the criterion of right. Besides, the most distinguished advocates of this theory, Dr. Paley and his followers, for instance, expressly limit its application to actions. It has no concern, according to them, with the intentions of the agent. But we have seen that it does not hold good as a test of actions; if we retain the criterion, then, we must in opposition to Paley himself, make use of it as the test of intentions. If we apply the test of utility at all, as the ultimate ground of our decisions, we must so apply it, as to show that the intended production of good is always right, as well as that the intended production of evil is always wrong. This last proposition, of course, we would not be supposed to deny; but we believe it on other grounds than those taken by the advocates of utility. But to consider the first proposition alluded to above, is the intentional production of good always right? Is every action, which I mean to be a useful one, therefore right? We deny that it is. To take a very familiar instance, the persecution of the primitive Christians by Paul, before his conversion. There is no doubt, he thought, that he was doing God service, by this action; and there is as little doubt that the ultimate effects of the persecutions endured by the infant church, were beneficial to its growth and to its virtues. But Paul never dreamed of justifying his conduct on the score of its utility, or of his sincere conviction of its utility. On the contrary, he regarded himself as one of the chief of sinners, on account of his crimes in persecuting the disciples. But taking utility as the test, we do not perceive that the Apostle was not fully justified.

Another instance to illustrate our views, may be found in the case of the assassin, as stated by Dr. Paley, for a different purpose. Suppose that an old man of worthless character is in possession of a large fortune, which I can attain by putting him to death, and employ for my own benefit and that of mankind. Why should not I knock the rich villain in the head, and do good with the money, of which he makes no use? The action, by the very terms of the statement, will be a beneficial one. My intentions in committing it, are with a single view to the benefit it will produce. There is no other way. But, says Dr. Paley, the action is unlawful, because a general rule to sanction such actions would be injurious. Be it so. But in this instance, what have I to do with general rules, if utility be my only guide? I know that the action will be useful, and that is all I want to know. What consequence is it to me, that a general rule, taken by others from my conduct, might in some future, uncertain cases, be injurious? I know not that such cases will ever occur, and if they do, they are nothing to me, let them be determined by those who are called to act upon them. Utility tells me to take this man's life for his money, and utility I will obey. We do not see that such reasoning can be set aside, allowing that the operation of the general rule in question would be injurious. But, still further, we cannot see how a general rule, formed from a particular beneficial action can be injurious. The general rule would comprehend only such actions as are precisely similar to the one upon which it is founded. If it be useful in a given case to take the life of an old man because I can make a better use of his money than he does himself, it would also be useful to take the lives of ten, twenty, thirty, or as many as were in similar circumstances. If the utility of one action makes it right, it is impossible that the utility of ten, twenty, or thirty actions precisely similar, should not also make them right. If the particular case be beneficial, the general rule must be beneficial also. But, the truth is, in cases of this kind we must have recourse to some criterion, less flexible, less vague, less uncertain than that of utility.

　　We have now seen that there are useful actions, which have no moral character whatever—actions, intended to be useful, which are wrong—and actions, intended to be wrong, committed with a criminal motive, which are useful. Hence it follows, that utility cannot be the legitimate criterion of right and wrong. That the dispositions and sentiments which are universally regarded as virtuous, are generally useful to their possessors and to mankind, we have not a shadow of doubt. We are certain that this element is common to all the motives and feelings which the collected sense of the human race has pronounced to be right; that it would be incalculably for the benefit of the world, if the actions which are agreed to be virtuous, were universally practised. But this is a very different thing—and it is utterly surprising that the difference has been so generally overlooked—from making the actual utility of actions, a criterion of their moral character. It is certainly one thing to say, that the practice of right actions would be generally useful; and another, and quite a different thing to say, that the fact of its utility determines an action to be right.

3.2

General Utilitarianism

GU tells us not to ask "What will happen if I do this in this case?" but "What would happen if everyone did this in such cases?" or, rather, "What would the consequences be in terms of good and evil if everyone did this in such cases?" The best known recent exponent of such a view is M. G. Singer, who espouses a kind of negative GU. Oversimplifying a bit, we can state Singer's view as follows: An act is wrong for me to do if the consequences of everyone's doing it in similar cases would be undesirable; otherwise, it is not wrong for me to do. This method of reasoning he calls the generalization argument, and in the following selection he tries to defend its use. Notice how he appeals to the generalization principle as well as to the principle of utility (in the negative form of not promoting undesirable consequences) in doing so.

Singer's argument in this selection consists largely of replying to possible objections to the generalization principle and the generalization argument. As you read it, you should consider whether Singer's defense of his version of GU is convincing to you, and whether there are other objections that he has not met. What does he mean by saying that "the generalization argument provides only a presumptive, and not a conclusive, reason for its conclusion"? What does it mean to call an argument "invertible" and/or "reiterable"? Finally, what is the major difference between Singer's generalization principle and Kant's categorical imperative?

GENERALIZATION IN ETHICS

Marcus G. Singer

The question "What would happen if everyone did that?" is one with which we are all familiar. We have heard it asked, and perhaps have asked it ourselves. We have some familiarity with the sort of context in which it would be appropriate to ask it. For instance, we under stand that it is either elliptical for or a prelude to saying, "If everyone did that, the consequences would be disastrous," and that this is often considered a good reason for concluding that one ought not to do that. The situations in which this sort of consideration might be advanced are of course exceedingly diverse. One who announces his intention of not voting in some election might be met by the question, "What would happen if no one voted?" If no one voted the government would collapse, or the democracy would be repudiated, and this is deemed by many to indicate decisively that everyone should vote. Again, one who disapproves of another's attempts to avoid military service might point out: "If everyone refused to serve, we would lose the war." The members of a discussion group, which meets to discuss papers presented by members, presumably all realize that each should take a turn in reading a paper, even if he does not want to and prefers to take part in the discussion only, because if everyone refused to read a paper the club would dissolve, and there would be no discussions. This sort of consideration would not be decisive to one who did not care whether the club dissolved. But it undoubtedly would be decisive to one who enjoys the meetings and wishes them to continue.

Each of these cases provides an example of the use or application of a type of argument which I propose to call *the generalization argument:* "If everyone were to do that, the consequences would be disastrous (or undesirable); therefore, no one ought to do that." Any argument of the form "The consequences of no one doing x would be undesirable; therefore every one ought to do x" is also, obviously, an instance of the generalization argument. Now the basic problem about this argument is to determine the conditions under which it is a good or valid one, that is to say, the conditions under which the fact that the consequences of everyone doing x would be undesirable provides a

From Mind, *LXIV (July, 1955), 361–62, 371–75. Reprinted by permission of the author and* Mind. *The substance of this essay, in revised and considerably expanded form, is contained in the author's book,* Generalization in Ethics *(New York: Alfred A. Knopf, 1961; 2nd ed., Atheneum, 1971). A selection from Singer's book is included in Section 3.4 of this volume.*

good reason for concluding that it is wrong for anyone to do x. I have formulated the problem in this way because there are conditions under which the generalization argument is obviously not applicable. Though the instances presented above are ones in which the consideration of the consequences of everyone acting in a certain way seems clearly relevant to a moral judgment about that way of acting, there are others in which this sort of consideration is just as clearly irrelevant. While "humanity would probably perish from cold if everyone produced food, and would certainly starve if everyone made clothes or built houses," it would be absurd to infer from this that no one ought to produce food or build houses.

It might be thought that this is a counter-example, which proves the generalization argument to be invalid or fallacious generally, and that the fallacy consists in arguing from "not everyone" to "no one," or from "some" to "all." But this would be a mistake. It is not always a fallacy to argue from "some" to "all." The belief that it is is merely a prejudice arising out of a preoccupation with certain types of statements. It is true that the generalization argument involves an inference from "not everyone has the right" to "no one has the right," from "it would not be right for everyone" to "it would not be right for anyone." This inference, however, is mediated by what I shall call "the generalization *principle*," that *what is right (or wrong) for one person must be right (or wrong) for any similar person in similar circumstances.*

Since the generalization argument presupposes and thus depends on the generalization principle, and since the generalization principle is certainly of considerable interest in its own right, I shall devote the next section—the major portion—of this paper to an attempt to determine the meaning and importance of this principle.[1] This will involve a consideration of the meaning and function of the qualification "similar persons in similar circumstances." Following this I shall take up the problem about the generalization argument mentioned above, by considering briefly certain fairly plausible objections to it and attempting to show that they are not decisive. This will go some distance towards the formulation of the conditions under which the generalization argument is valid.

1. The Generalization Principle

. . . the generalization principle can be formulated in any of the following ways. What is right for one person cannot be wrong for another, unless there is some relevant difference in their natures or

---

[1] [Most of this discussion has been omitted here.—EDS.]

circumstances. Or, what is right (or wrong) for one person must be right (or wrong) for everyone, if there is no reason for the contrary. Thus the claim that something that would not be right for everyone is right for a given person is one that must be justified. In the form peculiarly appropriate to the generalization argument, the principle may be stated: *If not everyone has the right to act in a certain way, then no one has the right to act in that way without a reason. . . .*

I have said that the generalization principle implies that an act which is right or wrong is right or wrong on "general grounds" and is therefore right or wrong for a class of persons. This class of persons is determined by the reasons in terms of which the act is right or wrong. This may appear to conflict with the fact that there are some acts which would be right for only one person. But there is really no conflict here. An act of this sort is still right for a class of persons in the sense that it would be right for anyone who meets certain conditions, even though these conditions may be such that just one person can meet them. The act is still right as an act of a certain *kind*, or as an instance of a certain class of acts. It may be right for A and for no one else to do act d in certain circumstances. Yet if B were similar to A in certain respects then it would be right for B to do d. (The act may be described in such a way that this last statement may seem silly. It would amount to saying "if B were A then. . . ." But this can be met by redescribing the act.) Furthermore, since d must be an act of a certain kind (if it were not it could not be described at all), it must be the case that it would be right for everyone similar to A to do an act of the same kind as d (to act in the same way) in similar circumstances.

The following example should make this clear. While it would not be wrong for Mr. Jones to have sexual relations with Mrs. Jones, it would (generally) be wrong for anyone else to do so, and certainly wrong for everyone else to do so. Here we have an act which is right for just one person. But there is no conflict with the generalization principle. This principle does not say that no one ought to do what not everyone ought to do. It says that no one ought to do what not everyone ought to do, without a reason or justification. Mr. Jones is justified in having sexual relations with Mrs. Jones by the fact that he is married to her. If he were not he would (presumably) not be justified in this, and anyone else who was married to Mrs. Jones would be justified in having sexual relations with her. Furthermore, this act is an act of a certain kind, and can be described in a more general way so as to bring this out. Instead of describing Mr. Jones's act as one of "having sexual relations with Mrs. Jones," it can be referred to as "having sexual relations with one's own wife." Everyone is justified in doing an act of this kind in similar circumstances—everyone has the right to have sexual relations with his own wife, though not with anyone else's. (This rule necessarily does not apply to women. This does not make it unfair or unjust. It can obviously be restated to cover this.) Mr. Jones is justified in having sexual relations with Mrs. Jones because she is his wife. This last statement is of course perfectly general. It can thus be seen to be a further application of the more general generalization principle.

2. The Generalization Argument

The fact that the generalization principle is involved in the generalization argument removes the ground from the claim that the latter involves a formal fallacy, that of arguing from "some" to "all." It would be fallacious to argue that, since not everyone has red hair, no one has red hair. But it is not necessarily fallacious to argue that, since not everyone has the right to act in a certain way, no one has the right to act in that way. The difference is that in the latter case we are dealing with moral judgments; and this latter inference is mediated by the generalization principle. That this is so is probably obscured by the fact that in applications of the argument the qualification "all similar persons in similar circumstances" is left inexplicit. But in valid applications of the argument this restriction is either implicitly understood or is indicated by various linguistic devices. For example, the argument "everyone ought to vote because if no one voted the government would collapse" is evidently meant to apply only to those legally permitted to vote. This is taken as understood. It is a further consequence of the generalization principle that the conclusion "no one has the right to do x" is really elliptical for "no one has the right to do x without a reason or justification." One can justify his failing or refusing to vote. Hence the generalization argument provides only a presumptive, and not a conclusive, reason for its conclusion.

Another objection to the generalization argument which has already been mentioned is that "humanity would probably perish from cold if everyone produced food, and would certainly starve if everyone made clothes or built houses." Since the consequences of everyone producing food would be undesirable, on the pattern of the generalization argument it would seem to follow that it is wrong for anyone to do so. But this actually does not follow. For consider what would happen if no one produced food. If no one produced food, everyone would starve. Hence on the same line of reasoning it might be argued that everyone ought to produce food. The argument that no one ought to produce food because of what would happen if everyone did can thus be met by the counter-argument that everyone ought to produce food because of what would happen if no one did. But a valid application of the generalization argument cannot be met by such a counter-argument. The argument that everyone ought to vote because of what would happen if no one did cannot be rebutted in this way.

In a case in which the consequences of everyone acting in a certain way would be undesirable, while the consequences of no one acting in that way would also be undesirable, I shall say that the argument can be *inverted*. Thus the argument is invertible with respect to producing food, building houses, and making clothes. Now in order for the generalization argument to have a valid application with respect to some action it is necessary that it not be invertible with respect to that action.

Consider the following possible objection: "If everyone ate at six o'clock there would be no one to perform certain essential functions, things which must be attended to at all times, and so on, with the net result that no one would be able to eat at six or any other time, and with various other undesirable consequences." Does it follow that no one has the right to eat at six o'clock? It should be noted that this argument in no way depends on the exact time specified. If we could argue that no one has the right to eat at six, we could argue that no one has the right to eat at five, or at seven, or at three minutes past two, and so on. We could therefore argue that no one has the right to eat at any time, that is to say, that no one has the right to eat.

In such a case as this the argument may be said to be *reiterable*. Note that there is no need to restrict ourselves to eating in order to obtain examples of a reiterable argument. Any action, such as walking, talking, sleeping, or drinking—even doing nothing at all—when particularized in this way, will do as well. Now any instance of the generalization argument that is reiterable is invalid. For any instance of the generalization argument that is reiterable is also invertible. For example, the argument from "not everyone has the right to eat at six o'clock to "no one has the right to eat at six o'clock," since it can be reiterated for any time, implies "no one has the right to eat." But if no one were to eat the consequences would be just as undesirable, presumably, as if everyone were to eat at the same time.

This last condition, that the argument be not reiterable, is closely tied up with the procedure by which one can justify his acting in a way in which it would be undesirable for everyone to act. One can justify his acting in that way by showing that he is a member of a certain class of persons such that if every member of that class were to act in that way the consequences would not be undesirable, or by showing that the circumstances of his action are such that the consequences of everyone acting in that way in those circumstances would not be undesirable. But the argument must not be reiterable with respect to the class of persons or circumstances selected. Otherwise the class in question would be "distinguished" by a characteristic in terms of which everyone would be an exception, and hence not really distinguished at all.

There is one other objection to the generalization argument, one which is, oddly enough, fairly popular, that must be disposed of. It is simply irrelevant to reply, "Not everyone *will* do it." What the argument implies is that if A has the right to do something, then everyone else (or everyone similar to A in certain respects) has this same right in a similar situation; and therefore if it is undesirable for everyone to have this right, it is undesirable for A to have it. (This, incidentally, is not to say that if the consequences of everyone acting in a certain way would be undesirable, then the consequences of some particular individual acting in this way would be undesirable. The consequences of any particular act of this kind, considered by themselves, may be beneficial.) Thus what has to be shown is how A is an exception. One is not shown to be an exception by the fact that the consequences of his acting in a certain way would not be the same as the consequences of everyone acting in that way. Nor is one shown to be an exception by the fact that not everyone will act in that way. For what such facts would show is that everyone is an exception, which is strictly nonsense.

Finally, it should, perhaps, be made clear that the application of the generalization argument presupposes, and does not by itself determine, that the consequences of everyone acting in a certain way would be undesirable. I have not here been concerned with the question how to determine the desirability or undesirability of a certain set of consequences. It is sufficient to have shown the argument to be *valid*. The question of the *soundness* of any particular application of it, that is to say, the question whether its premises are true, is something else again.

In the following selection A. C. Ewing discusses the use of the Generalization Argument, though without reference to Singer. Incidentally, he also explains the difference between Kant and GU. Between Singer and Ewing we get a very good discussion of the use in ethics of the common question, "What if everybody did that?"

WHAT IF EVERYBODY DID THAT?

A. C. Ewing

I must say something more on . . . the method which depends on asking what would happen if everybody acted like me, for this method certainly raises serious problems. Its paradoxical character is brought out

From Second Thoughts in Moral Philosophy (*London: Routledge & Kegan Paul Ltd., 1959). Reprinted by permission of the publisher.*

by asking what we should think of a doctor who knew that a particular patient was allergic to penicillin but, though believing it would have bad effects on him, still gave it on the ground that it would be a very bad thing if a general rule were made to the effect that nobody should have penicillin. What is the difference between this and declining, e.g. to break a promise where it would do good to break it on the ground that, if everybody broke their promises, it would do harm? It is certain that everybody will not break his promises whether I keep mine or not, and therefore it may be asked what is the sense of declining to do something beneficial not because of the consequences which the action will actually have but because of the consequences which would accrue if something else happened that we have no reason to think ever will happen and that will certainly not be brought about by our action. Yet this type of argument is used very commonly in favour of keeping rules. It must be distinguished carefully from two other types of argument which are easier to justify.

(1) The observance of a well-established general rule is thought usually to produce good effects but very occasionally bad ones, and where it is impracticable to ascertain beforehand about a particular case whether it belongs to the former or the latter class of cases, it may therefore well be best on purely utilitarian grounds to go on the principle that we should do what will at least most probably be beneficial and act according to the general rule. This would correspond to the case of a doctor who gave penicillin knowing that his patient might possibly be allergic to it, because he was unable to ascertain beforehand whether this was so or not, and hence thought it best to give what would probably be beneficial. This principle certainly has a very wide application in ethics. It is very commonly best to keep well-established general rules if for no other reason than that it would be extremely difficult to decide each case properly on its own merits and the attempt to do so would be liable to produce more harm than good, especially as the cases where we are most inclined to make exceptions to a good general rule are likely to be cases where we are biased because the law is felt as adverse to our own interests or those of a friend. On these grounds Moore, though a utilitarian, went so far as to say that we should "*always* conform to rules which are both generally useful and generally practised."[1] Even if we do not go so far as this, we must certainly admit that there is a strong utilitarian point here in favour of keeping to the well-established rules in most cases.

(2) In cases where a particular action of itself indisputably does harm it may be an effective means of making the person inclined to do it realize this more forcibly if we call attention to the consequences that would

---

[1] *Principia Ethica*, p. 164. I understand that he has not retained the view that it ought to be done *always*.

ensue if everybody acted like him. Thus we might say to somebody who was excessively and unnecessarily gloomy—What a miserable place the world would be if everybody were like you? Here the man's depressing attitude in any case produces an evil effect on those around him, and the point of the remark is merely to make him see this more clearly by suggesting how bad it would be if the effects of his action, already bad in any case, were multiplied indiscriminately. We can see good and evil better "writ large," as Plato taught. It is quite different from a case where the effects of the particular action prohibited seem good but the effects of widespread breaking of the general rule would clearly be evil.

Yet even in the latter class of cases reasonable and moral people would often none the less condemn the action, and if challenged as to why they did so would ask—What would happen if everybody broke the rule? For example, it is difficult to suppose that if the government were deprived of the amount I contribute in taxation it would lead to any diminution of social services or of any benefits conferred by the use of government funds, yet the amount I contribute certainly makes a perceptible difference to me. But supposing I therefore argued that more harm than good was done by taxing me and therefore I ought not to be taxed, the general attitude would be most unsympathetic. Again, while people have claimed on conscientious grounds that they ought not to be compelled to do military service, few, if any, would accept the argument of a man who claimed that he ought not to do it because he found it very unpleasant and dangerous and the addition of one man to the forces would not make any difference either to the prevention or winning of a war. In both cases the natural reaction would be to ask—What would happen if everybody acted as you propose to do? The argument has a very considerable resemblance to the one Kant treats as central to ethics. There is however also a considerable difference: for Kant the argument is *a priori* in that there is supposed to be some kind of contradiction, not necessarily a logical contradiction, in willing the universalization of the principles he condemns, but the argument as generally used appeals to consequences and contends that the consequences of the general adoption of a certain principle or breach of a certain rule would be very evil. But in both forms the argument seems endangered by the objection that it is unreasonable to settle the question by asking not what will happen if we act in the way proposed but what would happen if everybody acted like that, when we know they will not. How can it possibly be wrong to do something just because very evil consequences would follow if something else were to happen that in fact will not?

To this question it seems to me two answers may be given. In the first place there are two premises which any consistent universalistic utilitarian must hold, (1) that an act or class of acts is wrong if it does harm rather than good, (2) that, if it is right for me to do A, it will also be right for everybody else to do A under circumstances similar in all ethically relevant respects. Now in cases where the method I am discussing is employed the following argument may be used. It would be disastrous if everybody did A (broke the rule), so that by the first premiss this class of acts would be wrong; but if I were entitled to do A, it would follow from the second premiss that everybody might, so that the class of acts would not be wrong. From this it can be concluded that I ought not to do A, since the supposition that I might permissibly would lead to a contradiction. However, the conclusion of the argument, though it follows logically from premises which all utilitarians would admit, itself is incompatible with what is commonly regarded as the fundamental principle of utilitarianism, namely that the right act is always the one that will produce the greatest good, at least as far as can be foreseen. It involves the admission that act A may have better effects than act B and yet that it may be wrong to do it instead of B because it belongs to a class which has worse effects than the class to which belongs act B. So the utilitarian seems to be entangled in a contradiction unless he abandons the form of utilitarianism which considers only the effect of each single act as relevant and considers also classes of acts.

This he seems indeed bound to do in any case. For after all most of the "actions" of which we talk are really classes of minor actions. The principle I have discussed has an application also where we are concerned with a class of actions relating primarily to the agent's own interests.[2] Consider this case: A man has to pass an examination, although he is not sufficiently intelligent or interested in the subject for the experience of study in it to have appreciable intrinsic value. For any hour of study he could always think of an intrinsically much better way of spending his time. Now to decide to take any particular single hour off in such a pursuit will not endanger his chances of passing and therefore will always in itself be beneficial, but if therefore he took every hour off the result would certainly be failure. He can therefore deal with the matter reasonably only if he considers not merely the effect of any one of these decisions but the effect of the whole class. The situation is indeed not quite parallel to that with, e.g. breaking promises because we

---

[2] I do not mean that it applies in all cases where we are concerned with a class of actions. For in some such cases each minor act contributes sensibly to the value of the whole class, and in others they are all necessary if the purpose of the latter is to be achieved at all (e.g. where my purpose is to walk to a given point the omission of a single step would prevent me from arriving there if the step is worth taking for this purpose at all).

cannot say that he ought never to take an hour off except in grave emergencies, but it is certain that in regulating his work he must take account, not only of each particular decision as to work or leisure, but of the whole class of decisions. He must not drop his work each time that he considers the effects of an hour's break good but see that such decisions do not too much diminish the class of decisions to work. I may well be in a position in which I have to admit that it was wrong of me not to spend more time than I did on a given piece of work without being able to fix on any one of the alternative things I did and say that it was wrong to do this one.

But another factor is present in the case of rules the breach of which affects others more directly. It is that we consider it *unfair* to profit through others keeping a rule, as we obviously do profit if it can reasonably be argued that the effects of breaking the rule would be generally disastrous, and yet refuse to abide by it ourselves. Perhaps not to do this ought to be regarded as a *prima facie* duty over and above those specified by Ross, and certainly this idea of unfairness plays a very large part in our social morality. One who manages his life on the principle of always getting as much for himself as he can without taking his share in the burdens involved in producing it (or their equivalent in our economic system) is subjected to severe criticism on account of the inherent meanness of his attitude and not only because he does less good than he might.

These arguments bring out the limitations of the universalization method. It must not be used where there is a strong special reason for breaking the general law in the agent's case such that, if exceptions were made and made only when there were reasons as strong as this, it would be a good thing on the whole, for then we can no longer say that, if it were right for him to break it, it would be equally right to break it in all cases or in a sufficient number to cause disaster and that therefore it is not right for him to break it. And we could no longer contend that he is necessarily being unfair to others if he breaks it, for the argument presupposes that it would not cost him a much greater sacrifice than it costs others to keep it. (This is not to say that he is entitled to break it whenever keeping it would cost him an appreciably greater sacrifice than it costs others, for efficiency in practice requires general rules and understandings, the effects of which cannot precisely be measured in each particular case, and a good man will not be very anxious to measure exactly whether he does or does not lose more than others by keeping general rules.)

3.3

Rule-Utilitarianism

RU is also called "restricted," "indirect," or "modified" utilitarianism. Where GU tells us to determine what is right by asking, "What if everyone were to do that?" and trying to see what the results would be in terms of good and evil, RU tells us to ask what the *rules* call for, but insists that rules must be justified by the consequences of our accepting or conforming to them. That is, RU instructs us, not just to look straight at the utility of a proposed act, as AU does, and not to ask what the utility of everyone's doing it would be as GU does, but rather to go by the rules and inquire about utility only when determining whether a rule is valid.

There are several kinds of RU, but we need to distinguish only actual-rule-utilitarianism (ARU) and ideal-rule-utilitarianism (IRU). ARU holds that an action is right if it conforms to the accepted or prevailing moral rules and wrong if it does not, assuming that these rules are those whose acceptance and observance is for the greatest general good. IRU is of two kinds. One holds that an action is right if and only if it conforms to a set of rules, general *conformity* to which would maximize utility; the other, that an action is right if and only if it conforms to a set of rules, general *acceptance* of which would maximize utility.

In all its forms RU arises mainly as an attempt, by philosophers who are convinced of utilitarianism, to find a position that avoids the objections to AU made by deontologists like Butler, Ross, and Ripley—as we shall see in the essay by R. B. Brandt. RU was first formulated in the eighteenth century by George Berkeley and William Paley, but came to the fore again recently, largely because J. O. Urmson wrote an article on J. S. Mill in which he distinguished AU and RU and argued that RU was more tenable than AU and that Mill should be interpreted as an RU. This suggests that we should present Mill's position here. Actually, however, Mill's view is so ambiguous that we cannot put him under either AU or RU. Hence we include no selection from Mill in this chapter, even though he is the most interesting utilitarian writer of all. However, we include enough of Mill in Chapter 5, where we take up hedonism, to show what his theory is like and to provide an opportunity for discussing it. If desired, those selections may be studied at this point.

In this section we will study R. B. Brandt as a representative of RU. In the essay that follows he first attacks AU in much the same ways that Ripley and Ross do. Then, using Urmson, he explains and discusses two forms of RU, namely, ARU and IRU. He rejects the former and urges an IRU of the second kind distinguished above. (In an omitted part of his paper he contends that IRU of the first kind is equivalent to AU in practice and, hence, unsatisfactory).

In addition to considering Brandt's arguments for his version of IRU, note the problems he sees arising from the fact that existing societies (and persons) are imperfect. Note also his comments on justice at the beginning and end of his essay. The question of the role of the concept of justice in a theory of moral obligation will be taken up again in Section 3.4.

TOWARD A CREDIBLE FORM
OF UTILITARIANISM

Richard B. Brandt

In recent years, types of rule-utilitarianism have been the object of much interest. And for good reason. Act-utilitarianism, at least given the assumptions about what is valuable which utilitarians commonly make, has implications which it is difficult to accept.[1] It implies that if you have employed a boy to mow your lawn and he has finished the

Reprinted from Morality and the Language of Conduct, *edited by Hector-Neri Castaneda and George Nakhnikian, by permission of the Wayne State University Press. Copyright © 1963 by Wayne State University Press. Also used by permission of the author.*

---

[1] In this paper I propose to ignore that form of act-utilitarianism which proposes to close the gap between what seems to be right and the implications of act-utilitarianism, by asserting that such things as promise-keeping are intrinsically good. This form of theory has most recently been defended by Oliver Johnson in his *Rightness and Goodness* (The Hague: Martinus Nijhoff, 1959).

I am inclined to agree that there are some intrinsically good things which are not states of persons—for instance, equality of distribution of welfare. But act-utilitarians require to count further things—such as specific traits of character like truthfulness, or complexes like the-keeping-of-a-promise—as intrinsically good in order to square with reasonable convictions about what is right or wrong. But surely it is job and asks for his pay, you should pay him what you promised only if you cannot find a better use for your money. It implies that when you bring home your monthly pay-check you should use it to support your family and yourself only if it cannot be used more effectively to supply the needs of others. It implies that if your father is ill and has no prospect of good in his life, and maintaining him is a drain on the energy and enjoyments of others, then, if you can end his life without provoking any public scandal or setting a bad example, it is your positive duty to take matters into your own hands and bring his life to a close. A virtue of rule-utilitarianism, in at least some of its forms, is that it avoids at least some of such objectionable implications.

In the present paper I wish to arrive at a more precise formulation of a rule-utilitarian type of theory which is different from act-utilitarianism and which is not subject to obvious and catastrophic difficulties. To this end I shall, after an important preliminary discussion, begin by considering two formulations, both supported by distinguished philosophers, which, as I shall show, lead us in the wrong direction. This discussion will lead to a new formulation devised to avoid the consequences of the first theories. I shall then describe three problems [2] which the new theory seems to face, and consider how—by amendments or otherwise—these difficulties may be met. . . .

Accepted Rules vs. Justifiable Rules as the Test of Rightness

It is convenient to begin by taking as our text some statements drawn from an interesting article by J. O. Urmson. In this paper, Urmson sug-

---

contrary to the spirit of utilitarianism to decide the issue, say, whether a promise should be kept by appeal to such intrinsic values. One would have thought the utilitarian would test the merits of traits of character like truthfulness by examining whether they have good consequences rather than decide that there is an obligation to tell the truth by considering the intrinsic goodness of truthfulness. Should not the issue of the intrinsic goodness of truthfulness wait upon reasoning to show that it is a good thing to tell the truth? One who denies this is far from traditional utilitarian thought. In any case, can we seriously claim that the-keeping-of-a-promise is an intrinsic good? It would be absurd to hold that we can add to the value of the world by the simple device of making promises and then keeping them, irrespective of what is effected by the keeping of them. Presumably, then, what is held is rather that the-breaking-of-a-promise is intrinsically bad. But how will it be shown that precisely this is intrinsically bad? Suppose I promise to do something no one wants done, and everyone is greatly relieved when I fail to perform. Is this intrinsically evil?

The kind of utilitarianism I propose here to discuss is one with narrower commitments about what is intrinsically good—one which does not claim that specific kinds of action or specific traits of character (like truthfulness or fidelity) are intrinsically good or bad. This kind of utilitarianism is worth assessment even if my reasons for ignoring other types are unsound.

[2] [Two of which are omitted here.—Eds.]

gested that John Stuart Mill should be interpreted as a rule-utilitarian; and Urmson's opinion was that Mill's view would be more plausible if he were so interpreted. Urmson summarized the possible rule-utilitarian interpretation of Mill in four propositions, of which I quote the first two:

A. A particular action is justified as being right [in the sense of being morally obligatory] by showing that it is in accord with [is required by] some moral rule. It is shown to be wrong by showing that it transgresses some moral rule.

B. A moral rule is shown to be correct by showing that the recognition of that rule promotes the ultimate end.[3]

Urmson's first proposition could be taken in either of two ways. When it speaks of a "moral rule," it may refer to an *accepted* moral rule, presumably one accepted in the society of the agent. Alternatively, it may refer to a *correct* moral rule, presumably one the recognition of which promotes the ultimate end. If we ask in which way the proposed theory should be taken, in order to arrive at a defensible theory, part of the answer is that qualifications are going to be required, whichever way we take it. I think it more worthwhile and promising, however, to try to develop it in the second interpretation.

Various philosophers would make the opposite judgment about which interpretation is the more promising. And there is much to be said for their view, in particular the following points. First, we shall probably all agree that the moral rules accepted in a community often do fix real obligations on members of the community. For example, among ourselves it is taken for granted that primary responsibility for caring for an old man falls on his children, although in special cases it could fall elsewhere. On the other hand, suppose that our social system contained the rule—as that of the Hopi actually does—that this responsibility falls primarily on the children of a man's sisters, again with exceptions for special cases. It seems clear that in a social system like ours the children do have responsibility for their father, whereas in a social system like that of the Hopi they do not—the responsibility belongs to the children of the sisters. There are complications, to be sure; but in general we must say that when an institutional system specifies that responsibility falls in a certain place, then on the whole and with some exceptions and qualifications, that is where it really does lie. Any theory which denies this is mistaken; and if our second theory is to be plausible, it must be framed so as to imply this. Second, I think we should concede that if two persons are debating whether some act is right and one of them is able to show that

---

[3] J. O. Urmson, "The Interpretation of the Philosophy of J. S. Mill," *Philosophical Quarterly*, III (1953), 33–39.

it infringes on the accepted moral code of the community, the "burden of proof" passes to the other party. The fact that it is generally believed that a certain kind of action is wrong is prima facie evidence that it is wrong; it is up to persons who disagree to show their hand. Third, if a conscientious man is deliberating whether he is morally obligated to do a certain thing which he does not wish to do, I believe he will generally feel he must do this thing, even if he thinks that a correct moral code would not require him to, provided he concludes that many or most persons in his community would conclude otherwise. The reason for this is partly, I think, that a conscientious man will take pains to avoid even the appearance of evil; but the reason is also that a conscientious man will wish to make substantial allowances for the fact that he is an interested party and might have been influenced by his own preferences in his thinking about his obligations. He will therefore tend to hold himself to the received code when this is to his disadvantage.

Nevertheless, it is extremely difficult to defend Urmson's rule interpreted in this way, even when we hedge it with qualifications, as, for example, Toulmin did. In the first place, people do not *think* that anything like this is true; they think they are assessing particular cases by reference to objectively valid principles which they happen to know, and not simply by reference to a community code. Notice how we do not find it surprising that people with unusual moral principles, such as the immorality of killing and violence in all circumstances, come to distinctive conclusions about their own particular obligations, by no means drawing their particular moral judgments from the code of the community. The whole tradition emphasizing the role of conscience in moral thinking is contrary to the view that socially accepted principles are crucial for deciding what is right or wrong. In the second place, we frequently judge ourselves to have moral obligations either when we don't know what the community "standards" are, or when we think that in all probability there is no decided majority one way or the other: for instance, with respect to sexual behavior, or to declaration, to revenue officers, of articles purchased abroad or of one's personal income. Surely we do not think that in such situations the proper judgment of particular cases is that they are morally indifferent? Third, and perhaps most important, we sometimes judge that we have an obligation when we know that the community thinks we don't; and we sometimes think an act is right when the community thinks it wrong. For instance, we may judge that we have an obligation to join in seeking presidential clemency for a convicted Communist spy whom we regard as having received an unduly severe sentence because of mass hysteria at the time of his trial, although we know quite well that the communal code prescribes no favors for Communists. Again, we may think it not wrong to work on the

Sabbath, marry a divorced person, perform a medically necessary abortion, or commit suicide, irrespective of general disapproval in our group. Were these things *ever* objectively wrong, in view of being proscribed—even unanimously—by the community of the agent? (It may be replied that the "code" does not legislate for complex matters of these sorts, but only for more basic things, like Ross's list of prima facie obligations. But it is not clear what can be the basis for this distinction; the acts in question may be prohibited by law and would be reported by a visiting anthropologist as proscribed by the code.)

One might argue that the existence of an accepted moral rule is not sufficient to make particular actions wrong or obligatory but is a necessary condition. To say this, however, is to say that men have no obligation to rise above the commonplace morals of their times. Whereas in fact we do not think it right for men to be cruel to animals or to slaves in a society which condones this.

We cannot well say in advance that no thesis like Urmson's can play an important part in a defensible theory of morals, if it is interpreted in this first way. But the difficulties are surely enough to encourage experimenting with versions of the second interpretation. Let us turn to this.

For a start, we might summarize the gist of Urmson's proposal, construed in the second way, as follows: "An act is right if and only if it conforms with that set of moral rules, the recognition of which would have significantly desirable consequences." A somewhat modified version of this is what I shall be urging.

One minor amendment I wish to make immediately. I think we should replace the second clause by the expression, "the recognition of which would have the *best* consequences." This amendment may be criticized on the ground that the business of moral rules is with commanding or prohibiting actions whose performance or omission would be quite harmful if practiced widely, but not to require actions which just maximize benefits, especially if the benefit concerns only the agent. It may be said, then, that the amendment I propose is possibly a clue to *perfect* behavior but not to right behavior. But this objection overlooks an important point. We must remember that it is a serious matter to have a moral rule at all, for moral rules take conduct out of the realm of preference and free decisions. So, for the recognition of a certain moral rule to have good consequences, the benefits of recognition must outweigh the costliness of restricting freedom. Therefore, to recognize a moral rule restricting self-regarding behavior will rarely have the best consequences; rules of prudence should normally not be moral rules. Again, my proposal implies that moral rules will require services for other people only when it is better to have such services performed from a sense of obligation

than not performed at all; so the amendment does not commit us to saying that it is morally obligatory to perform minor altruistic services for
others.

But why insist on the amendment? The reason is that the original,
as I stated it (but not necessarily as Urmson intended it), is insufficiently
comparative in form. The implication is that a rule is acceptable so long
as it is significantly better than no regulation at all. But the effect of this
is tolerantly to accept a great many rules which we should hardly regard
as morally acceptable. Consider promises. There are various possible rules
about when promises must be kept. One such possible rule is to require
keeping all promises, absolutely irrespective of unforeseeable and uncon-
templated hardships on the promisee. Recognition of this rule might have
good consequences as compared with no rule at all. Therefore it seems
to satisfy the unamended formula. Many similar rules would satisfy it.
But we know of another rule—the one we recognize—with specifications
about allowable exceptions, which would have much better consequences.
If we are utilitarian in spirit, we shall want to endorse such a rule but
not both of these rules; and the second one is much closer to our view
about what our obligations are. The amendment in general endorses as
correct many rules which command our support for parallel reasons, and
refuses to endorse many others which we reject for parallel reasons. . . .

Rule Utilitariansm: A Second
Approximation

. . . the formulation we have suggested is itself open to interpretations that may lead to problems. How may we construe Urmson's proposal, so that it is both unambiguous and credible? Of course we do not
wish to go to the opposite extreme and take "recognition of" to mean
merely "doffing the hat to" without attempt to practice. But how shall
we take it?

I suggest the following as a second approximation.

First, let us speak of a set of moral rules as being "learnable" if
people of ordinary intelligence are able to learn or absorb its provisions,
so as to believe the moral propositions in question in the ordinary sense
of "believe" for such contexts. Next, let us speak of "the adoption" of a
moral code by a person as meaning "the learning and belief of its provisions (in the above sense) and conformity of behavior to these to the
extent we may expect people of ordinary conscientiousness to conform
their behavior to rules they believe are principles about right or obligatory behavior." Finally, let us, purely arbitrarily and for the sake of
brevity, use the phrase "maximizes intrinsic value" to mean "would pro-

duce at least as much intrinsic good as would be produced by any relevant alternative action." With these stipulations, we can now propose, as a somewhat more precise formulation of Urmson's proposal, the following rule-utilitarian thesis: "An act is right if and only if it conforms with that learnable set of rules, the adoption of which by everyone would maximize intrinsic value."

This principle does not at all imply that the rightness or wrongness of an act is contingent upon the agent's having *thought about* all the complex business of the identity of a set of ideal moral rules; it asserts, rather, that an act is right if and only if it *conforms* to such a set of rules, regardless of what the agent may think. Therefore the principle is not disqualified from being a correct principle about what is objectively right or wrong . . . for it makes rightness and wrongness a matter of the facts, and totally independent of what the agent thinks is right, or of what the agent thinks about the facts, or of the evidence the agent may have, or of what is probably the case on the basis of this evidence.

An obvious merit of this principle is that it gives expression to at least part of our practice or procedure in trying to find out what is right or wrong. For when we are in doubt about such matters, we often try to think out how it would work in practice to have a moral code which prohibited or permitted various actions we are considering. We do not, of course, ordinarily do anything as complicated as try to think out the *complete* ideal moral code; we are content with considering whether certain specific injunctions relevant to the problem we are considering might be included in a good and workable code. Nevertheless, we are prepared to admit that the whole ideal code is relevant. For if someone shows us that a specific injunction which we think would be an acceptable part of a moral code clearly would not work out in view of other provisions necessary to an ideal code, we should agree that a telling point had been made and revise our thinking accordingly.

In order to get a clearer idea of the kind of "set of rules" (with which right actions must conform) which could satisfy the conditions this rule-utilitarian principle lays down, let us note some general features such a set presumably would have. First, it would contain rules giving directions for recurrent situations which involve conflicts of human interests. Presumably, then, it would contain rules rather similar to W. D. Ross's list of prima facie obligations: rules about the keeping of promises and contracts, rules about debts of gratitude such as we may owe to our parents, and, of course, rules about not injuring other persons and about promoting the welfare of others where this does not work a comparable hardship on us. Second, such a set of rules would not include petty restrictions; nor, at least for the most part, would it contain purely prudential rules. Third, the rules would not be very numerous; an upper limit on quantity is set by the ability of ordinary people to learn them. Fourth, such a set of rules would not include unbearable demands; for their inclusion would only serve to bring moral obligation into discredit. Fifth, the set of rules adoption of which would have the best consequences could not leave too much to discretion. It would make concessions to the fact that ordinary people are not capable of perfectly fine discriminations, and to the fact that, not being morally perfect, people of ordinary conscientiousness will have a tendency to abuse a moral rule where it suits their interest. We must remember that a college dormitory rule like "Don't play music at such times or in such a way as to disturb the study or sleep of others" would be ideally flexible if people were perfect; since they aren't, we have to settle for a rule like "No music after 10 P.M." The same thing is true for a moral code. The best moral code has to allow for the fact that people are what they are; it has to be less flexible and less efficient than a moral code that was to be adopted by perfectly wise and perfectly conscientious people could be.

Should we think of such a moral code as containing only prescriptions for situations likely to arise in *everyone's* life—rules like "If you have made a promise, then . . ." or "If you have a parent living, then treat him thus-and-so"? Or should we think of it as containing distinct sets of prescriptions for *different roles or statuses,* such as "If you are a policeman, then . . ." or "If you are a physician, then . . ."? And if the ideal code is to contain different prescriptions for different roles and statuses, would it not be so complex that it could not be learned by people of ordinary intelligence? The answer to these questions is that the rule-utilitarian is not committed, by his theory, to the necessity of such special codes, although I believe he may well admit their desirability—admit, for instance, that it is a good thing for a physician to carry a rule in his mental kit, specially designed to answer the question, "Shall I treat a patient who does not pay his bill?" In any case, our rule-utilitarian theory can *allow* for such special rules. Nor is there a difficulty in the fact that people of normal intelligence could hardly learn all these special sets of rules. For we can mean, by saying that a code can be "learned" by people of ordinary intelligence, that any person can learn all the rules relevant to the problems *he* will face. A rule-utilitarian will not, of course, have in mind a moral code which in some part is secret—for instance, lawyers having a moral code known only to themselves, a code which it would be harmful for others to know about. For surely in the long run it could not have best consequences for a society to have a moral code, perhaps granting special privileges to some groups, which could not stand the light of public knowledge.

First Problem: Moral Codes
for an Imperfect Society

Our "second approximation" to a rule-utilitarian principle has proposed that an act is right if and only if it conforms with the requirements of a learnable moral code, the adoption of which by *everyone* would maximize utility—and meaning by "adoption of a code" the learning and belief that the code lays down the requirements for moral behavior; and conformity to it to the extent we may expect from people of *ordinary conscientiousness*.

The italicized words in the preceding paragraph indicate two respects in which the proposed test of rightness in a sense departs from reality. In actuality moral codes are not subscribed to by everybody in all particulars: there is virtual unanimity on some items of what we call "the code of the community" (such as the prohibition of murder and incest), but on other matters there is less unanimity (in the United States, the "code" permits artificial birth-control measures despite disapproval by many Catholics), and it is a somewhat arbitrary matter to decide when the disagreement has become so general that we ought not to speak of something as part of the code of the community at all. There is probably some measure of disagreement on many or most moral matters in most modern communities (and, surely, in at least many primitive communities). Furthermore, our proposal, in an effort to be definite about the degree of commitment involved in the "adoption" of a code, spoke of an "ordinary conscientiousness." This again departs from reality. Ordinary conscientiousness may be the exception: many people are extremely, perhaps even overly conscientious; at the other extreme, some people act as if they have developed no such thing as a conscience at all. It is characteristic of actual communities that there is a wide range in degrees of conscientiousness.

As a result of these departures from reality, our test for rightness savors a bit of the utopian. We are invited to think of different worlds, each populated by people of "ordinary conscientiousness," all of whom are inoculated with a standard moral code. We are to decide whether given types of action are right or wrong by considering which of these hypothetical communities would realize a maximum of value.

There is force in [our] proposal. In fact, if we are thinking of sponsoring some ideal, this conception is a useful one for appraising whatever ideal we are considering. Just as we might ask whether large military establishments or a capitalist economy would be suitable for the ideal community of the future, so we can ask whether certain features of our present moral code would be suitable in such a community. It may be that such a conception should play a large role in deciding what ultimate ideals we should espouse.

Nevertheless, this conception may, from its very framework, necessarily be unsuitable for deciding the rightness of actions in the real world. It appears that, in fact, this is the case with both of the features mentioned above.

First, the proposal is to test rightness by the desirability of a rule in a moral code among people of ordinary conscientiousness. Now, in a community composed of people of ordinary conscientiousness we do not have to provide for the contingency of either saints or great sinners. In particular, we do not have to provide for the occurrence of people like Adolf Hitler. In such a community, presumably, we could get along with a minimal police force, perhaps an unarmed police force. Similarly, it would seem there would be no value in a moral prescription like "Resist evil men." In the community envisaged, problems of a certain sort would presumably not arise, and therefore the moral code need not have features designed to meet those problems. Very likely, for instance, a moral code near to that of extreme pacifism would work at least as well as a code differing in its non-pacifism.

More serious is the flaw in the other feature: that the test of rightness is to be compatibility with the requirements of the moral code, adoption of which *by everyone* would maximize utility. The trouble with this is that it permits behavior which really would be desirable if everyone agreed, but which might be objectionable and undesirable if not everyone agreed. For instance, it may well be that it would have the best consequences if the children are regarded as responsible for an elderly parent who is ill or needy; but it would be most unfortunate if the members of a Hopi man's native household—primarily his sisters and their families—decided that their presently recognized obligation had no standing on this account, since the result would be that as things now stand, no one at all would take the responsibility. Again if everyone recognized an obligation to share in duties pertaining to national defense, it would be morally acceptable to require this legally; but it would hardly be morally acceptable to do so if there are pacifists who on moral grounds are ready to die rather than bear arms. And similarly for other matters about which there are existing and pronounced moral convictions.

It seems clear that some modifications must be made if our rule-utilitarian proposal is to have implications consistent with the moral convictions of thoughtful people. Unfortunately it is not clear just what the modifications should be. The one I am inclined to adopt is as follows. First, we must drop that part of our conception which assumes that people in our hypothetical societies are of ordinary conscientiousness. We want to allow for the existence of both saints and sinners and to have a moral code to cope with them. In order to do this, we had better move closer to Urmson's original suggestion. We had better drop the notion of "adoption" and replace it by his term "recognition," meaning by "recognition by all" simply "belief by all that the rules formulate moral requirements." Second, we must avoid the conception of the acceptance of all the rules of a given moral code by *everybody* and replace it by something short of this, something which does not rule out the problems created by actual convictions about morals. Doing so means a rather uneasy compromise, because we cannot sacrifice the central feature of the rule-utilitarian view, which is that the rightness of an act is to be tested by whether it conforms with rules the (somehow) general acceptance of which would maximize utility. The compromise I propose is this: that the test whether an act is right is whether it is compatible with that set of rules which, were it to replace the moral commitments of members of the *actual society* at the time, *except where there are already fairly decided moral convictions*, would maximize utility. . . .

Concluding Remarks

The principle with which we end is this: "An act is right if and only if it conforms with that learnable set of rules the recognition of which as morally binding—roughly at the time of the act—by everyone in the society of the agent, except for the retention by individuals of already formed and decided moral convictions, would maximize intrinsic value."

I wish to make three final comments on this principle.

First, one may ask whether a set of moral rules which would maximize intrinsic value in the way described would necessarily be a *just* set of rules. Surely, if the rules are not just, conformity with them will by no means guarantee that an action is right. A further inquiry must be made about whether additional requirements are needed to assure that moral rules are just. It may be that, as I have suggested elsewhere, none is called for if equality of some sort is an intrinsic good.

Second, if the proposed principle is correct, we can give at least a partial answer to a person who asks why he ought to perform actions he is obligated to perform, if they conflict with his self-interest. Perhaps a person who asks such a question is merely confused, and his query not worth our attention. But we can say to him that one reason for meeting his obligation is that by doing so he plays the game of living according to the rules which will maximize welfare. And this will be, at least partially, a satisfying answer to a man who is activated by love or sympathy or respect directed at other sentient beings generally.

Finally, some reflections on the employment of the principle. It is, perhaps, obvious that it is not necessary to advocate that everyone always bear the rule-utilitarian principle in mind in deciding what he ought to do. Not that it would be harmful—beyond the waste of time—to do so; for it is obvious that the clear moral obligations are prescribed by the principle. For example, only an instant's thought is required to see that it is socially useful to recognize the rule that solemn promises should be kept—doubtless with some qualifications. The rule's employment is important, however, in analyzing more difficult cases, in making clear whether a given moral rule should be qualified in a certain way. Of course, it would be foolish to suggest that application of the principle is an easy road to the resolution of moral problems. It may very often be that after most careful reflection along the lines suggested, the most that can be said is that a given action is probably the one which the principle requires. If so, if we accept the principle, we can go on to say that this action is probably the right one.

RU has been attacked in a variety of ways, on one side by AUs like J. J. C. Smart and on the other by deontologists. Ripley was in effect criticizing it when he discussed Paley in Section 3.1 above. In the following essay, Alan Donagan criticizes Brandt and other utilitarians from a deontological point of view that involves an interesting combination of Sidgwick and Kant.

IS THERE A CREDIBLE FORM
OF UTILITARIANISM? *

Alan Donagan

In his important essay, "Toward a Credible Form of Utilitarianism," Professor R. B. Brandt has shown convincingly that if utilitarianism is credible in any form, it is substantially in the version of rule-ultilitarianism that he delineates. While conceding that, in that form, utilitarianism is plausible, I shall try to show that it is not credible.

Following Brandt, I take utilitarianism to be generically a theory

From Michael D. Bayles, ed., Contemporary Utilitarianism *(Garden City, N.Y.: Doubleday & Company, Inc., Anchor Books, 1968). Reprinted by permission of the author and Michael D. Bayles.*

---

* The original draft of this paper was read on 24 March 1964 at a colloquium at the University of Pittsburgh, and subsequently at a seminar at Indiana University. It was intended for discussion, not publication; and it is with misgiving that I have consented to the publication of this amended version of it.

about what acts are right, what wrong; and specifically a theory that the rightness or wrongness of an act consists *in some way* in whether its consequences are better or worse than those of other acts which the agent could have done instead. The modification "in some way" is important. The early utilitarians, Bentham and the Mills [John Stuart Mill and his father, James Mill], did not treat it as the office of a moralist to calculate the consequences of individual acts, this murder or that lie, but only whether the consequences of classes of acts like murders or lies are better or worse than the consequences of the classes of alternative acts in which the agents refrain from murdering or lying.

Not all utilitarians have followed Bentham and the Mills in this. Professor J. J. C. Smart, for example, has argued that to "restrict" utilitarianism as in practice Bentham and the Mills did leads to absurdities; and that the only tenable form of utilitarianism is the "extreme" or "radical" doctrine that you ought never to do an individual act that will produce, on balance, more evil and less good than some alternative.[1] Following Brandt, I shall describe this position as "act-utilitarianism."

Act-utilitarianism has generally been put down as incredible, on the ground that in certain circumstances it enjoins as duties what virtually everybody considers to be criminal. To employ a hackneyed example: it might well be the case that more good and less evil would result from your painlessly and undetectedly murdering your malicious, old and unhappy grandfather than from your forbearing to do so: he would be freed from his wretched existence; his children would be rejoiced by their inheritances and would no longer suffer from his mischief; and you might anticipate the reward promised to those who do good in secret. Nobody seriously doubts that a position with such a consequence is monstrous.

To object that the conditions imagined in this example have never been fulfilled, even if the objection is true (which I doubt), would be beside the point. Moral theory is *a priori*, as clear-headed utilitarians like Henry Sidgwick recognized. It is, as Leibnitz would say, true of all possible worlds. A world in which some murders can be painless and undetected is certainly possible. And the notion that the reason why it would be wrong painlessly to murder your malicious, old, unhappy grandfather is that, in the actual world, you could not get away with it, if anything, is more monstrous than the view that such a murder would be permissible.

I therefore conclude that act-utilitarianism is incredible. . . .

Is rule-utilitarianism . . . as Brandt has more fully elucidated it

---

[1] J. J. C. Smart, "Extreme and Restricted Utilitarianism," *Philosophical Quarterly*, Vol. VI (1956), 344–54.

credible? I have already conceded that one argument against it will not hold water, namely, that it degenerates in practice into act-utilitarianisms because its moral rules are no more than rules of thumb. Nor shall I urge the classical objection: that there is no scientific way of carrying out the calculations of comparative consequences that all forms of utilitarianism require. True, this objection is dismissed too lightly by utilitarians, who tend not to distinguish their awareness that their convictions about the consequences of socially recognizing this rule or that are strong from their persuasion that such convictions must somehow be scientific. Nor, finally, shall I argue that, in our society, a rule-utilitarian's moral conclusions would necessarily be wrong. But that his conclusions may well be right is beside the point. As we have seen, whether a moral theory is true or false depends on whether its implications for all possible worlds are true. Hence whether utilitarianism is true or false cannot depend on how the actual world is.

Is it possible to specify a possible world in which rule-utilitarianism would have implications that are false?

It must be acknowledged at once that in no possible world does rule-utilitarianism have implications of the kind that are fatal to act-utilitarianism: implications that acts which virtually nobody seriously doubts to be evil, and which not even "enlightened Utilitarians" will openly praise, may be right if they can be done secretly. In any possible world, rule-utilitarianism excludes esoteric moral principles, and enjoins observance of moral rules without regard to whether or not they can be secretly broken. Unlike act-utilitarianism, rule-utilitarianism is not a monstrous theory; and, if it can be shown to be false, the considerations by which it is shown will be delicate.

There appear to be at least two kinds of consideration that present difficulties for rule-utilitarians: (1) the distinction between duties and supererogatory acts; and (2) the distinction between duties and certain excusable or nearly excusable wrongs.

(1) Consider the following possible situation: a fifth of the members of a society are lazy, idle, and irresponsible; their behavior causes them serious harm, yet coercing them to behave more responsibly would occasion grave evils; and, finally, if the rule, "It is the duty of every industrious and prudent person to set aside, according to his means, a small but appreciable portion of his income for the support of the lazy but needy," were adopted in the society in question, more good and less evil would result than if it were not adopted. I do not think that our society is of this kind, but, since such a society is certainly possible, a rule-utilitarian living in it would have no choice but to consider himself morally obliged to recognize the proposed rule.

Now I think that many would reject such a rule. I do not mean that they would necessarily refuse to set aside part of their income for the undeserving poor, but only that they would vehemently deny that they were obliged to do it. And would they not be right? Is not their action a palmary example of a supererogatory rather than an obligatory act?

One possible reply must be briefly mentioned and dismissed. It may be held that to demand that the industrious and prudent work for the idle and irresponsible is evil in itself, and that its evil is so grave that it outweighs all the other good consequences of accepting that demand. It is true, of course, that to give up part of your income when you neither desire to nor have any inducement to is an evil according to utilitarianism. But if the part of your income that is given up, although appreciable, is small, utilitarianism cannot recognize it as a grave evil. Ethical theories, e.g. some theories of natural rights, according to which any rule depriving a man, without return, of any part of his earned income would be a very grave evil, all violate the sense of utilitarianism.

Let me offer a second example with a less conservative flavor. Suppose that you have a neighbor who is indiscreet and foolish, and who confides to you that he is mortgaging everything he can in order to make a speculative investment which you are convinced would be disastrous. You believe that, if you expend much time and effort, you can dissuade him from making the investment; that nobody else will even try to dissuade him; and that the disaster you anticipate for him would be out of all proportion to the inconvenience and embarrassment you will suffer in dissuading him. Are you morally obliged to dissuade him? I do not deny that you ought to express your opinion that the investment he proposes would be disastrous, and to express it strongly; but, beyond that, is it your duty to embark on a lengthy and possibly embarrassing attempt to change his mind?

There can be little doubt that there would be more good and less evil in society as a whole if the rule were to be adopted: "It is the duty of everybody who has adequate reason to believe that the course of action which a neighbor proposes will be disastrous to that neighbor, that he can without grave inconvenience or embarrassment dissuade that neighbor from his proposed course, and that nobody else will, to dissuade him." Hence there can be little doubt that rule-utilitarianism entails that such a rule ought to be adopted in the actual world. And even if the actual world be not such that the consequences of adopting such a rule are beneficial, it is evident that such a world is possible. Yet I think that many would reject such a rule. Once again, I do not deny that those who reject it might set out to dissuade a foolish neighbor in such a case. But I for one would deny that I was morally obliged to do so; and would think that, if I did so, my act would be supererogatory.

(2) A second consideration against rule-utilitarianism may be found in what it implies about certain wrongs which are tempting and perhaps even excusable. Consider an example once unhappily employed by Sir David Ross: Can it ever be expedient, as Caiaphas held, that one man should die for the people? Is a judge morally obliged to procure a judicial murder if it should be for the public good?

Although many rule-utilitarians maintain that their position implies the falsity of Caiaphas's doctrine, it can hardly be doubted that a world in which the good of the people sometimes would require it is *possible*, and that, in such a world, rule-utilitarians would be committed to the position of Caiaphas. Consider the rule: "Judges must conform to the prescriptions of their judicial calling, except when, by departing from them, but not in such a way as to bring about even worse consequences, they can avert major calamities to their nation or to the world," which I shall, for brevity, call "Caiaphas's rule."

The calamity which Caiaphas himself tried to avert was (on one version) a rebellion against the authority of the Sanhedrin, and (on another) a Roman persecution of the Jewish people. Whether Caiaphas's unjust judgment did in fact avert either calamity may be doubted; but there is no reason to suspect his sincerity. And it is at least conceivable, in a world in which large nations bully small ones as a matter of course, that a large nation might threaten a small one with bombing, military occupation, and the like, unless some innocent person whose conduct had given offence was tried and condemned on a capital charge.

A rule-utilitarian might object that, since general recognition of Caiaphas's rule would so discredit the judiciary that public life would be mortally injured, there could be no circumstances in which the public good would be served by recognizing that rule. But it is not at all evident that to recognize Caiaphas's rule as a moral rule (not, of course, as a legal one) would seriously impair confidence in the judiciary. It is even likely, as the remarks of some French anti-Semites about the Dreyfus case suggest, that some would sleep more quietly in their beds if they knew that their judges would not be overscrupulous in national emergencies. However that may be, it cannot seriously be denied that there could be a society in which the general recognition of Caiaphas's rule would not discredit the judiciary.

There seems to be no other reason for contesting the conclusion that, in some possible social situations, rule-utilitarianism would require that Caiaphas's rule be adopted. And although I do not pretend that we might not excuse or palliate the wrong done by somebody who acted on that rule, it seems to me that such an implication must ruin rule-utilitarianism. However much certain judicial murders may be excused or even defended, they are *not* morally right.

A dedicated rule-utilitarian might reject both considerations I have offered against it. He might simply reject any distinction between obligatory and supererogatory good acts, and maintain that a sound moral code must, so far as it is practicable, ordain that in any situation a man ought to do the best act that he can do. And he might reject, as a survival of rule-idolatry, my conviction that no circumstances can make judicial murder right.

It must be confessed that when, as with rule-utilitarianism, moral theory contradicts moral intuition only in a few farfetched cases, moral intuition is far from a safe guide. Against act-utilitarianism it suffices; for act-utilitarianism if I am right about its implications, outrages moral intuition at almost every turn. Rule-utilitarianism, on the other hand, provides so persuasive a theoretical basis for common morality that when it contradicts some moral intuition, it is natural to suspect that intuition, not theory, is corrupt. Moral theory must account for common morality, which act-utilitarianism does not do; but individual moral intuitions are not sacrosanct. One important reason for inquiring into moral theory is to purify our moral beliefs.

The intuitive considerations I have offered against rule-utilitarianism can stand only if they point to a theory that justifies them; and I think they do. I cannot here expound that theory, but it is incumbent on me at least to indicate it. It is manifestly Kantian, and its character is sufficiently exhibited in two principles, for the formulation of which I shall draw upon Sidgwick and Kant.

(i) "It cannot be right for A to treat B in a manner in which it would be wrong for B to treat A, merely on the ground that they are different individuals, and without there being any difference between the natures or circumstances of the two which can be stated as a reasonable ground for the difference of treatment." [2]

(ii) "[R]ational beings stand under the *law* that each of them should treat himself and all others, *never merely as a means,* but always *at the same* time as an end in himself." [3]

Of these principles, (i) is a principle of equity fundamental to any rational morality, and (ii) has to do with the substance and scope of moral rules. . . .

In trying to support my two principles I should begin by investigating the presuppositions of the question, "On what principles does reason require you to act?" Such a question, we have seen, takes you beyond egoism. In asking it, you presuppose that you have charac-

---

[2] Henry Sidgwick, *The Methods of Ethics,* 7th ed. (London: Macmillan & Co., Ltd., 1962), p. 380.

[3] Immanuel Kant, *Grundlegung zur Metaphysik der Sitten,* 2nd ed., pp. 74–75; Pruss. Acad. ed., p. 433 (tr. H. J. Paton).

teristics by virtue of which rational claims can be made by others upon you and by you upon others. The primary moral claims arise from the acts of rational beings with respect to one another; and the principles of morality are concerned with how it is that the fact that two beings are rational should limit what is permissible for each to do with reference to the other. Since what gives rise to moral claims is rationality itself, not the degree in which it is present, from the point of view of morality, rational individuals will be equal as moral subjects, however they may differ in their characteristics. The value of each will be absolute. Hence my two principles.

Although I do not advance this sketch as a valid argument, I think that a valid argument of the kind sketched can be found. My reason for offering such a sketch, full of blunders though it doubtless is, was to elicit what is wrong with even the most plausible form of utilitarianism. Utilitarianism conceives our moral obligations to derive from the putative obligation to increase good and diminish evil, no matter what must be done to this or that individual. I wish to maintain, on the contrary, that moral obligations derive from the obligation to respect the independence and worth of every individual, no matter at what cost in good foregone and evil accepted. Violating the moral rights of this or that individual seldom in the end turns out well for others; but that is not why such violations are wrong.

3.4

Justice and Other Problems

There are many more points about utilitarianism that might be discussed. One question, which was mentioned briefly by both Brandt and Donagan, is raised by Sidgwick in the following paragraphs. Although very close to utilitarianism, he argues, in the first paragraph, that the principle of utility must be supplemented by a principle of distribution or justice. The second paragraph contains a statement of the principle of justice that he himself subscribed to. The question is whether he is right in contending that a separate principle of justice is necessary, and if so, whether his principle will do the job. One might also ask whether the line of thought mentioned by Brandt in his footnote—that a certain distribution of welfare, e.g., an equal one, is intrinsically good—could be used by a nonhedonistic utilitarian (AU or RU) as an answer to Sidgwick. Notice, incidentally, Sidgwick's comments on the Golden Rule.

UTILITARIANISM AND JUSTICE

Henry Sidgwick

There is one more point that remains to be noticed. It is evident that there may be many different ways of distributing the same quantum of happiness among the same number of persons; in order, therefore, that the Utilitarian criterion of right conduct may be as complete as

From The Methods of Ethics, *7th ed. (London: Macmillan & Co., Ltd., 1962). The first edition was published in 1874.*

possible, we ought to know which of these ways is to be preferred. This question is often ignored in expositions of Utilitarianism. It has perhaps seemed somewhat idle, as suggesting a purely abstract and theoretical perplexity, that could have no practical exemplification; and no doubt, if all the consequences of actions were capable of being estimated and summed up with mathematical precision, we should probably never find the excess of pleasure over pain exactly equal in the case of two competing alternatives of conduct. But the very indefiniteness of all hedonistic calculations . . . renders it by no means unlikely that there may be no cognisable difference between the quantities of happiness involved in two sets of consequences respectively; the more rough our estimates necessarily are, the less likely we shall be to come to any clear decision between two apparently balanced alternatives. In all such cases, therefore, it becomes practically important to ask whether any mode of distributing a given quantum of happiness is better than any other. Now the Utilitarian formula seems to supply no answer to this question: at least we have to supplement the principle of seeking the greatest happiness on the whole by some principle of Just or Right distribution of this happiness. The principle which most Utilitarians have either tacitly or expressly adopted is that of pure equality—as given in Bentham's formula, "everybody to count for one, and nobody for more than one." And this principle seems the only one which does not need a special justification; for, as we saw, it must be reasonable to treat any one man in the same way as any other, if there be no reason apparent for treating him differently.[1] . . .

. . . whatever action any of us judges to be right for himself, he implicitly judges to be right for all similar persons in similar circumstances. Or, as we may otherwise put it, "if a kind of conduct that is right (or wrong) for me is not right (or wrong) for some one else, it must be on the ground of some difference between the two cases, other than the fact that I and he are different persons." A corresponding proposition may be stated with equal truth in respect of what ought to be done to—not by—different individuals. These principles have been most widely recognised, not in their most abstract and universal form, but in their special application to the situation of two (or more) individuals similarly related to each other: as so applied, they appear in what is popularly known as the Golden Rule, "Do to others as you would have them do to you." This formula is obviously unprecise in

---

[1] It should be observed that the question here is as to the distribution of *Happiness*, not the *means of happiness*. If more happiness on the whole is produced by giving the same means of happiness to B rather than to A, it is an obvious and incontrovertible deduction from the Utilitarian principle that it ought to be given to B, whatever inequality in the distribution of the *means* of happiness this may involve.

statement; for one might wish for another's co-operation in sin, and be willing to reciprocate it. Nor is it even true to say that we ought to do to others only what we think it right for them to do to us; for no one will deny that there may be differences in the circumstances—and even in the nature—of two individuals, A and B, which would make it wrong for A to treat B in the way in which it is right for B to treat A. In short the self-evident principle strictly stated must take some such negative form as this; "it cannot be right for A to treat B in a manner in which it would be wrong for B to treat A, merely on the ground that they are two different individuals, and without there being any difference between the natures or circumstances of the two which can be stated as a reasonable ground for difference of treatment." Such a principle manifestly does not give complete guidance [2]—indeed its effect, strictly speaking, is merely to throw a definite *onus probandi* on the man who applies to another a treatment of which he would complain if applied to himself; but Common Sense has amply recognised the practical importance of the maxim: and its truth, so far as it goes, appears to me self-evident.

We cannot include a full set of selections on justice, representing all points of view. We have just quoted Sidgwick's statement of his formal principle of justice. This formal principle is compatible with both an equalitarian and a nonequalitarian conception of material justice. In passages already quoted in Chapter 2, Ross takes a meritarian position; for him justice is distributing good, not equally, but in accordance with merit or virtue. This is essentially Aristotle's view about distributive justice. Notice that he uses "equal" as simply another word for "just" or "proportional." His idea is that there is distributive justice if and only if the following ratio holds:

$$\frac{A's \text{ share of } x}{B's \text{ share of } x} = \frac{A's \text{ merit or virtue}}{B's \text{ merit or virtue}}$$

DISTRIBUTIVE JUSTICE

Aristotle

As the person who is unjust is unfair, and the thing which is unjust is unfair, it is clear that there is a certain mean in respect of unfairness, or inequality. This mean is that which is fair or equal; for whatever be

From Dr. J. E. Weldon, ed. and trans. *The Nicomachean Ethics of Aristotle (London: Macmillan & Co. Ltd., 1892).*

---

[2] [For further guidance, Sidgwick thinks we should appeal to the principle of utility.—EDS.]

the nature of an action that admits of excess or defect, it admits also of fairness or equality.

If then that which is unjust is unfair, that which is just is fair, as indeed every one sees without argument.

But since that which is fair or equal is a mean between two extremes, that which is just will in a certain sense be a mean. But fairness or equality implies two persons or things at least. It follows therefore that that which is just is a mean, that it is fair or equal and that it is relative to certain persons. It follows also that, inasmuch as it is a mean, it is a mean between certain extremes, viz. excess and defect, and that inasmuch as it is just, it is relative to certain persons. But, if so, then that which is just must imply four terms at least; for the persons relatively to whom it is just are two, and the things in which it consists are two likewise. Also, if the persons are equal, the things will be equal; for as one thing is to the other thing, so is one person to the other person. For if the persons are not equal, they will not have equal shares; in fact the source of battles and complaints is either that people who are equal have unequal shares, or that people who are not equal have equal shares, distributed to them. The same truth is clearly seen from the principle of merit; for everybody admits that justice in distributions is determined by merit of some sort; only people do not all understand the same thing by merit. The democrats understand [it to be free birth], the oligarchs wealth or nobility, and the aristocrats virtue.

Justice then is a sort of proportion; for proportion is not peculiar to abstract quantity, but belongs to quantity generally, proportion being equality of ratios and implying four terms at least.

Now it is plain that discrete proportion implies four terms; but the same is true of continuous proportion; for in continuous proportion one of the terms is used as two, and is repeated. Thus as A is to B, so is B to C; here B is repeated; consequently if B be set down twice, the terms of the proportion will be four.

That which is just then requires four terms at least, and an equality of ratio between them, the persons and the things being similarly divided. As then the term A is to the term B, so will C be to D, and consequently *alternando* as A is to C, so will B be to D. The whole therefore will bear the same ratio to the whole i.e. $A + C$ *will be to* $B + D$ *as* A *is to* B *or* C *to* D, but this is the combination which the distribution effects, and, if the terms be thus united, it is a just combination.

The conjunction therefore of A with C and of B with D is what is just in distribution, and this justice is a mean between the violations of proportion; for that which is proportionate is a mean, and that which is just is proportionate. Mathematicians call this kind of proportion geometrical; for in geometrical proportion the whole is to the whole as each of the separate terms is to each. But this proportion is not continuous, as no one arithmetical term can stand both for person and for thing.

That which is just then in this sense is that which is proportionate, and that which is unjust is that which is disproportionate. It follows that this disproportion may take the form either of excess or defect; and this is actually the case, for the author of the injustice has too much, and the victim has too little, of the good. In regard to evil the contrary is the case; for the lesser evil in comparison with the greater counts as a good, as the lesser evil is more desirable than the greater, and that which is desirable is a good, and that which is more desirable is a greater good.

This then, is one form of justice.

A moderate equalitarian theory of justice, which finds a place for the recognition of desert or merit as well as for liberty, is worked out by D. D. Raphael in the following essay. He is not a utilitarian, but gives substantial weight to considerations of utility.

JUSTICE AND LIBERTY

D. D. Raphael

II. The notion of justice has traditionally been divided into *(a)* distributive and *(b)* retributive or corrective justice. . . . I take distributive justice to refer to a principle of equality in some sense. The difficulty is to specify that sense. Retributive or corrective justice I take to refer to the claims of reparation and of desert. "Reparation" here is used in a wider sense than the normal, to mean both the making good of injury (the ordinary sense of "reparation") and the readiness to requite benefits that is implied in the obligation of gratitude. "Desert" refers primarily to the merit of virtue and the demerit of vice, in consequence of which the first is thought to call for reward and the second for punishment; the ideas of "merit" and "reward" (but rarely those of "demerit" and "punishment") are also extended to express the praise accorded to certain non-moral qualities and activities and to the benefits that are accordingly regarded as their due. I have distinguished reparation from desert only in order to ignore the former in what follows. For social theory, and in particular for the relation of justice to liberty, the principles of justice that are relevant are those of equality and desert.

From Proceedings of the Aristotelian Society, *N.S., LI (1950–51). Reprinted by permission of the author and* Proceedings of the Aristotelian Society.

Theorists who deny or ignore the alleged claim to equality some-times treat the claim of desert, i.e. the apportionment of happiness or the means to it in accordance with merit (or perhaps merit and ca-pacity), as *distributive* justice, since such apportionment is, in their view, the one proper principle of distribution. . . . Since I shall argue that there is, in the moral thinking of our society at least, a claim to equality other than the so-called "proportionate equality," I retain the name of distributive justice for the claim to equality, and I subsume the requital of desert, whether by way of reward or by way of punish-ment, under retributive justice. If this diversity of usage is confusing, we may speak simply of the alleged principle or claim of equality and the alleged principle or claim of desert. By a "moral claim" I mean noth-ing other than a moral obligation, considered as *what* is owed to the persons or person towards whom the obligation is felt. . . .

I propose to consider first, whether the concept of merit can be reduced to that of social utility; and secondly, whether there is a posi-tive claim to equality, and if so, in what sense. I shall argue that neither desert nor equality can be wholly reduced to considerations of social utility or absolutely rejected as valid moral claims. I shall maintain that both are, to a degree, independent moral claims in modern democratic thought. . . .

IV. I turn next to the principle of equality. Many people who would agree that the principle of desert may go hand in hand with the claims of liberty would deny that liberty is compatible with equality. The first difficulty is to decide whether there is any valid principle of equality. Nobody in his senses would say that the alleged claim to equality is a claim that all men *are* equal. The first of the "truths" that are "held to be self-evident" by the American Declaration of Independence is "that all men are born equal." Similarly the French Declaration of 1789 begins "Men are born free and equal." "Rubbish," retorts the realist who cannot recognize a metaphor when he sees one. "Ivan Ivanovitch is born with poor physique, poor brains, poor parents, and as a slave of Mr. Stalin; Henry Ford junior is born with good physique, good brains, a millionaire father, and as a free citizen of the free-enterprise U.S.A." Locke and Rousseau, the Pilgrim Fathers and the French Revolutionaries, the drafters and the signatories of the U.N.O. Declaration of Human Rights, all knew perfectly well that men are not born equal in endowments, possessions, or opportunities. What they and their declarations say is that men are equal in respect of their *rights*, i.e. that in some sense men have a claim to equality, not that they *are* equal.

It may be said that a claim to equality must depend on an existing equality. If men have a claim to be considered or treated equally, this can only be because they are already equal in some respect which involves an obligation to treat them equally in action affecting them. It is often held that the claim to equality depends on religious doctrine and is an illustration of the fact that the whole of morality does. The ideals of liberty, equality, and fraternity, that have made themselves felt in western civilization since the French Revolution, owe their origin, it is claimed, to Christianity and rest on Christian doctrine. That they originated with the religious doctrine I think we may admit. Whether they can logically be derived from it is more dubious. The justification for equal treatment despite natural inequality, it is said, is the fact that, in religious doctrine, we are all the children of God and are therefore brothers. But does this metaphor help? It says that I should treat every man as I treat my brothers, i.e. as love would prompt, and wishes to persuade me that this is my duty by affirming that, morally and religiously though not biologically, all men are my brothers; moral conduct towards other men, i.e. my duty to them, is therefore the same in content as my natural conduct to my natural brothers. But does a man always love each of his brothers *equally?* Or as much as he may love one or two of his friends, or his wife, or his children? His children— there, it might be said, is the point. God loves us all as his children, and he loves us equally. For if you ask a parent which of his children he loves best, he will tell you that he loves each of them equally. This is not always true; did not Jacob love Joseph best? But even if it is true, does it follow that because a father loves his children equally, they will love each other equally? No, it will be replied, but they *should*. The doctrine of the fatherhood of God and the consequent brotherhood of man, however, was meant to tell us *why* we should love each other equally. It was intended to do this by giving us reason to regard those who are not literally our brothers as if they were. But the use of the image does not necessarily convey with it the idea of equality. Where a group of people are literally of the same family, they may think that they *ought* to act with equal love to each of their brethren, but their kinship does not necessarily cause them to do so nor does it give them a reason why they ought to do so. A man may consider both that he has an obligation to treat his brothers equally and that he has an obligation to treat all men equally, but he may still ask why in *each* of the two cases. The fact that he and his brothers have a common parent who loves them equally seems irrelevant.

The religious doctrine so far considered, then, does not give a basis for the claim to equality. But perhaps we have not seized upon the crucial element in the doctrine. It may be argued that the principle of equality rests on the fact that all men are born equal as moral agents, as having the dignity of a moral being, i.e. of the capacity to be moral, and thus they are equal in the sight of God. Other theologians, I have been told, interpret "equality in the sight of God" as equality in sin; we are all born equally steeped in original sin. Whether or not we accept the latter interpretation of "equality in the sight of God," it is of course true that all men are potential moral agents and therefore have an equal "dignity" not possessed by beings incapable of morality. But this equality is not what an enslaved or downtrodden populace refers to in claiming equality of rights. The "rights" or claims of justice are claims to *happiness* (or the opportunity to pursue happiness, or the means to happiness). Nobody would say that the equality of all men as potential moral agents involves equal claims to happiness, and it is to be hoped that the upholders of original sin do not think that all men have equal claims to misery, that they are all *equally* damned. If we are to consider the relation between our *moral* natures and our claims to happiness, it seems more reasonable to say that moral achievement, not mere potentiality, is what counts in determining "rights" or claims; the non-egalitarian principle of desert supplies the connecting link.

It is for this reason that some moralists would deny the validity of any positive claim to equality. If men are equal only in moral potentiality, and if claims to happiness are determined by moral achievement, in which men are unequal, how can we say they have equal claims? Accordingly, it may be held, the principle of desert is the sole principle of "distributive justice" and there is no claim to equal distribution apart from this. "Distributive justice," the argument would run, following Aristotle, is a distribution according to merit; unequal shares to unequals, and equal shares to equals. Equal distribution is right only when there is equal merit.

To sustain this view, we must interpret "merit" widely. . . . Inequality, whether of liberty, wealth, opportunity, or other desirable things, may be justified by differences of moral merit, of economic "merit," or of natural "merit"; a man who has wilfully committed a crime "deserves" to be imprisoned; an enterprising manufacturer "deserves" the fruits of his success; a bright child "deserves" a good education. Taking "merit" in this wide sense, it may be claimed that just distribution is always in accordance with merit.

What, then, are we to say of claims to equality? That these, when justified, are always based on equal merit? This suggestion would cover only a proportion of the relevant instances. It may be held, however, that claims to equality are usually to be interpreted negatively as justified protests against particular inequalities, justified not because there is any positive claim to equality but because the inequality is not "deserved," i.e. has an improper ground. It is unjust that Aristides be selected for ostracism; that a businessman become rich by "profiteering," that is, by making large profits in circumstances in which the general interest is harmed by his "enterprise"; that a dull-witted Vere de Vere be selected for Eton in preference to a bright Smith. The ground of the particular inequality attacked is morally "irrelevant," while an existing "relevant" ground for differentiation is ignored. The objection is not to inequality as such but to the ground of differentiation. The unequal treatment has conflicted with merit, where "merit" can mean moral worth, social utility, or natural capacity. In these respects men are of unequal "worth," and their treatment or status, it may be held, should be in accordance with their different "worths." But throughout history unequal treatment has almost always far exceeded, or cut across, the differences of "worth." Some men are of lesser "worth" than the others, but none are so much less valuable than others that they should be their serfs, still less their slaves or chattels. Even where those treated as of less account have not been serfs but just a lower class, the higher class has seldom consisted of those who are more "worthy" in virtue, utility, or capacity; usually, membership of the privileged class has been based on birth or similar accidents. Accordingly, the argument might conclude, the cry for equality is really a cry against unjustified inequality; but if, *per impossibile,* human affairs could be so arranged that men were treated in accordance with their natural inequalities, all would be well. To treat them equally, however, when they are naturally unequal, is just as wrong as to exaggerate or to run directly counter to their natural inequalities.

This view of course smacks of the "aristocrat," the "superior person," and therefore in these days many of us have a prejudice against it. But it cannot be easily dismissed, and the difficulty of justifying a positive claim to equality in the face of natural inequality tempts one to think that it must be true. Further, it need not in practice lead to aristocracy, for a modern exponent of the theory may agree that if, like Plato, we try to adjust our human affairs to the degree of inequality conferred on men by nature we shall be sure to make a mess of it. The advice that the theory might offer for practice is this: "We should neither try to secure equality nor try to adjust treatment to nature. Both are impracticable. What we should do, and what successful reformers have in fact done, is to protest against and remove unjustified inequality, inequality that clearly goes against the inequalities of nature. If we stick to this task, we shall have plenty to do, and shall not be led into extravagant and impracticable paths."

As practical advice, I think this is sensible; and the view does contain a great part of the truth about equality. Where the cry for equality has reference to the claims of "worth," i.e. of moral merit, natural capacity, or social utility, it is not based on a positive belief in equality but is a negative plea against unjustified inequality. To this extent the claim to equality is negative.

But the theory, as expounded so far, omits one of the justifying grounds for unequal treatment, and this ground, paradoxical though it appears at first sight, points to a limited positive claim to equality. Unequal treatment may be justified, not only on account of the different "worths" of the recipients, but also on account of their different needs. We think it right to make special provision for those affected by special needs, through natural disability, such as mental or physical weakness, or through the slings and arrows of outrageous fortune, through sickness, unemployment, or destitute old age. Here, it would seem, we go *against* nature, and think ourselves justified in doing so. The unequal treatment meted out is in *inverse* proportion to natural inequalities. We attempt to remedy, so far as we can, the inequality of nature. Though in the mere provision of aid, monetary or other, we seem at first sight to do more for the needy person than for the normal, to make an unequal discrimination in favour of the former, the inequality of treatment is an attempt to reduce the existing inequality, to bring the needy person up to the same level of advantages as the normal. We try to make up for the natural inequality and to give the handicapped, so far as possible, equal opportunities and equal satisfactions to those possessed by the nonhandicapped.

It is, however, an exaggeration to say, without qualification, that justice here is a matter of going against nature. For in dealing with the handicaps with which some people are born, we usually cannot provide them with fully equal opportunities to those possessed by normal people. We can try, as the theory we are considering bids us, to see that their handicap is not allowed, by the social arrangements of man, to extend beyond what it naturally must be. In the past, for example, handicapped children were neglected while normal children were, for reasons of utility, given opportunity for development. We think that we ought to remedy the neglect, to give the handicapped child such opportunities for development as his natural capacities allow. We try to ensure that the inequalities of nature are not exaggerated, but we cannot remove the natural inequalities themselves.

Yet it would be a mistake to think that, because some natural handicaps cannot be removed, there is no obligation to remove those which we can. If we can cure congenital blindness, we think we have an obligation to do so. We do not think that illness should simply be left to take its natural course; sometimes "leaving it to nature" is the best way to cure illness, sometimes not, and we think we ought to take the course, natural or not, which will be most likely to effect the cure. Where a person's peculiar disadvantages are due to external causes, such as an economic slump, an earthquake, or a flood, we certainly think that we should remedy them and, if possible, prevent them.

The claim of need, then, involves a distribution not in accordance with existing differences but contrary to them. People do of course differ in their needs, so that the provision of satisfaction for them will be an unequal one. But strictly, the potential needs and desires of people, even the most fortunate, are unlimited. Although I have not the special need of an invalid for eggs, I could do with quite a lot. Although normal children do not have the special need of the handicapped child for special educational equipment and personal supervision, they could quite well do with better educational equipment and more personal supervision than they now receive. How do we determine when a need is a "special" need? Our recognition of "special" needs is a recognition that some persons, by reasons of nature or accident, fall below the normal level of satisfactions, below the level which most people enjoy and which we regard as essential for decent living. Our attempt to meet these special needs is an attempt to bring such people up to the normal level of satisfactions, or as near to it as we can. When we do more for the handicapped child or the disabled man, this is a recognition that they are at present unequal to (below) most people in capacity to earn their living and have a reasonably happy life. Our unequal (greater) provision of care for them is an attempt to reduce the existing inequality; we want, so far as we can, to bring them to a level of equality with others in capacity to enjoy their lives. Thus the basis of the claim of special need is really a recognition of a claim to equality. It is a positive moral claim taking its place with others such as the claims of moral worth, utility, and capacity. For note that this claim of need remains even if there is no other moral claim. The permanently disabled, the aged, the insane, have, we think, a claim to be taken care of, to a reasonable measure of comfort and happiness, even though they are incapable of making any return.

V. Having established that there is a positive claim to equality, let us now consider more directly its content. To what precisely do we regard people as having an equal claim? Equality of what? Of consideration, of opportunity, of material goods, or of happiness? Certainly to equality of consideration; i.e. we recognize the right of *everyone* to have his various claims considered. But this is only a way of saying that everyone *has* claims; it does not involve any additional content as the claim of distributive justice. We also recognize a claim to equality of opportunity, that is, a claim of every man to an equal chance of developing his capacities and pursuing his interests. Is there also a claim to equal distribution? That is, when material means to happiness are available, should they, in the absence of other claims, be distributed equally? The question may be put alternatively thus: have men a claim to equal happiness, or only to an equal chance of pursuing happiness?

In fact, of course, equal happiness cannot be secured. If, for instance, everyone were given the same amount of money, the different tastes of different persons, and the different costs of satisfying their tastes, would mean that the same amount of money would provide more happiness for some than for others; if I like beer and you like whisky, I should be able to say "Nunc est bibendum" more often than you. Again, some would, by luck or greater ability, soon turn their standard income into a larger one, while others would soon be paupers. However, this practical impossibility of providing equal happiness does not affect the theoretical question. For many obligations cannot in practice be fully satisfied. If, for example, it be held that we have an obligation to increase the sum of happiness or good, or to distribute happiness in accordance with merit, this is in practice often impossible. The relevant obligation is really to try to aim at or approach the proposed ideal.

Let us first see what is involved in "equality of opportunity." I think that this is bound up with the idea of liberty. The idea of liberty is, primarily, a negative one, the removal of restraints upon doing what one wishes. Such restraints may be imposed by the actions of other persons or may be due to natural obstacles. Social liberty refers to the removal of restraints by other persons. The restraints of nature may be external or internal. The Firth of Clyde prevents me from walking to Bute, and if I wish to get to Bute a ferry must be provided. But besides such external obstacles to the satisfaction of our desires, there are also internal restraints. If I want to be a champion tennis-player, I am restrained by the weakness of my sight. Of internal restraints, some can be removed, others cannot. I have not the natural endowment to become a good tennis-player, but I have the natural endowment to become a fair chess-player. Natural endowments, however, cannot always be exercised by their possessor without training and suitable environment; in the absence of these, they remain unfulfilled potentialities. My potential capacity to become a fair chess-player is subject to the natural restraint that, if left to itself without training and practice, it cannot be actualized. Suitable training and practice are the removal of the natural restraint on the exercise of natural potentialities. Two children may have the potentiality of becoming good craftsmen. If one is given the necessary training and suitable environment to enable him to develop his potentialities so as to lead a satisfying life and to be socially useful, he thereby receives opportunity to make the most of his capacities. If the other is not given such training, he is denied the opportunity to make the most of his capacities. Equal opportunity means, ideally, maximum opportunity for all to develop the potentialities they have, and failing that, the maximum that is possible in the face of, e.g. economic difficulties. The opportunity is to be equally, i.e. impartially, spread in the sense that discrimination in the provision of a particular type of opportunity for some and not for others should depend on the potentialities that the prospective recipients have, instead of depending on "irrelevant" considerations such as birth or wealth.

Social liberty . . . is the absence of restraint by other persons. The provision of opportunity, however, involves, not the absence of action by other persons, but its presence in the form of aid and training in the development of capacities. Liberal political philosophy concentrated on social liberty. But the mere absence of interference by others does not give full opportunities to all to pursue happiness in accordance with their capacities, because many capacities do not develop of themselves but need assistance. When Mill rests the claim to liberty on the value of "the development of individuality," he implies an extension of the old Liberal idea of liberty. It would be generally agreed by thoughtful people today that men have a moral claim not only to social liberty but also to liberty in the further sense of maximum development of potentiality. Equal liberty for all will not result in equal happiness, for men differ in their potentialities so that some will be more able than others to achieve happiness for themselves by the exercise of their developed capacities.

Let us now turn to the other suggested principle of equal satisfactions. There seems to be some claim that all should be given equal satisfactions to the extent that this is within our power, e.g. in the provision of material means to happiness. This principle would conflict with the principle of maximum opportunity for all, if the latter were taken to imply not only that a man should be enabled to develop his potentialities to the fullest extent but also that he should be allowed to use his developed capacities as he wishes for his own maximum enjoyment. The second of these two implications is required by the principle of social liberty, and the two together by a combination of the principle of maximum opportunity with the principle of social liberty. The principle of opportunity alone, however, need not necessarily be held to conflict with the principle of equal satisfactions, for a man might be enabled to develop his capacities but required to devote the fruits of his capacities to the common good; that is to say, he might be expected to retain or receive, for his own enjoyment, a roughly equal amount of material means to satisfaction as others, while any surplus material results of his exercise of capacity were distributed to others whose own capacities did not allow them to effect as much. This is the egalitarian position—from each according to his capacity, to each according to his needs. The position conflicts with the principle of maximum social liberty, but not with the principle of maximum opportunity.

In practice, however, neither the position of extreme Liberalism nor the position of extreme egalitarianism is acceptable in isolation. The egalitarian has to give some weight to social liberty for the sake of utility, that is, in order to provide incentives to production so that the needs which can be satisfied may be at a maximum. There is in fact no limit to the desires which can be satisfied, so that distribution "to each according to his needs" must always be below what could be done. Accordingly, certain desires, which are thought to be more fundamental than others, are distinguished by the name of "needs," and it is thought that these should be satisfied for all equally before further desires are satisfied for any. "Bread for all before there is jam for some." The jam, however, is not distributed equally. On the other hand, the Liberal position is rarely carried to the extreme conclusion, "each for himself and devil take the hindmost." Few adherents of the position would be content to let the weak and the aged starve to death. Some sort of basic minimum, ranging from the paltry assistance of the Poor Law to the ambitions of the "Beveridge Programme," is usually admitted, and this is a concession to the principle of equal satisfactions. Justice, then, is thought to require a basic minimum of equal satisfactions, unrelated to utility or to capacity. Above that line, room is left for individuals to do as they think fit. The position of the line is different in different societies and at different periods of history, depending both on economic circumstances and on the level of social morality. That it depends on economic circumstances is obvious enough. "A chicken in every pot" is impossible if a country cannot afford to raise or buy enough chickens. But it depends on the level of social morality too. Tom Paine proposed in 1797 the establishment of a national fund, from which everyone should receive £15 at the age of 21 and £10 at the age of 50 "to enable them to live without wretchedness and go decently out of the world." The country could have afforded this very limited scheme of "social security," depending as it did, like the Beveridge plan, on some redistribution of existing income, but most of the people who could influence social legislation at the time would have thought it wildly utopian. On the other hand, many people to-day would say that the Labour Government, in sticking to all the benefits of the Welfare State irrespective of whether the country can afford them at present, is allowing its moral fervour to outrun economic necessity.

Distributive justice, we have found, makes two claims of equality, first, equality of opportunity, that is, the greatest possible degree of opportunity for all impartially; and second, the provision of material means to satisfaction for all impartially, such provision in practice being limited, for utilitarian reasons, to a standard of basic needs.

The first of these principles depends partly on utility (since the development and exercise of a good many capacities is useful for the production of means to satisfaction for society at large), and partly on valuing self-development. This means that the development of capacity is regarded as a moral claim, reinforced by the claims of utility if the capacity is especially useful to society (as, e.g., technical skill or teaching ability is and the capacity for playing chess is not), and overridden by the claim of utility if the capacity is socially harmful (e.g. the capacity for burglary; we do not think we ought to provide schools of burglary for potentially successful burglars). Since people differ in capacities, and since some men are better endowed than others with a particular capacity, this claim for the development of capacity is not one for equality (except in the sense that it is a claim of everyone) but reflects the differences of nature. We speak of *"equal* opportunity" because in the past the opportunities provided for development have not been in accordance with the inequalities of nature but have either run counter to them for the private interests of some or else exaggerated them for the sake of general interest. Where opportunity was not confined to privilege, it depended on social utility; it was extended to those whose development would benefit society to an unusual degree. Thus there is no need to invoke justice in order to approve of the provision of free higher education for the gifted children of poor parents; social utility will require it no less. But the provision of equal opportunity for the handicapped, in mind or body, can often not be justified by utility.

The second element of distributive justice ensures that there is a basic minimum for all even if some of those affected could not achieve it by their own efforts. Here we "go against nature" in the sense that we rate basic needs above the capacity to satisfy them, and of course above social utility, for keeping alive the aged and the incurably sick is not economic. We think it is due to *them* as individuals.

The two principles of equality, like the principle of retributive justice, are chiefly concerned to protect the individual irrespective of general utility. One is a claim that each person be given such opportunity for development as his natural capacity allows, even though it may not always add to social utility (but we shall do still more for socially useful capacities because of their utility). The other is a claim for the satisfaction of basic needs (i.e. those regarded as essential for tolerable living) for each individual even though there may be no economic return. We think these two things are due to individuals as such, as being "ends-in-themselves." If, with Mill, we hold that the most important element in the idea of liberty is not the negative factor of the absence of restraint but the positive factor of valuing individuality, then the essential point of justice and that of liberty are identical.

Except for Singer, all utilitarians hold that we ought to promote good, directly or indirectly. Most deontologists would agree, as Ross does, though they would hasten to add that we have other duties too. Some writers insist, however, that we have no obligation to do positive good, not even a prima facie one. Doing good to others is, of course, not wrong on this view, but it is not morally required. It is a kind of gift by the doer, like going the second mile; it is not something he owes, not something another has a right to. This view is forcefully stated by Singer in an attack on what he calls the obverse principle of consequences.

After you examine Singer's criticism of beneficence as a duty, you will find G. J. Warnock defending that position in the selection following that of Singer. Are you convinced by Singer's position?

IS BENEFICENCE A DUTY?   .

Marcus G. Singer

The obverse of the principle of consequences, or what may also be called "the principle of consequences in its positive form," states that: "If the consequences of A's doing x would be desirable, then it is A's duty to do x." It may also be stated in its generalized form: "If the consequences of doing x are generally (or usually) desirable, then it is one's duty to do x," where "x" refers, not to a specific act in specific circumstances, but to a kind of action. But to simplify the argument, which will be complicated enough, let us consider this principle simply in the form in which it asserts: "If the consequences of A's doing x would be desirable *on the whole*, then A ought to do x." Now this principle, in one form or another, has had an extraordinarily wide acceptance, and is widely regarded as either intuitively or demonstratively certain. . . .

This principle, however, has been asserted much more frequently than it has been supported; it is usually not argued for at all, but left at the level of "self-evidence" or intuitive obviousness. This is unfortunate, for once it is so accepted the tendency is to leave its implications unexamined. Thus [Ross] says: "It seems self-evident that if there are things that are intrinsically good, it is *prima facie* a duty to bring them into existence rather than not to do so, and to bring as much of them into existence as possible," and adds that the proposition "that there is no *prima facie* duty to produce as much that is good as we can . . . hardly

From Generalization in Ethics (*New York: Alfred A. Knopf, Inc., 1961; 2nd ed., Atheneum, 1971). From Chapter 7, pp. 180–82, 184–89. Reprinted by permission of the author.*

admits of argument but seems to me plainly false." [1] Yet it is not at all self-evident, and there are actually fairly strong reasons against it. . . .

One major objection to this principle is that if consistently adhered to, it would lead to moral fanaticism, to the idea that no action is indifferent or trivial, that every occasion is momentous. That this is so is borne out by the fact that one supporter gladly accepts such a consequence: "It is obvious that any of the acts that we do has countless effects, directly or indirectly, on countless people, and the probability is that any act, however right it be, will have adverse effects (though these may be very trivial) on some innocent people. Similarly, any wrong act will probably have beneficial effects on some deserving people. Every act, therefore, viewed in some aspects, will be *prima facie* right, and viewed in others, *prima facie* wrong." [2] Now this, I submit with all due respect, is nothing less than absurd. Not every occasion of life is momentous, nor is every choice we make or thing we do. To suppose otherwise is to suppose that every occasion of life gives rise to a moral problem, and that everything we do requires justification, and this is simply false. One who consistently thought so would die from moral perplexity. Unless the question whether some act is right or wrong actually arises, through some conflict, either real or apparent, with some moral rule, it is senseless to raise it. For there would then be no possibility of answering it.

The problems to which this principle would give rise are exemplified by the problem of "the concert ticket": "Suppose I had one ticket for a concert, and suppose I knew that Q would appreciate the concert just as much as I should and no more. Ought I to give him my ticket or go myself?" This is a problem that logically arises on the principle presented. Yet there is absolutely no reason why I ought to give Q the ticket, and even if Q would appreciate the concert much more than I should, there would still be no reason. Of course, there *might* be a reason. If, for example, I had promised Q to give him the ticket, then there would be a reason; and if, for some reason, I was unable to go, and was unable or unwilling to sell the ticket, then there would be a reason. But to say that there might be a reason is not to say that there is, and given the circumstances described, there is no reason whatever. Indeed, to suppose that there is, and that I *ought* to give Q the ticket, say on the ground that this would be an instance of benevolence or generosity, would lead to an inescapable paradox. For, if I ought to give Q the ticket, then, for the very same reason, Q ought to give it right back to me, and the very same

---

[1] W. D. Ross, *The Right and The Good* (Oxford: The Clarendon Press, 1930), pp. 24, 25. On p. 27 it is asserted that, in virtue of "the general principle that we should produce as much good as possible," we have such duties as the duties of beneficence and self-improvement.

[2] Ross, *The Right and the Good,* p. 41.

reason would be a reason why we ought to spend the rest of the evening trading it back and forth, each insisting that the other have it, with the consequence that neither of us would get to the concert. If this is not lunacy, it is a good imitation of it. Of course, if I *want* to give Q the ticket, I have a perfect right to, supposing it is mine to give and that I have not promised it to anyone else. Given such conditions as these, there would be nothing wrong in my giving him the ticket, and if I have an especially generous disposition, I very well might. But likewise there would be nothing wrong in my not giving him the ticket, and if I do not want to, I have a perfect right not to. For Q has no claim on me, and in keeping the ticket myself I have not violated anyone's rights. To suppose otherwise would actually lead to contradiction. For I am not different from anyone else in this respect, and if I ought to give Q the ticket, then everyone else, in a similar situation, ought to act in the same way. But then it would follow that everyone ought to give whatever he has, and not just a concert ticket, to anyone else who would enjoy it as much or more. But this implies that whatever anyone does is wrong, for he *might* have done something better; and this is not just false—it is self-contradictory.

Some of the points I have just made clearly require elaboration, and this can best be given them by specifying as clearly as possible just what is involved in my denial that the obverse of the principle of consequences is a sound moral principle. In the first place, in denying that one has the duty to do that which would have good consequences, I am not saying that such action would be wrong. What I am saying is that one has the right not to, so long as the consequences of not doing so would not be undesirable. So what I am denying is that generosity or benevolence is a duty. No doubt benevolence is a good thing, and it would be a good thing if there were more of it; and no doubt an act of generosity or benevolence is praiseworthy and admirable. But this does not mean that it is obligatory.

In the second place, in denying that one has the duty to do that which would have good consequences, I am not denying that one often has the duty to do that which would *in fact* have good consequences. What I am denying is that one has the duty to do that which would have good consequences *for that reason alone*. If an act would have consequences that would be on the whole desirable, it does not follow that the act ought to be done. If the act ought to be done, it is for some other reason, and obviously there are many actions that are obligatory and which would also have good consequences.

In the third place, my denial of this principle must not be taken to mean that our duties are "merely negative," that there are no actions that one ought to *do* but only actions that one ought *not* to do, nor can it be taken to mean that one need not help others who are in need of help. On the contrary, that one has the duty to help others in need of help is a consequence of the principles already elaborated. And it follows from the principle of consequences in its *negative* form that a person may have the duty to sacrifice his time, his convenience, his interests, or even his life, in order to save the life or protect the interests of another. This will be so if the consequences of not doing so would be undesirable. It will not be so, however, if the consequences of not doing so would not be undesirable.

The fact is that these two principles, the principle of consequences and its obverse, coincide in most cases, and consequently in most cases would require the same conduct. It is most often the case that if an act is such that if it is *not* done the consequences would be on the whole *un*-desirable, then it is also such that if it *is* done the consequences would be on the whole desirable; and the converse proposition also holds. This fact, that these two principles usually coincide, may account for whatever plausibility the obverse principle may appear to have. For in a case where the consequences of doing some act would be desirable, on the whole, it is easy to suppose that this is the reason why it ought to be done; whereas the true explanation is that the consequences of not doing it would be (on the whole) undesirable.

But even though these two principles usually coincide, they do not do so always, and it is in the cases where they do not that the obverse principle breaks down and leads to the paradoxes mentioned. For it may hold true, in some instance, that the consequences of A's not doing x would be undesirable, in which case A ought to do x, even though the consequences of his doing x would not be positively desirable. It might be alleged that in such a case the consequences of A's doing x must necessarily be desirable, on the ground that in doing x the undesirable consequences of not doing it would have been avoided. This is a possible way of looking at the matter. Its only defect is that it would tend to make the two principles equivalent. And what I wish to insist on is that there is a genuine difference between what might be called positive loss and the absence of positive gain, between an act's being merely not harmful and its being positively beneficial. "To throw out of cultivation land already productive, is a *positive* loss. *Leaving* waste-land as it is, is merely the absence of a possible gain. The one procedure, if carried on to any considerable extent, would cause ruin to the occupiers, and distress to the whole community; the other is merely *negative,* and hurts nobody." [3] Given this difference, then, it is possible for some act not to be harmful

---

[3] Richard Whately, *Paley's Moral Philosophy: With Annotations* (London: John W. Parker & Son, 1859), pp. 100–101.

to anyone even though it is not beneficial to anyone, and it is possible for the consequences of not doing some act to be undesirable even though the consequences of doing it would not be positively desirable.

But then, in exactly the same way, it is possible for the consequences of doing some act to be positively desirable even though the consequences of not doing it would not be undesirable. Here again it might be alleged that the consequences of not doing it must be undesirable because the positive benefits of doing it would not have been achieved. In some cases this will be a solid consideration. But in many it is not. For though an act may not be beneficial to anyone (aside from the agent, who presumably wishes to perform it), it does not follow that it is hurtful to anyone. You would no doubt be benefited (though I am afraid not to any very great extent) if I assigned to you half my income; it does not follow that you would be harmed if I do not. Now it is in just these cases that there is not only not a coincidence between these two principles, but something of a conflict between them. For let us suppose that the consequences of A's doing x would be desirable; and let us also suppose that the consequences of his not doing x would (on the whole) not be undesirable. Then it follows from this last statement that A has the right not to do x, if he so chooses, and this conclusion conflicts with, and, I should say, outweighs, the conclusion that A ought to do x, derived from the obverse of the principle of consequences.

Let us now consider the obverse principle of consequences in relation to the generalization argument. Suppose that the consequences of A's doing x would be desirable. Does it follow that A ought to do x? There are at least two possibilities here. Suppose (1) that the consequences of no one's doing x would be undesirable. Then it follows that A ought to do x, but this follows from this application of the generalization argument, which implies that everyone (within the scope of the argument) ought to do x, and not from the obverse of the principle of consequences. On the other hand, suppose (2) that the consequences of everyone's doing x would be undesirable. Then it follows that no one ought to do x, without a reason; and this conclusion conflicts with that obtained from the obverse principle. One might have such a reason. But, as I have already argued, such a reason is not provided by the mere fact that the consequences of one's doing x would be desirable. It would have to be shown, in addition, that one's circumstances differ from those of others in some other respect than this.

So much, then, at least for the present, for the obverse of the principle of consequences. I do not think that any one of the arguments I have used against it is conclusive by itself. But taken together they have a cumulative force that I regard as considerable. And at least I may have succeeded in throwing some doubt upon it. If I have, then, though this will not have shown the obverse of the generalization argument to be unsound, it will have removed one of its means of support. . . .

Many other topics might be introduced here—topics such as rights, duties to self, the existence of absolute moral rules, the possibility of conflict between a principle of beneficence or utility and a principle of justice. Instead, we elect to present an interesting theory of obligation recently advanced by G. J. Warnock. It is interesting partly because he begins with a teleological view of the object or function of morality (much like that of Protagoras) and yet comes out with a nonutilitarian normative ethics that recognizes four moral "virtues" and four corresponding "principles." According to him, the general object of morality is to contribute to the betterment of the human predicament by seeking to countervail our limited sympathies for others and their potentially damaging effects. From this hypothesis he then derives his normative principles.

As you read this, you might look for the similarities and the differences between Warnock's view and that of W. D. Ross. Also, ask yourself whether Warnock's argument for beneficence would be an adequate reply to Singer's claim that beneficence is not a duty.

MORAL VIRTUES AND PRINCIPLES

G. J. Warnock

. . . We are operating with the idea that, "good dispositions" being crucially important to abatement of the ills inherent in the human predicament, one might with reason regard as specifically *moral virtues* those which, not being essentially, or even potentially, exclusively self-profiting, would tend to countervail those particular ills liability to which is to be laid at the door of the limitedness of human sympathies. So, if we seek further light on what these good dispositions would be, we need now to consider in a little more detail what those particular ills are—that is, in what ways, in consequence of the limitedness of human sympathies, people are typically *liable* to act so as to worsen, or not to act so as to ameliorate, the predicament.

The first step on this path, at any rate, seems an easy one to take. If I am exclusively, or even predominantly, concerned with the satisfaction of my own wants, interests, or needs, or of those of some limited group such as my family, or friends, or tribe, or country, or class, with whose interests and ends I am naturally disposed to sympathize, then I,

From The Object of Morality (London: Methuen & Co., Ltd., 1971). Reprinted by permission of the author and publisher.

other members of that group, or the group as a whole, may be naturally prone to act directly to the detriment of other persons, non-members of the group, or of other groups. I may be inclined, from competitiveness or mere indifference or even active malevolence, to do positive harm to others, whether in the form of actual injury to them, or of frustration and obstruction of the satisfaction of their wants, interests, and needs. There is here, that is to say, a liability to act simply *maleficently*—harmfully, damagingly—to others, quite directly, either out of sheer unconcern with the damage so inflicted, or even out of a positive taste for the infliction of damage on persons or groups outside the circle of one's sympathies. That being so, it can scarcely seem controversial to say that *one* of the "good dispositions" we are in search of will be the disposition to abstain from (deliberate, unjustified) maleficence. Of course, if we nominate this disposition as one of the moral virtues, it may reasonably be remarked that it is not, in a sense, very much of a virtue; a disposition, that is to say, not to act deliberately maleficently towards other persons, from sheer unconcern for or active malevolence towards them, is, one may hopefully suppose, just normally to be expected in normal persons, who accordingly come up for commendation on this account only if their non-maleficence is exceptional in degree, or maintained in the face of exceptional temptation, or provocation, or difficulty. However, the propensity *not* to act injuriously towards others whenever one has, or might have, some "natural" inclination to do so, while perhaps not specially creditable in ordinary circumstances, is still very clearly of fundamental importance; for it is obvious what a gangster's world we should find ourselves in without it —and indeed do find ourselves in, when and so far as this disposition is absent.

The next step seems also, in general terms, scarcely more problematic. If we need, and if humans in general do not just naturally, regularly, and reliably have, the disposition of non-maleficence, just the same can plainly be said of the disposition towards positive beneficence. The limitedness of sympathies tends often to make it not just natural to interest oneself directly in another's good; there is need, then, for cultivation of the disposition to do so, which will very often take the particular form of readiness to give *help* to others in their activities. It seems reasonable to hold, and indeed practically impossible not to hold, that responsibility for pursuit of an individual's good is primarily his own—partly for the reason that it is primarily for him to say (though of course he cannot say infallibly) what that good is, and partly for the plain, practical reason that, in normal circumstances, if everyone embroils himself persistently, however well-meaningly, in other people's concerns rather than his own, a considerable measure of chaos and cross-purposes is likely to ensue. There are, however, many ends a person may have which cannot be secured by his own efforts alone. There are common ends, to be ensured only by the co-operation of many. There are some persons who have particular claims upon the beneficence of particular other persons. And there are some persons who, though perhaps without any special claims, should be helped because their need of help is exceptionally great, or their ability to help themselves exceptionally restricted. Not much more than this could be said in quite general terms. People and societies clearly differ a good deal, for a variety of reasons, in their assessment of the proportion of time, talents, efforts, and resources that an individual should devote to ends and interests other than his own; moreover, what is required in this way, what there is scope for, depends very much on the organization and institutions of particular societies. How far, for instance, there is need and room for private charity will depend on the extent to which public provision is made for the relief of indigence. But it is worth remarking, I think, that disagreement on this issue is often disagreement on the facts, at least in part. It was once held, notoriously, that it is *in fact* most advantageous for everybody that each, by and large, should pursue and promote his own interest single-mindedly; and though this thesis no doubt was often disingenuously asserted by those who fancied their chances in the envisaged free-for-all, and indeed is certainly not true without qualification, it is still, I suppose, a question of fact, and an unsettled question, in what ways and to what extent it needs to be qualified. In any case we are not attempting to settle here exactly what, in one case or another, the proper exercise of this virtue would actually consist in; what here matters, and what in general terms seems scarcely disputable, is that, along with non-maleficence, it *is* a virtue.

What else? Well, so far we have laid at the door of "limited sympathies," and accordingly have affirmed the need to countervail, the inclination to act damagingly to others towards whom one is not "naturally" sympathetic, and not to act beneficently when such action is needed or claimed. I believe that we should now add, as an independent requirement, the disposition not to *discriminate*, as surely most humans have some natural propensity to do, to the disadvantage of those outside the limited circle of one's natural concern. If, for instance, twenty people have a claim upon, or are substantially in need of, some service or benefit that I can provide, it seems not enough merely to say that I should not refuse it; it must be added that I should not help or benefit some of them *less* merely because, for instance, I may happen to like them less, or be less well-disposed towards them. The general name for this good disposition is, I take it, fairness. Of course it is commonly supposed, and indeed it would be unrealistically inhuman not to suppose, that actual sympathies and natural ties quite often justify discriminatory treatment; nevertheless, it must be observed that these should issue in discriminatory treatment only when, as is not always the case, they do actually justify it. Once again it would be inappropriate and probably quite unprofitable to try here to specify in any detail what, in this case or that, the exercise of this good disposition would actually consist in; what matters here is merely the very general proposition that, as an essential corrective to the arbitrariness and inequality and depriva- tion liable otherwise to result from the haphazard incidence of limited sympathies, it surely *is* a "good disposition" to be ready, on appropriate occasions, to recognize the need for or claims to good, or to relief from ill, of those in whose good or ill one may have no natural concern whatever. And we may add that the importance of this virtue of fairness tends, evidently but interestingly, to increase with the increase of scope and occasions for its exercise. For very many people, after all, their power to help or harm others is actually so limited as probably to be confined, on most occasions, to persons who may well be within the circle of their natural concern; but as such power increases, it is increasingly likely to expand its scope over persons to whom one may personally be wholly indifferent, or even of whom one may know nothing at all. This is to say, surely truly, that the virtue of fairness—or, more formally, justice— is a more important virtue in, for instance, political rulers, judicial func- tionaries, commanders of armies, heads of institutions, and so on, than it is in the case of relatively obscure private persons, whose circum- stances may confront them with relatively little occasion to exercise it.

Then one more thing. If we consider the situation of a person, some- what prone by nature to an exclusive concern with his own, or with some limited range of, interests and needs and wants, living among other persons more or less similarly constituted, we see that there is one device in particular, very often remarkably easy to employ, by which he may be naturally more or less inclined to, so to speak, carve out his egoistical way to his own, and if necessary at the expense of other, ends; and that is *deception*. It is possible for a person, and often very easy, by doing things, and especially in the form of saying things, to lead other persons to the belief that this or that is the case; and one of the simplest and most seductive ways of manipulating and manœuvring other persons for the sake of one's own ends is that of thus operating self-interestedly upon their beliefs. Clearly this is not, necessarily, di- rectly damaging. We all hold from time to time an immense range and variety of false beliefs, and very often are none the worse for doing so; we are the worse for it only if, as is often not the case, our false belief leads or partly leads us actually to act to our detriment in some way. Thus, I do not necessarily do you any harm at all if, by deed or word, I induce you to believe what is not in fact the case; I may even do you good, possibly by way, for example, of consolation or flattery. Neverthe-less, though deception is thus not necessarily directly damaging, it is easy to see how crucially important it is that the natural inclination to have recourse to it should be counteracted. It is, one might say, not the implanting of false beliefs that is damaging, but rather the generation of the suspicion that they may be being implanted. For this undermines trust; and, to the extent that trust is undermined, all co-operative undertak-ings, in which what one person can do or has reason to do is dependent on what others have done, are doing, or are going to do, must tend to break down. I cannot reasonably be expected to go over the edge of a cliff on a rope, for however vital an object, if I cannot trust you to keep hold of the other end of it; there is no sense in my asking you for your opinion on some point, if I do not suppose that your answer will actually express your opinion. (Verbal communication is doubtless the most im-portant of all our co-operative undertakings.) The crucial difficulty is precisely, I think, that deception is so easy. Deliberately saying, for in-stance, what I do not believe to be true is just as easy as saying what I do believe to be true, and may not be discriminable from it by even the most practised and expert of observers; thus, uncertainty as to the cre-dentials of *any* of my performances in this respect is inherently liable to infect *all* my performances—there are, so to speak, no "natural signs," or there may be none, by which the untrustworthy can be distinguished from the veracious, so that, if any may be deceptive, all may be. Nor, obviously, would it be any use merely to devise some special formula for the purpose of explicitly signalling non-deceptive performance; for, if the performance may be deceptive, so also might be the employment of any such formula—it is easy to say "I really mean it," not really mean-ing it, and hence to say "I really mean it" without thereby securing be-lief. Even *looking* sincere and ingenuous, though perhaps slightly more difficult than simply saying that one is, is an art that can be learned. In practice, of course, though there may be very few persons indeed whom we take to be non-deceptive on all occasions, we do manage, and rightly, to trust quite a lot of the people quite a lot of the time; but this depends on the supposition that, while sometimes they may have special reasons, which with luck and experience and judgement we may come to under-stand, for resorting to deceptive performance on some occasions, they do not do so simply *whenever* it suits their book. If one could not make even this milder supposition, then co-operative involvement among per-sons would become, if not impossible, at any rate more or less useless and unreasonable—like political agreements between bourgeois poli-ticians and Marxists.

Parenthetically, I should like to mention here, though not to discuss, the curious case, which does also occur, of persons who, while seldom or perhaps even never deliberately speaking or acting, to suit their book, contrary to their real beliefs, seem to have the knack of so tailoring their beliefs as to suit their book. This singular propensity is, in a way, even more damaging than that of the common-or-garden liar; it is compatible, for one thing, with extreme self-righteousness; but, more importantly, while the liar for his own ends misrepresents the way things are, he may perfectly retain the capacity to realize how they are, and may thus be thought to be, in a sense, more redeemable than one whose capacity to see straight is itself corrupted. But we impinge here on self-deception, a complex topic.

We suggest, then, that, in the general context of the human predicament, there are these four (at least) distinguishable damaging, or non-ameliorative, types of propensity which tend naturally to emanate directly from "limited sympathies"—those of maleficence, non-beneficence, unfairness, and deception. If now we apply the supposition that the "object" of morality is to make the predicament less grim than, in a quasi-Hobbesian state of nature, it seems inherently liable to be, and to do so specifically by seeking to countervail the deleterious liabilities inherent in "limited sympathies," we seem to be led to four (at least) general types of good disposition as those needed to countervail the above-mentioned four types of propensity; and these dispositions will be, somewhat crudely named, those of non-maleficence, fairness, beneficence, and non-deception. We venture the hypothesis that these (at least) are fundamental *moral virtues*.

But we can now manipulate this conclusion a little. If it were agreed that we have here, in these "good dispositions," four moral virtues, it could scarcely be contentious to derive from this the proposition that we have here, by the same token, four fundamental moral *standards*, or moral *principles*. To have and to display, say, the moral virtue of non-deception could be said to be to regulate one's conduct in conformity to a *principle* of non-deception, or to refer to that as to a *standard* in one's practical decisions. But such a principle would be a principle of judgement as well as of decision. That is, if I accept a principle of non-deception, I may judge others to be morally condemnable in so far as (without excuse) their acts constitute breaches of it, or morally praiseworthy in so far as they (laudably) comply with it in practice. And thus we can say what a "moral reason" is. Namely, it is a consideration, about some person, or some person's character, or some specimen of actual or possible conduct, which tends to establish in the subject concerned conformity or conflict with a moral principle. That your act would inflict wanton damage on some other person would be a "moral reason" for judging that—at least "from the moral point of view"—you ought not so to act, since it tends to establish that your act would be in conflict with the moral principle of non-maleficence, or, to put just the same point in a different way, would be inconsistent with exercise of the moral virtue of non-maleficence. Moral "pros and cons" . . . will be those considerations, perhaps very complex and very numerous, concerning some particular case that comes up for judgement, which indicate respectively conformity to or conflict with some one or more moral principles.

. . . it seems to me that the "principles" we have sketchily elicited, and as to which we offer the hypothesis that they are basic *moral* principles, have to be accepted as independent principles, not reducible either to one another or to anything else. There is indeed, if I am right, some bond of union between them, as well as a very manifest *rationale* behind them—something, that is, that makes it possible coherently to explain why it is that they are grouped together as *moral* principles, and why compliance with them should constitute moral *virtue;* the suggestion is, namely, that they are alike in the respect that their voluntary recognition would tend to counteract the maleficent liabilities of limited sympathies, and in *that* way to work towards amelioration of the human predicament. However, though alike in this, they remain independent. For there is not *one* way in which beings of limited sympathies are inherently liable to act to each other's detriment, but *several* ways, and thus several independent "good dispositions" to be desiderated. This emerges, I think, reasonably clearly from what has been said. It would be just possible, I suppose, though extremely artificial, to class non-maleficence as a sub-species of beneficence; but it seems to me both more natural and more explicit to regard the principle of abstaining from avoidable and unjustified damage as *different* from that of doing solicited or unsolicited good. Abstaining from theft is not a special kind of philanthropy. Fairness, again, is a *different* requirement from that of non-maleficence, or of beneficence; it may often be the case that a maleficent act is unfair, but that is to say about it two things, not one thing; and even if, as may not always be the case, some act of fairness is also an act of beneficence, still the reason for judging it to be the first will not be the same as that for judging it to be the second. An act of deception, as we said before, is not necessarily maleficent; and again, if I benefit you in acting non-deceptively, to show that I do benefit you is a quite different matter from showing that I do not deceive you—even when these go together, they are not the same. To tell you the truth to the best of my ability is not at all the same thing as to tell you what I judge it would be of benefit to you to be told. It has been held that deception is always a breach of the principle of justice, but this again seems to me, though just possible, undesirably artificial; deception, I would think, is appropriately classed as unjust only if the victim has some sort of *special* claim, not merely that which any person has on any other person whatever, not to be deceived. It is perhaps specifically unfair for me to lie to you when you have trustingly favoured me with your confidence; but it is not in the same way *unfair* of me to deceive a total stranger.

There are two major reasons, I believe, why recognition of this fact of independence is of considerable importance. The first is theoretical. Philosophers, professionally in pursuit of systematic unity, and feeling (rightly in my view) that behind morality there is to be discerned an—in some sense—single *rationale*, seem often to have been taken with the idea that perhaps there is really just *one* fundamental moral principle. This seems to be an error. It may be that there is one, very general, end in view; but there is not, as one might put it, just one means to that end. And the second point is practical, or anyway less purely theoretical; it is that what I take to be the plurality and independence of moral principles implies that "moral reasons" may conflict. We are inveterately liable in any case to be perplexed in practice by conflicting considerations; even if, for instance, we are charged with the single requirement of selecting for an appointment the best instructor in philosophy, the circumstance of some applicant's exceptional philosophical ability may conflict with his obvious lack of interest in teaching, or inability to express himself comprehensibly to the student mind. Or again, an arbitrator's decision that would do justice to the claims of one party may sometimes, by exactly the same standard, imply injustice to the claims of another. But if, in morality, there are anyway independent principles, there is the obvious possibility that what conformity with one would require would involve conflict with another; there may, that is, be clear moral pros *and* cons in the very same case; and if that is so, it seems to me quite impossible to exclude the possibility that predicaments may arise which are, literally, morally insoluble. One would indeed wish to avoid this conclusion if possible, but I do not myself see how this possibility of genuine insolubility is to be excluded. It is clear that moral principles *may* point in opposite directions and I can discern no ground on which one could pronounce *in general* which, in such a case, is to predominate over another. This may indeed be possible in special cases. One may have, as a judge perhaps, a *special* commitment to justice, as a scholar to truth, or as a friend to beneficence. But still, if there is independence, there may be conflict; and if there may be conflict, there may be irresoluble perplexity. I do not know, however, that one need be particularly appalled by this conclusion; for even if there exists the possibility of irresoluble perplexity, I know of no reason for supposing, in the Existentialist manner, that irresoluble perplexity is *typical* of moral decision, or that the typical terminal process in morals is that of arbitrary choice. And one may add that even if, like the simple Utilitarian, one held that there was only one moral principle really, it would still have to be admitted that cases might arise in which considerations, weighed by that one principle alone, might point, with exactly equal force, in opposite directions. Thus reduction to a single principle, even if it were possible, would not wholly get us out of this difficulty, so far as it is one. . . .

3.5

The Ethics of Love

The Christian ethics of love (or agapism) is sometimes presented as an alternative to all of the normative theories so far discussed. Partly for this reason, and partly because it has been so important in the ethics of the Christian world—more important than any other ethical theory, including even utilitarianism, which probably grew out of it—we believe it desirable to include an exposition and discussion of it here.

The Christian ethics of love has its source in the following words of Jesus, though these were anticipated in the Old Testament.

> You shall love the Lord your God with your heart, and with all your soul, and with all your mind. This is the great and first commandment. And a second is like it, You shall love your neighbor as yourself. On these two commandments depend all the law and the prophets. [Matthew 22:37–40]

The idea is not solely Christian or Judeo-Christian, however, as is shown by the following quotation from the Chinese thinker, Mo Ti (c. 470–c. 391 B.C.; also called Mo Tzu):

> The question then is: what is the Will of Heaven like? The answer is: to love all men everywhere alike.[1]

It must also be pointed out that not all Christian ethics take the form of a pure ethics of love; for instance, the ethics of St. Thomas Aquinas or Joseph Butler does not. What the ethics of love says is that ultimately there is one and

---

[1] Mo Ti in E. R. Hughes, *Chinese Philosophy in Classical Times* (London: J. M. Dent & Sons, Ltd., 1942), p. 48.

only one moral command, obligation, or virtue: to love God and/or mankind. All other commands, obligations, or virtues are derived from this one. This is the position of the Protestant theologian Emil Brunner, at least in the selection reproduced here. In this selection he especially attacks "legalism" in ethics and comes close to espousing a kind of situational ethics or act-agapism, even though he rejects extreme "antinomianism" and has a place for rules and prohibitions. He also, incidentally, seems to subscribe to a divine command theory of right and wrong, which raises the question whether his basic principle is to obey God or to love Him (and man). Presumably, however, he thinks these two principles come to the same thing in practice if not in theory. It should also be observed that Brunner uses the term "good" in more than one sense. In some places it is clearer if one substitutes "right" for "good," for instance, when he says, "The Good is simply what God wills that we should do."

One question which should be considered in connection with Brunner's essay is: What is the relationship between the ethics of love and the divine command theory discussed in Section 2:4?

THE DIVINE IMPERATIVE

Emil Brunner

. . . the Christian conception of the Good differs from every other conception of the Good at this very point: that it cannot be defined in terms of principle at all.

Whatever can be defined in accordance with a principle—whether it be the principle of pleasure or the principle of duty—is legalistic. This means that it is possible—by the use of this principle—to pre-determine "the right" down to the smallest detail of conduct. We have already seen how this legalistic spirit corrupts the true conception of the Good from its very roots. The Christian moralist and the extreme individualist are at one in their emphatic rejection of legalistic conduct; they join hands, as it were, in face of the whole host of legalistic moralists; they are convinced that conduct which is regulated by abstract principles can never be good. But equally sternly the Christian moralist rejects the individualistic doctrine of freedom, according to which there is no longer any difference between "right" and "wrong." Rather, in the Christian view, that alone is "good" which is free from all caprice, which takes place in unconditional obedience. There is no Good save obedient behaviour, save the obedient will. But this obedience is rendered not to a law or a principle which can be known beforehand, but only to the free, sovereign will of God. The Good consists in always doing what God wills at any particular moment.

This statement makes it clear that for us the will of God cannot be summed up under any principle, that it is not at our disposal, but that so far as we are concerned the will of God is absolutely free. The Christian is therefore "a free lord over all things," [1] because he stands directly under the personal orders of the free Sovereign God. This is why genuine "Christian conduct"—if we may use this idea as an illustration— is so unaccountable, so unwelcome to the moral rigorist and to the hedonist alike. The moral rigorist regards the Christian as a hedonist, and the hedonist regards him as a rigorist. In reality, the Christian is neither, yet he is also something of both, since he is indeed absolutely *bound* and obedient, but, since he is bound to the *free* loving will of God, he is himself free from all transparent bondage to principles or to legalism. Above all it is important to recognize that even love is not a principle of this kind, neither the love which God Himself *has,* nor the love which He *requires.* Only God Himself defines love in His action. We, for our part, do not know what God is, nor do we know what *love* is, unless we learn to know God in His action, in faith. To be in this His Love, is the Commandment. Every attempt to conceive love as a principle leads to this result: it becomes distorted, either in the rigoristic, legalistic sense, or in the hedonistic sense. Man only knows what the love of God is when he sees the way in which God acts, and he only knows how he himself ought to love by allowing himself to be drawn by faith into this activity of God. . . .

The Good consists simply and solely in the fact that man receives and deliberately accepts his life as a gift from God, as life dependent on "grace," as the state of "being justified" because it has been granted as a gift, as "justification by faith." Only thus can we know the Will of God, that is, in this revelation of Himself in which He manifests Himself as disinterested, generous Love. . . .

He claims us for *His* love, not for an *idea* of love—and not for a conception of the divine love which can be gained from merely reading the Bible. He claims us for His present, living activity of love, which can only be, and must always remain, His work. Therefore we can never know beforehand what God will require. God's command can only be perceived at the actual moment of hearing it. It would denote a breaking away from obedience if we were to think of the Divine Command as one

---

[1] Luther: *Of the Freedom of a Christian Man (Von der Freiheit eines Christenmenschen).*

which had been enacted once for all, to be interpreted by us in particular instances. To take this life would mean reverting to the legalistic distortion of His love. Love would then have become a "principle." The *free* love of God requires us to remain *free*, that we may be freely at His disposal. *You* cannot say what it means to love here and now; *He* alone can tell you what this means for you at this moment.

The Good is simply what *God* wills that we should do, not that which we would do on the basis of a principle of love. God wills to do something quite definite and particular through us, here and now, something which no other person could do at any other time. Just as the commandment of love is absolutely universal so also it is absolutely individual. But just as it is absolutely individual so also it is absolutely devoid of all caprice. "I will guide thee with Mine eye." [2] No one can experience this "moment" save I myself. The Divine Command is made known to us "in the secret place." Therefore it is impossible for us to know it beforehand; to wish to know it beforehand—legalism—is an infringement of the divine honour. The fact that the holiness of God must be remembered when we dwell on His love means that we cannot have His love at our disposal, that it cannot ever be perceived as a universal principle, but only in the act in which He speaks to us Himself; even in His love He remains our *Master* and Lord. But He is our "Lord" in the sense that He tells us Himself what it means to "love," here and now. . . .

The abstract legalistic system of ethics, because ideas have no connexion with life, can only judge this connexion of the moral element with reward and punishment as heteronomy, as the perversion of the moral endeavour. "We ought to do the Good for the sake of the Good." It does not perceive that behind this phrase, "for the sake of the Good," there lies concealed, "for My sake." And it does not understand that the Good is done for the sake of the Good when it is done for the sake of God, in obedience to the Divine Command. We ought to obey God because He commands it, not because obedience means happiness and disobedience means unhappiness. Faith would not be faith, obedience would not be obedience, if things were otherwise. But obedience would not be obedience towards *God*, did we not know that His Command means life and His prohibition death. The primary concern is not that which refers to my Ego, to my life; no, the primary concern is this: that it is God's will, the will of Him to whom my life belongs. But that which refers to *me*, that which refers to *my* life, is the necessary second element for it concerns the will of Him who Himself is life—even *my* life. Obedience would be impure if this second element were made the first.

---

[2] Psalm xxxii. 8.

But it would be unreal, and indeed impossible, if this second element, as the second, were not combined with the first. We cannot do anything good which has no significance for life, and we cannot avoid anything evil, unless at the same time we know it to be harmful. It is not the question whether all morality is not mingled with self-interest—without self-interest nothing would concern us at all—but the question is this: is this self-interest regarded as founded in God or in myself? To do the Good for the sake of the Good is only a pale reflection of the genuine Good; to do the Good for the sake of God means to do the Good not because my moral dignity requires it, but because it is that which is commanded by God. . . .

To *love* a human being means to accept his existence, as it is given to me by God, and thus to love him *as he is*. For only if I love him thus, that is, as this particular sinful person, do I love *him*. For this is what he really is. Otherwise I love an idea—and in the last resort this means that I am merely loving myself. I can only love a person by allowing myself to be disturbed by him as he is, and wherever he may come into contact with me, in order that I may make his claim on life my own— and especially in that which does not coincide with my own desires. But if we love like this how can we forget that this our fellow-man is not what he ought to be, how can we forget what a goal has been made known even to him in Christ? . . . Therefore to include him within the love of Christ—and this alone is what it means to love truly—also means first of all to accept him, and then to try to lead him towards the goal he has not yet seen.

But even so the concrete situation has not been yet taken into account. Indeed "man," or "I, as man," does not really exist; rather my fellow-man meets me as the member of an order—in his particular "class" and "calling," just as I likewise meet him as the member of an order in my "class" and "calling." It is of course true that I am to meet him as my "Brother Man," just as if there were no "class" or "calling"; but I would not do any real service either to him or to the others to whom I am indebted, were I to ignore what the order in which we meet each other requires of us. I must render to him not only that which he requires, but also that which is in accordance with his "situation," which is always (although as it were in a reflection) *my* situation too. So far as motive is concerned the only valid reason for my interest in him is the fact that he is my brother. But *how* this is to be realized is determined by the concrete situation in which I have to deal with him in accordance with this actual situation, even when such action may simply consist in the fact that his situation must be altered. It is legalistic, abstract, Utopian idealism to leave out this concrete situation; it means giving no heed to the command of the Creator. But, on the other hand, it is lazy worldliness to do merely what is required by the claims of our order, without trying to attack all that is contrary to God within this situation with the whole energy of love.

. . . the Divine Command is *one* and one alone, namely, to acknowledge this God as the God who *is,* to know that He is *our* God; it is the "first commandment": "I am the Lord thy God, thou shalt have none other Gods but Me." That is: to believe in God as the only Centre, as the Origin and End of our life, upon whose love and grace alone our life is based, and in which it is made complete, to fear Him and to love Him. The love which God commands is the love which He Himself is and which He gives. To love Him truly means to let oneself be loved by Him; this is faith, and it is the fulfilment of the first Commandment.

We are never bidden to do anything else. "Love is the fulfilling of the law." [3] From this point of view this obedience-of-faith-in-love alone is the "moral"; everything else—from the ethical point of view—is technique, that is, the search for, and the use of, means which make this love real. The daring saying of Augustine: *Dilige et fac quod vis* [love and do as you please] simply means that love is the fulfilling of the law. But directly this Command becomes law it becomes a judgment on all our action. For which of us loves as God loves? The commandment of love cannot be realized as law, but only in faith in the love into which we are drawn and in which we are forgiven. We can love only "through the Holy Spirit," only when *God Himself* takes possession of us, by His love, and does *His* work through us.

"And the other is like unto it: Thou shalt love thy neighbour as thyself." [4] The love of God includes the love of man; therefore to be laid hold of by His will, to be freely obedient to His will, means to love our neighbour. There are no "duties towards God" and "duties towards man." There is only the *one* "duty": to love God. And this one duty of loving God is itself the other duty of loving our neighbour. The love of God, His surrender of Himself to man, comes to meet us in the Man Jesus. To love man means to be united to him in love. This alone is the Good. That mystical love of God which is severed from the love of man is something totally different, since it is not based upon the revelation of God in the man Jesus. God does not will to draw any love exclusively to Himself; He wills that we should love Him "in our neighbour."

Where this takes place, God's will is fulfilled—whatever else may happen. But this love is only possible where we do not take it for granted that we know what we owe our neighbour; this kind of love is only possible when we accept our "neighbour" as he is, in the concrete claims

[3] Rom. xiii. 10.
[4] Matt. xxii. 39.

laid upon us by the very fact of his existence, when we accept him, in fact, as given to us by God, when we look at him—in the language of Luther—as the "mask" of God, as one in whom God wills to come into touch with us. Love means the acceptance of love's "bonds," the state of "thraldom" to another. Just as we are held captive by the free, sovereign will of God through the Command of love, and have no right to transform the Command into a law, an independent principle, so also we are united to our neighbour by the Command of love, which excludes all legalistic general rules and every attempt to stereotype human relationships. Thus where our neighbour is concerned there are no isolated "duties," but only the *one* duty—to do to him what the love of God wills should be done to him here and now; thus to fulfil the claim which our neighbour has on us, as he is, here and now. It is love which does not steal, does not kill, does not lie, does not commit adultery, but does its best for its neighbour.

This is why God is always bidding us do some particular thing, something which cannot be done at any other time, something quite new. God's Command does not vary in *intention,* but it varies in *content,* according to the conditions with which it deals. The error of casuistry does not lie in the fact that it indicates the infinite variety of forms which the Command of love may assume; its error consists in deducing particular laws from a universal law in ever greater and more scrupulous detail; thus it is wrong because it turns the Divine Command into a Law, and then inevitably into the sum-total of all laws. Casuistry tries to imprison concrete life within a net of "cases" as though all could be arranged beforehand, and thinks it can do this by means of an exposition of the law which is modelled on the lines of a legal code, applied in a similar manner through derivation from a supreme principle. Love, however, is free from all this predefinition, for it means free for God, "relaxed as the arrow in the hunter's bow" (Thurneysen), in the Hand of God, and therefore free for our real neighbour. Love is "occasionalist." She does not know the Good beforehand—and by this very fact she is bound both to God Himself and to her actual neighbour.

The particular decision is not anticipated; it cannot be "looked up" in the ethical law-book. The whole responsibility rests upon the individual himself; this kind of love alone is free from heteronomy, as well as from the self-glorification of autonomy. Therefore in its external appearance it is "opportunistic," "lacking principles," while it too, and it alone, is free from all caprice. Each of its decisions is a "discovery," but each of such "discoveries"—if this love is true and real—is "something given." It is the end of the law, as it is also its fulfilment.

What, then, is the meaning and the function of the individual "commandments" in the Bible? whether those of the Decalogue or of the

Sermon on the Mount? Why is not the command of love sufficient? Why, instead of this, are we forbidden to kill, to steal, to commit adultery, and why are we told that even the lustful glance is adultery? This question requires a twofold answer. Firstly, the Commandments form part of the revelation of the Divine Will. We can only recognize God's will here and now . . . on the basis of the previous historical revelation. "It stands written." The non-legalistic character, the "occasionalism" of love ought never to be understood in the sense of fanaticism. We only know the will of God, here and now, on the basis of His revelation in the Scriptures, in Jesus Christ. The Commandments also belong to this revelation. They are witnesses to His revelation, as is everything in the Scriptures, but as such they are themselves revelation, indirectly, that is, when the Spirit quickens the "letter" into life. In His commandments, as in His promises, God shows us who He is and what He wills. . . .

Secondly, when we ask about the relation of these Commandments to the one Divine Command, we see that they are authentic "expositions" of the One Command. It is part of condescension of God towards our weakness that He does not merely tell us to do *one* thing, but a variety of things. "The Commandments" are the God-given examples of what His will and His love mean in the concrete situations of life. The Commandments—both of the Decalogue and of the Sermon on the Mount— are God-given paradigms of love, in which God wills that we should learn to practise what we have learned of the command to love.

Each of these commandments does two things: it makes the one Command concrete, and it also abstracts from concrete reality. It stands, so to speak, in the centre between the infinitely varied reality of life and the unity of the divine will of love. It shows us what love would mean in this or that more or less "special" but still general case, and it commands us to do this very thing. . . .

Therefore God only demands one thing: that we should live in His love. In His prophetic message Jesus summons men to "Love!" The apostolic exhortation, which points back to the gift of God in Christ, summons us to "Live in love." Or, still more plainly: to "*Remain* in love." For the apostolic exhortation is addressed to believers, that is, to those who are already in the love of God. This commandment transcends the contrast between mysticism and morality. It is the summons to remain within the giving of God, to return to Him again and again as the origin of all power to be good, or to do good. There are no "other virtues" alongside of the life of love. . . . Each virtue, one might say, is a particular way in which the person who lives in love takes the other into account, and "realizes" him as "Thou."

Only thus is the variety of the virtues to be understood aright. Truthfulness, for instance, is the special way of living in love, or of living in relation with others, which perceives or realizes the claim of the other man on my knowledge of the truth. Peaceableness is a particular way of living in relation with others in which I perceive the claim of the "Thou" for undisturbed fellowship with me. All these virtues are only really conceived in a personally actual, non-substantial manner, when they are conceived in terms of awareness of the claims of others, as a readiness to re-act, to respond to a definite call. Thus they are all *negative*, not positive, in character. They consist in having one's mind and heart open in a certain direction, but this does not imply that they possess positive content. All the virtues consist in "being ready." In this respect, too, the virtues cannot be defined in reply to the question *How?* but in reply to the question *Where?* The very fact that I—because I am living in love—am not self-centred and isolated, but am in touch with others, constitutes virtue in its varying forms. . . .

3.6

"None of the Above"

There are, of course, other ethical theories that are opposed to all of the theories covered so far, including the ethics of love. One of the most famous and radical of these is the view of Friedrich Nietzsche (1844–1900), who rejects all of the other views studied, except perhaps ethical egoism. We conclude this chapter with some selections from his works.

Among the questions raised by these selections are the following: Suppose Nietzsche is correct about the "genealogy" or origin of morals. Would it follow from this that people should stop being moral? What exactly would follow? What do you think of Nietzsche's claim in *Beyond Good and Evil* that "suffering . . . has produced all the elevations of humanity hitherto"? What do you think he means by his statement that "there is a distinction of rank between man and man"? Do you agree? Try to state Nietzsche's distinction between "master-morality" and "slave-morality" as clearly as you can. Finally, what sense do you make of his remark in the last paragraph that "there are altogether no moral facts"?

CRITIQUE OF MORALITY

Friedrich Nietzsche

THE GENEALOGY OF MORALS
[Preface, paragraphs 6 and 7] *

. . . Let us articulate that new claim: we need a critique of all moral values; the intrinsic worth of these values must, first of all, be called in question. . . . Nobody, up to now, has doubted that the "good" man represents a higher value than the "evil," in terms of promoting and benefiting mankind generally, even taking the long view. But suppose the exact opposite were true. What if the "good" man represents not merely a retrogression but even a danger, a temptation, a narcotic drug enabling the present to live at the expense of the future? More comfortable, less hazardous, perhaps, but also baser, more petty—so that morality itself would be responsible for man, as a species, failing to reach the peak of magnificence of which he is capable? What if morality should turn out to be the danger of dangers? . . .

Suffice it to say that ever since that vista opened before me I have been on the lookout for learned, bold and industrious comrades in arms —I am still looking. The object is to explore the huge, distant and thoroughly hidden country of morality, morality as it has actually existed and actually been lived, with new questions in mind and with fresh eyes. Is not this tantamount to saying that that country must be discovered anew? . . .

[First essay, paragraph 14] †

Will any one look a little into—right into—the mystery of how *ideals* are *manufactured* in this world? Who has the courage to do it? Come! Here we have a vista opened into these grimy workshops. Wait just a moment, dear Mr. Inquisitive and Foolhardy; your eye must first grow accustomed to this false changing light—Yes! Enough! Now speak! What is happening below down yonder? Speak out! Tell what you see, man of the most dangerous curiosity—for now *I* am the listener.

---

* *From* The Genealogy of Morals, *trans. Francis Golffing (Garden City, N.Y.: Doubleday & Company, Inc., Anchor Books, 1956). Reprinted by permission of the publisher.*

† *From* The Genealogy of Morals, *trans. Horace B. Samuel, Vol. 13 of* The Complete Works of Friedrich Nietzsche, *General Editor, Oscar Levy (1909–1911). New York: Russell & Russell, 1964. Reprinted with the permission of George Allen & Unwin, Ltd. and Russell & Russell, Publishers.*

"I see nothing, I hear the more. It is a cautious, spiteful, gentle whispering and muttering together in all the corners and crannies. It seems to me that they are lying; a sugary softness adheres to every sound. Weakness is turned to *merit*, there is no doubt about it—it is just as you say."

Further!

"And the impotence which requites not, is turned to 'goodness,' craven baseness to meekness, submission to those whom one hates, to obedience (namely, obedience to one of whom they say that he ordered this submission—they call him God). The inoffensive character of the weak, the very cowardice in which he is rich, his standing at the door, his forced necessity of waiting, gain here fine names, such as 'patience,' which is also called 'virtue'; not being able to avenge one's self, is called not wishing to avenge one's self, perhaps even forgiveness (for *they* know not what they do—we alone know what they do). They also talk of the 'love of their enemies' and sweat thereby."

Further!

"They are miserable, there is no doubt about it, all these whisperers and counterfeiters in the corners, although they try to get warm by crouching close to each other, but they tell me that their misery is a favour and distinction given to them by God, just as one beats the dogs one likes best; that perhaps this misery is also a preparation, a probation, a training; that perhaps it is still more something which will one day be compensated and paid back with a tremendous interest in gold, nay in happiness. This they call 'Blessedness.'"

Further!

"They are now giving me to understand, that not only are they better men than the mighty, the lords of the earth, whose spittle they have got to lick (*not* out of fear, not at all out of fear! But because God ordains that one should honour all authority)—not only are they better men, but that they also have a 'better time,' at any rate, will one day have a 'better time.' But enough! Enough! I can endure it no longer. Bad air! Bad air! . . .

BEYOND GOOD AND EVIL
[*Paragraphs 225, 228, 259, and 260*] *

Whether it be hedonism, pessimism, utilitarianism or eudaemonism, all those modes of thinking which measure the worth of things accord-

* *From* Beyond Good and Evil, trans. H. Zimmern, Vol. 12 of The Complete Works of Friedrich Nietzsche, *General Editor, Oscar Levy (1909–1911). New York: Russell & Russell, 1964. Reprinted with the permission of George Allen & Unwin, Ltd. and Russell & Russell, Publishers.*

ing to *pleasure* and *pain,* that is, according to accompanying circumstances and secondary considerations, are plausible modes of thought and naïvetés, which every one conscious of creative powers and an artist's conscience will look down upon with scorn, though not without sympathy. Sympathy for *you!*—to be sure, that is not sympathy as you understand it: it is not sympathy for social "distress," for "society" with its sick and misfortuned, for the hereditarily vicious and defective who lie on the ground around us; still less is it sympathy for the grumbling, vexed, revolutionary slave-classes who strive after power—they call it "freedom." *Our* sympathy is a loftier and further-sighted sympathy:— we see how *man* dwarfs himself, how *you* dwarf him! and there are moments when we view *your* sympathy with an indescribable anguish, when we resist it,—when we regard your seriousness as more dangerous than any kind of levity. You want, if possible—and there is not a more foolish "if possible"—*to do away with suffering;* and we?—it really seems that *we* would rather have it increased and made worse than it has ever been! Well-being, as you understand it—is certainly not a goal; it seems to us an *end;* a condition which at once renders man ludicrous and contemptible—and makes his destruction *desirable!* The discipline of suffering, of *great* suffering—know ye not that it is only *this* discipline that has produced all the elevations of humanity hitherto? The tension of soul in misfortune which communicates to it its energy, its shuddering in view of rack and ruin, its inventiveness and bravery in undergoing, enduring, interpreting, and exploiting misfortune, and whatever depth, mystery, disguise, spirit, artifice or greatness has been bestowed upon the soul—has it not been bestowed through suffering, through the discipline of great suffering? In man *creature* and *creator* are united: in man there is not only matter, shred, excess, clay, mire, folly, chaos; but there is also the creator, the sculptor, the hardness of the hammer, the divinity of the spectator, and the seventh day—do ye understand this contrast? And that *your* sympathy for the "creature in man" applies to that which has to be fashioned, bruised, forged, stretched, roasted, annealed, refined—to that which must necessarily *suffer,* and *is meant* to suffer? And *our* sympathy—do ye not understand what our *reverse* sympathy applies to, when it resists your sympathy as the worst of all pampering and enervation?—So it is sympathy *against* sympathy!—But to repeat it once more, there are higher problems than the problems of pleasure and pain and sympathy; and all systems of philosophy which deal only with these are naïvetés. . . .

I hope to be forgiven for discovering that all moral philosophy hitherto has been tedious and has belonged to the soporific appliances—and that "virtue," in my opinion, has been *more* injured by the *tediousness* of its advocates than by anything else; at the same time, however, I would not wish to overlook their general usefulness. It is desirable that as few people as possible should reflect upon morals, and consequently it is *very* desirable that morals should not some day become interesting! But let us not be afraid! Things still remain today as they have always been: I see no one in Europe who has (or *discloses*) an idea of the fact that philosophising concerning morals might be conducted in a dangerous, captious, and ensnarling manner—that *calamity* might be involved therein. Observe, for example, the indefatigable, inevitable English utilitarians: how ponderously and respectably they stalk on . . . in the footsteps of Bentham. . . . No new thought, nothing of the nature of a finer turning or better expression of an old thought, not even a proper history of what has been previously thought on the subject: an *impossible* literature, taking it all in all, unless one knows how to leaven it with some mischief. . . . In the end, they all want *English* morality to be recognised as authoritative, inasmuch as mankind, or the "general utility," or "the happiness of the greatest number,"—no! the happiness of *England*, will be best served thereby. They would like, by all means, to convince themselves that the striving after *English* happiness, I mean after *comfort* and *fashion* (and in the highest instance, a seat in Parliament), is at the same time the true path of virtue; in fact, that in so far as there has been virtue in the world hitherto, it has just consisted in such striving. Not one of those ponderous, conscience-stricken herding-animals (who undertake to advocate the cause of egoism as conducive to the general welfare) wants to have any knowledge or inkling of the facts that the "general welfare" is no ideal, no goal, no notion that can be at all grasped, but is only a nostrum,—that what is fair to one *may not* be fair to another, that the requirement of one morality for all is really a detriment to higher men, in short, that there is a *distinction of rank* between man and man, and consequently between morality and morality. They are an unassuming and fundamentally mediocre species of men, these utilitarian Englishmen, and, as already remarked, in so far as they are tedious, one cannot think highly enough of their utility. . . .

To refrain mutually from injury, from violence, from exploitation, and put one's will on a par with that of others: this may result in a certain rough sense in good conduct among individuals when the necessary conditions are given (namely, the actual similarity of the individuals in amount of force and degree of worth, and their co-relation within one organisation). As soon, however, as one wished to take this principle more generally, and if possible even as *the fundamental principle of society*, it would immediately disclose what it really is—namely, a Will to the *denial* of life, a principle of dissolution and decay. Here one must think profoundly to the very basis and resist all sentimental weakness: life itself is *essentially* appropriation, injury, conquest of the strange and weak, suppression, severity, obtrusion of peculiar forms, incorporation, and at the least, putting it mildest, exploitation;—but why should one for ever use precisely these words on which for ages a disparaging purpose has been stamped? Even the organisation within which, as was previously supposed, the individuals treat each other as equal—it takes place in every healthy aristocracy—must itself, if it be a living and not a dying organisation, do all that towards other bodies, which the individuals within it refrain from doing to each other: it will have to be the incarnated Will to Power, it will endeavour to grow, to gain ground, attract to itself and acquire ascendency—not owing to any morality or immorality, but because it *lives*, and because life *is* precisely Will to Power. On no point, however, is the ordinary consciousness of Europeans more unwilling to be corrected than on this matter; people now rave everywhere, even under the guise of science, about coming conditions of society in which "the exploiting character" is to be absent:—that sounds to my ears as if they promised to invent a mode of life which should refrain from all organic functions. "Exploitation" does not belong to a depraved, or imperfect and primitive society: it belongs to the *nature* of the living being as a primary organic function; it is a consequence of the intrinsic Will to Power, which is precisely the Will to Life.—Granting that as a theory this is a novelty—as a reality it is the *fundamental fact* of all history: let us be so far honest towards ourselves!

In a tour through the many finer and coarser moralities which have hitherto prevailed or still prevail on the earth, I found certain traits recurring regularly together, and connected with one another, until finally two primary types revealed themselves to me, and a radical distinction was brought to light. There is *master-morality* and *slave-morality;*—I would at once add, however, that in all higher and mixed civilisations, there are also attempts at the reconciliation of the two moralities; but one finds still oftener the confusion and mutual misunderstanding of them, indeed, sometimes their close juxtaposition—even in the same man, within one soul. The distinctions of moral values have either originated in a ruling caste, pleasantly conscious of being different from the ruled—or among the ruled class, the slaves and dependents of all sorts. In the first case, when it is the rulers who determine the conception "good," it is the exalted, proud disposition which is regarded as the distinguishing feature, and that which determines the order of rank. The noble type of man separates from himself the beings in whom the opposite of this exalted, proud disposition displays itself: he despises them. Let it at once be noted that in this first kind of morality the antithesis "good" and "bad" means practically the same as "noble" and "despicable";—the antithesis "good" and *"evil"* is of a different origin. The cowardly, the timid, the insignificant, and those thinking merely of narrow utility are despised; moreover, also, the distrustful, with their constrained glances, the self-abasing, the dog-like kind of men who let themselves be abused, the mendicant flatterers, and above all the liars:—it is a fundamental belief of all aristocrats that the common people are untruthful. "We truthful ones"—the nobility in ancient Greece called themselves. It is obvious that everywhere the designations of moral value were at first applied to *men,* and were only derivatively and at a later period applied to actions; it is a gross mistake, therefore, when historians of morals start questions like, "Why have sympathetic actions been praised?" The noble type of man regards *himself* as a determiner of values; he does not require to be approved of; he passes the judgment: "What is injurious to me is injurious in itself"; he knows that it is he himself only who confers honour on things; he is a *creator of values.* He honours whatever he recognises in himself: such morality is self-glorification. In the foreground there is the feeling of plenitude, of power, which seeks to overflow, the happiness of high tension, the consciousness of a wealth which would fain give and bestow:—the noble man also helps the unfortunate, but not—or scarcely—out of pity, but rather from an impulse generated by the super-abundance of power. The noble man honours in himself the powerful one, him also who has power over himself, who knows how to speak and how to keep silence, who takes pleasure in subjecting himself to severity and hardness, and has reverence for all that is severe and hard. "Wotan placed a hard heart in my breast," says an old Scandinavian Saga: it is thus rightly expressed from the soul of a proud Viking. Such a type of man is even proud of *not* being made for sympathy; the hero of the Saga therefore adds warningly: "He who has not a hard heart when young, will never have one." The noble and brave who think thus are the furthest removed from the morality which sees precisely in sympathy, or in acting for the good of others, or in *désintéressement,* the characteristic of the moral; faith in oneself, pride in oneself, a radical enmity and irony towards "selflessness," belong as definitely to noble morality, as do a careless scorn and precaution in presence of sympathy and the "warm heart."—It is the powerful who *know* how to honour, it is their art, their domain for invention. The profound reverence for age and for tradition —all law rests on this double reverence,—the belief and prejudice in favour of ancestors and unfavourable to newcomers, is typical in the morality of the powerful; and if, reversely, men of "modern ideas" believe almost instinctively in "progress" and the "future," and are more and more lacking in respect for old age, the ignoble origin of these "ideas" has complacently betrayed itself thereby. A morality of the ruling class, however, is more especially foreign and irritating to present-day taste in the sternness of its principle that one has duties only to one's equals; that one may act towards beings of a lower rank, towards all that is foreign, just as seems good to one, or "as the heart desires," and in any case "beyond good and evil": it is here that sympathy and similar sentiments can have a place. The ability and obligation to exercise prolonged gratitude and prolonged revenge—both only within the circle of equals,—artfulness in retaliation, *raffinement* of the idea in friendship, a certain necessity to have enemies (as outlets for the emotions of envy, quarrelsomeness, arrogance—in fact, in order to be a good *friend*): all these are typical characteristics of the noble morality, which, as has been pointed out, is not the morality of "modern ideas," and is therefore at present difficult to realise, and also to unearth and disclose. —It is otherwise with the second type of morality, *slave-morality*. Supposing that the abused, the oppressed, the suffering, the unemancipated, the weary, and those uncertain of themselves, should moralise, what will be the common element of their moral estimates? Probably a pessimistic suspicion with regard to the entire situation of man will find expression, perhaps a condemnation of man, together with his situation. The slave has an unfavourable eye for the virtues of the powerful; he has a scepticism and distrust, a *refinement* of distrust of everything "good" that is there honoured—he would fain persuade himself that the very happiness there is not genuine. On the other hand, *those* qualities which serve to alleviate the existence of sufferers are brought into prominence and flooded with light; it is here that sympathy, the kind, helping hand, the warm heart, patience, diligence, humility, and friendliness attain to honour; for here these are the most useful qualities, and almost the only means of supporting the burden of existence. Slave-morality is essentially the morality of utility. Here is the seat of the origin of the famous antithesis "good" and "evil":—power and dangerousness are assumed to reside in the evil, a certain dreadfulness, subtlety, and strength, which do not admit of being despised. According to slave-morality, therefore, the "evil" man arouses fear; according to master-morality, it is precisely the "good" man who arouses fear and seeks to arouse it, while the bad man is regarded as the despicable being. The contrast attains its maximum when, in accordance with the logical consequences of slave-morality, a shade of depreciation—it may be slight and well-intentioned —at last attaches itself to the "good" man of this morality; because, according to the servile mode of thought, the good man must in any case be the *safe* man: he is good-natured, easily deceived, perhaps a little stupid, *un bonhomme*. Everywhere that slave-morality gains the ascendency, language shows a tendency to approximate the significations of the words "good" and "stupid."—A last fundamental difference: the desire for *freedom*, the instinct for happiness and the refinements of the feeling of liberty belong as necessarily to slave-morals and morality, as artifice and enthusiasm in reverence and devotion are the regular symptoms of an aristocratic mode of thinking and estimating.—Hence we can understand without further detail why love *as a passion*—it is our European specialty—must absolutely be of noble origin; as is well known, its invention is due to the Provençal poet-cavaliers, those brilliant, ingenious men of the *"gai saber,"* to whom Europe owes so much, and almost owes itself.

THE GAY SCIENCE
[Paragraphs 283 and 290] *

Preparatory men. I welcome all signs that a more manly, a warlike, age is about to begin, an age which, above all, will give honor to valor once again. For this age shall prepare the way for one yet higher, and it shall gather the strength which this higher age will need one day— this age which is to carry heroism into the pursuit of knowledge and *wage wars* for the sake of thoughts and their consequences. To this end we now need many preparatory valorous men who cannot leap into being out of nothing—any more than out of the sand and slime of our present civilization and metropolitanism: men who are bent on seeking for that aspect in all things which must be *overcome;* men characterized by cheerfulness, patience, unpretentiousness, and contempt for all great vanities, as well as by magnanimity in victory and forbearance regarding the small vanities of the vanquished; men possessed of keen and free judgment concerning all victors and the share of chance in every victory and every fame; men who have their own festivals, their own weekdays, their own periods of mourning, who are accustomed to command with assurance and are no less ready to obey when necessary, in both cases equally proud and serving their own cause; men who are in greater danger, more fruitful, and happier! For, believe me, the secret of the greatest fruitfulness and the greatest enjoyment of existence is: to *live dangerously!* Build your cities under Vesuvius! Send your ships into uncharted seas! Live at war with your peers and yourselves! Be robbers and conquerors, as long as you cannot be rulers and owners, you lovers of knowledge! Soon the age will be past when you could be satisfied to live like shy deer, hidden in the woods! At long last the pursuit of knowledge will reach out for its due: it will want to *rule* and *own,* and you with it! . . .

One thing is needful. "Giving style" to one's character—a great and rare art! It is exercised by those who see all the strengths and weaknesses of their own natures and then comprehend them in an artistic plan until everything appears as art and reason and even weakness delights the eye. Here a large mass of second nature has been added; there a piece of original nature has been removed: both by long practice and daily labor. Here the ugly which could not be removed is hidden; there it has been reinterpreted and made sublime. . . . It will be the strong and domineering natures who enjoy their finest gaiety in such compulsion, in such constraint and perfection under a law of their own; the passion of their tremendous will relents when confronted with stylized, conquered, and serving nature; even when they have to build palaces and lay out gardens, they demur at giving nature a free hand. Conversely, it is the weak characters without power over themselves who *hate* the constraint of style. . . . They become slaves as soon as they serve; they hate to serve. Such spirits—and they may be of the first rank —are always out to interpret themselves and their environment as *free* nature—wild, arbitrary, fantastic, disorderly, astonishing; and they do well because only in this way do they please themselves. For one thing is needful: that a human being attain his satisfaction with himself— whether it be by this or by that poetry and art; only then is a human being at all tolerable to behold. Whoever is dissatisfied with himself is always ready to revenge himself therefor; we others will be his victims, if only by always having to stand his ugly sight. For the sight of the ugly makes men bad and gloomy.

Perhaps premature. . . . There is no morality that alone makes moral, and every ethic that affirms itself exclusively kills too much good strength and costs humanity too dearly. The deviants, who are so frequently the inventive and fruitful ones, shall no longer be sacrificed; it shall not even be considered infamous to deviate from morality, in thought and deed; numerous new experiments of life and society shall be made; a tremendous burden of bad conscience shall be removed from the world— these most general aims should be recognized and promoted by all who are honest and seek truth.[1]

---

[1] [*The Dawn* (Paragraph 164), from *The Portable Nietzsche* by Walter Kaufmann. Copyright 1954, © 1968 by The Viking Press, Inc. Reprinted by permission of The Viking Press, Inc., and Chatto & Windus Ltd., p. 81.—EDS.]

If we have our own *why* of life, we shall get along with almost any *how*. Man does *not* strive for pleasure; only the Englishman does.[2]

What is good? Everything that heightens the feeling of power in man, the will to power, power itself.
What is bad? Everything that is born of weakness.
What is happiness? The feeling that power is *growing*, that resistance is overcome.
Not contentedness but more power; not peace but war; not virtue but fitness. . . .[3]

My demand upon the philosopher is known, that he take his stand *beyond* good and evil and leave the illusion of moral judgment *beneath* himself. This demand follows from an insight which I was the first to formulate: that *there are altogether no moral facts*. Moral judgments agree with religious ones in believing in realities which are no realities. Morality is merely an interpretation of certain phenomena—more precisely, a misinterpretation. Moral judgments, like religious ones, belong to a stage of ignorance at which the very concept of the real and the distinction between what is real and imaginary, are still lacking; thus "truth," at this stage, designates all sorts of things which we today call "imaginings." Moral judgments are therefore never to be taken literally: so understood, they always contain mere absurdity. Semeiotically, however, they remain invaluable: they reveal, at least for those who know, the most valuable realities of cultures and inwardnesses which did not know enough to "understand" themselves. Morality is mere sign language, mere symptomatology: one must know what it is all about to be able to profit from it.[4]

---

[2] ["Maxims and Arrows" (Paragraph 12), in *Twilight of the Idols*, from *The Portable Nietzsche* by Walter Kaufmann. Copyright 1954, ©1968 by The Viking Press, Inc. Reprinted by permission of The Viking Press, Inc., and Chatto & Windus Ltd., p. 468.—EDS.]

[3] [*The Antichrist* (Paragraph 2), from *The Portable Nietzsche* by Walter Kaufmann. Copyright 1954, © 1968 by The Viking Press, Inc. Reprinted by permission of The Viking Press, Inc., and Chatto & Windus Ltd., p. 570.—EDS.]

[4] ["The 'Improvers' of Mankind" (Paragraph 1), in *Twilight of the Idols*. from *The Portable Nietzsche* by Walter Kaufmann. Copyright 1954, © 1968 by The Viking Press, Inc. Reprinted by permission of The Viking Press, Inc., and Chatto & Windus Ltd., p. 501.—EDS.]

Suggestions for Further Readings

3.1–3.3   Utilitarianism (AU, GU, and RU)

Blanshard, Brand. *Reason and Goodness.* New York: Macmillan, 1961, pp. 324–29.

Butler, Joseph. *Five Sermons.* Indianapolis: Bobbs-Merrill, 1950, pp. 87–90.

Gorovitz, Samuel, ed. *Utilitarianism with Critical Essays.* Indianapolis: Bobbs-Merrill, 1971.

Landesman, Charles. "A Note on Act Utilitarianism," *Philosophical Review,* LXXIII (1964), 243–47.

Lyons, David. *Forms and Limits of Utilitarianism.* Oxford: Clarendon Press, 1965.

Mabbott, J. D. "Moral Rules," *Proceedings of the British Academy,* XXXIX (1953), 97–118.

Smart, J. J. C. *An Outline of a System of Utilitarian Ethics.* Melbourne: Melbourne University Press, 1961.

————. "Extreme and Restricted Utilitarianism," *The Philosophical Quarterly,* VI (1956), 344–54.

Strang, Colin. "What If Everybody Did That?" in Baruch A. Brody, ed., *Moral Rules and Particular Circumstances* (Englewood Cliffs, N.J.: Prentice-Hall, 1970), pp. 135–44.

3.4   Justice

Bedau, H. A., ed. *Justice and Equality.* Englewood Cliffs, N.J.: Prentice-Hall, 1971.

Frankena, W. K. "Some Beliefs About Justice," The Lindley Lecture, University of Kansas, March 2, 1966. Lawrence, Kansas: University of Kansas Department of Philosophy, 1966.

Rashdall, Hastings. *The Theory of Good and Evil* (2nd ed.). Oxford: Clarendon Press, 1924.

3.5   Ethics of Love

Fletcher, Joseph. *Situation Ethics.* Philadelphia: Westminster Press, 1966.

Frankena, W. K. "Love and Principle in Christian Ethics," in Alvin Plantinga, ed., *Faith and Philosophy* (Grand Rapids, Mich.: Eerdmans, 1964), pp. 203–25.

Ramsay, Paul. *Deeds and Rules in Christian Ethics.* New York: Scribner's, 1967.

3.6   Nietzsche

Kaufmann, Walter. *Nietzsche: Philosopher, Psychologist, Antichrist.* Cleveland: The World Publishing Company, 1956.

4

MORAL VALUE
AND RESPONSIBILITY

Introduction

From now on we shall be dealing for the most part, though not entirely, with questions that can be answered in the same way by both
teleologists and deontologists—or in one way by some and in another
by others, regardless of their orientation toward teleology or deontology.
For example, both deontologists and teleologists can be determinists or
indeterminists, hedonists or nonhedonists, intuitionists or nonintuition-
ists.

In this chapter we shall be concerned with a kind of normative or
value judgment—more specifically, a kind of moral judgment—that was
barely noticed by Broad in his essay in Chapter 1, namely, judgments
of *moral value*. As Mill said, we not only judge the rightness or wrongness of actions, we also judge the moral goodness or badness of the agent
or of his motives and character. In fact, in morality we make two kinds
of judgments: (1) *deontic* judgments, in which we say that an action
is right, is wrong, is a duty, is obligatory, or ought or ought not to be
done; and (2) *aretaic* judgments, in which we say that a person, action,
motive, intention, or trait of character is morally good or bad, virtuous
or vicious, responsible, blameworthy, courageous, temperate, just, etc.
This is nicely pointed out in the selection by R. C. Cross and A. D.
Woozley in this chapter. In Chapters 2 and 3 we were mainly concerned
with different theories about the standards to be used in making deontic
judgments; here we shall deal with some views and problems about the
making of aretaic judgments, taking first judgments of moral value, then
judgments of moral responsibility.

4.1

Ethics of Virtue

We must at once notice that some moral philosophers and theologians have argued for an ethics of virtue, being, character, or ideals in opposition to an ethics of duty, doing, action, laws, principles, or rules. Our so-called new morality seems to favor the former. The issue may be understood as follows. As we have seen, there are two kinds of moral judgments, deontic and aretaic. Our actual morality—and most ethical theory—recognizes both kinds of judgment. Ross and Kant, for example, do this. It is often said, however, that aretaic judgments are primary in the morality and ethical theory of the Greeks, while deontic ones are primary in Christian and modern morality and moral philosophy. Whether or not this is historically true, it is possible to hold that deontic judgments should be regarded as primary in morality and aretaic ones as derivative or dispensable, or, alternatively, that aretaic judgments should be regarded as primary and deontic ones as derivative. If one holds the former, one has a deontic ethics or ethics of duty; if the latter, an aretaic ethics. But an aretaic ethics is not necessarily an ethics of virtue. To be an ethics of virtue, it must insist that moral judgments about actions, aretaic or deontic, are secondary to, and derivative from, aretaic judgments about agents or persons and their motives or traits. In short, for an ethics of virtue, what is basic in morality are judgments such as "Be just" or "Be sincere," or, more accurately, "Justice is a virtue" or "Sincerity is morally good."

It should also be noticed that, so far, we have been proceeding as if the ethics-of-duty approach is correct; this is because most modern moral philosophers, both teleologists and deontologists, have taken that approach. The utilitarians studied earlier are as much committed to an ethics of duty as the deontologists. But an ethics of virtue can also be either teleological or deontological; roughly, an ethics of virtue would be teleological if it holds that benevolence is the whole of virtue, deontological if it denies this and insists that there are other moral virtues as well, such as honesty or chastity.

Instead of adopting either an ethics of virtue or an ethics of duty that has a place for virtues and aretaic judgments, which is what philosophers have usually done, one might argue that a fully adequate morality should consist of two parts: an ethics-of-duty part for one sphere of life and an ethics-of-virtue part for another sphere of life, one sphere being subject to the call of duty, the other being outside or beyond that call. Such a view has a good deal of attractiveness—among other things, it makes it easy to find a place for saints and heroes and might be worked out in a variety of ways.

To round out our study of normative ethics then, we must provide a forum for discussion of the idea of an ethics of virtue. We do this, first, by presenting a passage from Plato, in which he definitely states an ethics of virtue (justice is merely an example of his general view, which includes three other cardinal virtues: wisdom, courage, and temperance), together with a commentary on it by R. C. Cross and A. D. Woozley; and, second, by including a selection in which Bernard Mayo, who himself subscribes to an ethics of principle, gives a very sympathetic exposition of the opposing position of those who emphasize ideals of virtue. In addition to the readings in this section, the selection from Kant in Chapter 2 indicates at least some of what he would say in opposition to an ethics of virtue.

In reading the selection from Mayo, you should also pay attention to what he says about ideals and about saints and heroes, topics that are important in their own right and independent of the issue of deontic versus aretaic ethics.

THE VIRTUE OF JUSTICE

Plato

. . . If the case is put to us, must we not admit that the just State, or the man who is trained in the principles of such a State, will be less likely than the unjust to make away with a deposit of gold or silver? Would any one deny this?

No one, he replied.

Will the just man or citizen ever be guilty of sacrilege or theft, or treachery either to his friends or to his country?

Never.

Neither will he ever break faith where there have been oaths or agreements?

From "The Republic," in The Dialogues of Plato, *3rd ed., trans. Benjamin Jowett (London: Oxford University Press, 1892).*

Impossible.

No one will be less likely to commit adultery, or to dishonor his father and mother, or to fail in his religious duties?

No one.

And the reason is that each part of him is doing its own business, whether in ruling or being ruled?

Exactly so.

Are you satisfied then that the quality which makes such men and such states is justice, or do you hope to discover some other?

Not I, indeed.

Then our dream has been realized; and the suspicion which we entertained at the beginning of our work of construction, that some divine power must have conducted us to a primary form of justice, has now been verified?

Yes, certainly.

And the division of labor which required the carpenter and the shoemaker and the rest of the citizens to be doing each his own business, and not another's, was a shadow of justice, and for that reason it was of use?

Clearly.

But in reality justice was such as we were describing, being concerned however, not with the outward man, but with the inward, which is the true self and concernment of man: for the just man does not permit the several elements within him [1] to interfere with one another, or any of them to do the work of others,—he sets in order his own inner life, and is his own master and his own law, and at peace with himself; and when he has bound together the three principles within him, which may be compared to the higher, lower, and middle notes of the scale, and the intermediate intervals—when he has bound all these together, and is no longer many, but has become one entirely temperate and perfectly adjusted nature, then he proceeds to act, if he has to act, whether in a matter of property, or in the treatment of the body, or in some affair of politics or private business; always thinking and calling that which preserves and cooperates with this harmonious condition, just and good action, and the knowledge which presides over it, wisdom, and that which at any time impairs this condition, he will call unjust action, and the opinion which preserves over it ignorance.

You have said the exact truth, Socrates.

Very good; and if we were to affirm that we had discovered the just

---

[1] [Plato believes that man's soul has three parts, the rational, the spirited, and the appetitive, and that justice involves their harmonious relationship.—EDS.]

man and the just State, and the nature of justice in each of them, we should not be telling a falsehood?

Most certainly not.

May we say so, then?

Let us say so.

And now, I said, injustice has to be considered.

Clearly.

Must not injustice be a strife which arises among the three principles —a meddlesomeness, and interference, and rising up of a part of the soul against the whole, an assertion of unlawful authority, which is made by a rebellious subject against a true prince, of whom he is the natural vassal,—what is all this confusion and delusion but injustice, and intemperance and cowardice and ignorance, and every form of vice?

Exactly so.

And if the nature of justice and injustice be known, then the meaning of acting unjustly and being unjust, or, again, of acting justly, will also be perfectly clear?

What do you mean? he said.

Why, I said, they are like disease and health; being in the soul just what disease and health are in the body.

How so? he said.

Why, I said, that which is healthy causes health, and that which is unhealthy causes disease.

Yes.

And just actions cause justice, and unjust actions cause injustice?

That is certain.

And the creation of health is the institution of a natural order and government of one by another in the parts of the body; and the creation of disease is the production of a state of things at variance with this natural order?

True.

And is not the creation of justice the institution of a natural order and government of one by another in the parts of the soul, and the creation of injustice the production of a state of things at variance with the natural order?

Exactly so, he said.

Then virtue is the health and beauty and well-being of the soul, and vice the disease and weakness and deformity of the same?

True.

And do not good practices lead to virtue, and evil practices to vice?

Assuredly.

Still our old question of the comparative advantage of justice and injustice has not been answered: Which is the more profitable, to be just and act justly and practise virtue, whether seen or unseen of gods and men, or to be unjust and act unjustly, if only unpunished and unreformed?

In my judgment, Socrates, the question has now become ridiculous. We know that, when the bodily constitution is gone, life is no longer endurable, though pampered with all kinds of meats and drinks, and having all wealth and all power; and shall we be told that when the very essence of the vital principle is undermined and corrupted, life is still worth having to a man, if only he be allowed to do whatever he likes with the single exception that he is not to acquire justice and virtue, or to escape from injustice and vice; assuming them both to be such as we have described?

Yes, I said, the question is, as you say, ridiculous. . . .

COMMENTARY ON PLATO

R. C. Cross & A. D. Woozley

About the fourth virtue, justice, [Plato] does speak at slightly more length. Attempts, such as were made in Book I, to characterise justice in terms of a man's conduct are misguided and place the emphasis in the wrong place, for conduct is only a sign or "image" of character. A man is just when the three elements of his soul are in their correct harmonious relationship under the overall rule of the rational element. Such a relationship will manifest itself in just conduct. Conversely, the practice of just conduct, through moral training and example, will serve to produce and maintain the relationship, but should not be confused with it. In this contrast between conduct and the character of which it is, or should be, the expression, Plato is underlining a distinction which is central to ethics. Some of our moral judgments are judgments about a man's conduct, regardless of his motives or his reasons for acting so; and to this sphere belong especially words like "right," "wrong," "ought" and "obligation." We say that a man has done what was right if his action conforms with what we accept as moral rules, wrong if it violates them. For example, in the ordinary situation where no problems arise over which there is reason for moral disagreement we may say that a man has done what was right if, having made a promise, he keeps it, that he has done wrong if he

From Plato's Republic (London: Macmillan & Co., Ltd., 1964; New York: St. Martin's Press, 1964). Reprinted by permission of the authors, Macmillan, London and Basingstoke, and St. Martin's Press.

breaks it. If one man keeps a promise out of respect for the sanctity of promises, and another keeps his promise because he thinks it will pay him to do so, or that he will suffer loss if he breaks it, we do not say that the first man's action was right, but the second's was not. If it is right to pay taxes and bills when they are due, to tell the truth when giving evidence under oath, to obey traffic lights when driving a car, to report for duty when called up into the army, etc., then your conduct is right when it is of the prescribed kind. In judging that what you did was right, or judging that you have done what you ought, we are judging you for your conduct, and are not interested in your motives or reasons. We shall not withdraw our assertion that you did what you ought, if we discover that your reasons for so acting were much less reputable than we may have at first supposed. But belief and knowledge about your reasons will determine a different kind of moral judgment which we make, judgment about you as a man, or about your conduct in relation to you as a man. And this is the sphere to which the "virtue" (and "vice") words belong: the general words like "good" and "bad" and the more specific virtue words like "generous," "honest," "courageous," "conscientious," etc., and vice words like "mean," "malicious," "untrustworthy," These are the words which we use in describing and assessing a man's character, and in appraising his conduct when we are not simply judging it externally by its conformity with (or violation of) a moral code of behaviour, but are judging it in relation to the man's reasons and motives for so acting. We approve of a man keeping his promise, whatever his reasons may be, but we shall not admire him if we know that his sole reason was fear of the consequences to himself of being caught breaking it. Plato's point is that in right conduct as such there is no virtue. If a man sticks to his job, or stays within his class, he is acting justly, but he is not on that account a just man: he may be sticking to his job because he can make more money out of it than at any other, because of fear of unemployment if he leaves it, because he will lose his house if he leaves it, or because it has been made a legal offence to leave it. He will be a just man, or his conduct will display justice, only if it is the manifestation of his inner self or character, and only if that inner self consists of the three elements in their correct relationship; real justice, then, characterises, not a man's behaviour, but the state of his soul, which will naturally manifest itself in his behaviour. . . .

ETHICS OF VIRTUE vs.
ETHICS OF PRINCIPLE

Bernard Mayo

Duty and Virtue

It has been said that the whole of Western philosophy is a set of footnotes to Plato. This is a pardonable half-truth for, say, metaphysics, but it is very far from true of moral philosophy. The philosophy of moral principles, which is characteristic of Kant and the post-Kantian era, is something of which hardly a trace exists in Plato. Plato speaks at great length of goodness and the good; we also speak of the word "good" as a moral word, but, . . . it is an evaluative and not an imperative word, and is less at home in the context of moral principles than are such words as "right" and "wrong." These words, on the other hand, do not occur in Platonic ethics. Plato says nothing about rules or principles or laws, except when he is talking politics. Instead he talks about virtues and vices, and about certain types of human character. The key word in Platonic ethics is Virtue; the key word in Kantian ethics is Duty. And modern ethics is a set of footnotes, not to Plato, but to Kant, and, more remotely, to the Old Testament and Roman Law. . . .

Doing and Being

Attention to the novelists can be a welcome correction to a tendency of philosophical ethics of the last generation or two to lose contact with the ordinary life of man which is just what the novelists, in their own way, are concerned with. Of course there are writers who can be called in to illustrate problems about Duty (Graham Greene is a good example). But there are more who perhaps never mention the words duty, obligation or principle. Yet they are all concerned—Jane Austen, for instance, entirely and absolutely—with the moral qualities or defects of their heroes and heroines and other characters. This points to a radical one-sidedness in the philosophers' account of morality in terms of principles: it takes little or no account of qualities, of what people *are*. It is just here that the old-fashioned word Virtue used to have a place; and

From Ethics and the Moral Life *(London: Macmillan & Co. Ltd., 1958; New York: St. Martin's Press, 1958). Reprinted by permission of the author, Macmillan, London and Basingstoke, and St. Martin's Press.*

it is just here that the work of Plato and Aristotle can be instructive. Justice, for Plato, though it is closely connected with acting according to law, does not *mean* acting according to law: it is a quality of character, and a just action is one such as a just man would do. Telling the truth, for Aristotle, is not, as it was for Kant, fulfilling an obligation; again it is a quality of character, or, rather, a whole range of qualities of character, some of which may actually be defects, such as tactlessness, boastfulness, and so on—a point which can be brought out, in terms of principles, only with the greatest complexity and artificiality, but quite simply and naturally in terms of character.

If we wish to enquire about Aristotle's moral views, it is no use looking for a set of principles. Of course we can find *some* principles to which he must have subscribed—for instance, that one ought not to commit adultery. But what we find much more prominently is a set of character-traits, a list of certain types of person—the courageous man, the niggardly man, the boaster, the lavish spender and so on. The basic moral question, for Aristotle, is not, What shall I do? but, What shall I be?

These contrasts between doing and being, negative and positive, and modern as against Greek morality were noted by John Stuart Mill; I quote from the *Essay on Liberty:*

> Christian morality (so-called) has all the characters of a reaction; it is, in great part, a protest against Paganism. Its ideal is negative rather than positive; passive rather than active; Innocence rather than Nobleness; Abstinence from Evil, rather than energetic Pursuit of the Good; in its precepts (as has been well said) "Thou shalt not" predominates unduly over "Thou shalt . . ." Whatever exists of magnanimity, highmindedness, personal dignity, even the sense of honour, is derived from the purely human, not the religious part of our education, and never could have grown out of a standard of ethics in which the only worth, professedly recognised, is that of obedience.

Of course, there are connections between being and doing. It is obvious that a man cannot just *be;* he can only be what he is by doing what he does; his moral qualities are ascribed to him because of his actions, which are said to manifest those qualities. But the point is that an ethics of Being must include this obvious fact, that Being involves Doing; whereas an ethics of Doing, such as I have been examining, may easily overlook it. As I have suggested, a morality of principles is concerned only with what people do or fail to do, since that is what rules are for. And as far as this sort of ethics goes, people might well have no moral qualities at all except the possession of principles and the will (and capacity) to act accordingly.

Principles and Ideals

When we speak of a moral quality such as courage, and say that a certain action was courageous, we are not merely saying something about the action. We are referring, not so much to what is done, as to the kind of person by whom we take it to have been done. We connect, by means of imputed motives and intentions, with the character of the agent as courageous. This explains, incidentally, why both Kantians and Utilitarians encounter, in their different ways, such difficulties in dealing with motives, which their principles, on the face of it, have no room for. A Utilitarian, for example, can only praise a courageous action in some such way as this: the action is of a sort such as a person of courage is likely to perform, and courage is a quality of character the cultivation of which is likely to increase rather than diminish the sum total of human happiness. But Aristotelians have no need of such circumlocution. For them a courageous action just is one which proceeds from and manifests a certain type of character, and is praised because such a character trait is good, or better than others, or is a virtue. An evaluative criterion is sufficient: there is no need to look for an imperative criterion as well, or rather instead, according to which it is not the character which is good, but the cultivation of the character which is right.

Dispositions of the special sort applicable to human beings are . . . in an important sense "elastic"; that is, from the information that someone is timid we cannot rigorously deduce that he will be frightened on a given occasion, as we can rigorously deduce from the solubility of sugar that it will dissolve when immersed in water. Timid people sometimes act courageously, that is, as courageous people behave; in general, people can act "out of character." Acting out of character is interestingly different from breaking a principle. There are no degrees about rule-breaking: the rule is either kept or broken. In terms of rules, all we are entitled to consider is the relation between an action (the subject of judgment) and a rule (the criterion of judgment), and the verdict is either Right or Wrong. But in considering action by an agent, we have to take into account as well a whole range of other actions by the agent, on the basis of which we form a judgment of character. Actions are "in character" or "out of character" in varying degrees, and, further, we can never state precisely what a person's character is. Instead of the extreme simplicity of the moral judgment based on a moral principle and an instance of conduct which either does or does not conform to that principle, we have a double complexity. Corresponding to the moral principle (which represents the conduct of an ideally righteous man) we have, instead, the idea of a virtue (which represents the conduct and conduct-tendency of an ideally good man). But whereas a man's action can be compared directly with the principle and only two possible verdicts result (or three, if we include "indifferent"), it cannot be compared in this way with the standard of virtue. For we cannot say exactly either how far the action is "in character" for the man, nor how far the character of the man matches or fails to match the ideal. It is not surprising that moral principles, with their superior logical manageability, have proved more attractive than moral ideals as material for ethical theory.

No doubt the fundamental moral question is just "What ought I to do?" And according to the philosophy of moral principles, the answer (which must be an imperative "Do this") must be derived from a conjunction of premises consisting (in the simplest case) firstly of a rule, or universal imperative, enjoining (or forbidding) all actions of a certain type in situations of a certain type, and, secondly, a statement to the effect that this is a situation of that type, falling under that rule. In practice the emphasis may be on supplying only one of these premises, the other being assumed or taken for granted: one may answer the question "What ought I to do?" either by quoting a rule which I am to adopt, or by showing that my case is legislated for by a rule which I do adopt. To take a previous example of moral perplexity, if I am in doubt whether to tell the truth about his condition to a dying man, my doubt may be resolved by showing that the case comes under a rule about the avoidance of unnecessary suffering, which I am assumed to accept. But if the case is without precedent in my moral career, my problem may be soluble only by adopting a new principle about what I am to do now and in the future about cases of this kind.

This second possibility offers a connection with moral ideals. Suppose my perplexity is not merely an unprecedented situation which I could cope with by adopting a new rule. Suppose the new rule is thoroughly inconsistent with my existing moral code. This may happen, for instance, if the moral code is one to which I only pay lip-service; if . . . its authority is not yet internalised, or if it has ceased to be so; it is ready for rejection, but its final rejection awaits a moral crisis such as we are assuming to occur. What I now need is not a rule for deciding how to act in this situation and others of its kind. I need a whole set of rules, a complete morality, new principles to live by.

Now according to the philosophy of moral character, there is another way of answering the fundamental question "What ought I to do?" Instead of quoting a rule, we quote a quality of character, a virtue: we say "Be brave," or "Be patient" or "Be lenient." We may even say "Be a man": if I am in doubt, say, whether to take a risk, and someone says "Be a man," meaning a morally sound man, in this case a man of sufficient courage. (Compare the very different ideal invoked in "Be a gentleman." I shall not discuss whether this is a *moral* ideal.) Here, too, we have the extreme cases, where a man's moral perplexity extends not merely to a particular situation but to his whole way of living. And now the question "What ought I to do?" turns into the question "What ought I to be?"—as, indeed, it was treated in the first place. ("Be brave.") It is answered, not by quoting a rule or a set of rules, but by describing a quality of character or a type of person. And here the ethics of character gains a practical simplicity which offsets the greater logical simplicity of the ethics of principles. We do not have to give a list of characteristics or virtues, as we might list a set of principles. We can give a unity to our answer.

Of course we can in theory give a unity to our principles: this is implied by speaking of a *set* of principles. But if such a set is to be a system and not a mere aggregate, the unity we are looking for is a logical one, namely the possibility that some principles are deductible from others, and ultimately from one. But the attempt to construct a deductive moral system is notoriously difficult, and in any case ill-founded. Why should we expect that all rules of conduct should be ultimately reducible to a few?

Saints and Heroes

But when we are asked "What shall I be?" we can readily give a unity to our answer, though not a logical unity. It is the unity of character. A person's character is not merely a list of dispositions; it has the organic unity of something that is more than the sum of its parts. And we can say, in answer to our morally perplexed questioner, not only "Be this" and "Be that," but also "Be like So-and-So"—where So-and-So is either an ideal type of character, or else an actual person taken as representative of the ideal, an exemplar. Examples of the first are Plato's "just man" in the Republic; Aristotle's man of practical wisdom, in the Nicomachean Ethics; Augustine's citizen of the City of God; the good Communist; the American way of life (which is a collective expression for a type of character). Examples of the second kind, the exemplar, are Socrates, Christ, Buddha, St. Francis, the heroes of epic writers and of novelists. Indeed the idea of the Hero, as well as the idea of the Saint, are very much the expression of this attitude to morality. Heroes and saints are not merely people who did things. They are people whom we are expected, and expect ourselves, to imitate. And imitating them means not merely doing what they did; it means being like them. Their status is not in the least like that of legislators whose laws we admire; for the character of a legislator is irrelevant to our judgment about his legislation. The heroes and saints did not merely give us principles to live by (though some of them did that as well): they gave us examples to follow.

Kant, as we should expect, emphatically rejects this attitude as "fatal to morality" (*Groundwork*, p. 76). According to him, examples serve only to render *visible* an instance of the moral principle, and thereby to demonstrate its practical feasibility. But every exemplar, such as Christ himself, must be judged by the independent criterion of the moral law, before we are entitled to recognize him as worthy of imitation. I am not suggesting that the subordination of exemplars to principles is incorrect, but that it is one-sided and fails to do justice to a large area of moral experience.

Imitation can be more or less successful. And this suggests another defect of the ethics of principles. It has no room for ideals, except the ideal of a perfect set of principles (which, as a matter of fact, is intelligible only in terms of an ideal character or way of life), and the ideal of perfect conscientiousness (which is itself a character-trait). This results, of course, from the "black-or-white" nature of moral verdicts based on rules. There are no degrees of rule-keeping and rule-breaking. But there certainly are degrees by which we approach or recede from the attainment of a certain quality or virtue; if there were not, the word "ideal" would have no meaning. Heroes and saints are not people whom we try to be *just* like, since we know that is impossible. It is precisely because it is impossible for ordinary human beings to achieve the same qualities as the saints, and in the same degree, that we do set them apart from the rest of humanity. It is enough if we try to be a little like them.

The Plurality of Moral Standards

Now there is a term which includes both principles of conduct and qualities of character: namely the term "standard." [Earlier] we spoke of "right" and "wrong" (the typical words of principle-verdicts) as belonging to imperative language, and of "good" and "bad" (the typical words of character-appraisal) as belonging to evaluative language. Some philosophers have failed to emphasise the differences between the two, while others have over-stressed them. Mr. Lamont, for example, in *The Value Judgment*, claims that evaluative words do not belong to morality at all, and are more at home in economics. It is better, I think, to retain "good" and "bad" within moral theory, and quite indispensable if we are to apply the terms to character-traits, that is, to speak of virtues at all. Economics is concerned with what we choose to have; the ethics of principles is concerned with what we choose to do; and the ethics of character is concerned with what we choose to be. It is true that the second involves no evaluation (being an "all-or-none" choice); but the third involves evaluation and scales of preferences, just as much as the first. We can arrange house, car, TV set, and so on, in order of preference; and so we can arrange in order or preference the characters of moral heroes and villains.

The point that different ethical theories each attend to a limited segment of the moral life, and overlook the rest, is well brought out in an interesting recent article [1] in which the author distinguishes between three different kinds of moral standard. These are, firstly, the "Self-Respect" standard, so-called because it is the standard below which we cannot fall without loss of self-respect; it expresses the minimum required of us as moral beings; and it is one in which we are blamed for failure but not praised for success. Notice how all these are negative features. This is the standard that corresponds with my discussion of rules and principles, where it is breaches or infringements that matter; what is right is only what is not against the rules; one is blamed for neglecting one's duty but not praised for doing it. Secondly there is the "Aspirational" standard, and this is not what one seeks merely to maintain, but what one seeks to achieve; not a minimum requirement, but a positive goal, and failure is no longer blameworthy, while success deserves praise. This is not a standard of principles, unless the "principles" are so difficult to live up to that we praise a man "of high principles," but this is really an allusion to character. Then there is a third standard, which corresponds to my Saints and Heroes: it is the "Inspirational" standard, the moral ideal or standard of perfection, which is not what we seek to maintain, nor yet to achieve, since it is unachievable. It is in the light of the example set by the finest men that we set our own moral targets.

---

[1] H. J. N. Horsburgh, "The Plurality of Moral Standards," *Philosophy* XXIX/No. 111 (October 1954,) 332–46.

4.2

Virtue and the Virtues

As we have indicated, even proponents of the ethics of duty usually think of the moral life as including the cultivation of certain virtues. Thus, whether we think in terms of ethics of duty or ethics of virtue, we will want to consider some views about the virtues to be cultivated. Views about this will, of course, vary. Ethical egoists, utilitarians, and deontologists will have different conceptions of what virtue and moral goodness are, and about what dispositions are virtues. Kant's view, again, is at least partly indicated in the selection in Chapter 2. For Ross, moral goodness in general is a disposition to act from a desire to do what is right, but there will also be a more specific moral virtue corresponding to each of his principles of prima facie duty (for instance, a disposition to tell the truth). For an act-utilitarian, there will be one cardinal virtue: benevolence. In a way this will be true for a rule-utilitarian also, but he may prefer to say that there are a number of moral virtues, roughly corresponding to the rules he takes to be conducive to the greatest general good.

In the following selections we present several views about the virtues. After Plato, the most famous view is that of Aristotle. He distinguishes between intellectual excellences or virtues and moral ones. The former are desirable states of the intellect—theoretical wisdom (intuitive and demonstrative knowledge) and practical wisdom. The latter are desirable states of the appetitive and sensitive parts of the soul. The following selection contains much of what Aristotle has to say about moral virtues. Notice that he sounds like an act-deontologist near the end.

THE MORAL VIRTUES

Aristotle

Inasmuch as happiness is an activity of soul in accordance with complete or perfect virtue, it is necessary to consider virtue, as this will perhaps be the best way of studying happiness. . . .

Virtue or excellence being twofold, partly intellectual and partly moral, intellectual virtue is both originated and fostered mainly by teaching; it therefore demands experience and time. Moral virtue on the other hand is the outcome of habit, and accordingly its name ($\eta\theta\iota\kappa\eta$ $\alpha\rho\epsilon\tau\eta$) is derived by a slight deflexion from habit ($\epsilon\theta\sigma$).[1] From this fact it is clear that no moral virtue is implanted in us by nature; a law of nature cannot be altered by habituation. . . . It is neither by nature then nor in defiance of nature that virtues are implanted in us. Nature gives us the capacity of receiving them, and that capacity is perfected by habit. . . . But the virtues we acquire by first exercising them, as is the case with all the arts, for it is by doing what we ought to do when we have learnt the arts that we learn the arts themselves; we become e.g., builders by building and harpists by playing the harp. Similarly it is by doing just acts that we become just, by doing temperate acts that we become temperate, by doing courageous acts that we become courageous. . . . It is by acting in such transactions as take place between man and man that we become either just or unjust. It is by acting in the face of danger and by habituating ourselves to fear or courage that we become either cowardly or courageous. It is much the same with our desires and angry passions. Some people become temperate and gentle, others become licentious and passionate, according as they conduct themselves in one way or another way in particular circumstances. In a word moral states are the results of activities corresponding to the moral states themselves. It is our duty therefore to give a certain character to the activities, as the moral states depend upon the differences of the activities. Accordingly the difference between one training of the habits and another from early days is not a light matter, but is serious or rather all-important. . . .

But it may be asked what we mean by saying that people must become just by doing what is just and temperate by doing what is tem-

From The Nicomachean Ethics of Aristotle, *trans. J. E. C. Weldon (London: Macmillan & Co., Ltd., 1892).*

---

[1] The approximation of $\epsilon\theta\sigma$ (habit) and $\eta\theta\sigma$ (character) cannot be represented in English.

perate. For if they do what is just and temperate, they are *ipso facto* proved, it will be said, to be just and temperate in the same way as, if they practise grammar and music, they are proved to be grammarians and musicians. . . .

But actions in accordance with virtue are not e.g. justly or temperately performed [merely] because they are in themselves just or temperate. It is necessary that the agent at the time of performing them should satisfy certain conditions, i.e. in the first place that he should know what he is doing, secondly that he should deliberately choose to do it and to do it for its own sake, and thirdly that he should do it as an instance of a settled and immutable moral state. If it be a question whether a person possesses any art, these conditions, except indeed the condition of knowledge, are not taken into account; but if it be a question of possessing the virtues, the mere knowledge is of little or no avail, and it is the other conditions, which are the results of frequently performing just and temperate actions, that are not of slight but of absolute importance. Accordingly deeds are said to be just and temperate, when they are such as a just or temperate person would do, and a just and temperate person is not merely one who does these deeds but one who does them in the spirit of the just and the temperate. . . .

. . . the virtues are neither emotions nor faculties [but] moral states. . . . But it is not enough to state merely that virtue is a moral state, we must also describe the character of that moral state.

It must be laid down then that every virtue or excellence has the effect of producing a good condition of that of which it is a virtue or excellence, and of enabling it to perform its function well. Thus the excellence of the eye makes the eye good and its function good, as it is by the excellence of the eye that we see well. Similarly, the excellence of the horse makes a horse excellent and good at racing, at carrying its rider and at facing the enemy.

If then this is universally true, the virtue or excellence of man will be such a moral state as makes a man good and able to perform his proper function well. We have already explained how this will be the case, but another way of making it clear will be to study the nature or character of this virtue.

Now in everything, whether it be continuous or discrete, it is possible to take a greater, a smaller, or an equal amount, and this either absolutely or in relation to ourselves, the equal being a mean between excess and deficiency. By the mean in respect of the thing itself, or the absolute mean, I understand that which is equally distinct from both extremes; and this is one and the same thing for everybody. By the mean considered relatively to ourselves I understand that which is neither too much nor too little; but this is not one thing, nor is it the same for everybody. Thus if 10 be too much and 2 too little we take 6 as a mean in respect of the thing itself; for 6 is as much greater than 2 as it is less than 10, and this is a mean in arithmetical proportion. But the mean considered relatively to ourselves must not be ascertained in this way. It does not follow that if 10 pounds of meat be too much and 2 be too little for a man to eat, a trainer will order him 6 pounds, as this may itself be too much or too little for the person who is to take it; it will be too little e.g. for Milo,[2] but too much for a beginner in gymnastics. It will be the same with running and wrestling; the right amount will vary with the individual. This being so, everybody who understands his business avoids alike excess and deficiency; he seeks and chooses the mean, not the absolute mean, but the mean considered relatively to ourselves.

Every science then performs its function well, if it regards the mean and refers the works which it produces to the mean. This is the reason why it is usually said of successful works that it is impossible to take anything from them or to add anything to them, which implies that excess or deficiency is fatal to excellence but that the mean state ensures it. Good artists too, as we say, have an eye to the mean in their works. But virtue, like Nature herself, is more accurate and better than any art; virtue therefore will aim at the mean;—I speak of moral virtue, as it is moral virtue which is concerned with emotions and actions, and it is these which admit of excess and deficiency and the mean. Thus it is possible to go too far, or not to go far enough, in respect of fear, courage, desire, anger, pity, and pleasure and pain generally, and the excess and the deficiency are alike wrong; but to experience these emotions at the right times and on the right occasions and towards the right persons and for the right causes and in the right manner is the mean or the supreme good, which is characteristic of virtue. Similarly there may be excess, deficiency, or the mean, in regard to actions. But virtue is concerned with emotions and actions, and here excess is an error and deficiency a fault, whereas the mean is successful and laudable, and success and merit are both characteristics of virtue.

It appears then that virtue is a mean state, so far at least as it aims at the mean.

Again, there are many different ways of going wrong; for evil is in its nature infinite, to use the Pythagorean figure, but good is finite. But there is only one possible way of going right. Accordingly the former is easy and the latter difficult; it is easy to miss the mark but difficult to hit it. This again is a reason why excess and deficiency are characteristics of vice and the mean state a characteristic of virtue.

---

[2] The famous Crotoniate wrestler.

"For good is simple, evil manifold."

Virtue then is a state of deliberate moral purpose consisting in a mean that is relative to ourselves, the mean being determined by reason, or as a prudent man would determine it.[3]

It is a mean state firstly as lying between two vices, the vice of excess on the one hand, and the vice of deficiency on the other, and secondly because, whereas the vices either fall short of or go beyond what is proper in the emotions and actions, virtue not only discovers but embraces the mean.

Accordingly, virtue, if regarded in its essence or theoretical conception, is a mean state, but, if regarded from the point of view of the highest good, or of excellence, it is an extreme.

But it is not every action or every emotion that admits of a mean state. There are some whose very name implies wickedness, as e.g., malice, shamelessness, and envy, among emotions, or adultery, theft, and murder, among actions. All these, and others like them, are censured as being intrinsically wicked, not merely the excesses or deficiencies of them. It is never possible then to be right in respect of them; they are always sinful. Right or wrong in such actions as adultery does not depend on our committing them with the right person, at the right time or in the right manner; on the contrary it is sinful to do anything of the kind at all. It would be equally wrong then to suppose that there can be a mean state or an excess or deficiency in unjust, cowardly or licentious conduct; for, if it were so, there would be a mean state of an excess or of a deficiency, an excess of an excess and a deficiency of a deficiency. But as in temperance and courage there can be no excess or deficiency because the mean is, in a sense, an extreme, so too in these cases there cannot be a mean or an excess or deficiency, but, however the acts may be done, they are wrong. For it is a general rule that an excess or deficiency does not admit of a mean state, nor a mean state of an excess or deficiency.

But it is not enough to lay down this as a general rule; it is necessary to apply it to particular cases, as in reasonings upon actions general statements, although they are broader, are less exact than particular statements. For all action refers to particulars, and it is essential that our theories should harmonize with the particular cases to which they apply.

We must take particular virtues then from the catalogue of virtues.

In regard to feelings of fear and confidence, courage is a mean state. On the side of excess, he whose fearlessness is excessive has no name, as

---

[3] [That is, moral virtue is a state of character consisting of a disposition to choose the mean relative to oneself in matters of action and feeling, the mean being determined by reason, or as a man of practical wisdom would determine it.—Eds.]

often happens, but he whose confidence is excessive is foolhardy, while he whose timidity is excessive and whose confidence is deficient is a coward.

In respect of pleasures and pains, although not indeed of all pleasures and pains, and to a less extent in respect of pains than of pleasures, the mean state is temperance, the excess is licentiousness. We never find people who are deficient in regard to pleasures; accordingly such people again have not received a name, but we may call them insensible.

As regards the giving and taking of money, the mean state is liberality, the excess and deficiency are prodigality and illiberality. Here the excess and deficiency take opposite forms; for while the prodigal man is excessive in spending and deficient in taking, the illiberal man is excessive in taking and deficient in spending.

(For the present we are giving only a rough and summary account of the virtues, and that is sufficient for our purpose; we will hereafter determine their character more exactly.)

In respect of money there are other dispositions as well. There is the mean state which is magnificence; for the magnificent man, as having to do with large sums of money, differs from the liberal man who has to do only with small sums; and the excess corresponding to it is bad taste or vulgarity, the deficiency is meanness. These are different from the excess and deficiency of liberality; what the difference is will be explained hereafter.

In respect of honour and dishonour the mean state is highmindedness, the excess is what is called vanity, the deficiency littlemindedness. Corresponding to liberality, which, as we said, differs from magnificence as having to do not with great but with small sums of money, there is a moral state which has to do with petty honour and is related to highmindedness which has to do with great honour; for it is possible to aspire to honour in the right way, or in a way which is excessive or insufficient, and if a person's aspirations are excessive, he is called ambitious, if they are deficient, he is called unambitious, while if they are between the two, he has no name. The dispositions too are nameless, except that the disposition of the ambitious person is called ambition. The consequence is that the extremes lay claim to the mean or intermediate place. We ourselves speak of one who observes the mean sometimes as ambitious, and at other times as unambitious; we sometimes praise an ambitious, and at other times an unambitious person. The reason for our doing so will be stated in due course, but let us now discuss the other virtues in accordance with the method which we have followed hitherto.

Anger, like other emotions, has its excess, its deficiency, and its mean state. It may be said that they have no names, but as we call one who observes the mean gentle, we will call the mean state gentleness. Among the extremes, if a person errs on the side of excess, he may be called passionate and his vice passionateness, if on that of deficiency, he may be called impassive and his deficiency impassivity. . . .

In the matter of truth then, he who observes the mean may be called truthful, and the mean state truthfulness. Pretence, if it takes the form of exaggeration, is boastfulness, and one who is guilty of pretence is a boaster; but if it takes the form of depreciation it is irony, and he who is guilty of it is ironical.

As regards pleasantness in amusement, he who observes the mean is witty, and his disposition wittiness; the excess is buffoonery, and he who is guilty of it a buffoon, whereas he who is deficient in wit may be called a boor and his moral state boorishness.

As to the other kind of pleasantness, viz. pleasantness in life, he who is pleasant in a proper way is friendly, and his mean state friendliness; but he who goes too far, if he has no ulterior object in view, is obsequious, while if his object is self interest, he is a flatterer, and he who does not go far enough and always makes himself unpleasant is a quarrelsome and morose sort of person.

There are also mean states in the emotions and in the expression of the emotions. For although modesty is not a virtue, yet a modest person is praised as if he were virtuous; for here too one person is said to observe the mean and another to exceed it, as e.g. the bashful man who is never anything but modest, whereas a person who has insufficient modesty or no modesty at all is called shameless, and one who observes the mean modest.

Righteous indignation, again, is a mean state between envy and malice. They are all concerned with the pain and pleasure which we feel at the fortunes of our neighbours. A person who is righteously indignant is pained at the prosperity of the undeserving; but the envious person goes further and is pained at anybody's prosperity, and the malicious person is so far from being pained that he actually rejoices at misfortunes. . . .

It is in some cases the deficiency and in others the excess which is the more opposed to the mean. Thus it is not foolhardiness the excess, but cowardice the deficiency which is the more opposed to courage, nor is it insensibility the deficiency, but licentiousness the excess which is the more opposed to temperance. There are two reasons why this should be so. One lies in the nature of the thing itself; for as one of the two extremes is the nearer and more similar to the mean, it is not this extreme, but its opposite, that we chiefly set against the mean. For instance, as it appears that foolhardiness is more similar and nearer to courage than cowardice, it is cowardice that we chiefly set against courage; for things which are further removed from the mean seem to be more opposite to it. This being one reason which lies in the nature of the thing itself, there is a second which lies in our own nature. It is the things to which we ourselves are naturally more inclined that appear more opposed to the mean. Thus we are ourselves naturally more inclined to pleasures than to their opposites, and are more prone therefore to licentiousness than to decorum. Accordingly we speak of those things, in which we are more likely to run to great lengths, as being more opposed to the mean. Hence it follows that licentiousness which is an excess is more opposed to temperance than insensibility.

It has now been sufficiently shown that moral virtue is a mean state, and in what sense it is a mean state; it is a mean state as lying between two vices, a vice of excess on the one side and a vice of deficiency on the other, and as aiming at the mean in the emotions and actions.

That is the reason why it is so hard to be virtuous; for it is always hard work to find the mean in anything, e.g., it is not everybody, but only a man of science, who can find the mean or centre of a circle. So too anybody can get angry—that is an easy matter—and anybody can give or spend money, but to give it to the right persons, to give the right amount of it and to give it at the right time and for the right cause and in the right way, this is not what anybody can do, nor is it easy. That is the reason why it is rare and laudable and noble to do well. Accordingly one who aims at the mean must begin by departing from that extreme which is the more contrary to the mean; he must act in the spirit of Calypso's advice,

"Far from this smoke and swell keep thou thy bark,"

for of the two extremes one is more sinful than the other. As it is difficult then to hit the mean exactly, we must take the second best course, as the saying is, and choose the lesser of two evils, and this we shall best do in the way that we have described, i.e. by steering clear of the evil which is further from the mean. We must also observe the things to which we are ourselves particularly prone, as different natures have different inclinations, and we may ascertain what these are by a consideration of our feelings of pleasure and pain. And then we must drag ourselves in the direction opposite to them; for it is by removing ourselves as far as possible from what is wrong that we shall arrive at the mean, as we do when we pull a crooked stick straight.

But in all cases we must especially be on our guard against what is pleasant and against pleasure, as we are not impartial judges of pleasure. Hence our attitude towards pleasure must be like that of the elders of the people in the *Iliad* towards Helen, and we must never be afraid of applying the words they use; for if we dismiss pleasure as they dismissed

Helen, we shall be less likely to go wrong. It is by action of this kind, to put it summarily, that we shall best succeed in hitting the mean.

It may be admitted that this is a difficult task, especially in particular cases. It is not easy to determine e.g. the right manner, objects, occasions, and duration of anger. There are times when we ourselves praise people who are deficient in anger, and call them gentle, and there are other times when we speak of people who exhibit a savage temper as spirited. It is not however one who deviates a little from what is right, but one who deviates a great deal, whether on the side of excess or of deficiency, that is censured; for he is sure to be found out. Again, it is not easy to decide theoretically how far and to what extent a man may go before he becomes censurable, but neither is it easy to define theoretically anything else within the region of perception; such things fall under the head of particulars, and our judgment of them depends upon our perception.

So much then is plain, that the mean state is everywhere laudable, but that we ought to incline at one time towards the excess and at another towards the deficiency; for this will be our easiest manner of hitting the mean, or in other words of attaining excellence.

To complete our sampling, we present a modern statement about the virtues involved in the moral life. (One Christian conception is briefly stated at the end of the Brunner selection in Chapter 3.) The following essay by the famous American philosopher John Dewey is a good example of a view of the virtues that goes with a pragmatic form of reflective morality. Much of his philosophy of education is implicit in it.

THE CONCEPTION OF VIRTUE IN REFLECTIVE MORALITY

John Dewey

In customary morality it is possible to draw up a list or catalogue of vices and virtues. For the latter reflect some definite existing custom, and the former some deviation from or violation of custom. The acts approved and disapproved have therefore the same definiteness and fixity as belong to the customs to which they refer. In reflective morality, a list of virtues has a much more tentative status. Chastity, kindness, honesty, patriotism, modesty, toleration, bravery, etc., cannot be given a fixed meaning, because each expresses an interest in objects and institutions which are changing. In form, *as* interests, they may be permanent, since no community could endure in which there were not, say, fair dealing, public spirit, regard for life, faithfulness to others. But no two communities conceive the objects to which these qualities attach in quite identical ways. They can be defined, therefore, only on the basis of *qualities characteristic of interest*, not on the basis of permanent and uniform objects in which interest is taken. This is as true of, say, temperance and chastity as it is of regard for life, which in some communities does not extend to girl babies nor to the aged, and which in all historic communities is limited by war with hostile communities.

Accordingly we shall discuss virtue through enumeration of traits which must belong to an attitude if it is to be genuinely an interest, not by an enumeration of virtues as if they were separate entities. (1) *An interest must be wholehearted.* Virtue is integrity, vice is duplicity. Sincerity is another name for the same quality, for it signifies that devotion to an object is unmixed and undiluted. The quality has a much broader scope than might at first seem to be the case.

Conscious hypocrisy is rare. Divided and inconsistent interest is common. Devotion that is complete, knowing no reservations and exceptions, is extremely difficult to attain. We imagine we are whole-hearted when we throw ourselves into a line of action which is agreeable, failing to notice that we give up or act upon an incompatible interest when obstacles arise. Whole-heartedness is something quite different from immediate enthusiasm and ardor. It always has an emotional quality, but it is far from being identical with a succession of even intense emotional likings for a succession of things into each of which we eagerly throw ourselves. For it requires consistency, continuity, and community of purpose and effort. And this condition cannot be fulfilled except when the various objects and ends which succeed one another have been brought into order and unity by reflection upon the nature and bearing of each one. We cannot be genuinely whole-hearted unless we are single-minded.

Hence (2) the interest which constitutes a disposition virtuous must be continuous and *persistent*. One swallow does not make a summer nor does a passing right interest, no matter how strong, constitute a virtue. Fair weather "virtue" has a bad name because it indicates lack of stability. It demands character to stick it out when conditions are adverse, as they are when there is danger of incurring the ill-will of others, or when it requires more than ordinary energy to overcome obstacles. The *vitality* of interest in what is reflectively approved is attested by persistence under unfavorable conditions.

A complete interest must be (3) *impartial* as well as enduring. Interest, apart from a character formed and fortified through reflection, is partial, and in that sense divided and, though unconsciously, insincere. A person readily tends to evince interest in the well-being of friends and members of his family, and to be indifferent to those with whom he is not bound by ties of gratitude or affection. It is easy to have one scale for determining interest in those of one's own nation and a totally different one for the regard of those of another race, color, religion, or nationality. Complete universality of interest is, of course, impossible in the sense of equality of strength or force of quantity; that is, it would be mere pretense to suppose that one can be as *much* interested in those at a distance with whom one has little contact as in those with whom one is in constant communication. But equity, or impartiality, of interest is a matter of quality not of quantity as in-iquity is a matter not of more or less, but of using uneven measures of judgment. Equity demands that *when* one has to act in relation to others, no matter whether friends or strangers, fellow citizens or foreigners, one should have an equal and even measure of value as far as the interests of the others come into the reckoning. In an immediate or emotional sense it is not possible to love our enemies as we love our friends. But the maxim to love our enemies as we love ourselves signifies that in our conduct we should take into account their interests at the same rate of estimate as we rate our own. It is a principle for regulating judgment of the bearings of our acts on the happiness of others.

Single-mindedness of purpose would be narrow were it not united to breadth and impartiality of interest. The conception that virtue resides in fundamental and thoroughgoing interest in approved objects accomplishes more than merely saving us from the identification of virtues with whatever is conventionally and currently prized in a particular community or social set. For it protects us from an unreal separation of virtuous qualities from one another. The mere idea of a catalogue of different virtues commits us to the notion that virtues may be kept apart, pigeonholed in water-tight compartments. In fact virtuous traits interpenetrate one another; this unity is involved in the very idea of integrity of character. At one time persistence and endurance in the face of obstacles is the most prominent feature; then the attitude is the excellence called courage. At another time, the trait of impartiality and equity is uppermost, and we call it justice. At other times, the necessity for subordinating immediate satisfaction of a strong appetite or desire to a comprehensive good is the conspicuous feature. Then the disposition is denominated temperance, self-control. When the prominent phase is the need for thoughtfulness, for consecutive and persistent attention, in order that these other qualities may function, the interest receives the name of moral wisdom, insight, conscientiousness. In each case the difference is one of emphasis only.

This fact is of practical as well as theoretical import. The supposition that virtues are separated from one another leads, when it is acted upon, to that narrowing and hardening of action which induces many persons to conceive of all morality as negative and restrictive. When, for example, an independent thing is made of temperance or self-control it becomes mere inhibition, a sour constraint. But as one phase of an interpenetrated whole, it is the positive harmony characteristic of integrated interest. Is justice thought of as an isolated virtue? Then it takes on a mechanical and quantitative form, like the exact meting out of praise and blame, reward and punishment. Or it is thought of as vindication of abstract and impersonal law—an attitude which always tends to make men vindictive and leads them to justify their harshness as a virtue. To the notion of courage there still adheres something of its original notion of fortitude in meeting an enemy. The Greeks broadened the conception to include all the disagreeable things which need to be borne but which one would like to run away from. As soon as we recognize that there can be no continuity in maintaining and executing a purpose which does not at some time meet difficulties and obstacles that are disagreeable, we also recognize that courage is no separate thing. Its scope is as wide as the fullness of positive interest which causes us in spite of difficulties to seek for the realization of the object to which the interest is attached. Otherwise it shrinks to mere stoical and negative resistance, a passive rather than an active virtue.

Finally, conscientiousness is sometimes treated as if it were mere morbid anxiety about the state of one's own virtue. It may even become a kind of sublimated egoism, since the person concentrates his thoughts upon himself, none the less egoistic because concerned with personal "goodness" instead of with personal pleasure or profit. In other cases, it becomes a kind of anxious scrupulosity which is so fearful of going wrong that it abstains as much as possible from positive outgoing action. Concern for the good is reduced to a paralyzing solicitude to be preserved from falling into error. Energy that should go into action is absorbed in prying into motives. Conscience, moral thoughtfulness, makes us cowards as soon as it is isolated from courage.

Another bad consequence of treating virtues as if they were separate from one another and capable of being listed one by one is the attempt to cultivate each one by itself, instead of developing a rounded and positive character. There are, however, in traditional teachings many reminders of the wholeness of virtue. One such saying is that "love is the fulfilling of the law." For in its ethical sense, love signifies completeness of devotion to the objects esteemed good. Such an interest, or love, is marked by temperance because a comprehensive interest demands a harmony which can be attained only by subordination of particular impulses and passions. It involves courage because an active and genuine interest nerves us to meet and overcome the obstacles which stand in the way of its realization. It includes wisdom or thoughtfulness because sympathy, concern for the welfare of all affected by conduct, is the surest guarantee for the exercise of *consideration*, for examination of a proposed line of conduct in all its bearings. And such a complete interest is the only way in which justice can be assured. For it includes as part of itself impartial concern for all conditions which affect the common welfare, be they specific acts, laws, economic arrangements, political institutions, or whatever.

Still on the issue of moral goodness and virtue, we find that, while Kant considers good will (that is, moral goodness or conscientiousness) to be a good thing and, indeed, the only thing that is good without qualification, some recent writers question whether its goodness is so great and even whether it is a virtue at all. This view and an answer to it are stated by A. Campbell Garnett in the following essay. Garnett presupposes a teleological ethics of duty or principle, but because he tries to do justice to the deontologists' claims, most of what he says could be accepted by a deontologist.

CONSCIENCE AND CONSCIENTIOUSNESS

A. Campbell Garnett

Professor Nowell-Smith tells a story of an Oxford don who thought it his duty to attend Common Room, and did so conscientiously, though his presence was a source of acute distress both to himself and others. This story is told in illustration of a discussion of the question whether conscientiousness is good without qualification. The philosopher's comment is "He would have done better to stay at home," and he reinforces this view with the historical judgment that "Robespierre would have been a better man (quite apart from the question of the harm he did) if he had given his conscience a thorough rest and indulged his taste for roses

From "Conscience and Conscientious Action," Rice University Studies, LI (1965). Reprinted by permission of Margaret E. Garnett, Rice University Studies, and Trinity University Press.

and sentimental verse." [1] The harm, in these cases, he points out, seems to spring, in part at least, from the very conscientiousness of these people, and he concludes that we have no reason for accepting the principle of the supreme value of conscientiousness and that there is nothing either self-contradictory or even logically odd in the assertion "You think that you ought to do A, but you would be a better man if you did B." [2]

This judgment, it should be noted, is a *moral* evaluation. "Better man" here means "ethically better." It explicitly excludes "better" in the sense of "more useful or less harmful to society" in the reference to Robespierre. Further, it is not restricted to the mere right or wrong of overt acts, saying, for example, that Robespierre would have done less that is objectively wrong if he had attended to his roses more and his conscience less, for it is a judgment on the moral character of the *man*, not merely on that of his overt acts, and moral judgments upon a man must take account of every feature of his personality concerned in the performance of his acts, i.e., his motives, intentions, character, beliefs, abilities and so forth. What we have here, therefore, is the contention that in some cases where conscientiousness would lead to more harm than good (as it may do in cases of mistaken moral judgments or other ignorance) a man may be a morally better man by stifling his conscience and doing what he believes he ought not to do. It is not claimed that this will always be true in such cases, and it is not denied that conscientiousness is to some degree a value. But it is denied that it is the only moral value, or a value with supreme authority above all others, or that it is an essential feature of all moral value.

These denials are not uncommon among contemporary moralists, but it should be noted that they constitute a rejection of the major tradition in moral philosophy, from Plato to the present day. They also conflict with the convictions of the common man expressed in such injunctions as "Let your conscience be your guide," "Do what you yourself believe to be right, not what others tell you," "Act on your own convictions," "Always act in accord with your own conscience," "To thine own self be true." Conscientiousness is firmness of purpose in seeking to do what is right, and to most people it seems to be the very essence of the moral life and a value or virtue in some sense "higher" or more important than any other. Among philosophers this view is notably expressed in Joseph Butler's doctrine of the "natural supremacy" of conscience and in Immanuel Kant's insistence that there is nothing good in itself, intrinsically good, save the good will, and that this consists in the will to do one's duty for duty's sake. There are, evidently, some complex

[1] P. H. Nowell-Smith, *Ethics* (London, 1954), p. 247.
[2] *Ibid.*, p. 253.

issues and confusions involved in these sharply varying positions and to clarify them we shall need to begin with an examination of what is involved in conscience itself. . . .

Analysis of Conscience

Conscience involves both a cognitive and an emotive or motivational element. The cognitive element consists in a set of moral judgments concerning the right or wrong of certain kinds of action or rules of conduct, however these have been formed. The emotive or motivational element consists of a tendency to experience emotions of a unique sort of approval of the doing of what is believed to be right and a similarly unique sort of disapproval of the doing of what is believed to be wrong. These feeling states, it is generally recognized, are noticeably different from those of mere liking or disliking and also from feelings of aesthetic approval and disapproval (or aesthetic appreciation) and from feelings of admiration and the reverse aroused by nonmoral activities and skills. They can become particularly acute, moving and even distressing, in the negative and reflexive form of moral disapproval of one's own actions and motives, the sense of guilt and shame. In this form (indeed in both forms) they may have some notably irrational manifestations, but the sense of shame also has a very valuable function as an inhibitory motive upon the person who contemplates the possibility of doing what he believes to be wrong.

These are the commonly recognized aspects of conscience, and they frequently function quite uncritically. Because of this uncritical emotive reaction conscience all too frequently moves people to approve or disapprove actions and rules concerning which adequate reflection would lead to a very different verdict, and sometimes it afflicts people with a quite irrational sense of guilt. These deplorable effects of some manifestations of conscience are a large part of the reason for its devaluation in the judgment of many modern moralists. What these thinkers rightly deplore is the uncritical emotive reaction which the person who experiences it calls his conscience, particularly when the emotive element in it inhibits any critical activity of the cognitive element. But it is not necessary, and it is not usually the case, that the emotive element in conscience stifles the critical, and there is no justification for jumping to the conclusion that conscience should be ignored. For critical ethical thinking is itself usually conscientiousness, and conscience can be trained to be habitually critical.

For clarity of thinking on this question we need to distinguish between the critical and the traditional conscience. The latter is uncritical.

Here the emotive element attaches to moral ideas accepted from the tradition without critical re-evaluation of them. Its strength lies in this perpetuation of tradition, but this is also the source of its errors. It is this blind but emotive perpetuation of an outgrown and mistaken condition that contemporary critics of the supreme evaluation of conscience, for the most part, are concerned to deplore. And thus far they are right. But one would be unfair to such critics if one were not to recognize that their efforts to point out the errors of the tradition are usually also conscientious and are not merely the echoing of another tradition. Sometimes their critical ideas are boldly new and very commonly they are presented with persistent and painstaking care and in spite of personal cost. Nietzsche and Marx, Schweitzer and Gandhi, as well as Robespierre, were thoroughly conscientious men. Their ideas were new but were held with great emotive strength and tenacity. The same is true of the prophets of Israel and the great moral innovators of other religions. Indeed, the outstanding examples of conscientious men are not the mere sustainers of a tradition but the thinkers who try to improve the tradition. . . .

It is not difficult to see how the cognitive element in conscience, the judgment of right and wrong, becomes critical. To some extent it must be so from the beginning. A favorite word in every child's vocabulary is "Why?" And especially does he ask for reasons when told that he *ought* to do something he does not want to do. If moral injunctions are accepted as such on mere authority it is because it is implicitly believed that the authority *has* good reasons for issuing them, or else that the demand or example of this authority is in itself a sufficient reason for obedience or conformity, as with kings and deities. Apart from authority, reasons for moral rules have to be found in their relevance to the needs and security and peace of the community and the well-being of the person himself. But always, it is a distinguishing mark of a *moral* rule that it is one for which it is believed that reasons can be given. Critical thinking about moral rules is therefore stimulated whenever the reasons presented seem inadequate, beginning with the child's "Why?" and whenever there is a conflict of rules.

This critical thinking at first accepts as its basic principles the sort of reasons customarily given for moral rules and injunctions—the traditions of the tribe, its peace, security, prosperity and honor, revelations from divine sources, and so forth. But at a higher level of critical thinking conflicts are found between these basic principles themselves, and man is directed to the philosophical task of thinking out the *most* basic of all principles—if any such can be found. The search may end in scepticism and confusion, but so long as the thinker is prepared to accept any reason at all as a reason why something "ought" (in the ethical sense) to be done he is also convinced that he ought to do that which his search for reasons has led him to believe that he ought to do. Further, the experience of finding reasons for rejecting old views and accepting new ones impresses upon him the need and value of the search. Thus, so long as he recognizes any moral reasons at all he must recognize a duty of continued critical examination of moral ideas. The critical conscience thus becomes its own stimulus to further critical thinking. Conscience takes the form of the firm conviction, not merely that one ought to do what one believes one ought to do, still less that one ought to do without question what one has been taught one ought to do, but that one ought to think for oneself as to what one really ought to do and then act on one's own convictions. And the emotive drive is apt to attach itself as firmly to this last formulation of the cognitive element in conscience as ever it does to the other two.

Conscience, Love and Personal Integrity

It is clear that the motivational element of conscience in its most developed form is not merely the continuing echo of approvals and disapprovals of specific rules and actions impressed upon us by the social environment of our childhood. Yet the emotive content is continuous through all the changes in the sort of action the contemplation of which arouses it. One can imagine a youth of the eighteenth century feeling strong moral approval of a man who challenges a dangerous opponent to a duel in defense of his wife's good name, and later, in his maturity, feeling similar moral approval of another man who faces social obloquy for his refusal to fight a duel in similar circumstances because he is opposed in principle to duelling. In both cases it is the manifestation of courage in defense of principle that calls forth the moral approval, but his judgment has changed as to the mode of action appropriate to such defense. We see that what has changed is the specific sort of action that calls forth approval and disapproval, while what remains the same is the specific sort of reason that is held to be appropriate for judging an action to be worthy of approval or disapproval. And this we would find to be true in general (if we had space to demonstrate it) through the whole process of critical re-examination of moral judgment. Moral approval and disapproval attach to whatever we find to have reasons for approval. These reasons, in the course of thinking, become more and more specifically formulated and more and more highly generalized into abstract principles of moral judgment and they are only changed as change is seen to be needed to bring them into consistency with one another. Emotive unwillingness to accept some of the consequences of this process of ethical thinking sometimes inhibits and distorts it, but through it all the emotive drives of approval and disapproval tend to attach themselves to whatever lines of action are thought to be characterized by the recognized reasons for such attitudes.

On account of the complexity of all their implications the exact and proper statement of these basic ethical principles is a matter of very great difficulty. Yet there is a degree of agreement as to general principle which is really remarkable considering the complexity of human conduct and the diversity of traditional moral judgment with which we start. Thus, there is almost universal agreement that the fact that an act may have bad consequences for some persons is a good reason for disapproving it, and the reverse if it would have good consequences. Similarly there are certain rules of justice that are generally recognized, such as that of impartiality in the distribution of goods and burdens, the keeping of contracts and promises, the making of reparations, and the equitable application of the law. Questions arise as to how far the duties of beneficence should go, as to what to do when principles conflict in practical application, as to whether all principles can be comprehended under some one principle, and so forth. But the general trend is clear. Moral approval and disapproval are moved by the thought of the effect of our actions upon the weal or woe of human beings. This is the root of conscience. If some conscientious thinkers, such as Nietzsche, seem to be an exception to this rule it is because they have developed unusual or paradoxical views of what really constitutes true human weal or woe, or how it can best be promoted.

This connection of conscience with reasons for action bearing on the effects of action on human well-being enables us to understand the distinctive feeling-tone of moral approval and disapproval—i.e., their difference from mere liking and disliking, and from other emotions such as the aesthetic, and from nonmoral admiration and its reverse. The moral emotions are often mingled with these others, but they are also different. There is in them a distinct element of concern for human welfare which is gratified by what promotes it and distressed at anything that seems injurious. For this reason the moral emotions have often been identified with sympathy, but they are not mere passive feeling states. There is in them an element of active concern for human values with an impulse to give help where it seems needed. For this reason these emotions are responsive to judgments about the effects of human action, bringing forth a positive response of approval to that which seems helpful and the reverse toward the hurtful. For this reason also moral approval is a gratifying emotion, inducing a favorable reaction, while moral disapproval is apt to become a source of distress and an occasion for anger. For moral approval, we can now see, is a specification in action of the most deeply satisfying of all human emotions, that of love, in its most general form of expression.

Moral approval, then, is a development of the basic social interest of man as a social animal, it is an expression of the general sympathetic tendency of concern for human values with special attention to those depending on the orderly life of the group. It is an expression of the desire to create and maintain those values. Its conflict with other motives is, therefore, a conflict of desires. But this particular conflict, the conflict of conscience (moral approvals and disapprovals) with other desires (temptations) is not just an ordinary conflict of desires. It is a conflict in which the integrity of the personality is peculiarly involved. In an ordinary conflict of desires, in which there is no moral issue, the best solution is for one of the desires to be completely set aside and fade into oblivion without regrets, the opposing interest being completely triumphant. And, for the integrity of the personality it does not matter which interest gives way. But if the conflict be between "conscience" (the interests involved in moral approval and disapproval) and "temptation" (some opposed interest or desire) then it does matter which triumphs. The integrity of personality is involved. It tends to dissolve as a person slips into the habit of doing things he believes to be wrong. He loses his self-respect and his firmness of purpose. For a time the sense of guilt depresses. Later it tends to be repressed. With these psychological repressions the personality tends to manifest either general weakness or the overcompensations which give a false impression of strength as they manifest themselves in irrational drives. The guilty conscience and the repressed conscience are at the root of most of the disorders of personality, whether the guilt itself be reasonably conceived or not.

It is evident, therefore, that the emotive or motivational element that manifests itself in conscience is rooted in conative tendencies or interests which are of basic importance in the life of man. This psychological conclusion has, in recent years, been strongly emphasized by a number of workers in the field of psychotherapy, notably by Erich Fromm, who argues strongly that only in what he calls the "orientation of productive love" [3] can the personality of man develop continuously and with the integrity necessary for mental health. From this conclusion concerning the psychological need of this type of orientation Fromm also develops a most important theory of conscience. What we have distinguished as the critical and uncritical (or traditional) conscience he distinguishes as the "authoritarian" and the "humanistic" conscience. The former he dismisses as the internalized voice of an external authority, but the latter, he maintains, is "the reaction of our total personality to its proper functioning

---

[3] Erich Fromm, *Man For Himself* (New York, 1947), pp. 92–107.

or disfunctioning. . . . Conscience is thus . . . the voice of our true selves which summons us . . . to live productively, to develop fully and harmoniously. . . . It is the guardian of our integrity." [4]

If Fromm's psychological analysis of the growth and structure of personality is accurate in essentials, and if our account of the growth of the critical conscience out of the uncritical is also correct, then we must recognize that conscience at every stage is, as Fromm says of the "humanistic" conscience, "the reaction of our total personality to its total functioning," its "voice" is the experience of the constraint of the personality as a whole, in its seeking of a growing creative expression with integrity or wholeness, upon the occasional and temporary impulses and desires which would tend to stultify its creativity and destroy its integrity. It is because doing what we believe we ought not is destructive of that integrity that conscience demands that we always act in accord with our own convictions; and it is because the fundamental orientation of human life is social and creative that ethical thinking tends, through the course of history, to clarify itself in the light of principles which tend to formulate moral judgments as expressions of impartial concern for human well-being.

The Authority of Conscience

It is time now to return to the question with which we started. Is it true that a man would sometimes be a better man (i.e., morally better) for refusing to obey his conscience rather than obeying it? It should be noted that the question is not whether the consequences to himself or to others might be better in general, but whether he would, himself, be a morally better man for acting in this way. This raises the question whether it is ever morally right to go against one's conscience. Is it ever right to do as you think you ought not to do? And this, again, is not the question whether conscience is always right in what it commands us to do, but whether it is ever right to disobey those commands, thus choosing to do what we believe to be wrong? The traditional answer is given by Joseph Butler in asserting the "natural supremacy" of conscience, which "magisterially asserts itself and approves and condemns." "Had it strength as it had right: had it power, as it had manifest authority, it would absolutely govern the world." [5] Against this we have the contemporary challenge voiced by Nowell-Smith.

One serious objection to this modern challenge to the traditional

---

[4] *Ibid.*, pp. 158–60.

[5] Joseph Butler, *Five Sermons* (New York, 1950), p. 41.

view is that it is necessarily futile and worse than futile, as a guiding principle of moral behaviour. It is futile because, though a man may believe that *perhaps,* in some cases, it *may* be that he would be a better man if he did not do what he believes he ought to do, he can never believe this in any particular case, for that would be to believe that he ought not to do this that he believes he ought to do, which is self-contradictory. Thus this piece of ethical theory is so paradoxical that it can never function as a guide to action. Further, it is worse than futile, for it implies, not merely that moral judgment may be mistaken (and therefore needs critical examination) but that the very effort not to do wrong may itself sometimes be wrong—that the conscientious effort to try to find out what is really right and act firmly in accord with one's own convictions, is sometimes wrong and we have no way of knowing when it is wrong. From this state of mind the only reasonable reaction is to abandon the ethical inquiry and the ethical endeavor and make the easiest and most satisfactory adjustment we can to the mores of the community and the practical exigencies of our personal situation.

The logical alternatives, therefore, are either to abandon the moral standpoint entirely, or to affirm, with Butler, the moral authority of every man's own conscience. The fact that judgments conscientiously made may be in error does not imply that this assertion of the sovereignty of the individual conscience must lead to either conflict or chaos. It rather avoids conflict, for each person, in asserting the rights of his own conscience, at the same time affirms the right of freedom of conscience for others. And it avoids chaos because, laying the injunction upon us to exercise continuous critical examination of our own moral judgments, it points us on the only possible way to consistency and order in moral judgment, by finding our errors and rectifying them. A community of people open-mindedly seeking the best formulation and reformulation of its moral rules, and abiding by its most intelligent findings, is more likely to maintain order with progress than one in which conscience operates in any other way, or in no way at all.

We must conclude, then, that if one were to accept Nowell-Smith's critique of conscience one could not apply it to the decision of any moral question in one's own conduct, and that its acceptance, if taken seriously, would be apt to have a deteriorating effect upon personal moral endeavor. But it is still possible to grant it theoretical credence and apply it to our evaluation of the moral value of the personality of others. This is what Nowell-Smith does in the cases of Robespierre and the Oxford don: Robespierre would have been a better man if he had indulged his taste for roses and sentimental verse rather than follow the demands of his conscience that he strive by whatever terrible means seemed necessary to carry through the program of the revolution; and the Oxford don would have been a better man if he had allowed his personal distaste for Common Room society to overcome his sense of duty which required him to attend it.

This is a judgment on the moral quality of the man as affected by his act of choice. The choice with which we are concerned is not that of his decision as to whether A or B is the right thing to do but his decision as to whether he would do what he believed to be the right thing or follow his personal wishes to do something that he found much more agreeable to himself. The latter act is the one he would do if he had not given any consideration to the effect of his actions on other people, or the needs of the social structure of which he is a part, except so far as his own interests were involved, and, coming as it does after he has considered these things and formed a judgment as to what they require of him, it is a decision to set aside the results of this thoughtful examination of the possible consequences of his conduct and do the thing he personally wants to do and would have done if he had never given the matter any ethical thought at all. When the issue is thus clearly stated it is very difficult to see how any thoughtful person could judge the unconscientious following of inclination to be the act of a better man, or an act that tends to make a better man, than the careful thinking and active self-determination involved in conscientiousness. It seems evident that those who have expressed the view that the following of personal inclination is sometimes morally better than conscientiousness are confusing this issue with another to which we must next give attention.

Conscientiousness and Other Values

For Immanuel Kant there was nothing good in itself, good without qualification, except a good will, and a good will, he explains, is good, not because it is a will to produce some good, or even the greatest possible good, but simply by reason of the nature of its volition as a will to do one's duty, a will to do what is conceived as right. Thus, for Kant, an action only has *moral* worth if it is done from a sense of duty, not from any inclination, even that of an impartial desire to promote general human well-being. Kant does not deny that good-natured inclinations have value, but he insists that the will to do one's duty has incomparably higher value and that it alone is of distinctly moral value. Kant's position here is an extreme one. Conscientiousness is regarded not merely as an essential part of moral value but as the only truly moral value and supreme among all values. Against this Nowell-Smith is not alone in protesting, and it is this rejection of the extravagant claim for conscientiousness as compared with other values, that seems to him to justify the notion that there are some occasions when some other value should be preferred and conscientiousness rejected.[6]

It is true, as Nowell-Smith says, that "we normally think of moral worth as meaning the worth of any virtuous motive and we normally think of sympathy and benevolence as virtuous motives." [7] It is also true, that, contrary to Kant, we normally judge a right action done out of sympathy and good will to be morally better than the same action would be if done solely from a sense of duty but without sympathy or good will.[8] These normal judgments I think we must fully endorse, but they do not involve the implication that a man can be morally justified (i.e., can be a "better man" than he otherwise would be) in performing an act, even of sympathy and good will (let alone indulging an interest in roses), which, in the circumstances, he regards as wrong.

There is a story told by Mark Twain of two ladies who lied to protect a runaway slave even though believing it wrong to do so and fearing that they might suffer in hell for their sin. In such a case we see a conflict, not merely of conscience with desire, but of the uncritical or traditional conscience with the critical. The deeper level of conscience, which they might well have called their "intuitions," urged the protection of the poor, frightened slave. They were not sufficiently capable of philosophical thinking to formulate a philosophical critique in support of their own deeper insights, so they remained superficially of the traditional opinion that their action was wrong. But their choice was actually a conscientious one, true to the deeper levels of conscience, and we tend to endorse their decision because it is endorsed by our consciences too. But this example (and others like it) is not a case of judging that the motives of love and sympathy were here better than conscientiousness, but of judging that the will to do good, seen as the very root of righteousness, is better than the will to conform to rules uncritically accepted as right. Such a judgment is far from the same as judging that the Oxford don would have been a morally better man for indulging his reluctance to attend Common Room than he would for conscientiously fulfilling what he believed to be his duty in the matter.

If we accept a teleological ethics then we recognize that the purpose of moral rules is to protect and promote the more important aspects of social well-being. We then see that the motives of love and sympathy, if sufficiently strong, enlightened and impartial, would achieve the pur-

---

6 Nowell-Smith, *op. cit.,* p. 245.

7 *Ibid.,* p. 246.

8 *Ibid.,* p. 259.

poses of moral rules better than the moral rules do, and would also achieve other good purposes beyond them. A world of saints would be a better world than a world of conscientious persons without mutual love and sympathy. Seeing this, though there are no saints, we endorse such elements of saintliness as there are (i.e., love and sympathy expressed in this enlightened and impartial way) and recognize them as morally good and as expressions of a better type of personality than one in which conscientiousness is found without these motives. But this recognition of the greater value of enlightened and impartial good will, or love, can never involve a rejection of conscientiousness in favor of such love, for such love includes and transcends all that conscientiousness stands for. Such love is the fulfilling of the law and the fulfilling, not the rejection, of the conscientiousness which supports the law. Thus, while a teleological ethics rejects Kant's apotheosis of the will to do one's duty as the only intrinsic moral value it does not lead to an endorsement of the view that we should sometimes judge a man as morally better for neglecting his conscience to indulge some other inclination. If, on the other hand, we were to accept a deontological ethics we should find that to speak of a conflict between conscientiousness and an enlightened and impartial love and sympathy (or any other good motive) as a conflict between different moral values involves a category mistake. For conscientiousness and other good motives, on this view, are not moral values in the same sense. An act of love is not made moral by the kind of consequences at which it aims. The only moral actions are those which intentionally adhere to intuitively discerned principles. So whatever value is attached to love and sympathy, it is not moral value. Moral value belongs alone to conscientiousness. Thus a man could never become morally better by rejecting the morally valuable motive of conscientiousness for some other motive to which only nonmoral value is attached. This deontological theory Nowell-Smith, I think rightly, rejects, but it is well to see that it, too, involves a rejection of his theory of the comparison of conscientiousness with other moral values.

Returning to the teleological point of view, and reflecting on the deontologist's claim, we can perhaps see the reason for the basic confusions that haunt people's minds on this question of the relative value of conscientiousness and impartial good will, or love. Conscientiousness is uniquely a moral motive in that its end is morality itself, the keeping of moral rules. All other motives, if without conscientiousness, are at best nonmoral (operating without concern for moral rules) or at worst immoral—consciously in opposition to them. This is true even of love and sympathy, simply as such. But if the teleological point of view is correct it is not true of love and sympathy *with a concern for impartiality*, for this latter is the very basis of moral rules and such love is of the essence of the moral life. Thus conscientiousness and impartial good will share together the unique character of being moral in the sense of being motivated by a concern for morality as such, the former for the rules which formulate it in lines of conduct, and the latter for the basic principle of impartial concern for human well-being in accordance with which the rules merely formulate the guiding lines. But this merely means that impartial good will is a motive characterized by the critical conscience, while conscientiousness without love, sympathy or good will is an operation of the traditional or uncritical conscience alone. Thus the motive that is of uniquely moral value and of supreme moral authority is love finding expression in the form of the critical conscience.

The main conclusions, therefore, of this paper may be summed up briefly thus: (1) Conscientiousness, if it be properly critical, is good without qualification, but an uncritical conscientiousness is not. (2) Since we cannot be saints we need to be conscientious, and this includes both the effort to find out what we really ought to do and the effort to do it to the best of our ability. (3) We should also cultivate the motive of impartial love or good will, for it functions as both an illuminating guide and support to our efforts to be conscientious and is itself of intrinsic moral value. (4) We can be righteous, and to that extent good, men merely by being conscientious, but we can be much better men by being not only conscientious but men in whom, without conflicting with conscience, the effort to be conscientious is made unnecessary by the outflow of spontaneous good will. These are very ordinary conclusions, but it takes clear thinking to keep them free from some very extraordinary objections.

One of the most desirable dispositions to cultivate, from a moral standpoint, is an intellectual virtue of a sort not recognized by Aristotle, namely, an ability or disposition to "realize" in imagination the lives, interests, feelings, etc., of others. The nature of this disposition and other points about it are forcefully stated, though in an old-fashioned rhetoric, by Josiah Royce (1855–1916) in a description of what he calls "the moral insight." One might almost take it as a description of the moral point of view.

THE MORAL INSIGHT

Josiah Royce

. . . [The following] is our reflective account of the process that, in some form, must come to every one under the proper conditions. In this process we see the beginning of the real knowledge of duty to others. The process is one that any child can and does, under proper guidance, occasionally accomplish. It is the process by which we all are accustomed to try to teach humane behavior in concrete cases. We try to get people to realize what they are doing when they injure others. But to distinguish this process from the mere tender emotion of sympathy, with all its illusions, is what moralists have not carefully enough done. Our exposition [tries] to take this universally recognized process, to distinguish it from sympathy as such, and to set it up before the gates of ethical doctrine as the great producer of insight.

But when we say that to this insight common sense must come, under the given conditions, we do not mean to say: "So the man, once having attained insight, must act thenceforth." The realization of one's neighbor, in the full sense of the word realization, is indeed the resolution to treat him as if he were real, that is, to treat him unselfishly. But this resolution expresses and belongs to the moment of insight. Passion may cloud the insight in the very next moment. It always does cloud the insight after no very long time. It is as impossible for us to avoid the illusion of selfishness in our daily lives, as to escape seeing through the illusion at the moment of insight. We see the reality of our neighbor, that is, we determine to treat him as we do ourselves. But then we go back to daily action, and we feel the heat of hereditary passions, and we straightway forget what we have seen. Our neighbor becomes obscured. He is once more a foreign power. He is unreal. We are again deluded and selfish. This conflict goes on and will go on as long as we live after the manner of men. Moments of insight, with their accompanying resolutions; long stretches of delusion and selfishness: That is our life.

To bring home this view . . . to the reader, we ask him to consider very carefully just what experience he has when he tries to realize his neighbor in the full sense that we have insisted upon. Not pity as such is what we desire him to feel. For whether or no pity happens to work in him as selfishly and blindly as we have found that it often does work, still not the emotion, but its consequences, must in the most favorable case give us what we seek. All the forms of sympathy are mere impulses.

From The Religious Aspects of Philosophy *(Boston: Houghton Mifflin Company, 1885).*

It is the insight to which they bring us that has moral value. And again, the realization of our neighbor's existence is not at all the discovery that he is more or less useful to us personally. All that would contribute to selfishness. In an entirely different way we must realize his existence, if we are to be really altruistic. What then is our neighbor?

We find that out by treating him in thought just as we do ourselves. What art thou? Thou art now just a present state, with its experiences, thoughts, and desires. But what is thy future Self? Simply future states, future experiences, future thoughts and desires, that, although not now existing for thee, are postulated by thee as certain to come, and as in some real relation to thy present Self. What then is thy neighbor? He too is a mass of states, of experiences, thoughts, and desires, just as real as thou art, no more but yet no less present to thy experience now than is thy future Self. He is not that face that frowns or smiles at thee, although often thou thinkest of him as only that. He is not the arm that strikes or defends thee, not the voice that speaks to thee, not that machine that gives thee what thou desirest when thou movest it with the offer of money. To be sure, thou dost often think of him as if he were that automaton yonder, that answers thee when thou speakest to it. But no, thy neighbor is as actual, as concrete, as thou art. Just as thy future is real, though not now thine, so thy neighbor is real, though his thoughts never are thy thoughts. Dost thou believe this? Art thou sure what it means? This is for thee the turning-point of thy whole conduct towards him. What we now ask of thee is no sentiment, no gush of pity, no tremulous weakness of sympathy, but a calm, clear insight. . . .

If he is real like thee, then is his life as bright a light, as warm a fire, to him, as thine to thee; his will is as full of struggling desires, of hard problems, of fateful decisions; his pains are as hateful, his joys as dear. Take whatever thou knowest of desire and of striving, of burning love and of fierce hatred, realize as fully as thou canst what that means, and then with clear certainty add: *Such as that is for me, so is it for him, nothing less.* If thou dost that, can he remain to thee what he has been, a picture, a plaything, a comedy, or a tragedy, in brief a mere Show? Behind all that show thou hast indeed dimly felt that there is something. Know that truth thoroughly. Thou hast regarded his thought, his feeling, as somehow different in sort from thine. Thou hast said: "A pain in him is not like a pain in me, but something far easier to bear." Thou hast made of him a ghost, as the imprudent man makes of his future self a ghost. Even when thou hast feared his scorn, his hate, his contempt, thou hast not fully made him for thee as real as thyself. His laughter at thee has made thy face feel hot, his frowns and clenched fists have cowed thee, his sneers have made thy throat feel choked. But that was only the social instinct in thee. It was not a full sense of his reality. Even so the little baby smiles back at one that smiles at it, but not because it realizes the approving joy of the other, only because it by instinct enjoys a smiling face; and even so the baby is frightened at harsh speech, but not because it realizes the other's anger. So, dimly and by instinct, thou has lived with thy neighbor, and hast known him not, being blind. Thou hast even desired his pain, but thou hast not fully realized the pain that thou gavest. It has been to thee, not pain in itself, but the sight of his submission, of his tears, or of his pale terror. Of thy neighbor thou hast made a thing, no Self at all.

When thou hast loved, hast pitied, or hast reverenced thy neighbor, then thy feeling has possibly raised for a moment the veil of illusion. Then thou hast known what he truly is, a Self like thy present Self. But thy selfish feeling is too strong for thee. Thou hast forgotten soon again what thou hadst seen, and hast made even of thy beloved one only the instrument of thy own pleasure. Even out of thy power to pity thou hast made an object of thy vainglory. Thy reverence has turned again to pride. Thou hast accepted the illusion once more. No wonder that in this darkness thou findest selfishness the only rule of any meaning for thy conduct. Thou forgottest that without realization of thy future and as yet unreal self, even selfishness means nothing. Thou forgottest that if thou gavest thy present thought even so to the task of realizing thy neighbor's life, selfishness would seem no more plain to thee than the love of thy neighbor.

Have done then with this illusion that thy Self is all in all. Intuition tells thee no more about thy future Self than it tells thee about thy neighbors. Desire, bred in thee by generations of struggle for existence, emphasizes the expectation of thy own bodily future, the love for thy own bodily welfare, and makes thy body's life seem alone real. But simply try to know the truth. The truth is that all this world of life about thee is as real as thou art. All conscious life is conscious in its own measure. Pain is pain, joy is joy, everywhere even as in thee. The result of thy insight will be inevitable. The illusion vanishing, the glorious prospect opens before thy vision. Seeing the oneness of this life everywhere, the equal reality of all its moments, thou wilt be ready to treat it all with the reverence that prudence would have thee show to thy own little bit of future life. What prudence in its narrow respectability counseled, thou wilt be ready to do universally. As the prudent man, seeing the reality of his future self, inevitably works for it; so the enlightened man, seeing the reality of all conscious life, realizing that it is no shadow, but fact, at once and inevitably desires, if only for that one moment of insight, to enter into the service of the whole of it. . . . Lift up thy eyes, behold that life, and then turn away and forget it as thou canst; but if thou hast known that, thou hast begun to know thy duty.

4.3

Responsibility
and Freedom of the Will

Besides saying of people that their acts are right or wrong, or that they or their motives are morally good or bad, we also make judgments of *responsibility* about them and their actions. These judgments of responsibility are central in morality. In fact, we usually think that we cannot make moral judgments, aretaic or deontic, about a man or his actions unless he is responsible for what he does. The crucial questions, then, are these: When is a man responsible for his actions? When may he be held responsible for what he has done? Is he responsible for his character traits?

One of the first (and still one of the most generally accepted) answers to these questions is that of Aristotle. He says, in effect, that a person is responsible for his action if it is "voluntary," and then explains when an action is voluntary and when it is not. He also contends that both virtue and vice are voluntary and, hence, that we are responsible for our moral character.

WHEN IS A PERSON RESPONSIBLE?

Aristotle

As virtue is concerned with emotions and actions, and such emotions and actions as are voluntary are the subjects of praise and blame, while

From The Nicomachean Ethics of Aristotle, *trans. J. E. C. Welldon (London: Macmillan & Co. Ltd., 1892).*

such as are involuntary are the subjects of pardon and sometimes even of pity, it is necessary, I think, in an investigation of virtue to distinguish what is voluntary from what is involuntary. It will also be useful in legislation as bearing upon the honours and punishments which the legislator assigns.

It is generally admitted that acts done under compulsion, or from ignorance, are involuntary. But an act is compulsory, if its origin is external to the agent or patient, i.e., if it is one in which the agent or the patient contributes nothing, as e.g., if the wind, or people who have us in their power, were to carry us in a certain direction. But if an action is done from fear of greater evils or for some noble end, e.g., if a tyrant, who had our parents and children in his power, were to order us to do some shameful act, on condition that, if we did it, their lives should be spared, and, if not, they should be put to death, it is a question whether such action is voluntary or involuntary. The case of throwing goods overboard during a storm at sea is similar; for although nobody would voluntarily make such a sacrifice in the abstract, yet every sensible person will make it for his own safety and the safety of his fellow passengers. Actions like this, although they are of a mixed character, are more like voluntary than involuntary actions, as they are chosen at the time of performing them, and the end or character of an action depends upon the choice made at the moment of performing it. When we speak then of an action as voluntary or involuntary, we must have regard to the time at which a person performs it. The person whose actions we are considering acts voluntarily; for in actions like his the original power which sets the instrumentality of his limbs in motion lies in himself, and when the origin of a thing lies in a person himself, it is in his power either to do it or not to do it. Such actions then are practically voluntary, although in the abstract they may be said perhaps to be involuntary, as nobody would choose any such action in itself.

Such actions are at times subjects of praise, when people submit to something that is shameful or painful for the sake of gaining what is great and noble; or in the contrary case they are the subjects of censure, as it is only a bad man who would submit to what is utterly shameful, if his object were not noble at all, or were indifferent. There are also some actions which are pardonable, although not laudable, as when a person is induced to do what is wrong by such causes as are too strong for human nature and do not admit of resistance. Yet it is probable that there are some actions where compulsion is an impossibility; a person would rather suffer the most dreadful form of death than do them. Thus the reasons which constrained Alcmæon in Euripides to murder his mother are clearly ridiculous.

It is sometimes difficult to determine what ought to be chosen or endured for the sake of obtaining or avoiding a certain result. But it is still more difficult to abide by our decisions; for it generally happens that, while the consequence which we expect is painful, the act which we are constrained to do is shameful, and therefore we receive censure or praise according as we yield or do not yield to the constraint.

What class of actions then is it that may be rightly called compulsory? Actions it may be said are compulsory in the abstract, whenever the cause is external to the agent and he contributes nothing to it. But if an action, although involuntary in itself, is chosen at a particular time and for a particular end, and if its original cause lies in the agent himself, then, although such an action is involuntary in itself, it is voluntary at that time and for that end. Such an action however is more like a voluntary than an involuntary action; for actions fall under the category of particulars, and in the supposed case the particular action is voluntary.

. . . It might be argued that whatever is pleasant or noble is compulsory, as pleasure and nobleness are external to ourselves and exercise a constraint upon us; but if that were so, every action would be compulsory, as these are the motives of all actions in us all. Again, if a person acts under compulsion and involuntarily, his action is painful to him; but if the motives of his action are pleasure and nobleness, it is pleasant. It is ridiculous to lay the blame of our wrong actions upon external causes, rather than upon the facility with which we ourselves are caught by such causes, and, while we take the credit of our noble actions to ourselves, to lay the blame of our shameful actions upon pleasure. It seems then that an action is compulsory if its origin is external to the agent, i.e. if the person who is the subject of compulsion is in no sense contributory to the action.

An action which is due to ignorance is always non-voluntary; but it is not involuntary, unless it is followed by pain and excites a feeling of regret. For if a person has performed an action, whatever it may be, from ignorance, and yet feels no distress at his action, it is true that he has not acted voluntarily, as he was not aware of what he was doing, but on the other hand, he has not acted involuntarily, so long as he feels no pain.

If a person who has acted from ignorance regrets what he has done, it may be said that he is an involuntary agent; but, if he does not regret it, his case is different; and he may be called a non-voluntary agent, for, as there is this difference, it is better that he should have a special name.

It would seem, too, that there is a difference between acting from ignorance and doing a thing in ignorance. Thus, if a person is intoxicated or infuriated, he is not regarded as acting from ignorance, but as acting from intoxication or fury; yet he does not act consciously but in ignorance.

It must be admitted then that every vicious person is ignorant of what he ought to do, and what he ought to abstain from doing, and that ignorance is the error which makes people unjust and generally wicked. But when we speak of an action as involuntary, we do not mean merely that a person is ignorant of his true interest. The ignorance which is the cause of involuntary action, as distinguished from that which is the cause of vice, is not such ignorance as affects the moral purpose, nor again is it ignorance of the universal; for this is censurable. It is rather ignorance of particulars, i.e. ignorance of the particular circumstances and occasion of the action. Where this ignorance exists, there is room for pity, and forgiveness, as one who is ignorant of any such particular is an involuntary agent.

It will perhaps be as well then to define the nature and number of these particulars. They are

1. the agent,
2. the act,
3. the occasion or circumstances of the act.

Sometimes also

4. the instrument, e.g. a tool,
5. the object, e.g. safety, and
6. the manner of doing an act, e.g. gently or violently.

Nobody but a madman can be ignorant of all these particulars. It is clear that nobody can be ignorant of the agent; for how can a person be ignorant of himself? But a person may be ignorant of what he is doing, as when people say that a word escaped them unawares or that they did not know a subject was forbidden, like Aeschylus when he revealed the mysteries, or that he only meant to show the working of a weapon when he discharged it, like the man who discharged the catapult. Again, a person may take his son for an enemy like Merope, or a pointed foil for a foil that has its button on, or a solid stone for a pumice stone, or he may kill somebody by a blow that was meant to save him, or he may deal a fatal blow while only intending, as in a sparring match, to give a lesson in the art of dealing a blow. As there may be ignorance in regard to all these particular circumstances of an action, it may be said that a person has acted involuntarily, if he was ignorant of any one of them, and especially of such particulars as seem to be most important, i.e. of the circumstances of the action, and of its natural result. But if an action is to be called involuntary in respect of such ignorance, it is necessary that it should be painful to the agent and should excite in him a feeling of regret.

As an action is involuntary if done under compulsion or from ignorance, it would seem to follow that it is voluntary if the agent originates it with a knowledge of the particular circumstances of the action. For it is perhaps wrong to say that actions which are due to passion or desire are involuntary. For in the first place upon that hypothesis none of the lower animals can any more be said to act voluntarily, nor can children; and secondly is it to be argued that nothing which we do from desire or passion is voluntary? or are our noble actions done voluntarily, and our shameful actions involuntarily? Surely the latter view is ridiculous, if one and the same person is the author of both kinds of action. But it would seem irrational to assert that such things as ought to be the objects of desire are desired involuntarily; and there are certain things which ought to be the occasions of anger, and certain things such as health and learning, which ought to be the objects of desire. Again, it seems that what is involuntary is painful, but what is done from desire is pleasant. Again, what difference is there, in respect of involuntariness, between errors of reason and errors of passion? It is our duty to avoid both; but the irrational emotions seem to be as truly human as the reason itself and therefore we are as truly responsible for our emotions as for our reasoning. Such actions then as proceed from passion and desire are not less the actions of the man than rational actions; it is absurd therefore to regard these as involuntary. . . .

Virtue and vice are both alike in our own power; for where it is in our power to act, it is also in our power to refrain from acting, and where it is in our power to refrain from acting, it is also in our power to act. Hence if it is in our power to act when action is noble, it will also be in our power to refrain from acting when inaction is shameful, and if it is in our power to refrain from acting when inaction is noble, it will also be in our power to act when action is shameful. But if it is in our power to do, and likewise not to do, what is noble and shameful, and if so to act or not to act is as we have seen to be good or bad, it follows that it is in our power to be virtuous or vicious. The saying

"None would be wicked, none would not be blessed,"

seems to be partly false and partly true; for while nobody is blessed against his will, vice is voluntary.

. . . we punish a person for mere ignorance, if it seems that he is responsible for it. Thus the punishments inflicted on drunken people who commit a crime are double, as the origin of the crime lies in the person himself, for it was in his power not to get drunk, and the drunkenness was the cause of his ignorance.

Again, we punish people who are ignorant of any legal point, if they ought to know it, and could easily know it. Similarly in other cases we punish people, whenever it seems that their ignorance was due to carelessness; for they had it in their power not to be ignorant, as they might have taken the trouble to inform themselves. It will perhaps be argued that a person is of such a character that he cannot take the trouble; but the answer is that people are themselves responsible for having acquired such a character by their dissolute life, and for being unjust or licentious, as their injustice is the consequence of doing wrong, and their licentiousness of spending their time in drinking and other such things. For a person's character depends upon the way in which he exercises his powers. . . .

Again, it is irrational to assert that one who acts unjustly does not wish to be unjust, or that one who acts licentiously does not wish to be licentious. If a person, not acting in ignorance, commits such actions as will make him unjust, he will be voluntarily unjust. But it does not follow that, if he wishes, he will cease to be unjust and will be just, any more than it follows that a sick man, if he wishes, will be well. It may happen that he is voluntarily ill through living an incontinent life, and disobeying his doctors. If so, it was once in his power not to be ill; but, as he has thrown the opportunity away, it is no longer in his power. . . .

If then, as is generally allowed, the virtues are voluntary (for we are ourselves, in a sense, partly responsible for our moral states, and it is because we possess a certain character that the end which we set before ourselves is of a certain kind), it follows that our vices too must be voluntary, as what is true of one is equally true of the other. . . .

As Aristotle says, it is only voluntary actions and traits that are *subject* to praise and blame. Now another question arises. What more must be true for a person to be *worthy* of praise or blame for what he does or is? Must, for example, his motive or motives be good or bad? Such questions are briefly dealt with by A. C. Ewing in the next selection.

WHEN IS A PERSON BLAMEWORTHY?

A. C. Ewing

In discussing actions we have so far been discussing the principles according to which we decide which action it is best to choose to do in a given situation, i.e. which action is externally the right one. But there is another way, equally ethical, of looking at actions. We look at them in

From Teach Yourself Ethics *(London: Teach Yourself Books Ltd., 1953). Reprinted by perimssion of the publisher.*

this second way when we consider whether the agent deserves praise or blame, and here we think of motives rather than effects, of the inner rather than the outer side. The contrast between the two aspects of an action appears most clearly when we consider the case of a man who does something wrong in all good faith because he mistakenly thinks it right. It is apparent to every thinking person in a war where people on both sides fight with a good conscience believing that they are doing what is right, or in any case where a person acts with good intentions but makes a terrible mistake as to the consequences to be anticipated from what he does. Confronted with such cases we do not blame the agent morally for acting as he did except in so far as we think him morally responsible for his beliefs, though of course we may still blame him intellectually, i.e. call him a fool. This distinction raises some difficulties. It is a recognized principle of ethics that it is always our duty to do what after proper consideration we think we ought to do, but suppose we are mistaken, then we by this principle ought to do something which is wrong and which therefore we ought not to do. Is not this a contradiction? It would be if we were not using two different senses of "ought" (and correspondingly of "right," "wrong," "duty"). Whether we are mistaken or not in our beliefs, there is clearly no morally permissible alternative to doing what we think we ought, provided we add a reservation, hard to define, about sufficient consideration. For, if we do not thus act, we cannot be acting out of moral motives but are on the contrary going against the moral principle in us, and so we ought to be blamed and not praised even if the action happens to be externally right, for that is only a matter of luck, since we did it not because it was right but thinking it wrong. Even if we accept the authority of somebody else, we do so on our own moral responsibility, and are only entitled to do so if we think him more likely to be right than ourselves. Yet the mere possibility of enquiring whether we ought to perform an action implies that there is a sense in which an action may still be wrong even if it is done with the best possible motives in the conviction that it is right. If what we thought right were automatically the right thing to do in all senses, there would be no point in devoting trouble and care to finding out what was right. We cannot answer the question what we ought to do in this other sense by pointing merely to our actual opinions and our motives. Granted that our motive is to do what is right, we still have to find out what is right. It was the nature of the principles relating to the answer to this question that [was discussed] above, let us now turn to the question of moral blame.

Here one naturally starts by laying down the principle which I have already mentioned, namely, that we cannot be morally blamed if we do what we think right, "act in accordance with our conscience" as the phrase is. The question is not however quite so simply answered as it might seem. A man may think his conscience tells him to do the most outrageous things, as did many Nazis. Suppose Hitler believed that he was doing his duty when he inflicted appalling sufferings on the Jews and other unfortunate people and violated almost every canon of morals. Is he to escape all moral blame because he somehow deluded himself into thinking that all the abominable things he wanted to do were right or actually his duty? If he had this knack of deluding himself into believing that everything he did was right, does it follow that he was morally less blameworthy than are most people, who have a better ideal but constantly fall below it, as according to themselves have very many who would be accounted saints or almost saints? The reply would be made that Hitler was at any rate morally at fault in neglecting his duty of trying to consider properly what really was right before he acted as he did, but it is quite possible that it may not have occurred to him that he had not considered the question sufficiently, and then by the above principle he could not be blamed for neglecting that duty. But could he really escape all moral blame in this fashion? I am not therefore altogether satisfied with the above, usually accepted, principle.

But, even if we do accept it, it is important to recognize a distinction between two kinds of mistake which lead people to make wrong decisions as to what they ought to do. One kind of mistake relates to matters of fact, as when, e.g. a doctor through an error of judgement gives medicine that does harm rather than good, or a man breaks an agreement because he has genuinely misunderstood its import. Such an error is certainly not morally blameworthy unless due to negligence or avoidable prejudice, however much it may show lack of intelligence. But there is another kind of error which consists not in mistake as to matters of fact but in mistaken judgments of value. Such errors, whether morally blameworthy in the strict sense or not, at least disclose what we may call a moral defect in the person concerned. The latter is at any rate in a morally less desirable state than he would be in if he did not make such errors, whether it is "his fault" or not. An example of the first kind of error is given by a man who says something false because he thinks it true, of the second by a man who says something false because he underestimates the evil of lying or by one who attaches little value to any but "material" goods. Whether they could help it or not, it must be admitted that such men are in a lower state morally than they would be if they were free from these grave moral errors. Perhaps this is only because they are at an earlier stage of development or perhaps it is because they have knowingly done wrong in the past, but in any case they are in this state, however they got there.

For any action to have moral merit it is required not merely that it should be externally what the agent thinks right after due consideration, but that its motives should be good. What is a good and what a bad motive? There is no doubt that the desire to do one's duty because it is one's duty—I disagree with Kant in seeing no reason for not calling it a desire—is a good motive, but it is not the only one. Love for a particular person, benevolence, the desire for knowledge, the desire to create what is beautiful also can reasonably claim this title, and it is hard to refuse them it. Yet they may all lead us into evil courses on occasion if there is not at the back of our minds a moral consciousness which prevents this, so that the strictly moral motive, the desire to do what is right as such, though it need not and should not or indeed could not always be our motive, should always in a sense be present potentially. But whether a man has acted from the right motives or not on a particular occasion depends not only on the nature of the desires involved in themselves but on the context. Suppose as examiner I consciously gave a candidate a first-class mark out of love for him or out of a desire to give him pleasure (benevolence). Now love and benevolence are as such good in themselves, but I certainly could not be said to have acted from the right motives, and consequently even if he deserved such a mark my action would be morally bad, though not so bad as if I had given a third-class mark to a candidate out of the evil desire to cause him pain.[1] In either case the motive from which I acted ought to have had no influence at all in deciding the man's class. In other cases I might be blamed not because I acted from a motive which ought not to have influenced me at all, but because my action was not affected by other motives which ought also to have influenced me. This would be the case if I were motivated strongly by a desire for the welfare of a friend but indifferent to suffering brought on others by the way in which I sought to further that welfare. To say that a man's motive is wrong is therefore by no means necessarily to say that he is acting from a desire which is intrinsically evil. The only intrinsically evil desires are desires to produce things evil-in-themselves for their own sake, of which the most common (if not the only one) is the desire to inflict pain in anger or hatred on someone who has offended the agent. An action consciously and preventably influenced by such a desire is always blameworthy even if it be externally right, and even if it be also influenced by moral motives, as might well be the case with a person administering punishment. It is not equally clear that the desire to produce what is good in itself is always intrinsically good, for my pleasure is good in itself, yet the desire for pleasure for oneself does not seem to be intrinsically good. . . .

---

[1] Some philosophers, however, while agreeing that actions externally right but done from bad motives are morally bad, would prefer not to call them "wrong," v. Ross, *The Right and the Good*, pp. 4–6, and *Foundations of Ethics*, p. 114 ff., discussed in my *Definition of Good*, pp. 137–44.

So there are various ways in which even an externally right act may be blameworthy because it is wrongly motivated. On the other hand we cannot say that moral blameworthiness depends only on motives, since a man may out of a good motive do something which he believes to be wrong, e.g. steal out of love. Further, the degree of blameworthiness for a wrong act depends also on the strength of the temptation to do it: a man would be blamed much less for killing another unjustifiably if he did it to save his own life than if he did it to steal from the other extra beer and tobacco money, and a man is less blameworthy if owing to peculiar psychological causes a desire which would be slight in most men has become intensely strong in him. Also, other things being equal, the degree of blameworthiness will increase in proportion to the clarity with which the culprit realizes his action to be wrong. Thus, if it is a necessary condition of moral blameworthiness in the fullest sense that the agent should be conscious that he is acting wrongly, the degree of blameworthiness will increase in proportion to the clarity of this consciousness and the unsuitability of the motive, while it will decrease in proportion to the strength of the temptation. . . .

The most controversial question about responsibility and blame, however, is this: Is a person responsible and subject to moral judgment, praise, or blame for his action only if he did it freely—in the sense that his doing the action was not determined by previous causes, including, perhaps, his own beliefs, desires, and traits of character? Some philosophers say yes to this question, others no. The debate is an old one and is today as lively as ever. For, if the answer to this question is yes *and* if determinism is true, then no one is responsible and, hence, praiseworthy or blameworthy for what he does; and, if this is true, it looks as if no moral judgments can be appropriately passed on anyone; a conclusion that would render morality an essentially wrongheaded enterprise. Thus, there are two questions: (1) Is determinism true? and (2) If determinism is true, does it follow that man is neither free nor responsible? Since (1) is important for ethics only if the answer to (2) is affirmative, the main question is (2).

We present here three recent contributions to this debate. In the first, Paul Edwards takes a hard determinist position, holding (a) that determinism is true, and (b) that determinism is incompatible with moral responsibility, as this is understood by reflective people. Perhaps the most important question to ask yourself when reading Edwards's essay is this: Do you agree with his presupposition that having originally chosen one's own character is a logical prerequisite for being morally responsible?

HARD AND SOFT DETERMINISM

Paul Edwards

In his essay "The Dilemma of Determinism," William James makes a distinction that will serve as a point of departure for my remarks. He there distinguishes between the philosophers he calls "hard" determinists and those he labels "soft" determinists. The former, the hard determinists, James tells us, "did not shrink from such words as fatality, bondage of the will, necessitation and the like." He quotes a famous stanza from Omar Khayyám as representing this kind of determinism:

> With earth's first clay they did the last man knead,
> And there of the last harvest sowed the seed.
> And the first morning of creation wrote
> What the last dawn of reckoning shall read.

Another of Omar's verses expresses perhaps even better the kind of theory that James has here in mind:

> Tis all a checker-board of nights and days,
> Where destiny with men for pieces plays;
> Thither and thither moves, and metes, and slays,
> And one by one back to the closet lays.

James mentioned no names other than Omar Khayyám. But there is little doubt that among the hard determinists he would have included Jonathan Edwards, Anthony Collins, Holbach, Priestley, Robert Owen, Schopenhauer, Freud, and also, if he had come a little earlier, Clarence Darrow.

James of course rejected both hard and soft determinism, but for hard determinism he had a certain respect: the kind of respect one sometimes has for an honest, straightforward adversary. For soft determinism, on the other hand, he had nothing but contempt, calling it a "quagmire of evasion." "Nowadays," he writes, "we have a *soft* determinism which abhors harsh words, and repudiating fatality, necessity, and even predetermination, says that its real name is 'freedom.'" From his subsequent observations it is clear that he would include among the evasionists not only neo-Hegelians like Green and Bradley but also Hobbes and Hume and Mill; and if he were alive today James would undoubtedly include Schlick and Ayer and Stevenson and Nowell-Smith, not to mention some of the philosophers present in this room.

The theory James calls soft determinism, especially the Hume-Mill-Schlick variety of it, has been extremely fashionable during the last twenty-five years, while hardly anybody can be found today who has anything good to say for hard determinism. In opposition to this contemporary trend, I should like to strike a blow on behalf of hard determinism in my talk today. I shall also try to bring out exactly what is really at issue between hard and soft determinism. I think the nature of this dispute has frequently been misconceived chiefly because many writers, including James, have a very inaccurate notion of what is maintained by actual hard determinists, as distinct from the bogey men they set up in order to score an easy victory.

To begin with, it is necessary to spell more fully the main contentions of the soft determinists. Since it is the dominant form of soft determinism at the present time, I shall confine myself to the Hume-Mill-Schlick theory. According to this theory there is in the first place no contradiction whatsoever between determinism and the proposition that human beings are sometimes free agents. When we call an action "free" we never in any ordinary situation mean that it was uncaused; and this emphatically includes the kind of action about which we pass moral judgments. By calling an action "free" we mean that the agent was not compelled or constrained to perform it. Sometimes people act in a certain way because of threats or because they have been drugged or because of a posthypnotic suggestion or because of an irrational overpowering urge such as the one that makes a kleptomaniac steal something he does not really need. On such occasions human beings are not free agents. But on other occasions they act in certain ways because of their own rational desires, because of their own unimpeded efforts, because they have chosen to act in these ways. On these occasions they are free agents although their actions are just as much caused as actions that are not deemed free. In distinguishing between free and unfree actions we do not try to mark the presence and absence of causes but attempt to indicate the *kind* of causes that are present.

Secondly there is no antithesis between determinism and moral responsibility. When we judge a person morally responsible for a certain action, we do indeed presuppose that he was a free agent at the time of the action. But the freedom presupposed is not the contracausal freedom about which indeterminists go into such ecstatic raptures. It is nothing more than the freedom already mentioned—the ability to act according to one's choices or desires. Since determinism is compatible with freedom in this sense, it is also compatible with moral responsibility. In other words, the world is after all wonderful: we can be determinists and yet go on punishing our enemies and our children, and we can go on blaming ourselves, all without a bad intellectual conscience.

Mill, who was probably the greatest moralizer among the soft determinists, recognized with particular satisfaction the influence or alleged influence of one class of human desires. Not only, for example, does such a lowly desire as my desire to get a new car influence my conduct. It is equally true, or so at least Mill believed, that my desire to become a more virtuous person does on occasion influence my actions. By suitable training and efforts my desire to change my character may in fact bring about the desired changes. If Mill were alive today he might point to contemporary psychiatry as an illustration of his point. Let us suppose that I have an intense desire to become famous, but that I also have an intense desire to become a happier and more lovable person who, among other things, does not greatly care about fame. Let us suppose, furthermore, that I know of a therapy that can transform fame-seeking and unlovable into lovable and fame-indifferent character structures. If, now, I have enough money, energy, and courage, and if a few other conditions are fulfilled, my desire may actually lead to a major change in my character. Since we can, therefore, at least to some extent, form our own character, determinism according to Mill is compatible not only with judgments of moral responsibility about this or that particular *action* flowing from an unimpeded desire, but also, within limits, with moral judgments about the *character* of human beings.

I think that several of Mill's observations were well worth making and that James's verdict on his theory as a "quagmire of evasion" is far too derogatory. I think hard determinists have occasionally written in such a way as to suggest that they deny the causal efficacy of human desires and efforts. Thus Holbach wrote:

> You will say that I feel free. This is an illusion, which may be compared to that of the fly in the fable, who, lighting upon the pole of a heavy carriage, applauded himself for directing its course. Man, who thinks himself free, is a fly who imagines he has power to move the universe, while he is himself unknowingly carried along by it.

There is also the following passage in Schopenhauer:

> Every man, being what he is and placed in the circumstances which for the moment obtain, but which on their part also arise by strict necessity, can absolutely never do anything else than just what at that moment he does do. Accordingly, the whole course of a man's life, in all its incidents great and small, is as necessarily predetermined as the course of a clock.

Voltaire expresses himself in much the same way in the article on "Destiny" in the *Philosophical Dictionary*.

> Everything happens through immutable laws, . . . everything is necessary. . . . "There are," some persons say, "some events which are necessary and others which are not." It would be very comic that one part of

the world was arranged, and the other were not; that one part of what happens had to happen and that another part of what happens did not have to happen. If one looks closely at it, one sees that the doctrine contrary to that of destiny is absurd; but there are many people destined to reason badly; others not to reason badly; others not to reason at all, others to persecute those who reason. . . .

. . . I necessarily have the passion for writing this, and you have the passion for condemning me; both of us are equally fools, equally the toy of destiny. Your nature is to do harm, mine is to love truth, and to make it public in spite of you.

Furthermore there can be little doubt that Hume and Mill and Schlick were a great deal clearer about the relation between motives and actions than the hard determinists, who either conceived it, like Collins, as one of logical necessity or, like Priestley and Voltaire and Schopenhauer, as necessarily involving coercion or constraint.

But when all is said and done, there remains a good deal of truth in James's charge that soft determinism is an evasion. For a careful reading of their works shows that none of the hard determinists really denied that human desires, efforts, and choices make a difference in the course of events. Any remarks to the contrary are at most temporary lapses. This, then, is hardly the point at issue. If it is not the point at issue, what is? Let me at this stage imagine a hard determinist replying to a champion of the Hume-Mill theory: "You are right," he would say, "in maintaining that some of our actions are caused by our desires and choices. But you do not pursue the subject far enough. You arbitrarily stop at the desires and volitions. We must not stop there. We must go on to ask where *they* come from; and if determinism is true there can be no doubt about the answer to this question. Ultimately our desires and our whole character are derived from our inherited equipment and the environmental influences to which we were subjected at the beginning of our lives. It is clear that we had no hand in shaping either of these." A hard determinist could quote a number of eminent supporters. "Our volitions and our desires," wrote Holbach in his little book *Good Sense,* "are never in our power. You think yourself free, because you do what you will; but are you free to will or not to will; to desire or not to desire?" And Schopenhauer expressed the same thought in the following epigram: "A man can surely do what he wills to do, but he cannot determine what he wills."

Let me turn once more to the topic of character transformation by means of psychiatry to bring out this point with full force. Let us suppose that both A and B are compulsive and suffer intensely from their neuroses. Let us assume that there is a therapy that could help them, which could materially change their character structure, but that it takes a great deal of energy and courage to undertake the treatment. Let us suppose that

A has the necessary energy and courage while *B* lacks it. *A* undergoes the therapy and changes in the desired way. *B* just gets more and more compulsive and more and more miserable. Now, it is true that *A* helped form his own later character. But his starting point, his desire to change, his energy and courage, were already there. They may or may not have been the result of previous efforts on his own part. But there must have been a first effort, and the effort at that time was the result of factors that were not of his making.

The fact that a person's character is ultimately the product of factors over which he had no control is not denied by the soft determinists, though many of them don't like to be reminded of it when they are in a moralizing mood. Since the hard determinists admit that our desires and choices do on occasion influence the course of our lives, there is thus no disagreement between the soft and the hard determinists about the empirical facts. However, some hard determinists infer from some of these facts that human beings are never morally responsible for their actions. The soft determinists, as already stated, do not draw any such inference. In the remainder of my paper I shall try to show just what it is that hard determinists are inferring and why, in my opinion, they are justified in their conclusion.

I shall begin by adopting for my purposes a distinction introduced by C. A. Campbell in his extremely valuable article "Is Free Will a Pseudo-Problem?" [1] in which he distinguishes between two conceptions of moral responsibility. Different persons, he says, require different conditions to be fulfilled before holding human beings morally responsible for what they do. First, there is what Campbell calls the ordinary unreflective person, who is rather ignorant and who is not greatly concerned with the theories of science, philosophy, and religion. If the unreflective person is sure that the agent to be judged was acting under coercion or constraint, he will not hold him responsible. If, however, he is sure that the action was performed in accordance with the agent's unimpeded rational desire, if he is sure that the action would not have taken place but for the agent's decision, then the unreflective person will consider ascription of moral responsibility justified. The fact that the agent did not ultimately make his own character will either not occur to him, or else it will not be considered a sufficient ground for withholding a judgment of moral responsibility.

In addition to such unreflective persons, continues Campbell, there are others who have reached "a tolerably advanced level of reflection."

Such a person will doubtless be acquainted with the claims advanced in some quarters that causal law operates universally; or/and with the theories

---

[1] *Mind*, 1951.

of some philosophies that the universe is throughout the expression of a single supreme principle; or/and with the doctrines of some theologians that the world is created, sustained and governed by an Omniscient and Omnipotent Being.

Such a person will tend to require the fulfillment of a further condition before holding anybody morally responsible. He will require not only that the agent was not coerced or constrained but also—and this is taken to be an additional condition—that he "could have chosen otherwise than he actually did." I should prefer to put this somewhat differently, but it will not affect the main conclusion drawn by Campbell, with which I agree. The reflective person, I should prefer to express it, requires not only that the agent was not coerced; he also requires that the agent *originally chose his own character*—the character that now displays itself in his choices and desires and efforts. Campbell concludes that determinism is indeed compatible with judgments of moral responsibility in the unreflective sense, but that it is incompatible with judgments of moral responsibility in the reflective sense.

Although I do not follow Campbell in rejecting determinism, I agree basically with his analysis, with one other qualification. I do not think it is a question of the different senses in which the term is used by ignorant and unreflective people, on the one hand, and by those who are interested in science, religion, and philosophy, on the other. The very same persons, whether educated or uneducated, use it in certain contexts in the one sense and in other contexts in the other. Practically all human beings, no matter how much interested they are in science, religion, and philosophy, employ what Campbell calls the unreflective conception when they are dominated by violent emotions like anger, indignation, or hate, and especially when the conduct they are judging has been personally injurious to them. On the other hand, a great many people, whether they are educated or not, will employ what Campbell calls the reflective conception when they are not consumed with hate or anger—when they are judging a situation calmly and reflectively and when the fact that the agent did not ultimately shape his own character has been vividly brought to their attention. Clarence Darrow in his celebrated pleas repeatedly appealed to the jury on precisely this ground. If any of you, he would say, had been reared in an environment like that of the accused or had to suffer from his defective heredity, *you* would now be standing in the dock. . . . Darrow nearly always convinced the jury that the accused could not be held morally responsible for his acts; and certainly the majority of the jurors were relatively uneducated.

I have so far merely distinguished between two concepts of moral responsibility. I now wish to go a step farther and claim that only one of them can be considered, properly speaking, a moral concept. This is not an easy point to make clear, but I can at least indicate what I mean. We do not normally consider just any positive or negative feeling a "moral" emotion. Nor do we consider just any sentence containing the words "good" or "bad" expressions of "moral" judgment. For example, if a man hates a woman because she rejected him, this would not be counted as a moral emotion. If, however, he disapproves, say, of Senator McCarthy's libelous speech against Adlai Stevenson before the 1952 election because he disapproves of slander in general and not merely because he likes Stevenson and dislikes McCarthy, his feeling would be counted as moral. A feeling or judgment must in a certain sense be "impersonal" before we consider it moral. To this I would add that it must also be independent of violent emotions. Confining myself to judgments, I would say that a judgment was "moral" only if it was formulated in a calm and reflective mood, or at least if it is supported in a calm and reflective state of mind. If this is so, it follows that what Campbell calls the reflective sense of "moral responsibility" is the only one that qualifies as a properly moral use of the term.

Before I conclude I wish to avoid a certain misunderstanding of my remarks. From the fact that human beings do not ultimately shape their own character, I said, it *follows* that they are never morally responsible. I do not mean that by reminding people of the ultimate causes of their character one makes them more charitable and less vengeful. Maybe one does, but that is not what I mean. I mean "follow" or "imply" in the same sense as, or in a sense closely akin to, that in which the conclusion of a valid syllogism follows from the premises. The effectiveness of Darrow's pleas does not merely show, I am arguing, how powerfully he could sway the emotions of the jurors. His pleas also brought into the open one of the conditions the jurors, like others, consider necessary on reflection before they hold an agent morally responsible. Or perhaps I should say that Darrow *committed* the jurors in their reflective nature to a certain ground for the ascription of moral responsibility.

It will be convenient to introduce our second and third authors together. Charles A. Baylis presents the soft determinist position that (a) determinism is true, (b) determinism is compatible with moral freedom and responsibility, and (c) indeterminism is not compatible with them. He assumes a teleological theory of obligation in some of his statements, but this is not essential to soft determinism.

The third author, Roderick M. Chisholm, agrees with Baylis that indeterminism is inconsistent with moral freedom and responsibility, but contends that this is true of determinism too. He also believes that determinism is false. He therefore defends a position that may be called self-determinism, which resembles the position Baylis ascribes to Kant. On this view, it is the self that causes one to do what one does, but the self is not determined to do what it does by any causes or events, past, present, or future. It is not even determined, at least not completely, by one's beliefs, desires, and previously acquired character.

Two notes are necessary: (1) The Edwards referred to by Chisholm is not Paul Edwards, but an eighteenth-century American named Jonathan; and Jonathan Edwards was a soft determinist, and not a hard one as Paul says he was. (2) Baylis interprets Moore as thinking that determinism is not consistent with moral responsibility and obligation, whereas Chisholm interprets Moore as thinking the opposite. This is because Moore changed his mind somewhat, and Chisholm is talking about Moore's earlier view, Baylis about his later position. In any case, it will help in reading and using these two selections if one notices that Chisholm holds the view Baylis ascribes to Moore and that Baylis holds the view Chisholm ascribes to Moore. In fact, in reading Baylis one can substitute "Chisholm" for "Moore," and in reading Chisholm, "Baylis" for "Moore."

DETERMINISM AND MORAL OBLIGATION

Charles A. Baylis

Even though the view is difficult if not impossible to prove, there appears to be a growing belief in determinism as applied to human choice. Rare indeed is the psychologist who would deny that every voluntary human action is motivated. The average layman, too, expects the behavior of his fellow men to be explainable. If someone acts peculiarly he asks at once, "Why?" "What led him to do that?" And he would hesitate to take you seriously if you told him that the action is strictly unexplainable.

Determinism in this sense does *not* imply fatalism. It is, roughly, the view that every human choice occurs in accordance with some law of a causal or functional sort. It implies that an individual's choice in any given circumstances is determined, determined by such factors as the kind of person he is, his habits, his disposition, his intelligence, his emotional drives, his desires, and his aversions. Complete knowledge of the relevant laws, the situation, and the person concerned would make

From "Rational Preference, Determinism, and Moral Obligation," The Journal of Philosophy, XLVII, No. 3 (February 2, 1950). Reprinted by permission of the author and The Journal of Philosophy.

possible accurate prediction of his choice. But it does not follow from this view, as Jerome Frank urges in *Fate and Freedom,* that human values and human purposes are irrelevant and can affect neither this choice nor the future. Just the contrary is true. Because human beings can be educated to be influenced less by emotion and more by rational considerations, it is possible to make human choices and their consequences progressively better as human wisdom develops.

Though Frank's fears are unfounded, G. E. Moore and others echo Kant in urging that determinism confronts us with a more serious difficulty. Moore, in his reply to critics in *The Philosophy of G. E. Moore,* insists that we take seriously the classical dictum, "I ought implies I can." He states that, if determinism is true, there is no sense of freedom with which he is acquainted according to which we could have done anything other than what we did do. Hence he does not see how, if determinism is true, we could justify the statement that we were under moral obligation to have acted otherwise. Moore urges that we should not be satisfied with the reply that we could have acted otherwise had we chosen to do so. Nor, he adds, is it a satisfactory answer that we could have chosen otherwise had we wanted or preferred so to choose. Somewhere along the line our choice of an action or our choice of a choice is determined. Taking all the concrete circumstances of the situation and of our own nature into account we recognize that our action could not have differed from what it was. How then, he asks, can it be true that we ought to have acted or chosen otherwise?

It is the thesis of this paper that all the types of freedom required for moral obligation and moral responsibility do in fact exist and are compatible with determinism. If Moore is asking for an indeterministic type of freedom, he is asking for something that would make moral responsibility and obligation impossible. In order to substantiate this thesis, it will be necessary to analyze the notion of moral obligation, to distinguish a number of different types of freedom, and to take account of the distinction between retributive and non-retributive responsibility.

There is, of course, a weak sense of "ought" in which there is much that we ought to do that we can not do. This is the sense in which "X ought to be" is equivalent to "It would be better if X were." In this sense war and mosquitoes and hurricanes ought not to occur and there ought to be much more beauty and health and good weather than there is. Since some of these "oughts" call for goods beyond human control, it is clear that they do not involve moral obligation in any human sense.

It might seem reasonable to demand that among the various things we could do—if we wished—we should choose the best possible alternative. But this would still impose on human beings the impossible task of always knowing the objectively best. Which alternative is best depends on the relative value of the consequences of our different possible choices. Since human knowledge of the future is only probable, our beliefs as to what is best will often be incorrect, even though they are based on correct assessment of all the relevant available evidence. Because of this limitation on our knowledge, though it would sometimes be better if we were to do what *is* best, we are under moral obligation not to do that but to do what we *believe to be best,* grounding our belief on sound judgment in the light of the available evidence. The right thing for us to do is to act in this way.

This sense of moral obligation can be stated more precisely as follows: Among the various alternative actions which it is possible for a person in given circumstances to do if he chooses, his choice ought to be effectively determined by two factors: (1) moral interest, that is, desire to do what is right, and (2) sound judgment, that is, correct assessment of the available evidence as to the relative values of the various alternatives. Let us call a choice that is determined by moral interest, *moral,* and one which is based on sound judgment, *sound.* A choice which is both moral and sound, we can call for brevity a *wise* choice. The essence of moral obligation, then, is to act wisely, to act, as Aristotle expressed it, as "the wise and right-minded man" would act. Our important voluntary actions should result from sound moral choices.

Does this sense of moral obligations meet Moore's difficulty satisfactorily? We *ought* to choose wisely, but *can* we choose wisely? We can in the sense that sometimes we do. We have a capacity for so choosing. At times we are in fact moved to a decision by our moral interest, and at some of these times our beliefs as to what is right are well-grounded. In general, human beings are capable of being moved by moral ideals and are capable of reasoning correctly. There are, of course, occasions on which we are ruled by non-moral or even immoral interests, and there are instances in which our reasoning is far from sound. Sometimes, perhaps, we deliberately choose what we know to be wrong; sometimes, as the saying goes, we think not with our heads but with our hearts—with our blood as the Nazis would have said; sometimes we succumb to irrational impulses, conscious or unconscious; sometimes we are simply fatigued or inattentive; occasionally we may be under the influence of alcohol or a drug, or of some more deep-seated disability such as a neurosis. In such instances, taking all the circumstances into account, including our own condition, there is a sense in which we couldn't have acted otherwise. We did the best—as well as the worst—which we could have done in that specific case. But these more or less impermanent disabilities are not incompatible with our general ability to choose wisely, an ability which is demonstrated under more favorable circumstances by sound moral choices. We do indeed have the capacity to be immoral and irrational. Who would deny it? But also we have the capacity to reason correctly and to want so strongly what we believe to be right that this moral interest becomes our dominant motive.

An important thing to note here is the distinction between possession of a general ability and the inhibition of that ability in particular circumstances. Consider an analogous situation in the physical realm. We say of the human eye that it is capable of seeing a certain star if normal eyes under standard conditions can discern it. We do not say that the human eye loses this capacity because certain eyes are weak or inflamed, or because clouds obscure the star. We do of course say that the star is invisible under these special circumstances, that is, when concealed by clouds, or when the sole observer has defective eyes, but we still agree that in general this star is visible to the naked eye. The situation is similar with regard to the human ability to choose morally. In particular cases a person with a weak, poorly developed moral sense, or with his mind inflamed by passion, may be unable to choose wisely. But this is not incompatible with the fact—attested by actual wise choices—that in general people do have this capacity. People whose moral and intellectual development comes up to certain standards, confronted with situations not too unusual in their difficulty, can and do choose wisely. In this sense we *can* do what we are under moral obligation to do. In particular instances where we are unwise, we fail to live up to the best of which we are in general capable. We fall short of our ideals, ideals that on other occasions we succeed in realizing. Falling short, we reproach ourselves and are reproached by others. This reproach, as well as other treatment we may receive, sometimes so changes us that on other similar occasions we are wise enough to act wisely.

Another important consideration in meeting Moore's difficulty has been suggested by Ross (*Foundations of Ethics,* pp. 240–46). When we say "we *can* do either *a* or *b* or *c*," there is implicitly included the tacit proviso "if our interest in *a* or *b* or *c* outweighs our interest in either of the others." If the only thing that kept us from doing what was right was the weakness of our interest in acting rightly, we still say that we could have done what was right, that is, we could have, had we been somewhat more interested. Now, having only a weak interest in the right, so that confronted with a choice between what we believe to be right and what we believe to be wrong, our interest in acting rightly is not strong enough to overcome the attractions of some wrong course of action, is precisely what we mean by having a weak moral character, by being immoral. Hence, even though in one sense we could not have done other than what we did do, if the only factor that kept us from doing what

was right was our weak good will, we and others are justified in label-
ling us immoral for acting as we did. For we have just demonstrated
that our moral fibre is too weak to be effective.

A similar problem to be solved in a similar way arises when, though
we do what we believe to be right, we err in our belief and resultant
action not through lack of moral stamina but through failure to judge
correctly the probable value of various alternatives. Let us suppose that
at our best we could have judged them correctly, but that through fatigue we erred.

Here we can reply that we recognize that to live up to our moral
obligations we must be at our best, not only morally but also intellectually. In this instance having slipped intellectually because we were tired,
we were not at our best. Hence, we did not do what we ought to have
done and could have done had we not been tired. We are not immoral,
we are not even stupid, but we did make an unsound judgment. We
might well counsel ourselves to be sure not to be fatigued when, in
the future, we have important decisions to make. If, later, we knowingly disregard this advice, we shall then be immoral.

If the above account is substantially correct, we can give a significant meaning under deterministic assumptions to such a statement
as "I ought not to have done what I did do; I ought to have acted
wisely." This would be true in the sense that:

1. I could have done what I ought had I chosen to do so.
2. I could have chosen wisely, had I wanted to; I would have
   wanted to had it pleased me so to want; and so on.
3. If my choice was unwise because of my weak interest in doing
   what is right, my failure to do my duty was a direct reflection
   of my moral weakness and reveals me as being to that extent
   immoral.
4. If my unwise choice was due to unsound judgment it reflects
   another weakness of my own, a failure to be as mentally alert,
   logically cogent, and free from irrational motivation as I sometimes am.
5. In my action I failed to live up to my ideal of myself. I did not
   think as soundly or choose as wisely as would the self that I
   aspire to be, and sometimes succeed in being.
6. There are changes in my character, which, if made earlier, would
   have led me to choose wisely, and which, if made now, will
   enable me to choose more wisely on another similar occasion.

The fifth point is of special significance because it provides, I
think, some additional confirmation of the view I have presented, by
suggesting a new interpretation of the famous Kantian distinction be-

tween the empirical self and the intelligible self. A person's choice in any specific instance is determined by his actual or, if you like, his empirical self, with all its weaknesses, moral and intellectual. But the ideal or intelligible self to which he aspires is a soundly reasoning moral self. Sometimes these two selves coalesce. As a person's moral and intellectual powers develop the choices of his empirical self come to coincide more and more frequently with the choices which would be made by the wise and right-minded self which is his ideal. Most of us achieve enough maturity to make some wise choices, but not enough to overcome all temptations. However, our capacity for further development is without apparent limit.

On the supposition that determinism is true, to what extent is an individual responsible for his choices, wise or unwise? To what extent are they due to him rather than to some other factor in the situation? To the extent that they are determined by his own nature, to the degree that they result from his character. It is commonly agreed that a person's choice is a function of the situation with which he is confronted and of his personality as it reacts to that situation. In different situations the same individual will react differently. Confronted by the same situation, different individuals will respond variously, depending on their characters. A fool will respond foolishly, a wise man wisely. An unwise choice in any given set of circumstances indicates either a lack of sound judgment or a deficiency of moral interest. If determinism be true, then, all external factors being what they are, it is a tautology to say that a man's choice is due to his own nature. And since his nature characterizes him, he is responsible for his choices.

If it be asked who or what is responsible for his character, the determinist's answer is that it is due to the interplay of many factors, his own earlier choices, his environment and associates, his education, his home training, his heredity. These in turn are determined by earlier factors. To ask for an ultimate source of responsibility is like asking for a first cause. Perhaps there is not any. Indeed if determinism be true there can be none. In any event a man is today the kind of man he is, no matter what the influences were which made him that way. He is the sort of person who, because of his character, chooses as he does. The first responsibility for his choices rests squarely on him.

If on the other hand the kind of freedom that Moore seems to demand, freedom from determining motives, be actual, then such indeterminism would result in complete lack of responsibility. For if our choices be independent of every aspect of our character, they are capricious, and entirely outside of our control. We do not, I submit, want that kind of free will. It would be like possessing an auto which goes off the road for no reason at all. To own a car which may be wrecked by a blowout or a broken steering gear is bad enough, but to own one which can smash into the ditch or suddenly climb a telephone pole for no reason at all would be intolerable. When we ask what was responsible for an accident we are asking for the cause of that accident. To say there is no cause is to say nothing was responsible. Similarly, it is bad enough to find that some weak or undesirable trait of our character has led us astray. Knowing what was responsible we can at least take steps to improve our character. But if our fault was not due to any aspect of our nature, if there were nothing we could have done in the past or can do now which would make us behave better, we are helpless. And being helpless, we can not be held responsible. What is responsible for any occurrence, including human choice, is the cause of that occurrence. If indeterminism be true, if some choices are uncaused, then nothing and no one is responsible for them.

If determinism be true, is punishment of unwise choices or reward of wise choices profitable? In a non-retributive sense, yes. If a man's character leads him to commit grievously anti-social deeds, his social group will judge correctly that he is the kind of person who makes such unwise choices and they will be justified in restraining him, by imprisonment or other means, until he can be re-educated so that he will make better choices. He has shown by his action that he is the kind of man whom society can not safely allow at large. On the other hand, retributive punishment or reward, the allocation to an individual of his "just deserts," is unjustified under either determinism or indeterminism. In the former case, though a man's actions are due to his character, his character is due largely to others and hence deserves itself neither reward nor punishment. In the latter case, since his action was not the consequence of anything, there is nothing appropriate to be rewarded or punished.

In less serious cases, where restraint is unjustified, to what extent ought a person to blame himself or to be blamed by others for his unwise decisions? To the extent that a wise or right-minded man would blame him. The aim, presumably, is to help him and others to make better choices in the future. Blame and praise will be of some benefit. But reforming an adult is difficult. There is much to indicate that the basic formative influences on human character occur in early childhood. It seems clear therefore that the major lesson to be learned from adult errors of choice is that we ought to modify the environment and training of young children so that more of them will develop, to a greater degree than is common today, freedom from dominance by irrational or immoral motives. To the extent that we train the next generation to respond to sound reasoning and moral motives, members of it will approach the goal of always choosing as a wise or right-minded man would choose, of always living up to their moral obligations.

HUMAN FREEDOM AND THE SELF

Roderick M. Chisholm

A staff moves a stone,
and is moved by a hand,
which is moved by a man.

ARISTOTLE, *Physics,* 256a.

The metaphysical problem of human freedom might be summarized in the following way: "Human beings are responsible agents; but this fact appears to conflict with a deterministic view of action—the view that every event that is involved in an act is caused by some other event. And it also appears to conflict with the view that some of the events that are essential to the act are not caused at all." To solve the problem, I believe, we must make somewhat far-reaching assumptions about the self or the agent—about the man who performs the act. . . .

Let us consider some deed, or misdeed, that may be attributed to a responsible agent: one man, say, shot another. If the man *was* responsible for what he did, then, I would urge, what was to happen at the time of the shooting was something that was entirely up to the man himself. There was a moment at which it was true, both that he could have fired the shot and also that he could have refrained from firing it. And if this is so, then, even though he did fire it, he could have done something else instead. (He didn't find himself firing the shot "against his will," as we say.) I think we can say, more generally, then, that if a man is responsible for a certain event or a certain state of affairs (in our example, the shooting of another man), then that event or state of affairs was brought about by some act of his, and the act was something that was in his power either to perform or not to perform.

But now if the act which he *did* perform was an act that was also in his power *not* to perform, then it could not have been caused or

From "Human Freedom and the Self," the Lindley Lecture given at the University of Kansas, April 23, 1964, revised by the author. Reprinted by permission of the author and the University of Kansas, Department of Philosophy. (An earlier version of the lecture was published by the Department of Philosophy of the University of Kansas in 1964.)

determined by any event that was not itself within his power either to bring about or not to bring about. For example, if what we say he did was really something that was brought about by a second man, one who forced his hand upon the trigger, say, or who, by means of hypnosis, compelled him to perform the act, then since the act was caused by the *second* man it was nothing that was within the power of the *first* man to prevent. And precisely the same thing is true, I think, if instead of referring to a second man who compelled the first one, we speak instead of the *desires* and *beliefs* which the first man happens to have had. For if what we say he did was really something that was brought about by his own beliefs and desires, if these beliefs and desires in the particular situation in which he happened to have found himself caused him to do just what it was that we say he did do, then, since *they* caused it, *he* was unable to do anything other than just what it was that he did do. It makes no difference whether the cause of the deed was internal or external; if the cause was some state or event for which the man himself was not responsible, then he was not responsible for what we have been mistakenly calling his act. If a flood caused the poorly constructed dam to break, then, given the flood and the constitution of the dam, the break, we may say, *had* to occur and nothing could have happened in its place. And if the flood of desire caused the weak-willed man to give in, then he, too, had to do just what it was that he did do and he was no more responsible than was the dam for the results that followed. (It is true, of course, that if the man is responsible for the beliefs and desires that he happens to have, then he may also be responsible for the things they lead him to do. But the question now becomes: *is* he responsible for the beliefs and desires he happens to have? If he is, then there was a time when they were within his power either to acquire or not to acquire, and we are left, therefore, with our general point.) . . .

There is one standard objection to all of this and we should consider it briefly.

The objection takes the form of a stratagem—one designed to show that determinism (and divine providence) is consistent with human responsibility. The stratagem is one that was used by Jonathan Edwards and by many philosophers in the present century, most notably, G. E. Moore.[1]

One proceeds as follows: The expression (a) He could have done otherwise, it is argued, means no more nor less than (b) if he had chosen to do otherwise, then he would have done otherwise. (In place

---

[1] Jonathan Edwards, *Freedom of the Will* (New Haven, 1957); G. E. Moore, *Ethics* (Home University Library, 1912), Chapter Six.

of "chosen," one might say "tried," "set out," "decided," "undertaken," or "willed.") The truth of statement (b), it is then pointed out, is consistent with determinism (and with divine providence); for even if all of the man's actions were causally determined, the man could still be such that, *if* he had chosen otherwise, then he would have done otherwise. What the murderer saw, let us suppose, along with his beliefs and desires, *caused* him to fire the shot; yet he was such that *if*, just then, he had chosen or decided *not* to fire the shot, then he would not have fired it. All of this is certainly possible. Similarly, we could say, of the dam, that the flood caused it to break and also that the dam was such that, *if* there had been no flood or any similar pressure, then the dam would have remained intact. And therefore, the argument proceeds, if (b) is consistent with determinism, and if (a) and (b) say the same thing, then (a) is also consistent with determinism; hence we can say that the agent *could* have done otherwise even though he was caused to do what he did do; and therefore determinism and moral responsibility are compatible.

Is the argument sound? The conclusion follows from the premises, but the catch, I think, lies in the first premise—the one saying that statement (a) tells us no more nor less than what statement (b) tells us. For (b), it would seem, could be true while (a) is false. That is to say, our man might be such that, if he had chosen to do otherwise, then he would have done otherwise, and yet *also* such that he could not have done otherwise. Suppose, our murderer was of this sort; first, he would have done otherwise *only* if he had chosen to do otherwise; and, secondly, he *could not have chosen* to do otherwise. Then the fact that he also happens to be such that, *if* he had chosen not to shoot, he would not have shot, would make no difference. For, in the circumstances imagined he could not have done anything other than just what it was that he did do. In a word: from our statement (b) above ("If he had chosen to do otherwise, then he would have done otherwise"), we cannot make an inference to (a) above ("He could have done otherwise") unless we can *also* assert: (c) He could have chosen to do otherwise. And therefore, if we must reject this third statement (c), then, even though we may be justified in asserting (b), we are not justified in asserting (a). If the man could not have chosen to do otherwise, then he would not have done otherwise—*even if* he was such that, if he *had* chosen to do otherwise, then he would have done otherwise.

I suggest that, if the man could have done otherwise, then these things are true: first, if he had undertaken, endeavored, or set out to do otherwise, then he would have done otherwise; and, secondly, there was no sufficient causal condition for his not thus undertaking, endeavoring, or setting out to do otherwise.[2] If this is true, then the ascription of responsibility conflicts with a deterministic view of human action.

Perhaps there is less need to argue that the ascription of responsibility also conflicts with the view that the act, or some event essential to the act, is not caused at all. If, say, the motion of the finger was caused by the flexing of the muscles, if the flexing of the muscles was caused by some other change within the man's brain, and if the change within the brain was not caused at all, if it was fortuitous or capricious, happening so to speak out of the blue, then presumably no one was responsible for the act.

We must not say that every event involved in the act is caused by some other event; and we must not say that the act is something that is not caused at all. The possibility that remains, therefore, is this: We should say that at least one of the events that are involved in the act is caused, not by any other events, but by something else instead. And this something else can only be the agent—the man. If there is an event that is caused, not by other events, but by the man, then there are some events involved in the act that are not caused by other events. But if the event in question is caused by the man then it *is* caused and we are not committed to saying that there is something involved in the act that is not caused at all.

But this, of course, is a large consequence, implying something of considerable importance about the nature of the agent or the man.

If we consider only inanimate natural objects, we may say that causation, if it occurs, is a relation between *events* or *states of affairs*. The dam's breaking was an event that was caused by a set of other events—the dam being weak, the flood being strong, and so on. But if a man is responsible for a particular deed, then, if what I have said is true, there is some event, or set of events, that is caused, *not* by other events or states of affairs, but by the agent, whatever he may be. . . .

One may object . . . : "You say that whenever a man does anything, then there is some event A, presumably a change within the man's own state, which is caused only by the man. But if A was not caused by any other event, then A was not brought about by any *other* change within the agent. You cannot say, therefore, what the man's causing A consists of."

It is true that we cannot say what the man's causing A "consists of." To the question "What is it for a man to cause an event A to happen?" we can answer only by saying "Just that—he causes A to happen."

---

[2] I have attempted to spell this out in more detail in "He Could Have Done Otherwise," in Myles Brand, ed., *The Nature of Human Action* (Glenview, Ill., Scott, Foresman and Company, 1970).

But this does not mean that the concept of a man's causing something to happen is muddled or obscure.

Indeed, we may plausibly say—and there is a respectable philosophical tradition to which we may appeal—that the notion of causation by an agent is *more* clear than that of causation by an event, and that it is only by understanding our own causal efficacy as agents that we can grasp the concept of *cause* at all. Hume may be said to have shown that we do not derive the concept of *cause* from what we perceive of external things. How, then, do we derive it? The most plausible suggestion, it seems to me, is that of Reid, once again: namely, that "the conception of an efficient cause may very probably be derived from the experience we have had . . . of our own power to produce certain effects." [3] If we did not understand the concept of agent causation, we would not understand the concept of event causation.

One may object, finally: "If the agent makes a certain event A happen, then, in addition to the event A, there is the event which is the agent's making A happen. What is the status of *that* event? Either it was caused by some other event, or it was not caused at all, or it was caused by the agent. But if it was caused by some other event, you cannot hold the agent responsible for it. And if it wasn't caused at all, you cannot hold him responsible for it. Therefore you must say that whenever a man makes anything happen, he makes it happen that he makes that thing happen. But this, surely, is absurd. There may be occasions on which I cause myself to do something. I may leave a reminder on the table in order to bring it about that I will do a certain thing tomorrow. But ordinarily I do not cause myself to do the things I do; I just do them. And from this it follows that it would be a mistake to say that, whenever a man makes anything happen, he makes it happen that he makes that thing happen."

When a man thus leaves a reminder on the table, he does something for the purpose of causing himself to do a certain other thing later. And in this sense it is true to say that ordinarily a man does not cause himself to do the things he does. For a man's ordinary actions are such that it is not necessary for him to do other things for the purpose of causing himself to perform them. But this is quite consistent with the thesis that, whenever a man does perform an act, he causes it to happen that he performs that act. For, as we have seen, it is one thing to say merely that a man makes a certain event X happen, and it is another thing to say that he makes X happen for the purpose of making some other event happen. From the fact that he makes X happen, it does not follow that he makes anything happen for the purpose of making X

---

[3] Reid, *Works,* p. 524.

happen. And so a man may make it happen that he performs a certain action without thereby doing anything for the purpose of causing himself to perform that action. Therefore, from the fact that most acts are such that the agent doesn't have to do anything for the purpose of causing himself to get them done, it does not follow that it is a mistake to say that, whenever a man makes anything happen, he makes it happen that he makes that thing happen. . . .

If we are responsible, and if what I have been trying to say is true, then we have a prerogative which some would attribute only to God: each of us, when we really act, is a prime mover unmoved. In doing what we do, we cause certain events to happen, and nothing and no one, except we ourselves, causes us to cause those events to happen. . . .

Suggestions for Further Reading

4.1–4.2   MORAL VIRTUE

AQUINAS, ST. THOMAS. *Summa Theologica* (Vol. II, Questions LV–LXII).

DONNELLY, JOHN, and LEONARD LYONS, eds. *Conscience.* New York: Alba House, 1973.

FRANKENA, W. K. "Prichard and the Ethics of Virtue," *The Monist,* LIV (1970), 1–17.

STRAWSON, P. F. "Social Morality and Individual Ideal," *Philosophy,* XXXVI (1961), 1–17. Reprinted in Kenneth Pahel and Marvin Schiller, eds., *Readings in Contemporary Ethical Theory* (Englewood Cliffs, N.J.: Prentice-Hall, 1970), pp. 344–59.

URMSON, J. O. "Saints and Heroes," in A. I. Melden, ed., *Essays in Moral Philosophy* (Seattle: University of Washington Press, 1958), pp. 198–216.

4.3   DETERMINISM AND RESPONSIBILITY

BEARDSLEY, E. L. "Determinism and Moral Perspectives," *Philosophy and Phenomenological Research,* XXI (1960), 1–20.

BEROFSKY, BERNARD, ed. *Free Will and Determinism.* New York: Harper & Row, 1966.

HOOK, SIDNEY, ed. *Determinism and Freedom in the Age of Modern Science.* New York: New York University Press, 1958.

5

INTRINSIC VALUE
AND THE GOOD LIFE

Introduction

What C. D. Broad in Chapter 1 called the theory of value has two main parts. This is because words like "good," "desirable," and "bad" have both moral and nonmoral uses. We were concerned with the theory of moral value in the first part of Chapter 4; now we shall take up problems and points of view in the theory of nonmoral value, though some of these have already been broached by Broad, Epicurus, Kant, Bentham, and Nietzsche.

The most important nonmoral judgments are (a) those in which we say that something is instrumentally good or good as a means to something else, and (b) those in which we say that something is intrinsically good, good in itself, or good as an end and not just because of its consequences. Since the judgments in (a) presuppose judgments in (b), we shall focus on the latter. In other words, the discussions of this chapter will be concerned with questions about what is good, desirable, or worthwhile in itself. The problem is not about the meaning of "good," but only about what things are good in themselves.

5.1

Hedonism:
First Line of Debate

Broad distinguished monistic and pluralistic theories of what is intrinsically good and took hedonism as his main example of the former. But a monistic theory of value, such as Nietzsche's theory that the good is power, may be non-hedonistic. Pluralistic theories will, of course, be nonhedonistic. In any case, the main issue in the theory of intrinsic value is the question of hedonism vs. nonhedonism—whether or not pleasure is the only thing that is intrinsically good. Hedonists equate happiness with pleasure and then equate pleasure with the good. Nonhedonists may or may not equate happiness with pleasure, but they always reject the equation of the good with pleasure. It should be observed that hedonists need not say that "good" *means* "pleasure" (and usually do not hold this); they only need to hold that what is good in itself is pleasant and vice versa, or a bit more accurately, that the things that are intrinsically good are so if, and only if, they are pleasant, and that they are good *because* of their pleasantness. Hedonists sometimes argue for this thesis by claiming that pleasure alone is the ultimate object of human desire. In other words, they sometimes defend ethical hedonism on the basis of psychological hedonism. This is done, for example, by the Epicureans and by Mill. Correspondingly, non-hedonists sometimes argue that ethical hedonism is false because psychological hedonism is false—pleasure is not the only ultimate goal of human striving, they argue. Aristotle and Nietzsche, for example, hold this position. Sometimes, however, hedonists and antihedonists debate the issue on other, nonpsychological, grounds by trying to show straight-out, without asking what we desire or aim at, that pleasure alone is or is not intrinsically good. Plato, Sidgwick, Moore, Rashdall, Ross, and R. M. Blake all do this.

For an example of an ethical hedonist who rests his position on psychological hedonism, we could look back at Cicero's statement of Epicurus's theory. Another example is contained in the following passages from *Utilitarianism* by John Stuart Mill (1806–73). Mill states the position of the hedonistic utilitarian and then defends hedonism against one family of objections, explaining much of his interesting philosophy of the good life and its attainment at the same time. Among other things, he introduces his famous thesis that pleasures differ in value because of their quality and not just because of the quantity of pleasure involved. Finally, he gives his equally famous "proof" that pleasure alone is good as an end.

DEFENSE OF HEDONISM

John Stuart Mill

Answer to Some Objections

. . . The creed which accepts as the foundation of morals "utility" or the "greatest happiness principle" holds that actions are right in proportion as they tend to promote happiness, wrong as they tend to produce the reverse of happiness. By happiness is intended pleasure, and the absence of pain; by unhappiness, pain, and the privation of pleasure. To give a clear view of the moral standard set up by the theory, much more requires to be said; in particular, what things it includes in the ideas of pain and pleasure; and to what extent this is left an open question. But these supplementary explanations do not affect the theory of life on which this theory of morality is grounded—namely, that pleasure and freedom from pain are the only things desirable as ends; and that all desirable things (which are as numerous in the utilitarian as in any other scheme) are desirable either for the pleasure inherent in themselves, or as means to the promotion of pleasure and the prevention of pain.

Now such a theory of life excites in many minds, and among them in some of the most estimable in feeling and purpose, inveterate dislike. To suppose that life has (as they express it) no higher end than pleasure—no better and nobler object of desire and pursuit—they designate as utterly mean and groveling; as a doctrine worthy only of swine, to whom the followers of Epicurus were, at a very early period, contemptuously likened; and modern holders of the doctrine are occasionally made the subject of equally polite comparisons by its German, French, and English assailants.

From Utilitarianism *(London, 1863).*

. . . I do not, indeed, consider the Epicureans to have been by any means faultless in drawing out their scheme of consequences from the utilitarian principle. To do this in any sufficient manner, many Stoic, as well as Christian, elements require to be included. But there is no known Epicurean theory of life which does not assign to the pleasures of the intellect, of the feelings and imagination, and of the moral sentiments, a much higher value as pleasures than to those of mere sensation. It must be admitted, however, that utilitarian writers in general have placed the superiority of mental over bodily pleasures chiefly in the greater permanency, safety, uncostliness, etc., of the former—that is, in their circumstantial advantages rather than in their intrinsic nature. And on all these points utilitarians have fully proved their case; but they might have taken the other and, as it may be called, higher ground with entire consistency. It is quite compatible with the principle of utility to recognize the fact that some kinds of pleasure are more desirable and more valuable than others. It would be absurd that, while, in estimating all other things, quality is considered as well as quantity, the estimation of pleasures should be supposed to depend on quantity alone.

If I am asked what I mean by difference of quality in pleasures, or what makes one pleasure more valuable than another, merely as a pleasure, except its being greater in amount, there is but one possible answer. Of two pleasures, if there be one to which all or almost all who have experience of both give a decided preference, irrespective of any feeling of moral obligation to prefer it, that is the more desirable pleasure. If one of the two is, by those who are competently acquainted with both, placed so far above the other that they prefer it, even though knowing it to be attended with a greater amount of discontent, and would not resign it for any quantity of the other pleasure which their nature is capable of, we are justified in ascribing to the preferred enjoyment a superiority in quality so far outweighing quantity as to render it, in comparison, of small account.

Now it is an unquestionable fact that those who are equally acquainted with and equally capable of appreciating and enjoying both, do give a most marked preference to the manner of existence which employs their higher faculties. Few human creatures would consent to be changed into any of the lower animals for a promise of the fullest allowance of a beast's pleasures; no intelligent human being would consent to be a fool, no instructed person would be an ignoramus, no person of feeling and conscience would be selfish and base, even though they should be persuaded that the fool, the dunce, or the rascal is better satisfied with his lot than they are with theirs. They would not resign what they possess more than he for the most complete satisfaction

of all the desires which they have in common with him. If they ever
fancy they would, it is only in cases of unhappiness so extreme that to
escape from it they would exchange their lot for almost any other, however undesirable in their own eyes. A being of higher faculties requires
more to make him happy, is capable probably of more acute suffering,
and certainly accessible to it at more points, than one of an inferior
type; but in spite of these liabilities, he can never really wish to sink
into what he feels to be a lower grade of existence. We may give what
explanation we please of this unwillingness; we may attribute it to pride,
a name which is given indiscriminately to some of the most and to some
of the least estimable feelings of which mankind are capable: we may
refer it to the love of liberty and personal independence, an appeal to
which was with the Stoics one of the most effective means for the in-
culcation of it; to the love of power or to the love of excitement, both of
which do really enter into and contribute to it; but its most appropriate
appellation is a sense of dignity, which all human beings possess in one
form or other, and in some, though by no means in exact, proportion to
their higher faculties, and which is so essential a part of the happiness
of those in whom it is strong that nothing which conflicts with it could
be otherwise than momentarily an object of desire to them. Whoever
supposes that this preference takes place at a sacrifice of happiness—
that the superior being, in anything like equal circumstances, is not happier than the inferior—confounds the two very different ideas of happiness and content. It is indisputable that the being whose capacities of
enjoyment are low has the greatest chance of having them fully satisfied; and a highly endowed being will always feel that any happiness
which he can look for, as the world is constituted, is imperfect. But he
can learn to bear its imperfections, if they are at all bearable; and they
will not make him envy the being who is indeed unconscious of the
imperfections, but only because he feels not at all the good which those
imperfections qualify. It is better to be a human being dissatisfied than
a pig satisfied; better to be Socrates dissatisfied than a fool satisfied.
And if the fool, or the pig, are of a different opinion, it is because they
only know their own side of the question. The other party to the comparison knows both sides.

It may be objected that many who are capable of the higher pleasures occasionally, under the influence of temptation, postpone them to
the lower. But this is quite compatible with a full appreciation of the
intrinsic superiority of the higher. Men often, from infirmity of character,
make their election for the nearer good, though they know it to be the
less valuable; and this no less when the choice is between two bodily
pleasures than when it is between bodily and mental. They pursue
sensual indulgences to the injury of health, though perfectly aware that

health is the greater good. It may be further objected that many who
begin with youthful enthusiasm for everything noble, as they advance in
years, sink into indolence and selfishness. But I do not believe that those
who undergo this very common change voluntarily choose the lower
description of pleasures in preference to the higher. I believe that, before they devote themselves exclusively to the one, they have already
become incapable of the other. Capacity for the nobler feelings is in
most natures a very tender plant, easily killed, not only by hostile influences, but by mere want of sustenance; and in the majority of young
persons it speedily dies away if the occupations to which their position
in life has devoted them, and the society into which it has thrown them,
are not favorable to keeping that higher capacity in exercise. Men lose
their high aspirations as they lose their intellectual tastes, because they
have not time or opportunity for indulging them; and they addict themselves to inferior pleasures, not because they deliberately prefer them,
but because they are either the only ones to which they have access, or
the only ones which they are any longer capable of enjoying. It may be
questioned whether any one who has remained equally susceptible to
both classes of pleasures, ever knowingly and calmly preferred the lower,
though many, in all ages, have broken down in an effectual attempt to
combine both.

From this verdict of the only competent judges, I apprehend there
can be no appeal. On a question which is the best worth having of two
pleasures, or which of two modes of existence is the most grateful to the
feelings, apart from its moral attributes and from its consequences, the
judgment of those who are qualified by knowledge of both, or, if they
differ, that of the majority among them, must be admitted as final. And
there needs be the less hesitation to accept this judgment respecting the
quality of pleasures, since there is no other tribunal to be referred to
even on the question of quantity. What means are there of determining
which is the acutest of two pains, or the intensest of two pleasurable
sensations, except the general suffrage of those who are familiar with
both? Neither pains nor pleasures are homogeneous, and pain is always
heterogeneous with pleasure. What is there to decide whether a particular pleasure is worth purchasing at the cost of a particular pain,
except the feelings and judgment of the experienced? When, therefore,
those feelings and judgment declare the pleasures derived from the higher
faculties to be preferable *in kind,* apart from the question of intensity,
to those of which the animal nature, disjoined from the higher faculties,
is susceptible, they are entitled on this subject to the same regard.

I have dwelt on this point, as being a necessary part of a perfectly
just conception of utility or happiness considered as the directive rule
of human conduct. But it is by no means an indispensable condition to

the acceptance of the utilitarian standard; for that standard is not the agent's own greatest happiness, but the greatest amount of happiness altogether; and if it may possibly be doubted whether a noble character is always the happier for its nobleness, there can be no doubt that it makes other people happier, and that the world in general is immensely a gainer by it. Utilitarianism, therefore, could only attain its end by the general cultivation of nobleness of character, even if each individual were only benefited by the nobleness of others, and his own, so far as happiness is concerned, were a sheer deduction from the benefit. But the bare enunciation of such an absurdity as this last renders refutation superfluous.

According to the greatest happiness principle, as above explained, the ultimate end, with reference to and for the sake of which all other things are desirable—whether we are considering our own good or that of other people—is an existence exempt as far as possible from pain, and as rich as possible in enjoyments, both in point of quantity and quality; the test of quality and the rule for measuring it against quantity being the preference felt by those who, in their opportunities of experience, to which must be added their habits of self-consciousness and self-observation, are best furnished with the means of comparison. This, being, according to the utilitarian opinion, the end of human action, is necessarily also the standard of morality, which may accordingly be defined "the rules and precepts for human conduct," by the observance of which an existence such as has been described might be, to the greatest extent possible, secured to all mankind; and not to them only, but, so far as the nature of things admits, to the whole sentient creation.[1]

Against this doctrine, however, arises another class of objectors who say that happiness, in any form, cannot be the rational purpose of human life and action; because, in the first place, it is unattainable; and they contemptuously ask, What right hast thou to be happy?—a question which Mr. Carlyle clenches by the addition, What right, a short time ago, hadst thou even to be? Next they say that men can do without happiness; that all noble human beings have felt this, and could not have become noble but by learning the lesson of Entsagen, or renunciation; which lesson, thoroughly learnt and submitted to, they affirm to be the beginning and necessary condition of all virtue.

The first of these objections would go to the root of the matter were it well founded; for if no happiness is to be had at all by human beings, the attainment of it cannot be the end of morality or of any rational conduct. Though, even in that case, something might still be said for

---

[1] [Note that here Mill appears to be an ideal rule-utilitarian. In the first paragraph of this selection, however, he writes more as an act-utilitarian would.—Eds.]

the utilitarian theory, since utility includes not solely the pursuit of happiness, but the prevention or mitigation of unhappiness; and if the former aim be chimerical, there will be all the greater scope and more imperative need for the latter, so long at least as mankind think fit to live, and do not take refuge in the simultaneous act of suicide recommended under certain conditions by Novalis. When, however, it is thus positively asserted to be impossible that human life should be happy, the assertion, if not something like a verbal quibble, is at least an exaggeration. If by happiness be meant a continuity of highly pleasurable excitement, it is evident enough that this is impossible. A state of exalted pleasure lasts only moments or in some cases, and with some intermissions, hours or days, and is the occasional brilliant flash of enjoyment, not its permanent and steady flame. Of this the philosophers who have taught that happiness is the end of life were as fully aware as those who taunt them. The happiness which they meant was not a life of rapture; but moments of such, in an existence made up of few and transitory pains, many and various pleasures, with a decided predominance of the active over the passive, and having as the foundation of the whole not to expect more from life than it is capable of bestowing. A life thus composed, to those who have been fortunate enough to obtain it, has always appeared worthy of the name of happiness. And such an existence is even now the lot of many, during some considerable portion of their lives. The present wretched education and wretched social arrangements are the only real hindrance to its being attainable by almost all.

The objectors perhaps may doubt whether human beings, if taught to consider happiness as the end of life, would be satisfied with such a moderate share of it. But great numbers of mankind have been satisfied with much less. The main constituents of a satisfied life appear to be two, either of which by itself is often found sufficient for the purpose: tranquility and excitement. With much tranquility, many find that they can be content with very little pleasure; with much excitement, many can reconcile themselves to a considerable quantity of pain. There is assuredly no inherent impossibility of enabling even the mass of mankind to unite both, since the two are so far from being incompatible that they are in natural alliance, the prolongation of either being a preparation for, and exciting a wish for, the other. It is only those in whom indolence amounts to a vice that do not desire excitement after an interval of repose; it is only those in whom the need of excitement is a disease that feel the tranquility which follows excitement dull and insipid, instead of pleasurable in direct proportion to the excitement which preceded it. When people who are tolerably fortunate in their outward lot do not find in life sufficient enjoyment to make it valuable to them, the cause generally is caring for nobody but themselves. To those who have neither public nor private affections, the excitements of life are much curtailed, and in any case dwindle in value as the time approaches when all selfish interests must be terminated by death; while those who leave after them objects of personal affection, and especially those who have also cultivated a fellow-feeling with the collective interests of mankind, retain as lively an interest in life on the eve of death as in the vigor of youth and health. Next to selfishness, the principal cause which makes life unsatisfactory is want of mental cultivation. A cultivated mind—I do not mean that of a philosopher, but any mind to which the fountains of knowledge have been opened, and which has been taught, in any tolerable degree, to exercise its faculties—finds sources of inexhaustible interest in all that surrounds it: in the objects of nature, the achievements of art, the imaginations of poetry, the incidents of history, the ways of mankind, past and present, and their prospects in the future. It is possible, indeed, to become indifferent to all this, and that too without having exhausted a thousandth part of it, but only when one has had from the beginning no moral or human interest in these things, and has sought in them only the gratification of curiosity. . . .

Of What Sort of Proof
the Principle of Utility Is Susceptible

It has already been remarked that questions of ultimate ends do not admit of proof, in the ordinary acceptation of the term. To be incapable of proof by reasoning is common to all first principles, to the first premises of our knowledge, as well as to those of our conduct. But the former, being matters of fact, may be the subject of a direct appeal to the faculties which judge of fact—namely, our senses and our internal consciousness. Can an appeal be made to the same faculties on questions of practical ends? Or by what other faculty is cognizance taken of them?

Questions about ends are, in other words, questions what things are desirable. The utilitarian doctrine is that happiness is desirable, and the only thing desirable, as an end; all other things being only desirable as means to that end. What ought to be required of this doctrine, what conditions is it requisite that the doctrine should fulfil—to make good its claim to be believed?

The only proof capable of being given that an object is visible is that people actually see it. The only proof that a sound is audible is that people hear it; and so of the other sources of our experience. In like manner, I apprehend, the sole evidence it is possible to produce that anything is desirable is that people do actually desire it. If the end which the utilitarian doctrine proposes to itself were not, in theory and in practice, acknowledged to be an end, nothing could ever convince any person that it was so. No reason can be given why the general happiness is desirable, except that each person, so far as he believes it to be attainable, desires his own happiness. This, however, being a fact, we have not only all the proof which the case admits of, but all which it is possible to require, that happiness is a good; that each person's happiness is a good to that person, and the general happiness, therefore, a good to the aggregate of all persons. Happiness has made out its title as *one* of the ends of conduct, and consequently one of the criteria of morality.

But it has not, by this alone, proved itself to be the sole criterion. To do that, it would seem, by the same rule, necessary to show, not only that people desire happiness, but that they never desire anything else. Now it is palpable that they do desire things which, in common language, are decidedly distinguished from happiness. They desire, for example, virtue and the absence of vice, no less really than pleasure and the absence of pain. The desire of virtue is not as universal, but it is as authentic a fact as the desire of happiness. And hence the opponents of the utilitarian standard deem that they have a right to infer that there are other ends of human action besides happiness, and that happiness is not the standard of approbation and disapprobation.

But does the utilitarian doctrine deny that people desire virtue, or maintain that virtue is not a thing to be desired? The very reverse. It maintains not only that virtue is to be desired, but that it is to be desired disinterestedly, for itself. Whatever may be the opinion of utilitarian moralists as to the original conditions by which virtue is made virtue, however they may believe (as they do) that actions and dispositions are only virtuous because they promote another end than virtue, yet this being granted, and it having been decided, from considerations of this description, what *is* virtuous, they not only place virtue at the very head of the things which are good as means to the ultimate end, but they also recognize as a psychological fact the possibility of its being, to the individual, a good in itself, without looking to any end beyond it; and hold that the mind is not in a right state, not in a state conformable to utility, not in the state most conducive to the general happiness, unless it does love virtue in this manner—as a thing desirable in itself, even although, in the individual instance, it should not produce those other desirable consequences which it tends to produce, and on account of which it is held to be virtue. This opinion is not, in the smallest degree, a departure from the happiness principle. The ingredients of happiness are very various, and each of them is desirable in itself, and not merely when considered as swelling an aggregate. The principle of utility does not mean that any given pleasure, as music, for instance, or any exemption from pain, as for example health, is to be looked upon as means to a collective something termed happiness, and to be desired on that account. They are desired and desirable in and for themselves; besides being means, they are a part of the end. Virtue, according to the utilitarian doctrine, is not naturally and originally part of the end, but it is capable of becoming so; and in those who love it disinterestedly it has become so, and is desired and cherished, not as a means to happiness, but as a part of their happiness.

To illustrate this further, we may remember that virtue is not the only thing originally a means, and which if it were not a means to anything else would be and remain indifferent, but which by association with what it is a means to comes to be desired for itself, and that too with the utmost intensity. What, for example, shall we say of the love of money? There is nothing originally more desirable about money than about any heap of glittering pebbles. Its worth is solely that of the things which it will buy; the desires for other things than itself, which it is a means of gratifying. Yet the love of money is not only one of the strongest moving forces of human life, but money is, in many cases, desired in and for itself; the desire to possess it is often stronger than the desire to use it, and goes on increasing when all the desires which point to ends beyond it, to be compassed by it, are falling off. It may, then, be said truly that money is desired not for the sake of an end, but as part of the end. From being a means to happiness, it has come to be itself a principal ingredient of the individual's conception of happiness. The same may be said of the majority of the great objects of human life: power, for example, or fame, except that to each of these there is a certain amount of immediate pleasure annexed, which has at least the semblance of being naturally inherent in them—a thing which cannot be said of money. Still, however, the strongest natural attraction, both of power and of fame, is the immense aid they give to the attainment of our other wishes; and it is the strong association thus generated between them and all our objects of desire which gives to the direct desire of them the intensity it often assumes, so as in some characters to surpass in strength all other desires. In these cases the means have become a part of the end, and a more important part of it than any of the things which they are means to. What was once desired as an instrument for the attainment of happiness has come to be desired for its own sake. In being desired for its own sake it is, however, desired as *part* of happiness. The person is made, or thinks he would be made, happy by its mere possession; and is made unhappy by failure to obtain it. The desire of it is not a different thing from the desire of happiness any more than the love of music or the desire of health. They are included in happiness. They are some of the elements of which the desire of happiness is made up. Happiness is not an abstract idea but a concrete whole; and these are some of its parts. And the utilitarian standard sanctions and approves their being so. Life would be a poor thing, very ill provided with sources of happiness, if there were not this provision of nature by which things originally indifferent, but conducive to, or otherwise associated with, the satisfaction of our primitive desires, become in themselves sources of pleasure more valuable than the primitive pleasures, both in permanency, in the space of human existence that they are capable of covering, and even in intensity.

Virtue, according to the utilitarian conception, is a good of this description. There was no original desire of it, or motive to it, save its conduciveness to pleasure, and especially to protection from pain. But through the association thus formed it may be felt a good in itself, and desired as such with as great intensity as any other good; and with this difference between it and the love of money, of power, or of fame, that all of these may, and often do, render the individual noxious to the other members of the society to which he belongs, whereas there is nothing which makes him so much a blessing to them as the cultivation of the disinterested love of virtue. And consequently, the utilitarian standard, while it tolerates and approves those other acquired desires, up to the point beyond which they would be more injurious to the general happiness than promotive of it, enjoins and requires the cultivation of the love of virtue up to the greatest strength possible, as being above all things important to the general happiness.

It results from the preceding considerations that there is in reality nothing desired except happiness. Whatever is desired otherwise than as a means to some end beyond itself, and ultimately to happiness, is desired as itself a part of happiness, and is not desired for itself until it has become so. Those who desire virtue for its own sake desire it either because the consciousness of it is a pleasure, or because the consciousness of being without it is a pain, or for both reasons united; as in truth the pleasure and pain seldom exist separately, but almost always together—the same person feeling pleasure in the degree of virtue attained, and pain in not having attained more. If one of these gave him no pleasure, and the other no pain, he would not love or desire virtue, or would desire it only for the other benefits which it might produce to himself or to persons whom he cared for.

We have now, then, an answer to the question, of what sort of proof the principle of utility is susceptible. If the opinion which I have now stated is psychologically true—if human nature is so constituted as to desire nothing which is not either a part of happiness or a means of happiness, we can have no other proof, and we require no other, that these are the only things desirable. If so, happiness is the sole end of human action, and the promotion of it the test by which to judge of all human conduct; from whence it necessarily follows that it must be the criterion of morality, since a part is included in the whole.

And now to decide whether this is really so, whether mankind do desire nothing for itself but that which is a pleasure to them, or of which the absence is a pain, we have evidently arrived at a question of fact and experience, dependent, like all similar questions, upon evidence. It can only be determined by practised self-consciousness and self-observation, assisted by observation of others. I believe that these sources of evidence, impartially consulted, will declare that desiring a thing and finding it pleasant, aversion to it and thinking of it as painful, are phenomena entirely inseparable or rather two parts of the same phenomenon; in strictness of language, two different modes of naming the same psychological fact; that to think of an object as desirable (unless for the sake of its consequences) and to think of it as pleasant are one and the same thing; and that to desire anything except in proportion as the idea of it is pleasant, is a physical and metaphysical impossibility.

So obvious does this appear to me that I expect it will hardly be disputed; and the objection made will be, not that desire can possibly be directed to anything ultimately except pleasure and exemption from pain, but that the will is a different thing from desire; that a person of confirmed virtue or any other person whose purposes are fixed carries out his purposes without any thought of the pleasure he has in contemplating them or expects to derive from their fulfilment, and persists in acting on them, even though these pleasures are much diminished by changes in his character or decay of his passive sensibilities, or are outweighed by the pains which the pursuit of the purposes may bring upon him. All this I fully admit and have stated it elsewhere as positively and emphatically as anyone. Will, the active phenomenon, is a different thing from desire, the state of passive sensibility, and, though originally an offshoot from it, may in time take root and detach itself from the parent stock, so much so that in the case of an habitual purpose, instead of willing the thing because we desire it, we often desire it only because we will it. This, however, is but an instance of that familiar fact, the power of habit, and is nowise confined to the case of virtuous actions. Many indifferent things which men originally did from a motive of some sort, they continue to do from habit. Sometimes this is done unconsciously; the consciousness coming only after the action; at other times with conscious volition, but volition which has become habitual and is put in operation by the force of habit, in opposition perhaps to

the deliberate preference, as often happens with those who have contracted habits of vicious or hurtful indulgence. Third and last comes
the case in which the habitual act of will in the individual instance is
not in contradiction to the general intention prevailing at other times,
but in fulfilment of it; as in the case of the person of confirmed virtue
and of all who pursue deliberately and consistently any determinate end.
The distinction between will and desire thus understood is an authentic
and highly important psychological fact; but the fact consists solely
in this—that will, like all other parts of our constitution, is amenable to
habit, and that we may will from habit what we no longer desire for
itself, or desire only because we will it. It is not the less true that will,
in the beginning, is entirely produced by desire; including in that term
the repelling influence of pain as well as the attractive one of pleasure.
Let us take into consideration no longer the person who has a confirmed
will to do right, but him in whom that virtuous will is still feeble,
conquerable by temptation, and not to be fully relied on; by what means
can it be strengthened? How can the will to be virtuous, where it does
not exist in sufficient force, be implanted or awakened? Only by making the person *desire* virtue—by making him think of it in a pleasurable
light, or of its absence in a painful one. It is by associating the doing
right with pleasure, or the doing wrong with pain, or by eliciting and
impressing and bringing home to the person's experience the pleasure
naturally involved in the one or the pain in the other, that it is possible
to call forth that will to be virtuous which, when confirmed, acts without any thought of either pleasure or pain. Will is the child of desire, and
passes out of the dominion of its parent only to come under that of habit.
That which is the result of habit affords no presumption of being intrinsically good; and there would be no reason for wishing that the purpose of virtue should become independent of pleasure and pain were
it not that the influence of the pleasurable and painful associations
which prompt to virtue is not sufficiently to be depended on for unerring
constancy of action until it has acquired the support of habit. Both in
feeling and in conduct, habit is the only thing which imparts certainty;
and it is because of the importance to others of being able to rely absolutely on one's feelings and conduct, and to oneself of being able to
rely on one's own, that the will to do right ought to be cultivated into
this habitual independence. In other words, this state of the will is a
means to good, not intrinsically a good; and does not contradict the
doctrine that nothing is a good to human beings but in so far as it is
either itself pleasure or a means of attaining pleasure or averting pain.

But if this doctrine be true, the principle of utility is proved. Whether
it is so or not, must now be left to the consideration of the thoughtful
reader.

What Mill says in the preceding selections has been much discussed. One of his sharpest critics was G. E. Moore. In the following paragraphs Moore argues against Mill on both logical and psychological grounds. After reading Moore, you may wish to reread the relevant passages in Mill and consider what, if anything, Mill or his defenders might say in response.

CRITICISM OF MILL'S HEDONISM

G. E. Moore

. . . "Good," [Mill] tells us, means "desirable," and you can only find out what is desirable by seeking to find out what is actually desired. . . .

Well, the fallacy in this step is so obvious, that it is quite wonderful how Mill failed to see it. The fact is that "desirable" does not mean "able to be desired" as "visible" means "able to be seen." The desirable means simply what *ought* to be desired or *deserves* to be desired; just as the detestable means not what can be but what ought to be detested and the damnable what deserves to be damned. Mill has, then, smuggled in, under cover of the word "desirable," the very notion about which he ought to be quite clear. "Desirable" does indeed mean "what it is good to desire"; but when this is understood, it is no longer plausible to say that our only test of *that,* is what is actually desired. Is it merely a tautology when the Prayer Book talks of *good* desires? Are not *bad* desires also possible? . . .

Well, then, the first step by which Mill has attempted to establish his Hedonism is simply fallacious. He has attempted to establish the identity of the good with the desired, by confusing the proper sense of "desirable," in which it denotes that which it is good to desire, with the sense which it would bear if it were analogous to such words as "visible." If "desirable" is to be identical with "good," then it must bear one sense; and if it is to be identical with "desired," then it must bear quite another sense. . . .

Let us try to analyse the psychological state which is called "desire." That name is usually confined to a state of mind in which the idea of some object or event, not yet existing, is present to us. Suppose, for instance, I am desiring a glass of port wine. I have the idea of drinking such a glass before my mind, although I am not yet drinking it. Well, how does pleasure enter in to this relation? My theory is that it enters

From Principia Ethica *(London: Cambridge University Press, 1903). Reprinted by permission of Cambridge University Press.*

in, in this way. The *idea* of the drinking causes a feeling of pleasure in my mind, which helps to produce that state of incipient activity, which is called "desire." It is, therefore, because of a pleasure, which I already have——the pleasure excited by a mere idea—that I desire the wine, which I have not. And I am ready to admit that a pleasure of this kind, an actual pleasure, is always among the causes of every desire, and not only of every desire, but of every mental activity, whether conscious or sub-conscious. I am ready to *admit* this, I say: I cannot vouch that it is the true psychological doctrine; but, at all events, it is not *primâ facie* quite absurd. And now, what is the other doctrine, the doctrine which I am supposing held, and which is at all events essential to Mill's argument? It is this. That when I desire the wine, it is not the wine which I desire but the pleasure which I expect to get from it. In other words, the doctrine is that the idea of a pleasure *not actual* is always necessary to cause desire; whereas my doctrine was that the *actual* pleasure caused by the idea of something else was always necessary to cause desire. It is these two different theories which I suppose the Psychological Hedonists to confuse: the confusion is, as Mr. Bradley puts it,[1] between "a pleasant thought" and "the thought of a pleasure." It is in fact only where the latter, the "thought of a pleasure," is present, that pleasure can be said to be the *object* of desire, or the *motive* to action. On the other hand, when only a pleasant thought is present, as, I admit, *may* always be the case, then it is the object of the thought—that which we are thinking about—which is the object of desire and the motive to action; and the pleasure, which that thought excites, may, indeed, cause our desire or move us to action, but it is not our end or object nor our motive.

Well, I hope this distinction is sufficiently clear. Now let us see how it bears upon Ethical Hedonism. I assume it to be perfectly obvious that the idea of the object of desire is not always and only the idea of a pleasure. In the first place, plainly, we are not always conscious of expecting pleasure, when we desire a thing. We may be only conscious of the thing which we desire, and may be impelled to make for it at once, without any calculation as to whether it will bring us pleasure or pain. And, in the second place, even when we do expect pleasure, it can certainly be very rarely pleasure *only* which we desire.

. . . For instance, granted that, when I desire my glass of port wine, I have also an idea of the pleasure I expect from it, plainly that pleasure cannot be the only object of my desire; the port wine must be included in my object, else I might be led by my desire to take worm-

---

wood instead of wine. If the desire were directed *solely* towards the pleasure, it could not lead me to take the wine; if it is to take a definite direction, it is absolutely necessary that the idea of the object, from which the pleasure is expected, should also be present and should control my activity. The theory then that what is desired is always and only pleasure must break down: it is impossible to prove that pleasure alone is good, by that line of argument. But, if we substitute for this theory, that other, possibly true, theory, that pleasure is always the cause of desire, then all the plausibility of our ethical doctrine that pleasure alone is good straightway disappears. For in this case, pleasure is not what I desire, it is not what I want: it is something which I already have, before I can want anything. And can any one feel inclined to maintain, that that which I already have, while I am still desiring something else, is always and alone the good?

But now let us return to consider another of Mill's arguments for his position that "happiness is the sole end of human action." Mill admits, as I have said, that pleasure is not the only thing we actually desire. "The desire of virtue," he says, "is not as universal, but it is as authentic a fact, as the desire of happiness." And again, "Money is, in many cases, desired in and for itself." These admissions are, of course, in naked and glaring contradiction with his argument that pleasure is the only thing desirable, because it is the only thing desired. How then does Mill even attempt to avoid this contradiction? His chief argument seems to be that "virtue," "money" and other such objects, when they are thus desired in and for themselves, are desired only as "a part of happiness." Now what does this mean? Happiness, as we saw, has been defined by Mill, as "pleasure and the absence of pain." Does Mill mean to say that "money," these actual coins, which he admits to be desired in and for themselves, are a part either of pleasure or of the absence of pain? Will he maintain that those coins themselves are in my mind, and actually a part of my pleasant feelings? If this is to be said, all words are useless: nothing can possibly be distinguished from anything else; if these two things are not distinct, what on earth is? We shall hear next that this table is really and truly the same thing as this room; that a cab-horse is in fact indistinguishable from St Paul's Cathedral; that this book of Mill's which I hold in my hand, because it was his pleasure to produce it, is now and at this moment a part of the happiness which he felt many years ago and which has so long ceased to be. Pray consider a moment what this contemptible nonsense really means. "Money," says Mill, "is only desirable as a means to happiness." Perhaps so; but what then? "Why," says Mill, "money is undoubtedly desired for its own sake." "Yes, go on," say we. "Well," says Mill, "if money is desired for its own sake, it must be desirable as an end-in-itself: I have said so myself." "Oh," say we, "but you also said just now that it was only desirable as a means." "I own I did," says Mill, "but I will try to patch up matters, by saying that what is only a means to an end, is the same thing as a part of that end. I daresay the public won't notice." And the public haven't noticed. Yet this is certainly what Mill has done. He has broken down the distinction between means and ends, upon the precise observance of which his Hedonism rests. And he has been compelled to do this, because he has failed to distinguish "end" in the sense of what is desirable, from "end" in the sense of what is desired: a distinction which, nevertheless, both the present argument and his whole book presupposes.

. . . I [also] wish to shew that Mill's admissions as to quality of pleasure are either inconsistent with his Hedonism, or else afford no other ground for it than would be given by mere quantity of pleasure.

It will be seen that Mill's test for one pleasure's superiority in quality over another is the preference of most people who have experienced both. A pleasure so preferred, he holds, is more desirable. But then, as we have seen, he holds that "to think of an object as desirable and to think of it as pleasant are one and the same thing." He holds, therefore, that the preference of experts merely proves that one pleasure is pleasanter than another. But if that is so, how can he distinguish this standard from the standard of quantity of pleasure? Can one pleasure be pleasanter than another, except in the sense that it gives *more* pleasure? "Pleasant" must, if words are to have any meaning at all, denote some one quality common to all the things that are pleasant; and, if so, then one thing can only be more pleasant than another, according as it has more or less of this one quality. But, then, let us try the other alternative, and suppose that Mill does not seriously mean that this preference of experts merely proves one pleasure to be pleasanter than another. Well, in this case what does "preferred" mean? It cannot mean "more desired," since, as we know, the degree of desire is always, according to Mill, in exact proportion to the degree of pleasantness. But, in that case, the basis of Mill's Hedonism collapses, for he is admitting that one thing may be preferred over another, and thus proved more desirable, although it is not more desired. . . .

Mill's judgment of preference, so far from establishing the principle that pleasure alone is good, is obviously inconsistent with it. He admits that experts can judge whether one pleasure is more desirable than another, because pleasures differ in quality. But what does this mean? If one pleasure can differ from another in quality, that means, that *a* pleasure is something complex, something composed, in fact, of pleasure *in addition to* that which produces pleasure. . . .

Aristotle is an example of a philosopher who agrees with Epicurus, Bentham, and Mill (and with Eudoxus, whom he discusses) that the good is what we aim at or desire, but who denies that what we finally aim at is pleasure. Although he holds that our ultimate goal is for happiness (eudaimonia), he insists that happiness is excellent or virtuous activity of the soul, not pleasure. He believes that such activity is accompanied by pleasure, but thinks it is good because it is desired, not because it is pleasant, and that it is desired for its own sake (though he talks as if he regards the question of whether we desire life for the sake of pleasure or pleasure for the sake of life as unimportant). He also argues that happiness consists primarily of the speculative activity of contemplation (or, more generally, of excellent intellectual activity), and only secondarily, if at all, of morally virtuous action.

THE GOOD IS EXCELLENT ACTIVITY

Aristotle

[*From Book I*]

Every art and every scientific inquiry, and similarly every action and purpose, may be said to aim at some good. Hence the good has been well defined as that at which all things aim. But it is clear that there is a difference in the ends; for the ends are sometimes activities, and sometimes results beyond the mere activities. . . .

If it is true that in the sphere of action there is an end which we wish for its own sake, and for the sake of which we wish everything else, and that we do not desire all things for the sake of something else (for, if that is so, the process will go on *ad infinitum*, and our desire will be idle and futile) it is clear that this will be the good or the supreme good. Does it not follow then that the knowledge of this supreme good is of great importance for the conduct of life, and that, if we know it, we shall be like archers who have a mark at which to aim, we shall have a better chance of attaining what we want? But, if this is the case, we must endeavour to comprehend, at least in outline, its nature, and the science or faculty to which it belongs. . . .

As every knowledge and moral purpose aspires to some good, what is in our view the good at which the political science aims, and what is

From The Nicomachean Ethics of Aristotle, *trans. J. E. C. Welldon (London: Macmillan & Co. Ltd., 1892).*

the highest of all practical goods? As to its name there is, I may say, a general agreement. The masses and the cultured classes agree in calling it happiness, and conceive that "to live well" or "to do well" is the same thing as "to be happy." But as to the nature of happiness they do not agree, nor do the masses give the same account of it as the philosophers. The former define it as something visible and palpable, e.g. pleasure, wealth, or honour; different people give different definitions of it, and often the same person gives different definitions at different times; for when a person has been ill, it is health, when he is poor, it is wealth, and, if he is conscious of his own ignorance, he envies people who use grand language above his own comprehension. Some philosophers on the other hand have held that, besides these various goods, there is an absolute good which is the cause of goodness in them all.

. . . As it appears that there are more ends than one and some of these, e.g. wealth, flutes, and instruments generally we desire as means to something else, it is evident that they are not all final ends. But the highest good is clearly something final. Hence if there is only one final end, this will be the object of which we are in search, and if there are more than one, it will be the most final of them. We speak of that which is sought after for its own sake as more final than that which is sought after as a means to something else; we speak of that which is never desired as a means to something else as more final than the things which are desired both in themselves and as means to something else; and we speak of a thing as absolutely final, if it is always desired in itself and never as a means to something else.

It seems that happiness preeminently answers to this description, as we always desire happiness for its own sake and never as a means to something else, whereas we desire honour, pleasure, intellect, and every virtue, partly for their own sakes (for we should desire them independently of what might result from them) but partly also as being means to happiness, because we suppose they will prove the instruments of happiness. Happiness, on the other hand, nobody desires for the sake of these things, nor indeed as a means to anything else at all.

We come to the same conclusion if we start from the consideration of self-sufficiency, if it may be assumed that the final good is self-sufficient. But when we speak of self-sufficiency, we do not mean that a person leads a solitary life all by himself, but that he has parents, children, wife, and friends, and fellow-citizens in general, as man is naturally a social being. But here it is necessary to prescribe some limit; for if the circle be extended so as to include parents, descendants, and friends' friends, it will go on indefinitely. Leaving this point, however, for future investigation, we define the self-sufficient as that which, taken by itself, makes life desirable, and wholly free from want, and this is our conception of happiness.

Again, we conceive happiness to be the most desirable of all things, and that not merely as one among other good things. If it were one among other good things, the addition of the smallest good would increase its desirableness; for the accession makes a superiority of goods, and the greater of two goods is always the more desirable. It appears then that happiness is something final and self-sufficient, being the end of all action.

Perhaps, however, it seems a truth which is generally admitted, that happiness is the supreme good; what is wanted is to define its nature a little more clearly The best way of arriving at such a definition will probably be to ascertain the function of Man. For, as with a flute-player, a statuary, or any artisan, or in fact anybody who has a definite function and action, his goodness, or excellence seems to lie in his function, so it would seem to be with Man, if indeed he has a definite function. Can it be said then that, while a carpenter and a cobbler have definite functions and actions, Man, unlike them, is naturally functionless? The reasonable view is that, as the eye, the hand, the foot, and similarly each several part of the body has a definite function, so Man may be regarded as having a definite function apart from all these. What then, can this function be? It is not life; for life is apparently something which man shares with the plants; and it is something peculiar to him that we are looking for. We must exclude therefore the life of nutrition and increase. There is next what may be called the life of sensation. But this too, is apparently shared by Man with horses, cattle, and all other animals. There remains what I may call the practical life of the rational part of Man's being. But the rational part is twofold; it is rational partly in the sense of being obedient to reason, and partly in the sense of possessing reason and intelligence. The practical life too may be conceived of in two ways,[1] viz., either as a moral state, or as a moral activity: but we must understand by it the life of activity, as this seems to be the truer form of the conception.

The function of Man then is an activity of soul in accordance with reason, or not independently of reason. Again the functions of a person of a certain kind, and of such a person who is good of his kind e.g. of a harpist and a good harpist, are in our view generically the same, and this view is true of people of all kinds without exception, the superior excellence being only an addition to the function; for it is the function of a harpist to play the harp, and of a good harpist to play the harp well. This being so, if we define the function of Man as a kind of life, and this

---

[1] In other words life may be taken to mean either the mere possession of certain [dispositions] or their active exercise.

life as an activity of soul, or a course of action in conformity with reason, if the function of a good man is such activity or action of a good and noble kind, and if everything is successfully performed when it is performed in accordance with its proper excellence, it follows that the good of Man is an activity of soul in accordance with virtue or, if there are more virtues than one, in accordance with the best and most complete virtue. But it is necessary to add the words "in a complete life." For as one swallow or one day does not make a spring, so one day or a short time does not make a fortunate or happy man. . . .

[From Book X]

. . . let us review the various doctrines of pleasure.

Eudoxus held that pleasure was the good, because he saw that all things, whether rational or irrational, make pleasure their aim. He argued that in all cases that which is desirable is good, and that which is most desirable is most good; hence the fact of all things being drawn to the same object is an indication that that object is the best for all, as everything discovers what is good for itself in the same way as it discovers food; but that that which is good for all, and is the aim of all, is the good.

His theories were accepted, not so much for their intrinsic value as for the excellence of his moral character; for he was regarded as a person of exemplary temperance. It seemed then that he did not put forward these views as being a votary of pleasure, but that the truth was really as he said. He held that this truth resulted with equal clearness from a consideration of the opposite of pleasure; for as pain is something which everyone should avoid, so too its opposite is something which everybody should desire. He argued that a thing is in the highest degree desirable, if we do not desire it for any ulterior reason, or with any ulterior motive, and this is admittedly the case with pleasure; for if a person is pleased, nobody asks the further question, What is his motive in being pleased? a fact which proves that pleasure is desirable in itself. And further that the addition of pleasure to any good, e.g. to just or temperate conduct, renders that good more desirable, and it follows that if the good is augmented by a thing, that thing must itself be a good.

It seems then that this argument proves pleasure to be a good, but not to be a good in a higher sense than anything else; for any good whatever is more desirable with the addition of another good than when it stands alone. It is by a precisely similar argument that Plato tries to prove that pleasure is not the good. Pleasure (he says) is not the chief good, for the pleasant life is more desirable with the addition of prudence than without it; but if the combination is better, pleasure is not the good, as the good itself cannot be made more desirable by any addition.

But it is clear that, if pleasure is not the good, neither can anything else be which is made more desirable by the addition of any absolute good. What is it then which is incapable of such addition, but at the same time admits of our participating in it? For it is a good of this kind which is the object of our research.

People who argue on the other hand that that which all things aim at is not a good may be said to talk nonsense; for we accept the universal opinion as true, and one who upsets our trust in the universal opinion will find it hard to put forward any opinion that is more trustworthy. If it were only unintelligent beings that longed for pleasure, there would be something in what he says; but if intelligent beings also long for it, how can it be so? It is probable that even in the lower creatures there is some natural principle which is superior to the creatures themselves, and aims at their proper good. . . .

But if the instance of immoral pleasures be adduced to prove that pleasure is a bad thing, we may answer that these are not really pleasant. They may be pleasant to people who are in a bad condition, but it must not be inferred that they are pleasant except to such people, any more than that things are healthful or sweet or bitter in themselves, because they are so to invalids, or that things are white, because they appear so to people who are suffering from ophthalmia.

Perhaps the truth may be stated thus: Pleasures are desirable, but not if they are immoral in their origin, just as wealth is pleasant, but not if it be obtained at the cost of turning traitor to one's country, or health, but not at the cost of eating any food, however disagreeable. Or it may be said that pleasures are of different kinds, those which are noble in their origin are different from those which are dishonourable, and it is impossible to enjoy the pleasure of the just man without being just, or that of the musician without being musical, and so on. . . .

Again, nobody would choose to live all his life with the mind of a child, although he should enjoy the pleasures of childhood to the utmost, or to delight in doing what is utterly shameful, although he were never to suffer pain for doing it. There are many things too upon which we should set our hearts, even if they brought no pleasure with them, e.g. sight, memory, knowledge, and the possession of the virtues; and if it be true that these are necessarily attended by pleasures, it is immaterial, as we should desire them even if no pleasure resulted from them. It seems to be clear then that pleasure is not the good, nor is every pleasure desirable, and that there are some pleasures which are desirable in themselves, and they differ in kind or in origin from the others.

Again, every sense exercises its activity upon its own object, and the activity is perfect only when the sense itself is in a sound condition, and the object is the noblest that falls within the domain of that sense; for this seems to be preeminently the character of the perfect activity. We may say that it makes no difference whether we speak of the sense itself or of the organ in which it resides as exercising the activity; in every instance the activity is highest when the part which acts is in the best condition, and the object upon which it acts is the highest of the objects which fall within its domain. Such an activity will not only be the most perfect, but the most pleasant; for there is pleasure in all sensation, and similarly in all thought and speculation, and the activity will be pleasantest when it is most perfect, and it will be most perfect when it is the activity of the part being in a sound condition and acting upon the most excellent of the objects that fall within its domain.

Pleasure perfects the activity, but not in the same way in which the excellence of the sense or of the object of sense perfects it, just as health is the cause of our being in a healthy state in one sense and the doctor is the cause of it in another.

It is clear that every sense has its proper pleasure; for we speak of pleasant sights, pleasant sounds and so on. It is clear too that the pleasure is greatest when the sense is best, and its object is best; but if the sentient subject and the sensible object are at their best, there will always be pleasure so long as there is a subject to act and an object to be acted upon.

When it is said that pleasure perfects the activity, it is not as a state or quality inherent in the subject but as a perfection superadded to it, like the bloom of youth to people in the prime of life.

So long then as the object of thought or sensation and the critical or contemplative subject are such as they ought to be, there will be pleasure in the exercise of the activity; for this is the natural result if the agent and the patient remain in the same relation to each other. . . .

It may be supposed that everybody desires pleasure, for everybody clings to life. But life is a species of activity and a person's activity displays itself in the sphere and with the means which are after his own heart. Thus a musician exercises his ears in listening to music, a student his intellect in speculation, and so on.

But pleasure perfects the activities; it therefore perfects life, which is the aim of human desire. It is reasonable then to aim at pleasure, as it perfects life in each of us, and life is an object of desire.

Whether we desire life for the sake of pleasure or pleasure for the sake of life, is a question which may be dismissed for the moment. For it appears that pleasure and life are yoked together and do not admit of separation, as pleasure is impossible without activity and every activity is perfected by pleasure.

If this be so, it seems to follow that pleasures are of different kinds, as we hold that things which are different in kind are perfected by things which are themselves different in kind. . . .

Now the pleasures of the intellect are different from the pleasures of the senses, and these again are different in kind from one another. It follows that the pleasures which perfect them will also be different. . . .

Again, as the activities differ in goodness and badness, some being desirable, some undesirable, and some neither the one nor the other, so it is with pleasures, as every activity has its proper pleasure. Thus the pleasure which is proper to a virtuous activity is good, and that which is proper to a low activity is vicious. For the desires of what is noble are themselves laudable, the desires of what is disgraceful are censurable. . . .

. . . the same things give pleasure to some people and pain to others, to some they are painful and hateful, to others pleasant and lovable. This is true of sweet things; the same things do not seem sweet to a person in a fever and to a person in good health, nor does the same thing seem hot to an invalid and to a person in a good physical condition. It is much the same with other things as well.

But in all these cases it seems that the thing really is what it appears to the virtuous man to be. But if this is a true statement of the case, as it seems to be, if virtue or the good man *qua* good is the measure of everything, it follows that it is such pleasures as appear pleasures to the good man that are really pleasures, and the things which afford him delight that are really pleasant. It is no wonder if what he finds disagreeable seems pleasant to somebody else, as men are liable to many corruptions and defilements; but such things are not pleasant except to these people, and to them only when they are in this condition.

It is clear then that we must not speak of pleasures which are admitted to be disgraceful as pleasures, except in relation to people who are thoroughly corrupt. But the question remains, Among such pleasures as are seen to be good, what is the character or nature of the pleasures that deserve to be called the *proper* pleasures of Man? It is plain, I think, from a consideration of the activities; for the activities bring pleasures in their train. Whether then there is one activity or there are several belonging to the perfect and fortunate man, it is the pleasures which perfect these activities that would be strictly described as the *proper* pleasures of Man. All other pleasures are only in a secondary or fractional sense the pleasures of Man, as are all other activities.

After this discussion of . . . pleasure it remains to give a sketch of happiness, since we [regard] happiness as the end of human things. We shall shorten our account of it if we begin by recapitulating our previous remarks.

We said that happiness is not a moral state; for, if it were, it would be predicable of one who spends his whole life in sleep, living the life of a vegetable, or of one who is utterly miserable. If then we cannot accept this view if we must rather define happiness as an activity of some kind, as has been said before, and if activities are either necessary and desirable as a means to something else or desirable in themselves, it is clear that we must define happiness as belonging to the class of activities which are desirable in themselves, and not desirable as means to something else; for happiness has no want, it is self-sufficient.

Again, activities are desirable in themselves, if nothing is expected from them beyond the activity. This seems to be the case with virtuous actions, as the practice of what is noble and virtuous is a thing desirable in itself. It seems to be the case also with such amusements as are pleasant, we do not desire them as means to other things. . . .

The reason why [amusements] are regarded as elements of happiness is that people who occupy high positions devote their leisure to them. But such people are not, I think, a criterion. For a high position is no guarantee of virtue or intellect, which are the sources on which virtuous activities depend. And if these people, who have never tasted a pure and liberal pleasure, have recourse to the pleasures of the body, it must not be inferred that these pleasures are preferable; for even children suppose that such things as are valued or honoured among them are best. It is only reasonable then that, as men and children differ in their estimate of what is honourable, so should good and bad people.

As has been frequently said, therefore, it is the things which are honourable and pleasant to the virtuous man that are really honourable and pleasant. But everybody feels the activity which accords with his own moral state to be most desirable, and accordingly the virtuous man regards the activity in accordance with virtue as most desirable.

Happiness then does not consist in amusement. It would be paradoxical to hold that the end of human life is amusement, and that we should toil and suffer all our life for the sake of amusing ourselves. For we may be said to desire all things as means to something else except indeed happiness, as happiness is the end or perfect state.

It appears to be foolish and utterly childish to take serious trouble and pains for the sake of amusement. But to amuse oneself with a view to being serious seems to be right, as Anacharsis says; for amusement is a kind of relaxation, and it is because we cannot work for ever that we need relaxation.

Relaxation then is not an end. We enjoy it as a means to activity; but it seems that the happy life is a life of virtue, and such a life is serious, it is not one of mere amusement. . . .

[Since] happiness consists in virtuous activity, it is only reasonable to suppose that it is the activity of the highest virtue, or in other words, of the best part of our nature. Whether it is the reason or something else which seems to exercise rule and authority by a natural right, and to have a conception of things noble and divine, either as being itself divine or as relatively the most divine part of our being, it is the activity of this part in accordance with its proper virtue which will be the perfect happiness.

It has been already stated that it is a speculative activity, i.e. an activity which takes the form of contemplation. This is a conclusion which would seem to agree with our previous arguments and with the truth itself; for the speculative is the highest activity, as the intuitive reason is the highest of our faculties, and the objects with which the intuitive reason is concerned are the highest of things that can be known. It is also the most continuous; for our speculation can more easily be continuous than any kind of action. We consider too that pleasure is an essential element of happiness, and it is admitted that there is no virtuous activity so pleasant as the activity of wisdom or philosophic reflexion; at all events it appears that philosophy possesses pleasures of wonderful purity and certainty, and it is reasonable to suppose that people who possess knowledge pass their time more pleasantly than people who are seekers after truth.

Self-sufficiency too, as it is called, is preeminently a characteristic of the speculative activity; for the wise man, the just man, and all others, need the necessaries of life; but when they are adequately provided with these things, the just man needs people to whom and with whom he may do justice, so do the temperate man, the courageous man and everyone else; but the wise man is capable of speculation by himself, and the wiser he is, the more capable he is of such speculation. It is perhaps better for him in his speculation to have fellow-workers; but nevertheless he is in the highest degree self-sufficient.

It would seem too that the speculative is the only activity which is loved for its own sake as it has no result except speculation, whereas from all moral actions we gain something more or less besides the action itself.

Again, happiness, it seems, requires leisure; for the object of our business is leisure, as the object of war is the enjoyment of peace. Now the activity of the practical virtues is displayed in politics or war, and actions of this sort seem incompatible with leisure. . . .

If then political and military actions are preeminent among virtuous actions in beauty and grandeur, if they are incompatible with leisure and aim at some end, and are not desired for their own sakes, if the activity of the intuitive reason seems to be superior in seriousness as being speculative, and not to aim at any end beyond itself, and to have its proper pleasure, and if this pleasure enhances the activity, it follows that such self-sufficiency and power of leisure and absence of fatigue as are possible to a man and all the other attributes of felicity are found to be realized in this activity. This then will be the perfect happiness of Man, if a perfect length of life is given it, for there is no imperfection in happiness. But such a life will be too good for Man. He will enjoy such a life not in virtue of his humanity but in virtue of some divine element within him, and the superiority of this activity to the activity of any other virtue will be proportionate to the superiority of this divine element in man to his composite or material nature.

If then the reason is divine in comparison with the rest of Man's nature, the life which accords with reason will be divine in comparison with human life in general. Nor is it right to follow the advice of people who say that the thoughts of men should not be too high for humanity or the thoughts of mortals too high for mortality; for a man, as far as in him lies, should seek immortality and do all that is in his power to live in accordance with the highest part of his nature, as, although that part is insignificant in size, yet in power and honour it is far superior to all the rest.

It would seem too that this is the true self of everyone, if a man's true self is his supreme or better part. It would be absurd then that a man should desire not the life which is properly his own but the life which properly belongs to some other being. The remark already made will be appropriate here. It is what is proper to everyone that is in its nature best and pleasantest for him. It is the life which accords with reason then that will be best and pleasantest for Man, as a man's reason is in the highest sense himself. This will therefore be also the happiest life.

It is only in a secondary sense that the life which accords with other, i.e. non-speculative, virtue can be said to be happy; for the activities of such virtue are human, they have no divine element. Our just or courageous actions or our virtuous actions of any kind we perform in relation to one another, when we observe the law of propriety in contracts and mutual services and the various moral actions and in our emotions. But all these actions appear to be human affairs. It seems too that moral virtue is in some respects actually the result of physical organization and is in many respects closely associated with the emotions. Again, prudence is indissolubly linked to moral virtue, and moral virtue to prudence, since the principles of prudence are determined by the moral virtues, and moral rectitude is determined by prudence. But the moral virtues, as being inseparably united with the emotions, must have to do with the composite or material part of our nature, and the virtues of the composite part of our nature are human, and not divine, virtues. So too therefore is the life which accords with these virtues; so too is the happiness which accords with them. . . .

We conclude then that happiness is coextensive with speculation, and that the greater a person's power of speculation, the greater will be his happiness, not as an accidental fact but in virtue of the speculation, as speculation is honourable in itself. Hence happiness must be a kind of speculation.

5.2

Hedonism:
Second Line of Debate

As we have shown, some philosophers try to settle the question of what is good as an end, not by asking what we desire as an end but, more directly, by asking simply what we do or what we would judge to be intrinsically good when we reflect carefully. Moore thought that this was the proper method to use, as Sidgwick did. But Sidgwick remained a hedonist, arguing that when we think carefully, we must agree that things are intrinsically good only insofar as they are pleasant or contain pleasure ("pleasurable consciousness"). Moore, however, denied this, holding that even if pleasure is intrinsically good, there are also other things that are intrinsically good, such as beauty, knowledge, and personal affection. In fact, he insisted that while it is probable that pleasure is a part of most experiences or wholes that are intrinsically good, the intrinsic value of an experience or whole need not depend entirely on the amount of pleasure it contains. He even argued that "from the fact that no value resides in one part of a whole, considered by itself, we cannot infer that all the value belonging to the whole does reside in the other part, considered by itself." [1] That is, even if the knowing of something, considered by itself, is not intrinsically good, unless it is pleasant, it does not follow that the intrinsic value of the knowing is all due to the pleasantness. This point is what he calls the principle of organic unities in the following summary of his argument against Sidgwick's hedonism.

It seems to me, then, that if we place fairly before us the question: Is consciousness of pleasure the sole good? the answer must be: No. And with

---

[1] G. E. Moore, *Principia Ethica* (Cambridge: Cambridge University Press, 1903), p. 95.

this the last defence of Hedonism has been broken down. In order to put the question fairly we must isolate consciousness of pleasure. We must ask: Suppose we were conscious of pleasure only, and of nothing else, not even that we were *conscious,* would that state of things, however great the quantity, be very desirable? No one, I think, can suppose it so. On the other hand, it seems quite plain, that we do regard as very desirable, many complicated states of mind in which the consciousness of pleasure is combined with consciousness of other things—states which we call "enjoyment of" so and so. If this is correct, then it follows that consciousness of pleasure is not the sole good, and that many other states, in which it is included as a part, are much better than it. Once we recognise the principle of organic unities, any objection to this conclusion, founded on the supposed fact that the other elements of such states have no value in themselves, must disappear. And I do not know that I need say any more in refutation of Hedonism.[2]

For the rest, Moore's arguments are nicely summarized in the following selection from an essay by R. M. Blake. Here Blake accepts Moore's procedure and uses it in defending hedonism against Moore.

WHY NOT HEDONISM?

R. M. Blake

. . . Fundamental ethical principles, in fact, as Mr. Moore so properly insists, are accepted or rejected on intuitive grounds. The most that any adherent of any ethical system can do by way of persuading another to accept his theory is to state its fundamental principles as clearly and adequately as possible, to take care that these are properly interpreted, and that the issues are not obscured by any confusion with irrelevant or inconsistent doctrines, to exhibit the implications of these principles and their consistency or inconsistency with other human beliefs, and then simply to appeal to the reflective judgment of his hearer. . . .

For my own part, when I subject to such a test the fundamental principles of hedonistic ethics, they appear to me to ring true. Indeed, it seems to me to be actually self-evident that all pleasurable experience is ultimately good. It does *not* seem to me self-evident that *nothing but*

From "Why Not Hedonism? A Protest," International Journal of Ethics, XXXVII, No. 1 (1926). Reprinted by permission of the University of Chicago Press. Copyright 1926 by the University of Chicago Press.

[2] *Ibid.*

pleasurable experience is ever ultimately good; but much careful reflection has hitherto failed to reveal anything else which *does* seem to me ultimately good. Again, it is not self-evident to me that the intrinsic value of a whole is necessarily always in proportion to the amount of ultimate good which it contains; but in every instance which I have ever considered it has always seemed to me that this is actually the case. Consequently I am forced to adopt a hedonistic position. If other men judge these matters differently I know of no way of "refuting" them; but, on the other hand, I have never been able to see that any of the considerations advanced in opposition to hedonism constitute a refutation of *it*.

From what has been said, however, it is obvious that there may be perfectly *legitimate* criticisms of hedonism—those, namely, which consist simply in presenting for judgment "hard cases" concerning which it is thought that the only conclusion consistent with hedonistic principles will nevertheless, on careful reflection, be rejected. But such criticisms, however legitimate in method, have never actually seemed to me in the least conclusive. Such force as they at first sight sometimes appear to have always turns out to arise, so far as I can see, from some confusion of thought which still clouds the issue. Once these confusions are cleared away, I never seem to find in these "hard cases" anything incompatible with the truth of hedonism.

Any adequate consideration of this phase of the matter would lead us too far afield to allow of our undertaking it on the present occasion with any degree of fulness. I shall therefore simply illustrate the way in which it seems to me possible to dispose of such hard cases by the examination of a few upon which Mr. Moore chiefly depends, and which I hope will be more or less typical. The following is an instance which he believes will persuade us that even wholes containing no pleasure may be intrinsically valuable: "Let us imagine one world exceedingly beautiful. Imagine it as beautiful as you can . . . and then imagine the ugliest world you can possibly conceive. Imagine it simply one heap of filth," and then suppose that no one ever can or does receive pleasure or displeasure from either world in any respect or degree whatever. "Would it not be well to do what we could to produce [the beautiful world] [1] rather than the other?" Would not the former be intrinsically better than the latter? Now I ask myself whether this case does not derive most of its apparent force from the circumstance that the reader who makes this imaginative comparison very naturally revolts from the image of the ugly world and at the same time takes pleasure in the thought of the beautiful world, and that he neglects explicitly to notice

---

[1] [Blake's brackets.—EDS.]

and to discount this fact. I also ask myself whether the reader is not influenced, and his judgment unconsciously perverted, by the fact that we can scarcely compare these two imaginary worlds without the thought that the beautiful world obviously possesses greater pleasure-producing *potentialities* than the ugly one; by the fact that it is difficult to compare these two imaginary worlds without reference to the consideration that the one world provides, for any conscious being that might sometime be introduced upon the scene, a better basis for enjoyment than does the other. Once I carefully notice and discount such sources of bias, I entirely fail, for my own part, to see any superior value in the beautiful world.

Another of Mr. Moore's examples—one of those which to his mind "constitute a *reductio ad absurdum* of the view that intrinsic value is always in proportion to quantity of pleasure," is as follows. If this hedonistic principle is true, it "involves our saying . . . that a world in which absolutely nothing except pleasure existed—no knowledge, no love, no enjoyment of beauty, no moral qualities—must yet be intrinsically better —better worth creating—provided only the total quantity of pleasure in it were the least bit greater, than one in which all these things existed *as well as* pleasure." This instance seems almost deliberately framed to confuse the issue; for it is very difficult in considering the matter to remember that, if we are not illegitimately to introduce into our second world an additional increment of pleasure, by "enjoyment of beauty" we must here distinctly mean merely *contemplation* of beauty, wholly divorced from any element of pleasure. Moreover, it is difficult to keep our minds wholly free from the thought of the greater hedonic potentialities of a world possessing so many elements which in our experience are fruitful sources of enjoyment, as compared with a world from which these sources are eliminated. Once I clear my mind from such confusing associations, however, I feel no further difficulty in reaching the hedonistic conclusion.

Mr. Moore also points out that the hedonistic theory compels us to assert that "the state of mind of a drunkard, when he is intensely pleased with breaking crockery, is just as valuable, in itself—just as well worth having, as that of a man who is fully realizing all that is exquisite in the tragedy of King Lear, provided only the mere quantity of pleasure in both cases is the same." Here again, once I carefully abstract from all tacit reference to the differing promise and potentiality of these two states of mind, from all larger thought of their vastly differing significance for the total lives of these men and of their fellows, I find myself quite clearly committed to the hedonistic view of the matter.

I thus do quite clearly embrace the conclusion which Mr. Moore thinks self-evidently mistaken, "that if we *could* get as much pleasure in

the world, without needing to have any knowledge, or any moral qualities, or any sense of beauty, as we can get *with* them, then all these
things would be entirely superfluous." But I also quite as heartily agree
with Mr. Moore that "the question is quite incapable of proof either
way," and that "if anybody, after clearly considering the issue, does
come" to the contrary conclusion, "there is no way of proving that he
is wrong." My point simply is that there is no short and easy way with
hedonism, and that the cavalier way in which it is commonly treated is
wholly unreasonable and unjust.

In the *Philebus* Plato discuses both the view that pleasure is the good and
the view that knowledge is the good, arguing that neither is correct. In Plato's
view the good life is a "mixed" life containing various kinds of knowledge and
some, but not all, kinds of pleasures. The necessary ingredients in it, however,
are beauty, truth, and measure or virtue. To some extent his position and arguments anticipate Moore's, but his emphasis on pattern is important. In fact, we
might take Plato's theory as a way of fitting hedonism, Aristotle, and Moore into
a more comprehensive theory of the good life. If you find yourself agreeing with
Plato that the good is a "mixed" life, you might find it worthwhile to try to
list the ingredients that *you* think it should contain.

PHILEBUS

Plato

. . . *Socrates.* Well then, by Zeus, let us proceed, and I will make
what I believe to be a fair summary of the argument.

Protarchus. Let me hear.

Socrates. Philebus says that pleasure is the true end of all living
beings, at which all ought to aim, and moreover that it is the chief good
of all, and that the two names "good" and "pleasant" are correctly given
to one thing and one nature; Socrates, on the other hand, begins by
denying this, and further says, that in nature as in name they are two,
and that wisdom partakes more than pleasure of the good. Is not and
was not this what we were saying, Protarchus?

Protarchus. Certainly.

Socrates. And is there not and was there not a further point which
was conceded between us?

From The Dialogues of Plato, *3rd ed., trans. Benjamin Jowett (London: Oxford
University Press, 1892).*

Protarchus. What was it?

Socrates. That the good differs from all other things.

Protarchus. In what respect?

Socrates. In that the being who possesses good always everywhere and in all things has the most perfect sufficiency, and is never in need of anything else.

Protarchus. Exactly.

Socrates. And did we not endeavour to make an imaginary separation of wisdom and pleasure, assigning to each a distinct life, so that pleasure was wholly excluded from wisdom, and wisdom in like manner had no part whatever in pleasure?

Protarchus. We did.

Socrates. And did we think that either of them alone would be sufficient?

Protarchus. Certainly not.

Socrates. And if we erred in any point, then let any one who will, take up the enquiry again and set us right; and assuming memory and wisdom and knowledge and true opinion to belong to the same class, let him consider whether he would desire to possess or acquire,—I will not say pleasure, however abundant or intense, if he has no real perception that he is pleased, nor any consciousness of what he feels, nor any recollection, however momentary, of the feeling,—but would he desire to have anything at all, if these faculties were wanting to him? And about wisdom I ask the same question; can you conceive that any one would choose to have all wisdom absolutely devoid of pleasure, rather than with a certain degree of pleasure, or all pleasure devoid of wisdom, rather than with a certain degree of wisdom?

Protarchus. Certainly not, Socrates; but why repeat such questions any more?

Socrates. Then the perfect and universally eligible and entirely good cannot possibly be either of them?

Protarchus. Impossible.

Socrates. Then now we must ascertain the nature of the good more or less accurately, in order, as we were saying, that the second place may be duly assigned?

Protarchus. Right.

Socrates. Have we not found a road which leads towards the good?

Protarchus. What road?

Socrates. Supposing that a man had to be found, and you could discover in what house he lived, would not that be a great step towards the discovery of the man himself?

Protarchus. Certainly.

Socrates. And now reason intimates to us, as at our first beginning, that we should seek the good, not in the unmixed life but in the mixed.

Protarchus. True.

Socrates. There is greater hope of finding that which we are seeking in the life which is well mixed than in that which is not?

Protarchus. Far greater. . . .

Socrates. Tell me first;—should we be most likely to succeed if we mingled every sort of pleasure with every sort of wisdom?

Protarchus. Perhaps we might.

Socrates. But I should be afraid of the risk, and I think that I can show a safer plan.

Protarchus. What is it?

Socrates. One pleasure was supposed by us to be truer than another, and one art to be more exact than another.

Protarchus. Certainly.

Socrates. There was also supposed to be a difference in sciences; some of them regarding only the transient and perishing, and others the permanent and imperishable and everlasting and immutable; and when judged by the standard of truth, the latter, as we thought, were truer than the former.

Protarchus. Very good and right.

Socrates. If, then, we were to begin by mingling the sections of each class which have the most of truth, will not the union suffice to give us the loveliest of lives, or shall we still want some elements of another kind?

Protarchus. I think that we ought to do what you suggest.

Socrates. Let us suppose a man who understands justice, and has reason as well as understanding about the true nature of this and of all other things.

Protarchus. We will suppose such a man.

Socrates. Will he have enough of knowledge if he is acquainted only with the divine circle and sphere, and knows nothing of our human spheres and circles, but uses only divine circles and measures in the building of a house?

Protarchus. The knowledge which is only superhuman, Socrates, is ridiculous in man.

Socrates. What do you mean? Do you mean that you are to throw into the cup and mingle the impure and uncertain art which uses the false measure and the false circle?

Protarchus. Yes, we must, if any of us is ever to find his way home.

Socrates. And am I to include music, which, as I was saying just now, is full of guesswork and imitation, and is wanting in purity?

Protarchus. Yes, I think that you must, if human life is to be a life at all.

Socrates. Well, then, suppose that I give way, and, like a doorkeeper who is pushed and overborne by the mob, I open the door wide, and let knowledge of every sort stream in, and the pure mingle with the impure?

Protarchus. I do not know, Socrates, that any great harm would come of having them all, if only you have the first sort.

Socrates. Well, then, shall I let them all flow into what Homer poetically terms "a meeting of the waters"?

Protarchus. By all means.

Socrates. There—I have let them in, and now I must return to the fountain of pleasure. For we were not permitted to begin by mingling in a single stream the true portions of both according to our original intention; but the love of all knowledge constrained us to let all the sciences flow in together before the pleasures.

Protarchus. Quite true.

Socrates. And now the time has come for us to consider about the pleasures also, whether we shall in like manner let them go all at once, or at first only the true ones.

Protarchus. It will be by far the safer course to let flow the true ones first.

Socrates. Let them flow, then; and now, if there are any necessary pleasures, as there were arts and sciences necessary, must we not mingle them?

Protarchus. Yes; the necessary pleasures should certainly be allowed to mingle.

Socrates. The knowledge of the arts has been admitted to be innocent and useful always; and if we say of pleasures in like manner that all of them are good and innocent for all of us at all times, we must let them all mingle?

Protarchus. What shall we say about them, and what course shall we take?

Socrates. Do not ask me, Protarchus; but ask the daughters of pleasure and wisdom to answer for themselves.

Protarchus. How?

Socrates. Tell us, O beloved—shall we call you pleasures or by some other name?—would you rather live with or without wisdom? I am of opinion that they would certainly answer as follows:

Protarchus. How?

Socrates. They would answer, as we said before, that for any single class to be left by itself pure and isolated is not good, nor altogether possible; and that if we are to make comparisons of one class with another and choose, there is no better companion than knowledge of things in general, and likewise the perfect knowledge, if that may be, of ourselves in every respect.

Protarchus. And our answer will be:—In that ye have spoken well.

Socrates. Very true. And now let us go back and interrogate wisdom and mind: Would you like to have any pleasures in the mixture? And they will reply:—"What pleasures do you mean?"

Protarchus. Likely enough.

Socrates. And we shall take up our parable and say: Do you wish to have the greatest and most vehement pleasures for your companions in addition to the true ones? "Why, Socrates," they will say, "how can we? seeing that they are the source of ten thousand hindrances to us; they trouble the souls of men, which are our habitation, with their madness; they prevent us from coming to the birth, and are commonly the ruin of the children which are born to us, causing them to be forgotten and unheeded; but the true and pure pleasures, of which you spoke, know to be of our family, and also those pleasures which accompany health and temperance, and which every Virtue, like a goddess, has in her train to follow her about wherever she goes,—mingle these and not the others; there would be great want of sense in any one who desires to see a fair and perfect mixture, and to find in it what is the highest good in man and in the universe, and to divine what is the true form of good—there would be great want of sense in his allowing the pleasures, which are always in the company of folly and vice, to mingle with mind in the cup."—Is not this a very rational and suitable reply, which mind has made, both on her own behalf, as well as on the behalf of memory and true opinion?

Protarchus. Most certainly.

Socrates. And still there must be something more added, which is a necessary ingredient in every mixture.

Protarchus. What is that?

Socrates. Unless truth enter into the composition, nothing can truly be created or subsist.

Protarchus. Impossible.

Socrates. Quite impossible; and now you and Philebus must tell me whether anything is still wanting in the mixture, for to my way of thinking the argument is now completed, and may be compared to an incorporeal law, which is going to hold fair rule over a living body.

Protarchus. I agree with you, Socrates.

Socrates. And may we not say with reason that we are now at the vestibule of the habitation of the good?

Protarchus. I think that we are.

Socrates. What, then, is there in the mixture which is most precious, and which is the principal cause why such a state is universally beloved by all? When we have discovered it, we will proceed to ask whether this omnipresent nature is more akin to pleasure or to mind.

Protarchus. Quite right; in that way we shall be better able to judge.

Socrates. And there is no difficulty in seeing the cause which renders any mixture either of the highest value or of none at all.

Protarchus. What do you mean?

Socrates. Every man knows it.

Protarchus. What?

Socrates. He knows that any want of measure and symmetry in any mixture whatever must always of necessity be fatal, both to the elements and to the mixture, which is then not a mixture, but only a confused medley which brings confusion on the possessor of it.

Protarchus. Most true.

Socrates. And now the power of the good has retired into the region of the beautiful; for measure and symmetry are beauty and virtue all the world over.

Protarchus. True.

Socrates. Also we said that truth was to form an element in the mixture.

Protarchus. Certainly.

Socrates. Then, if we are not able to hunt the good with one idea only, with three we may catch our prey; Beauty, Symmetry, Truth are the three, and these taken together we may regard as the single cause of the mixture, and the mixture as being good by reason of the infusion of them.

Protarchus. Quite right.

Socrates. And now, Protarchus, any man could decide well enough whether pleasure or wisdom is more akin to the highest good, and more honourable among gods and men.

Protarchus. Clearly, and yet perhaps the argument had better be pursued to the end.

Socrates. We must take each of them separately in their relation to pleasure and mind, and pronounce upon them; for we ought to see to which of the two they are severally most akin.

Protarchus. You are speaking of beauty, truth, and measure?

Socrates. Yes, Protarchus, take truth first, and, after passing in review mind, truth, pleasure, pause awhile and make answer to yourself,—as to whether pleasure or mind is more akin to truth.

Protarchus. There is no need to pause, for the difference between them is palpable; pleasure is the veriest impostor in the world; and it is said that in the pleasures of love, which appear to be the greatest, perjury is excused by the gods; for pleasures, like children, have not the least particle of reason in them; whereas mind is either the same as truth, or the most like truth, and the truest.

Socrates. Shall we next consider measure, in like manner, and ask whether pleasure has more of this than wisdom, or wisdom than pleasure?

Protarchus. Here is another question which may be easily answered; for I imagine that nothing can ever be more immoderate than the transports of pleasure, or more in conformity with measure than mind and knowledge.

Socrates. Very good; but there still remains the third test: Has mind a greater share of beauty than pleasure, and is mind or pleasure the fairer of the two?

Protarchus. No one, Socrates, either awake or dreaming, ever saw or imagined mind or wisdom to be in aught unseemly, at any time, past, present, or future.

Socrates. Right.

Protarchus. But when we see some one indulging in pleasures, perhaps in the greatest of pleasures, the ridiculous or disgraceful nature of the action makes us ashamed; and so we put them out of sight, and consign them to darkness, under the idea that they ought not to meet the eye of day.

Socrates. Then, Protarchus, you will proclaim everywhere, by word of mouth to this company, and by messengers bearing the tidings far and wide, that pleasure is not the first of possessions, nor yet the second, but that in measure, and the mean, and the suitable, and the like, the eternal nature has been found.

Protarchus. Yes, that seems to be the result of what has been now said.

Socrates. In the second class is contained the symmetrical and beautiful and perfect or sufficient, and all which are of that family.

Protarchus. True.

Socrates. And if you reckon in the third class mind and wisdom, you will not be far wrong, if I divine aright.

Protarchus. I dare say.

Socrates. And would you not put in the fourth class the goods which we were affirming to appertain specially to the soul—sciences and arts and true opinions as we call them? These come after the third class, and form the fourth, as they are certainly more akin to good than pleasure is.

Protarchus. Surely.

Socrates. The fifth class are the pleasures which were defined by us as painless, being the pure pleasures of the soul herself, as we termed them, which accompany, some the sciences, and some the senses.

Protarchus. Perhaps.

Socrates. And now, as Orpheus says,

"With the sixth generation cease the glory of my song."

Here, at the sixth award, let us make an end; . . .

5.3

Satisfaction,
Happiness, and the Good Life

The debate between the hedonists and their opponents in general concerned the identification of pleasure or satisfaction with what is good as an end. It seems worthwhile at this point to present two selections from recent philosophers that may help us to organize our own thoughts on the matter.

Brand Blanshard, who writes with Plato, Aristotle, Moore, and hedonism in mind and recognizes the principle of organic unities, attempts to find a theory that combines the truths on both sides of the debate. His answer is that the good life is a combination of pleasure or satisfaction and "fulfillment of impulse-desire" or "flowering of powers." Note the way in which his theory provides, among other things, an alternative to Mill's theory concerning quality of pleasure.

SATISFACTION, FULFILMENT, AND THE GOOD

Brand Blanshard

The kind of consideration on which we are embarking is so different from our earlier analyses that it may be well to set down briefly and at once the view of goodness that will gradually emerge from it. We

From Reason and Goodness *(London: George Allen and Unwin Ltd., 1961).* *Reprinted by permission of the author and publisher.*

shall hold that only experiences are directly or immediately good. When they are good intrinsically, they perform a double function: they fulfil an impulse, drive or need, and in so doing they give satisfaction or pleasure. Both components, fulfilment and satisfaction, are necessary, and they vary independently of each other. But both are always partial in the sense that they apply to a limited set of needs; and they are always provisional or incomplete, so that goodness is a matter of degree. It is to be measured against an ideal good, which is the kind of life which would fulfil and satisfy wholly.

Every point here is controversial. It is obvious that this view of goodness and the good is bound up with a theory of how the mind is constituted, of how values arise in experience, and of how they are connected with needs and impulses.

. . . nothing is good for us if we can take no satisfaction in it. It must hence be admitted that even love and understanding would be without value for us if we found no satisfaction in them. And it is easy to argue that since, when you add satisfaction you have goodness and when you subtract it you do not, the goodness lies in the satisfaction solely, and hence all that is good in human goods could be generated or abolished by redirecting our satisfactions.

But the case is not so simple. Such an argument confuses a necessary with the sufficient condition of goodness. You cannot argue validly that because a certain factor is necessary to a certain result, it is therefore the only contributor to that result. For instance, you cannot argue that since giving water to a plant makes it grow, and withholding water makes it die, water is the whole secret of its life and growth. By such logic you could equally prove that the whole secret lay in air or light or soil, any of which conclusions would contradict the first. The truth is that these things are all equally necessary, and taken alone, equally insufficient. Similarly, it is true that the boy who, through some chance rebuff, takes no interest in music, will find no good in it. But what exactly does that show? Does it show that the whole good of the music, even as he experiences it, lies in the satisfaction he takes in it, so that the goodness depends solely on his liking or disliking it? This clearly does not follow. All it does show is that the boy's satisfaction in music is one condition of his finding it good. Similarly with our case of instinct. If nature had turned out even more "red in tooth and claw" than she has shown herself to be and had spawned a tiger with human craft and cunning, it might have regarded St. Francis with indifference or contempt except as a somewhat unappetizing form of prey. But while we are endowing our super-cat with so much cunning, we might as well give it enough to see its own inconsequence in arguing from the lack of satisfaction in the Franciscan life to the worthlessness of that life for those who do find it satisfying. We saw long ago that the goodness of music or love does not lie in an abstract quality, identical in both, which somehow attach to them. Neither is it exhausted in the fact that someone finds them satisfying. The goodness is a function of the satisfaction plus something else.

Thus, *what makes things desirable is not exhausted in the fact that they are desired, or what makes them satisfactory in the fact that they satisfy.* The very notion that the goodness lies in the satisfaction or pleasure alone as distinct from the object, shows that one is trying to introduce into a value experience a kind of distinctness of parts that is found only outside it. There is no trouble in distinguishing the water you give to the plant from the later growth to which it contributes. But can you distinguish in the same sharp way within an experience of music, for example, the enjoyment from what is enjoyed, so that you can locate the value of the whole in one part rather than the other? If A and B sit side by side listening to Beethoven, and A is utterly indifferent while B is deeply stirred, are we to say that B hears exactly what A heard, only with the addition of a stirring emotion? That is surely to put the case too mechanically. The music and the appreciation of it are so blended that B would probably say that A *could* not have heard what he did without being stirred. On the other hand, the notion that A or anyone else could know what B found good in the experience merely by knowing in the abstract that he was enjoying something and without any notion that *what* satisfied him was music, and indeed this particular music, would seem grotesque. What has value is neither the music nor the satisfaction as abstracted from each other, but the two in this particular union. Whoever experienced that union would be in possession of the value. . . .

We have said that our desires grow out of our satisfactions, and that our inventory of ideal goods is drawn up by our desires. We must qualify this later to make clear the sense in which the desirable exceeds the desired. Still, what we genuinely desire is a fairly reliable index to what we take as good. It has often been held that in our inventory of goods there is only one kind of article. What we desire, it has been argued, is satisfaction—not the experience of knowing or loving or doing, but the feeling of pleasure or satisfaction in it; and then the step is short to saying that since satisfaction is the only thing desired, it is the only thing that is good. To be sure, the inference is not a compelling one. It is conceivable that everyone should in fact desire pleasure and pleasure only, and also that there should be things other than pleasure which, if we came to know about them, we should desire and regard as good. But this mere theoretic possibility has not weighed greatly with moralists. The doctrine of psychological hedonism, that we desire only pleasure, seems always to have been accompanied by ethical hedonism, the doctrine that pleasure is the only good; that one is the real foundation of the other. To see that the first is false is to leave the other baseless. And psychological hedonism *is* false. It ought to have died once for all of the wounds inflicted on it by Butler. But it seems to be as irrepressible as the phoenix, and has cropped up again and again, to be successively scotched with elegance by Sidgwick, Rashdall, Broad, and many others. For anything I shall say of it here, it may go on with these reincarnations; the criticisms already offered seem to me decisive. We desire to eat food, and not merely to have the pleasure of eating; we desire to hear music, and play games, and understand, not merely to gain satisfaction out of objects and activities themselves indifferent. And if our goods reflect the content of our desires, we see again that those goods are not exhausted in pleasure or satisfaction. They consist of satisfying experiences as wholes.

Our major goods answer to the main types of impulse-desire. One major drive has been much studied by philosophers, namely the impulse to know, and its career may serve as a suggestion of what we should probably find if we studied other drives in similar detail. Instinctive curiosity, which passes on at a higher level into the desire for understanding, is a distinguishable impulse with an end of its own. That end is not at all what the pragmatists have supposed; it is not an impulse to do something to things, for example to make them over into something more satisfying to our non-cognitive impulses; that is to confuse the impulse to know in fatal fashion with impulses of a different kind. Knowing is of course an activity, but its end is contemplation, not action. The desire to know is the desire to see things as they are. Now such seeing is and must be more than a mere registry of fact. What we want is not only to know, but to understand, that is, lay hold of the connections among facts that make them intelligible. Thought at its simplest is judgment, and in the most rudimentary judgment we are grasping a linkage between terms. That linkage as it stands may be unintelligible to us. "That cat purrs"; with this we have entered the field of judgment. But from the first there is awaking within such judgment the spirit of inquiry; we have connected the purring with the cat; can we connect it more specifically with anything else about the cat? In short, why does the cat purr? With that question we have begun our career in science and philosophy. The intellectual quest from the lowest judgment to the most complicated theories of modern physics may be regarded as one persisting effort to answer the question, Why? To answer it calls for a continually widening knowledge and a continual re-ordering of that knowledge in the direction of consistency and inter-dependence of parts, for the end sought by the theoretic impulse is an intelligible whole. Every advance toward such understanding brings satisfaction. We repeat, however, that it is not satisfaction merely that the impulse is seeking, but that which will satisfy it, namely this partic-ular kind of light. But neither is it light merely; for what is the point of a knowledge in which one takes no satisfaction? What is sought is something which, because of its special character, fulfils the aim of the cognitive impulse, and which because of this fulfilment, satisfies. This double service of fulfilling and of satisfying is what makes knowledge good. It is also what makes anything good.

How many of these conative drives of impulse-desire, with their varying ends, can be distinguished in human nature? The point is a controversial one which we shall make no attempt to settle. . . .

It will now be clear what are the virtue and weakness of those theories which, following Hobbes, would equate the good with what is in fact favoured, liked, or desired. Their virtue lies in the major insight that good is somehow connected with satisfaction. This insight is enough to eliminate the "eternal goods" of Nicolai Hartmann and Dean Inge, existing in sublime indifference whether they will ever be wanted or not. On the other hand, there are two conspicuous weaknesses in these theories. First, they fail to take due account of the elastic and expansive character of desire, because they fail to connect it with the fundamental teleology of mind. Mind just *is*, in the view here taken, a set of activities directed to ends. It is these ends alone that are, or would be, good with-out qualification, for only they are fully satisfactory; that is, in them alone would the activities that constitute mind gain fulfilment and satis-faction. But at any given stage of our advance, these ends are indefinitely far ahead. Hence to take the objects in which our desires, cognitive, moral, or aesthetic, find satisfaction at the moment, and call them good without qualification, is to freeze into immobility what in its very nature is in motion and self-creative. It is true that what satisfies is so far, good. But if present satisfaction is looked at in the light of the history and prospects of mind, it is equally true to say that what satisfies is never good. There is no real paradox here. There is only the requirement that we see things in perspective, that we view the career of mind as the long pilgrimage that it actually is, in which the values of a given time offer us, not a continuing stay, but rather a halting-place for the night. Once we see this plainly, we cannot go on saying without quali-fication that whatever is liked or desired is thereby good.

The second error is to infer that because the good must satisfy, its goodness varies with satisfaction or pleasure alone. This is untrue be-cause goodness depends also on fulfilment, and fulfilment is not the same as satisfaction. Fulfilment is achieving the end that our impulse is seeking; satisfaction is the feeling that attends this fulfilment. We see the difference clearly in Spinoza's account of the *conatus* toward "adequate ideas." What the *conatus* seeks is a comprehensive view of things, so ordered internally as to satisfy the logical sense. This comprehension or understanding is that which, when it comes, will fulfil the impulse or desire, but this fulfilment is not the same as the satisfaction felt in its coming. If the goodness of knowledge is to be attained, both must be present, since it is a function of the two jointly. The error of the satisfaction theories is to suppose it to be the function of feeling alone. If it were, the only way in which good could be increased would be to alter the factor of feeling. That it can be thus increased we may agree. An insight achieved with delight is more worth having than the same insight without it. But good can also be augmented by enlarging the insight itself, even though the satisfaction remains the same. To solve the problem of free will would be far more worth achieving than to know the name of one's neighbour down the street, even though, at the moment, one had no more interest in one than in the other, and would get equal satisfaction from them. It would be more worth achieving because it would provide a more complete fulfilment of the desire to understand one's world. It is entirely possible that the ecstasy felt by some primitive beater of a tom-tom is a more intense satisfaction than that of an accomplished musician playing a masterpiece. But it is hard to see why for that reason we should have to call it better. In spite of the high authority of Sidgwick, we cannot reduce the good of an experience to the pleasure it gives us, nor can we even take this, with McTaggart, as an accurate index of the good. It is one of two variables in whose presence the good lies jointly, and which may vary independently of each other.

It is an argument of weight for this view that it clears up in straightforward manner the old difficulty of the hedonists about the quality and quantity of pleasure. Bentham, Mill and Sidgwick all maintained that what made an experience good and measured the amount of its goodness was the pleasure it contained. But when Mill worked out the implications of this view, he found it leading on to an absurdity from which any sensible person must recoil. It is entirely possible that if you took equal intervals in the life of Socrates and that of a moron, indeed even that of a pig, the amount of pleasure felt by the moron or the pig would be greater than that of Socrates. If pleasure were the sole component in goodness, their lives for that period should therefore be better than that of the Socratic life. Mill agreed with his critics that this was absurd. He therefore introduced a second component which he called *quality* of pleasure, and held that the higher quality of Socrates' pleasure outweighed the greater quantity of the porcine pleasure. Most later moralists have recognized that this would not do. A man is not really making pleasure the sole criterion of good if he admits that, of two experiences, the second may be more pleasant and yet less good. Mill thus ended in self-contradiction.

On the theory here proposed, the difficulty is dealt with as follows: the feeling of satisfaction or pleasure taken in an experience *is* a condition of its goodness; in this the insight of the hedonists was sound. But it is one condition only, and there is another. This other is the fulfilment of impulse-desire. Socrates' life was better than that of the pig or the moron because it involved a fulfilment of impulse-desire, a development and flowering of powers, beyond the reach of commonplace minds, and of course still further beyond the reach of the animal mind. Comparison in this respect is possible because the three levels of life are not simply discontinuous; the desires for knowledge and companionship, for example, that were fulfilled so remarkably in the life of Socrates are sturdily at work in the plainest citizen and are at least stirring in the form of impulse well down in the animal scale. It is therefore entirely intelligible to say that Socrates' life was the best, whether it was the most pleasant or not. The place taken in Mill's theory by quality of pleasure, is taken in ours by fulfilment of impulse-desire. This can no longer be confused with pleasure, since it is recognized as a different dimension; and while higher and lower rank among the qualities of pleasure has proved a most obscure notion, degrees of fulfilment of the same impulse-desire is a straightforward and indeed inevitable notion. An old puzzle of ethical theory thus receives a clear solution.

The good, in the sense of the ethical end, is the most comprehensive possible fulfilment and satisfaction of impulse-desire. By a comprehensive fulfilment I mean one that takes account not only of this or that desire, but of our desires generally, and not only of this or that man's desires, but of all men's. That there is and must be such a good, supreme over all others, we can see by considering how conflicts are resolved. Two distinct and important trends of impulse-desire have been repeatedly mentioned, the cognitive and the aesthetic, each with its special type of good, measured by its own immanent standard. Suppose these two conflict. Suppose that a youth has interests and talents for philosophy on the one hand, and music on the other, and feels drawn in both directions, but that one or the other must be sacrificed, if proficiency is to be reached in either. In any concrete case he would no doubt need to take into account the importance of these two activities to his community, but by way of taking one difficulty at a time, let us exclude these considerations. The youth must then decide the conflict by considering his good as a whole. He will have to ask himself the question, How may I, as a person who can gain some measure of fulfilment through each of these channels, gain most of this on the whole—by making myself a philosopher, by making myself a musician, or by making myself some sort of hybrid between them? And if he is really free in the matter, the obvious way to settle it is to take stock of his interests and powers. If he has a very strong interest and bent for speculative analysis, and a feeble enjoyment and skill in music, then, as between these two, the choice will be easy; his good will be in philosophy, since he would find a completer fulfilment there. If the reverse holds, the choice will similarly go to music. But the case in fact may well be harder; he may discover an approximately equal bent for each. Then, if he must drop one or the other, he will consider which of the two would carry with it the larger range of subsidiary satisfactions. The two walks of life will involve different incomes, associates, surroundings, holidays, hours of work and freedom; the one activity may stimulate and support more fruitfully than the other all sorts of minor interests, scientific, political, and literary. In practice he will probably select one or the other as his principal business and try to keep the other alive in a secondary role.

If all this is very obvious—and I must admit that it seems so to me —it none the less shows how naturally our theory of the good explains what is involved in such major choices. I cannot think that other theories do so with equal naturalness. There are moralists who would say that philosophy as such is better or higher than music, whereas neither of them in the abstract has any value at all; where they do have value, it is only as an activity in somebody's mind. Hence, if one is to compare them, one must compare certain amounts of each, realized in individual lives and in particular circumstances. One may gain a far greater fulfilment and happiness through being a good farmer than through being a bad philosopher; indeed William James complained that our graduate schools were full of the bald-headed and the bald-hearted, who were the ruins of excellent farmers. . . . Professor Perry would say that the goodness resolves itself into the fact of awaking interest, and the hedonists that it resolves itself into the fact of being pleasant, whereas we hold that the content is as indispensable to the goodness as the interest or the pleasure. Dr. Ewing holds that if in a given case the philosopher's experience is better than the musical, that means that it is more fitting to favour it. I agree that this is more fitting, but think it possible to go further and say why it is more fitting. Many moralists of weight, such as Rashdall, Moore, and Ross, would say that the goodness of either type of experience is a simple, unanalysable quality or attribute. I do not consider it unanalysable. There is always, I think, some content that fulfils impulse-desire, and a feeling of satisfaction attendant on this fulfilment. Goodness is neither the fulfilment apart from the satisfaction nor the satisfaction apart from the fulfilment; it is the two in union. If a synonym is wanted, perhaps the best is satisfactoriness.

Though this account of the good lays stress on desire, it is not so much on *de facto* desire, the want or wish of the moment, as on reflective desire, the desire that emerges after correction by thought and experience. The good is what brings fulfilment and its attendant pleasure to desire of this self-amending kind. These desires arise because we are the sort of beings we are, and wisdom lies in making them more accurately and fully expressive of human nature; "our aims," said Emerson, "should be mathematically adjusted to our powers." There is nothing novel in such an account of the good; indeed it is as old as the Greeks. We shall not try to show this by chapter and verse. It will perhaps be enough to quote a passage in which A. E. Taylor sets out the drift of the ethical thought of Plato and Aristotle. In philosophy there are no authorities, but at least there is some comfort in having such august names on one's side. Taylor notes that

> εὐδαιμονία [eudaimonia], for both of them, is not primarily getting something which I desire; it is living the kind of life which I have been constructed to live, doing the "work of man," and if we want to know what life rather than any other should be pronounced εὐδαιμων, we have to begin by asking what is the "work" which man, and only man, in virtue of his very constitution, can do. It is true, no doubt, that Plato holds that all of us also do desire εὐδαιμονία, if only most of us were not as unaware as we are of the real nature of our most deep-seated desires. But the very reason why we all have this insuperable *desiderium naturale* for a certain kind of life is that it is the life we have been constructed by God or by Nature to lead. We are unhappy, without clearly knowing why, so long as we are living any other kind of life, for the same reasons that a fish is unhappy out of water. The true way to discover what it is that we really want out of life is to know what kind of life we have been sent into the world to lead. We do not lead that life as a "means" to the "enjoyable results" of doing so, any more than the fish lives in the water, or the bird in the air as a means to the pleasure of such a life; we enjoy the pleasure (as the tenth book of the *Nicomachean Ethics* explains) because we are living the kind of life for which we were made.[1]

The following passage is part of Hastings Rashdall's discussion of hedonism. His own view is that pleasure is *a* good but not *the* good, not the only good. The highest good for him, as for Kant, is virtue, but "many other things—intellectual cultivation and intelligent action, aesthetic cultivation, emotions of various kinds—are also good and of more intrinsic value than mere pleasure." [2]

---

[1] *Mind, Vol.* 48 (1939) 280.

[2] Hastings Rashdall, *The Theory of Good and Evil*, Vol. 2, 2nd ed. (Oxford: The Clarendon Press, 1924), p. 37.

Pleasure is an element in everything that is good, but value is not proportional to pleasantness. Having said this, he goes on in our passage to distinguish pleasure and happiness in an interesting way. Then, still more interestingly, he suggests that the good or well-being cannot be equated even with happiness. The good or ideal life, he argues, will contain something else besides pleasure or even happiness, viz. "good will, knowledge, thought, the contemplation of beauty, love of other persons and of what is best in them."

HAPPINESS, PLEASURE, AND THE GOOD

Hastings Rashdall

There is another concept which seems to demand a brief treatment in this connexion—that of happiness. If we repudiate the hedonistic identification of pleasure and happiness, what account, it may be asked, are we to give of the latter? If we regard pleasure as part, though not the whole, of the life that has supreme value, is not this last, it may be suggested, very much what we mean by happiness? If we attempt (apart altogether from theory) to analyse what as a matter of fact we commonly mean when we talk of happiness, the answer will, I think, be something of this kind. Happiness represents satisfaction with one's existence as a whole—with the past and the future as well as with the immediate present. Happiness certainly cannot be identified with pleasure, not even with the higher or more refined kinds of pleasure. It is possible to get an enormous amount of pleasure into one's life—of pleasures that are recognized as having a value and even a high value—and yet to be on the whole unhappy through the presence of desires which are unsatisfied, dissatisfaction with the past, anxiety as to the future, unfulfilled aspirations, baffled hopes and the like.[1] It is possible to endure a considerable amount of hardship, of positive pain both bodily and mental,

From The Theory of Good and Evil, *2nd ed. (Oxford: The Clarendon Press, 1924). Reprinted by permission of The Clarendon Press, Oxford.*

---

[1] This distinction between happiness and pleasure is no doubt present to the minds of those who make the end of life to be satisfaction of a "timeless self." But, apart from other objections, happiness, though it is distinguished from pleasure (*a*) by being commonly attributed only to some considerable period of a man's life and (*b*) by involving the satisfaction of desires which "look before and after," the satisfaction of the more permanent and dominant aims and desires of a man's life, is still

and yet to be on the whole happy; though we should certainly say that the removal or mitigation of those pains would add to the happiness even of those who are most "self-sufficient for happiness."

There is therefore a difference between happiness and pleasure. And yet it is impossible without paradox to dissociate the idea of happiness altogether from that of pleasure. A happy life must include some pleasure: all happiness is pleasurable, though not all pleasure is happiness. The pleasure which is an essential part of happiness is no doubt pleasure of the kind which is most dependent upon the man himself and least dependent upon circumstances—the kind of pleasure which, as Aristotle contended, the higher activities necessarily bring with them. But happiness is by no means altogether independent of external circumstances: there must, as Aristotle puts it, be that unimpeded exercise of the higher faculties which is very much dependent upon circumstances. Happiness depends largely upon health, upon suitable work, upon a congenial marriage: and these are emphatically things which are not in our own power. It is true that some kinds of ill health or of uncongenial environment are in some men compatible with a considerable measure of happiness; and the people who are most capable of such happiness are, no doubt, on the whole the best men. But nobody would contend, "except when defending a thesis," that those complaints which bring extreme depression with them as a mere physiological consequence are compatible with any high degree of happiness. And there are "blows"—public or private calamities, failures, bereavements—which make the recovery of happiness impossible to most men; nor can it be laid down as a general proposition that all good men are happy. To say how far a bad man can be happy would involve pushing the definition of an essentially vague conception further than it is commonly pushed. We should have to talk of different kinds or different senses of happiness. The bad man is no doubt generally unhappy because any better desires that he has are unsatisfied, and because very often his desires and inclinations are of a kind that are incompatible with one another, so that one part or aspect of his nature is always unsatisfied: his life has no wholeness or unity. But this is not perhaps always the

---

emphatically something in time. Some people, it is probable, would say that parts of their life have been happy, other parts unhappy, and most people that some parts have been more happy or less unhappy than others. The objections which I make below to regarding even a sublimated happiness as *the* end may be urged also to the attempt to make the end consist in satisfaction of any kind. It is true no doubt that any experience which we pronounce valuable must give satisfaction, but to make satisfaction the end almost inevitably suggests that things are valuable in proportion as they satisfy this or that individual's actual desires, irrespective of their nature, whereas in fact we feel that it is better to be "a human being dissatisfied than a pig satisfied; better to be Socrates dissatisfied, than a fool satisfied" (Mill, *Utilitarianism*, p. 14).

case: the bad man no doubt cannot get the same happiness as the good man, but he may get what he wants, and so may attain a kind of happiness. At all events we may say that, though, on the whole, goodness tends to make people happy (far more generally than it tends to increase the sum of their pleasures), men are not happy in proportion to their goodness. We cannot, therefore, without using words in unusual and unnatural senses, so far sublimate the idea of happiness as to identify it with the end of life in general, with consciousness that has value, with Well-being. It is a most important element no doubt in true Well-being—a far more important one than pleasure; or (if we say that happiness is a particular kind of pleasure) it is a far more valuable kind of pleasure than any other, and far more inseparable than most other pleasures from the goods to which we ascribe the very highest value. And yet it is not by itself *the* good. We cannot say that it actually includes all forms of pleasure that are valuable, high intellectual or aesthetic development or even goodness, though the most complete kind of happiness may presuppose the last. Still less, when the good is unattainable, can we say that, among goods or elements of the good, happiness is always the one that possesses the most value, or is the one to which all others should be sacrificed. The noblest kinds of self-devotion do involve a real sacrifice not merely of pleasure but of happiness.

Happiness has this much in common with the good—that for most of us it represents an ideal which we can hardly say that we have ever enjoyed in the undiluted and unruffled fullness which we picture to ourselves as possible and desirable; that we can only form an ideal conception of it by putting together, amplifying, idealizing moments or periods or elements of our actual experience, supposing them continuously prolonged, and leaving out all that disturbed or qualified the joyous moments while they were actually there. Perfect happiness is no doubt an ideal, but it is a different ideal from that of perfect Well-being. It is an ideal which, at least for people who have in their way higher desires and aspirations, is closely connected with the highest elements in life, but still it cannot safely be made the sole and direct object of pursuit by each individual for himself. Perfect Well-being would doubtless include perfect happiness, but it would include much more than we ordinarily mean by happiness. The idea of happiness can no more be dispensed with in any concrete account of the ideal life than the idea of pleasure, and can equally little be identified with that of value. It is not the whole of the ideal life, but an element or an aspect of it. The ideal life or the good is an ultimate conception which does not admit of further definition, and the content of which we can only express by enumerating the various elements or aspects of it, and then explaining in what way they are to be combined. Among these elements happiness and pleasure are both included, but they are not the whole; though no doubt the kind of happiness and the kind of pleasure which do enter into the ideal life are inseparable from those other elements of it which we call goodness or the good will, knowledge, thought, the contemplation of beauty, love of other persons and of what is best in them.

5.4

Other Conceptions of the Good

Other writers agree that the good life or well-being cannot be equated with pleasure or happiness, but take very different views from those of Plato, Aristotle, Moore, or Rashdall—views much like those of the objectors to hedonism that Mill had in mind. Such writers suggest that, at least for some people, the good life may consist of power, finding one's deepest impulse and following it, doing what one thinks is right, being honest, devoting oneself to a cause, or renunciation of desire—even if, and maybe because, these involve risk, uncertainty, danger, or suffering. One example is Nietzsche, quoted in Chapter 3. Other examples are given in the following passages. The first, from the Bhagavad-Gita, puts the highest value on renunciation of desires and illumination of mind.

THE GOOD IS ENLIGHTENMENT

Bhagavad-Gita

Arjuna:

Krishna, how can one identify a man who is firmly established and absorbed in Brahman? In what manner does an illumined soul speak? How does he sit? How does he walk?

From The Bhagavad-Gita, *trans. Swami Probhavananda and Christopher Isherwood (Hollywood, Calif.: The Marcel Rodd Co., 1944).*

Sri Krishna:

He knows bliss in the Atman
And wants nothing else.
Cravings torment the heart:
He renounces cravings.
I call him illumined.

Not shaken by adversity,
Not hankering after happiness:
Free from fear, free from anger,
Free from the things of desire.
I call him a seer, and illumined.

The bonds of his flesh are broken.
He is lucky, and does not rejoice:
He is unlucky, and does not weep.
I call him illumined.

The tortoise can draw in its legs:
The seer can draw in his senses.
I call him illumined.

The abstinent run away from what they desire
But carry their desires with them:
When a man enters Reality,
He leaves his desires behind him.

Even a mind that knows the path
Can be dragged from the path:
The senses are so unruly.
But he controls the senses
And recollects the mind
And fixes it on me.
I call him illumined.

Thinking about sense-objects
Will attach you to sense-objects;
Grow attached, and you become addicted;
Thwart your addiction, it turns to anger;
Be angry, and you confuse your mind;
Confuse your mind, you forget the lesson of experience;
Forget experience, you lose discrimination;
Lose discrimination, and you miss life's only purpose.

When he has no lust, no hatred,
A man walks safely among the things of lust and hatred.
To obey the Atman
Is his peaceful joy:
Sorrow melts
Into that clear peace:
His quiet mind
Is soon established in peace.

The uncontrolled mind
Does not guess that the Atman is present:
How can it meditate?
Without meditation, where is peace?
Without peace, where is happiness?
The wind turns a ship
From its course upon the waters:
The wandering winds of the senses
Cast man's mind adrift
And turn his better judgment from its course.
When a man can still the senses
I call him illumined.

The recollected mind is awake
In the knowledge of the Atman
Which is dark night to the ignorant:
The ignorant are awake in their sense-life
Which they think is daylight:
To the seer it is darkness.

Water flows continually into the ocean
But the ocean is never disturbed:
Desire flows into the mind of the seer
But he is never disturbed.
The seer knows peace:
The man who stirs up his own lusts
Can never know peace.
He knows peace who has forgotten desire.
He lives without craving:
Free from ego, free from pride.

This is the state of enlightenment in Brahman:
A man does not fall back from it
Into delusion.

Even at the moment of death
He is alive in that enlightenment:
Brahman and he are one.

In the next passage the speaker in Dostoevsky's *Notes from the Underground* states, in a rather extreme but striking way, the more or less existentialist view that a man's highest good is merely independence of choice—"doing his own thing," in the sense of doing what *he* decides to do, sane or insane. The speaker may not necessarily be expressing Dostoevsky's own view. But even if he does not, he may be expressing *your* view, or the view of someone close to you. Is he?

THE MOST PRECIOUS THING
FOR MAN

Fyodor Dostoevsky

Oh, tell me, who first declared, who first proclaimed, that man only does nasty things because he does not know his own real interests; and that if he were enlightened, if his eyes were opened to his real normal interests, man would at once cease to do nasty things, would at once become good and noble because, being enlightened and understanding his real advantage, he would see his own advantage in the good and nothing else, and we all know that not a single man can knowingly act to his own disadvantage. Consequently, so to say, he would begin doing good through necessity. Oh, the babe! Oh, the pure, innocent child! Why, in the first place, when in all these thousands of years has there ever been a time when man has acted only for his own advantage? What is to be done with the millions of facts that bear witness that men, *knowingly*, that is, fully understanding their real advantages, have left them in the background and have rushed headlong on another path, to risk, to chance, compelled to this course by nobody and by nothing, but, as it were, precisely because they did not want the beaten track, and stubbornly, wilfully, went off on another difficult, absurd way seeking it almost in the darkness. After all, it means that this stubbornness and willfulness were more pleasant to them than any advantage. Advantage! What is advantage? And will you take it upon yourself to define with perfect accuracy in exactly what the advantage of man consists of? And what if it so happens that a man's advantage *sometimes* not only may, but even must, consist exactly in his desiring under certain conditions what is harmful to himself and not what is advantageous. And if so, if there can be such a condition then the whole principle becomes worthless. What do you think—are there such cases? You laugh; laugh away, gentlemen, so long as you answer me: have man's advantages been calculated with perfect certainty? Are there not some which not only have been included but cannot possibly be included under any classification? After all, you, gentlemen, so far as I know, have taken your whole register of human advantages from the average of statistical figures and scientific-economic formulas. After all, your advantages are prosperity, wealth, freedom, peace—and so on, and so on. So that a man who, for instance, would openly and knowingly oppose that whole list would, to your thinking, and indeed to mine too, of course, be an obscurantist or an absolute madman, would he not? But, after all, here is something amazing: why does it happen that all these statisticians, sages and lovers of humanity, when they calculate human advantages invariably leave one out? They don't even take it into their calculation in the form in which it should be taken, and the whole reckoning depends upon that. There would be no great harm to take it, this advantage, and to add it to the list. But the trouble is, that this strange advantage does not fall under any classification and does not figure in any list. For instance, I have a friend. Bah, gentlemen! But after all he is your friend, too; and indeed there is no one, no one, to whom he is not a friend! When he prepares for any undertaking this gentleman immediately explains to you, pompously and clearly, exactly how he must act in accordance with the laws of reason and truth. What is more, he will talk to you with excitement and passion of the real normal interests of man; with irony he will reproach the short-sighted fools who do not understand their own advantage, for the true significance of virtue; and, within a quarter of an hour, without any sudden outside provocation, but precisely through that something internal which is stronger than all his advantages, he will go off on quite a different tack—that is, act directly opposite to what he has just been saying himself, in opposition to the laws of reason, in opposition to his own advantage—in fact, in opposition to everything. I warn you that my friend is a compound personality, and therefore it is somehow difficult to blame him as an individual. The fact is, gentlemen, it seems that something that is dearer to almost every man than his greatest advantages must really exist, or (not to be illogical) there is one most advantageous advantage (the very one omitted of which we spoke just now) which is more important and more advantageous than all other advantages, for which, if necessary, a man is ready to act in opposition to all laws, that is, in opposition to reason, honor, peace, prosperity—in short, in opposition to all those wonderful and useful things if only he can attain that fundamental, most advantageous advantage which is dearer to him than all.

"Well, but it is still advantage just the same," you will retort. But excuse me, I'll make the point clear, and it is not a case of a play on words, but what really matters is that this advantage is remarkable from the very fact that it breaks down all our classifications, and continually shatters all the systems evolved by lovers of mankind for the happiness of mankind. In short, it interferes with everything. But before I mention this advantage to you, I want to compromise myself personally, and therefore I boldly declare that all these fine systems—all these theories for explaining to mankind its real normal interests, so that inevitably striving to obtain these interests, it may at once become good and noble —are, in my opinion, so far, mere logical exercises! Yes, logical exercises. After all, to maintain even this theory of the regeneration of mankind by means of its own advantage, is, after all, to my mind almost the same thing as—as to claim, for instance, with Buckle, that through civilization mankind becomes softer, and consequently less bloodthirsty, and less fitted for warfare. Logically it does not seem to follow from his arguments. But man is so fond of systems and abstract deductions that he is ready to distort the truth intentionally, he is ready to deny what he can see and hear just to justify his logic. I take this example because it is the most glaring instance of it. Only look about you: blood is being spilled in streams, and in the merriest way, as though it were champagne. Take the whole of the nineteenth century in which Buckle lived. Take Napoleon—both the Great and the present one. Take North America—the eternal union. Take farcical Schleswig-Holstein. And what is it that civilization softens in us? Civilization only produces a greater variety of sensations in man—and absolutely nothing more. And through the development of this variety, man may even come to find enjoyment in bloodshed. After all, it has already happened to him. Have you noticed that the subtlest slaughterers have almost always been the most civilized gentlemen, to whom the various Attilas and Stenka Razins could never hold a candle, and if they are not so conspicuous as the Attilas and Stenka Razins it is precisely because they are so often met with, are so ordinary and have become so familiar to us. In any case if civilization has not made man more bloodthirsty, it has at least made him more abominably, more loathsomely bloodthirsty than before. Formerly he saw justice in bloodshed and with his conscience at peace exterminated whomever he thought he should. And now while we consider bloodshed an abomination, we nevertheless engage in this abomination and even more than ever before. Which is worse? Decide that for yourselves. It is said that Cleopatra (pardon the example from Roman history) was fond of sticking gold pins into her slave-girls' breasts and derived enjoyment from their screams and writhing. You will say that that occurred in comparatively barbarous times; that these are barbarous times too, because (also comparatively speaking) pins are stuck in even now; that even though man has now learned to see more clearly occasionally than in barbarous times, he is still far from having *accustomed* himself to act as reason and science would dictate. But all the same you are fully convinced that he will inevitably accustom himself to it when he gets completely rid of certain old bad habits, and when common sense and science have completely re-educated human nature and turned it in a normal direction. You are confident that man will then refrain from erring *intentionally,* and will, so to say, willy-nilly, not want to set his will against his normal interests. More than that: then, you say, science itself will teach man (though to my mind that is a luxury) that he does not really have either caprice or will of his own and that he has never had it, and that he himself is something like a piano key or an organ stop, and that, moreover, laws of nature exist in this world, so that everything he does is not done by his will at all, but is done by itself, according to the laws of nature. Consequently we have only to discover these laws of nature, and man will no longer be responsible for his actions and life will become exceedingly easy for him. All human actions will then, of course, be tabulated according to these laws, mathematically, like tables of logarithms up to 108,000, and entered in a table; or, better still, there would be published certain edifying works like the present encyclopedic lexicons, in which everything will be so clearly calculated and designated that there will be no more incidents or adventures in the world.

Then—it is still you speaking—new economic relations will be established, all ready-made and computed with mathematical exactitude, so that every possible question will vanish in a twinkling, simply because every possible answer to it will be provided. Then the crystal palace will be built. Then—well, in short, those will be halcyon days. Of course there is no guaranteeing (this is my comment now) that it will not be, for instance, terribly boring then (for what will one have to do when everything is calculated according to the table?) but on the other hand everything will be extraordinarily rational. Of course boredom may lead you to anything. After all, boredom even sets one to sticking gold pins into people, but all that would not matter. What is bad (this is my comment again) is that for all I know people will be thankful for the gold pins then. After all, man is stupid, phenomenally stupid. Or rather he is not stupid at all, but he is so ungrateful that you could not find another like him in all creation. After all, it would not surprise me in the least, if, for instance, suddenly for no reason at all, general rationalism in the midst of the future, a gentleman with an ignoble, or rather with a reactionary and ironical, countenance were to arise and, putting his arms akimbo, say to us all: "What do you think, gentlemen, hadn't we better kick over all that rationalism at one blow, scatter it to the winds, just to send these logarithms to the devil, and to let us live once more according to our own foolish will!" That again would not matter; but what is annoying is that after all he would be sure to find followers—such is the nature of man. And all that for the most foolish reason, which, one would think, was hardly worth mentioning: that is, that man everywhere and always, whoever he may be, has preferred to act as he wished and not in the least as his reason and advantage dictated. Why, one may choose what is contrary to one's own interests, and sometimes one *positively ought* (that is my idea). One's own free unfettered choice, one's own fancy, however wild it may be, one's own fancy worked up at times to frenzy— why that is that very "most advantageous advantage" which we have overlooked, which comes under no classification and through which all systems and theories are continually being sent to the devil. And how do these sages know that man must necessarily need a rationally advantageous choice? What man needs is simply *independent* choice, whatever that independence may cost and wherever it may lead. Well, choice, after all, the devil only knows . . .

You see, gentlemen, reason, gentlemen, is an excellent thing, there is no disputing that, but reason is only reason and can only satisfy man's rational faculty, while will is a manifestation of all life, that is, of all human life including reason as well as all impulses. And although our life, in this manifestation of it, is often worthless, yet it is life nevertheless and not simply extracting square roots. After all, here I, for instance, quite naturally want to live, in order to satisfy all my faculties for life, and not simply my rational faculty, that is, not simply one-twentieth of all my faculties for life. What does reason know? Reason only knows what it has succeeded in learning (some things it will perhaps never learn; while this is nevertheless no comfort, why not say so frankly?) and human nature acts as a whole, with everything that is in it, consciously or unconsciously, and, even if it goes wrong, it lives. I suspect, gentlemen, that you are looking at me with compassion; you repeat to me that an enlightened and developed man, such, in short, as the future man will be, cannot knowingly desire anything disadvantageous to himself, that this can be proved mathematically. I thoroughly agree, it really can—by mathematics. But I repeat for the hundredth time, there is one case, one only, when man may purposely, consciously, desire what is injurious to himself, what is stupid, very stupid—simply in order *to have the right* to desire for himself even what is very stupid and not to be bound by an obligation to desire only what is rational. After all, this very stupid thing, after all, this caprice of ours, may really be more advantageous for us, gentlemen, than anything else on earth, especially in some cases. And in particular it may be more advantageous than any advantages even when it does us obvious harm, and contradicts the soundest conclusions of our reason about our advantage—because in any case it preserves for us what is most precious and most important—that is, our personality, our individuality. Some, you see, maintain that this really is the most precious thing for man; . . .

In our last passage of this section John Wild provides an example of an existential and phenomenological approach to the question of the good (and the right). One typical stance of those who take such an approach—and much of our new morality and contemporary culture does—emphasizes not so much pleasure, satisfaction, or happiness, that is, the content of our lives, as the form, manner, or style of this content; that is, *how* we do what we do in living. Thus, it is often said that what matters is being honest, sincere, or autonomous. Wild puts the emphasis on *authenticity* as the existential value and explains what he thinks an authentic life would be like. He also describes the stages that he believes each of us tends to go through in the development of our ethical norms. Does his description fit your own experience?

AUTHENTIC EXISTENCE

John Wild

In this paper, I shall examine a new approach to "ethics" and "value theory" which is emerging from recent studies in phenomenology and existential philosophy. It is characteristic of this approach to use such terms as *real, genuine,* and especially *authentic* in a peculiar normative sense. Such usage is found in Kierkegaard,[1] Heidegger's *Sein und Zeit,*[2] Merleau-Ponty,[3] and other existentially oriented thinkers. I believe that it is based on the recognition of a new kind of "value" and a new kind

From John Wild, "Authentic Existence, A New Approach to Value Theory" from An Invitation to Phenomenology, *ed. by James M. Edie, pp. 59-71, 77. Copyright © 1965 by Quadrangle/The New York Times Book Co. Reprinted by permission of Mrs. Catherine A. Wild and Quadrangle/The New York Times Book Co.*

[1] Cf. R. Bretall, *A Kierkegaard Anthology,* selection from *Either/Or,* pp. 105–6; *Purity of Heart,* p. 280; *The Point of View,* pp. 331–32, *et passim.*

[2] Halle, 3rd ed., Sec. 9, pp. 42–43.

[3] *Phenomenology of Perception,* New York, p. 380.

of "norm" which have been neglected in traditional ethical theory. But in the authors I have mentioned, the use of *authentic* and *authentic existence* is still obscure and confused. My aim in this paper is to clarify the meaning of these terms by contrasting them with traditional theories in such a way as to bring out the novel direction in which they are moving. In the first section (1) I shall deal briefly with "existential values," as they may be called initially, and then at greater length in the second section (2) with existential norms.

Existential Values

Let us begin by considering the theory of objective values which originated in the thought of Plato and Aristotle, which dominated ethical theory until modern times, and is still alive and influential. According to this theory, the world is a cosmic order including inorganic things, plants, animals, and a divine first cause that is fixed for all time. Man occupies a special position in this hierarchical order between the non-rational animals and the first cause. Each individual is endowed with a fixed nature, consisting of vegetative, animal, and rational faculties, which remains the same throughout his history, and which sets the natural end—the realization of these faculties or powers. This process of realization demands that certain acts be performed under the conditions laid down by the structure of the cosmos. Thus power over inorganic and living things must be obtained to enable the organism to survive, food and shelter to enable it to grow and live in health, and education to nurture the rational faculties.

The faculty of reason can understand the objective nature of this human end, and of the external conditions that must be met. It can then lay down the general pattern of virtuous action leading to happiness, and can calculate the special means required to reach this natural end in special circumstances. Evil acts are those which fail to meet the natural conditions and lead to frustration. Any act is good insofar as it furthers self-realization. Freedom is identified with rational action of this kind. This is the ethics of natural law, and those many versions of self-realization ethics which have developed from it.

They are all subject to various criticisms which may be briefly summarized as follows. In the first place, there are cogent reasons for doubting that the world in which we exist is a single cosmic order established by external causes quite independent of all human interpretation, and fixed for all time. This fails to take account of the well-known differences between the worlds of different peoples and those of different individuals in societies with a respect for personal freedom. It also fails to recognize the rise and decline of these different worlds in the course of human history. In the second place, these criticisms would seem to indicate the presence of subjective factors, like freedom of interpretation and freedom of the will, which do not belong in the objective perspectives of reason and science.

The third objection follows directly from the second. Is not this traditional theory involved in a onesided intellectualism which faces very basic criticisms of which we need mention only two? First, in the light of psychological analysis, is it possible now to defend the traditional conception of a perfectly detached human reason which can escape from every influence coming from will, feeling, and factors in the surrounding culture? Second, does this conception do justice to the range and depth of human freedom? If it were true, would it not enslave us to a rigid pattern that would obstruct creative thought and action?

Finally, in the fourth place, we may mention a final objection that summarizes the rest. According to this intellectualistic theory, my self has been bestowed upon me in advance. It is simply a condition that requires to be realized by meeting other external conditions in a course of action whose general pattern, at least, has already been determined. But if this is true, in what sense can I call this self, and the life that I live, my own? I think of myself as in some sense the author of my way of life, and as responsible for it. This is certainly part of what we mean by the term *authentic*.[4] Grave doubts can be raised as to whether the traditional view we are examining can find any place for the "values" to which this term refers.

The traditional theory we have examined holds that being can be identified with objects present before the senses and the mind. Even the process of self-realization can be objectively studied and analyzed. Hence we may refer to this type of theory as *objectivistic* in its methods and conclusions. The difficulties we have summarized have led to the development of an opposed view which we may call *subjectivistic*, and which we may briefly characterize as follows.

The subjectivist denies that man is originally endowed with any fixed self or nature. The self of an individual person and the shared semi-self of a nation, or people, are constituted by their acts in history. As Sartre puts it: "man is nothing other than he makes himself to be."[5]

---

[4] According to the *Oxford Universal Dictionary* (rev. ed., 1955), this term may mean "really proceeding from its reputed source or author"; and also "real, actual [opposed to pretended]." [Brackets in the original.—EDS.] At this point we are referring to the first of these meanings. As we proceed, we shall also make use of the second.

[5] "l'homme n'est rien d'autre que ce qu'il se fait." *L'Existentialism est un Humanism*, Paris, 1946, p. 22.

He does not exist in a cosmic order that is already fixed and established. He exists in a world that is organized around the chosen projects of his people which he freely accepts, or around his own projects that he has freely chosen. Apart from man, there is no world, no meaning, and no value. He creates them and projects them around him, as a lantern projects its surrounding light. The objective facts of nature and the laws of science impose no conditional norms upon us, for, in themselves, they are meaningless and neutral to value. Their value or disvalue will depend upon the projects we choose.

Neither are there any existential norms imposed on our subjective freedom, save freedom itself. Even not to choose is a mode of choice —namely to follow the choice of others. So we are condemned to be free. It belongs to the human condition and therefore seems to operate, for Sartre, as a norm. It is always bad to sacrifice this freedom, to become sticky and congealed, or to sacrifice the freedom of others. But there are no other existential norms. Man is free to choose any project which appeals to him, and to organize a world of meaning around it. This choice is purely arbitrary, for there is no independent understanding to guide it. Any possible interpretation arises from a previous, arbitrary choice. With the possible exception of freedom, there are no universal norms. One choice is no better and no worse than another.

This view, very close to what is commonly called *relativism,* is open to several difficulties which may be summarized as follows. In the first place, questions may be raised as to whether it does justice to the element of hard facticity that belongs to every phase of our human existence in the world. Thus it may be true that I am not endowed at birth with a fixed nature that needs only to be realized. But I am endowed with a living body which requires certain objects, like food and shelter, to remain alive. Sartre has to recognize "a human universality of condition." [6] Universal conditions, in which man always finds himself, cannot be evaded, or refused, without falling into fantasy or pretense. They point to "universal values" which need to be objectively recognized and provided for all men by technology.

But the living body exists in the possibility of becoming a self. This also is part of the human condition. It points to existential values, as they have been called, of a very different kind, like freedom, which Sartre also recognizes as universal. But is freedom the only value of this kind? Or are there others, such as the finding of meaning, and responsibility? If so, Sartre says nothing about them. Can these existential values be understood in the same way as objective values? Can they be realized or achieved in the same way? Sartre does not carefully con-

---

[6] *Ibid.*, p. 67.

sider these questions. Furthermore, existential conditions and values must be known, if our acts are not to go astray. But, according to Sartre, there is no meaning, no understanding that is independent of our choice. This leads to a onesided voluntarism which makes all decisions equally blind and arbitrary. But we distinguish such choices from those that are reasonable and informed. How is this distinction to be explained?

We may summarize these objections to subjectivism, and the closely associated doctrine of relativism, by making a final point. If my life project, and the meanings derived from it, result from an arbitrary choice taking no account of the actual situation I am in, nor the necessary conditions of human existence, two possibilities confront me. On the one hand, I may cling to my project in words and imagination, but let others support me by their oriented action. On the other hand, I may try actively to achieve my arbitrary project by "reasonable" acts which are really inconsistent with it. In the first case, I am inactive and lose myself. In the second, I deceive myself and become divided. In either case, my project is a sham and a pretense, or in one sense of these words, unreal or unauthentic.[7]

We have now examined two types of value theory, the objectivistic and the subjectivistic, and have suggested reasons for believing that there are certain existential values, as we have called them, which neither theory is in a position to recognize. In common language, we refer to these values by the terms *authentic, unauthentic,* and their synonyms. Let us now try to clarify the meanings of these words in contrast to those of the objective and subjective values we have considered.

These existential values are concerned with the process of becoming ourselves in the world. But they involve a new approach to the traditional notions of "world," "becoming," and "self," and new values founded upon these findings. The world is thought of neither as an independent cosmic order to which we must passively adapt, nor as many fields of meaning organized around arbitrarily chosen projects. It is rather the emerging sense of a history in which man struggles for existence and meaning among the independent things and agencies among which he has been thrown. They present him with factors of brute facticity, both within and outside of himself, which must be taken account of, if he is to survive and act. But they also offer him the possibility of global interpretations supporting projects that make sense to him.

The process of world interpretation, therefore, can be reduced neither to a passive reception of meanings already established, nor to the arbitrary imposition of subjective categories on an indeterminate

---

[7] Cf. footnote 4, second meaning.

stuff. It is rather a mutual give and take in which our human answers are either rejected as unworkable, or silently accepted as possible by the events of history. This process has resulted in innumerable versions of the world which have come and gone. Those which are closed and fanatical become isolated and cease to develop, though, under favorable conditions, they may last for long periods of time. Those, on the other hand, which remain open to *the world,* of which they know that they are versions, have often grown and achieved results of universal significance. Openness to the world and the achievement of meaningful world versions which take account of the facts are, therefore, existential values of universal importance.

The self is not given as a set of fixed properties determining potentialities that merely need to be realized in achieving a natural end. This self is never realized, since it is always unfinished and incomplete. Neither is it created *ex nihilo* by the arbitrary choices of an isolated subject. It is given, with the living body, as a possible way of existing in the world, which is open to individuals living in a technologically advanced and free society. This possibility may be either refused or actively accepted and chosen. If it is chosen, it must meet certain existential conditions which operate as norms. Since the self is not a subject which can be separated from the world in which it exists, some distance from the established cultural world must be achieved, from which an interpretation may be worked out, and a personal project formed. In the light of this world of meaning, which makes sense to some individual or group, the actual situation must then be taken over in a responsible manner. By meaningful action of this kind, new sense may be infused into crystallized situations, and new world versions may be formed.

Such processes of becoming cannot be reduced to a mere succession of present states. Man is stretched out ecstatically into the future and the past. Hence each of the phases of time, past, present, and future, makes its own peculiar contribution to this process. If any one of these becomes rigid and isolated from the rest, the whole development becomes congealed and, under pressure, it disintegrates. Hence we can say that freedom (the gaining of distance from ourselves), the working out of global meanings, responsible action, and temporal integrity are conditions of human becoming which apply to all men. Insofar as we come to understand them through philosophical reflection, or concrete examples in history and literature, we can recognize them as existential values of a peculiar and distinctive kind. In contrast with those we have considered, we can distinguish them as being neither externally imposed upon us nor established by arbitrary decree.

If it is asked how this is possible, we may answer that values of this kind become established as norms by a peculiar process of interchange between cognitive and conative factors in man, which is altogether absent in the establishment of objective and subjective norms. If we may be permitted to use an analogy, we may say that these latter values are set up through a "dialogue" in which one partner dominates the interchange. Whatever the other one says or does, he remains unaffected and returns the same fixed answer. In the case of existential values, however, there is a reciprocal interdependence between the revealed possibilities of meaning (value) and our modes of active response. Each of these affects the other, and a real development may occur on both sides. This does not take place in the case of subjective or objective values, as we shall now briefly indicate.

It would be futile to deny that basic projects and versions of the world are sometimes set up by an arbitrary decree. When this happens, as Sartre has pointed out, the choice suddenly erupts with no preceding, noetic guidance. Such guidance is, indeed, impossible if, as the subjectivist theory maintains, meaning and understanding depend upon a preceding project as their originative source. Once a project is chosen, a world of value and meaning is ordered around it. If the situation shifts and new knowledge comes in, no basic change is required—only a certain amount of ingenuity to fit it into the closed world that is already established. There is no mutual give and take between the active and the revealing powers. There is no genuine dialogue; but only a onesided monologue in which desire and will are dominant. Historical versions of voluntarism have defended theories of this kind, and Heidegger comes close to such a view in his early work *Sein und Zeit*.[8] If consistently maintained, it leads to various forms of relativism and fanaticism which are, as a matter of fact, mutually reinforcing.

Until modern times, dominant trends in classical and mediaeval philosophy maintained that all real values are founded on actual conditions in man and the things around him which can be brought before the senses and the mind as present objects. This dogmatic view has been seriously undermined by modern criticism. Nevertheless there are certain values of this kind, like useful artifacts, which can be objectively analyzed and produced by technological calculation and equipment. Values of this kind are based on factual conditions into which we have been thrown. These conditions work on us causally to generate various needs, that of food, for example, which work on us as norms demanding recognition and satisfaction.

Such objective norms, imposed on us by alien forces, continue to operate in the same way, whatever our response may be. If we come

---

[8] "But on what basis does Dasein disclose itself in resoluteness? . . . *Only* the resolution itself can give the answer." *Being and Time*, tr. Robinson and Macquarrie, New York, 1962, p. 345.

to understand them and pay attention to their demands, they may lead us to bodily health. On the other hand, if we try to ignore and to violate them, they will make us miserable and will ultimately destroy us. This makes a difference to us. But it makes no difference to the objective conditions which maintain their causal operations in the same way in either case. Here again there is no mutual give and take between the revealing and active powers. There is only a onesided monologue in which the objective conditions and the understanding that reveals them are completely dominant. When generalized, this attitude leads to theories of intellectualism and determinism which dilute human action and freedom.

Let us now turn to the process by which existential norms are constituted, where something like a genuine dialogue takes place. These norms are not founded on objective conditions which are continuously in act. They are possible ways of meaningful existence which lie before us as men. But they do not rest on an arbitrary choice. They belong to the human condition into which we have been thrown, and if they are to be achieved, they must be achieved in an actual world with all its objective and independent factors. But this process of existential achievement is not to be confused with the realization of a given self in a world that is fixed and finished. The personal self is not given at the beginning. I am a possibility to be achieved, so far as this is possible. But as long as I exist, I am unfinished and incomplete.

Neither is the world in which I may become myself ever finished. It is open, and if I am to become myself, I must work out a version of the world that both fits the facts and is also meaningful to me. These existential possibilities are not imposed upon me by the causal action of alien forces. They are patterns of meaning which act on me only by the appeal of a global significance. But this appeal makes sense only to one who is ready to listen, and requires an active answer to be understood. Hence, as we have suggested, the process through which existential possibilities become normative for me, and finally elicit meaningful action in a concrete situation, involve something like a real dialogue. There is a mutual give and take between the active and revealing factors of human care, in which neither one dominates over the other, and in which there is a genuine development on both sides.

Let us now try to analyze the normal course of such a development. . . .

The Development of Existential Norms

We are concerned to analyze the active-revealing process by which abstract values become norms, and finally bring forth meaningful action.

Of course this can happen in many ways, either slowly or rapidly, with many separate stages, or with several of these telescoped together. Nevertheless there are certain well-marked steps that seem to be essential, and which we shall try to trace through in the following analysis and the illustration that follows. In times of cultural stability, it is possible for meaningful action and a meaningful world to develop in close union with the process through which the individual learns his mother tongue, and is assimilated into his own culture. But this is less common, and when it occurs, at least some of the stages which we shall note must be passed through in a mixed form. We shall be concerned here rather with the more usual process which must be undergone by an adult individual, already assimilated, who seeks to become himself, and to work out a way of life of his own.

(1) If such an individual is to do something more than play the roles that have been assigned to him by the culture into which he has been born, he must first gain a certain distance from these roles. From this distance, he may reflect upon them, and may come to see that they are not his own. This insight will be expressed by a general dissatisfaction with the way of life that his culture has imposed upon him.

(2) This dissatisfaction will enable him to glimpse certain possibilities ahead of him which he had not seen before. These possibilities will at first appear to him as abstract ways of supporting general ends, like the welfare of mankind, not demanding specific sacrifices, nor touching him directly in his concrete way of life. At this initial stage of becoming himself, they will not repel him. In this general form, they will first appeal to him, and lead him away from his accepted way of life.

(3) But this revelation of abstract possibilities will die away without an active answer. If this answer occurs, it will take the form of a growing detachment from his established way of life, which will seek escape in forgetfulness and distraction. The new possibility that is drawing him away is still general and not specific. As such, it does not yet repel. It merely brings forth a certain restlessness and attracts him from a majestic distance, like a gleaming star in the sky.

(4) But if this restlessness is maintained, the abstract possibility will become clearer, and will be brought closer to him. As the person reflects upon it, he will see it contract into a real possibility that touches him at this moment. This is a crucial phase of the history when the issue hangs in the balance. This real possibility may be rejected, in which case the dialogue may cease, as he abandons himself. Or on the other hand, he may give an active answer.

(5) This answer, if it is given, will take the form of a new sort of anxiety expressing a tension between the old way of life into which he has fallen and the new way now looming before him. As it draws closer

to his existence, it will not only attract; it will also repel, as it touches the substance of his being.

(6) If he can sustain this tension, the real possibility will soon be revealed in a sharper and clearer form. It will become an obligation, a demand for specific action here and now, that is expressed in the stronger language of necessity—*I ought* and *I must*. The real possibility is revealed as a norm coming even nearer to an emerging self, and demanding a specific answer here and now.

(7) Unless this normative appeal is refused, which may happen at any time, the answer will take the form of a specific, isolated act in the particular situation now confronting the agent. This act may bear a certain limited significance in the particular situation confronting him. But it is intended as the beginning of a personal way of life with a total significance which it does not yet possess. It is only a fragment in response to a fragmentary situation. How does this limited intention fit together with the intentions of other acts just performed and to be performed in the future? How can these isolated ideas be fitted together in a total world that makes sense? This feeling of meaninglessness pervades the whole scene, and the project may end then and there. The isolated normative act is a cry for integral meaning that calls for a revealing answer.

(8) If this answer is given, the dialogue will proceed in the form of a search for global meaning that will make sense to the active project now under way. It is not a question of uniting ideas together into an abstract system. It is rather a question of fitting them together in a way that will be capable of guiding meaningful action in the concrete world. Even if the pattern is familiar and already established, it will be seen in a new light when it is thought through by an active agent caught up in a novel situation, and related to his life project. This revelation of global meaning calls for an answer.

(9) If the agent listens, his answer will no longer take the form of an isolated response to a partial situation. It will rather be an act bearing global significance. It will be the beginning of a new way of life in a new world of meaning, the becoming of a self that can be called his own. This phase of the dialogue is over, and a new phase will begin. . . .

Authentic action is the expression of a very finite freedom. But it does not enslave us to norms that are externally imposed, since it takes them over, and lifts them up into a world of meaning that we have thought through and authorized for ourselves. There is a real sense in which these meaningful acts are mine. But they have not been laid down by an arbitrary decree, since they take account of the facts and make them meaningful precisely as they stand. Acts demanded of me by external norms, which I do not understand, are not mine. I am not the author of them. Hence they are unauthentic. Meanings which fail to take account of real conditions and existent facts make lasting action impossible. Hence they also are unauthentic—a hollow pretense and a sham.

In this paper I have tried to clarify the concepts of authenticity and the unauthentic which characterize a new approach to ethics which is coming to light in the investigations of phenomenology. This includes a notion of values as the central structures of a global world of meaning that is neither subjective nor objective. It has uncovered existential norms, as we have called them, which are imposed neither by external conditions over which we have no control, nor by arbitrary decrees having no relation to the facts. These values and norms may elicit modes of meaningful action of which man himself is really the author, with no pretense or sham. Following ordinary linguistic usage, we may properly call such action genuinely human, or authentic.

Suggestions for Further Reading

5.0 INTRINSIC GOODNESS

EWING, A. C. *The Definition of Good.* New York: Macmillan, 1947.

LEWIS, C. I. *The Ground and Nature of the Right.* New York: Columbia University Press, 1955 (Chapter IV).

5.1–5.3 HEDONISM AND NONHEDONISM

BRANDT, R. B. *Ethical Theory.* Englewood Cliffs, N.J.: Prentice-Hall, 1959. (Chapters XII and XIII).

———. "Rational Desires," *Proceedings of the American Philosophical Association,* XLIII (1970), 43–64.

Ross, W. D. *The Right and the Good.* Oxford: Clarendon Press, 1930 (Chapters V and VI).

5.4 OTHER CONCEPTIONS OF THE GOOD

GRENE, MARJORIE. "Authenticity: An Existential Virtue," *Ethics,* LXII (1952), 266–74.

HUXLEY, ALDOUS. *The Perennial Philosophy.* New York: Harper & Row, 1970.

NEUMANN, ERICH. *Depth Psychology and a New Ethic.* New York: Harper & Row, 1973.

PARKER, DEWITT. *The Philosophy of Value.* Ann Arbor, Mich.: University of Michigan Press, 1957 (Chapters IV–VII).

ROGERS, CARL. *On Becoming a Person.* Boston: Houghton Mifflin, 1961 (Chapters VIII and IX).

WARNOCK, MARY. *Existentialist Ethics.* New York: St. Martin's, 1967.

WOLFF, R. P. *The Poverty of Liberalism.* Boston: Beacon Press, 1968 (Chapter V).

6

MEANING
AND JUSTIFICATION

Introduction

So far we have been concerned mainly with questions of what we called normative ethics, namely, questions about what is morally right or wrong or good or bad (Chapters 2–4), or about what is intrinsically good or bad (Chapter 5). There are, however, a number of fundamental questions of a rather different sort that may be asked: "Aren't the answers to questions about what is morally right or good relative or even arbitrary?" "Can any answers to these questions ever be justified (and if so, how)?" "Anyway, why should one be moral or do what is morally right at all?" These questions, and others like them, are much asked and discussed today, especially by students, some of whom assume a skeptical or even hostile position toward the whole business of making or acting on moral and value judgments. Although they are so prominent today, such questions are not entirely new; they were asked by the Sophists and the skeptics of ancient Greece. They are, in fact, the main questions of meta-ethics, and must now be taken up. We begin with the problem of justifying ethical judgments.

We often justify an ethical judgment by giving reasons for it. For example, if I say X is right or good, and you ask me why, I may reply by pointing out that X will keep a promise, do someone a favor, or be pleasant. Then I adduce a fact as my reason for my ethical judgment.

Here my "X is right (or good)" is a particular judgment. But it is natural for us to appeal to factual beliefs about man and the world even in justifying more general and more ultimate ethical convictions. Epicurus did this (and Mill did too, in a way) when he argued that pleasure is the good because it is what we all seek. In another way, the author of I John 4:7–11 did it when he wrote:

> Beloved, let us love one another: for love is of God. . . . if God so loved us, we ought also to love one another.

Not only is it natural to make such an appeal to psychological, metaphysical, or theological premises in defending ethical goals and principles, it seems impossible to justify our basic ethical beliefs without the use of such factual premises. Yet there are problems about justifying them in this way. One of the first to notice this was David Hume. In a much quoted and much discussed paragraph that forms part of Hume's case for emotivism (his thesis that moral judgments are not the work of reason but of feeling or sentiment), he says,

> I cannot forbear adding to these reasonings an observation, which may, perhaps, be found of some importance. In every system of morality which I have hitherto met with, I have always remarked, that the author proceeds for some time in the ordinary way of reasoning, and establishes the being of a God, or makes observations concerning human affairs; when of a sudden I am surprised to find, that instead of the usual copulations of propositions, *is* and *is not*, I meet with no proposition that is not connected with an *ought*, or an *ought not*. This change is imperceptible; but is, however, of the last consequence. For as this *ought*, or *ought not*, expresses some new relation or affirmation, it is necessary that it should be observed and explained; and at the same time that a reason should be given, for what seems altogether inconceivable, how this new relation can be a deduction from others, which are entirely different from it. But as authors do not commonly use this precaution, I shall presume to recommend it to the readers; and am persuaded, that this small attention would subvert all the vulgar systems of morality, and let us see that the distinction of vice and virtue is not founded merely on the relations of objects, nor is preceived by reason.[1]

In this passage Hume points out that if a person tries to proceed from a factual premise (an Is) to an ethical conclusion (an Ought), he must at least explain how and why he can do this, for Ises and Oughts are prima facie very different. He may even have thought that it is logically impossible to infer an Ought from premises that are all Ises, for he concludes that Oughts cannot be established by reason alone. But however this may be, many philosophers after Hume—writers as different from

---

[1] David Hume, *Treatise of Human Nature* (first published in London, 1739; many subsequent editions), Book 3, Part 1, Section 1, last paragraph.

one another as Henry Sidgwick, Josiah Royce, James Balfour, M. J. Adler, and R. M. Hare—have considered it obvious that Oughts cannot be derived from Ises alone, and some of them have referred to this principle as Hume's Law.

Because it appears that basic Oughts cannot be justified unless they can be derived from Ises, some people who accept the No-Ought-from-an-Is dictum conclude that basic ethical judgments must be arbitrary and unjustifiable; in fact, this view is very common today, especially among the noncognitivists that we will study later. It is suggested by Broad's rather skeptical remarks quoted in Chapter 1, and is forcefully asserted by Brian Medlin.

> I believe that it is now pretty generally accepted by professional philosophers that ultimate ethical principles must be arbitrary. One cannot derive conclusions about what should be merely from accounts of what is the case; one cannot decide how people ought to behave merely from one's knowledge of how they do behave. To arrive at a conclusion in ethics one must have at least one ethical premiss. This premiss, if it be in turn a conclusion, must be the conclusion of an argument containing at least one ethical premiss. And so we can go back, indefinitely but not for ever. Sooner or later, we must come to at least one ethical premiss which is not deduced but baldly asserted. Here we must be a-rational; neither rational nor irrational, for here there is no room for reason even to go wrong.[2]

Must we agree with this popular position? The Naturalists and Intuitionists think not. Before we come to them, however, we must notice that there is still another alternative worth considering. Bentham and Mill both say, in passages already quoted, that basic ethical principles (such as that of utility) are incapable of proof by reasoning. They also reject the view that any such principles are intuitive or self-evident. Yet they insist that basic ethical principles are not matters of arbitrary choice, as so many today believe they are. They argue instead that it is possible to advance a rational case for one (and only one) ethical principle, namely, the principle of utility—and we have already reviewed much of this argument in Chapters 3 and 5.

---

[2] Brian Medlin, "Ultimate Principles and Ethical Egoism," *Australasian Journal of Philosophy* XXXV (1957), 111.

6.1

Ethical Naturalism and Definism

One way of dealing with the problem of justifying statements about what is right or good (Oughts) is to ask what "right" and "good" mean. The idea, which would have been insisted on by Socrates, is that if we know what "right," "good," and "ought" mean, then we can see whether or not such judgments can be justified and if so, how. For example, if "good" means "desired," then we can show that X is good by showing that it is desired; and if "right" means "commanded by God," then we can show that Y is right by showing that God commands it. In fact, following this line of thought, we might even point out that we can proceed logically from Ises to Oughts if we can define "right" and "good" in some appropriate way, i.e. if we can reduce Oughts to, or translate them into, Ises. This is the position adopted by the definists, including the ethical naturalists. A definist is one who regards the basic concepts or terms of ethics as definable or translatable by the use of non-ethical terms (psychological, metaphysical, or theological, for example). Naturalists hold that they can be defined by using empirical or scientific terms (nonmetaphysical and nontheological).

We might consider Aristotle to be an example of a definist. Looking back to the Aristotle selection in Chapter 5, we can interpret him as defining the good as what we all aim at, and then arguing that happiness (or excellent activity) is the good because it is what we all aim at. Then he justifies the statement that happiness is the good by appeal to a psychological fact about human nature. And if we ask him why we should regard that at which we all aim as the good, he answers that this is true by definition, true because "good" means "what we aim at." At any rate, for a definist, the basic thing in ethics is always a definition. He claims his basic ethical principle to be true by definition,

370

and given this, he can prove the rest. In this way he thinks he can solve the problem of justification, at least if definitions are not necessarily arbitrary or relative.

A naturalist may, however, be a relativist, or subjectivist, if, for example, he thinks that "right" means "approved of by the speaker" or "demanded by my society." But, if he defines "good" as Aristotle seems to, or "right" as "fitting in with the direction of human evolution," then he is an objectivist or absolutist, assuming his definition to have general validity.

Proponents of the divine command theory of ethics are sometimes definists. C. F. Henry (quoted in Chapter 2) seems to be one, though he can hardly be called a naturalist. Definists who are naturalists include William James, F. C. Sharp, and Brand Blanshard, and possibly Aristotle, Aquinas, and Bentham. Our example will be R. B. Perry. In the following selection, Perry first defines the general concept of "value." Next, he defines "morality," "morally good," "right," and other moral terms. He then points out that if we define the moral good as harmonious happiness, then this becomes the moral standard by which we judge and act. He ends by giving us reasons for adopting this standard.

VALUE AND MORALITY

Ralph Barton Perry

The Definition of Value

The question, "What does 'value' mean?" is not the same as the question "What things have value?" Though the two questions are often confused, the difference is evident when attention is called to it. The statement that "a sphere is a body of space bounded by one surface all points of which are equally distant from a point within called its center" is different from the statement that "the earth is (or is not) a sphere." The statement that peace is a condition in which societies abstain from the use of violence in settling their disputes, is different from the statement that the world is (or is not) now at peace. And similarly, a statement, such as is proposed below, of what value is, differs from the statement that peace is valuable.

If the second of each of these pairs of statements is to be definitive and accurate it is clearly advisable to have in mind the first. If, in other words, one is to know whether peace is or is not valuable, it is well to know what 'valuable' is: in other words, to know what it is that is stated

From Realms of Value: A Critique of Human Civilization *(Cambridge, Mass.: Harvard University Press, 1954). Reprinted by permission of the publisher. Copyright, 1954, by the President and Fellows of Harvard College.*

about peace when it is stated that it is valuable. But while the question raised by the second statement depends on an answer to the question raised by the first, the two questions are not the same question. And it is the first question with which the present inquiry is primarily concerned. In other words, theory of value ascribes value to things only in the light of what 'value' means.

Some philosophers, unfortunately, put the question concerning value in the form "What *is* meant by 'value'?" or "What *does* one mean by 'value'?" as though that meaning were already determined, and it was only necessary to call attention to it. Those who approach the matter in this way are accustomed to challenge a proposed definition of value by saying, "But this is not what is meant by 'value' " or "This is not what one means by 'value'." The fact is, however, that there is no such established and universal meaning. Different people mean different things in different contexts. The problem is not to discover a present meaning— there are only too many meanings.

The problem is not solved, however, by simply enumerating these many meanings. This job is already done by the unabridged dictionaries which list, in fine print, all the varieties of meaning which appear in literature and ordinary speech. Theory of value is in search of a preferred meaning. The problem is to define, that is, *give* a meaning to the term, either by selecting from its existing meanings, or by creating a new meaning.

But one must not then leap to the conclusion that this giving of a meaning to the term 'value' is an arbitrary matter, dictated by the caprice, or mere personal convenience, of the author. One can, it is true, make the term mean "anything one likes," but this would not advance knowledge, or be of the slightest importance, or be capable either of proof or of disproof. The man who said "When I say 'value' I mean a purple cow" would not even be listened to, unless by a psychiatrist or a kindergarten teacher. There must, in other words, be a control or set of criteria, by which the definition is justified or rejected.

According to the definition of value here proposed, *a thing—any thing—has value, or is valuable, in the original and generic sense when it is the object of an interest—any interest. Or, whatever is an object of interest is ipso facto valuable.* Thus the valuableness of peace is the characteristic conferred on peace by the interest which is taken in it, for what it is, or for any of its attributes, effects, or implications.

Value is thus defined in terms of interest, and its meaning thus depends on another definition, namely, a definition of interest. The following is here proposed: interest is *a train of events determined by expectation of its outcome.* Or, *a thing is an object of interest when its being expected induces actions looking to its realization or non-realization.*

Thus peace is an object of interest when acts believed to be conducive to peace, or preventive of peace, are performed on that account, or when events are selected or rejected because peace is expected of them.

Both of these definitions require clarification and elaboration; but these summary statements will suffice for the present purpose of indicating the criterion by which the definitions are to be justified. These criteria are three in number, namely, *linguistic, formal,* and *empirical.* When the definition is challenged it must defend itself on three grounds: its use of words; the clarity, definiteness, tenability, and fruitfulness of the concepts which it employs; and its capacity to describe certain facts of life, to which it refers, and by which it is verified. . . .

The Meaning of Morality

Morality is man's endeavor to harmonize conflicting interests: to prevent conflict when it threatens, to remove conflict when it occurs, and to advance from the negative harmony of non-conflict to the positive harmony of coöperation. Morality is the solution of the problem created by conflict—conflict among the interests of the same or of different persons. The solution of the personal problem lies in the substitution for a condition of warring and mutually destructive impulses a condition in which each impulse, being assigned a limited place, may be innocent and contributory. For the weakness of inner discord it substitutes the strength of a unified life in which the several interests of an individual make common cause together. The same description applies to the morality of a social group, all along the line from the domestic family to the family of nations.

Such a moralization of life takes place, insofar as it does take place, through organization—personal and social. This crucial idea of organization must not be conceived loosely, or identified with organism. In organism, as in a work of art, the part serves the whole; in moral organization the whole serves the parts, or the whole only for the sake of the parts. The parts are interests, and they are organized in order that they, the constituent interests themselves, may be saved and fulfilled.

When interests are thus organized there emerges an interest of the totality, or moral interest, whose superiority lies in its being greater than any of its parts—greater by the principle of inclusiveness. It is authorized to speak for all of the component interests when its voice is their joint voice. The height of any claim in the moral scale is proportional to the breadth of its representation. What suits all of a person's interests is exalted above what merely suits a fraction; what suits everybody is exalted above what merely suits somebody. . . .

Morality conceived as the harmonization of interests for the sake of the interests harmonized can be described as a cult of freedom. It does not force interests into a procrustean bed, but gives interests space and air in which to be more abundantly themselves. Its purpose is to provide room. And ideally the benefits of morality are extended to all interests. Hence moral progress takes the double form, of liberalizing the existing organization, and of extending it to interests hitherto excluded. Both of these principles have important applications to the "dynamics" of morality, or to the moral force in human history. The extension of moral organization is made possible by increase of contact and interaction, which, however, then multiplies the possibilities of conflict. Hence the peculiar destiny of man, whose ascent is rendered possible by the same conditions which make possible his fall. There can be no development of a unified personality or society without the risk of inner tensions; no neighborhood, nation, or society of all mankind, without the risk of war.

Morality as progressive achievement requires the integration of interests. They cannot be simply added together. If they are to compose a harmonious will that represents them all, they must be brought into line. At the same time, if such a will is truly to embrace them, which is the ground of its higher claim, they must themselves accept the realignment. Morality is an integration of interests, in which they are rendered harmonious without losing their identity. The procedure by which this is effected is the method of *reflective agreement*, appearing in the personal will, and in the social will.

The Interpretation of Moral Concepts

There are certain terms of discourse, such as 'good', 'right', 'duty', 'responsibility', and 'virtue', which are commonly recognized as having to do with morality, and to which a theory of morals must assign definite meanings.

Two meanings have already been assigned to the term 'good'. In the most general sense, it means the character which anything derives from being the object of any positive interest: whatever is desired, liked, enjoyed, willed, or hoped for, is *thereby* good. In a special sense, 'morally good' is the character imparted to objects by interests harmoniously organized. . . .

An object . . . is *morally good* in the special sense when the interest which makes it good satisfies the requirement of harmony, that is, innocence and coöperation. This requirement may be met in one or both of two ways. In the first place, it may qualify any interest when that interest is governed by a concern for other interests. Thus the object of a person's sensuous enjoyment acquires a moral character when it is governed by his concern for his health or practical achievements; and a person's ambition acquires a moral character when it is governed by his concern for the interests of other persons. Or, in the second place, the moral requirement may qualify a special interest—the moral interest— by having harmony as its object.

In other words, one may state of any object of interest that it is morally good when the interest is endorsed by other interests; and one may state that a total life in which all interests endorse one another is morally good when it is the object of the moral will.

The "good life," morally speaking, may be described as a condition of *harmonious happiness*—a condition in which, through the increase and coöperation of its members, all interests tend to be positive. This description throws light on the meaning of the familiar but obscure idea of "happiness," and on the traditional claim of happiness to rank as the supreme moral end.

Happiness is attributed to a person as a whole, as distinguished from his momentary or partial interests. He is happy insofar as every outlook is auspicious; he can face many prospects and face them all cheerfully. His present interest is accompanied by a sense of the applause of all his other interests, brought into consciousness by imagination and reflection. . . .

As happiness reflects a harmony of interests, so unhappiness is an effect of conflict, as when a man is said to be "at war with himself." Insofar as this condition prevails, each interest sees the others as its enemies, and is moved to defeat them. Each positive interest—each enjoyment or prosperous achievement—then begets a negative interest on behalf of the other interests which it jeopardizes.

The application of similar principles to inter-personal relations gives meaning to such expressions as 'the general good'. The happiness of a society or a family, or nation, or mankind, is morally good insofar as its personal members live together as friends, so that each regards the others' interests as harmless or helpful to his own. The interests of the several members are so happily attuned that each person in willing his own happiness wills also the happiness of his fellows. The happiness enjoyed is the happiness of each; its sociality lies in the fact that the several happinesses are conditioned by benevolence. The happy society is a society of happy men, who derive happiness from one another's happiness.

It is generally conceded that as the personal good is morally better than the good of one of its constituent interests, so the social good is morally better than the personal, and the good of mankind than that of any narrower human group. Interpreted in terms of harmonious happiness and the standard of inclusion, this means that the greater harmonies must include the lesser harmonies. There must be a harmony of harmonies. . . .

According to the theory here proposed, 'right' means conduciveness to moral good, and 'wrong' means conduciveness to moral evil: the one to harmony, and the other to conflict. So construed, right and wrong are dependent and instrumental values. That which is right or wrong may, however, like all objects of dependent interests, come to be loved or hated for its own sake, and thus acquire *intrinsic* value. . . .

An act is right when it conduces to the moral good, that is, to harmonious happiness; and it is wrong when it conduces to disharmony. The right may conduce to the good as antecedent cause to subsequent effect, as when a humane act leads to the happiness of the other party; or as part to whole, as when a man's humane act is embraced within his happiness, or when a man best serves a happy society by being happy himself. In both cases, whether the act "makes for," or "goes into the making of," its rightness consists in its *contributing* to harmonious happiness. This is the root meaning of 'right' and 'wrong.' . . .

The full meaning of substantive "rights" can be understood only in the context of polity and law, in which this idea plays a fundamental role. It is, however, a basic moral concept, and should receive its initial interpretation here.

Rights are sometimes considered axiomatic, but in a consequential theory such as is here proposed they must be explained by their conduciveness to the good life. Harmonious happiness is justified by its provision for the several interests which it harmonizes. The claim which *each* of these interests has upon the bounty of the whole is its "right." Harmonious happiness is achieved by organization, and it sets limits to the interests for which it provides. A right is therefore not the unrestricted demand of the component interest but a *right* demand—a demand the fulfillment of which is consistent with the fulfillment of other demands. Each interest is entitled to an area within which it enjoys liberty to follow its own inclination; but it is a limited area, bounded by the areas of other interests within a system which provides for all interests. . . .

There is a basic idea common to 'ought', 'duty', 'moral obligation', and 'moral imperative'. To clarify the subject it is necessary not only to provide such a basic meaning, but also to account for various shades of meaning and meaninglessness.

On the level of everyday discourse what ought to be done is what is called for by some end; it is the converse of the right. The moral ought is what is called for by the end of the moral good, that is, by harmonious happiness. The act which ought to be performed may or may not be a necessary or sufficient condition of the good. The obligatory act may or may not be a unique act; in any given situation there may be many acts which satisfy the condition of conducing to the good, one of which ought to be performed.

That moral obligation is commonly expressed in the form of a command and therefore in the imperative voice is an accident, due to the fact that right action is associated with political, parental, or other authority. Or, the imperativeness of obligation may be an after effect of the logical necessity by which the rightness of the act was inferred from its consequences. Just as the "thou shalt" may remain after the authority has ceased to utter it, so the "therefore" or tone of necessity may remain in after the premises have disappeared.

The term 'duty' is applied primarily to the moral agent, and only secondarily to acts which are "in the line of duty." It is a stronger term than 'ought' since it is associated with an implied promise by which the agent has bound himself. When it is said that every right has its associated duty, it is meant that in claiming his benefit as a moral right he has committed himself to allotting some equivalent benefit on the other party. If he does not fulfill his part, not only as beneficiary but as benefactor, he incurs the charge of inconsistency, as well as the justifiable resentment of the other beneficiary. There are as many duties as there are rights, and there are as many rights as there are moral systems with delimited spheres and mutual engagements. There are duties as well as rights associated with every role in organized society—the parent, the neighbor, the soldier, the employer and worker, or the citizen.

When it is said that an act "ought" to be performed, it is meant that the act is called for by some good to which the act is conducive. . . .

The Proof of the Moral Standard

The moral good has been defined as harmonious happiness, or as that organization of interests in which each enjoys the non-interference and support of the others, whether within the personal life or the life of society. This becomes the moral "first principle." It sets the standard by which objects are deemed morally good or bad, and is the premise from which right, duty, and virtue are to be derived. It provides the most general predicate of moral judgment and the basic concept of moral knowledge. How is it to be proved? The moral philosopher is compelled not only to produce evidence, but to decide what kind of evidence may properly be demanded. . . .

Subject to these generalities which characterize all knowledge, there are two kinds of moral knowledge, derivative and basic. When an act of homicide is judged to be wrong it is ordinarily sufficient to call it 'murder'. That is deemed sufficient, since it is assumed that murder is wrong. This judgment may be subsumed under some other accepted generalization, such as the right to life, or the goodness of security and order. But if one follows this line from premise to premise, and if one avoids circularity, one arrives eventually at an ultimate premise or first premise which cannot be similarly deduced.

The application to the standard of harmonious happiness is evident. It is judged that things are morally right and wrong, good and bad, obligatory and forbidden, judged by the standard of harmonious happiness. There are two judgments, the judgment which adopts the standard, and the judgment which applies it. The fundamental question of moral knowledge is the question of the proof of the first or basic judgment. It is a judgment about a standard, and to the effect that a specific standard, such as harmonious happiness, occupies a peculiar place among standards, and is entitled to be designated as "the moral standard." This is not a moral judgment in the sense of assigning such predicates as 'good,' 'right,' and 'ought.' Moral theory, whether it asserts that the ultimate moral standard is happiness, or that the moral right or good is indefinable, or that duty is obedience to God, or that the right is the reasonable, stands outside the whole circle of such judgments, and makes non-moral statements about them.

The first condition which such a theory must satisfy is that the proposed standard should be in fact a standard, or qualified to be a standard. If harmonious happiness can be truly affirmed to be the moral standard, it must so agree with human nature and the circumstances of human life that men can adopt it by education, persuasion, and choice; and, having adopted it, can govern their conduct in accordance with its requirements. It must be qualified to serve as a criterion by which human interests, acts, characters, and organizations can be classified and ranked. The evidence that it satisfied these requirements will be found in the fact that it is so adopted and employed.

If, however, harmonious happiness is to be proved to be *the* moral standard, to the exclusion of other standards for which a similar claim is made, it must possess further and unique qualifications. Otherwise it will be merely one standard among many, differing only historically. There would be no ground of persuasion by which the adherent of another standard could be converted to this standard. It could be judged *in terms* of this standard, but there could be no judgment *between* them. The standard of harmonious happiness would have no *theoretical* precedence. . . .

But there still remain arguments to be advanced in its support—

arguments which, though they may not satisfy everybody, at least have the merit of being appropriate to the thesis which is to be proved.

In the first place, the standard of harmonious happiness is *capable* of being agreed on—both theoretically and practically. It satisfies the requirement of cognitive universality and objectivity; that is, it is the same for all knowers who address themselves to the subject. Since the norm of harmonious happiness acknowledges all interests, its affirmation is free from the so-called "personal equation." As the astronomer recognizes all stellar facts regardless of the accidents of the observer's history, and thus overcomes the geocentricism which has led men to affirm that the heavens move about a stationary earth, so the theory of harmonious happiness overcomes that egocentricism which has led moral observers to subordinate all interests to their own, or to those of their neighborhood, class, or nation. It embraces human perspectives within a total system of relationships. It places itself in all points of view, and fits them together. It discovers alien and remote interests, and makes allowance for the ignorance which it cannot wholly dispel. It is impartial. It says, in effect, that since it is interest as such which generates good, and a harmonious relation of interests which constitutes moral good, to him who makes the judgment *his* interest is just one among the rest. Since the principle of harmonious happiness deals with the nature of interest in general, and with its types of relationship, it is applicable to all interests and persons. . . . [It] is the only norm which promises benefits to each interest *together with* all other interests. It does not rob Peter to pay Paul, but limits Peter in order to pay both Peter and Paul. . . .

Making due allowance for the possibility of error in general, and for the degree of its probability in any particular field of inquiry, it may properly be argued for any theory that it agrees with widespread opinion.

The theory here proposed reaffirms the standard virtues of antiquity —courage, temperance, wisdom, and justice. The good of harmonious happiness requires, like any end, a brave will that is not dismayed by obstacles, and effort sustained without complaint through long stretches of time. It requires a moderation of appetites lest in their excessive indulgence they should rob one another. It requires enlightened mediating judgments, that is, a true representation of ends and an intelligent choice of means. It requires a distribution of goods to each interest in accordance with a judgment which represents all interest. Christianity did not reject these virtues, but added faith, hope, and love; and these, also, are endorsed by the present theory. Harmonious happiness is an ideal and if an ideal is to be pursued there must be a steadfast belief in its attainability by means that lie beyond present knowledge, and a confidence in its actual attainment in the future. The pursuit of the harmonious happiness of all requires a sympathetic concern for one's fellow men—a sensitiveness to their pains or frustrations and an impulse to help.

Other funded moral wisdom falls into line. The most generally accepted of all maxims, the Golden Rule, is justified because the harmonious happiness of all requires that each man shall put himself in the place of other men, and recognize their interests, however cold and remote, as of the same coin with those warm and intimate interests which he calls his own. Veracity signifies the need of communication as the condition of all human intercourse. Honesty is that keeping of agreements which is essential to security and to concerted plans. Selfishness is that preoccupation with the narrower interests of self, family, class, or nation which obstructs the longer and wider vistas demanded by universal happiness.

These maxims and virtues are not invariably accepted. They are sometimes defied and they are frequently ignored. It cannot, however, be said that they are peculiar to Western Europe, or to capitalistic societies, or to Christianity, or to the modern world. They cross all such divisions, and when, as today, life is organized on a wider scale, to include all nations, all dependent and backward groups, and all hitherto unprivileged persons and classes, it is to this body of moral opinion that men appeal. Equally significant is the fact that when men differ as to the specific applications of moral opinion it is to the standard of harmonious happiness that they look for common ground. And it is by this standard that men criticize and justify their major social institutions—conscience itself, polity, law, economy—and by which they define the places in human society that are to be allotted to art, science, education, and religion. . . .

It is no disproof of the present doctrine of harmonious happiness to point out that men are not harmoniously happy, or are inharmoniously unhappy. All that needs to be proved is that there is a prolonged and widespread attempt to be harmoniously happy; that men are capable of such an attempt; that they can and do take steps in the direction of harmonious happiness; and that they can and do measure their steps by the standard of harmonious happiness. The fundamental claim for the present view is that it describes a peculiarly widespread, fundamental, and persistent human pursuit for which 'moral' is the most appropriate name.

6.2

Intuitionism

Intuitionism offers us another way of avoiding the conclusion that basic ethical beliefs are arbitrary or unjustifiable. Intuitionists agree that Oughts cannot be logically inferred from Ises. To establish an ethical conclusion, they insist, one must have at least one ethical premise. What, then, about one's basic ethical premises? Are these necessarily arbitrary? The intuitionist's answer is that some ethical propositions are intuitive or self-evident. They cannot be inferred from nonethical premises and, hence, cannot be *proved,* but they are not therefore arbitrary; they are indemonstrable all right, but they are, so to speak, self-justifying to anyone who clearly understands them. We express such a view in our Declaration of Independence when we say, "We hold these truths to be self-evident."

Intuitionists must then also reject definism of all sorts. In fact, they argue that the basic concepts or properties of ethics are indefinable, irreducible, or simple and unique. Intuitionism is sometimes called nonnaturalism because it insists that ethical concepts or properties are not only simple and indefinable, but also nonempirical; that is, they are not discovered by sensation or introspection, as yellowness and pleasantness are. In short, intuitionism holds that (1) the basic terms of ethics stand for indefinable nonnatural properties, and (2) the basic propositions of ethics are intuitive or self-evident.

This view was first worked out, not by Sidgwick, as Moore thought, but by Richard Price and Thomas Reid in the eighteenth century (and possibly by Plato). It was held in recent times by Sidgwick, Rashdall, Prichard, Carritt, Ross, Laird, Broad, Ewing, Blake, and, in continental Europe, by Scheler, Hartmann, and others. Moore has been the most important representative of twentieth-century intuitionism. He takes the property of being good in itself as basic in ethics, arguing very forcefully that it is simple and indefinable, and that, therefore, basic judgments about what is good in itself are uninferable, intuitive, and self-evident.

THE SUBJECT-MATTER OF ETHICS

G. E. Moore

6. What, then, is good? How is good to be defined? Now, it may be thought that this is a verbal question. A definition does indeed often mean the expressing of one word's meaning in other words. But this is not the sort of definition I am asking for. Such a definition can never be of ultimate importance in any study except lexicography. If I wanted that kind of definition I should have to consider in the first place how people generally used the word "good"; but my business is not with its proper usage, as established by custom. I should, indeed, be foolish, if I tried to use it for something which it did not usually denote: if, for instance, I were to announce that, whenever I used the word "good," I must be understood to be thinking of that object which is usually denoted by the word "table." I shall, therefore, use the word in the sense in which I think it is ordinarily used; but at the same time I am not anxious to discuss whether I am right in thinking that it is so used. My business is solely with that object or idea, which I hold, rightly or wrongly, that the word is generally used to stand for. What I want to discover is the nature of that object or idea, and about this I am extremely anxious to arrive at an agreement.

But, if we understand the question in this sense, my answer to it may seem a very disappointing one. If I am asked "What is good?" my answer is that good is good, and that is the end of the matter. Or if I am asked "How is good to be defined?" my answer is that it cannot be defined, and that is all I have to say about it. But disappointing as these answers may appear, they are of the very last importance. To readers who are familiar with philosophic terminology, I can express their importance by saying that they amount to this: That propositions about the good are all of them synthetic and never analytic; and that is plainly no trivial matter. And the same thing may be expressed more popularly, by saying that, if I am right, then nobody can foist upon us such an axiom as that "Pleasure is the only good" or that "The good is the desired" on the pretence that this is "the very meaning of the word."

From Principia Ethica *(London: Cambridge University Press, 1903). Reprinted by permission of Cambridge University Press.*

7.   Let us, then, consider this position. My point is that "good" is a simple notion, just as "yellow" is a simple notion; that, just as you cannot, by any manner of means, explain to any one who does not already know it, what yellow is, so you cannot explain what good is. Definitions of the kind that I was asking for, definitions which describe the real nature of the object or notion denoted by a word, and which do not merely tell us what the word is used to mean, are only possible when the object or notion in question is something complex. You can give a definition of a horse, because a horse has many different properties and qualities, all of which you can enumerate. But when you have enumerated them all, when you have reduced a horse to his simplest terms, then you can no longer define those terms. They are simply something which you think of or perceive, and to any one who cannot think of or perceive them, you can never, by any definition, make their nature known. It may perhaps be objected to this that we are able to describe to others, objects which they have never seen or thought of. We can, for instance, make a man understand what a chimaera is, although he has never heard of one or seen one. You can tell him that it is an animal with a lioness's head and body, with a goat's head growing from the middle of its back, and with a snake in place of a tail. But here the object which you are describing is a complex object; it is entirely composed of parts, with which we are all perfectly familiar—a snake, a goat, a lioness; and we know, too, the manner in which those parts are to be put together, because we know what is meant by the middle of a lioness's back, and where her tail is wont to grow. And so it is with all objects, not previously known, which we are able to define: they are all complex; all composed of parts, which may themselves, in the first instance, be capable of similar definition, but which must in the end be reducible to simplest parts, which can no longer be defined. But yellow and good, we say, are not complex: they are notions of that simple kind, out of which definitions are composed and with which the power of further defining ceases.

8.   When we say, as Webster says, "The definition of horse is 'A hoofed quadruped of the genus Equus,'" we may, in fact, mean three different things. (1) We may mean merely: "When I say 'horse,' you are to understand that I am talking about a hoofed quadruped of the genus Equus." This might be called the arbitrary verbal definition: and I do not mean that good is indefinable in that sense. (2) We may mean, as Webster ought to mean: "When most English people say 'horse,' they mean a hoofed quadruped of the genus Equus." This may be called the verbal definition proper, and I do not say that good is indefinable in this sense either; for it is certainly possible to discover how people use a word: otherwise, we could never have known that "good"

may be translated by "gut" in German and by "bon" in French. But (3) we may, when we define horse, mean something much more important. We may mean that a certain object, which we all of us know, is composed in a certain manner: that it has four legs, a head, a heart, a liver, etc., etc., all of them arranged in definite relations to one another. It is in this sense that I deny good to be definable. I say that it is not composed of any parts which we can substitute for it in our minds when we are thinking of it. We might think just as clearly and correctly about a horse, if we thought of all its parts and their arrangements instead of thinking of the whole: we could, I say, think how a horse differed from a donkey just as well, just as truly, in this way, as now we do, only not so easily; but there is nothing whatsover which we could so substitute for good; and that is what I mean, when I say that good is indefinable.

9.   But I am afraid I have still not removed the chief difficulty which may prevent acceptance of the proposition that good is indefinable. I do not mean to say that *the* good, that which is good, is thus indefinable; if I did think so, I should not be writing on Ethics, for my main object is to help towards discovering that definition. It is just because I think there will be less risk of error in our search for a definition of "the good," that I am now insisting that *good* is indefinable. I must try to explain the difference between these two. I suppose it may be granted that "good" is an adjective. Well "the good," "that which is good," must therefore be the substantive to which the adjective "good" will apply: it must be the whole of that to which the adjective will apply, and the adjective must *always* truly apply to it. But if it is that to which the adjective will apply, it must be something different from that adjective itself; and the whole of that something different, whatever it is, will be our definition of *the* good. Now it may be that this something will have other adjectives, beside "good," that will apply to it. It may be full of pleasure, for example; it may be intelligent; and if these two adjectives are really part of its definition, then it will certainly be true, that pleasure and intelligence are good. And many people appear to think that, if we say "Pleasure and intelligence are good," or if we say "Only pleasure and intelligence are good," we are defining "good." Well, I cannot deny that propositions of this nature may sometimes be called definitions; I do not know well enough how the word is generally used to decide upon this point. I only wish it to be understood that that is not what I mean when I say there is no possible definition of good and that I shall not mean this if I use the word again. I do most fully believe that some true proposition of the form "Intelligence is good and intelligence alone is good" can be found; if none could be found, our definition of *the* good would be impossible. As it is, I believe *the* good to be definable; and yet I still say that good itself is indefinable.

10. "Good," then, if we mean by it that quality which we assert to belong to a thing, when we say that the thing is good, is incapable of any definition, in the most important sense of that word. The most important sense of "definition" is that in which a definition states what are the parts which invariably compose a certain whole; and in this sense "good" has no definition because it is simple and has no parts. It is one of those innumerable objects of thought which are themselves incapable of definition, because they are the ultimate terms by reference to which whatever *is* capable of definition must be defined. That there must be an indefinite number of such terms is obvious, on reflection; since we cannot define anything except by an analysis, which, when carried as far as it will go, refers us to something, which is simply different from anything else, and which by that ultimate difference explains the peculiarity of the whole which we are defining: for every whole contains some parts which are common to other wholes also. There is, therefore, no intrinsic difficulty in the contention that "good" denotes a simple and indefinable quality. There are many other instances of such qualities.

Consider yellow, for example. We may try to define it, by describing its physical equivalent; we may state what kind of light-vibrations must stimulate the normal eye, in order that we may perceive it. But a moment's reflection is sufficient to shew that those light-vibrations are not themselves what we mean by yellow. *They* are not what we perceive. Indeed we should never have been able to discover their existence, unless we had first been struck by the patent difference of quality between the different colours. The most we can be entitled to say of those vibrations is that they are what corresponds in space to the yellow which we actually perceive.

Yet a mistake of this simple kind has commonly been made about "good." It may be true that all things which are good are *also* something else, just as it is true that all things which are yellow produce a certain kind of vibration in the light. And it is a fact, that Ethics aims at discovering what are those other properties belonging to all things which are good. But far too many philosophers have thought that when they named those other properties they were actually defining good; that these properties, in fact, were simply not "other," but absolutely and entirely the same with goodness. This view I propose to call the "naturalistic fallacy" and of it I shall now endeavour to dispose.

11. Let us consider what it is such philosophers say. And first it is to be noticed that they do not agree among themselves. They not only say that they are right as to what good is, but they endeavour to prove that other people who say that it is something else, are wrong. One, for instance, will affirm that good is pleasure, another, perhaps, that good is that which is desired; and each of these will argue eagerly to prove that the other is wrong. But how is that possible? One of them says that good is nothing but the object of desire, and at the same time tries to prove that it is not pleasure. But from his first assertion, that good means the object of desire, one of two things must follow as regards his proof:

(1) He may be trying to prove that the object of desire is not pleasure. But, if this be all, where is his Ethics? The position he is maintaining is merely a psychological one. Desire is something which occurs in our minds, and pleasure is something else which so occurs; and our would-be ethical philosopher is merely holding that the latter is not the object of the former. But what has that to do with the question in dispute? His opponent held the ethical proposition that pleasure was the good, and although he should prove a million times over the psychological proposition that pleasure is not the object of desire, he is no nearer proving his opponent to be wrong. The position is like this. One man says a triangle is a circle: another replies "A triangle is a straight line, and I will prove to you that I am right: *for*" (this is the only argument) "a straight line is not a circle." "That is quite true," the other may reply; "but nevertheless a triangle is a circle, and you have said nothing whatever to prove the contrary. What is proved is that one of us is wrong, for we agree that a triangle cannot be both a straight line and a circle: but which is wrong, there can be no earthly means of proving, since you define triangle as straight line and I define it as circle"—Well, that is one alternative which any naturalistic Ethics has to face; if good is *defined* as something else, it is then impossible either to prove that any other definition is wrong or even to deny such definition.

(2) The other alternative will scarcely be more welcome. It is that the discussion is after all a verbal one. When A says "Good means pleasant" and B says "Good means desired," they may merely wish to assert that most people have used the word for what is pleasant and for what is desired respectively. And this is quite an interesting subject for discussion: only it is not a whit more an ethical discussion than the last was. Nor do I think that any exponent of naturalistic Ethics would be willing to allow that this was all he meant. They are all so anxious to persuade us that what they call the good is what we really ought to do. "Do, pray, act so, because the word 'good' is generally used to denote actions of this nature": such, on this view, would be the substance of their teaching. And in so far as they tell us how we ought to act, their teaching is truly ethical, as they mean it to be. But how perfectly absurd is the reason they would give for it! "You are to do this, because most people use a certain word to denote conduct such as this." "You are to say the thing which is not, because most people call it lying." That is an argument just as good!—My dear sirs, what we want to know from

you as ethical teachers, is not how people use a word; it is not even, what kind of actions they approve, which the use of this word "good" may certainly imply: what we want to know is simply what *is* good. We may indeed agree that what most people do think good, is actually so; we shall at all events be glad to know their opinions: but when we say their opinions about what *is* good, we do mean what we say; we do not care whether they call that thing which they mean "horse" or "table" or "chair," "gut," or "bon" or "ἀγαθός", we want to know what it is that they so call. When they say "Pleasure is good," we cannot believe that they merely mean "Pleasure is pleasure" and nothing more than that.

12.   Suppose a man says "I am pleased"; and suppose that is not a lie or a mistake but the truth. Well, if it is true, what does that mean? It means that his mind, a certain definite mind, distinguished by certain definite marks from all others, has at this moment a certain definite feeling called pleasure. "Pleased" *means* nothing but having pleasure, and though we may be more pleased or less pleased, and even, we may admit for the present, have one or another kind of pleasure; yet in so far as it is pleasure we have, whether there be more or less of it, and whether it be of one kind or another, what we have is one definite thing, absolutely indefinable, some one thing that is the same in all the various degrees and in all the various kinds of it that there may be. We may be able to say how it is related to other things: that, for example, it is in the mind, that it causes desire, that we are conscious of it, etc., etc. We can, I say, describe its relations to other things, but define it we can *not*. And if anybody tried to define pleasure for us as being any other natural object; if anybody were to say, for instance, that pleasure *means* the sensation of red, and were to proceed to deduce from that that pleasure is a colour, we should be entitled to laugh at him and to distrust his future statements about pleasure. Well, that would be the same fallacy which I have called the naturalistic fallacy. That "pleased" does not mean "having the sensation of red," or anything else whatever, does not prevent us from understanding what it does mean. It is enough for us to know that "pleased" does mean "having the sensation of pleasure," and though pleasure is absolutely indefinable, though pleasure is pleasure and nothing else whatever, yet we feel no difficulty in saying that we are pleased. The reason is, of course, that when I say "I am pleased," I do *not* mean that "I" am the same thing as "having pleasure." And similarly no difficulty need be found in my saying that "pleasure is good" and yet not meaning that "pleasure" is the same thing as "good," that pleasure *means* good, and that good *means* pleasure. If I were to imagine that when I said "I am pleased," I meant that I was exactly the same thing as "pleased," I should not indeed call that a naturalistic fallacy, although it would be the same fallacy as I have called natu-

ralistic with reference to Ethics. The reason of this is obvious enough. When a man confuses two natural objects with one another, defining the one by the other, if for instance, he confuses himself, who is one natural object, with "pleased" or with "pleasure" which are others, then there is no reason to call the fallacy naturalistic. But if he confuses "good," which is not in the same sense a natural object, with any natural object whatever, then there is a reason for calling that a naturalistic fallacy; its being made with regard to "good" marks it as something quite specific, and this specific mistake deserves a name because it is so common. As for the reasons why good is not to be considered a natural object, they may be reserved for discussion in another place. But, for the present, it is sufficient to notice this: Even if it were a natural object, that would not alter the nature of the fallacy nor diminish its importance one whit. All that I have said about it would remain quite equally true: only the name which I have called it would not be so appropriate as I think it is. And I do not care about the name: what I do care about is the fallacy. It does not matter what we call it, provided we recognise it when we meet with it. It is to be met with in almost every book on Ethics; and yet it is not recognised: and that is why it is necessary to multiply illustrations of it, and convenient to give it a name. It is a very simple fallacy indeed. When we say that an orange is yellow, we do not think our statement binds us to hold that "orange" means nothing else than "yellow," or that nothing can be yellow but an orange. Supposing the orange is also sweet! Does that bind us to say that "sweet" is exactly the same thing as "yellow," that "sweet" must be defined as "yellow"? And supposing it be recognised that "yellow" just means "yellow" and nothing else whatever, does that make it any more difficult to hold that oranges are yellow? Most certainly it does not: on the contrary, it would be absolutely meaningless to say that oranges were yellow, unless yellow did in the end mean just "yellow" and nothing else whatever—unless it was absolutely indefinable. We should not get any very clear notion about things, which are yellow—we should not get very far with our science, if we were bound to hold that everything which was yellow, *meant* exactly the same thing as yellow. We should find we had to hold that an orange was exactly the same thing as a stool, a piece of paper, a lemon, anything you like. We could prove any number of absurdities; but should we be the nearer to the truth? Why, then, should it be different with "good"? Why, if good is good and indefinable, should I be held to deny that pleasure is good? Is there any difficulty in holding both to be true at once? On the contrary, there is no meaning in saying that pleasure is good, unless good is something different from pleasure. It is absolutely useless, so far as Ethics is concerned, to prove, as Mr. Spencer tries to do, that increase of pleasure coincides with increase of life, unless good *means* something different from either life or pleasure. He might just as well try to prove that an orange is yellow by shewing that it always is wrapped up in paper.

13. In fact, if it is not the case that "good" denotes something simple and indefinable, only two alternatives are possible: either it is a complex, a given whole, about the correct analysis of which there may be disagreement; or else it means nothing at all, and there is no such subject as Ethics. In general, however, ethical philosophers have attempted to define good, without recognising what such an attempt must mean. They actually use arguments which involve one or both of the absurdities considered in § 11. We are, therefore, justified in concluding that the attempt to define good is chiefly due to want of clearness as to the possible nature of definition. There are, in fact, only two serious alternatives to be considered, in order to establish the conclusion that "good" does denote a simple and indefinable notion. It might possibly denote a complex, as "horse" does; or it might have no meaning at all. Neither of these possibilities has, however, been clearly conceived and seriously maintained, as such, by those who presume to define good; and both may be dismissed by a simple appeal to facts.

(1) The hypothesis that disagreement about the meaning of good is disagreement with regard to the correct analysis of a given whole, may be most plainly seen to be incorrect by consideration of the fact that, whatever definition be offered, it may be always asked, with significance, of the complex so defined, whether it is itself good. To take, for instance, one of the more plausible, because one of the more complicated, of such proposed definitions, it may easily be thought, at first sight, that to be good may mean to be that which we desire to desire. Thus if we apply this definition to a particular instance and say "When we think that A is good, we are thinking that A is one of the things which we desire to desire," our proposition may seem quite plausible. But, if we carry the investigation further, and ask ourselves "Is it good to desire to desire A?" it is apparent, on a little reflection, that this question is itself as intelligible, as the original question "Is A good?"— that we are, in fact, now asking for exactly the same information about the desire to desire A, for which we formerly asked with regard to A itself. But it is also apparent that the meaning of this second question cannot be correctly analysed into "Is the desire to desire A one of the things which we desire to desire?": we have not before our minds anything so complicated as the question "Do we desire to desire to desire to desire A?" Moreover any one can easily convince himself by inspection that the predicate of this proposition—"good"—is positively different from the notion of "desiring to desire" which enters into its subject: "That we should desire to desire A is good" is *not* merely equivalent to "That A

should be good is good." It may indeed be true that what we desire to desire is always also good; perhaps, even the converse may be true: but it is very doubtful whether this is the case, and the mere fact that we understand very well what is meant by doubting it, shews clearly that we have two different notions before our minds.

(2) And the same consideration is sufficient to dismiss the hypothesis that "good" has no meaning whatsoever. It is very natural to make the mistake of supposing that what is universally true is of such a nature that its negation would be self-contradictory: the importance which has been assigned to analytic propositions in the history of philosophy shews how easy such a mistake is. And thus it is very easy to conclude that what seems to be a universal ethical principle is in fact an identical proposition; that, if, for example, whatever is called "good" seems to be pleasant, the proposition "Pleasure is the good" does not assert a connection between two different notions, but involves only one, that of pleasure, which is easily recognised as a distinct entity. But whoever will attentively consider with himself what is actually before his mind when he asks the question "Is pleasure (or whatever it may be) after all good?" can easily satisfy himself that he is not merely wondering whether pleasure is pleasant. And if he will try this experiment with each suggested definition in succession, he may become expert enough to recognise that in every case he has before his mind a unique object, with regard to the connection of which with any other object, a distinct question may be asked. Every one does in fact understand the question "Is this good?" When he thinks of it, his state of mind is different from what it would be, were he asked "Is this pleasant, or desired, or approved?" It has a distinct meaning for him, even though he may not recognise in what respect it is distinct. Whenever he thinks of "intrinsic value," or "intrinsic worth," or says that a thing "ought to exist," he has before his mind the unique object—the unique property of things—which I mean by "good." Everybody is constantly aware of this notion, although he may never become aware at all that it is different from other notions of which he is also aware. But, for correct ethical reasoning, it is extremely important that he should become aware of this fact; and, as soon as the nature of the problem is clearly understood, there should be little difficulty in advancing so far in analysis. . . .

14. My objections to Naturalism are then, in the first place, that it offers no reason at all, far less any valid reason, for any ethical principle whatever; and in this is already fails to satisfy the requirements of Ethics, as a scientific study. But in the second place I contend that, though it gives a reason for no ethical principle, it is a *cause* of the acceptance of false principles—it deludes the mind into accepting ethical principles, which are false; and in this it is contrary to every aim of Ethics. It is

easy to see that if we start with a definition of right conduct as conduct
conducive to general happiness; then, knowing that right conduct is
universally conduct conducive to the good, we very easily arrive at the
result that the good is general happiness. If, on the other hand, we once
recognise that we must start our Ethics without a definition, we shall be
much more apt to look about us, before we adopt any ethical principle
whatever; and the more we look about us, the less likely are we to adopt
a false one. It may be replied to this: Yes, but we shall look about us
just as much, before we settle on our definition, and are therefore just as
likely to be right. But I will try to shew that this is not the case. If we
start with the conviction that a definition of good can be found, we start
with the conviction that good *can mean* nothing else than some one
property of things; and our only business will then be to discover what
that property is. But if we recognise that, so far as the meaning of good
goes, anything whatever may be good, we start with a much more open
mind. Moreover, apart from the fact that, when we think we have a
definition, we cannot logically defend our ethical principles in any way
whatever, we shall also be much less apt to defend them well, even if
illogically. For we shall start with the conviction that good must mean
so and so, and shall therefore be inclined either to misunderstand our
opponent's arguments or to cut them short with the reply, "This is not
an open question: the very meaning of the word decides it; no one can
think otherwise except through confusion." . . .

86. . . . I [have] tried to shew what "good"—the adjective "good"—
means. This appeared to be the first point to be settled in any treatment
of Ethics, that should aim at being systematic. It is necessary we should
know this, should know what good means, before we can go on to consider what is good—what things or qualities are good. It is necessary we
should know it for two reasons. The first reason is that "good" is the
notion upon which all Ethics depends. We cannot hope to understand
what we mean, when we say that this is good or that is good, until we
understand quite clearly, not only what "this" is or "that" is (which the
natural sciences and philosophy can tell us) but also what is meant by
calling them good, a matter which is reserved for Ethics only. Unless
we are quite clear on this point, our ethical reasoning will be always
apt to be fallacious. We shall think that we are proving that a thing is
"good," when we are really only proving that it is something else; since
unless we know what "good" means, unless we know what is meant by
that notion in itself, as distinct from what is meant by any other notion,
we shall not be able to tell when we are dealing with it and when we
are dealing with something else, which is perhaps like it, but yet not
the same. And the second reason why we should settle first of all this
question "What good means?" is a reason of method. It is this, that we

can never know on what *evidence* an ethical proposition rests, until we know the nature of the notion which makes the proposition ethical. We cannot tell what is possible, by way of proof, in favour of one judgment that "This or that is good," or against another judgment "That this or that is bad," until we have recognised what the nature of such propositions must always be. In fact, it follows from the meaning of good and bad, that such propositions are all of them, in Kant's phrase, "synthetic": they all must rest in the end upon some proposition which must be simply accepted or rejected, which cannot be logically deduced from any other proposition. This result, which follows from our first investigation, may be otherwise expressed by saying that the fundamental principles of Ethics must be self-evident. But I am anxious that this expression should not be misunderstood. The expression "self-evident" means properly that the proposition so called is evident or true, *by itself* alone; that it is not an inference from some proposition other than *itself*. The expression does *not* mean that the proposition is true, because it is evident to you or me or all mankind, because in other words it appears to us to be true. That a proposition appears to be true can never be a valid argument that true it really is. By saying that a proposition is self-evident, we mean emphatically that its appearing so to us, is *not* the reason why it is true: for we mean that it has absolutely no reason. It would not be a self-evident proposition, if we could say of it: I cannot think otherwise and therefore it is true. For then its evidence or proof would not lie in itself, but in something else, namely our conviction of it. That it appears true to us may indeed be the *cause* of our asserting it, or the reason why we think and say that it is true: but a reason in this sense is something utterly different from a logical reason, or reason why something is true. Moreover, it is obviously not a reason of the same thing. The *evidence* of a proposition to us is only a reason for *our holding it* to be true: whereas a logical reason, or reason in the sense in which self-evident propositions have no reason, is a reason why the *proposition itself* must be true, not why we hold it so to be. Again that a proposition is evident to us may not only be the reason why we do think or affirm it, it may even be a *reason* why we ought to think it or affirm it. But a reason, in this sense too, is not a logical reason for the truth of the proposition, though it is a logical reason for the rightness of holding the proposition. In our common language, however, these three meanings of "reason" are constantly confused, whenever we say "I have a reason for thinking that true." But it is absolutely essential, if we are to get clear notions about Ethics or, indeed, about any other, especially any philosophical, study, that we should distinguish them. When, therefore, I talk of Intuitionistic Hedonism, I must not be understood to imply that my denial that "Pleasure is the only good" is *based* on my Intuition of its falsehood.

My Intuition of its falsehood is indeed *my* reason for *holding* and declaring it untrue; it is indeed the only valid reason for so doing. But that is just because there is *no* logical reason for it; because there is no proper evidence or reason of its falsehood except itself alone. It is untrue, because it is untrue, and there is no other reason: but I *declare* it untrue, because its untruth is evident to me, and I hold that that is a sufficient reason for my assertion. We must not therefore look on Intuition, as if it were an alternative to reasoning. Nothing whatever can take the place of *reasons* for the truth of any proposition: intuition can only furnish a reason for *holding* any proposition to be true: this however it must do when any proposition is self-evident, when, in fact, there are no reasons which prove its truth.

6.3

Debate about
Naturalism and Intuitionism

Moore's criticism of definism and defense of intuitionism stimulated much debate about his arguments, as well as about naturalism and intuitionism themselves. This debate eventuated in theories that were neither naturalistic nor intuitionistic. In this section we present readings that will both illustrate this discussion and serve as a basis for considering the positions and arguments involved.

Moore's main weapons against the definists were the open question argument, stated in (1) under §13 of the above selection (see p. 389), and the naturalistic fallacy charge; most of the debate focused on them. In the following selection, Perry's reply to one of Moore's followers, Mary E. Clarke, we can see at least part of what one naturalist's answer to Moore would be. Perry does not mention the open question argument or the naturalistic fallacy, but he is in effect indicating how he would deal with them.

Ralph Barton Perry

. . . Since there is no way of naming [the value-property] [1] except by words whose denotation is highly equivocal, it is hard even to point to it. I have tried in entire good faith to find it. When Miss Clarke tries to

From "Value as Simply Value," Journal of Philosophy, XXVIII, No. 19 (September 10, 1931). Reprinted by permission of the Journal of Philosophy.

---

[1] [Perry is referring to the intuitionist theory that value is a unique, indefinable property.—Eds.]

find it, or discover whether it attaches to this or that, I try with her, in the hope that I can at least discover what it is that she is looking for. And I always end by concluding that when she finds value, as she at times somewhat hesitatingly does, she is finding that this or that moves or attracts her. At any rate, when I feel that I have found a value, it is because, as in the esthetic experience, I have felt a thrill; or because I have felt the stirring of desire or will; or because I have seen a causal relation, direct or indirect to the interest of sentient beings. . . .

Now when I am unable to find for myself what other people allude to, I should perhaps regard myself as having some defective receptivity, in the case of color-blindness. This possibility I admit, and there is nothing more to be done about it, except to console myself with the reflection that I am in good company. But there is another and to me more acceptable possibility, namely, that the thing is not there. In this case I must account for the fact that very respectable and trustworthy people think they find it. The explanation lies, I believe, in the effect of words.

I can not resist the feeling that those who hold the view that "valuable" means just valuable, are the victims of verbalism. They must be supposed to contend that there is a familiar meaning needing only a generally accepted name to be easily recognizable. In that case it should be easy to agree on "value" as its authorized philosophical name. I suspect, however, that the reverse is the case, that it is the name that is in search of a meaning.

My doubts are strengthened by Professor Clarke's explicit appeal to verbal usage. We are told that "in ordinary speech the adjective 'valuable,' in the intrinsic sense, means what ought to be an object of value is an object which ought to be for its own sake." Now I strongly doubt whether the term "valuable" is used at all in ordinary speech in what the author would regard as "the intrinsic" sense. I submit that the only widely current use of the term "valuable" is economic. . . . But this current economic meaning is precisely what Miss Clarke and her fellow-proponents would most emphatically reject. . . .

The persistent impression that there is a meaning of "valuable" attaching uniquely to that word, and incapable of being expressed by any other word or combination of other words, seems to me to betray a philosophical superstition to the effect that where there's a common word there's a common meaning, and where there's a unique word there's a unique meaning. Now those who rely on verbal usage and on common sense should make a special study of them, which is scarcely to be expected, since if they had made such a study they probably would not have relied on them. Even without such a special study it is evident that meanings undergo perpetual change, by degradation, associative saturation, ellipsis, or shifting of context; and it is not possible to tell from the face of a particular verbal statement at what phase of such changes it stands. Meanings also express different degrees of directness. Thus attributive judgments, such as "S is R," may express the belief "S is said to be R"; or, "S has certain characters which are commonly taken to be the sign of R"; or "S is what people call R, whatever that means." In all of these cases the user of the letter "R" may mean nothing by it except the letter "R." It is quite possible, and is no doubt frequently the case, that a word is widely used that has no meaning whatever, being merely a verbal echo, or an obsolete habit.

The verbalism connected with the present use of the term "value" is peculiarly scandalous because, in the generalized sense in which it is now used, it is a new and technical word; a word which has recently acquired vogue as the result of a reorganization of philosophy, in which different fields of inquiry have been consolidated to form a new province. "Value" has been adopted as the flag or emblem of this new province, to indicate a hope of articulating or bringing to light a unifying concept. Under the circumstances it is absurd to appeal to the existing or traditional meaning of the term as though it represented some universal, familiar, and ancestral experience. As for my own use of the term, I can only say that I chose it because while its general associations were relevant its meaning was equivocal. It struck me as a good term to give a meaning *to*, rather than as a term already having a determinate meaning to which it was only necessary to call attention. I was further influenced by the fact that the word could be used as verb, noun, or adjective; as well as by the fact that it could be qualified by "positive" and "negative," when one wished to generalize the relation of polarity.

I can not help suspecting that the dissatisfaction with definitions such as the proposed definition of value in terms of interest, is in part the inevitable nostalgia which is the effect of all definition. It changes meanings, even if it does no more than to elucidate, clarify, or analyze them. Those who are attached by habit to old and undefined meanings miss them. Something is lost, even if it be nothing but the familiar darkness, obscurity, and inarticulateness. If a term is invented to indicate a problem, and if the problem is solved, then the term has lost its problematic meaning, and there is a feeling that *this* which we now have is not what we were *then* talking about.

There are, furthermore, purely verbal associations which the new set of words in which the definition is framed does not and can not possess. In the broad sense no new combination of words can be the "equivalent" of an old word. Assuming "rational animal" to be a definition of man, the effect of substituting the one expression for the other in English literature would produce a surprising and distinctly unpleasant effect. This bathos of definition is peculiarly marked in the case of words highly charged with emotional meanings. Thus, for example, there is no metaphysical definition "God" that can possibly satisfy those who have worshipped God; and this dissatisfaction has nothing to do with the correctness of the definition.[2]

We are here confronted, also, with the whole problem of analysis. The has-been-analyzed is not the same as the to-be-analyzed,—otherwise there would be no point in analysis. This transformative character of analysis does not help us to distinguish the analyzable from the non-analyzable. When "triangle" is analyzed into "plane formed by the intersection of three straight lines," it is no longer *just triangle*. It is to be noted that all subject-matter is "simple" before analysis, in the sense in which a question mark is simple. Knowledge spreads from an initial point, namely, a locus of interrogation. I assume, however, that things are what they appear to be when we get through knowing them, rather than what they appear to be at the moment of attack. I am quite willing to admit that when "good" or "beautiful" is analyzed into object-desired or object-enjoyed, it is no longer *just* beauty and goodness. There is no doubt a something about value which is not precisely the same as object-of-interest, but I am prepared to admit this only provided my critics are willing to admit that the same is true of *all* analysis; and that so far as this line of argument is concerned, value is as analyzable as anything else. If difficulties connected with analysis prove so serious as to compel us to abandon the notion altogether, then the analysis of value will have to go with the rest; but that is another matter, which we are not called upon to decide here. . . .

Moore's arguments and conclusions were also discussed by people who rejected both naturalism and intuitionism. These people agree with Moore that "That which is P is good" is always a significant nonanalytic sentence, but they deny that it follows that "good" stands for an indefinable, nonnatural property. One example is R. M. Hare, who in the following reading, restates Moore's argument in nonintuitionist terms.

---

[2] Similarly, by translating value into terms of interest, and interest into "anticipatory responses which are in accord with the unfulfilled phases of a governing set," Professor Charner M. Perry evidently counts upon the reader's feeling that *value* has somehow been conjured away. There is an effect of absurdity created by the substitution of definitions for the original terms. The same effect can always be produced by substituting the results of scientific or philosophical thought for the terms of familiar discourse and unanalyzed experience. . . .

R. M. Hare

. . . Let us then ask whether "good" behaves in the way that we have noticed for the same reason that "rectangular" does; in other words, whether there are certain characteristics of pictures which are defining characteristics of a good picture, in the same way as "having all its angles 90 degrees and being a rectilinear plane figure" are defining characteristics of a rectangle. Moore thought that he could prove that there were no such defining characteristics for the word "good" as used in morals. His argument has been assailed since he propounded it; and it is certainly true that the formulation of it was at fault. But it seems to me that Moore's argument was not merely plausible; it rests, albeit insecurely, upon a secure foundation; there is indeed something about the way in which, and the purposes for which, we use the word "good" which makes it impossible to hold the sort of position which Moore was attacking, although Moore did not see clearly what this something was. Let us, therefore, try to re-state Moore's argument in a way which makes it clear why "naturalism" is untenable, not only for the moral use of "good" as he thought, but also for many other uses.

Let us suppose for the sake of argument that there are some "defining characteristics" of a good picture. It does not matter of what sort they are; they can be a single characteristic, or a conjunction of characteristics, or a disjunction of alternative characteristics. Let us call the group of these characteristics C. "P is a good picture" will then mean the same as "P is a picture and P is C." For example, let C mean "Having a tendency to arouse in people who are at that time members of the Royal Academy (or any other definitely specified group of people), a definitely recognizable feeling called 'admiration'." The words "definitely specified" and "definitely recognizable" have to be inserted, for otherwise we might find that words in the *definiens* were being used evaluatively, and this would make the definition no longer "naturalistic." Now suppose that we wish to say that the members of the Royal Academy have good taste in pictures. To have good taste in pictures means to have this definitely recognizable feeling of admiration for those pictures, and only those pictures, which are good pictures. If therefore we wish to say that the members of the Royal Academy have good taste in pictures, we have, according to the definition, to say something which means the same as saying that they have this feeling of admiration for pictures which have a tendency to arouse in them this feeling.

Now this is not what we wanted to say. We wanted to say that they

From The Language of Morals *(Oxford: The Clarendon Press, 1952). Reprinted by permission of The Clarendon Press, Oxford.*

admired good pictures; we have succeeded only in saying that they admired pictures which they admired. Thus if we accept the definition we debar ourselves from saying something that we do sometimes want to say. What this something is will become apparent later; for the moment let us say that what we wanted to do was to *commend* the pictures which the members of the Royal Academy admired. Something about our definition prevented our doing this. We could no longer commend the pictures which they admired, we could only say that they admired those pictures which they admired. Thus our definition has prevented us, in one crucial case, from commending something which we want to commend. That is what is wrong with it.

Let us generalize. If "P is a good picture" is held to mean the same as "P is a picture and P is C," then it will become impossible to commend pictures for being C; it will be possible only to say that they are C. It is important to realize that this difficulty has nothing to do with the particular example that I have chosen. It is not because we have chosen the wrong defining characteristics; it is because whatever defining characteristics we choose, this objection arises, that we can no longer commend an object for possessing those characteristics.

. . . it is not true to say that the means used to upset naturalistic definitions of value-terms could be used equally to upset any definition. Value-terms have a special function in language, that of commending; and so they plainly cannot be defined in terms of other words which themselves do not perform this function; for if this is done, we are deprived of a means of performing the function. But with words like "puppy" this does not apply; one may define "puppy" in terms of any other words which will do the same job. Whether two expressions will do the same job is decided by reference to usage. And since what we are trying to do is to give an account of the word "good" as it *is* used—not as it *might* be used if its meaning and usage were changed—this reference is final. It is therefore no answer to the above argument to claim that a "naturalist" might if he pleased define "good" in terms of some characteristics of his choice. Such an arbitrary definition is quite out of place here; the logician is, it is true, at liberty to define his own technical terms as he pleases, provided that he makes it clear how he is going to use them. But "good" in this context is not a technical term used for talking about what the logician is talking about; it itself *is* what he is talking about; it is the object of his study, not the instrument. He is studying the function of the word "good" in language; and so long as he wishes to study this, he must continue to allow the word the function which it has in language, that of commending. If by an arbitrary definition he gives the word a different function from that which it now has, then he is not studying the same thing any longer; he is studying a figment of his own devising.

Naturalism in ethics, like attempts to square the circle and to "justify induction," will constantly recur so long as there are people who have not understood the fallacy involved. It may therefore be useful to give a simple procedure for exposing any new variety of it that may be offered. Let us suppose that someone claims that he can deduce a moral or other evaluative judgment from a set of purely factual or descriptive premises, relying on some definition to the effect that V (a value-word) means the same as C (a conjunction of descriptive predicates). We first have to ask him to be sure that C contains no expression that is covertly evaluative (for example "natural" or "normal" or "satisfying" or "fundamental human needs"). Nearly all so-called "naturalistic definitions" will break down under this test—for to be genuinely naturalistic a definition must contain no expression for whose applicability there is not a definite criterion which does not involve the making of a value-judgment. If the definition satisfies this test, we have next to ask whether its advocate ever wishes to commend anything for being C. If he says that he does, we have only to point out to him that his definition makes this impossible, for the reasons given. And clearly he cannot say that he never wishes to commend anything for being C; for to commend things for being C is the whole object of his theory.

Another example of a nonintuitionist criticism of naturalism is the following passage by Carl Wellman, who is much influenced by Hare and similar writers. He interprets the naturalistic fallacy charge as an accusation that the naturalist reduces the ethical to the nonethical. Wellman states that the charge is correct; the naturalists are making a very fundamental mistake. He adds that the intuitionists are making the same mistake because they also think that such judgments as "X is good" and "Y is right" are descriptive, in the sense that they simply say that X and Y have a certain property (in this case, an indefinable nonnatural one).

Carl Wellman

. . . At last we are prepared to return to our consideration of ethical naturalism. This view stands charged with committing a very serious mistake, the naturalistic fallacy. The essence of this error consists in re-

From The Language of Ethics (Cambridge, Mass.: Harvard University Press, 1961). Reprinted by permission of the author and publisher. Copyright 1961 by the President and Fellows of Harvard College.

ducing the ethical to the nonethical. I believe that this charge is justified. Ethical naturalism holds that ethical words stand for empirical characteristics. If this is so, ethical sentences turn out to be simply one more form of empirical description. The statement that x is good, for example, asserts that x has a certain empirical characteristic; it describes the nature of the object x. Fine. Any inquisitive mind will be delighted to have this information about the nature of the object. But this knowledge of the nature of the object leaves open the question of whether the object is to be chosen. It is this practical problem of whether to choose the object which is the primary ethical problem. It appears that on the naturalistic interpretation of ethical sentences *no* ethical statement ever constitutes an answer to this central ethical question. To my mind this is an intolerable position and should be rejected.

. . . Ethical judgments are not descriptions of objects and actions. It is unlikely that our language would be unable to formulate such an important range of human judgments. Moreover, there are many sentences which seem on the face of it to express ethical judgments. Very probably, then, there are some sentences which put our ethical judgments into words. It would follow that, although these ethical sentences can claim objective validity, their meaning is not descriptive. This, I take it, is the real point of the naturalistic fallacy. To hold that ethical sentences are a special kind of description is to deny their ethical status. The best comment was made by Moore himself: "Immensely the commonest type of truth, then, is the one which asserts a relation between two existing things. Ethical truths are immediately felt not to conform to this type, and the naturalistic fallacy arises from the attempt to make out that, in some roundabout way, they do conform to it."[1] This is an excellent analysis of what causes the intuitionist to make the very same mistake with which he charges the naturalist. He is led to believe that, either because of their meaningfulness or their objective validity, ethical sentences must be some peculiar form of description. I have tried to argue that this is not so. It is basically mistaken to hold that the meaning of ethical sentences is descriptive.

Finally, we must consider two closely related arguments that are often used against naturalism, intuitionism, or both. One was stated by Hume as another part of his argument for emotivism.

---

[1] G. E. Moore, *Principia Ethica*, p. 124.

David Hume

If morality had naturally no influence on human passions and actions, it were in vain to take such pains to inculcate it; and nothing would be more fruitless than that multitude of rules and precepts with which all moralists abound. Philosophy is commonly divided into *speculative* and *practical;* and as morality is always comprehended under the latter division, it is supposed to influence our passions and actions, and to go beyond the calm and indolent judgments of the understanding. And this is confirmed by common experience, which informs us that men are often governed by their duties, and are deterred from some actions by the opinion of injustice, and impelled to others by that of obligation.

Since morals, therefore, have an influence on the actions and affections, it follows that they cannot be derived from reason; and that because reason alone, as we have already proved, can never have any such influence. Morals excite passions, and produce or prevent actions. Reason of itself is utterly impotent in this particular. The rules of morality, therefore, are not conclusions of our reason.

No one, I believe, will deny the justness of this inference; nor is there any other means of evading it, than by denying that principle on which it is founded. As long as it is allowed, that reason has no influence on our passions and actions, it is in vain to pretend that morality is discovered only by a deduction of reason. An active principle can never be founded on an inactive; and if reason be inactive in itself, it must remain so in all its shapes and appearances, whether it exerts itself in natural or moral subjects, whether it considers the powers of external bodies, or the actions of rational beings.

From Treatise of Human Nature *(London, 1739).*

The second argument in question has been stated by P. H. Nowell-Smith, among others. He uses it here only against intuitionism, but it would obviously apply to naturalism as well. In a way, the point that he, Wellman, and others make is that for the intuitionist, an Ought is still a kind of Is because all it does is ascribe a simple nonnatural property to something—or state a simple nonnatural fact about it.

P. H. Nowell-Smith

Moral knowledge is represented by intuitionists as knowledge that a certain object has a certain characteristic. To learn a moral truth is like learning that Henry VIII had six wives or that α Centauri is 4½ light years away. The difference between moral characteristics and those that we learn about in science and in history is marked by calling them non-natural. But moral judgements are treated as descriptions of features of the universe, and the fact that these features are so peculiar as to merit the epithet "non-natural" in no way affects the status of moral judgements as descriptions. . . .

The intuitionist's answer to the question "why should I be moral?"—unless, like Prichard, he rejects it as a senseless question—is that, if you reflect carefully, you will notice that a certain act has two characteristics, (a) that of being obligatory and (b) that of producing a maximum of good or of being a fulfilment of a promise or the payment of a debt, etc. . . .

Moreover, if you have noticed these characteristics you will feel a special moral emotion of obligation; and you will not feel this special emotion if you have not noticed the characteristics.

But suppose all this has taken place. I have noticed the right-making characteristic and the rightness; and I feel the emotion of obligation. Does it follow that I ought to do the action towards which I feel the emotion? If Hume's argument is valid at all, is it not equally valid against this deduction? It cannot be evaded by merely calling the characteristic and the emotion "non-natural"; copious use of this epithet serves only to disguise Hume's gap, not to bridge it.

. . . a world of non-natural characteristics is revealed to us by a third faculty called "*intuition.*" . . . And from statements to the effect that these exist no conclusions follow about what I *ought to do.* A new world is revealed for our inspection; it contains such and such objects, phenomena, and characteristics; it is mapped and described in elaborate detail. No doubt it is all very interesting. If I happen to have a thirst for knowledge, I shall read on to satisfy my curiosity, much as I should read about new discoveries in astronomy or geography. Learning about "values" or "duties" might well be as exciting as learning about spiral nebulae or waterspouts. But what if I am not interested? Why should I *do* anything

From Ethics   (*London: Penguin Books Ltd.,* © *P. H. Nowell-Smith, 1954*). *Reprinted by permission of the author and publisher.*

about these newly-revealed objects? Some things, I have now learnt, are
right and others wrong; but why should I do what is right and eschew
what is wrong? . . .

　　Of course the question "Why should I do what I see to be right?"
is . . . an absurd one. . . . [But this question,] which [is] absurd when
words are used in the ordinary way, would not be absurd if moral words
were used in the way that intuitionists suppose. . . . But if "X is right"
and "X is obligatory" are construed as statements to the effect that X has
the non-natural characteristic of rightness or obligatoriness, which we
just "see" to be present, it would seem that we can no more deduce "I
ought to do X" from these premises than we would deduce it from "X is
pleasant" or "X is in accordance with God's will." A gap of which ordinary
language knows nothing has been created between "X is obligatory on
me" and "I ought to do it." . . .

6.4

Noncognitive
or Nondescriptivist Theories

Intuitionism was also criticized on epistemological grounds. People questioned not only its assumption that "good" and "right" stand for properties, but also its notions of indefinability, nonnaturalness, a priori concepts, self-evident truths, and the like. The upshot of all this discussion was that most moral philosophers rejected both naturalism and intuitionism. Some, especially in the 1930s, turned to "the emotive theory of ethics" as a third alternative. The emotive theory was not new then, having been held in the eighteenth century by Hutcheson, Hume, and Adam Smith, and in the early twentieth century by Santayana and Russell, but it gained a popularity it had never had before. Its leading exponent was Charles L. Stevenson, but we have space for only one example of twentieth-century emotivism here, and have selected the following reading from A. J. Ayer because he took a somewhat simpler, if more extreme, position. This reading should make clear what emotivism involves. Notice that Ayer uses Moore's open question argument against naturalism and definism.

AN EMOTIVE THEORY OF ETHICS

A. J. Ayer

. . . it is our business to give an account of "judgements of value" which is both satisfactory in itself and consistent with our general empiricist principles. We shall set ourselves to show that in so far as statements of value are significant, they are ordinary "scientific" statements; and that in so far as they are not scientific, they are not in the literal sense significant, but are simply expressions of emotion which can be neither true nor false. In maintaining this view, we may confine ourselves for the present to the case of ethical statements. . . . What we are interested in is the possibility of reducing the whole sphere of ethical terms to non-ethical terms. We are enquiring whether statements of ethical value can be translated into statements of empirical fact.

That they can be so translated is the contention of those ethical philosophers who are commonly called subjectivists, and of those who are known as utilitarians. For the utilitarian defines the rightness of actions, and the goodness of ends, in terms of the pleasure, or happiness, or satisfaction, to which they give rise; the subjectivist, in terms of the feelings of approval which a certain person, or group of people, has towards them. Each of these types of definition makes moral judgements into a sub-class of psychological or sociological judgements; and for this reason they are very attractive to us. For, if either was correct, it would follow that ethical assertions were not generically different from the factual assertions which are ordinarily contrasted with them; and the account which we have already given of empirical hypotheses would apply to them also.

Nevertheless we shall not adopt either a subjectivist or a utilitarian analysis of ethical terms. We reject the subjectivist view that to call an action right, or a thing good, is to say that it is generally approved of, because it is not self-contradictory to assert that some actions which are generally approved of are not right, or that some things which are generally approved of are not good. And we reject the alternative subjectivist view that a man who asserts that a certain action is right, or that a certain thing is good, is saying that he himself approves of it, on the ground that a man who confessed that he sometimes approved of what was bad or wrong would not be contradicting himself. And a similar argument is fatal to utilitarianism. We cannot agree that to call an action right is to say that of all the actions possible in the circumstances it would cause,

From Language, Truth and Logic (*London: Victor Gollancz Ltd, 1936; New York: Dover Publications, Inc., 1950). Reprinted by permission of the author and the publishers.*

or be likely to cause, the greatest happiness, or the greatest balance of pleasure over pain, or the greatest balance of satisfied over unsatisfied desire, because we find that it is not self-contradictory to say that it is sometimes wrong to perform the action which would actually or probably cause the greatest happiness, or the greatest balance of pleasure over pain, or of satisfied over unsatisfied desire. And since it is not self-contradictory to say that some pleasant things are not good, or that some bad things are desired, it cannot be the case that the sentence "x is good" is equivalent to "x is pleasant," or to "x is desired." And to every other variant of utilitarianism with which I am acquainted the same objection can be made. And therefore we should, I think, conclude that the validity of ethical judgements is not determined by the felicific tendencies of actions, any more than by the nature of people's feelings; but that it must be regarded as "absolute" or "intrinsic," and not empirically calculable.

If we say this, we are not, of course, denying that it is possible to invent a language in which all ethical symbols are definable in non-ethical terms, or even that it is desirable to invent such a language and adopt it in place of our own; what we are denying is that the suggested reduction of ethical to non-ethical statements is consistent with the conventions of our actual language. That is, we reject utilitarianism and subjectivism, not as proposals to replace our existing ethical notions by new ones, but as analyses of our existing ethical notions. Our contention is simply that, in our language, sentences which contain normative ethical symbols are not equivalent to sentences which express psychological propositions, or indeed empirical propositions of any kind. . . .

In admitting that normative ethical concepts are irreducible to empirical concepts, we seem to be leaving the way clear for the "absolutist" view of ethics—that is, the view that statements of value are not controlled by observation, as ordinary empirical propositions are, but only by a mysterious "intellectual intuition." A feature of this theory, which is seldom recognized by its advocates, is that it makes statements of value unverifiable. For it is notorious that what seems intuitively certain to one person may seem doubtful, or even false, to another. So that unless it is possible to provide some criterion by which one may decide between conflicting intuitions, a mere appeal to intuition is worthless as a test of a proposition's validity. But in the case of moral judgements, no such criterion can be given. Some moralists claim to settle the matter by saying that they "know" that their own moral judgements are correct. But such an assertion is of purely psychological interest, and has not the slightest tendency to prove the validity of any moral judgement. For dissentient moralists may equally well "know" that their ethical views are correct. And, as far as subjective certainty goes, there will be nothing to choose between them. When such differences of opinion arise in connection with an ordinary empirical proposition, one may attempt to resolve them by referring to, or actually carrying out, some relevant empirical test. But with regard to ethical statements, there is, on the "absolutist" or "intuitionist" theory, no relevant empirical test. We are therefore justified in saying that on this theory ethical statements are held to be unverifiable. They are, of course, also held to be genuine synthetic propositions.

Considering the use which we have made of the principle that a synthetic proposition is significant only if it is empirically verifiable, it is clear that the acceptance of an "absolutist" theory of ethics would undermine the whole of our main argument. And as we have already rejected the "naturalistic" theories which are commonly supposed to provide the only alternative to "absolutism" in ethics, we seem to have reached a difficult position. We shall meet the difficulty by showing that the correct treatment of ethical statements is afforded by a third theory, which is wholly compatible with our radical empiricism.

We begin by admitting that the fundamental ethical concepts are unanalysable, inasmuch as there is no criterion by which one can test the validity of the judgements in which they occur. So far we are in agreement with the absolutists. But, unlike the absolutists, we are able to give an explanation of this fact about ethical concepts. We say that the reason why they are unanalysable is that they are mere pseudo-concepts. The presence of an ethical symbol in a proposition adds nothing to its factual content. Thus if I say to someone, "You acted wrongly in stealing that money," I am not stating anything more than if I had simply said, "You stole that money." In adding that this action is wrong I am not making any further statement about it. I am simply evincing my moral disapproval of it. It is as if I had said, "You stole that money," in a peculiar tone of horror, or written it with the addition of some special exclamation marks. The tone, or the exclamation marks, adds nothing to the literal meaning of the sentence. It merely serves to show that the expression of it is attended by certain feelings in the speaker.

If now I generalise my previous statement and say, "Stealing money is wrong," I produce a sentence which has no factual meaning—that is, expresses no proposition which can be either true or false. It is as if I had written "Stealing money!!"—where the shape and thickness of the exclamation marks show, by a suitable convention, that a special sort of moral disapproval is the feeling which is being expressed. It is clear that there is nothing said here which can be true or false. Another man may disagree with me about the wrongness of stealing, in the sense that he may not have the same feelings about stealing as I have, and he may quarrel with me on account of my moral sentiments. But he cannot, strictly speaking, contradict me. For in saying that a certain type of action is right or wrong,

I am not making any factual statement, not even a statement about my own state of mind. I am merely expressing certain moral sentiments. And the man who is ostensibly contradicting me is merely expressing his moral sentiments. So that there is plainly no sense in asking which of us is in the right. For neither of us is asserting a genuine proposition.

What we have just been saying about the symbol "wrong" applies to all normative ethical symbols. Sometimes they occur in sentences which record ordinary empirical facts besides expressing ethical feeling about those facts: sometimes they occur in sentences which simply express ethical feeling about a certain type of action, or situation, without making any statement of fact. But in every case in which one would commonly be said to be making an ethical judgement, the function of the relevant ethical word is purely "emotive." It is used to express feeling about certain objects, but not to make any assertion about them.

It is worth mentioning that ethical terms do not serve only to express feeling. They are calculated also to arouse feeling, and so to stimulate action. Indeed some of them are used in such a way as to give the sentences in which they occur the effect of commands. Thus the sentence "It is your duty to tell the truth" may be regarded both as the expression of a certain sort of ethical feeling about truthfulness and as the expression of the command "Tell the truth." The sentence "You ought to tell the truth" also involves the command "Tell the truth," but here the tone of the command is less emphatic. In the sentence "It is good to tell the truth" the command has become little more than a suggestion. And thus the "meaning" of the word "good," in its ethical usage, is differentiated from that of the word "duty" or the word "ought." In fact we may define the meaning of the various ethical words in terms both of the different feelings they are ordinarily taken to express, and also the different responses which they are calculated to provoke.

We can now see why it is impossible to find a criterion for determining the validity of ethical judgements. It is not because they have an "absolute" validity which is mysteriously independent of ordinary sense-experience, but because they have no objective validity whatsoever. If a sentence makes no statement at all, there is obviously no sense in asking whether what it says is true or false. And we have seen that sentences which simply express moral judgements do not say anything. They are pure expressions of feeling and as such do not come under the category of truth and falsehood. They are unverifiable for the same reason as a cry of pain or a word of command is unverifiable—because they do not express genuine propositions.

Thus, although our theory of ethics might fairly be said to be radically subjectivist, it differs in a very important respect from the orthodox subjectivist theory. For the orthodox subjectivist does not deny, as we do, that the sentences of a moralizer express genuine propositions. All he denies is that they express propositions of a unique non-empirical character. His own view is that they express propositions about the speaker's feelings. If this were so, ethical judgements clearly would be capable of being true or false. They would be true if the speaker had the relevant feelings, and false if he had not. And this is a matter which is, in principle, empirically verifiable. Furthermore they could be significantly contradicted. For if I say, "Tolerance is a virtue," and someone answers, "You don't approve of it," he would, on the ordinary subjectivist theory, be contradicting me. On our theory, he would not be contradicting me, because, in saying that tolerance was a virtue, I should not be making any statement about my own feelings or about anything else. I should simply be evincing my feelings, which is not at all the same thing as saying that I have them.

The distinction between the expression of feeling and the assertion of feeling is complicated by the fact that the assertion that one has a certain feeling often accompanies the expression of that feeling, and is then, indeed, a factor in the expression of that feeling. Thus I may simultaneously express boredom and say that I am bored, and in that case my utterance of the word, "I am bored," is one of the circumstances which make it true to say that I am expressing or evincing boredom. But I can express boredom without actually saying that I am bored. I can express it by my tone and gestures, while making a statement about something wholly unconnected with it, or by an ejaculation, or without uttering any words at all. So that even if the assertion that one has a certain feeling always involves the expression of that feeling, the expression of a feeling assuredly does not always involve the assertion that one has it. And this is the important point to grasp in considering the distinction between our theory and the ordinary subjectivist theory. For whereas the subjectivist holds that ethical statements actually assert the existence of certain feelings, we hold that ethical statements are expressions and excitants of feeling which do not necessarily involve any assertions.

We have already remarked that the main objection to the ordinary subjectivist theory is that the validity of ethical judgements is not determined by the nature of their author's feelings. And this is an objection which our theory escapes. For it does not imply that the existence of any feelings is a necessary and sufficient condition of the validity of an ethical judgement. It implies, on the contrary, that ethical judgements have no validity.

There is, however, a celebrated argument against subjectivist theories which our theory does not escape. It has been pointed out by Moore that if ethical statements were simply statements about the speaker's feelings, it would be impossible to argue about questions of value.[1] To take a typical example: if a man said that thrift was a virtue, and another replied that it was a vice, they would not, on this theory, be disputing with one another. One would be saying that he approved of thrift, and the other that *he* didn't; and there is no reason why both these statements should not be true. Now Moore held it to be obvious that we do dispute about questions of value, and accordingly concluded that the particular form of subjectivism which he was discussing was false.

It is plain that the conclusion that it is impossible to dispute about questions of value follows from our theory also. For as we hold that such sentences as "Thrift is a virtue" and "Thrift is a vice" do not express propositions at all, we clearly cannot hold that they express incompatible propositions. We must therefore admit that if Moore's argument really refutes the ordinary subjectivist theory, it also refutes ours. But, in fact, we deny that it does refute even the ordinary subjectivist theory. For we hold that one really never does dispute about questions of value.

This may seem, at first sight, to be a very paradoxical assertion. For we certainly do engage in disputes which are ordinarily regarded as disputes about questions of value. But, in all such cases, we find, if we consider the matter closely, that the dispute is not really about a question of value, but about a question of fact. When someone disagrees with us about the moral value of a certain action or type of action, we do admittedly resort to argument in order to win him over to our way of thinking. But we do not attempt to show by our arguments that he has the "wrong" ethical feeling towards a situation whose nature he has correctly apprehended. What we attempt to show is that he is mistaken about the facts of the case. We argue that he has misconceived the agent's motive: or that he has misjudged the effects of the action, or its probable effects in view of the agent's knowledge; or that he has failed to take into account the special circumstances in which the agent was placed. Or else we employ more general arguments about the effects which actions of a certain type tend to produce, or the qualities which are usually manifested in their performance. We do this in the hope that we have only to get our opponent to agree with us about the nature of the empirical facts for him to adopt the same moral attitude towards them as we do. And as the people with whom we argue have generally received the same moral education as ourselves, and live in the same social order, our expectation is usually justified. But if our opponent happens to have undergone a different process of moral "conditioning" from ourselves, so that, even when he acknowledges all the facts, he still disagrees with us about the moral value of the actions under discussion, then we abandon the at-

---

[1] Cf. *Philosophical Studies*, "The Nature of Moral Philosophy."

tempt to convince him by argument. We say that it is impossible to argue with him because he has a distorted or undeveloped moral sense; which signifies merely that he employs a different set of values from our own. We feel that our own system of values is superior, and therefore speak in such derogatory terms of his. But we cannot bring forward any arguments to show that our system is superior. For our judgement that it is so is itself a judgement of value, and accordingly outside the scope of argument. It is because argument fails us when we come to deal with pure questions of value, as distinct from questions of fact, that we finally resort to mere abuse.

In short, we find that argument is possible on moral questions only if some system of values is presupposed. If our opponent concurs with us in expressing moral disapproval of all actions of a given type t, then we may get him to condemn a particular action A, by bringing forward arguments to show that A is of type t. For the question whether A does or does not belong to that type is a plain question of fact. Given that a man has certain moral principles, we argue that he must, in order to be consistent, react morally to certain things in a certain way. What we do not and cannot argue about is the validity of these moral principles. We merely praise or condemn them in the light of our own feelings.

If anyone doubts the accuracy of this account of moral disputes, let him try to construct even an imaginary argument on a question of value which does not reduce itself to an argument about a question of logic or about an empirical matter of fact. I am confident that he will not succeed in producing a single example. And if that is the case, he must allow that its involving the impossibility of purely ethical arguments is not, as Moore thought, a ground of objection to our theory, but rather a point in favour of it.

Emotivism is one kind of noncognitivism or antidescriptivism. All such theories hold that ethical judgments are not, or at least not primarily, statements in which a property, definable or indefinable, natural or nonnatural, is ascribed to an object—their job is fundamentally a very different one. Such a theory was suggested in the last paragraph of the Nietzsche selection in Chapter 3. Another theory of this sort is that of existentialists like Sartre, Camus, or Olafson. Existentialism is somewhat different from emotivism. It holds ethical judgments to be not so much expressions of one's emotions, sentiments, or attitudes as expressions of one's will, choice, or decision. We could quote Sartre here, but a somewhat similar position has been formulated much more clearly by R. M. Hare. Hare rejects naturalism and intuitionism (and all kinds of "descriptivism") on grounds such as those given in Section 6.3; he also rejects emotivism on the grounds that it neglects the principle of universalizability and, in general, provides too little place for reasoning in ethics. His view is sometimes called prescriptivism. In the following statement of it Hare explains his views about what moral reasoning and morality are, about why we need moral rules, and about moral education. In passing, he also restates his argument against the descriptivists.

WHAT MORALITY IS

R. M. Hare

. . . moral reasoning has to involve the will (which is an old-fashioned way of saying that moral judgements, or the most important and typical part of them, are prescriptive; and that this fact places a restriction on the kinds of reasoning that could possibly have a moral conclusion: it has to be the kind of reasoning in which and by which we come to prescribe something). I want now to clear away a common misconception about the view which I have just adumbrated. In what follows I am certainly not going to say that *factual statements about* what people will or want or prescribe can supply the missing ingredient in our moral reasoning, which will enable us to reach moral conclusions by a form of argument revealed by philosophers. To say this would be to invite obvious objections. We should still be trying to get moral conclusions from factual premises, which is forbidden by the third premiss which I accepted—namely, from factual premises about what people want, etc. It would also incur the charge of subjectivism; we should be deriving moral conclusions from the fact that somebody had a certain subjective attitude; and against such a procedure there are well-known objections which I shall not rehearse. Not that my own view is a form of objectivism either; in so far as the terms 'objectivism' and 'subjectivism' still have a use in moral philosophy, they refer to two equally mistaken views, which, indeed, share a common defect—namely the assimilation of moral judgements to purely descriptive, factual statements. If moral judgements were purely factual or descriptive, it would be possible to ask whether the facts they stated were subjective facts about the speaker, or objective facts about whatever he was describing. But if they are not purely factual—if there is an element in their meaning which is not descriptive—it makes no sense to ask, of this element, whether it conveys something objective or subjective. What it conveys is something that could not be either objective or subjective.

There is, however, an even more important objection to the view that moral reasoning is founded upon statements of fact about what people will or want or prescribe. One of the most essential features of moral reasoning is that, in the course of it, and because of it, our desires, or what we will, can *change;* facts about a man's desires cannot, therefore, be used as a fixed datum from which he reasons to a moral conclusion. However, it is easy to confuse this mistaken proposal with that which I shall be making, and so I would ask you to be attentive to the difference. We find ourselves, and we find other people, with certain desires; this is where we start. So far there is no difference between my view and the mistaken, subjectivist view I have just mentioned. These desires, if expressed, would be expressed in the form not of statements (this is the first difference), but of prescriptions—of *singular* prescriptions of the form 'Let me do *x*' or 'Let me have *y* done to me'. But (and this is the second difference) we do not *reason from* these desires or these prescriptions; we *operate upon* them by subjecting them to a certain requirement: the requirement that what we desire or prescribe for ourselves, we have to desire or prescribe for anyone else in like situations. Our singular prescriptions have to be, as it has been put, 'universalised'. When faced with this requirement—a requirement laid upon us by the nature or meaning of the moral concepts—we shall abandon some of our desires. They will not go through this sieve. By this I do not mean that we shall necessarily abandon them *qua* desires—we may still go on *wanting* to have the only remaining drink of water in this part of the desert; but we shall not be able to think that we *ought* to take it (we shall not be able to accept this implicitly *universal* prescription for *anyone* in our position) because we cannot desire or prescribe that anyone else should take it at the cost of ourselves going thirsty. The *appetites* may remain unchanged by the exercise of reason; but if we are, in Kantian terms, seeking to will something as a universal law, or, as Aristotle put it, willing and acting in accordance with a principle (*kata logon tâs orexeis poioumenoi kai prâttontes*),[1] we shall subordinate these appetites to the rational will. And if we are reasoning morally—if we are seeking an answer to the question 'What *ought* I to do?'—that is a discipline to which we have to submit. It is a discipline laid upon us, analytically, by the meaning of the word 'ought', which is to be discovered by a purely conceptual enquiry. This much philosophy can contribute.

I have said that when faced with the requirement to universalise, we shall abandon some of our desires, or subordinate them to the rational will. Shall we thus, inevitably, be led, as Kant seems to have thought, to a single unique system of moral principles? I do not think so; what I

---

[1] *Eth. Nic.* 1095 a10.

think will be achieved is something more modest. In matters in which no conflicts of interest arise between people, I can see this method leading to very different sets of principles. In matters where interests do conflict, which form the greater part of the moral problems that most trouble us, I think that all but a very few people, if any at all, will be led to moral principles which resemble, with relatively minor variations, those which are commonly accepted in most societies. The reason for this is that, in order to diverge from this norm, in matters in which conflicts of interest arise, one would have to be not only a person with very extraordinary desires, but one who was prepared to stick to these desires at the cost of the abnegation of desires which for nearly everybody are among their strongest. An example would be a person who has the most intense desire to torture people for his own enjoyment, and is not prepared to subordinate this desire to any others; he is prepared to accept and indeed welcome a principle which allows him to do this, even if it also allows other people, correspondingly, to torture him for *their* enjoyment in similar circumstances, were such circumstances to occur. And remember that the circumstances would have to be similar in this respect also, that he would have as strong a desire not to be tortured as his victim now has. For this reason an ordinary masochist would not do as an example of the sort of person we are looking for.

The practical value of the method of reasoning I have sketched is enhanced if such people are, as I think they are, extremely rare; but it does not rest entirely on such a supposition; for it may, I think, be at least assumed that in a *great many* of the moral problems which trouble us, *most* people will be brought by this method, if once they understand the moral concepts well enough to grasp it, to agree with one another in their universalised prescriptions or desires or wills; and we shall then have a basis for moral agreement, and for these people (that is to say nearly all of us) the moral problems will have been solved.

I could, if I had time, illustrate the practical utility of the method I have outlined by applying it to some particular moral problem that vexes us. I have done this elsewhere; but in what remains of this lecture I am going to ask a different sort of practical question, on which also these theoretical remarks have a bearing. If the nature of morality is as I have described it, how does that affect its future? Indeed, has it a future? Nobody who looks about him and listens and reads a little can fail to be struck by the prevalence, nowadays, of an attitude to which I have already referred, and which I am going to call 'amoralism'. This attitude is, as I said, not confined to intellectuals, but permeates our society. Or perhaps, when I say that amoralism permeates our society, I am taking things too much at their face value. Perhaps what permeates our society is not strictly speaking amoralism. It is something more complicated. Amoralism is a refusal to make moral judgements or ask moral questions. But what, I think, permeates our society is rather a pose of amoralism which can be assumed only by those who either misconceive the nature of morality, or do not think very clearly, or do not get too deeply involved in life. Scratch an amoralist of this spurious sort, or on the other hand get him to think clearly about some matter which concerns him closely, and he will start to moralise, though he may not call it that. The real amoralist, like the man who is really prepared to universalise his desire to torture people for his own enjoyment, is such a rarity that he need not claim much of the attention of people whose concern for the future of morality is a practical one.

What makes people into amoralists of this spurious sort? I think that the most important factor is a misunderstanding of what morality is. I have given my own account of what it is; but what the 'amoralist' is rejecting is not the sort of thing that I have been describing. That is why I say that he misconceives the nature of morality. There are a lot of rules which have come down to us which we do indeed, in a sense, call moral rules or principles, and which say that we ought, or (more commonly) ought not, to do this or that. These rules, which are what the amoralist means by morality, are of a highly general sort; they characterise the kinds of action which we ought to do or abstain from in very simple ways, without exceptions or qualifications. Those who admire these principles, and insist that we should have them, often seem to make it a requirement that to count as a moral principle a principle should not be merely universal in the logical sense (for of course even a very complicated and specific principle could be universal in that sense, provided that it made no essential reference to individuals), but should, to put it crudely, not be above twelve words or so long. Admittedly, even some of the prohibitions of the Decalogue are longer than this; but not the ones that are always being quoted.

I am not against these simple principles as guides; indeed, it is very important to have them if we are not going to succumb to all kinds of temptations and special pleadings; but all the same I have some sympathy with the 'amoralist'. He looks at the complexities of the world as we actually find it, and at the changes that are constantly occurring in our environment—changes often undreamt of by those who first formulated these simple rules—and it becomes only too obvious to him that to observe these rules always would lead us to do things such that, when we reflect upon them in the light of particular cases which either do or could occur, we cannot possibly approve of them. There thus arises a demand for the justification of these general rules—a demand which their advocates are not able to meet. Moral philosophers have throughout the centuries been trying to satisfy it, and nearly everyone thinks that they have failed. So inevitably the 'amoralist' asks, 'Why have moral rules at all?'

It is in the context of moral education that the problem is most acute. We constantly hear parents complaining of the amoralism of their children. This is nothing new; it has been going on at least since Socrates' day. But perhaps the problem makes itself felt most acutely at times like the present, when education, and therefore sophistication, is relatively widespread. The parents—let us face it—are on the losing side. They have themselves acquired (who knows how?) these moral rules, and they pay at least lip-service to them. But when it comes to justifying them they are at a loss. They try to pass on to their children the habit of obedience to these rules; but as soon as their children reach the age at which they begin to think morally (though probably they do not call it 'morally') for themselves, they start questioning the rules, and a certain rising percentage of them, finding no justification which convinces them, will not merely reject particular items from among them, but throw over the whole enterprise of 'morality' (as they call it) altogether. And there is nothing much the parents can do about this. For it is inherent in the parent-child relation that both parties to it are growing steadily older, and the balance of power is thus inexorably shifting. In this argument, the children are certainly going to have the last word. The only weapon the parent has is moral education; and this he is quite unable to wield, because he does not know what morality is, and therefore has no idea what he is trying to inculcate.

I have often heard moral philosophers reproached for doing nothing to remedy this situation; and the reproach is justified. So let us consider two different ways in which as moral philosophers we might try to help. The first way is that which has been advocated, at any rate implicitly, by the kind of moral philosophers whom I am calling descriptivists, who have always throughout the history of the subject been in the majority, and are still prevalent in all the main philosophical schools. The second is that which I myself think more helpful.

What the descriptivist thinks is needed is a way of proving to the young—or at least of getting them to agree—that the things that have been thought right and wrong up to now are, in fact, right and wrong. Once the young have accepted this, they will behave as they should. The two most popular kinds of descriptivism have been the kinds that are conveniently labelled intuitionism and naturalism—though philosophers are so sophisticated nowadays that it would be hard to tie either of these '-ism'-labels to any well-trained modern philosopher with assurance. Both kinds of descriptivism treat moral judgements as statements of fact differing, as regards their factuality, not at all from any other statements of fact. I am, I know, speaking now in a most unprofessionally and indeed unprofessorially crude way. Their purpose is to enable us to say to those who are in moral perplexity, and also to those who doubt or reject the standard moral rules, that these rules have a status like, for example, the fact that ice is lighter than water or even the fact that seven and five make twelve. We can, they think, ascertain the truth of moral statements without doing anything beyond making ourselves conversant with the meanings of the moral words and then using our faculties. The intuitionist thinks that we can ascertain these moral facts directly by the exercise of a special faculty called moral intuition. The naturalist thinks that we can ascertain them indirectly; once we understand properly the meanings of the moral words, we shall see that moral judgements are either equivalent to, or at least entailed by, certain statements of empirical fact; and the truth of these latter we can ascertain in the ordinary way. I have, as I said, put these positions extremely crudely, and I am sure that in this crude form nobody in my audience is going to admit that he holds either of them; but I have not myself found the refinements upon them which have been elaborated any more helpful than the crude versions—only more elusive. So I shall speak about the crude versions, in the assurance that what I say about them will apply, given a few more twists, to their more subtle modern developments.

I am not going to rehearse the well-known arguments against intuitionism and naturalism at the theoretical level; I have done it before, and others have done it better, and I have nothing to add. What I am going to do is to show that, even if intuitionism or naturalism or other forms of descriptivism were theoretically unimpeachable, they would still utterly fail to produce the practical results which are expected of them. We may admit for the sake of argument that there is a sense of moral judgements in which we can ascertain their truth by exercising a faculty for which 'moral intuition' might be a possible name; or we may admit that there is a sense of moral judgements in which they really do follow analytically from certain statements of empirical fact. But if this is the sense of moral judgements that we are going to teach the young, we shall be having no effect upon their conduct.

Let us suppose that we read in the newspaper that, as happens from time to time, some young men have, just for kicks, unscrewed a section of railway line in the middle of a tunnel, or the like. We can quite easily teach the young—even those young men themselves who do these things—that it is wrong to do this sort of thing, provided that we are using a sense of 'wrong' in which our demonstrations work. And they will work if it is either the case that this sense of 'wrong' makes it analytic to say that the gratuitous endangering of life is wrong, or that the feeling of revulsion which all normally educated people have when they contemplate such acts is itself a sufficient indication that the acts are wrong. But what shall we have gained if we get everyone to agree that in one of these senses of 'wrong' the acts are wrong? As I said, even the criminals themselves may admit this. But in admitting this, they will only have been admitting a fact without any essential bearing on their conduct. They can readily allow that the act does arouse the familiar feeling of revulsion; but they may say that they find this feeling of revulsion, and the thought that everyone who reads about their act in the newspapers will experience it, exciting—that is just what attracts them about the act. It is perhaps the knowledge that the act is wrong in this sense that makes it worth doing. Or they may agree that to endanger the lives of a trainload of people is wrong—indeed, if they have learnt some philosophy, they may agree that it is analytic to say that it is wrong—in perhaps the only sense of 'wrong' with which they are familiar, its descriptive sense. But this is also a sense in which one can quite easily say, 'Wrong: so what?' And that is what they will say.

So if we were following the descriptivists of either sort in our moral education, we should have taught the next generation a use of the moral words in which it was tolerably easy to establish that certain acts are right or wrong, but in which the knowledge that they were right or wrong would be without any necessary bearing on people's conduct. Indeed, that is what many well-meaning parents, abetted by many well-meaning clergymen, schoolmasters and even moral philosophers, have already succeeded in doing. Their children and pupils know perfectly well that all sorts of things, from growing their hair long to extra-marital sex and to murder, are wrong; but they do not see that that is any reason for abstaining from them. They have, as in Kierkegaard's fable,[2] mistaken the wig for the man. There is something very pathetic about these descriptivist families, of whom I have been acquainted with many; having quite failed to diagnose the disease which afflicts them, they often come to moral philosophers for more of the same useless remedy.

But what is the disease which afflicts them? Simply that they have never learnt that the only sense of moral words which matters in the moral life is their prescriptive sense. These is a sense of 'wrong' in which to think that an act is wrong is *eo ipso* to be disposed to refrain from doing it—a sense, even, in which if you think it wrong you *will* refrain from doing it unless you succumb to irresistible temptation. If we could teach people to use 'wrong' in this sense, we should have at least achieved the object of ensuring that, so far as in them lay, they

---

[2] *Concluding Unscientific Postscript,* s.f.

would refrain from what they thought wrong. But we should have done this at a cost: the cost of not predetermining the content of their moral judgements. No moral judgements of substance can, in this sense of the moral words, be passed off as analytic, or self-evident. This amounts to saying that, in teaching them to use the moral words in this way, we are tying their actions to their moral judgements, but setting them free to make their own moral judgements. What I am urging is that this cost has to be accepted, if morality is to survive. For although all of us have to go through a stage (sometimes called the stage of heteronomy) in which we get our moral judgements made for us, we have, if we are going to grow up morally, to reach the stage at which we make them for ourselves.

But, it may be asked, what guarantee is there that, once set free, they will not prescribe universally that people should cause train-crashes if they find it exciting? Simply that if they did this they would be prescribing that they themselves should be thus endangered by any-body who found it exciting, if and when they travel in trains. Of course they may not think of this, for people are often thoughtless. But the problem of making them think about the consequences of their actions for other people—of what it is like to be in the situations in which they are putting other people—is not a philosophical one. If anybody does give sufficient thought and imagination to the situations of the other people with whom he comes into contact, and treats them as if it were he that was in those situations, he will not prescribe universally that people should cause train-crashes in tunnels for fun unless he himself genuinely wants this to be done, even when he is a passenger. Indeed, not even this is enough; for he has to want it to be done, even when he is a passenger *and* wants there not to be a crash as much as the pas-sengers in this train, which he is causing to crash, want there not to be a crash.

I am not pretending that philosophy can solve all the problems of moral education. That would be pressing the claims of my subject too far. I am claiming only that it can remove one serious obstacle to suc-cess, namely ignorance of what we are trying to achieve. If once we understand what morality is—that it is not the same thing as conformity, but is the endeavour of a free agent to find for himself principles which he can accept as binding on all alike—then we shall be on the way to solving the many problems which remain. We are trying to educate peo-ple so that they, first of all, think about, and are able to assess reliably, the consequences of their actions for other people. So, although moral judgements are not, in the narrow sense, statements of fact, knowledge of the facts is of overwhelming importance in moral thinking; it is safe to say that by far the greatest number of people slip up in their moral thinking through ignorance or neglect of the facts. But secondly, they have to give as much weight to the interests of these other people as to their own interests; for unless they do this, they will not be universalising their prescriptions. To say that sole (or even preponderant) weight should be given to my interests just because they are mine is to utter a prescription which in principle defies universalisation. For to say that I should give sole weight to everybody's interests just because they are his is to contradict myself. It is logically impossible to give most-favoured treatment to everybody. To say, on the other hand, that *everybody* should give sole weight to *his own* interests, just because they are his, is, indeed, to utter a self-consistent universal prescription; but it is one which hardly anybody is going to accept once he has considered the effects which compliance with it by others would have on his own interests. For he would be implicitly prescribing to others to put him in the cooler. If he really thinks this, he must desire, or at any rate be content, that they should put him in the cooler—provided only that he realises the undoubted fact that to put him in the cooler is in the interests of nearly everybody with whom he comes in contact, if he is really prescribing and following a principle of complete neglect of other people's interests.

Let us, without claiming historical accuracy, call this last position the Nietzschean position, and admit that it is logically self-consistent; but let us add, since this is intended as a practical lecture, that Nietzscheans are not likely to trouble us in practice, any more than the other two kinds of logically possible eccentrics that I mentioned earlier. There will be plenty who err through ignorance or neglect of the facts; and there are non-philosophical disciplines whose business it is to put them right. There will also be plenty who are insensitive or lacking in imagination; literature and drama can perhaps do something for the education of these—but the character of their human environment in their families and schools is more important. Others are suffering from psychological defects, such that they cannot be brought to attend to the facts, or to other people as people like themselves, or to think clearly what they are saying or doing. The psychologists can, perhaps, find out eventually what to do about them. But the man who claims to be a Nietzschean, and is free from these three defects, is almost certainly suffering from conceptual confusion; for him, a clearer philosophical understanding of the words he is using is the remedy. If there are any factually well-informed, sensitive and imaginative, psychologically undisturbed and clear-thinking people who are Nietzscheans, I have yet to hear of their existence.

What, then, is the practical advice which I, as a philosopher, have to offer to those who are concerned, as to some extent we are all concerned, with the moral education of our successors? What is the distinctive relevance of philosophy to moral education—for of course there are many other contributions that are needed, some of which I have mentioned? The distinctive contribution of the philosopher is to make us clearer, if he can, about what morality *is;* and the practical advice I have to give is, that unless we know that, we shall only fumble in our efforts to teach it.

6.5

Relativism

This is a good point at which to look at relativism, partly because a belief in relativism is one of the usual grounds of emotivism and noncognitivism in ethical theory, but primarily because relativism is, in any case, one of the main obstacles to be faced by anyone who thinks that ethical judgments can be justified in some intersubjectively valid way. Relativism is not new, though it is widespread in our culture and social sciences today; in fact, it goes back to the Greek Sophists and Skeptics who appealed to the apparent variety of ethical beliefs in different cultures as a basis for their views. There are three things that may be called relativism:

1. the view that cultures and individuals differ in their basic moral and nonmoral value judgments;
2. the view that different kinds of action and ways of living are morally right, intrinsically good, etc., for different societies or individuals to engage in; and
3. the view that differences in basic moral and value judgments cannot be resolved in any rational or objective way, and that each of the judgments involved must be regarded as equally valid.

Here, (1) is a question of fact; (2) is an ethical judgment, no more and no less objectively valid than others; (3) is a meta-ethical theory. It is often held that (1) is true and that it follows that (2) and (3) are true; but (1) is not so obviously true as some social scientists and students think, and even if it is true, neither (2) nor (3) necessarily follows from it. For our present purposes, the interesting question is whether (3) can be established.

One of the most philosophically careful and anthropologically informed discussions of this question is that of R. B. Brandt. In the following selection he argues, in a qualified and tentative way, first for (1), and then for (3), which he calls nonmethodological relativism. He ends by suggesting that the scope of such relativism is much more limited than is generally realized. If you have studied the social sciences in recent years, it might be interesting for you to ask yourself if any new light has been shed on (1) since Brandt wrote this in 1959. The readings in Section 6.6 and 6.7 also have important points to make about (3).

DISAGREEMENT AND
RELATIVISM IN ETHICS

Richard B. Brandt

Are There Ultimate Disagreements
About Ethical Principle?

No one seriously doubts that there are differences of ethical principle. . . . However, there is a question about these differences, and its answer is controversial. In order to mark this question, let us use the phrase "*ultimate* difference of ethical principle," and let us then ask ourselves whether some of the differences we have been describing can be considered ultimate differences of principle.

What is meant by an "ultimate" difference of principle? Consider first an example of conflicting evaluations of a particular action. Suppose Smith gives his father an overdose of sleeping pills, resulting in death. Suppose further that Jones hears of this event, but thinks no worse of Smith for this reason, because he knows that Smith's father was dying from cancer and in a very painful condition, and he believes Smith's act was done as an act of mercy. We might say he thinks Smith's act was right, because it was of the kind *ABC*. Suppose, now, that Brown also learns of Smith's act, but, unlike Jones, he thinks it was wrong. Brown knows that Smith's father was wealthy and that Smith was penniless, and he believes Smith's act was done to expedite the transfer of his father's property to him. Brown, then, thinks Smith's act was wrong, since he assumes that it was of the kind *ADE*. Brown and Jones, then, differ in their appraisal of the act, but possibly they do not differ at all in their ethical principles, but only in their factual beliefs about the properties of the act. It may well be that Brown and Jones both agree that all acts of the kind *ABC* are right, and that all acts of the kind *ADE* are wrong. In this case, we do not wish to say there was any *ultimate* disagreement between them.

Let us now turn to disagreements about ethical principles. We said that the Romans decidedly did not think it right to put one's parents to death. In some of the Eskimo groups, however, this is thought proper. One observer has told of an Eskimo who was getting ready to move camp, and was concerned about what to do with his blind and aged father, who was a burden to the family. One day the old man expressed a desire to go sealhunting again, something he had not done for many years. His son readily assented to this suggestion, and the old man was dressed warmly and given his weapons. He was then led out to the seal grounds and was walked into a hole in the ice, into which he disappeared.[1] The Romans, we may expect, would have been shocked at this deed. The Eskimos think it right, in general, to drown a parent who is old and a burden; the Romans, we guess, think this is wrong. The Romans, we may say, think that all acts of the kind *ABC* are wrong; the Eskimos deny this.

But may it not be that the Eskimos and the Romans in some sense have different acts in mind? Suppose that Eskimos, through their experience with the hardships of living, think of parricide as being normally the merciful cutting short of a miserable, worthless, painful old age. And suppose the Romans think of parricide as being normally the getting rid of a burden, or a getting one's hands on the parent's money—an ungraceful, selfishly motivated aggression against one whose care and sacrifices years ago have made the child's life a rich experience. The Eskimos are more-or-less unconsciously taking for granted that putting a parent to death is euthanasia under extreme circumstances; the Romans are more-or-less unconsciously taking for granted that putting a parent to death is murder for gain. In this case, although the Romans and the Eskimos may use the very same words to describe a certain sort of act—and then may express conflicting ethical appraisal of it—actually in some sense they have in mind quite different things. The Eskimos, perhaps, are accepting something of the kind *ABCD;* the Romans are condemning something of the kind *ABFG.* In this situation, we do not want to say there is necessarily any ultimate disagreement of principle between them.

When, then, do we want to say there is ultimate disagreement about ethical principles? Let us suppose that A thinks that anything of the kind *FGH* is wrong; and let us suppose that B denies this. But now, let us suppose further that there is some property *P* that A is more-or-

---

[1] G. de Poncins, *Kabloona* (New York: Reynal & Hitchcock, 1941).

less consciously supposing that everything has, if it is of the kind *FGH*, whereas B does *not* more-or-less consciously suppose that everything of the kind *FGH* has *P*. Furthermore, let us suppose that if A ceased to believed that things that are *FGH* are also *P*, he would *cease* to believe that they are wrong; and also that if B began to believe that things that are *FGH* are also *P*, he would *begin* to believe that they are wrong. In this case, we shall say there is *not ultimate* disagreement, in respect of the ethical principle about things that are *FGH*. But if, as far as conscious beliefs are concerned, A thinks all things of a certain kind right, and B denies this, and there is no more-or-less conscious belief having the status described, then we shall say there *is* ultimate disagreement of principle between A and B.

It is theoretically quite important whether there is ultimate disagreement about ethical principles. It is important for critical ethics because, if there is *no* ultimate disagreement, then all ethical disputes are in principle capable of solution by the methods of science; for all we should have to do, to resolve a dispute, is first to find the ethical principles common to both parties, and then to use observation to determine how these principles apply to the case at hand.[2] But the matter is equally important for psychology. Many psychologists have assumed that we must so conceive the process of learning beliefs and attitudes that it can happen that people arrive at ethical convictions between which there is an ultimate clash; whereas other psychologists do not believe this is the case, thinking rather that conflicting ethical assessments are always a consequence of different cognitive fields, of different apprehensions of or beliefs about the properties of the thing being assessed.

It is not easy to answer the question whether there is ultimate disagreement on ethical principles between different groups. Most of the comparative material assembled, for instance by Westermarck, is of little value for this purpose, for in large part what it tells us is simply whether various peoples approve or condemn lying, suicide, industry, cleanliness, adultery, homosexuality, cannibalism, and so on. But this is not enough. We need, for our purpose, to know how various peoples *conceive* of these things. Do they eat human flesh because they like its taste, and do they kill slaves merely for the sake of a feast? Or do they eat flesh because they think this is necessary for tribal fertility, or be-

---

[2] By no means all the problems of critical ethics would be solved, however, although there would probably be decidedly less interest in them. For instance, whether or not there are disagreements, there is still the question of the sense in which ethical statements can be justified, or in which there is evidence for them. One can still be puzzled about what one could do to settle an ethical dispute, if one *did* arise.

Even if there is ultimate disagreement, however, all ethical disputes are still in principle capable of solution by the methods of science, if some form of naturalism is true.

cause they think they will then participate in the manliness of the person eaten? Perhaps those who condemn cannibalism would not do so if they thought that eating the flesh of an enemy is necessary for the survival of the group. If we are to estimate whether there is ultimate disagreement of ethical principle, we must have information about this, about the beliefs, more or less conscious, of various peoples about what they do. However, the comparative surveys seldom give us this.

In view of the total evidence, then, is it more plausible to say that there is ultimate disagreement of ethical principle, or not? Or don't we really have good grounds for making a judgment on this crucial issue?

First of all, we must report that no anthropologists, as far as the writer knows, today deny that there is ultimate disagreement—although doubtless many of them have not posed the question in exactly the above form. (*Almost* no philosophers deny it either.) This seems a matter of importance, because, even if they have not explicitly argued the matter out, their intuitive impression based on long familiarity with some non-Western society should carry considerable weight. However, we must concede that no anthropologist has offered what we should regard as really an adequate account of a single case, clearly showing there is ultimate disagreement in ethical principle. Of course, we must remember that this lack of information is just as serious for any claim that there is world-wide *agreement* on some principle.

Nevertheless, the writer inclines to think there is ultimate ethical disagreement, and that it is well established. Maybe it is not very important, or very pervasive; but there is some. Let us look at the matter of causing suffering to animals. It is notorious that many peoples seem quite indifferent to the suffering of animals. We are informed that very often, in Latin America, a chicken is *plucked alive*, with the thought it will be more succulent on the table. The reader is invited to ask himself whether he would consider it justified to pluck a chicken alive, for this purpose. Or again, take the "game" played by Indians of the Southwest (but learned from the Spaniards, apparently), called the "chicken pull." In this "game," a chicken is buried in the sand, up to its neck. The contestants ride by on horseback, trying to grab the chicken by the neck and yank it from the sand. When someone succeeds in this, the idea is then for the other constestants to take away from him as much of the chicken as they can. The "winner" is the one who ends up with the most chicken. The reader is invited to ask himself whether he approves of this sport. The writer had the decided impression that the Hopi disapproval of causing pain to animals is much milder than he would suppose typical in suburban Philadelphia—certainly much milder than he would feel himself. For instance, children often catch birds and make "pets" of them. A string is tied to their legs, and they are then "played" with. The birds seldom survive this "play" for long: their legs are broken, their wings pulled off, and so on. One informant put it: "Sometimes they get tired and die. Nobody objects to this." Another informant said: "My boy sometimes brings in birds, but there is nothing to feed them, and they die." [3] Would the reader approve of this, or permit his children to do this sort of thing?

Of course, these people might believe that animals are unconscious automata, or that they are destined to be rewarded many times in the afterlife if they suffer martyrdom on this earth. Then we should feel that our ethical principles were, after all, in agreement with those of these individuals. But they believe no such thing. The writer took all means he could think of to discover some such belief in the Hopi subconscious, but he found none. So probably—we must admit the case is not definitively closed—there is at least one ultimate difference of ethical principle. How many more there are, or how important, we do not say at present.

Possibly we need not go as far afield as Latin America or the Hopi to establish the point. The reader *may* have argued some ethical point with a friend until he found that, as far as he could tell, there were just some matters of principle on which they disagreed, which themselves could not be debated on the basis of any further common ground. In this case, the conclusion is the same. Note, however, that we say only "may have argued." Some people say they cannot remember ever having had such an experience; and perhaps the reader has not. In this case, we do not need to go afield.

It is obvious that if there is *ultimate* disagreement of ethical opinion between two persons or groups, there is also disagreement in *basic* principles—if we mean by "basic ethical principle" . . . the principles we should have to take as a person's ethical premises, if we represented his ethical views as a deductive system. We have so defined "ultimate disagreement" that a difference in the ethical theorems of two persons or groups does not count as being "ultimate" if it can be explained as a consequence of identical ethical premises but different factual assumptions of the two parties. Since ultimate ethical disagreements, then, cannot be a consequence of the factual assumptions of the parties, it must be a consequence of their ethical premises. Hence, there is also disagreement in "basic" principles. Our conclusion from our total evidence, then, is that different persons or groups sometimes have, in fact, conflicting basic ethical principles.

---

[3] See the writer's *Hopi Ethics: A Theoretical Analysis* (Chicago: University of Chicago Press, 1954), pp. 213–15, 245–46, 373.

The significance of this conclusion for "ethical relativism" we shall assess at a later stage. . . .

Nonmethodological Relativism: Relativism "Proper"

. . . Essentially the issue is this: If one informed (and so on) attitude in fact never clashes with another attitude that is equally qualified, both of course being directed at the same act or thing, then one person can never correctly claim, "*x* is wrong," when someone else can correctly say, "*x* is not wrong." *Valid* ethical statements would then never conflict, and relativism would be false.

Relativism is right, then . . . if "qualified" . . . attitudes toward the same act or event can be conflicting.[4]

Well, can they, or can they not? Or what should we believe?

The simplest way to answer these questions, of course, is just to find two individuals, both qualified in the relevant ways, and observe whether in fact one wants, abhors, feels obligated to do, demands from others, feels indignant or disgusted at, admires, or prefers things, actions, or events to which the other individual takes an opposite attitude. It is difficult, though, ever to be certain that such individuals are before us. How can we be sure that all the relevant facts are believed by both, and that neither needs to be disabused of false beliefs? How can we be sure that all the relevant considerations are present to the minds of both, with requisite vividness? Perhaps, of course, individuals on occasion may with reason be said to approximate to these conditions. It seems preferable, however, not to rest one's argument on such possible cases.

There is an indirect method for answering our question. Consider a parallel: that we feel free to make statements about how gases *would* behave at an absolute-zero temperature, although we have not actually observed gases in this state. Why? We draw inferences from relevant causal laws. The same is true in our case. If we have good reason to believe causal laws, to the effect that a person's attitudes are not a function solely of his information (or its vividness) and his state of personal needs or wishes (at the time) and his normalcy, then we have so much reason to think that "qualified" attitudes occasionally vary. If we happen to know precisely the nature of these laws, we may be able to specify the conditions under which such variation will occur. Psychological the-

---

4 [By a "qualified" attitude or judgment Brandt means one that is impartial, informed, normal, and compatible with having a consistent set of general principles. For elaboration see R. B. Brandt, *Ethical Theory*, pp. 244–52.—EDS.]

ory and experiment, then, are the most obvious source for an answer to our question.

Unfortunately, psychological theories do not provide a uniform answer to our question. Gestalt theory would lead us to believe that attitudes ("ought" experiences) to a situation will be identical, if the situation is identically understood, and personal needs and interests do not play a distorting or blinding role. Psychoanalytic theory and Hullian learning theory, however, provide a different answer. According to these theories, two attitudes, equally "qualified" in the sense of occurring in minds with equal information (and so on), can be conflicting, depending on the history of the development of the persons: their past identifications, their past rewards and punishments. The doctors, then, disagree. But how does the currently available experimental evidence look? Does it favor the view of either theory, on this particular point? To this our answer must be: There is no *certainly* correct reading of the evidence, but it *appears* to favor the relativist answer to our question, for there is some reason to think that fundamental orientations may be adopted from parents in early life, and that these may have a permanent influence on attitudes; that identifications, emotional relations with important figures in one's life, and feelings of security play a role in the development of one's values; that certain things or events may be highly valued in compensation for the inaccessibility of other satisfactions at an earlier period, or as a result of deprivations. Then, if these things are true, we can specify some occurrences in the life of an individual that would have the effect that his attitudes now, whatever the information (and so on) of his present state of mind, would be different from what they would have been had his earlier experiences been different. Individuals with relevantly different earlier experiences, then, may be expected to have different attitudes, despite identical qualifications with respect to knowledge, impartiality, and so forth.[5]

On the whole, then, the relativist is better able to claim the support of contemporary psychological theory and research than is his adversary. However, the issue is not closed.

---

[5] We should not, however, overlook the possibility that an individual might, if he knew that an attitude of his was a result of some type of early experience (for example, a high valuation of knowledge being a result of the unsatisfactoriness of his personal relations at an earlier period of development), to some extent lose this attitude. In other words, perhaps self-understanding in the sense of understanding the genesis of one's own values is a fact relevant to what one's present attitudes will be. It is possible that any two individuals, otherwise equally "qualified," would in fact always have the same attitudes toward everything at the conclusion of a careful psychological treatment in which each acquired complete self-understanding. Is there evidence, from psychoanalysts or other specialists in personality theory, that points in this direction? The writer does not know.

The facts of anthropology are also relevant to our question, and in the following way. In the first place, we have already noticed [in a section of *Ethical Theory* which is not included in our selection—Eds.] that studies of cultural change in primitive societies suggest that facts like personal conflicts and maladjustments, the attitudes of one's close relatives (for example, whether favorably oriented toward White civilization), and personal success in achieving status in one's group or outside one's group (for example, with White men) play an important role in the development of the values of adults. This finding is some support for our reading of the observational evidence of psychology. In the second place, there is the fact that various groups have different values. The mere fact that different ethical standards exist in different societies, of course, by itself proves nothing relevant to our present problem. Nevertheless, something important is proved if the facts bear testimony that different standards can prevail even if different groups have the *same beliefs* about the relevant event or act, and if there is no reason to suppose that the group standards reflect group differences in respect of other "qualifications." (We must remember that attitudes common to a group cannot usually be discounted as being a result of personal interest or of an abnormal frame of mind.) The fact of variation of group standards, in these circumstances, would tend to show that attitudes are a function of such variables, that attitudes could differ even if our "ideal qualifications" were all met.

Is there such variation of group standards? We have seen that there is one area of ethical opinion where there is diversity in appraisal and at the same time possible identity of belief about the action—that about the treatment of animals. On the whole, primitive groups show little feeling that it is wrong to cause pain to animals, whereas the columns of *The New York Times* are testimony to the fact that many persons in the U.S.A. take a vigorous interest in what goes on in slaughterhouses. We have already mentioned some details about the attitudes of primitive groups [in *Ethical Theory*, not included here—Eds.]. Nevertheless, we cannot be sure that attitudes of the groups here in question really do fulfill our "qualifications" equally well. Primitive peoples rarely make pets of the animals they maltreat. There is at least some question whether they have a vivid imagination of what the suffering of an animal is like, comparable to that of the authors of letters to the *Times*. The writer has assured himself by personal investigation that there is no definite discrepancy between the Hopi *beliefs*, about the effects of maltreating animals, and those of what seems a representative sample of educated White Americans. Degrees of *vividness* of belief, however, do not lend themselves to objective investigation, and it is not clear how we may definitely answer questions about them, either way. Perhaps the sanest conclusion is just to say that, as far as can be decided objectively, groups do sometimes make divergent appraisals when they have identical beliefs about the objects, but that the difficulties of investigation justify a healthy degree of skepticism about the conclusiveness of the inquiry.

The fact that objective inquiry is difficult naturally works both ways. It prevents us from asserting confidently that, where there are differences of appraisal, there is still identity of factual belief. But equally it prevents us from denying confidently that there is identity of belief, where appraisals differ.

The anthropological evidence, taken by itself, then, does not give a *conclusive* answer to our question. At the present time, the anthropologist does not have two social groups of which he can say definitely: "These groups have exactly the same beliefs about action A, on all points that could be seriously viewed as ethically relevant. But their views—attitudes—about the morality of the acts are vastly different." Whether, everything considered, the relativist reading of the facts is not the more balanced judgment, is another question. The writer is inclined to think it is the better judgment.

If we agree that the ethical standards of groups are not a function solely of their beliefs (or the vividness of these), it is reasonable to suppose that "ideally qualified" attitudes may well conflict with respect to the very same act or event. To say this is to say that there is reason to suppose that nonmethodological relativism is correct.

Ethical Universals

Thus far we have talked as if the truth of nonmethodological relativism were a black-and-white matter: either there are conflicts of justified ethical judgment in certain conditions or there are not. If there are, then relativism is correct; if there are not, then relativism is mistaken.

But to talk in this way is to conceive of the issue too indiscriminately, for it overlooks the fact that, whereas some conflicting ethical judgments may be equally valid in some areas of living and thinking, the same may not be the case in other areas. In other words, whereas it may be true that conflicting opinions are equally valid on the subject of cruelty to animals or sexual behavior, the same may not at all be the case when we come to topics like human rights.

There are some more detailed questions, then, that we may well ask ourselves. For instance, we may ask: Is relativism true for *all* topics of moral assessment, for perhaps fifty per cent, or perhaps for only one per cent? Or again, is relativism true for all topics except perhaps for those about which we have no strong feelings anyway, or is it true also for some topics (for example, slavery) of strong concern to us? Or, and this is obviously the most important issue, on *exactly which topics* are conflicting ethical views supportable, and on which topics must we say that all valid views are in agreement?

The last of these questions will be matter for inquiry in the following chapters of this book, for in large part the job of answering it is the job of normative ethics. If, after examination of the facts, we conclude that there cannot be two valid opinions on some principles, we shall have shown by implication that there are many specific matters for which a relativistic view is indefensible. Of course, our examination may have the contrary effect. We may find out that some arguments, which have been thought to establish some ethical principles beyond question, really do not do so; and hence we must conclude that, as far as we can see, the field for valid disagreement is much wider than had been thought.

The less specific questions—about the proportion of topics on which there may be conflicting but equally valid opinions, and about the relative importance of the topics on which conflicting moral views appear to be defensible—are of secondary import. Nevertheless, it is of interest to know the opinion of social scientists on these issues.

On this matter there has been a marked change of opinion among social scientists in the past twenty years. There was a time when anthropologists like Ruth Benedict proclaimed the equal validity of the most diverse modes of living and ideals for humanity. The megalomania of the Kwakiutl, the repressed sobriety of the Pueblo, and the paranoia of the Dobuan culture were different value systems; but it would be ethnocentric, she thought, to make judgments about the relative merits of the systems. Since that time, however, anthropologists have turned attention to the similarities between societies, and to the functioning of social systems, to the analysis of institutions in terms of their capacity to minister to essential human wants and the maintenance of the social group as a continuing entity. These new interests have led to the following results.

First, it has come to be agreed that certain features of a culture system are essential for the maintenance of life, and that a system of values that permits and sanctions these forms is inevitable in society.[6] For instance, every society must provide for mating and for the rearing of offspring. Again, it must provide for the education of the offspring in the

---

[6] See D. F. Aberle, *et al.*, "The Functional Prerequisites for a Society," *Ethics*, LIX (1949), 100–111.

performance of those tasks that are necessary for survival. Moreover, in a complex society there must be differentiation of jobs, assignment of individuals to these jobs and the means for training them for adequate performance, and provision of motivation to do the jobs. Sufficient security must be provided to prevent serious disruption of activities, for example, security against violent attack. And so on.

It must be no surprise, therefore, to find that certain institutional forms are present in all societies: such as the family with its responsibilities for training children and caring for the aged, division of labor between the sexes (and occupational differences in more complex societies), games or art or dance, and so on.[7]

Second, anthropologists have come to find much more common ground in the value systems of different groups than they formerly did. As Professor Kluckhohn recently put it:

> Every culture has a concept of murder, distinguishing this from execution, killing in war, and other "justifiable homicides." The notions of incest and other regulations upon sexual behavior, of prohibitions upon untruth under defined circumstances, of restitution and reciprocity, of mutual obligations between parents and children—these and many other moral concepts are altogether universal.[8]

There are other universals we could mention: disapproval of rape, the ideal for marriage of a lifelong union between spouses, the demand for loyalty to one's own social group, recognition that the interests of the individual are in the end subordinate to those of the group. Ralph Linton wrote that "all societies attach high value to reciprocity and to fair dealing"—with some exceptions, such as *caveat emptor*. Again, parents are universally expected to train children; the child, for his part, is expected to be obedient and to render care in the old age of his parents. Knowledge is universally valued, as is the escape from the pressures of reality provided by games, literature, art, dance, and music.[9]

At the same time, anthropologists agree that, to quote Kluckhohn, "variation rages rampant as to details of prescribed behavior, instrumentalities, and sanctions." Linton wrote, "If universal values exist, they must be sought for at the level of the deepest and most generalized conceptual

---

[7] See G. P. Murdock, "The Common Denominator of Cultures," in R. Linton (ed.), *The Science of Man in the World Crisis* (New York: Columbia University Press, 1945); and C. Kluckhohn, "Universal Categories of Culture," in A. L. Kroeber (ed.), *Anthropology Today* (Chicago: University of Chicago Press, 1953).

[8] C. Kluckhohn, "Ethical Relativity: Sic et Non," *Journal of Philosophy*, LII (1955), 663–77.

[9] See Ralph Linton, "The Problem of Universal Values," in R. F. Spencer (ed.), *Method and Perspective in Anthropology* (Minneapolis: University of Minnesota Press, 1954).

values, those which stand in closest relation to the individual needs and social imperatives shared by the whole of mankind." [10]

Linton has also suggested that *basic* values tend to be more matters of universal agreement than do superficial values:

> In any study of values, it soon becomes evident that the values held by a particular society are arranged in a hierarchy of importance, strong emotional affect being associated with some, little emotional affect with others. Those with which strong affect is associated tend to be reflected in numerous concepts and behavior patterns. They are usually associated with the satisfaction of the basic needs of individuals, both physical and psychological, and the fulfillment of the conditions necessary for the continuation and effective functioning of societies. They may be termed *basic values*. At the other end of the scale lie values which find very limited expression and carry little emotional affect. Such would be the transitory value attaching to a particular style of clothing while it was in fashion. These may be termed *superficial values*. Between these two extremes lie a continuous series of values carrying varying degrees of emotional affect and expressed in culture patterns of varying number and functional importance.
>
> A comparative study of a large number of cultures indicates that the *basic values* of all societies include many of the same elements. Differences increase as one moves toward the superficial end of the scale. [11]

This is not to say there are no divergencies between groups on fundamental matters. Raymond Firth reports that human life has only a small sentimental value among the Chinese and the Tikopia; but even so, he remarks that "in all human societies there is a basic moral view that it is good as a general rule to attempt to preserve human life." [12]

What is proved by these observations of anthropologists? First, that there is much agreement about values, especially important values, which provides some basis for the resolution of disputes, even if we set aside completely considerations of validity, and assume there is no such thing as a "valid" value. Second, some values, or some institutions with their supporting values, are so inevitable, given human nature and the human situation in society as they are, that we can hardly anticipate serious questioning of them by anybody—much less any conflicting "qualified attitudes," that is, conflicting attitudes that are informed (and so on).

Thus, ethical relativism may be true, in the sense that there are *some* cases of conflicting ethical judgments that are equally valid; but it would be a mistake to take it as a truth with pervasive scope. Relativism as an

---

[10] *Ibid.*, p. 152. It is not made quite clear what Linton means by a "conceptual" value. One example he gives is the value of "modesty," which can take numerous quite different forms. A conceptual value, he says, may not be consciously recognized by the group that has it. Presumably, it is a *general preference* that the the anthropologist finds it fruitful to postulate, to account for classes of cultural phenomena.

[11] Mimeographed report, "Cultural Relativity," October, 1951.

[12] *Elements of Social Organization* (London: Watts & Co., 1951), p. 201.

emphasis is misleading, because it draws our attention away from the central identities, from widespread agreement on the items we care most about. Furthermore, the actual agreement on the central things suggests the possibility that, with better understanding of the facts, the scope of agreement would be much wider.

6.6

Toward a Satisfactory
Theory of Justification

Many recent philosophers who have no wish to return either to intuitionism or to definism of the sort Moore had in mind also reject emotivism of the Ayer-Stevenson kind, existentialism, and Hare's prescriptivism. They believe that these latter views put too much emphasis on autonomy, freedom, prescriptivity, practicality, attitude, decision, disagreement, and relativity, and not enough on reason, objectivity, or consensus. In particular, they object to the idea that moral judgments and principles are ultimately matters of individual attitude or decision that may vary indefinitely from person to person and involve disagreements that are finally irresolvable. Some of them are still emotivists or noncognitivists but look, as Hume did, for some way of providing more objectivity or rationality. Others are "descriptivists" or "neonaturalists," looking for a form of naturalism that has satisfactory answers to the arguments of Moore and the noncognitivists. All hold that ethical judgments are objectively justifiable in ways or to a degree not recognized by most relativists or by earlier twentieth-century noncognitivism.

There are a number of writers one could mention here and a number of lines of thought that might be presented. Somewhat arbitrarily, we have selected four: Findlay, Baier, Nielsen, and Warnock. In our first selection, J. N. Findlay, who was an emotivist when he wrote it, argues for a limited form of absolutism or objectivism in ethics. He explains his view of what an ethical judgment is, and discusses not only the justification of moral judgments, but also that of judgments about what is good or worthwhile in itself.

ETHICAL JUDGMENTS AND
THEIR JUSTIFICATION

J. N. Findlay

I

Few features in regard to our moral judgements have proved more distressing to philosophers, or have seemed more hopelessly to obstruct their efforts to build up a science of ethics, than our plain inability to reach agreement on many moral questions. There seem to be, by contrast, in other fields of discourse, methods of settling arguments which are both intelligible and final. We can, for instance, bring most mathematical arguments to an end by calculation, that is, by operating continuously on our symbols (according to a set of rules that follow from their meanings) until some satisfactory result emerges. And we can likewise settle most disputes concerning objects in the realm of nature, if we can only succeed in placing ourselves where we can use our senses or our instruments to make appropriate observations. But in the field of morals such methods do not seem to be available: there do not seem to be any acknowledged, easy ways of reaching answers that everyone will find acceptable. The situation seems, in fact, to be so desperate that some have had recourse, in dealing with their moral problems, to certain wholly private operations, described by them in terms of "feeling" or "immediate intuition"; these are, unfortunately, quite worthless from the point of view of settling arguments, since no one else can be quite sure what they involve, or whether, in a given instance, they have been properly performed. And there are others who have sought a remedy for their difficulties by assuming, rather uselessly, that while it may be impossible for *us* to know whether we have the right answers to our moral questions, yet there nevertheless *are* a comprehensive set of right answers, "laid up" in some realm or mind or medium to which we have no means of access. And there are yet others who have simply ceased to worry about the hopeless character of disputes in ethics, and have even found a reason for this hopelessness: our ethical utterances have their origin in private feelings, which vary without principle from one man to another; it is not meaningful to say that any of these feelings are true or valid, or that others are the opposite.

From "Morality by Convention," Mind, LIII (April, 1944). Reprinted by permission of the author and Mind. [Professor Findlay wishes to add that he no longer believes (1974) that our use of the term 'ethical' creates a distinctive group of ethical reactions, but rather that the existence of such a distinctive group creates our use of the term 'ethical'.—EDS.]

Against the boundless nihilism of these doctrines, we shall attempt to argue that there is not, in fact, and cannot be, that wide variety of ethical feeling and opinion, that some have imagined possible, and that men only have assumed such variability because they simply have not understood, or have not analysed, what we really *mean* by saying that a feeling or opinion is an ethical one. And we shall also try to argue that we have, in morals, many quite definite methods by which our questions may be approached and dealt with, that a substantial range of questions can be satisfactorily disposed of by these methods, and that certain residual questions, which remain unanswered in this manner, are quite incapable of receiving any answers. . . .

Before we pass on to these questions, we may align ourselves, quite definitely, with a theory of the moral judgement which has been put forward recently by the so-called positivists, but which was also stated, in a less clear manner, by writers of the sentimental school in the eighteenth century. This is the view which holds it to be the function of an ethical statement, particularly in regard to certain crucial words occurring in it—words such as "good," "bad," "right," "wrong," "ought," "duty," and so on—to *evince* or *express* the sentiments of the speaker. A man who makes an ethical statement, and uses some of these peculiar words, is not, while he uses them, trying to "discover objects as they stand in nature, without addition or diminution":[1] he is rather trying to give voice to the demands and feelings which the notion of such objects arouses in him. . .

II

That moral judgements are emotional, is the truth which really underlies Moore's well-known doctrine of the "naturalistic fallacy." For what this doctrine really succeeds in bringing out, is the profound disparity between our ethical judgements, which evince attitudes, and all those other judgements which describe objects in the world around us, which tell us where they are, when they happen, how big or small they are, how long they last, how they are shaped and coloured, and even what they think or feel. These questions differ totally from ethical questions: it is only when we know (or have imagined) answers to them, that we are in a position to raise the genuinely ethical questions: "Is it a good thing for this to be like this?" or "Would it be a good thing if this were the case?" and so forth. Even questions of the type called "metaphysical," which try to penetrate beyond experience and the world of nature, but which nevertheless resemble empirical questions, and which leave experi-

---

[1] Hume, *An Inquiry Concerning the Principles of Morals,* Appendix I.

ence at quite definite points: these questions, too, are plainly quite different from ethical questions.

But though Moore made it very clear, in his early expositions, that there *was* a difference between such ethical and such non-ethical questions, he never in the least succeeded in saying what that difference really was. For though he held that the predicate "good" could neither be reduced nor analysed, he did not tell us how this made it so fundamentally different from all those very numerous non-ethical predicates which are equally irreducible and equally incapable of analysis. And though he also maintained that ethical predicates accrued to objects as secondary consequences of their "nature" (in a somewhat narrow sense of "nature"), he again failed to show how this rendered them fundamentally different from many non-ethical predicates, "simplicity" for instance, which are, to an equal extent, secondary and consequential. But if we make it the essential function of our ethical words and phrases to evince or voice the feelings and demands which the thought of certain objects arouses in us, we shall have no difficulty in understanding why ethical and non-ethical utterances are so widely different, and why no combination of the latter could ever conceivably yield us an exact equivalent of the former. . . .

We may, however, point to one respect in which all the sentimental schools have gone seriously astray; that is, in thinking that, because our ethical judgements had their origin in feeling, there could be no limit to their possible objects. They often speak as if it would be possible to have ethical emotions in regard to absolutely *anything*, and to voice one's sentiment in the corresponding judgement. Or if they have conceded any limit to the objects of our ethical emotions, they have tended to ascribe this to some merely constitutional bias, to some accident of our human make-up, or to some mere contingency of circumstance or of "social conditioning." They have never for a moment imagined that there might be definite *claims* involved in moral attitudes, claims capable of being tested, and capable, through the outcome of such testing, of rendering the attitudes in question either justifiable or unjustifiable. . . .

VI

We may now pass on to sketch another trait of our ethical responses which some might thing unduly narrowing in its effect. We shall deliberately restrict the object of our ethical reactions to those voluntary acts *that have some bearing on the welfare of sentient beings.* Either these acts may actually be productive (or destructive) of welfare, or they may aim at ends which would, if realized, have some influence on welfare, or they merely *mean* to achieve welfare (or the opposite) in ways that may be quite misguided. These differences are interesting, and would occupy separate compartments in a systematic ethical treatise, but this is obviously not the place to dwell upon them. We shall only rule that actions, in order to be morally commendable or censurable, must have some tendency to help or injure somebody, even if only in the imagination of the agent.

In laying down this ruling we are not coming out baldly in favour of some form of utilitarianism. For we have laid down no principles with regard to the distribution of welfare: we have not decided whether anyone's welfare is to be preferred to anyone else's in given circumstances, or whether every man's welfare is to be equally regarded. Nor have we made one of those depressing, blanket statements to the effect that welfare must be heaped up into as large a pile as possible, regardless of the precise persons who are to experience this welfare. Nor are we questioning in any way that some personal claims may be too sacred to be set aside on any ground of *general* welfare: we are only saying that even such personal claims are *claims to welfare*. Even when someone feels bound to carry out some promise to a dead friend, this can, we rule, only be an ethical experience in so far as he regards the dead as being capable of a sort of posthumous welfare. To do so is not absurd, for, whether one has experiences after death or not, to be a person whose wishes will be posthumously disregarded and overridden, is not, to that extent, to be "well off."

We rule, accordingly, that moral feelings are, in their developed form, invariably bound up with the notion of actual or intended benefit or harm to someone. In legislating in this manner, we are deliberately not taking account of, and failing to cover many attitudes of savages and civilized people which would, in common parlance, be denominated "ethical." The life of savages is full of very bizarre, unmotivated prohibitions and imperatives, whether of marrying, eating or performing certain ceremonies, in which some act seems ultimately and mysteriously right or wrong, without being apparently connected with anyone's welfare. And there are doubtless many members of more civilized communities who venerate similar taboos in certain regions of behaviour. But we should not be saying anything very questionable if we were to hold that all such attitudes tended to lose their grip on reflective minds once it became quite clear that certain acts, previously censured or commended, had absolutely *no* effects on welfare. The welfare involved might be gross and material, or spiritual and impalpable, but if an action had no bearing on any sort of well-being, we should certainly feel inclined to cease praising or condemning it. Or, if we went on doing so, we should feel disposed to say that our feelings were no longer ethical. Or, alternatively, we might continue to react ethically to some action which seemed, at first, to have no bearing on welfare, because we discovered it to have some subtle, long-term influence on welfare which was not obvious at the first glance. It is clear that, even in savages, the majority of the feelings that we call "ethical" are concerned with acts that *have* an influence on welfare; e.g. where one man steals his neighbour's landmark or has intercourse with his wife or robs him or breaks faith with him. So that we find it profitable to rule that only those acts are proper objects of an ethical reaction which have some bearing on welfare, allowing meanwhile that there may be many "undeveloped" and "distorted" ethical reactions in which this relevance to welfare is slurred over or ignored. When we call the latter "ethical reactions," we are stressing their manifold affinities with what we should unhesitatingly call "ethical reactions," but we add the qualifications "undeveloped" or "distorted" to show that they have some features which make us hesitate to call them "ethical reactions."

VII

We may now proceed to fix a number of traits of ethical reactions which will give rise to much less question than the relation to welfare we have just considered. We may lay down, first of all, that there is involved in every ethical reaction a *demand* that a certain primary response to conduct should be *tested* by a process of reflection, as well as a *claim* that this primary response will be able to survive this process. Both this primary response to conduct, and this secondary demand and claim with regard to this primary response, may be ruled to be essential elements of an ethical reaction.

The reflection which our ethical reaction demands in this manner is an exhaustive and intense examination of what we commonly call "the facts and values of the case." We test some response to conduct by probing into or reviewing *all* the circumstances of some action, the persons who are involved in it, the means employed to compass it, as well as all its probable or certain consequences. Only if our response survives such testing, and is not liquidated in the process, do we denominate it "true" and "valid." And only if our reaction includes, in addition to a certain primary response to conduct, the *claim* that this response can be validated in this manner, can we denominate the whole reaction "ethical" at all.

We also test our responses to conduct by trying either to *perceive palpably*, or to *imagine very vividly*, all the circumstances thus reviewed in thought: our response must not only survive the most lucid knowledge, but also the most vivid imagination. Above all, we try to enter sympathetically, with as much vividness as possible, into the feelings of all the persons involved in the action, and to conceive the situation as it must appear to them. We also test a response to conduct by trying to review, and feel keenly, all increments of spiritual or material benefit or injury (assessed according to some standard, and in some manner, which we need not consider here) of every circumstance and consequence of the action. Only if our response withstands such tests can we call it a justifiable response. We should not be experiencing an ethical reaction unless, in addition to experiencing such a response, we also claimed that this response was justifiable in this manner. . . .

VIII

We may now lay down that every ethical reaction involves the further demand that our primary response to conduct (which is also a part of it) *should be acceptable to other people.* When we speak ethically, we are not merely voicing some private upset of our own, as some have rather simple-mindedly imagined; we are addressing our utterance to the world at large, we are endeavouring to legislate for men in general, we are, to some extent, displaying an authoritarian and intolerant spirit. Often, indeed, we show ourselves as crudely masterful: we use the somewhat clumsy violence of praise and blame, or of reward and punishment, or the milder violence of ethical persuasion and exhortation, in order to impose our attitude on others. But even where our proselytism is not overt, or has been curbed for reasons of politeness or of policy, we should not be responding ethically at all, if there were not some modicum of this deep intolerance in our attitude. Even a moral attitude which is tentative, which readily yields to other men's persuasion, pretends faintly, while it lasts, that it is final and authoritative. The same holds good, of course, for certain other types of attitude, our attitude to the beautiful, for example, or to "the really worth-while things of life." In these fields, too, we cannot rest content while others fail to share our feelings: we experience a powerful *nisus* to convert dissenters. But few would question that this essentially intolerant and authoritarian pose was far more characteristic of our moral attitudes than of our axiological or aesthetic ones.

We may lay down, further, in close connection with this trait, that every ethical reaction submits itself to a process of *testing by the attitudes and sentiments of other persons.* Not only do we *demand* that others should accept our attitudes, we also positively *expect* that they will do so. And if, at first, they do not seem to share our feelings, we think that this is so, only because they have, as yet, been insufficiently reflective. We think that they have not yet dwelt upon the matter long enough, that they have not yet pictured all its aspects with sufficient vividness, or that they have not adequately taken account of the various values, the items of material or spiritual benefit or injury, that are involved in it. We tend to think that, if they would only carry out the searching scrutiny that we press for, they can hardly fail to reach complete agreement with us. In all such cases, we make our appeal above the unreflective heads of "present company," to the "great company of reflective persons," wherever they may be situated in space or time; we do this all the more emphatically that present company proves unsympathetic. But we should not be speaking ethically at all, if we were not making our appeal to some such company, if we were not submitting our immediate, primary attitude to some form of social testing. . . .

IX

We may now lay down a feature of the ethical reaction which, more than any other, determines its content and its flavour, the feature, namely, that an ethical reaction claims *impartiality*, that it aspires to be *unbiassed*, to *take no sides* among the persons who may be involved in some action. This is the feature brought out in so masterly a manner by Adam Smith, who has located an "impartial spectator" as the moral subject in our bosoms, a spectator who has sympathy with *all* the parties to an action, and yet divests himself of fear or favour in regard to *any*. It also comes out in the Kantian principle that we can only will something *morally*, if we are also prepared to will it *universally*. And it comes out in the three Sidgwickian maxims of equity and benevolence: that one man's well-being deserves as much consideration as another's, that what is right for one man cannot be wrong for others, if their circumstances are identical, and that it cannot be right for one man to treat another in a way in which it would be wrong for that other man, whose circumstances are similar, to treat the first man. These rules and axioms were not made known to us by any supernormal intuition, nor is it in any way queer that every ethical consciousness should acknowledge them; we simply should not *call* a set of feelings "ethical" in which they were not followed or approved. A man might find it personally amusing to see one person riding roughshod over others, he might even demand and love brutality and ruthlessness, but it would be quite impossible to keep to our accepted use of terms, and still maintain that these were *ethical* reactions. It is plainly only by a very liberal stretch of usage that the codes sponsored by Thrasymachus or Nietzsche, or those upheld by various lesser, later persons, could be described as ethical codes. . . .

All moral attitudes are, by their nature, levelling and egalitarian: they tolerate no differences and no degrees for which no very cogent reasons can be given. All these facts simply render silly those arguments which suggest that there might very well be people who approved morally of torturing innocent persons, or of committing other similar enormities, and that no one could do more than harry or abuse them for their very singular moral taste. Whereas, if anyone approved of such acts, he could not, on our ruling, be responding ethically at all, since no one could maintain that he was even attempting to achieve impartiality. Or, if we said he was attempting to achieve impartiality, he would be failing so grossly, that no one could regard his feelings or his judgements as anything but totally unjustifiable.

X

So far we have been showing that the moral responses of different people, must, since they are *moral* responses, agree in very many ways, and that the testing processes to which they are subjected must bring them into ever closer harmony. But we have still left open a somewhat dangerous avenue of variability: different people may not take the same view of human welfare, or of the factors which compose it. For we have said that acts, in order to be ethically relevant, must have some bearing upon welfare, and, if men differed widely in their view of welfare, their moral attitudes might also differ very widely. Two sets of moral attitudes that were both well-considered, stable, unbiassed, and acceptable in a given social setting, might yet be utterly at variance if they built on notions of welfare that were widely different. If some people could be of the opinion that welfare consisted entirely in editing Greek authors and visiting fashionable watering-places, while others found it wholly comprehended in trout-fishing and lion-taming, we could scarcely hope for much agreement in their ethical responses. And some have seriously argued as if such differences were thinkable. Whereas we shall attempt to show that there are processes of appraisal, very similar in many ways to the moral tests we have just dealt with, by which we can determine whether anything is "genuinely worth while," and how high we may rank it among human goods. And we shall also try to make plain that certain views of well-being can be shown by these tests to be utterly invalid, and that we have, in fact, a very narrow range of liberty in determining the content of well-being.

What is, in fact, the attitude behind the statement that some experience or way of living is "really worth having," or the contrary? Plainly it involves a state of satisfaction or dissatisfaction, which will be actual if the experience or way of life is actual, and hypothetical if it is imaginary. But it is not, as an attitude, exhausted by such feelings, nor does it merely seem to hold for one occasion, or for one person only. Quite obviously it also includes claims and expectations, which may be tested, and by which it may be validated or invalidated. A man who thinks some way of life to be authentically worth while, thinks, in the first place, that it will not cease to satisfy him, however long he ponders on it, and however long he continues to see it in relation to the whole of life, or to other ways of living. It must not merely be a satisfactory form of living: it must also be a source of *stable and enduring satisfaction*. And if, after a due course of reflection and comparison, it shows itself as paltry and meretricious, or if we find it varying inconsequently in our estimation, then our original appraisal must be withdrawn.

To hold a way of life to be genuinely worth while means, further, that we think it will be able to establish itself in the regard of *all* who have sufficiently experienced it, or who have thought about it long enough; we also think that it will be able to *maintain* itself in the regard of all such persons. Our estimate accordingly subjects itself, by virtue of its nature as an estimate of well-being, to a form of social testing. Not only do we *wish* to communicate our attitude to others, to lead them to set store by whatever we cherish ourselves: we also positively *expect* that they will do so, if they will only try our cherished ways of living long enough, so that they "really know what they are like." It is in such a spirit that we recommend to others the satisfactions of the adventurous life, or of the life of intellectual effort, or of self-sacrificing love. And, if our estimate finds no echo in the bosoms of our contemporaries or our neighbours, then we appeal to the judgement of *all* reflective persons, wherever they may be situated in space or time, and firmly trust that *they* will corroborate us.

That this communicability to others is a touchstone of authentic value, shows itself also in the fact that, in endeavouring to assess such value, we try, as far as possible, to divest ourselves of any merely personal preferences that we could never hope to render catholic. No one would hold, for instance, that beagling, playing cards and having wilful love-affairs were in themselves intrinsically valuable, since there must necessarily be many who have absolutely no taste for these amusements. Only what *everyone* must inevitably cherish, or come to cherish, can be genuinely worth while. The importance of communicability also shows itself in the great seriousness with which we trouble to *discuss* our way of life with others; we take the mere fact that someone says or feels that something is worth while, as evidence that it really *is* worth while. There is, in the unemotional sciences, no such value attaching to the mere multiplication of heads and voices. We are now in a position to see that, by virtue of the testing they receive, our estimates of the genuinely worth while must always tend to greater uniformity. For every estimate that is neither stable nor communicable will tend to be discredited and abandoned, while those that fluctuate only slightly, and are readily shared by others, will thereby come to be more firmly fixed and justified.

We should not, however, be giving a complete account of welfare, unless we touched upon the difference, so puzzling to philosophers, between the *higher* and the *lower* forms of welfare. Some ways of living do not merely seem satisfactory, they also seem *to have dignity;* we should sometimes choose them even if they were not so intensely satisfactory as other, less distinguished forms of living. Mill's talk about the quality of pleasures, his well-known dictum about Socrates dissatisfied and a pig satisfied, are sufficient to describe the situation. But, from our point of view, we cannot merely take this difference for granted; we must discover the *attitude* that underlies it. For to say that something has dignity, that it represents a higher way of living, is to evince or express a certain emotional attitude in regard to it, and we cannot interpret the utterances in question without understanding the nature of this attitude. What is, in fact, our attitude when we say that something has dignity?

Once we raise this question, the answer leaps to view: the "higher things" are things that we do not merely prize, but that we are also *able to admire.* There are, in welfare, elements so needful that they form its indispensable core, but there are other things that we only begin to demand when these primary goods are present, things which seem in some way to be rare or fine or difficult, and which accordingly attract our admiration. The higher ways of living are *admired* ways of living, not merely satisfactory ones. Accordingly, when we attempt to grade the various forms of life and experience, we have to remember that there are at least two ways of grading them, according as we find them merely satisfactory, and according as we find them admirable. We have, in short, *mere* well-being and the *higher* well-being. (And there may very well, in addition, be other forms of well-being, which correspond to such attitudes as awe or passionate love, and which we might qualify by such adjectives as "sublime," "glorious" and so forth: we could scarcely hope to cover, in one comprehensive scale of values, the very numerous, mutually incomparable forms of human bliss and blessedness.)

We shall now proceed to point to certain necessary and inevitable agreements in our preferences both in the sphere of mere welfare and in the sphere of the higher well-being. It is not hard to see, first of all, that if we eliminate all questions of higher and lower, and look on ways of living as merely satisfactory, and if we are careful to discard all merely personal preferences and idiosyncrasies, there is nothing left to make a way of living satisfactory to *us* but the fact that it is actually satisfactory to someone. The *content* of a way of life thereupon becomes irrelevant: the *fact* that it is satisfactory alone remains significant. We are, in short, brought back to common hedonism, which seems, in consequence, to be the one unquestionably correct account of what we have described as "mere welfare." For one could not make stamp-collecting or horse-breeding integral parts of welfare, since many find them utterly boring, and since no one who took the trouble to divest himself of any personal likings could discover the ghost of a reason why anyone who *didn't* care for them *should* care for them. But even those who have divested themselves of personal likings in the matter, still find it satisfactory that those who actually care for horse-breeding or stamp-collecting should devote themselves to these activities, merely *because* they find them agreeable or satisfactory. The activities themselves therefore lack what we may call "interpersonal value," but the fact that something is personally valuable and agreeable to someone, *has* interpersonal value. The source of pleasure doesn't count for impartial judges, but the pleasure itself does.

Even if we turn to certain standard acts, which all or most men find highly agreeable, the acts of eating or having sexual intercourse, for instance, we are still unable to regard these as integral parts of welfare since we can so readily *imagine* beings who would not find them pleasant. And no one could find a reason why anyone who *didn't* find them pleasant *should* find them so. But even those who didn't find them pleasant, would necessarily, in so far as they were impartially sympathetic, be agreeably affected by the pleasure of those who found them pleasant. There is also another good reason for excluding these generally pleasurable acts from welfare: our liking for them is utterly unstable. They may, at a given moment, seem all-important and supremely sweet, but in a flash they are capable of becoming distasteful or indifferent. It is only the pleasurableness of the activities that does not pall, not the activities themselves. It seems therefore that only pleasantness, and freedom from unpleasantness, will qualify as marks of our lower form of well-being, when this is assessed by judges who have divested themselves of all tastes and preferences that are not necessarily shared by everybody.

Turning, however, to our higher form of well-being, we shall try to show that here, too, there must be *much* inevitable agreement. For it is not possible to admire everything: some ways of living are simply not a possible object of this attitude. One could not, for example, think that enormous dignity attached to a life of brainless tea-drinking punctuated with mild gambling. To awaken admiration a way of life must, at the least, be *extraordinary* in some manner: it must be rare in its strength, in its purity, in its thoroughness, or unusual in its harmony or range. It must achieve or perform *more* in a certain direction than is normally achieved or performed: it cannot represent a merely humdrum or average level of accomplishment.

If some way of living is then to be rated as a higher form of well-being, it must, further, be able to *keep* our admiration, however long we think about it, and however clearly we see it in relation to other ways of living. Activities whose rarity soon wears off, or which only arouse wonder when our experience is limited, would certainly not deserve incorporation in a list of higher goods. It is further plain that nothing could be regarded as a higher form of welfare which we could not *unreservedly* admire, or which was essentially mixed up with other things that we could not help shunning or despising. Thus military glory could obviously never be reckoned among the higher forms of welfare, though equally obviously there is an immense amount of higher welfare involved in it.

We may lay down further, just as we did in other cases, that justifiable admiration is always capable of communication: things *truly* admirable are things that *all* reflective persons will ultimately come to admire. Is it unreasonable to suggest that the higher goods whose listing has been so prominent a feature of recent ethical discussion, really represent a well-attested summing-up of the ways of living that are enduringly, unmixedly and necessarily admirable to everyone? For practically everyone would agree that knowledge, contemplation of beauty, personal affection and moral virtue are to be included among the higher goods. Profound and penetrating intellectual vision, enjoyment of rare harmonies of form or rare felicities of expression, passionate and profound personal love and understanding, and determined choice of what is right and proper: these, and a few other similar things, are undoubtedly to be included among the higher forms of well-being. Nor need we fear that any of them could ever lose our admiration: for, by the use of such adjectives as "passionate," "profound" and "rare," we have ensured that they must always lie on the upper borderline of our experience (wherever that may be); they never could, accordingly, become commonplace or facile.

XI

We may now claim to have established that the ethical judgements of different people, although they express emotions, must necessarily agree in many ways, and that they must also necessarily tend towards greater and greater agreement. We have tried to show that they cannot have that boundless variability which some have thought inevitable in emotional expressions. . . .

It is now, however, time to stress another aspect of the matter. We must emphasize that there are many differences in morals that we simply cannot compose or settle, and that there are also many moral questions which will never have one satisfactory answer. And it is just because a realist ethics might lead us to suppose that every ethical question has some definite answer (although we may not know it), that such a theory becomes so definitely misleading. For the techniques by which we test our moral judgements are plainly quite incapable of leading to precise results in countless cases of doubt and conflict. And it is altogether unhelpful to suppose that there are objective differences where we are quite unable to draw distinctions.

We may, in fact, point to *two* major zones of indeterminacy in the moral field: the zone of *justice,* where we balance and compare the claims of different persons, and the zone of *welfare,* where we balance and compare the claims of different sorts of well-being. Must I keep faith with A, though B and C will suffer in consequence? How great a possible benefit to B and C would justify a breach of faith with A? These, and countless other similar questions may be regarded as "posers" of justice, and it is only too plain that we shall *never* be able to answer them. Again we may ask: Is virtuous ignorance preferable to unvirtuous (not necessarily vicious) knowledge? And how much virtue is equivalent to a certain depth and range of knowledge? These, and innumerable other similar questions may be regarded as "posers" of welfare, and it is again plain that they are *wholly* unanswerable. Indeed a mere perusal of the ethical literature of the present century would show the utter hopelessness of these inquiries: whatever the ethical questions on which we may at length achieve agreement, we shall *never* agree on these. There is, of course, a "sound man's judgement" in these dubious territories, to which many thinkers, following Aristotle, have appealed, but this is surely nothing but the very sensible proceeding of making up one's mind, and shaping one's conduct, quite arbitrarily in circumstances where self-torturing conscientiousness would be utterly profitless. There may, of course, be a heuristic value in postulating that there *are* answers to every ethical question, but we must remember that the heuristic value of false assumptions can be much exaggerated, both in this and in other fields of investigation. . . .

To save space, we shall assume Kurt Baier's position to be sufficiently presented by Kai Nielsen in the course of his discussion of it in the following essay. Nielsen effectively indicates how, in their opposition to emotivism and relativism, many people like Baier are looking for a way to show that moral judgments are, or at least may be, objectively valid. He then explains Baier's line of thought and defends it against Paul Taylor's charge of ethnocentrism—a charge that might also be applied (by the emotivists or Hare, for example) to Perry, Hume, Findlay, and Warnock. The issue involved here requires some explanation. Roughly, we can say that a moral judgment is any normative or value judgment made from the moral point of view, and morality is the business of making or acting on moral judgments. The question is this: How is the moral point of view to be defined? The line taken by Hare and many others is that one is taking the moral point of view if and only if one's judgments and decisions are accompanied by certain sorts of feelings, by a willingness to universalize, and/or by a rating of supreme importance or highest priority. In opposition to this, Baier, Nielsen, Findlay, Warnock, and Perry maintain that some reference to the content, matter, or reasons considered is part of taking the moral point of view. For Baier and Perry, this takes the form of saying that a rule isn't moral unless it is, or is thought to be, for the good of everyone alike; for Findlay, Warnock, and Nielsen, it takes the form of saying that morality and moral judgments involve consideration of facts about the welfare of sentient beings, including others besides oneself. Taylor's criticism, with which Hare and the emotivists would agree, is that if one takes this line, one is building a certain morality (say, ours) into the definition of morality itself. Nielsen contends that this is not true in any objectionable sense and supports an objectivist theory of moral judgments along Baier's lines.

ON MORAL TRUTH

Kai Nielsen

When we reflect philosophically about morality we are very typically concerned with determining whether we can have any knowledge of good and evil, whether any moral claims have an objective rationale; that is to say, in thinking about the foundations of moral belief, we want very much to know whether any ethical code or any moral claim at all can be shown to be objectively justified.

In making such an inquiry, we run into trouble right away. What does it mean to say that moral claims can be objectively justified? Pre-

From "Studies in Moral Philosophy," in American Philosophical Quarterly *Monograph Series, Monograph #1 (Oxford: Basil Blackwell, with the cooperation of the University of Pittsburgh, 1968). Reprinted by permission of the author and publisher.*

sumably it means that some moral claims are objective. But what does *that* mean? Some moral philosophers write as if moral judgments or moral statements would be objective if and *only* if moral values had a real existence apart from any reference to a human mind or to human attitudes. But now we are surely up queer street, for moral values are not objects like a table or even like an electron. To speak of moral values is to speak of what is good or right *to do,* or to *have done,* or what is good to seek, or of what one ought to be or to have been. But then we are surely not talking of what exists but of what is *to be* brought into existence. Sometimes we do indeed make assertions about what is the case when we make moral judgments, e.g., when we assert that someone has an admirable character, but moral utterances usually involve a *telling to,* not a *telling that.* (In talking about the past we are talking about what to have done.) Given this peculiarity of moral discourse, it is absurd to think of moral values as some peculiar sort of "non-natural object" or of norms as existing in some odd noumenal realm. If we note the actual uses of moral discourse we will immediately recognize that it is absurd to think of moral values as existing either apart from or as being dependent on human minds. Talk of existence cannot gain a foothold here. Moral values are neither natural nor non-natural objects. To ask whether in that sense they are objective is like asking whether a wife is unmarried. Such a request is self-refuting because it is nonsensical.

Yet, as Westermarck recognized, though he was not entirely free of the above kind of confusions, there are other, quite separable elements in the concept of an objective moral judgment that perhaps can be satisfied. First, if someone is claiming that the statements "*x* is good" or "*x* is wrong" are objective statements, he is claiming, at the very least, that such statements are not reducible to *x* is *thought* to be good or *x* is *thought* to be wrong. If our moral claims are objective, they must be something of which we could correctly say that though people *think* so and so is wrong, they are mistaken, for it is not wrong. There are people who think that the earth is flat but their thinking so does not make the earth flat. Only if we can get beyond "thinking makes it so" can we be justified in claiming that there are objective moral claims.

Westermarck adds another condition that must be satisfied if moral judgments can be correctly said to be objective. This is the condition that some moral judgments can be true and others false. To believe in the objectivity of morals is to believe that some moral statements are true. In short, to correctly claim that a certain "course of conduct is objectively right, it must be thought to be right by all rational beings who judge truly of the matter and cannot, without error, be judged to be wrong." Now we must be careful here to use the word "rational" in a non-moralistic way, if we are to avoid going in a short and vicious circle.[1] In short, to assert "*x* is objectively right" and "*x* is objectively speaking the best thing to do" is to give one to understand that statements asserting that *x* is objectively right or that *x* is objectively speaking the best thing to do are true and that they are thought to be true by all rational beings who properly consider the matter. But apart from difficulties about "rational" and "properly consider the matter," there are notorious difficulties about saying moral statements are true or false. I want here to consider these difficulties.

Most emotivists and other non-descriptivists claim that it is misleading to say that fundamental moral statements are either true or false.[2] They readily admit that it is linguistically quite in order to say of certain very typical moral statements that they are true or false. In that way they differ very markedly from commands or imperatives or mere expressions of emotion. A. J. Ayer puts this general point very well when he remarks:

> For, as the English language is currently used—and what else, it may be asked, is here in question?—it is by no means improper to refer to ethical utterances as statements; when someone characterizes an action by the use of an ethical predicate, it is quite good usage to say that he is thereby describing it; when someone wishes to assent to an ethical verdict, it is perfectly legitimate for him to say that it is true, or that it is a fact, just as if he wished to dissent from it, it would be perfectly legitimate for him to say that it was false. We should know what he meant and we should not consider that he was using words in an unconventional way.[3]

Ayer stresses all this, but he still argues, as have many others, that it is logically misleading to follow ordinary usage here. These non-descriptivists are recommending a new way of speaking that will be, so they think, logically speaking less misleading than the old way of speech. Ayer argues that when we consider carefully the actual use of moral language—its depth grammar rather than its surface grammar—we will see that moral utterances, even when declarative in form, are not verifiable or even confirmable. If I say "The dog is in the snow," "The Russians are invading Alaska," or "Frustrated people tend to respond with aggression" you know what facts count in establishing the truth or falsity of my claim. These statements assert certain quite empirically identifiable states of

---

[1] It is used in a moralistic way in the following examples. "A rational man will never simply use people to further his own interests," "A rational man will not pursue his own lesser good at the expense of the greater good of his society," "A rational man will be fair in his dealings with others."

[2] I say *most,* for C. L. Stevenson makes it quite evident that he does not think it is misleading. See C. L. Stevenson, *Facts and Values* (New Haven, 1963), pp. 214–20.

[3] A. J. Ayer, "On the Analysis of Moral Judgments" in Milton Munitz (ed.), *A Modern Introduction to Ethics* (New York, 1958), p. 537.

affairs which, if the asserted state of affairs in question actually does exist, will establish the truth of my claim. If it does not exist then my claim can quite correctly be said to be false. My attitudes, my interests, do not at all affect the truth or falsity of what I assert. I may hate to see dogs romping in the snow, I may fear the Russians coming to Alaska, I may deplore the fact that frustrated people keep the whole cycle going by responding aggressively, but all the same the facts are what they are no matter how I or anyone else may feel about them. But how do we verify or confirm, falsify, or disconfirm "Dogs ought to be allowed to romp in the snow," "The Russians ought not to invade Alaska," or "Frustrated people ought not to become aggressive"? We can and do give reasons for these statements, but what would it be like to verify the statements as distinct from verifying whether some of the factual statements given as supporting reasons are true? There seem to be no facts that we can point to that would verify such statements; and if there is no *conceivable* direct verification of them then we cannot sensibly speak of an indirect verification of them either, for where nothing could conceivably count as direct verification the phrase "indirect verification" could have no meaning. If this is so, we do not know what it would be like for such claims to be true, for we do not know what we would have to apprehend to make them true or, for that matter, false. Because of this, Ayer argues, we had better, for philosophical purposes at least, amend ordinary language and stop speaking of moral statements as true or false.

This, and more complex considerations as well, have counted heavily in favor of the "no truth" account of moral discourse. But there are difficulties here as well. Even if, as with descriptive statements, there are no facts that moral statements simply describe—even if there is nothing like ' "The cat is on the mat' is true" if and only if the cat is on the mat'— it does not follow that it is not proper to say that statements of logically diverse kinds are true. Mathematical and logical statements are true; more generally there are analytic truths even though such a "correspondence theory" will not begin to work for them. Just as we recognize factual truths and logical truths, why cannot we recognize moral truths as well?

It is here where the good reasons approach and Kurt Baier's analysis in particular can be of considerable help. Baier thinks he has a way around our problem. His first move is indirect. It consists (1) in showing how we determine the truth of claims about what is legal or customary, and (2) in showing how very different moral concepts are from legal concepts or from mere customs. To find out whether it is true that it is illegal for Caucasians and Negroes to marry in Mississippi, we need only to find out what the law is in Mississippi and how this bears on U.S. Federal laws; to find out whether it is customary for white men to flirt with Negro girls in Mississippi, we need only determine what the practice is in Mississippi.

Once we discover what the law is or what the custom is, we have un-equivocally settled the question of the truth of our legal claim or our claim about what is customary. But this is not so with moral questions. If we make a moral claim, if we assert "It is immoral to prevent Cau-casians and Negroes from marrying in Mississippi or anyplace else" or "It is wrong for white men to flirt with Negro girls when they cannot marry them, have no intention of marrying them, and do not even treat them as persons," the truth or falsity of these claims is *not* decided and cannot be decided simply by discovering what are the moral convictions of the group. Morality differs radically from law and custom here. If I know what is demanded or prohibited by the moral code of my society, I do *not* thereby know what is right in my society or elsewhere. Once a person knows what the law or custom of his own or some other culture is, he cannot intelligibly ask whether his convictions about what is legal or customary in *that culture* are true, but this is not so for morality. How then do we determine whether a moral conviction is true?

Baier's answer is very simple: "Our moral convictions are true if they can be seen to be required or acceptable from the moral point of view." [4] When we say that a moral judgment is true we endorse that judgment; we endorse it as a judgment that is rationally warranted; and when the judgment in question is a moral judgment, to say that it is rationally war-ranted comes to acknowledging it as acceptable from the moral point of view.

But what is it for something to be acceptable from the moral point of view? What is it to take the moral point of view? In Chapter 8 of his *The Moral Point of View*, Baier explicates what it is to take "the moral point of view." To take the moral point of view, three conditions must be satisfied.

1. We must adopt rules of conduct not as rules of thumb designed to promote our own individual interests, but as matters of principle. As Baier points out, "this involves conforming to the rules whether or not doing so favors one's own or anyone else's aim." [5]
2. A moral agent must adopt rules to which not only he and his friends conform as a matter of principle, but rules to which everyone can con-form as a matter of principle. Moral rules are meant for everybody.[6]

   There are four subsidiary conditions which need to be noted under this condition.

---

4 Kurt Baier, *The Moral Point of View* (Ithaca, New York, 1958), pp. 183–84. In my "History of Ethics," vol. III, *Encyclopedia of Philosophy*, ed. by Paul Edwards (New York, 1967), pp. 109–12, I have given a general characterization of the good reasons approach and tried to place it in contemporary ethical theory.

5 Kurt Baier, *op. cit.*, p. 191.

6 *Ibid.*, p. 195.

    a. It must be possible to teach a moral rule to everybody.

    b. It must be a rule such that its purpose would not be defeated if everyone acted on it.

    c. It must be a rule such that it would not be defeated if a person let it be known that he adopted it.

    d. It must not be a rule such that it would be literally impossible for everyone to act in accordance with it .

3. Moral rules must be rules which are adopted for the good of everyone alike. The principle of impartiality or justice is involved here, since the interests of all people must be furthered, or at least given equal consideration when some moral rule has to be overridden. Baier gives us a case to make clear exactly what it is that he means. This condition excludes from morality any set of rules "which enrich the ruling class at the expense of the masses." [7] It excludes any rule that is not reversible. This is to say, the behaviour in question "must be acceptable to a person whether he is at the 'giving' or 'receiving' end of it." [8]

One further point is important in considering what it is to take the moral point of view. When one takes the moral point of view one must, when one has a specific moral perplexity, review the *facts* in the light of one's moral convictions.[9] The important thing to see here is that if one is reasoning morally, one must attend to the facts relevant to the case.

According to Baier, we can determine true from false moral statements by determining which statements are *acceptable* from the moral point of view. If a statement is acceptable from the moral point of view, it is true; if not, not. Only certain rules of conduct will satisfy these conditions. This means that no moral statement can be true unless it is made in accordance with and acceptable from the point of view of those norms which incapsulate the moral point of view.

This view, if correct, would give us some moral truths, some knowledge of good and evil. But Baier's view and the good reasons approach generally has not escaped thorough criticism. It has been thought by many in some way to enshrine, as *the* logic of moral discourse, the rather limited moral views of some particular men at a particular time and place. Paul Taylor has made this reaction specific and penetrating in his striking article "The Ethnocentric Fallacy." [10] Taylor argues that Baier's effort is reduced in essence to the claim that a moral claim is true only if it is made in accordance with the moral principles of liberal Western society, but these principles in turn are not testable—nothing establishes their truth

---

    [7] *Ibid.,* p. 201.

    [8] *Ibid.,* p. 202

    [9] *Ibid.,* p. 185.

    [10] Paul Taylor, "The Ethnocentric Fallacy," *The Monist,* vol. 47 (1963), pp. 563–84.

or falsity. But to argue in this way—to argue as Baier does—is, Taylor argues, to commit the ethnocentric fallacy.

Let me explain exactly what Taylor means when he makes this claim. Baier, Taylor argues, defines "the moral point of view" in terms of the moral code of liberal Western Society.

> As a logical consequence of his definition, all moral convictions which do not accord with those of that particular society are false. But this assumes that one set of moral convictions are true, and does not tell us how we know *this*. In fact, by making moral knowledge relative to or dependent upon these convictions, it places the convictions themselves beyond truth and falsity and hence renders them arbitrary.[11]

This challenge of Taylor's is a powerful one—a challenge that cannot in some form or other but occur to any thoughtful reader of Baier's book. Let us take a close look at Taylor's incisive arguments.

Taylor points out that "if we define the word 'moral' in terms of an impartial set of rules, according to which no act is right unless reversible, then it become *self-contradictory* to talk of the moral code of a society which, for example, places women in a subordinate position to men." [12] But if we adopt this definition, we in effect make the truth of someone's moral convictions "relative to the moral code of what might be dubbed 'liberal Western society'—the society which had adopted a moral code embodying principles of justice, impartiality, and brotherhood extending to all human beings." [13] At this point Taylor drives home his most crucial point. For all his sophistication, Baier has been very culture-bound, very ethnocentric in his characterization of the moral point of view. Taylor remarks that the above liberal code of conduct

> . . . is only one among many. However deeply our own conscience and moral outlook may have been shaped by it, we must recognize that other societies in the history of the world have been able to function on the basis of other codes. There are societies with caste systems, societies which practice slavery, societies in which women are treated as inferior to men and so on. To claim that a person who is a member of one of those societies and who knows its moral code, nevertheless does not have true moral convictions is, it seems to me, fundamentally correct. But such a claim cannot be justified on the ground of Baier's concept of the moral point of view, for that is to assume that the moral code of liberal Western society is the only genuine morality. This renders it nonsensical to talk about alternative moral codes, unless we place "moral" in brackets or quotation marks . . . to indicate that such codes are somehow alleged to be moral but are not genuinely so.[14]

---

[11] *Ibid.*, p. 565.
[12] *Ibid.*, pp. 568–69.
[13] *Ibid.*, p. 570.
[14] *Ibid.*

To proceed in this ethnocentric way, Taylor argues, produces the very reverse effect of what Baier was after. Baier wanted to show how one could correctly assert that the moral convictions of a society, including his own, could be false. But given this ethnocentric definition of "the moral point of view" and given Baier's definition of "moral truth," moral truth comes to depend on which codes of which societies are referred to. If a moral claim is acceptable from the point of view of Western liberal morality, it is true; if not, it is false. This is a perfect rationalization for ethnocentrism. Moreover, it will now become senseless to ask whether a person's moral convictions are true if they are acceptable from the point of view of liberal Western morality. But this is itself, Taylor argues, surely nonsense for if this were so (1) "Act x is forbidden by the moral code of society S, but is it really wrong?" would become equivalent to (2) "Act x is forbidden by the moral code of society S, but is it forbidden by the moral code of liberal Western society?" But the two questions are not equivalent. (2) could be settled in the way we settle questions of what is customary or what is legal, but, as Baier has shown himself, we do not and cannot settle moral questions in this way. Furthermore (1) would make sense when asked of any society, but (2) does not make sense when society S is liberal Western society. Thus (1) and (2) are very different questions.

Surely Taylor is right *if* to take the "moral point of view" is to take a point of view wherein we must, to be even *reasoning morally*, have the ideal of the brotherhood of all men. There have been plenty of societies that have had moral codes that did not even remotely have this ideal. As Westermarck points out,

> Primitive peoples carefully distinguish between an act of homicide committed within their own community and one where the victim is a stranger: while the former is in ordinary circumstances disapproved of, the latter is in most cases allowed and often considered worthy of praise. And the same holds true of theft and lying and the infliction of other injuries. Apart from the privileges granted to guests, which are always of very short duration, a stranger is in early society devoid of all rights.[15]

Westermarck, utilizing a wealth of empirical material, goes on to show how in Greek society, Roman society, among the early Teutonic groups, through the Middle Ages and down into the seventeenth century in Europe, similar moral conceptions were very widespread. Even today, Westermarck points out, such ideas are not entirely dead within Western culture. Modern moral philosophers argue against it, but such tribal moral beliefs—beliefs which come to the fore during wartime and in times of political and economic pressure—are surely not dead among us. As norma-

---

[15] Edward Westermarck, *Ethical Relativity* (London, 1932), p. 197.

tive ethicists, as moralists, we may surely deplore such "moralities" and seek to argue for a universalistic morality in which the ideal of brotherhood and beneficence is extended to all men, but plainly such alternative moral codes and moral conceptions do exist.

Certainly this is a powerful attack. In a very plain sense of "adopted for the good of everyone alike" not all rules that as a matter of linguistic propriety can be properly called "moral rules" or "moral principles" enshrine such an intent.

Yet this is not the whole tale. What Baier says about the third condition for the moral point of view, perhaps with a little stretching in the direction of Hare, can be interpreted in a way that does not fall prey to the ethnocentric fallacy.

A key to what I want to claim here lies in Baier's Kantian claim that moral judgments must be reversible. When we say that a moral claim must be reversible, we are saying that whatever is to count as "a moral claim" must be acceptable to the agent whether he is on the giving or receiving end of it. Now it has been argued that this reversibility is not analytically linked with what it is for something to count as "a moral statement." After all, people have said, "Women should not vote," "Black men should not live in the same apartment blocks as white men," "The ruling classes have a right to enrich themselves at the expense of the masses," "Germans deserve one kind of treatment, Jews another," "People who are shipwrecked may be plundered." But, it has been argued, clearly non-reversible and neanderthal though they be, that these judgments are unequivocally moral judgments. It is, Taylor and others have argued, not a necessary condition for something's being a moral judgment that it be reversible. In thinking that it is, so the argument runs, Baier and Kant reveal an ethnocentric understanding of morality.

I want to argue that these examples not withstanding, reversibility *is* such a necessary condition and this Kantian claim, *properly understood,* does not commit us to an ethnocentric view of morality. There remains a very crucial sense in morals—in which even people who hold such apparently non-reversible views as the anti-Femininist, the racist and the Nazi quoted above, if they are reasoning morally at all, must be applying the criterion of reversibility. Consider this snatch of a dialogue:

A: Women should not vote. They must always remain in a subordinate place in our society.

B: If you were a woman you wouldn't say that.

A: No indeed I wouldn't. I would be quite justified in maintaining that if I were a woman I would have the right to vote, but I still would say that other women ought not to vote.

B: But then it isn't "being a woman" that should disqualify one from voting, but "being a certain kind of a person." There is something about *you* that entitles you, whether you are or are not a woman, to vote and the women whom you say should not vote lack that quality.

A: No, I'm not saying anything of the kind. There is—I confess— nothing distinctive about me. I am just saying that women *ought* not to vote. But I am *not* at all willing to say that if I were a woman, in all relevant respects like the women whom I say should not vote, that then *I* should not vote.

When A replies in this way he is saying something that is not intelligible as a bit of moral or normative discourse. It is in this sense that reversibility is a necessary requirement of the moral point of view. But such a limitation does not make it self-contradictory, as Taylor thinks, to set forth a moral code that places women in a subordinate position to men. Neanderthals who so argue will come up with some spurious factual claim that women are somehow either naturally or, as a matter of sociological fact, inferior to men and cannot therefore be given the responsibility of voting. But if such a man is reasoning morally, he must—logically must—be prepared to admit that if he were a woman or were inferior in the same specified way, then he too ought not to be allowed to vote. If he is not prepared to so reason, we would not *understand* what he could mean by saying that he was making a *moral* claim. He would not be playing the moral language game. He would not be thinking as a moral agent. The same thing can be said for the other examples I gave. They do not count against the contention that moral judgments must be reversible. This requirement of reversibility is but a facet of universalizability or the generalization principle, a principle that Taylor himself takes to be analytically tied to anything that could count as a normative judgment.[16] It is, Taylor rightly argues, analytic to "say that whatever is right or wrong for one person is right or wrong for every similar person in similar circumstances." In this sense all normative judgments and *a fortiori* all moral judgments must be reversible, and in *that sense,* impartial. As moral agents, we must be committed to such an idea of impartiality.

Yet we must not forget what both Hare and Taylor have stressed, that this requirement *by itself* does not determine the *content* of any moral judgment. It does not, by itself, block a tribal morality. Greeks can (and have) said of Barbarians that they ought not to have the rights of Greeks; Germans can (and have) said of Jews that they do not have the rights of Germans. But to say this, and make their remarks intelligible as moral

---

[16] Paul Taylor, *op. cit.*, pp. 575–76.

remarks, they must contend that there is something about Barbarians or Jews that makes them different from Greeks and Germans.

But, as Westermarck and more recently Hare have recognized, once we dwell on and take to heart this generalizing feature of moral discourse, it becomes very difficult—if we are at all clear-headed—to be a tribalist in ethics, for if Barbarians, Jews, Negroes, women, the proletariat, and the like are not to have the treatment the tribalist claims for himself, there must—logically must—be something about them that justifies that difference in treatment. That is, there must be something that the maker of the moral judgment would acknowledge as justifying a like treatment for him if that characteristic could be correctly attributed to him. It takes a very fanatical and irrational German to be prepared—to really be prepared—to put himself and all his family into the concentration camp if it turns out that they are Jews. We could play the little trick on him Hare proposes. First, by forged documents we get him to believe that he really is what the Nazis would call a Jew and then, if in true fanatical fashion he agrees that he and his family should have a first-class ticket to the gas chambers, we prove to him that the documents are forged and then ask him, what reason he has for claiming in the first place that he and his family should be gassed and why moments later he has changed his mind. What has changed about him and his family that justifies freeing them from this torment? Does he really see or notice anything about his family and children or about his own person in the two different situations that would justify a switch in treatment? He can, of course, continue to say that it is their "Jewishness/non-Jewishness" that justifies the switch in treatment, but then he is really caught up in obscurantism and mystagogy, for our very trick has shown that there is nothing empirically detectable about being a Jew that is relevant to his moral claim. Perhaps Jewishness is a non-natural intuitable, totiresultant quality supervening on all Jews and only on Jews.

In sum, I have tried to argue, as against Taylor, that Baier's characterization of the moral point of view can be interpreted in such a way that it does not commit the ethnocentric fallacy. I have, as Taylor has, concentrated on Baier's third condition, but now I shall show that the first two conditions do not commit Baier to identifying morality with liberal Western morality and that the three conditions, taken in conjunction with Baier's claim that in reasoning morally we must attend to the facts, give us adequate criteria for deciding when a moral judgment is true.

Let us consider Baier's second condition, namely his contention that a rule, to count as a "moral rule," must be one to which everyone can conform and a rule must be meant for everybody. Our prior discussion should have made it evident that condition two is plausible only under a rather distinctive interpretation. That is, we have to give a distinctive reading of "rule meant for everybody" or "rule to which everyone can conform as a matter of principle." My above remarks about reversibility make it plain how and in what way moral rules are meant for everybody and are rules to which one can conform as a matter of principle. If something is a moral rule it must apply to like people in like circumstances. If it is all right for a starving Brazilian farmer to steal in order to keep alive, if he can't get the means of life in any other way, then it would be all right for anyone like this farmer and in the same kind of situation to steal. In that way, and without ethnocentrism, moral rules are for everyone. But this does not commit us to the absurdity that psychotics and mentally defective people can conform to them, but only to claiming that if, and when, such people can act as moral agents, then they too must, in the relevant circumstances, act in certain prescribed ways.

If a "rule" to have the logical status of "a moral rule" must be universalizable in the manner I have described, it clearly must be a rule that can be taught to anyone capable of moral agency to whom the moral rule correctly applies. If a moral rule applies to men of a certain sort, distinctively situated, this commits us to the assertion that when certain conditions obtain they ought to do what the rule enjoins; and this, in turn, implies that they can do it. But surely a necessary condition for their following the rule is that they understand it. Thus the moral rule must be teachable to the men to whom it correctly applies. But in specifying these men we must specify them by pointing to the fact that they have certain determinate characteristics, and *universalizability* commits us to saying that the moral rule in question must apply to anyone who has these characteristics. This would hold for anything recognizable as "a moral rule." This is a plausible, if somewhat reduced, reading of Baier's claim that a moral rule must be teachable to everybody. I am saying rather that it must be capable of being taught to everyone to whom it can be correctly applied.

Baier's first condition poses more difficulties. Some have thought that there are, or at least can be, "egoistic moralities," but Baier tells us that to adopt the moral point of view is to conform to rules whether or not conforming to them promotes our self-interest. If something counts as a "moral rule" or as a "moral claim" it must (and the force of the "must" here is logical) override self-interest.

That this is so and why it is so is plain enough when we think of the *raison d'être* or, more modestly and more appropriately, a central *raison d'être*, for having a moral code—*any* moral code at all. Any society needs some device for impartially adjudicating conflicts of interest. Society is necessary for human beings, and when human beings live together, band together in a society with at least the minimal cooperation this implies, they will have conflicts of interest. If, when such conflicts occur, each man were to seek to further his self-interest alone, there would be the kind of conflict and chaos in society that no reasonable man could desire. In fact, if men were to act in this way, it would not even be correct to speak of them as living together in society. Thus to live together, to further one of the main ends of morality, men must adopt rules which override self-interest. To take the moral point of view of necessity involves conforming to such rules. But to conform to such rules is not simply to commit oneself to liberal Western morality. It is rather to adopt a point of view that is and must be implicit in all moral reasoning.

We are not out of the dark woods yet. Granting that moral judgments must be universalizable, granting that in the sense specified they must be for the good of everyone alike, we still do not know and cannot determine *what* is for the good of everyone alike, until we can determine something of the content of "for the good of everyone alike." Until we can do this we can hardly be said to have any knowledge of good and evil or any moral truth.

What is it for something to be for the *good* of everyone alike or even for something to be good for me or good period? If we leave the content of "good" unspecified in stating the moral point of view, then if two moralists both adopt the moral point of view and make logically incompatible moral judgments both of which are—under these circumstances—acceptable from the moral point of view, because they both satisfy Baier's three conditions, then we would have two logically incompatible moral judgments both of which, according to Baier's specifications, would be true. But it is a self-contradiction to assert that two logically incompatible assertions could both be true. Baier would surely add, but, of course, two mutually incompatible statements cannot be true, but the problem remains that if we accept his explication of "moral truth" there is no possible way of determining which of the two mutually incompatible moral statements are true.

An example may make my claim clearer. Suppose A claims that wives ought not to have lunch alone with men who are not their husbands, and B claims that this is absurdly medieval, that it is perfectly all right for a woman to have lunch alone with a man who is not her husband. Now these two judgments are both moral judgments, both satisfy Baier's three conditions and they are logically incompatible. We should want to say that they both can't be true, but given Baier's account, as explicated above, we could not possibly say which moral statement was true.

The way out here is to realize that in characterizing the moral point of view, we must *not* speak of "the good of everyone alike" in such a way that "good" is used so that it can have *just any* content. But when we claim "good" must have a certain content, we again run the risk of committing the ethnocentric fallacy. It is tempting to argue that in adopting the moral point of view, we attribute a certain content to "good" but not everyone would use "good" in this way; there are, as J. O. Urmson argues, alternative and often conflicting criteria for "good." But we must —if we follow Baier—specify moral truth with reference to the moral point of view and here we find that once we consider "good-making criteria," we get a relativity in the very specification of the moral point of view that defeats Baier's claim that we can develop an objective test for the truth of moral statements.

The question I want to ask here is this: Are the "good-making criteria" used in such moral appraisals all *that* relative? When we are trying to develop a rational criterion for deciding whether certain actions, rules or practices are good or bad, we are concerned with whether they are, more than any of their alternatives, in the best interests of everyone; and in talking of the best interests of everyone, we are talking about their most extensive welfare and well-being. Now, if you like, you may call "general welfare" and "human well-being" grading labels or evaluative terms or prescriptive terms or normative terms or what you will, but they are, all the same, so tied to certain descriptive criteria that actions, rules or practices which did not satisfy these criteria could not be properly said to be in the general welfare or to serve the human well-being.[17] Practices or rules which sanctioned starving everyone to the point where the human animal could just barely keep alive, prohibited all sexual relations, constantly interrupted people's sleep to the point where they were just capable of keeping alive, made both play and work impossible and destroyed all human affection, could not possibly be correctly said to be in the general welfare and serve human well-being. And if they could not serve human well-being or be in the general welfare they could not be in the best interests of everyone and if they could not be in the best interests of everyone they could not be for the good of everyone alike and if they could not be for the good of everyone alike they could not be compatible with the moral point of view.

Such criteria give content to the moral point of view and make it impossible for both the judgments of A and B to be true. Furthermore, while such an explication of "for the good of everyone alike" *may* commit what has been called the "naturalistic fallacy," it does not commit

---

[17] In this context see also my "Appraising Doing the Thing Done," *The Journal of Philosophy*, vol. 57 (1960); "Progress," *The Lock Haven Review*, no. 7 (1965); "On Looking Back at the Emotive Theory," *Methodos*, vol. 14 (1962); and "Problems of Ethics," vol. III, *Encyclopedia of Philosophy*, ed. by Paul Edwards (New York, 1967), pp. 130–32.

the "ethnocentric fallacy." To accept such criteria about human welfare or human well-being does not commit us to liberal Western morality or even to Western morality, it is part of *any* morality.

It could be argued that what I have said above is mistaken; such a conception of "general welfare" or "human well-being" is still ethnocentric, for Buddhists striving after nirvana and Plains Indians on the vision quest regard certain forms of behavior as supremely desirable even though they run contrary to what I have said is in the general welfare or for human well-being. After all, we can have an "ethic of renunciation." Someone with such an ethic, it is natural to argue, would have a concept of the general welfare very different from the one just put before you. As such ascetics conceive of man's deepest well-being and welfare, we have something that sharply conflicts with what I have said. Such renunciation, they would argue, in reality serves men's deepest well-being and is for the general welfare. "General welfare" and "human well-being" are essentially contested concepts.

This objection to my argument will not do. It will not show that my criterion is ethnocentric, for such behavior was never advocated as a basis for social action or as a way of life for *all* Buddhists or *all* Plains Indians to adopt. It was prescribed for the holy man and not for the ordinary Plains Indian or the ordinary Buddhist. Such behavior did not, even for the holy man, serve as criteria for what was for *human* well-being or in the *general* welfare. Here their criteria overlap with the criteria used by what Taylor calls "liberal Western morality"; and the overlap includes the criteria I gave. There is no good reason to think such criteria are ethnocentric.

There is a further consideration that deserves attention here. As we noted before, in adopting the moral point of view, we are committed, when we are able to review the facts carefully, to clarifying these facts for ourselves before making decisions, advocating certain moral rules, or supporting certain moral practices. Now where there *seems* to be some alteration or qualification of the criteria for human well-being that I have offered, it has been in the service of some superstitious, ideological, or wildly metaphysical scheme. That nirvana can be attained, that there is a numinosity answering to the Indian's quest, is either false or without factual significance.[18] Attention to the facts, including the understanding we would achieve if we attained even a minimum of conceptual

---

[18] My remark here may seem brusque and dogmatic, but I could hardly develop my arguments for it here, though I have in some detail in my "On Speaking of God," *Theoria*, vol. 28 (1962), Part 2; "Religious Perplexity and Faith," *The Crane Review*, vol. 8 (1965); "God-Talk," *Sophia*, vol. 3 (1964); "On Fixing the Reference Range of 'God'," *Religious Studies*, vol. 2 (1966); and in my book *The Quest for God* (forthcoming).

clarity, would lead us to reject such seeming alterations and qualifications of Baier's characterization of the moral point of view. To carry out moral reasoning fully, we must attend carefully to the non-moral facts and we must seek to be clear-headed. If we are clear-headed and do attend to the facts, we will not go on the vision quest or seek or even expect to attain nirvana.

We must also note that moral judgments are judgments that are ideally made in the light of a full knowledge of the relevant facts and they must, logically must, be made in the light of the facts that it is reasonable to expect the moral agent to have in his possession when he must make his moral decision or render judgment. To take the moral point of view is to reason in this way and it is to use "good" in the relevant contexts with this factual content. Since this is so, it cannot be the case that two logically incompatible moral judgments, like A's and B's about wives' dining with men who are not their husbands, could both be acceptable from the moral point of view. They have different consequences for human well-being and, everything being equal, if A's judgment is such that it would, if followed, make for greater general welfare than B's, then only A's judgment is acceptable from the moral point of view; and, if there are no other alternatives acceptable from the moral point of view here, then A's judgment is required from the moral point of view and *a fortiori* true.

The concept of good is sufficiently vague and moral reasoning is sufficiently complex to make it the case that for a wide and important range of cases, we cannot determine what we ought to do with any objectivity. But there are also standard cases and contexts in which we can determine moral truth—that is, we can determine how we ought to act from the moral point of view. Moreover, given a sophisticated and a determined application of moral reasoning and an extensive knowledge of man and his world, our knowledge of good and evil can constantly expand. The concept of truth has an application in morals and we have definite ways of determining truth in morality.

It will now be clear that the question about the definition of morality and the moral point of view is central to recent discussion of the possibility of justifying moral judgments objectively. May we and must we say that moral judgment is by definition concerned, in one way or another, with human good or harm, needs, wants, interests, or happiness? If so, then facts about such things are logically relevant to moral conclusions, and moral Oughts have a basis in objective facts. Like Findlay, Baier, and Nielsen, G. J. Warnock answers the question in the affirmative. Earlier in the book from which the following selection is taken, Warnock discussed and rejected intuitionism, emotivism, and prescriptivism. In the present reading he criticizes attempts by Hare and others to define morality wholly without reference to facts of the kind mentioned above, and explains his own position. Then, in the rest of the book he goes on to suggest that some kind of naturalism may be true after all.

THE CONCEPT OF MORALITY

G. J. Warnock

What Does "Moral" Mean?

The question which is in effect raised by such reflections as these is really a very fundamental one and it has been given, it seems to me, far less attention than it deserves. When philosophers discuss moral principles, moral judgment, moral discourse generally, *what* are they discussing? What does "moral" mean? What distinguishes a moral view from views of other kinds? I think it must be quite clear that there is no easy answer to these questions; and yet, until they are answered, it seems that moral philosophers cannot really know what they are talking about, or at any rate, perhaps no less importantly, cannot be sure whether or not they are all talking about the same thing. It is, indeed, pretty clear that, historically, they have not been. Kant, for instance, takes it for granted that the "moral law" imposes upon all rational beings unconditional, categorical demands to do and forbear—demands that are binding without any regard to human inclinations, purposes, desires, or interests, that have nothing essentially to do with human happiness, and call only for the absolute obedience of "the good will"; his problem is to explain how there can be demands of that kind. But for Hume, for example, this problem does not arise at all. For it does not enter his head that there *are* any demands of that kind; on the contrary, he takes it entirely for granted that moral views give direct expression to human preferences and desires, and that it is the essence of a moral system to promote the interests, the general harmony and well-being, of human communities. That being so, it is of course entirely inevitable that their accounts of "moral discourse" should be widely divergent; for it is not really the same thing that they are seeking to give an account of.

Now it is possible, I think, to distinguish at least four types of factors each of which has been taken, either alone or in conjunction with one or more of the others, as centrally characteristic of morality. First, it has occasionally been suggested that what is really distinctive

From Contemporary Moral Philosophy (*London: Macmillan & Co Ltd, 1967; New York: St. Martin's Press, 1967). Reprinted by permission of the author and Macmillan, London and Basingstoke, and St. Martin's Press.*

of a moral view is, to put it somewhat crudely, the way in which those who take that view feel about it. There is, it is said, a special sense of being *required* to act in a certain way, not by any external pressure or sanction, but rather by one's own consciousness of the sense of wrongdoing, of the guilt and self-reproach, that non-performance would incur. It is clear that there is not nothing in this; but it is perhaps equally clear that this can hardly be, by itself, a sufficient criterion of morality. It is not merely—though of course this is true—that a person may, for one reason or another, come to attach this psychological penumbra of guilt and self-reproach to performances, or non-performances, which are as a matter of fact entirely unobjectionable; for that is to say no more than that a person's moral feelings may sometimes be irrational. It is rather that a man may himself come to recognise that his sense of guilt and self-reproach is irrational and misplaced; and in that case, while the feelings may unfortunately prove very persistent, he presumably does not take their persistence as a ground for continuing to regard the issue, whatever it may be, as a moral one. It is possible, that is, as it were to detach one's feelings from the question whether some course of conduct is morally objectionable—to have the feelings appropriate to morally objectionable behaviour, and yet genuinely not to believe that one's behaviour is morally objectionable. But if so, then the occurrence or non-occurrence of certain feelings, the presence or absence of the characteristic sense of guilt, cannot be a sufficient criterion of a moral view.

Second, it has been held—less often, perhaps, explicitly than by implication—that, for any person, his moral principles and standards are to be identified as those which are in fact dominant in the conduct of his life. This is the view which is at least implicit in Hare's prescriptivism—"A man's moral principles, in this sense, are those which, in the end, he accepts to guide his life by." But this, as we mentioned before, looks highly paradoxical in this unqualified form. It is true, no doubt, that there are many good people whose lives are ultimately guided by their moral principles; but, on this view, we should be obliged to say that this was true, and even necessarily true, of everybody, or at least of everybody who has any principles at all; and surely that is wrong. Surely there have been individuals, and even whole societies, of whom or of which we should want to say that moral principles did not play any large part in their lives—that, perhaps, both their ideals of conduct and their actual conduct were shaped in accordance with standards that were not *moral* standards at all. Homer, in approving the ferocity, guile, and panache of the warrior chieftain, might be said to have been employing moral standards different from our own; but he might just as well, or better, be said not to have been employing moral standards at all.

We must, I think, regard as inadequate on just the same grounds the idea that a man's moral principles are *simply* those, whatever they may be, which he "prescribes" for everyone alike; for surely we should wish to leave open the possibility of saying that some persons, and even some societies, though perhaps they "prescribe" universally, nevertheless do not see things from "the moral point of view."

Finally, then, we may turn to the idea that morality should be somehow characterised, so to speak, by its subject-matter—the idea that what makes a view a *moral* view is, not the psychological penumbra by which it is surrounded, nor its predominance in the life of its proponent, but primarily its content, what it is about, the range or type of considerations on which it is founded. The detailed working out of this idea, so far as any has been done, has taken various forms. It has been suggested, in the spirit of utilitarianism, that rules of morality are by definition those whose observance is at any rate believed to promote the "greatest happiness," and whose violation is thought liable to increase the sum of human misery. Others have argued that we should seek the essence of morality, not in the notion of the promotion of happiness, but rather in that of the satisfaction of human needs, or of the reconciliation and promotion of human interests. Now it is surely hard to deny that there is very great plausibility in such views for must it not surely be supposed, by anyone who claims to be propounding a moral principle, that observance of the principle he propounds would do some sort of *good*, and that breaches of it would do some sort of *harm*? If we ask a man why he holds the moral views that he expresses, must he not try to show, by way of justification, that the things he commends are in some sense or other *beneficial*, that the things he condemns are in some sense or other *damaging*? If he were to make no attempt to explain his position in such terms, what reason could there for for making, or for accepting, the supposition that the views in question were moral views?

Has Morality a "Content"?

Let us now try, then, to survey our present problem from another angle. What does "moral" mean? How are we to identify those principles which are moral principles, or to recognise that species of discourse which is moral discourse? We have just mentioned briefly—no doubt one could extend the list—four possible "marks" of a moral view: its psychological penumbra; its actual importance in the individual's conduct of his life; its "universalisability"; and its general topic—human happiness or interests, needs, wants, or desires. Now there is an important distinction to be found within the items on this list, and one that would continue to be of great importance however our somewhat sketchy list might be extended. This distinction is that between those "marks" which do, and those which do not, assign to moral discourse a characteristic content, or subject-matter. In our short list, the first three items are thus distinguished from the fourth. For a view to which a certain psychological penumbra is attached may be a view *about* anything at all; and if a "moral" view is to be thus identified, there will be nothing that morality, *ex officio*, so to speak, is about. Similarly, a principle which is actually dominant in the conduct of a life, or one which is "prescribed universally" for all alike, may be a principle *about* anything at all; and if moral principles are to be thus identified, again there will be nothing that morality is essentially about. Our fourth item, however, is quite different in this respect; for by this "mark" we shall identify as a moral view a view which is, in one way or another, *about* what is good or bad for people, what they want or need, what promotes or detracts from their happiness, well-being, or satisfaction; and if a moral view is to be *thus* identified, its psychological penumbra may be seen as an open question, and likewise the question whether a man who holds it is actually guided, or demands that others should be guided, predominantly by it in the actual conduct of life. The issue is this: which questions do we take to be answerable *a priori*? Is it true *a priori* that moral views predominate in the conduct of life, and a matter for investigation with what topics, in this instance or that, such views are concerned? Or is it true *a priori* that moral views are concerned with certain topics, and a matter for enquiry what role in life (or in discourse) such views, in this instance or that, may be found to play?

In this essay I cannot hope, and do not propose to try, to answer these questions, but only to call attention to what I take to be the urgent need for their further investigation. For it will be obvious that, for the purposes of moral theory, it is of the first importance that they should be answered—on the answer that is given to these questions will depend one's whole conception of what moral philosophy is called upon to do. Is it one's task to elucidate what one might call the formal character of moral discourse, its general character as a system of "prescriptions," or "evaluations"? Or is one to attempt to elucidate the *content* of morals, to describe in outline and to make distinctions within the general range of phenomena to which moral concepts are applicable? But the questions I have raised are important, I believe, not only for this reason; they are important, here and now, for the additional reason that recent moral philosophers have, often tacitly, answered them quite differently, and very seldom debated the question how they should be answered. Thus one sees moral theories which are not merely quite different, but actually aiming to do, in principle, quite different things; yet the difference of principle, I think, has been seldom recognised and, for that reason, scarcely ever discussed.

My own view (if it is worth expressing a view which one does not then try seriously to examine) is that morality *has* some at least roughly specifiable content. Looking again at our sketchy list of four possible "marks" of a moral view, a moral judgment, a moral principle, the suggestion that I would myself be inclined to hazard is that while each is doubtless *relevant* to the characterisation of "the moral," some form or other of the fourth is likely to turn out to be by far the most centrally important. It is probably true that there is, for very many people, a characteristic way of feeling about the rights and wrongs of conduct in certain cases, a way of feeling which goes with what they take to be moral issues; but apart from the possibility, mentioned above, that such feelings may occur in cases which even the subject himself does not seriously believe to involve moral issues, would one not be inclined also to say that a special way of feeling about certain issues is consequential upon, rather than definitive of, their character as *moral* issues? Rather similarly, it would seem to me more natural to say that, for very many people, certain principles play a predominant role in their own conduct, and are applied universally in judgment of the conduct of others, *because* they are believed to be moral principles, rather than, in reverse as it were, that their being moral principles *consists in* their being treated as overriding and of general application. On the other hand, it appears at least enormously plausible to say that one who professes to be making a moral judgment *must* at least profess that what is in issue is the good or harm, well-being or otherwise, of human beings —that what he regards as morally wrong is somehow damaging, and what he regards as morally right is somehow beneficial. There is no doubt at all that, apart from its high degree of vagueness, this would not be a sufficient characterisation of moral judgment; nevertheless it does appear to me to mention a feature which, in one way or another, any intelligible theory must recognise to be of central importance.[1]

---

[1] It might be objected that, in suggesting that a concern with human benefit or harm is essential to anything deserving the name of moral view, one is illicitly incorporating some kind of utilitarian "humanism" into the very definition of morality. Would not this suggestion be indignantly repudiated by, for instance, the religious believer, for whom the foundation of morality is the Word of God? But I am inclined to think that such an objection would be unsound. For I suspect that religious views differ from "humanist" views, not by denying the essential moral relevance of human benefit or harm, but rather by incorporating very different beliefs as to what really is good or bad for human beings. The religious believer finds in a supernatural order a whole extra dimension of pre-eminently important gains and losses, benefits and harm; his difference with the non-believer is not on the question whether these are of moral significance, but simply on the question whether they are real or chimerical. He might also wish to expand what might be called the moral population to include moral beings supposed not to be human; but to this, if there are such beings, no one surely will object.

6.7

Why Be Moral?

This too is an old question, raised by the Greek Sophists and elaborately dealt with by Plato in the *Republic*. It is a question that seems natural to ask if one has begun to think and is told that something is morally right, wrong, or obligatory, especially if doing or not doing it is contrary to one's desires or contrary to what one takes to be in one's interest. It is a difficult question, not only to answer, but even to understand; some have even held it to be a pseudoquestion, natural maybe but not sensible. (See, for example, the passages from Nowell-Smith in Section 6.3.) In any case, the literature dealing with it is vast, and we can barely sample it. The question has already been broached in a number of previous readings in this book, such as those on egoism, those from Plato's *Republic* and *Protagoras*, and those by Kant, Mill, Garnett, and Nowell-Smith. To focus on it more clearly in this section, we have selected another essay by Nielsen, who takes our question to be a sensible one—if it is not construed as asking "Why morally should one be moral?" He points out that the question actually comprises two questions, discusses various attempts to answer each of them, and advances his own replies. To the second and more crucial question "Why should *I* be moral?" he terms his reply "subjectivism," and ends by arguing that we should not be troubled because no better answer seems available.

WHY SHOULD I BE MORAL?

Kai Nielsen

I

Why . . . be moral? We need initially to note that this question actually ought to be broken down into two questions, namely, 1) "Why should people be moral?" or "Why should there be a morality at all?" and 2) "Why should I be moral?" As will become evident, these questions ought not in the name of clarity, to be confused. But they have been run together; in asking for a justification for the institution of morality both questions are relevant and easily confused. "Why be Moral?" nicely straddles these questions. In this section I shall first examine some traditional, and I believe unhelpful, answers to the above general questions. There the general question is not broken down as it should be and in examining these views I shall not break it down either. After noting the difficulties connected with these approaches, I shall state what I believe to be a satisfactory answer to the question, "Why should there be a morality at all?" and indicate why it leaves untouched the harder question, "Why should I be moral?". . .

What good reasons are there for being moral? And if there are good reasons for being moral are they sufficient or decisive reasons?

There is a short, snappy answer to my question. The plain man might well say: "People ought to be moral because it is wicked, evil, morally reprehensible not to be moral. We have the very best reasons for being moral, namely that it is immoral not to be moral." The plain man (or at the very least the plain Western Man and not *just* the ordinary Oxford Don) would surely agree with Bradley "that consciousness, when unwarped by selfishness and not blinded by sophistry is convinced that to ask for the Why? is simple immorality. . . ." The correct answer to the question: "Why Be Moral?" is simply that this is what we ought to do.

This short answer will not do, for the plain man has failed to understand the question. A clear-headed individual could not be asking for *moral* justification for being moral. This would be absurd. Rather he is asking the practical question: why should people be bound by the conventions of morality at all? He would not dispute Baier's contention that "it is generally believed that when reasons of self-interest conflict with moral reasons, then moral reasons override those of self-interest." It is

From Methodos, XV, No. 59–60 (1963). Reprinted by permission of the author.

perfectly true that the plain man regards moral reasons as superior to all others and it is, of course, in accordance with reason to follow superior or overriding reasons, but if a clear-headed man asks "Why should we be moral?" he is challenging the very grading criteria those ordinary convictions rest on. He would acknowledge that it is indeed morally reprehensible or wicked not to act morally. But he would ask: "So what?" And he might even go on to query: "What is the good of all this morality anyway? Are not those Marxists and Freudians right who claim that the whole enterprise of morality is nothing but an ideological device to hoodwink people into *not* seeking what they really want? Why should people continue to fall for this conjuring trick? To call someone 'wicked' or 'evil' is to severely grade them down, but why should people accept any *moral* grading criteria at all?"

There are several traditional replies to this. But all of them are unsatisfactory.

One traditional approach advocated by Plato and Bishop Butler, among others, claims that people should be moral because they will not be happy otherwise. Being moral is at least a necessary condition for being happy.

For Butler the argument takes the following form. Human beings are so constituted that they will, generally speaking, act morally. When they don't act morally they will clearly recognize they were mistaken in not doing so. The human animal has a conscience and this conscience not only causes people to act in a certain way, but is in fact a *norm* of action. Conscience guides as well as goads; the deliverances of conscience are both action-evoking and a source of moral knowledge. Conscience tells the moral agent what to do even in specific situations. It clearly and unequivocally tell him to always act morally and he is so constituted that if he ignores the dictates of his conscience he will not be happy. In other words, Butler agrees with Plato in claiming that Thrasymachus and other amoralists are fundamentally mistaken about the true interests of a human being.

That it is in the human animal's best interest to live virtuously is no more established by Butler than it is by Plato. Plato is reduced to analogy, myth and mystagogy and, as Duncan-Jones points out, Butler is finally pushed to concede that "full acceptance of the conclusion that human nature is satisfiable and only satisfiable by virtue depends on revelation." In the face of what clearly seem to be genuine exceptions to the claim that it is in the individual's self-interest always to act morally, Butler is driven to remark: "All shall be set right at the final distribution of things.". . .

There is a more defensible answer to the question: "Why should people be moral?" It was first urged (in the Western World, at least) by Epicurus; later it was developed and given its classical forceful statement by Hobbes. Bertrand Russell elaborates it in his own way in his *Human Society in Ethics and Politics* (1955) and Kurt Baier has clearly elucidated and defended Hobbes' argument in his *The Moral Point of View* (1958). This Hobbesian argument, which within its proper scope seems to me conclusive, can readily be used to meet the objections of those "tough-minded" Marxists and Freudians who do not want the usual fare of "sweetness and light."

Hobbes points out that as a matter of fact the restless, malcontent, foraging human animal wants "The commodious life"; that is, he wants above all peace, security, freedom from fear. He wants to satisfy his desires to the maximum extent, but one of the very strongest and most persistent of these desires is the desire to be free from the "tooth and claw" of a life in which each man exclusively seeks his own interest and totally neglects to consider the interests of others. In such a situation life would indeed be "nasty, brutish and short." We could not sleep at night without fear of violent death; we could not leave what we possessed without well-warranted anxiety over its being stolen or destroyed. Impulses and inclinations would be held in check only when they would lead to behavior detrimental to the individual's own interest. Where people's interests conflict, each man would (without the institution of morality) resort to subterfuge or violence to gain his own ends. A pervasive Dobuan-like suspicion would be normal and natural . . . even rational in such a situation. Every individual would be struggling for the good things of life and no rule except that of his own self-interest would govern the struggle. The universal reign of the rule of exclusive self-interest would lead to the harsh world that Hobbes called "the state of nature." And, as Baier puts it, "At the same time, it will be clear to everyone that universal obedience to certain rules overriding self-interest would produce a state of affairs which serves everyone's interest much better than his unaided pursuit of it in a state where everyone does the same." Baier goes on to point out that "the very *raison d'être* of a morality is to yield reasons which override the reasons of self-interest in those cases when everyone's following self-interest would be harmful to everyone."

When we ask: why should we have a morality—any morality, even a completely conventional morality—we answer that if everyone acts morally, or generally acts morally, people will be able to attain more of what they want. It is obvious that in a moral community more good will be realized than in a non-moral collection of people. Yet in the interest of realizing a commodious life for all, voluntary self-sacrifice is sometimes necessary; but the best possible life for everyone is attainable only if people act morally; the greatest possible good is realizable only when everyone puts aside his own self-interest when it conflicts with the common good. . . .

II

Yet an answer to the question "Why should people be moral?" does not meet one basic question that the thorough-going sceptic may feel about the claims of morality. The "existing individual" may want to know why *he,* as an individual, ought to accept the standards of morality when it is not in *his* personal interest to do so. He may have no doubt at all about the general utility of the moral enterprise. But *his* not recognizing the claims of morality will not greatly diminish the total good. Reflecting on this, he asks himself: "Why should *I* be moral when I will not be caught or punished for not acting morally?". . .

Such an individual egoist cannot be refuted by indicating that his position cannot be a moral position. He may grant the overall social good of morality and he may be fully aware that "Why should I do my duty?" cannot be a moral question—there is indeed no room at all for that question as a moral question, but an individual egoist is not trying to operate within the bounds of morality. He is trying to decide whether or not he should *become* a moral agent or he may—in a more theoretical frame of mind—wonder if any *reason* can be given for his remaining a moral agent. Prichard is quite right in arguing that the *moral* agent has no choice here. To assert "I'll only be moral when being moral is in my rational interest" is to rule out, in a quite *a priori* fashion, the very possibility of one's being moral as long as one has such an intention. To be a moral agent entails that one gives up seriously entertaining whether one should deliberately adopt a policy of individual egoism. "X is moral" entails "X will try to do his duty even when so acting is not in his personal interest." Thus we must be very *careful* how we take the individual egoist's question: his question is, "Should I become moral and give up my individual egoism or shall I remain such an egoist?" If he decides to remain an individual egoist he will have made the decision that *he* ought to behave like a man of good morals when and only when such behavior is in his own personal interest. Now what grounds (if any) have we for saying that a man who makes such a decision is mistaken or irrational? What (if any) intellectual mistake has he made? . . .

Can such an individual egoist be shown to be wrong or to be asking a senseless question? What arguments can be given for an affirmative answer to the question: "Should I be moral?". . .

Must we say at this juncture that practical reasoning has come to an end and that we must simply *decide* for ourselves how to act? Is it just that, depending on what attitudes I actually happen to have, I strive to be one sort of a person rather than another without any sufficient rational guides to tell me what I am to do? Does it come to just that —finally? Subjectivists say (at such a juncture) that there are no such guides. And this time there seems to be a strong strand of common sense or hardheaded street wisdom to back up the subjectivists' position.

I do not believe that we are that bad off. There are weighty considerations of a mundane sort in favor of the individual's taking the moral point of view. But I think the subjectivists are right in claiming that it is a mistake to argue that a man is simply irrational If he does not at all times act morally. It is indeed true that if a man deliberately refuses to do what he acknowledges as morally required of him, we do say he is Irrational or better unreasonable. But here "irrational" and "unreasonable" have a distinctively *moral use*. There are other quite standard employments of the word in which we would not say that such a man is irrational. In all contexts the word "irrational" has the evaluative force of strongly condemning something or other. In different contexts the criteria for what is to be called "irrational" differ. In Toulmin's terms the criteria are field-dependent and the force of the word is field-independent. In saying a man acts irrationally in not assenting to any moral considerations whatsoever we need not be claiming that he makes any mistakes in observation or deduction. Rather we are condemning him for not accepting the moral point of view. But he is asking why he, as an individual in an ongoing community, should always act as a moral agent. He is not asking for *motivation* but for a *reason* for being a morally good man. He wants to know what intellectual mistake the man who acts non-morally must make. To be told such a man is immoral and in *that sense* is unreasonable or irrational is not to the point.

The subjectivist I am interested in contends that in the nature of the case there can be no reasons here for being moral rather than nonmoral. One must just *decide* to act one way or another without reasons. There is much to be said for the subjectivist's claim here but even here I think there are rational considerations in favor of an individual's opting for morality.

III

Before I state and examine those considerations I would like to show how two recent tantalizingly straight-forward answers will not do. Baier has offered one and Hospers the other.

Baier says that when we ask "Why should I be moral?" we are asking "Which is the course of action supported by the best reasons?" Since we can show along Hobbesian lines that men generally have better reasons for being moral than for being non-moral the individual has "been given a reason for being moral, for following moral reasons rather than any other. . . ." The reason is simply that "they are better reasons than any other." *But in the above type situation,* when I am asking "Why should I be moral?" I am not concerned with which course of action is supported by the best reasons *sans phrase* or with what is the best thing to do for all concerned. I am only concerned with what is a good reason *for me.* I want to know what is the best thing *for me* to do; that is, I want to know what will make for *my* greatest good.

Baier might point out that an individual has the best reasons for acting morally because by each man's acting morally the greatest possible good will be realized. Yet, if the reference is to men severally and not to them as a group, it might well be the case that an individual's acting immorally might in effect further the total good, for his bad example might spur others on to greater acts of moral virtue. But be that as it may, the individual egoist could still legitimately reply to Baier: "All of what you say is irrelevant unless realization of the greatest total good serves *my* best interests. When and only when the reasons for all involved are also the best reasons for me am I personally justified in adopting the moral point of view."

We can, of course, criticize a so-called ethical egoist for translating the question "What is the best thing to do" into the question "What is the best thing *for me* to do." In morality we are concerned with what is right, what is good and what is supported by the best reasons, *period;* but recall that the *individual* egoist is challenging the sufficiency of moral reasons which we, as social beings, normally grant to the moral enterprise. (We need to reflect on the sense of "sufficiency" here. The egoist is not challenging the point of having moral codes. He is challenging the sufficiency of the moral life as a device to enhance *his* happiness. But is this "a goal of morality"? It is not.) He is asking for reasons for *his* acting morally and unfortunately Baier's short answer does not meet the question Baier sets out to answer, though as I have already indicated it does answer the question, "Why should people be moral?"

Hospers has a different argument which, while wrong, carries a crucial insight that takes us to the very heart of our argument. Like Baier, Hospers does not keep apart the question "Why should I be moral?" from "Why should people be moral?" After giving a psychological explanation of what motivates people to be moral, Hospers considers what *reasons* there are for being moral.

Virtue is its own reward and if an act is indeed right this is a sufficient reason for performing the act. We have been operating on the wrong assumption—an assumption that we inherited from Plato—namely, that if it isn't in our interest to behave morally we have no reason to do it. But it does not follow that if a right action is not in our interest we have no reason for doing it. If we ask "Why should we do this act rather than other acts we might have done instead" the answer "Because it is the right act" is, says Hospers, "the best answer and ultimately the only answer." [1]

It is indeed true that *if we are reasoning from the moral point of view* and if an act is genuinely the right act to do in a given situation, then it is the act we should do. Once a moral agent knows that such and such an action is the right one *to do in* these circumstances he has *eo ipso* been supplied with the reason for doing it. But in asking "Why should I be moral?" an individual is asking why *he* should (non-moral sense of "should") reason as a moral agent. He is asking, and *not* as a moral agent, what reason there is for his doing what is right.

It is at this point that Hospers' reply—and his implicit defense of his simple answer—exhibits insight. It will, Hospers points out, be natural for an individual to ask this question only when "the performance of the act is *not* to his own interest." [2] It is also true that *any* reason we give other than a reason which will show that what is right is in his rational self-interest will be rejected by him. Hospers remarks "What he wants, and he will accept no other answer, is a self-interested reason" for acting as a moral agent.[3] But this is like asking for the taste of pink for "the situation is *ex hypothesi* one in which the act required of him is contrary to his interest. Of course it is impossible to give him a reason *in accordance with his interest for acting contrary* to his interest." [4] I have a reason for acting in accordance with my interest which is contrary to my interests" is a contradiction. The man who requests an answer to "Why should I do what is right when it is not in my interest?" is making a "self-contradictory request." We come back once more to Prichard and Bradley and see that after all our "question" is a logically absurd one— no real question at all. The person asking "the question" cannot "without self-contradiction, accept a reason of self-interest for doing what is contrary to his interest and yet he will accept no reason except one of self-interest." [5]

---

[1] John Hospers, *Human Conduct: An Introduction to the Problems of Ethics* (New York, 1961), p. 194.

[2] *Ibid.,* p. 194.

[3] *Ibid.*

[4] *Ibid.*

[5] *Ibid.,* p. 195

His "question" is no real question at all but at best a non-rational expression of a personal predicament. Our problem has been dissolved —the "common sense core of subjectivism" has turned out to be the core of the onion.

But has it really? Is any further question here but a confused request for *motivation* to do what we know we have the best reasons for doing? Let us take stock. Hospers has in effect shown us: 1) That x's being right entails *both* x should be done (where "should" has a moral use) and there is (from the moral point of view) a *sufficient reason* for doing x ("I ought to do what is right" is a tautology where "ought" is used morally); 2) That from the point of view of self-interest the only reasons that can be sufficient reasons for acting are self-interested reasons. This again is an obvious tautology. The man asking "Why should I do what is right when it is not in my self-interest?" has made a self-contradictory request *when he is asking this question as a self-interested question.*

These two points must be accepted, but what if an individual says: As I see it, there are two alternatives: either I act from the moral point of view, where logically speaking I must try to do what is right, or I act from the point of view of rational self-interest, where again I must seek to act according to my rational self-interest. But is there any *reason* for me always to act from one point of view rather than another when I am a member in good standing in a moral community? True enough, Hospers has shown me that *from the moral point of view* I have no alternative but to try to do what is right and from a *self-interested point of view* I have no rational alternative but to act according to what I judge to be in my rational self-interest. But what I want to know is what I am to do: Why adopt one point of view rather than another? Is there a good reason *for me*, placed as I am, to adopt the moral point of view or do I just arbitrarily choose, as the subjectivist would argue?

I do not see that Hospers' maneuver has shown this question to be senseless or an expression of a self-contradictory request. Rather his answer in effect brings the question strikingly to the fore by showing how from the moral point of view "Because it's right" must be a sufficient answer, and how it cannot possibly be a sufficient answer from the point of view of self-interest or from the point of view of an individual challenging the sufficiency of the whole moral point of view, as a personal guide for his actions. It seems that we have two strands of discourse here with distinct criteria and distinct canons of justification. We just have to make up our minds which point of view we wish to take. The actual effect of Hospers' argument is to display in fine rational order the common sense core of subjectivism: *at this point* we just choose and there can be no reasons for our choice.

It will not do for Hospers to argue that an individual could not rationally choose a non-moral way of life or ethos, for in choosing to act from a self-interested vantage point an individual is not choosing a way of life; he is, instead, adopting a personal policy of action in a very limited area for himself alone. Such an individual might well agree with Hospers that a rational way of life is one, the choice of which, is (1) free, (2) enlightened, and (3) impartial.[6] This remark, he could contend, is definitive of what we *mean* by "a rational way of life. An intelligent egoist would even urge that such a way of life be adopted but he could still ask himself (it any single individual, living in a community committed to such a way of life to act in accordance with it." (This need not be a question which logically speaking requires a self interested answer. An existing individual is trying to make up his mind what he is to do.)

To reply, "If it's rational then it should be done," is to neglect the context-dependent criteria of both "rational" and "should." There are both moral and non-moral uses of "should" and "rational." In the above example Hospers is using "rational" in a moralistic sense; as Hospers puts it, "Let me first define 'rationality' with regard to a way of life" and while a way of life is not exhausted by moral considerations it essentially includes them. Only if "rational" and "should" belong to the same strand of discourse is "If it is rational then it should be done" analytic. Something could be rational from the moral point of view (morally reasonable) and yet imprudent (irrational from the point of view of self-interest). If we were asking what we should do in terms of self-interest, it would not follow in this case that we should do what is rational in the sense of "morally reasonable." Conversely, where "What is rational" means "What is prudent" it would not follow that what is rational is what, morally speaking, we ought to do.

Thus, it seems to me that neither Baier's nor Hospers' answers will do. We are left with our original question, now made somewhat more precise, "Is there a good reason for me as an individual in a moral community to always act morally no matter how I am placed?" There is no room *in morality* for this question but this question can arise when we think about how to act and when, as individuals, we reflect on what ends of action to adopt. But as a result of Hospers' analysis, must we now say that here we must 1) simply make a choice concerning how to act or 2) where there is no live question concerning how to act it is still the case that there can be no non-question begging justification for an individual, were he faced with such a choice, to act one way rather than another? (Of course there is the very best *moral* justification for his acting as a moral agent. But that is not our concern here, for here we are asking: why reason morally?)

---

[6] *Ibid.,* p. 585.

Here the pull of subjectivism is strong—and at this point it has an enlightened common sense on its side. But I think there is something more to be said that will take the bite out of such subjectivism. In trying to bring this out, I am in *one sense* going back to Plato. It is, of course, true that we can't ask for a self-interested reason for doing what is right where *ex hypothesi* the action is not in our self-interest. But in actual moral situations it is not so clear what is in our self-interest and what is not, and often what is *apparently* in our self-interest is really not. Part of my counter to the subjectivist, and *here* I am with Plato, is that if a man decides *repeatedly* to act non-morally where he thinks he can get away with it, he will not, as a very general rule, be happy.

This isn't the whole of my case by any means, but I shall start with this consideration.

IV

Suppose that I, in a fully rational frame of mind, am trying to decide whether or not to adopt individual egoism as my personal policy of action. I ask myself: "Should I pursue a selfish policy or should I consider others as well even when in my best judgment it doesn't profit me?" In my deliberation I might well ask myself: "Will I really be happy if I act without regard for others?" And here it is natural to consider the answer of the ancients. Plato and Aristotle believe that only the man who performs just actions has a well-ordered soul. And only the man with a well-ordered soul will be "truly happy." If I am thrown off course by impulse and blind action I will not have a well-ordered soul; I will not be genuinely happy. But the alternative I am considering is not between impulsive blind action and rational, controlled action, but between two forms of deliberate, rationally controlled activity. Why is my soul any less well-ordered or why do I realize myself (to shift to Bradley's idiom) any the less if I act selfishly than if I act morally? If it is replied, "You will 'realize yourself more' because most people have found that they are happiest when they are moral," I can again ask: "But what has that to do with me? Though I am one man among men, I may not in this respect be like other men. Most people have neurotic compulsions about duties and are prey to customary taboos and tribal loyalties. If I can free myself from such compulsions and superstitions will I be any the less happy if I am selfish? I should think that I would be happier by being intelligently selfish. I can forget about others and single-mindedly go after what I want."

To this last statement Plato and Aristotle would reply that by always acting selfishly a man will not fully realize his distinctively human *areté*. By so acting, he simply will not be responding in a fully human way. We say of a man that he is a "good man, a truly happy man" when he performs his function well, just as we say a tranquilizer is a "good tranquilizer" when it performs its function well; that is to say, when the tranquilizer relaxes the tense, harrassed individual. But can we properly talk about human beings this way? We do speak of a surgeon as "a good surgeon" when he cures people by deftly performing operations when and only when people need operations. Similarly, a teacher is "a good teacher" if he stimulates his students to thought and to assimilate eagerly "the best that has been thought and said in the world." We can indeed speak of the *areté* or "virtue" of the teacher, fireman, preacher, thief or even . . . of the wife or unmarried girl. People have certain social roles and they can perform them ill or well. "In this sense we can speak of 'a good husband,' 'a good father,' 'a good Chancellor of the Exchequer,' . . ." but . . . hardly of "a good man." People, *qua* human beings, do not seem to have a function, purpose, or role. A child can sensibly ask: "What are hammers for?", "What are aspirins for?", "What are dentists for?" but if a child asks "What are people for?" we must point out to him that this question is not really like the others. "Daddie, what are people for?" is foolish or *at the very least*—even for the Theist—an extremely amorphous question. At best we must quickly strike some religious attitude and some disputed cosmology must be quickly brought in, but no such exigency arises for the cosmologically neutral question, "Daddie, what are napkins for?" or "Daddie, what are policemen for?" After all, what is the function of man *as such*? In spite of all his hullabalo about it, is not Sartre correct in claiming that man has no "essence"—no *a priori* nature—but that human beings are what human beings make of themselves? If a human being acts in an eccentric or non-moral way are we really entitled to say he is any less of a human being?

If we counter that we are indeed entitled to say this, and we then go on to say, "By not acknowledging that we are so entitled, we are in effect overriding or ignoring man's 'distinctively human qualities'" are we not now using "distinctively human qualities" primarily as a grading label? In such contexts, isn't its actual linguistic function primarily moral? We are disapproving of a way of acting and attempting to guide people away from patterns of behavior that are like this. If we say the consistently selfish man is less human than the moral man, are we not here using "less human" as a moral grading label and not just as a phrase to describe men? "More human," on such a use, would not be used to signify those qualities (if there are any) which are common to and distinctive of the human animal; but would be used as an honorific moral label. And *if* it is used *only* to describe how people have behaved then it is perfectly possible for me to ask, "Why should I be more human rather than less?"

Most moderns would not try to meet the question "Why should I be moral?" in this Greek way, though they still would be concerned with that ancient problem, "How should I live in order to be truly happy?" A rational man might make this elementary prudential reflection: "If I am thoroughly and consistently selfish and get caught people will treat me badly. I will be an outcast, I will be unloved, all hands will be on guard against me. I may even be retaliated against or punished as an 'irredeemable moral beast.' All of this will obviously make me suffer. Thus, I better not take up such a selfish policy or I will surely be unhappy."

At this point it is natural to take a step which, if pushed too far, cannot but lead to a "desert-island example." It is natural to reply: "Clearly it would be irrational to *appear* selfish. But I don't at all propose to do that. I only propose to look out for 'number one' and only 'number one.' I will do a good turn for others when it is likely, directly or indirectly, to profit me. I will strive to appear to be a man of good morals and I will do a good deed when and only when it is reasonable to believe there will be some personal profit in it. Surely, a policy of unabashed, outright selfishness would be disastrous to me. Obviously, this is something I will strive to avoid. But I shall keep as the maxim of *my* actions: Always consider yourself first. Only do things for others, when by so acting, it will profit you, and do not be frankly selfish or openly aggressive except in those situations where no harm is likely to befall you for so acting. Take great pains to see that your selfishness is undetected by those who might harm you."

But, at this point our hypothetical rational egoist would need to consider the reply: "You will regret acting this way. The pangs of conscience will be severe, your superego will punish you. Like Plato's tyrant you will be a miserable, disordered man. Your very mental health will be endangered."

Imperceptibly drawing nearer to a desert-island example, the egoist might reply: "But the phrase 'mental health' is used to describe those well adjusted people who keep straight on the tracks no matter what. I don't intend to be 'healthy' *in that sense*. And, I do not recognize the *authority* of conscience. My conscience is just the internalized demands of Father and Tribe. But why should I assent to those demands, when it doesn't serve my interests? They are irrational, compulsive moralistic demands, and I shall strive to free myself from them."

To this it might be countered, "Granted that conscience has no moral or even rational authority over *you*, you unfortunate man, but practically speaking, you cannot break these bonds so easily. Consciously you may recognize their lack of authority but unconsciously they have and always will continue to have—in spite of all your ratiocination—a dominating grip on you. If you flaunt them, go against them, ignore them, it will cost you your peace of mind, you will pay in psychic suffering, happiness will be denied you. But as a rational egoist happiness is supposedly your goal. And it is wishful thinking to think some psychiatrist will or can take you around this corner. Neither psychoanalysis nor any other kind of therapy can obliterate the 'voice of the superego.' It can at best diminish its demands when they are *excessive*. Your conditioning was too early and too pervasive to turn your back on it now. If you are rational you will not struggle in such a wholesale fashion against these ancient, internalized demands. Thus, you should not act without regard to the dictates of morality if you really want to be happy."

It is at this stage that the rational egoist is likely to use his visa to Desert Island. He might say: "But if I had the power of Gyges [7] and that power included the power to still the nagging voice of my superego, would it not then be reasonable for me to always act in my own self-interest no matter what the effect on others? If there was some non-harmful pill—some moral tranquilizer—that I could take that would 'kill' my conscience but allow me to retain my prudence and intelligence why then, under those circumstances, should I act morally rather than selfishly? What good reason is there for me in that situation to act morally if I don't *want* to?"

It is not sufficient to be told that if most people had Gyges' ring (or its modern, more streamlined, equivalent) they would go on acting as they do now. The question is not "What would most people do if they had Gyges' ring?" or even "What would I do if I had Gyges' ring?" The question is rather, "What should I do?" At this point can *reasons* be found which would convince an intelligent person that even in this kind of situation, he ought to act morally? That is, would it serve his "true interests" (as Plato believes) for him to be moral, even in the event these conditions obtained?

It is just here, I believe, that subjectivism quite legitimately raises its ugly head. If the above desert-island situation did in fact obtain, I think we would have to say that whether it would or would not be in your "true interests" to be moral or non-moral would depend on the sort of person you are. With the possible exception of a few St. Anthony's, we are, as a matter *of fact*, partly egoistic and partly other-regarding in our behaviour. There can be no complete non-personal, objective justification for acting morally rather than non-morally. In certain circumstances a person of one temperament would find it in his interests to act one way and a person of another temperament to act in another. We have two policies of action to choose from, with distinct criteria of appropriateness and which policy of action will make us happy will depend on the sort of person we *happen* to be.

---

[7] [According to the myth in Plato's *Republic*, Gyges found a magical ring that could make him invisible and, thus, able to escape punishment for any misdeeds.— EDS.]

It is here that many of us feel the "existential bite" of our question. Students, who are reasonably bright and not a little versed in the ways of the world, are often (and rightly) troubled by the successive destruction of first psychological egoism and then ethical egoism. They come to see that individual egoism can't be a moral view, but they feel somehow cheated; somehow, in some way, they sense that something has been put over on them. And I think there is a point to this rather common and persistent feeling and I have tried, in effect, to show what this is. I would *not*, of course, claim that it is always the "Why-should-I-be-moral?" question that troubles a reflective student at this juncture but frequently, like Glaucon and Adeimantus, the student wants to know why, as a solitary flesh and blood individual, he should be moral. He *feels* that he should be moral, but is he somehow being duped? He wants a *reason* that will be a good and sufficient reason for his being moral, quite apart from *his* feelings or attitudes about the matter. He does not want to be in the position of finally having to decide, albeit after reflection, what sort of person to strive to be. It seems to me that the subjectivists are right in suggesting that this is just what he finally can't avoid doing, that he doesn't have and can't have *the kind* of objectivity he demands here. We need not have existentialist dramatics here, but we do need to recognize the logical and practical force of this point. Most rationalistic and theological ethical theories seem to me mythmaking devices to disguise this *prima facie* uncomfortable fact.

V

But need we despair of the rationality of the moral life once we have dug out and correctly placed this irreducible element of choice in reasoning about human conduct? Perhaps some will despair but since it is not the job of a philosopher to be a kind of universal Nannie I don't think he need concern himself to relieve this despair. But, I think, if he will remind people of the exact point on the logical map where this subjectivism correctly enters and make them once more aware of the map as a whole they will—now be able to see the forest as well as the trees—be less inclined to despair about the rationality of their acting morally. If one is willing to reason morally, nothing we have said here need upset the objectivity and rationality of moral grading criteria. More importantly here, to admit subjectivism at this point does not at all throw into doubt the Hobbesian defense of the value of morality as a social practice. It only indicates that *in the situation* in which an *individual* is 1) very unlikely to be caught, 2) so rationally in control that he will be very unlikely to develop habits which would lead to his punishment, and

3) is free from the power of his conscience, it might, just might, (if he were a certain kind of person) make him happier to be non-moral than moral. But this is not the usual bad fellow we meet on the streets and the situation is anything but typical.

A recognition of the irrelevance of desert-island examples will provide further relief from moral anxiety, over such subjectivism. . . .

Our "Gyges-ring situations" are just such desert-island cases. In fact, . . . the Gyges-ring example in the *Republic* is a paradigm of all such desert-island arguments.

"Would I be happier if I were intelligently selfish in a situation in which I could free myself from guilt feelings, avoid punishment, loss of love, contempt of family and friends, social ostracism, etc?" To ask this is to ask a desert-island question. Surely we can and do get away with occasional selfish acts—though again note the usual burden of guilt—but given the world as it is, a deliberate, persistent though cunning policy of selfishness is very likely to bring on guilt feelings, punishment, estrangement, contempt, ostracism and the like. A clever man might avoid one or another of these consequences but it would be very unlikely that he could avoid them all or even most of them. And it is truistic to remark that we all want companionship, love, approval, comfort, security and recognition. It is very unlikely that the consistently selfish man can get those things he wants. At this point, it may be objected: "But suppose someone doesn't want those things, then what are we to say?" But this is only to burgeon forth with another desert-island example. The proper thing to reply is that people almost universally are not that way and that in reasoning about whether I should or should not be selfish, I quite naturally appeal to certain very pervasive facts (including facts about attitudes) and do not, and need not, normally, try to find an answer that would apply to all conceivable worlds and all *possible* human natures. To think that one must do so is but to exhibit another facet of the genuinely irrational core of rationalism.

VI

It seems to me that the above considerations count heavily against adopting a thoroughly consistent policy of individual egoism. But do such considerations at all touch the individual who simply, on occasion, when his need is great, acts in a way that is inconsistent with the dictates of morality? Will such a person always be happier—in the long run—if he acts conscientiously or is this a myth foisted on us, perhaps for good social reasons, by our religions and moralities? Are all the situations desert-island situations in which we can reasonably claim that there could be rational men who would be happier if they acted non-morally rather than morally or in which we would have to say that any decision to act one way rather than another is a matter of arbitrary choice? Are there paradigm cases which establish the subjectivist's case—establish that it is altogether likely that some clear-headed people will be happier if, in some non-desert-island circumstances, they deliberately do what they acknowledge is wrong and or in some non-desert-island circumstances some people must just decide in such circumstances what they are to do?

Let us examine three *prima facie* cases.

Suppose a man, believing it to be wrong, decides to be unfaithful to his wife when it is convenient, non-explosive and unlikely to be discovered. Usually it is not, on the part of the knight-errant husband, a deliberate and systematic policy but it might be and sometimes is. Bored husbands sometimes day-dream that this is a return to paradise, that is to say, it might earn, at least in anticipation, a good score in a felicific calculus. In order to make the example sufficiently relevant to the argument, we must exclude those cases in which the husband believes there is nothing wrong in this behavior and/or gives reasons or rationalizations to excuse his behavior. I must also exclude the guilty weak-willed man with the Pauline syndrome. The case demands a man who deliberately—though with sufficiently prudent moderation—commits adultery. It is important for our case that he believes adultery to be immoral. Nonetheless, while believing people ought not to be adulterers, he asks himself, "Should I continue to live this way anyway? Will I really be happier if I go the way of St. Paul?" He does not try to universalize his decision. He believes that to choose to remain an adulterer is immoral, but the immoral choice remains for him a live option. Though people may not put all this to themselves so explicitly, such a case is not an impossibility. People may indeed behave in this way. My example is not a desert-island one. I admit there is something odd about my adulterer that might make him seem like a philosophical *papier maché* figure. There is also something conceptually odd about saying that a man believes x to be wrong and yet, without guilt or ambivalence and without excusing conditions, rationally decides to do x. With good reason we say, "If he knows it to be wrong or really believes it to be wrong, he will (everything else being equal) try to avoid it." Still there is a sense in which he could say he believes x to be wrong even though he seeks x. The sense is this: he would not wish that people generally choose or seek x. When this is the case he says "x is wrong" even though he makes a frank exception of himself without attempting to morally justify this exception. It is important to note that this is a *special* though perfectly intelligible use on my part of "He believes it to be wrong." While it withdraws one essential feature, namely that non-universalisable exceptions are inadmissable, it retains something of the general sense of what we mean by calling something morally wrong.

Yet, for the sake of the argument at least, let us assume that we do not have a desert-island case. Assuming then that there are such men, is their doing what is wrong here also for *them* the personally disadvantageous thing? Can any individual who acts in such a way ever be reasonably sure he won't be caught—that one of the girls won't turn up and make trouble, that he won't run into an acquaintance at the wrong time? Even if these seem to be remote possibilities, can he ever be free enough from them in his dream life? And if his dreams are bothersome, if he develops a rather pervasive sense of uneasiness, is it really worth it? He must again consider the power of his conscience (superego) even though he rationally decided to reject its authority. Will it give him peace? Will the fun be worth the nagging of his conscience? It is difficult to *generalize* here. Knowledge of oneself, of people, of human psychology and of imaginative literature is all extremely relevant here. I think the individual egoist can correctly argue that it is not *always* clear that he would be unhappier in such a situation if he did what was wrong. A great deal depends on the individual and the exact particular circumstance but the moralist who says it is never, or hardly ever, the case that a person will be happier by pursuing a selfish policy certainly overstates his case.

Let me now take a different paradigm for which much the same thing must be said. It is important to consider this new case because most people would label this man a "veritable moral beast" yet he stands to gain very much from acting immorally. The case I have in mind is that of a very intelligent, criminally experienced, well-equipped, non-masochistic but ruthless kidnapper. He is a familiar type in the movies and thrillers. Now, Hollywood to the contrary, why should it not sometimes be the case that such a kidnapper will be happier if he is successful? Indeed, he may have a murder on his hands but the stakes are very high and when he is successful he can live in luxury for the rest of his life. With good reason our *folklore* teaches he would not be happier. It is of the utmost value to society that such behavior be strenuously disapproved. And given the long years of conditioning we are all subject to, it remains the case that most people (placed in the position of the kidnapper) would not be happier with the successful completion of such a kidnapping if it involved murdering the kidnapped child. But then most people are not kidnappers. They have very different personalities. Such brutalities together with fear of detection would haunt them and it is probably the case that they also haunt many kidnappers. But if the kidnapper were utterly non-moral, very, very clever, etc., why wouldn't *he* really be happier? He could live in comfort; he could marry, have children and attain companionship, love, approval, etc. "Well," we would say, "his conscience would always bother him." But, particularly with modern medical help, which he could now well afford, would it bother him enough? "Well, there would always be the awful possibility of detection and the punishment that might follow." But, if the stakes were high enough and if he were clever enough might it not be better than a life of dull routine, poverty or near poverty? And think of the "kicks" he would get in outwitting the police? We all have a little adventure in our souls. "But"—the dialogue might go on—"if he were intelligent enough to pull off this job successfully, he would certainly be intelligent enough to avoid poverty and to avoid making his living in a routine, boring way." The dialogue could go on interminably but I think it is clear enough again that even here there is no one decisive, clearcut answer to be given. The case for morality here is stronger than in the previous paradigm, but it is still not decisive. Yet there are paradigms in which doing what is clearly wrong (and understood by the individual in question to be wrong) is in the rational self-interest of some individuals. Our first more typical paradigm is not completely clear, but the following third and less typical paradigm given by Hospers is a clearer example of a case in which it is in a man's self-interest not to do what is right.

> There is a young bank clerk who decides, quite correctly, that he can em-
> bezzle $50,000 without his identity ever being known. He fears that he
> will be underpaid all his life if he doesn't embezzle, that life is slipping by
> without his ever enjoying the good things of this world; his fiancee will not
> marry him unless he can support her in the style to which she is ac-
> customed; he wants to settle down with her in a suburban house, surround
> himself with books, stereo hi-fi set, and various *objets d'art,* and spend a
> pleasant life, combining culture with sociability; he never wants to com-
> mit a similar act again. He does just what he wanted to do: he buys a house,
> invests the remainder of the money wisely so as to enjoy a continued in-
> come from it, marries the girl, and lives happily ever after; he doesn't
> worry about detection because he has arranged things so that no blame
> could fall on him; anyway he doesn't have a worrisome disposition and is
> not one to dwell on past misdeeds; he is blessed with a happy temperament,
> once his daily comforts are taken care of. The degree of happiness he now
> possesses would not have been possible had he not committed the im-
> moral act.[8]

Clearly it was in his rational self-interest to do what is wrong.

Someone might claim that it is too much to expect that he could arrange things so that no blame would fall on him. This could happen
only in desert-island type situations. But unless we began to have the
doubts characteristic of traditional epistemologists about "the blame

---

[8] John Hospers, *Human Conduct,* pp. 180–81.

could not fall on him," there are plenty of cases in which crimes of this general sort are carried out with success. There is no good reason to think such an individual in such circumstances would not be happier.

But it is also crucial to recall that our cases here only involve certain specific acts that do go against the requirements of morality. The cultured despiser of morals we described in the last section is a man who rejects the authority of *all* moral considerations and systematically pursues a selfish policy in all things. Thus, we would need to project risks similar to those of the wayward husband and the kidnapper through his entire life. But are there really any realistic paradigms for such generalized egoistic behavior that would hold any attraction at all for a rational man? I doubt very much that there are. Yet, our three paradigms indicate that for *limited patterns of behavior*, no decisively good reasons can be given to some individuals that would justify their doing the moral thing in such a context. (It would be another thing again if they repeatedly acted in that way. Here the case for morality would be much stronger.)

In pointing this out, the subjectivist is on solid ground. But it is also true that even here it is not just a matter of "paying your money and taking your choice," for what it would be rational for you to do depends, in large measure, on what sort of person you are and on the particular circumstances into which you are cast .

There is a further more general and more important consideration. Even if large groups of people read and accepted my argument as correct, even if it got favorable billing by Luce publications, it still remains very unlikely that kidnapping and crime would increase one iota. For the most part, people get their standards not from ethical treatises or even scriptural texts or homely sayings but by idealizing and following the example of some living person or persons. Morality or immorality does not typically (or perhaps even ever) arise from precept or argument but from early living examples. The foundations of one's character are developed through unconscious imitation way before perplexity over morality can possibly arise. Unless a man is already ready to run amuck, he will not be morally derailed by the recognition that in deliberating about how to act one finally must simply decide what sort of a person one wishes to be. Since most people are not ready to go amuck, the truth of my argument will not cause a housing shortage in hell.

There are further considerations that will ameliorate this subjectivism. It seems reasonable to say that in different societies the degree of subjectivism will vary. All societies are interested in preserving morality; they have a quite natural and rationally justifiable vested interest in their moral codes. Now, as societies gain a greater know-how, and particularly as they come to understand man and the structure of society better, it seems reasonable to assume they can more effectively protect their vested interests. In other words, I believe, it is reasonable to assume that it will become increasingly difficult to be successfully non-moral as a society gains more knowledge about itself and the world.

This also poses a puzzle for the intelligent individual egoist. In such advancing culture-studying cultures, it will become increasingly more difficult for *him* to be non-moral. But it is in his rational interest for *others* to be moral so he should not oppose this more efficient enforcement of morality. And if he does choose to oppose it, it is very probable that he will suffer a fate not unlike Camus' stranger.

More generally, it will not be in the interest of the individual egoist to oppose morality and even if he, and others like him, do find that it pays to act non-morally their failure to act morally will of necessity be so moderate that the set of social practices that help make up morality will not be disturbed in any extensive way. (This puts the point very modestly). And, if too many go the way of the rational individual egoist, then it will no longer pay to be non-moral so that large numbers of individual egoists, if they are rational, will become men of good morals.

Though the plain man committed to the moral point of view will probably not jump with joy over this state of affairs, I think the considerations in the last three paragraphs give him genuine grounds for being sanguine. The subjectivism I have pin-pointed need not create a generation of "despairing philosophers" even if my argument is accepted as completely sound.

Suggestions for Further Reading

GENERAL INTRODUCTIONS

BRANDT, R. B. *Ethical Theory.* Englewood Cliffs, N.J.: Prentice-Hall, 1959 (especially Chapters VII-XI). Includes chapters on naturalism, nonnaturalism, and noncognitivism.

HUDSON, W. D. *Modern Moral Philosophy.* New York: Doubleday, 1970. Includes chapters on intuitionism, emotivism, prescriptivism, and descriptivism.

ROYCE, JOSIAH. *The Religious Aspect of Philosophy.* Boston: Houghton Mifflin, 1885 (especially Chapters II and III). An older perspective on the discussion.

WARNOCK, G. J. *Contemporary Moral Philosophy.* New York: St. Martin's, 1967. Includes chapters on naturalism, intuitionism, emotivism, and prescriptivism.

Suggestions for Further Reading

(Sections 6.1–6.4 are arranged in historical rather than alphabetical order.)

6.1 ETHICAL NATURALISM AND DEFINISM

JAMES, WILLIAM. "The Moral Philosopher and the Moral Life" (first published in 1891), in *Essays in Pragmatism* (New York: Hafner, 1948), pp. 65–87.

SHARP, F. C. *Ethics.* New York: The Century Co., 1928.

PEPPER, S. C. *The Sources of Value.* Berkeley: University of California Press, 1958 (especially Chapters I and XIII).

BLANSHARD, BRAND. *Reason and Goodness.* New York: Macmillan, 1961.

6.2 INTUITIONISM

EWING, A. C. *The Definition of Good.* New York: Macmillan, 1947.

HUDSON, W. D. *Ethical Intuitionism.* New York: St. Martin's, 1967.

6.3 DEBATE ABOUT NATURALISM AND INTUITIONISM

FRANKENA, W. K. "The Naturalistic Fallacy," *Mind*, XLVIII (1939), 103–14. Reprinted in Kenneth Pahel and Marvin Schiller, eds., *Readings in Contemporary Ethical Theory* (Englewood Cliffs, N.J.: Prentice-Hall, 1970), pp. 32–43.

PRIOR, A. N. *Logic and the Basis of Ethics.* London: Oxford University Press, 1949.

STRAWSON, P. F. "Ethical Intuitionism," *Philosophy*, XXIV (1949), 23–33. Reprinted in R. B. Brandt, ed., *Value and Obligation* (New York: Harcourt, Brace & World, 1961), pp. 347–57.

HUDSON, W. D., ed. *The Is-Ought Question.* New York: St. Martin's, 1969.

6.4 NONCOGNITIVE OR NONDESCRIPTIVE THEORIES

HUME, DAVID. *Enquiry Concerning the Principles of Morals*, ed. L. A. Selby-Bigge (2nd ed.). Oxford: Clarendon Press, 1902. [pp. 272–74 (Section IX, Part I) and 285–91 (Appendix I)]

REID, THOMAS. *Essays on the Active Powers of Man.* (Essay V, Chapter VII.) [first published in 1788]). Reprinted in D. D. Raphael, ed., *British Moralists* (Oxford: Clarendon Press, 1969), II, 265–310. A critique of Hume's emotivism by an intuitionist.

STEVENSON, C. L. "The Emotive Meaning of Ethical Terms," *Mind*, XLVI (1937), 14–31. Reprinted in Kenneth Pahel and Marvin Schiller, eds., *Readings in Contemporary Ethical Theory* (Englewood Cliffs, N.J.: Prentice-Hall, 1970), pp. 44–60.

———. *Ethics and Language.* New Haven: Yale University Press, 1944.

SARTRE, JEAN-PAUL. *Existentialism and Humanism.* London: Methuen, 1948.

HARE, R. M. *Freedom and Reason.* New York: Oxford University Press, 1963.

6.5 RELATIVISM

BENEDICT, RUTH. *Patterns of Culture.* New York: Pelican Books, 1946 (Chapter VII).

Herskovits, M. J. *Cultural Anthropology.* New York: Knopf, 1955 (Chapter XIX).

Ladd, John, ed. *Ethical Relativism.* Belmont, Calif.: Wadsworth, 1973. A helpful anthology that includes both philosophers and social scientists.

Mandelbaum, Maurice. *The Phenomenology of Moral Experience.* Baltimore: Johns Hopkins, 1969 (Chapter V).

Stace, W. T. *The Concept of Morals.* New York: Macmillan, 1962 (Chapters I and II).

Taylor, P. W. "Four Types of Ethical Relativism," *Philosophical Review*, LXII (1954), 500–16.

———. *Normative Discourse.* Englewood Cliffs, N.J.: Prentice-Hall, 1961 (Chapters III–VI).

Wellman, Carl. "The Ethical Implications of Cultural Relativity," *Journal of Philosophy*, LX (1963), pp. 169–84.

6.6 Toward a Satisfactory Theory of Justification

Aiken, H. D. "Morality and Ideology," in R. T. De George, ed., *Ethics and Society* (Garden City, N.Y.: Doubleday, 1966), pp. 149–72.

———. *Reason and Conduct.* New York: Knopf, 1962 (Chapters III, IV, V, and VIII).

Baier, Kurt. *The Moral Point of View* (abridged ed.). New York: Random House, 1965.

Ewing, A. C. *Second Thoughts in Moral Philosophy.* London: Routledge & Kegan Paul, 1959 (Chapters I and II).

Findlay, J. N., "The Methodology of Normative Ethics," in *Language, Mind and Value* (London: Allen & Unwin, 1963), pp. 248–56.

Mayo, Bernard. *Ethics and the Moral Life.* New York: St. Martin's, 1958 (Chapters IV and V).

Wallace, G., and A. D. M. Walker, eds. *The Definition of Morality.* London: Methuen, 1970.

6.7 Why Be Moral?

Gauthier, D. P., ed. *Morality and Rational Self-Interest.* Englewood Cliffs, N.J.: Prentice-Hall, 1970 (Part III).

Pahel, Kenneth, and Marvin Schiller, eds. *Readings in Contemporary Ethical Theory.* Englewood Cliffs, N.J.: Prentice-Hall, 1970. (Section Four) See especially the paper by J. C. Thornton.

Phillips, D. Z. "Does It Pay to be Good?" *Proceedings of the Aristotelian Society*, LXV (1964–1965), 45–60. Reprinted in J. J. Thomson and Gerald Dworkin, eds., *Ethics* (New York: Harper & Row, 1968), pp. 261–78.

Scriven, Michael. *Primary Philosophy.* New York: McGraw-Hill, 1966, pp. 238–65.

Singer, M. G. *Generalization in Ethics.* New York: Atheneum, 1971 (Chapter X).

Taylor, P. W. *Normative Discourse.* Englewood Cliffs, N.J.: Prentice-Hall, 1961, pp. 142–50.

EPILOGUE

It has been a long, sometimes difficult, and perhaps inconclusive process to examine and evaluate the thoughts and arguments, from Plato to the twentieth century, that are included in this anthology. We have tried to present the beginning student of ethics with the best and most helpful philosophical reflections on the subject that are known to us. We do not, however, expect to have the last word on the subject or to present a single and completely satisfactory answer to the main questions of ethics. We believe that there is much truth and insight in the readings we have presented, but in the final analysis we invite you to consider these words of T. S. Eliot:

> . . . These are only hints and guesses,
> Hints followed by guesses; and the rest
> Is prayer, observance, discipline, thought and action.[1]

---

[1] T. S. Eliot, "The Dry Salvages," in *The Complete Poems and Plays, 1909–1950* (New York: Harcourt Brace Jovanovich, 1952), p. 136. Reprinted by permission of the publishers.

INDEX